The Soul *of* SCREENWRITING

The Soul *of* SCREENWRITING

On Writing, Dramatic Truth, and Knowing Yourself

Keith Cunningham

continuum

NEW YORK • LONDON

2008

The Continuum International Publishing Group Inc
80 Maiden Lane, New York, NY 10038

The Continuum International Publishing Group Ltd
The Tower Building, 11 York Road, London SE1 7NX

www.continuumbooks.com
www.keithcunningham.net

Illustrations by Manuel Ehrenfeld

Printed in the United States of America

Library of Congress Cataloging-in-Publication Data

Cunningham, Keith.
The soul of screenwriting : on writing, dramatic truth, and knowing yourself / Keith Cunningham.
p. cm.
Includes bibliographical references and index.
ISBN-13: 978-0-8264-2868-4 (hbk. : alk. paper)
ISBN-10: 0-8264-2868-1 (hbk. : alk. paper)
ISBN-13: 978-0-8264-2869-1 (pbk. : alk. paper)
ISBN-10: 0-8264-2869-X (pbk. : alk. paper) 1. Motion picture authorship. I. Title.

PN1996.C828 2008
808'.066791—dc22

2008022026

Contents

Preface

THIS BOOK IS ABOUT THE ART OF SCREENWRITING—AND MORE: storytelling, the structure of meaning, and the creative imperative unique to our species. It is, in fact, impossible to imagine humans—human consciousness—without stories. Just as language and the capacity to dream are structured into our biological system, stories, like dreams, are the spontaneous and inevitable products of our nature. The fact that stories, via movies, television, the Internet, and other media, now constitute a truly global industry is in no way surprising. Nor do the new media alter the fundamental storytelling impulse. This new media environment does indeed generate new challenges that bring the screenwriter's creative process, and her capacity for reflective insight, to the fore. Consequently, forging a unity of creative process and creative technique is the focus of this new approach to screenwriting.

The Soul of Screenwriting is an outgrowth of many seminars, hundreds really, spanning almost a quarter century and five continents. The story development models presented here have undergone continuous testing, evolution, and enrichment through dialogue with my collaborators, other screenwriters, and my students. Julian Friedmann, my agent, and David Barker at Continuum have had faith in the project since I presented it to them, and they have my enduring thanks.

Now, as this book goes forth into the world, three individuals who have nourished my understanding of story come vividly to mind.

First, there is Marty Matthews, late Professor Emeritus of Biochemistry at the University of Chicago. I think of this work as a step in an ongoing dialogue about form and meaning. An octogenarian, Marty's sparkling eyes were full of great questions about the nature of life. He was haunted by Pirandello's play *Six Characters in Search of an Author* because he felt that, like the characters in the play, the world of organic molecules wanted to communicate to *him*, so intimate was his relation to his lifelong research. Marty had repeated, impeccably cinematic visions of threading his way through an ancient, labyrinthine temple to arrive at a great stone wall covered with flaming hieroglyphs. He knew this was the language of life itself, yet the glyphs always faded before he could decipher them. Like an ancient seer, Marty would pose everyone he knew the following question: "What is a story such that it can heal a wound; what is a wound such that a story can heal it?" This elusive question still guides me onward.

Along with Marty, my thoughts go to the best friend of my youth, Freeman Pittman, taken too early from this world by Lou Gehrig's disease. At the age of nine, we discovered Homer's *Iliad* and *Odyssey* together. Through Freeman, I came to see stories as worlds one can enter, worlds with infinite extension. We open out these story "fields" by drawing them, painting them, retelling them, questioning them. Freeman was gifted with an effortless grace in the multimodal expression of story fields through art.

And very present in my mind is my longtime collaborator, seminar partner, and friend, Tom Schlesinger. Many years ago, our girlfriends brought us together one winter's night in a Mexican restaurant in Chicago, El Sol, and we began a conversation that has never abated. Tom, mentioned so often in the book, deserves equal credit for the elaboration of our concepts and creative techniques.

Along with Tom, I want to give a special thanks to my other close collaborator in writing and teaching, Daniel Speck of Munich. My brother Bruce and my dear friend Andrea De Micheli in Milan have given me important encouragement and support over the years, and I could not have accomplished the work without the generosity of Nina Schneider, who transcribed many of the chapters. I am likewise grateful for the staunch backing of professional institutions that have sponsored the seminars for many years. In this regard, I'd like to thank Jochen Bentz of the Koelner Filmhaus and Dr. Ruth Blaes of the ARD/ZDF Medienakademie.

Bringing together the techniques of storytelling for the screen with the psychology of the creative process has been a life's work for me. I have been guided and enriched by contacts with members of the international community of Analytical Psychology, most notably Mario Jacoby and Jan and Murray Stein in Zurich, my stimulating conversations with whom over the years has helped me sustain the effort. I also want to thank analysts and teachers Catherine Moreau of Les Arcs, France, and Florence Wiedemann of Dallas. My first contact with the world of Jungian psychology was through my professor of performance arts at Northwestern University, Leland Roloff, to whom I owe a lasting debt.

From that important formative period, the university days, I must mention three other persons, contact with whom has had an impact to this day. It was my friend Susan Goldberg who first insisted I start reading Joseph Campbell, and it was my soul-sister Rebecca Armstrong who was instrumental in my meeting Campbell for the first time. That was to be a turning point in my life. And, back in an almost mythical past, there is the great muse-figure of Anaïs Nin, who, in one brief, illuminating moment, conveyed to me the essence of living with soul.

Part I

THE LIVING STORY

1

The Night of the King Coho

Imagine the pattern of shadows cast by leaves on a white wall, moving in a soft breeze. An electric-blue damselfly darts from point to point on the wall, now in sunlight, now in shade, as though tracing an invisible design.

PATTERNS HAVE ALWAYS FASCINATED ME: the day as a pattern, the year as a larger pattern; the small town where I grew up as a pattern, the great city nearby as a larger pattern. Knowledge as a patterned set for organizing experience into cognizable patterns. One day as a child—I was probably playing in the yard, studying shadows—I made up my mind that all of reality is made of patterns, a web of interwoven patterns. And it seemed that the patterns of things were as real as the things themselves.

Of course, this is a counterpart of the age-old mythological idea of the "music of the spheres," which signifies the harmony of all things within a cosmic order or pattern.

But it seems to have come spontaneously to me out of my own experience. Later I encountered Gregory Bateson's "pattern that connects." Obviously, there were meta patterns, very large patterns that described or controlled many other patterns. Patterns connected human behavior and animal behavior, biology and psychology, economy and nationalism, physics and metaphysics.

Creative Process and Created Product as an Interlocking Pattern

For me, storytelling, cinema, and psychology were never three separate things, but parts, branches, of a broader meta-pattern. It is the unique perspective of this book that it makes visible a core pattern, one that unites the dynamics of storytelling and the technique of screenwriting with the creative process of the screenwriter. As you will see, it is really what the writer experiences in the act of writing that ultimately shapes the story. Powerful and compelling screenplays, the ones audiences remember, come from writers who engage with their stories with intensity and authenticity. In reality, it is not possible to separate the technique from the person who is going to use it. This book is designed to give you both the screenwriting techniques and the creative rapport you need to realize your full potential as a writer. We are putting the writer in the center of the picture, where she belongs.

It has not always been possible to go into a bookstore and find a vast shelf of titles on screenwriting. When I was a film school student, back in the early 1970s, there was not a single book available that was exclusively devoted to the craft of screenwriting, as distinguished from theater. I recall that in film school the lecture we were given on dialogue lasted less than five minutes:

> Dialogue serves three functions: to advance the plot, reveal character, and get a laugh. If a line of dialogue does one of these, it's an okay line; if it does two, it's a good line. And if it hits all three, it's a great line.

That was it! It's hard for us to realize today that before the generation of Lucas, Spielberg, and Coppola, the film business was not primarily learned in school, but on the job. The craft of screenwriting was gleaned from watching experienced writers do it, by adapting techniques from the theater, or simply by the seat of one's pants. As long as the "Hollywood style" of the studios dominated, the stylistic genres and standards were generally known. And when the studio system loosened up in the 1960s, there was a fertile period of experimentation.

A more disciplined approach to screenwriting started to emerge in books at the end of the seventies. The first book credited with having a broad influence on the industry was Syd Field's *Screenplay* (1979). The tone of the book suggested that it was the last word on the subject; in fact it was the first word. Field deserves substantial credit for putting the first road into the territory. But the understanding of how screenplays manage to convey so much meaning to the audience in so little time is evolving. It will continue to evolve. All of the books and seminars make some small or large contribution to that. What is important for you as a reader, I believe, is whether an approach speaks to you, awakens or enhances your creative capacity, and gives you the tools to apply that creativity to your screenwriting in a productive way.

Books on screenwriting are full of information. Sometimes there are breakthroughs on the information level. The Sixteen Story Steps model presented in this book is such a breakthrough. It is a new, more detailed understanding of dramatic structure, based on the universal storytelling functions a screenplay must fulfill if it is to be complete and create a powerful dramatic unity onscreen. The Sixteen Story Steps makes the hidden structures of Act II, the underground springs and tectonics of that vast terrain, visible to the screenwriter in a way they never have been before. This is an objective advance. But what really makes a great screenwriter is not something on the information or "head" level. There is no hidden formula, no trade secret a screenwriting guru can promise you, that you can apply mechanically to get a winner every time. If that were all it took, every movie would be a hit.

There is something fundamentally incomplete, if not misleading, in trying to teach screenwriting in terms of models that are thought of mechanically as templates into which to fit your story idea. It is especially misleading to try to learn from a few "perfect" examples, like *Chinatown*, *Witness*, *Terminator 2*, or *Titanic*. It is the easiest thing in the world to take a finished product that has already been a smash success and extol it as a perfect model. One simply ignores the *process*: what it took to get there!

Some inexperienced screenwriters and development executives, raised on a diet of perfect models, can be led into absurdities. I was once asked to rewrite a thriller that was not working, but to whose concept the producers were very attached. The project had already been given a green light for production, though the script had not yet been written. I was in the unfortunate position of having to tell them that their treatment (a twenty-five-page detailed synopsis) was a complete mess. The story was not even structured as a thriller, a fact of which the producers were unaware. If I were going to write a new treatment, I told them, I would have to have free rein to throw out whatever was necessary and start basically from scratch. The producer's response was: "Fine, fine. Whatever you want; you're the writer. Just bring me *Chinatown* in two weeks."

This is not really story development; it's name-brand thinking that comes from excluding the creative process from the discussion. *Chinatown* is a brand name, just like Budweiser or BMW. The brand name evokes the glamour of a "perfect" product that will guarantee market success. This producer perhaps did not know that while writing *Chinatown*, the screenwriter Robert Towne spent months at a time coming to the studio every day to lament that the story wasn't working, he was blocked, it was no use, and so on. Fortunately those working with him had the good sense—and the understanding of the creative process—to support him through that difficult period. The result is indeed a wonderful screenplay.

But it wasn't wonderful until it had been through a long and arduous trial of errors and revisions. During the long stretch of the process, *Chinatown* was not working . . . yet. Take a look at a middle draft of *Witness*, an Oscar winner for best screenplay: there are still awkward subplots that ultimately had to be removed. Or take a look at a middle draft of the climactic scene in *Ordinary People*, another Oscar winner. As the scene is written, it's a dramatic failure: rather than allowing Conrad to discover the truth, we have the psychiatrist explaining it all to him. It becomes the psychiatrist's scene when it should be Conrad's. Fortunately, the scene went through further revisions. Screenwriting is a long journey. Even the most gifted screenwriters get lost along the way. Getting lost, too, is part of the journey. Therefore, to treat the resulting movies as models of perfection while ignoring the process is a rather mean self-deception.

A second problem in overemphasizing hit movies like *Chinatown* as teaching aids is that, while they are inspiring, they are also limiting. General observations may carry over from the "perfect" model, but as soon as we must work on the more detailed level of actually writing a script, we're in trouble. Can we expect strategies that work for *Chinatown* to apply to *Angel at My Table*? "The devil is in the details" is an apt old saw. And the devil is that the closer we look, the more a screenplay's development challenges become distinctly unique. If it is your job to write or develop *this* particular story, at a certain point it becomes necessary to leave generalities behind. Each story must ultimately work on its own terms, not on borrowed terms.

So there is an essential component to screenwriting that cannot be contained in formulas, no matter now grand they may sound. Up to the present time, that essential component of successful screenwriting has never been fully acknowledged and integrated. This is quite strange, because the overlooked factor is *the screenwriter himself!* What the writer experiences in the act of writing has never been taken into account—but, after all, this is where the screenplay comes from: the writer's here-and-now experience while working on the story. Information—left-brain concepts and techniques about how to handle plot structure, character development and orchestration, the dynamics of scenes and sequences—is all necessary. But it is what we *do* with the information that makes for really fine screenwriting. Screenwriters need technique the way golfers need technique. Of course the golfer must be aware to keep his head down, not to turn his elbow in, and to let the momentum of the club guide the follow-through. However, if he has to "think" his way through it, he will freeze. The swing will never be natural. The golfer has to forget technique, meaning move beyond technique to the point where technique is integrated into who he is. And this is true of the screenwriter as well.

Good screenwriting is more than hitting the big "plot points" with exciting action. Good screenwriting also has integrity and authenticity. It has a "voice," and because it has a voice, it speaks to the audience. To gain a voice, the writer needs the heat of creative imagination: passion, commitment, enthusiasm, a drive to know the truth of the characters, a drive to get to the core of the dramatic conflict without resorting to escapism. These are qualities of the heart. Could screenwriting be, adapting Carlos Castaneda's phrase, "a path with heart"? The keystone premise of this book is that screenwriting can indeed be a path with heart.

Screenwriting Is Storytelling

It is perhaps impossible to write a book without having an agenda. There are usually several agendas, stated and unstated. The stated agenda becomes the text on the cover of the book. The unstated agenda becomes the *subtext*, an implicit fantasy the writer invites the reader to enter and share. I prefer to lay my agenda on the table and trust the reader's own powers of judgment. My agenda is that storytelling is one of our most fundamental and universal human capacities. We are all storytellers. We all want to tell our stories and experience ourselves as being heard. Those of us who choose storytelling through movies and other media as a profession are people who have been touched by stories, who feel compelled to use stories as our way of understanding ourselves and the world around us. We may indeed feel ourselves caught up in those large stories an entire society consciously or unconsciously tells itself about itself, the stories about where we come from and where we're going. In movies, as a popular entertainment, the story is a lens through which we collectively look at ourselves. The storyteller does not stand on the outside of this process and look in; he is part of the process, it pulls him along. The screenwriter as storyteller becomes a vehicle for the story as much as its author. Storytellers, like other artists and creatively intuitive individuals, might be pictured as the lookouts on the masthead of a ship, the first to warn of rocks off the starboard bow. They are the ones who cry out that the long-sought landfall is finally visible on the horizon. Storytelling thus has a long and sacred tradition.

Screenwriting is a natural extension of that. The movies are the medium, but in the end it comes down to human beings trying to communicate with one another about this life we share. Screenwriting is both technically and creatively demanding. It is the human context, however, that gives it meaning. This human context is the agenda. We value stories because they have meaning, and meaning makes human life possible.

The Soul of Screenwriting grows out of the seminars I have been leading for years with my colleague Tom Schlesinger. Our collaboration began in 1980. Over that extended period, one striking disconnect has remained constant. This is the difference between the ways screenwriting has been presented in books and seminars and the way it actually feels to sit down and write a screenplay. There is still a tendency to view the screenplay as a product divorced from the creative process. There is also a parallel disconnect between the way producers and development executives talk about screenplays and the way writers conceptualize and talk about their own work.

In both cases, the gulf is between seeing the screenwriting process from the outside and from the inside. From the outside, a screenplay is an object, a product, a thing: raw material to be shaped into a movie production like steel sheeting is shaped into an auto body. From the inside, from the writer's own perspective, the screenplay is a monster, a troupe of dancing girls, a chimera that comes to stay and takes over the house for months at a time. It upsets meals, changes sleep rhythms, destroys love relationships or begets others. The screenplay demands attention, plays seductive games, refuses to cooperate. Lacking a common awareness and appreciation of this difference, screenwriters and producers have a tough time communicating. Successful screenplay development, unlike writing a novel, demands clear communication among the entire story development team.

Misunderstandings based on these fundamentally different perspectives can quickly lead a project into "development hell": wasted time, effort, and money—and cancelled projects. Creating the concepts and pragmatic means to balance the demands of product and process, and to enhance communication within the development team, became central to the seminars Tom and I have been leading. An exclusively left-brain approach that treats the screenplay in a mechanistic way, as a machine to be assembled and fine-tuned, simply does not give writers what they need. Furthermore, mechanistic approaches are deceptive, because the control fantasies they imply in fact take writers out of their creative center. Only an approach balancing the two sides, the process and the product, does justice to the reality that the screenwriter has to work with day after day.

Tom and I came together from different backgrounds and perspectives, though we discovered we had grown up only a few miles apart. Tom had gotten off to a fast start as a screenwriter out of UCLA, selling or optioning his first two scripts. Difficulties with a third, however, led to a creative block. In an effort to get some guidance during his struggles, Tom had turned to more experienced screenwriters for advice. At the time we met, he was engaged in interviewing a number of America's top screenwriters, including Paul Schrader, Buck Henry, and Waldo Salt, about their working methods. Those interviews became a series of articles for *Film Quarterly*. What emerged from them as a leitmotif was the power of storytelling at the heart of the screenwriter's work. Each of these very successful screenwriters was a natural, gifted, even compulsive storyteller. Tom's questions about writing technique were answered by way of personal anecdotes that were engaging, humorous, and insightful. Storytelling emerged as the core aptitude behind screenwriting technique—more than a skill: a life attitude. Great screenwriters use words and images, just like the rest of us. But they *think* in stories.

At the time, I was approaching storytelling from another direction. Like most eager film school students, my ambition was to become a director. But after I had not found financial backing for an independent feature project, I turned to camera and gaffing work to make my living. It was in those first years of freelance activity that I had two encounters that altered my life's direction. The first of these was meeting mythologist Joseph Campbell for the first time, in 1976. Because of common friends, I was privileged to spend private, friendly time with Campbell on that occasion, sipping scotch with him in his hotel room. I had had a lifelong interest in mythology and the patterns of human culture, so there was much to discuss. No one at that time had publicly made a connection between mythic structure and screenplay structure. But Joseph Campbell had in fact identified and mapped out the archetypal meta-structure of story that links myth and drama together. This meeting in itself had a very mythic quality for me, and I kept up the contact with Campbell until his death in 1987. Within a month of that first meeting, my life had changed in startling ways. The year after meeting Campbell, I was introduced to the work of psychologist Jean Houston, herself also friends with Campbell and an indefatigable leader of the human potential movement. Over the next five years I did intensive training with Jean. Much of this work had to do with accessing and bringing forth those deep stories that guide the lives of productive individuals and societies. Jean's methods were deeply intertwined with theater and dramatization. Variations of some of her experiential exercises are still part of my seminars and are incorporated into this book.

Thus my approach to storytelling was already based on my understanding of the perennial, archetypal structure of stories, and the very lively and playful ways of working with the psyche I had learned with Jean Houston. As Tom and I explored what we had in common, we intuitively felt we were holding important pieces of a new understanding that we had yet to visualize and put together. We were being challenged on both professional and personal levels to integrate what was deep inside us with our way of working as filmmakers. It was a challenge to contribute a new insight to our profession by asking the basic questions about screenwriting in new and fresh ways.

The first public expression of our perspective was a weekend workshop for the American Film Institute in New York in April 1984. Joseph Campbell was still alive at the time; his interviews with Bill Moyers had yet to appear on PBS and his work was unknown to the general public. My lecture at that workshop on the Hero's Journey archetype and its application to screenwriting is, to my knowledge, the first public presentation of Campbell's work to the filmmaking community. The weekend also included interviews with David Mamet and other leading screenwriters. Through this event and subsequent seminars in California, Tom and I shaped our material, in dialogue with other writers, and especially by becoming more aware of what happens in the day-to-day process of writing. As writers ourselves, it made sense that the lived reality should be the proving ground for theory.

The Story Field: Four Compass Points

As a result of many interactions and reflections, a very small group of fundamental principles emerged. They formed an irreducible core that became the basis of our seminars and of this book.

1. **Stories Are Energy.** It is the energy within a story that shapes the story and gives it form. What is this "energy" we are talking about? A screenplay as such is but a stack of paper or bits in a computer file. The real story is a virtual reality that exists in the hearts and minds of the tellers and hearers. Stories are a manifestation of the psyche, of the human spirit. This is a natural process. It is in our nature to create forms to hold our experience so that we can both become conscious of it and share it with others. When we say that the energy is "within" the story, what we really mean is that the story condenses the psychic energy of a larger field of possibilities and gives it form. The form is

the energy and the energy is the form. This inborn urge to form is the root of both language and art.

The "story field" is comprised of all of the possible associations and combinations of material relevant to the story. Every fairy tale has multiple variations, but they all draw from the same story field. The same holds true for every love story, every thriller. One way of working with story energy, of interacting with the story field, is to actively shape it by willpower toward a chosen goal: the production which will be shot and the market to which it will be addressed. But willpower also has its downside. Ego-pushing is a stressful process and leaves stress marks both on the story development process and on the resulting movie. Using willpower to channel our energy indeed allows us greater focus. Consciousness becomes like a bright spotlight, but much of creative value is left beyond the reach of its narrow beam. We miss much of the inherent potential in the story field.

Another way of working with story energy is *allowing*: allowing the story to emerge. When allowed to develop out of its own inner dynamics, its inherent tensions and conflicts, a story seems to spontaneously shape itself. That is to say, intuitive processes that normally work in the background of consciousness take the lead. There are many screenwriters, playwrights, and novelists who enter into an allowing state of consciousness where scenes readily appear as an "objective" reality, and where the characters speak for themselves as though they were real people. This creative flow requires an attitude of non-intervention and receptivity: getting out of the way of the emerging story. In story development, both aspects work together like right and left hands. In story development, as we shall discuss throughout this book, asking the right, focused questions helps open the story up. Questions further the energy flow both within the story and between the creative partners, while "dictating to the story" or being narrowly judgmental tends to close the story energy down.

This makes the point that the energy in stories is the energy of *relationship*. Here we are not only referring to other people with whom we share our stories, though that is also important; we have all noticed that our stories come out differently depending on whom we tell them to, and of course relationship in this sense applies to the audience as well. But we also have a direct relationship with the story itself and the field from which it emerges. There is a call and response between something deep in the story and something deep in ourselves. The story comes into our homes, into our bedrooms, and lives with us. We become infatuated with it or alienated from it. The story energy can suddenly dry up, and then it can become impossible to write anything with conviction. This does not happen because we lack the right technique; it is a relationship problem. We are out of rapport with the story.

2. **Energy Radiates.** This is a basic, universal quality of energy. Like the sun's light and warmth, like ripples from a stone thrown into a pond, energy moves

out in all directions. If we are especially full of energy when we arrive at work in the morning, the people around us respond to it and reflect it back to us. It may pick up their own energy level. Of course, negative energy radiates as well. When we arrive at work radiating rage or envy, those around us are going to reflect that back as well. Energy is energy.

It is absolutely no different, we shall see, with our characters. Each is a radiating center of energy whose actions ripple out into the world of the story. Each character is an authentic center, just as we experience ourselves to be. Those radiating energy waves interact and cause turbulence, conflict. Waves of conflict move back and forth between protagonist and antagonist, impacting everyone in what we shall be calling the Emotional Network of the screenplay.

Energy is also radiating from the writer into the story and from the story back to the writer. The quality of this energy is ultimately radiated out to the audience through the energy of the actors' performances and every other aspect of the production. Producers and studio executives often repeat that the screenplay is the "raw material" for the production. I find this to be an inapt analogy. I think it would be fairer to say that the screenplay contains within its pages, on an energy level, the "genetic coding" for the unfolding of the entire production. If the screenwriter hasn't put that energy into the screenplay, the director, actors, and crew won't get energy from it.

3. **Parallel Journeys.** When we see how story energy shapes our work as screenwriters, we notice that the story takes us on a journey. It is a journey from a concept about a movie to a screenplay that is fully real in dramatic terms. It is a journey into the unknown, and along the way our "concepts about" are going to have to bite the dust as they give way to realities. It is a journey shaped by the excitement and infatuation of our first steps into the territory and our projective fantasy about how great it will be when we are done. The journey is also shaped by the weariness of extra drafts and frustrating or belligerent development meetings.

   We noted earlier that Joseph Campbell's work in mythology revealed a meta-structure to myths that has been found to apply to drama as well. It turns out that the journey the writer undertakes in writing the screenplay is a direct analogue to the journey the hero of the drama travels within the screenplay. This may seem intuitively obvious, but when Tom and I first promoted this idea, many people found it revolutionary. The screenwriter goes on a parallel journey along with the hero, down into wounds and fears, down into the unknown. It is a journey of creative breakdown and breakthrough, and there is a point-for-point correspondence between the mythic Hero's Journey and the writer's creative journey.

   This is great news for screenwriters. It means that rather than spending our energy heroically battling to overcome our low moods, our inertia, our anxiety and hopelessness when the screenplay is going nowhere, we can use all these reactions productively. We can choose to remain attentively disengaged from these feelings and, finding the parallels, use them to sharpen our understanding of our characters. When we realize that what we are feeling is a direct analogue to what our character is feeling at that point in the story, we can feed our own moods right back into the screenplay. The concrete situation will of course be different—we may actually not be on a runaway train headed for a mountain curve! But an underlying situation/pattern will be similar. And so we don't need to be afraid of anything: not of unproductive days, not of frustrating meetings, not of creative blocks. It all takes on meaning in the context of parallel journeys. The challenge is rather to look and discover, without bias, what the inner connection may be. This is the fundamental work of becoming conscious of what we are doing as writers and why we are doing it. In the process, yes, we become better writers. We become more aware in our personal lives as well. Using our professional craft to build consciousness is what can make screenwriting a path with heart.

Finally, this principle of parallel journeys also applies to the audience. The audiencc also goes on a journey, an aesthetic and emotional journey. They ride on that roller-coaster in sympathy or identification with the main character. Through the vehicle of the hero, as well as through the total expressiveness of the movie, the audience takes into themselves the fruits of the writer's experience. If the writer has arrived at something authentic and true through her journey, the audience will pick it up. If the writer is just going through the motions or following a formula, the audience will feel it.

4. **Uncertainty Is the Starting Point.** Screenwriting is a risky business because it is a journey whose outcome cannot be known beforehand. Books and seminars that offer "guaranteed" formulas or trade secrets are popular because they implicitly promise to relieve the creative risk. Models are helpful, but ultimately the writer is on his own. Day after day, he has to face the blank page or the blank computer screen. Each new scene, each new line of dialogue, is an unknown. Right now, it doesn't matter that you have written half a dozen treatments and scene outlines. Right now, you have to be in the present moment along with the characters, and when you are really in the present, you honestly don't know what is going to happen next. You aren't thinking about that. You surrender to what psychologist Mihály Csíkszentmihályi terms the "flow" experience.[1] When you are in the creative flow, *then* the characters have a chance to speak for themselves. *Then* the writing has a chance to be authentic, fresh, and powerful. Tom Schlesinger formulates it this way: "Powerful and authentic screenwriting is predicated on your ability to be with uncertainty, to sit with the thoughts and feelings that arise when you face the blank computer screen." We can have wonderful models and a

1. Csíkszentmihályi, Mihály, *Creativity: Flow and the Psychology of Discovery and Invention* (New York: Harper Collins, 1996).

perfect outline, but if we fail to grasp this basic principle, we won't make it over the long haul of writing an authentic, compelling screenplay.

Herein lies a source of tension between screenwriters on one hand and producers and development executives on the other. These latter live with the tremendous risks of the production, both financial and professional, on their shoulders. They are naturally invested in reducing risk. Writers often fail to appreciate how much producers are pressured by studio executives, distributors, market trends, the competition. It is natural for producers to want to know the outcome ahead of time and to control it as much as possible. This leads them to a certain logic about stories. We could call it a left-brain logic. Left-brain thinking tends to be more linear and goal-oriented. Meanwhile, the screenwriter *must* let herself go into the unknown if the writing is to have any vitality at all. This is a much more intuitive right-brain process. The producer tends to expect delivery on the treatment. He is geared toward the *product*. The screenwriter is geared toward the *process*. An essential dialogue must take place between these two perspectives or the story development effort will break down.

If these four basic principles—*Stories Are Energy*, *Energy Radiates*, *Parallel Journeys*, and *Uncertainty Is the Starting Point*—were merely academic, there would be no need to mention them. But they identify what we are actually doing as writers day after day, scene after scene, draft after draft. Thus these principles both come before concepts and models and follow after them. They come before in the sense that we already have these principles inside us; they are part of our basic psychic makeup. They follow after in that, once we have learned the "mechanics" of screenwriting, it is our contact with these fundamental principles that determine the extent to which we can "inhabit" the technique and make it truly our own, the same way a golfer makes the swing his own.

This book itself is in fact structured as a journey for the reader. It is a journey toward connecting our work with our authentic inner life: the way we think and feel and live. If we are professional writers, our knowledge of our craft, our knowledge of ourselves, and our knowledge of human nature are our primary professional tools. This is what we use to make our living. Like any real professionals, it is not enough for us to know how to make our tools work; we also need to know *why* they work the way they do. We realize that the how and the why are intimately connected. We can understand much better how to make Act II of our screenplay work when we understand the underlying dynamics that cause it to take the shape it does. Along the way, we also discover that a screen story is not a *thing*. It is a three-dimensional stream of meaning. And it is alive.

Night of the King Coho

Moments of new beginning are thought to have a special character. There is both opportunity and peril. Beginnings create a truly archetypal field that cannot be rationally explained away. When human beings start a new undertaking that involves risk, they invariably call upon ritual to draw good luck and protection. Birthdays are greeted with songs and cakes, weddings with complex ritual ceremonies. Contract-signings and ship-launchings call for champagne. In many cultures, the precise quality of that moment of beginning is thought to foretoken in seed form the entire later development. Seers are summoned; the stars are consulted.

The moment my friend Tom and I began our work together, the moment we received our Call to Adventure, so to speak, was marked by such an archetypal quality. We had spent a weekend at an intensive training with Jean Houston; from there we traveled to Chicago for the International Film Festival. It was the last day of the festival, and we took part in an event where Toshiro Mifune received a lifetime achievement award. Mifune's name evokes the "field" of the action-hero, in the noblest sense of that phrase. That night we found ourselves at a retro screening of a Burt Lancaster swashbuckler with the wonderful title *The Flame and the Arrow*. This was one of those classics kids used to be able to catch every Saturday afternoon. It featured Lancaster as a heroic Lombardian patriot named Dardo, battling for freedom against the arrogant Austrians. Dardo had a small son named Rudy, whom he had to rescue at the climax. The spectacular stunts, escapes, and sword fights involved climbing on curtains and swinging from chandeliers. This was an old-fashioned movie that satisfied without falling into pretentiousness or self-parody. As the credits rolled, Tom noticed that Waldo Salt, who had written *Midnight Cowboy* (the movie that had inspired Tom to become a screenwriter), had written *The Flame and the Arrow* as well. Waldo was later to be important in the development of our own concepts.

A movie like *The Flame and the Arrow* is such a rollicking good time that when you come out of it you feel like leaping down the steps and dueling with rapiers on the edge of a rampart. Tom and I were in this boisterous mood as we walked from the gothic library building on the Northwestern University campus, where the movie was shown, toward the parking lot, built on the Lake Michigan landfill. Acres of landfill had been landscaped around a pond fed by the lake. It was a windless, misty night as we skirted the edge of the pond, caught in a movie-induced reverie. Suddenly there was an uproar of voices and commotion in the dark. Three fishermen were shouting to each other in Korean. We could see one straining with his fishing rod as his fellows jumped among their gear for a net and a flashlight. The rod was bent almost double and the line zigzagged like lightning over the water as the beam from a powerful flashlight illuminated it. Still, nothing could be seen beneath the dark surface. You didn't need to know Korean to get they were shouting for him to hang on.

It was a primal scene my friend and I had been given to witness. We stood there mesmerized. Something glimmered in the water and we all shouted as one in different languages. It was big. A fin broke the surface and we shouted again. The fisherman was almost pulled into the drink. Then, seeming played out, the fish drifted near the stony shore and we got our first sight of a king coho salmon nearly three feet long. But just as one of the men lunged forward down the steep embankment with his net, the salmon took off again. The guy reaching with the net was caught off balance and tumbled in headfirst. The coho was still fighting as the man pulled himself out of the water.

In the end, the king gave in and gave himself up. Too tired to continue the fight, he was reeled into the shallows. But, exhausted as the coho was, it took all three men to haul him out of the water. The net was useless. It was meant for little lake perch, not this steely monster. With great effort and a cascade of Korean exclamations, the three men at last pulled and pushed the coho up onto the grass.

Silence fell again as the three men bent over, hands on knees, gazing as this "ancient of days" gulped feebly at the air. There were old scars on the silver torso and fungus lesions around the mouth. The great silver eyes were still alive, still looking. What were they seeing? The salmon suddenly flipped and writhed. One of the men clubbed him three times on the head, and that was that. A spell that had united us all for a moment in what the Spanish call *duende*, that spell that binds the bull, the torero, and the spectators together in a sense of shared passion, was broken. The three Koreans started to talk again, doubtless about the wonderful salmon steaks they were going to have and how this fish would feed their families for a week. Tom and I congratulated the men. They waved back with shy, astonished pride.

We didn't say much as we finally arrived at the parking lot and went on our way. But that moment had bonded us. From that night on, we somehow knew we had work to do together—though we had yet to discover what it was. The king coho became a touchstone for us as that work grew over the years. It had the power of a myth. We had glimpsed a small portion of an infinite mystery, one that connected us back to the archetypal moment of "beginnings," and we could feel ourselves fed and refreshed from the "other side." Such lived moments have nothing to do with rationality, but they are decisive.

So, why tell this story? What does this have to do with screenwriting? Why drag myths and babbling Korean fishermen into it? First, it is an example of how life can speak directly to us at key moments, if we are willing to listen. Perhaps you can recall some similar experience in your own life when you felt in touch with life's mystery through a serendipitous event. Or you may think of a moment when you were "called" to a new work or new adventure—perhaps to take up screenwriting. These moments are doubly alive, and they speak a universal language we can all understand. Second, we must believe that the stories we tell make a difference to those who hear them. Movies certainly do have an impact, and we must hope it is a decent one. Entertainment has become America's largest industry and most ubiquitous export. As markets merge and trade barriers fall, national, ethnic, and regional culture forms are disappearing like endangered species. The stories we put out into the marketplace have multiple levels of impact, including that of crowding out many traditional forms of expression. These old cultures may have become economically insignificant and nonviable, but they nevertheless contained the lives of the people, distilled into enduring forms.

Now we wield an overwhelming market power, but can we create stories that are, if not enduring, at least satisfying to the soul? Sometimes we hear a screenwriter or director pronounce themselves to be the "mythmakers of our time." We should not be too hasty to proclaim ourselves so. We are ever the sorcerer's apprentice, the Mickey Mouse character, *not* the sorcerer. As Joseph Campbell has cautioned, we cannot know what the new myth will be any more than we can predict what we will dream tonight. Connecting with our own authentic depths as storytellers is perhaps our only security against spending untold millions on the utterly trivial and sentimental.

Myths cannot be ordered off a menu or created by committee. They are not corporate accomplishments. Corporate culture is a saga of warring clans, their appetites and triumphs. It tends to produce pseudo-myths, mechanical myths, full of sound and fury, signifying merely their own puissance. Mythmaking, if it is to happen, requires the other factor not under our control. Something must come from the "other side," from the dark dimension of soul. The world must conspire along with us. Great stories make us feel more alive because they are born in moments of heightened aliveness. They are brimming over with aliveness. That aliveness touches something deep in us. We could all name movies that have touched us in this way. It is my guess that we have chosen to write screenplays rather than sell shoes or real estate because we have been so touched.

What we can do as screenwriters, to come closer to the region where the great stories are, is to let the story we are writing carry us away. Let it sweep us out of our comfort zone and into the unknown the way Odysseus and his sailors were blown clear off the map to strange lands. We go, like Odysseus, craftily—armed with our craft. The craft of screenwriting is the necessary preparation for a deeper encounter with aliveness. The fisherman has all the tools of his trade: lines, hooks, nets, gloves. But when he throws his line into the dark water, he can never be sure he will not snag the whale that swallowed Jonah.

2

Mirrored in the Story

> Creativity is the encounter of the intensely conscious human being with his or her world.
>
> *—Rollo May*

Outside Encountering Inside

OUR APPROACH BEGINS with seeing the screenplay and the creative process of the writer as the outside and the inside of a single process. In every other art—music, dance, painting, pottery—it is generally accepted that product is inseparable from process. But with screenwriting the necessary link, the continuous flow between process and product, has been kept in the background. One reason for this is that movies are thought of as "manufactured" as much as "created." Metaphors of the screenplay as "raw material" for the director are most common. There are competing agendas and perspectives at work in the development of any screenplay. Added to this is a second factor we have already alluded to: that writers and producers come to the project with different backgrounds, expectations, and temperaments. It sometimes takes an effort to appreciate the impact of the screenwriter's process on the finished product.

One fact we can all agree upon, however, is that the screenplay does not write itself. A story concept is not a screenplay. A verbal pitch to a producer is not a screenplay—many ideas that pitch well turn out to be un-writeable. The pitch is merely short enough to highlight exciting elements while concealing underlying structural flaws. Exposés (two- to six-page synopses), story treatments, and story outlines are not yet screenplays. We can learn much from them; we can feel we know where we are headed. But until we work our way through the entire story in screenplay format, we have not yet had the experience of hearing the characters speak for themselves, we have not had scenes appear before our eyes that are absolutely compelling and dramatically necessary—and not in the treatment. Until we start the screenplay itself, we have not had to endure the fundamental creative conflict between what we have planned—and may have contracted to—and what we experience as real and dramatically true right now, in the present, as we are working. Therefore we are forced, in our own best interest, to be concerned with the creative process and what goes on there.

As a creative act, writing a screenplay is not a sprint; it's more like running a marathon. The virtues and self-disciplines of a marathon runner—practice, patience, stamina, perseverance, the ability to focus inwardly on the finish line even when it is not visible, and dedication—also pertain to the screenwriter. And to these qualities we must also add that of *creative courage*. Creative courage, as psychologist Rollo May suggests, is our capacity for encounter, our capacity to draw something new and significant out of ourselves through the shock of confronting the "other." So, we may ask: what must we encounter as screenwriters that requires courage?

First, there is the continuous encounter with the unknown in the process of writing, day by day, scene by scene. We shall refer to this unknown in a later section as "creative darkness." It takes courage to admit that we do not know what the next line of dialogue will be until the character speaks it. This is a wonderful and scary freedom.

A second area of encounter for which we need creative courage is our encounter with the truth as it confronts us through our story. Stories are inevitably about human values and motivations, malice as well as idealism. Many screenplays remain unfinished because the writer unconsciously resists letting the full truth in the story emerge. This area of creative courage, or lack of it, is bound up with the issues of authenticity versus escapism. And intimately connected with the question of authenticity is our encounter with ourselves. Drama does have its own organic structure of internal consistency. Characters tend to move toward destinies they have created for themselves, and not all such destinies are pretty. When we as writers try to go against the truth or consistency of a character in order to make the story "work out," we always end up playing a false note. We end up with an unmotivated action or corny, clichéd lines of dialogue. Those we work with are going to point this out to us. They will criticize our writing, as they should, but we will probably take it personally. And, if it is a valid criticism, we *should* take it personally—not to react out of false pride but to help ourselves see our creative blind spots. The false note can be seen as a symptom that we have stepped away from the truth. We have escaped. There is an old Chinese proverb to this effect:

> If the arrow goes astray, the archer is deluded.

Writing is a continuous confrontation with self. Escapism happens when the writer tries to run away from some difficult or uncomfortable reality presented by a scene. Of course, escapism is an option. The screenwriter's escapism is related to the broader cultural escapism that lulls us all. Escapism as I define it here is not to be equated with myth, fantasy, science fiction, or the suspension of disbelief legitimate to storytelling. Escapism means not dealing honestly with the issues you raise. It is frankly easier to cue the carpet of saxophone music and move to a standard love scene where all the emotions are prepackaged, rather than staying with the more edgy and awkward expressions of vulnerability that might better fit the characters. Not many love scenes achieve the individuality, presence, and genuine (because deeply motivated) passion of the famous love scenes in *Chinatown*, *Don't Look Now*, and *Hiroshima Mon Amour*, but those that do stand out as superior achievements.

As we screenwriters are confronted with our characters' egoisms, ambivalences, and shadowy motives, we are likewise confronted with our own. We may believe we are driven by a simple ambition to stand up at the podium and receive our Oscar, but while writing we come face to face with the consequences of our characters' ambitions. It was ambition, after all, that led Macbeth to murder his lord, his best friend, and many innocent people. We have to connect to Macbeth's level of ambition in order to write *Macbeth*. Macbeth is in me! What we write about comes out of us and re-enters us in a creative loop. That's where the creative courage comes in. Some screenwriters decline to write thrillers because their personal experience of the story's shadow world touches them too deeply. Imagine Hannibal Lecter taking up a secret residence in your house for two to three months, the time it takes to write a typical screenplay draft. No one in your family can see him but you, yet everyone feels his presence. Your kids find you distracted; your spouse finds you cold. Is it only their imagination, or *has* something chilling entered your family's life? What do you do when you discover the inhuman coldness of a Hannibal in yourself? Where do you put it, where do you hide it, during dinner when everyone is looking at you?

For, as poets, storytellers, and psychologists have repeated, you cannot encounter something unless it is already in you. What appears to come from without will not register in consciousness unless it corresponds to something within. We are mirrored in the stories we tell. Stories, in the broadest sense, are a living language that makes meaning possible. Just think for a moment how wonderful it is that we can reflect ourselves to ourselves through stories, myths, images, symbols, art, and science. These are vehicles of consciousness. Frank McConnell reminds us that stories are "still the best version of 'self-help' our civilization has invented."[2]

Yet if story is a vehicle that reflects our aspirations and glories, it is also a dark mirror that reflects our failings, our unlived life, and the whole psychological problem of the shadow. How many of us have not said, secretly, along with Ahab, "I would strike the sun if it insulted me!" How many of us have not fantasized, like Don Corleone in *The Godfather*, about making someone "an offer he can't refuse"? How many of us have not, in some momentary fit of blind rage, dreamed, along with the glorious Hannibal, of tearing someone's face off? The

---

2. McConnell, Frank, *Storytelling and Mythmaking* (New York: Oxford University Press, 1979), 3.

hazards and pitfalls of growth as well as the rewards: stories mirror our entire human nature, including the parts we prefer not to look at.

This is a simple acknowledgment of the situation we have as screenwriters. It is not something we need to become anguished or depressed about. Rather, it is something to be handled in a spirit of serious play. Play always involves the capacity to be in two places at once: here in the real world and also in the make-believe world. As Joseph Campbell has noted, the "mask" of play places us in a paradox. The men in elaborate lion costumes in an African ritual simultaneously *must be* and *must not be* the lions they represent. They must let themselves go and really embody the lion spirit and power or the ceremony will not be convincingly alive, but at the same time, they cannot be so taken up in the role that they lose their human consciousness. Somewhere inside, they must recall that it is only "for play." This dual attitude is required of us as well.

Play (and screenwriting as play) is a temporary and partial dissociation. We lose some of our usual ego-control in the process and there is a possibility of losing sight of the limits. Wherever play is, there is also the possibility of *abduction*. Abduction simply means "getting carried away." But what actually happens when we get carried away? Where are we carried away to? It appears that at these moments of abduction some other part of our psyche takes over from our usual, reasonable self. Campbell describes an incident where a professor was working in his study while his two small children played make-believe on the floor with some wooden matchsticks. One matchstick was for Sleeping Beauty, one was for the Prince, and then there was a burnt matchstick for the Wicked Witch. The children had been engrossed in their play and the professor in his work for some minutes when suddenly there was a disturbance. The professor's daughter came running to him, crying, "Take the witch away, daddy! I don't want the witch anymore!"

She had been abducted by the witch. This little girl had slipped over the border from play into something else. The matchstick had literally *become* the witch, meaning that the girl was no longer able to differentiate between them. From this we can guess that the girl herself had become overidentified with Sleeping Beauty, and by so doing she had lost the sense of play. We know we have lost the sense of play when it's not fun anymore or when we feel out of the creative flow and stuck in some way. Feeling stuck is an indication that, like this small girl, we have been abducted or carried away by some part of our psyche. We have lost some measure of consciousness and psychic freedom in terms of perspective and flexibility. Often we enter an overpowering mood or get seized by an overpowering conviction. What makes a linebacker risk a certain fifteen-yard penalty by grabbing a facemask? At exactly what point does a boisterous crowd after a ball game become a mob breaking windows and looting? At exactly what point does playful innuendo in a conversation become interpreted as intrusive? At exactly what point does a lovers' quarrel become physical abuse? These situations all inhabit the ambiguous liminal space of the little girl's burnt matchstick.

Creativity, which is a playful activity, comes, by its very nature, with this ambiguous territory. No screenwriting formula, no witty aphorisms from a screenwriting guru, can take the inherent shiftiness out of the process of writing. Obviously, knowing our craft and feeling comfortable with it helps us reduce unnecessary performance anxiety, but it cannot relieve us of the anxiety of facing the unknown. Creating will always remain an ambiguous adventure, full of shadows. Trying to will ourselves through sheer pragmatism into believing that a screenplay is a sort of machine made up of objective parts or elements makes matters worse than they need to be. By constraining the play element in creation, "boot-camp" willpower takes us out of our creative center and divides us against ourselves. It breeds conflict and denial. Screenwriting and making movies will always be a risky business. There is not a single executive in Hollywood today who can predict with certainty what will be a hit a year from now. The shadowy and uncontrollable aspects of creativity are simply part of our professional territory. Working with them skillfully is part of our professional craft.

One very important thing we can do to support ourselves as writers is to learn how to work with our own process more consciously and cooperatively. We can learn to expand the range of territories in which we can play seriously without getting abducted by the witches we will inevitably encounter along the way. As we learn to bring more of ourselves to our screenwriting while retaining the dual perspective necessary for play (to *feel like* the lion without *becoming* the lion), our writing becomes in fact sharper, more authentic, and more powerful. We become able to handle stronger dramatic truths without getting thrown off-center. We cultivate a balanced and individual approach to models, techniques, and the entire business of screenwriting. We drop false modesty and false pride about our screenwriting because we are engaged and nourished by the flow experience of the act itself.

When we consider screenwriting as a process in itself and not as merely a means to an end, we encounter the screenwriter's journey. This is not simply a day trip to a colorful land of mythic figures. It is certainly not a question of packing a screenplay with spurious fantasy elements, which is another form of escapism. The screenwriter's journey does not take us *away from* our writing but deeper *into* it. It is a journey with real stakes because if we take a wrong turn or have a failure of nerve along the way, the consequence is an unachieved screenplay, critical failure, or even seeing our half-finished opus handed over to another writer. As my partner and I began to lead our first seminars years ago, we came to call the synthesis of the process and product aspects the storytelling perspective. Oral storytelling naturally brings together the process and product in one act. We discover the story in the act of shaping it; we shape it in the act of discovering it. Oral storytelling gives us instantaneous feedback from our audience. We develop a gut sense for when our story is working or not working. We know immediately, if we are willing to be sensitive to it, when we are hung up, out of the flow, or have lost the sense of play.

We are all storytellers. Stories have a universal meta-structure of meaning that speaks to all of us. We are born into this world with the ability to recognize and respond to stories just as we are born with the ability to recognize the meta-structures of language. Stories are a language in themselves, a language made up of events, actions, and gestures rather than letters and words. From the moment we begin to say "Mama," we are activating language centers in the brain—and at the same time we are beginning to tell stories. Screenwriting is an extension of that first act. No matter how demanding and technical a screenplay may become, we are always in the lineage of storytelling that goes back as far as language. We tell stories because they help us make meaning. We do it to entertain. We do it because the creative itch takes us. The movies are the medium the stories pass through on the way from me to you. The medium offers its own playful opportunities and satisfactions. At root it is an involuntary act, an act of soul.

It does turn out that telling our stories aloud is a very good way to shape them and discover what they are really about. We find out what we have to say through the act of saying it. The audience, our listener, lets us know how much exposition we need, whether the dramatic intensity is rising, whether the dramatic stakes are clear. When we can engage our listeners in this way, we can pull out from the told story a strong and clear throughline, the essential thread that holds beginning, middle, and end together, which we can use later as we pitch the story as a potential movie project. Story pitching (telling the story in a session that may last an hour or be as brief as thirty seconds) is a specialized language with its own codes. The storyline we pitch to producers is ideally the product, the quintessence, of our process of storytelling. Once our stories have been tested in the fire of their telling, then they may be strong enough to take the greater heat of a pitch session with a producer or studio development executive.

Encounter and Craft

There are tens of thousands of film stories pitched every year, but few really great movies come out of it. Why is that? Great stories emerge from the conjunction of great craft and intense encounter—"the encounter of an intensely conscious human being with his or her world," as Rollo May puts it. The key quality that allows us to hold craft and encounter together is our capacity to contain the intensity while giving voice to it. This is what the writer's journey is all about. When we can contain what is both in the story and in ourselves—not imprison or deny it—and let our great craft serve that intensity, then we have the possibility of using technique with insight and grace. We have the possibility of allowing that intensity to carry us out of our petty concerns into the mythic dimension, where the great stories come from. Like Jonah swallowed by the whale, we are taken up in something much larger than ourselves.

Great stories have broken through to another level, one that affects us all. It is not just a question of winning and losing. Yes, the hero may win the race and get the girl in the end—or he may not. But we can sense that the great story has other dimensions of meaning. After centuries, the stories of Oedipus and Lear, Ahab and Sleeping Beauty, Antigone and Isis still appear inexhaustible in their meaning. This is something very mysterious. They are not all winners by any means. But there is a kind of "call and response" between something deep within the story and something deep within ourselves. Not all great stories make us feel happy, but they make us feel more alive. They make us aware of the life that lives through us. We could all name movies that have touched us in this deep and mysterious way. For me, those movies include very early experiences of *The Mummy*, *Moby Dick*, and *Vertigo*, as well as most of Chaplin, *2001: A Space Odyssey*, Terrence Malick's *Days of Heaven*, Krzysztof Kieslowski's *Double Life of Veronique*, Clint Eastwood's *Unforgiven*, and *American Beauty*. Please take a moment to name for yourself some favorite movies that have touched you deeply. One sign of such a movie is that you can walk into a room where the movie is playing and be instantly absorbed by it. It still feels fresh and alive even if you haven't seen it for twenty years. We resonate with the story. We are compelled by it, not because of a well-timed series of shocks and explosions, but because of something subtler we can't quite put our finger on.

We can't put our finger on this magic something because the movie is speaking directly to the mythic dimension in ourselves, which is largely unconscious. This is part of the mirroring function of stories. We sense that the movie tells us something universally true. Maybe it captures the spirit of our particular time. The movie may have captured something in our own deepest spirit as well. It speaks the language of soul. We are impelled to see it over and over again. Movies that carry great stories may keep their power for generations, as long as the psychic current between story and audience continues to flow.

Screenplays with this mythic dimension strike a deep chord in those who read them. They are alive even before the "talent" is attached. Great stories with a mythic dimension cannot be created by committee. It is questionable whether they can be *willed* into being at all. As a matter of fact, the screenwriter may experience such a story as an intrusion, a revelation, something thrust upon him against his will. Great stories go beyond craft to the degree that every creative breakthrough takes us into the territory of what precisely we *do not* know, and for which craft is but the necessary preparation.

The mythic dimension of stories lands us at the bedrock questions of life. This is how screenwriter and playwright John Patrick Shanley expresses his sense of this bedrock:

> Who am I? This is a courageous question. As a writer and as a man I am involved in one central struggle—to discover and accept who I am. I believe all fear has its roots in denial. I have, at one time or another, denied everything. Every fact of my specific life. My parents, my Bronx origin, my Americanness, my Irishness, my appetites, my morality, my need for love and acceptance, my jealousy, my violence, my anger.

Screenwriting is storytelling, and storytelling takes us on a journey that changes our perspective. If we are open to the journey, we are carried beyond our old confines into a deeper dimension of life. By telling our stories we cease to be identical with the image we see reflected in the mirror, with the social masks we wear for others, or even with the role of screenwriter. We find a broader, more comprehensive point of view of life.

It has been my experience as a writer, consultant, and teacher that the screenplay we are working on takes us into exactly the issues we need to face at this moment—betrayal, forgiveness, vulnerability, independence, belonging, whatever it may be. The screenplay has an infallible way of getting into our blind spots and burrowing down into our shadow territory. This is a sign that the story has something to teach *us*, though normally we notice nothing until the story breaks down, we get a writer's block, and are forced to examine what went wrong. I want to emphasize that the problem is virtually never one of technique alone. Working out what is wrong in the screenplay always requires the writer to change some attitude. Looking back, it is evident to me that every screenplay I have worked on, whether an original or a commission, was an X-ray of my soul. It exposes me rather completely. In some way I have to admit the story knew me better than I knew myself. The screenplay became my teacher.

This should not be surprising when we consider that the story comes out of the writer. But it is important to personalize this and make it real for yourself through direct experience. Every proposal needs to be tested to see if it's true for *you*. Therefore I invite you to try a small exercise. Think of it as a piece of "internal software" that can help you sharpen yourself as a writer. You shall encounter a series of *Internal Software* exercises throughout the book.

Internal Software: The Café of Inner Voices

- Take just a few minutes and list some current issues or crises in your life. These may be as big as whom to marry or as minor as the fact that you have just run out of dog food. What is the feeling-tone of each?[3]
- As you do this, notice if you are breathing or not. Be aware of where the tension is in your body. We often do not notice, but feelings express themselves through the body. This is true of us as well as our characters.

Continued

3. *Feeling-tone* denotes not a specific emotion but a "state of feeling." We commonly speak of states of mind; a state of feeling or feeling-tone is the condition in our bodies we become aware of evoked by a memory, a color, or a piece of music. We experience it in the body, but not in any one specific place. Each person will have a unique feeling-tone or felt-sense related to the same stimulus, such as a song.

- Pick out the one issue that seems to have the most energy, the one that is the "juiciest."
- Now, for about five minutes, write down what all the interior voices have to say about the problem. Do this as quickly and spontaneously as possible. Don't worry about what voice belongs to whom. Imagine a café table with all these inner characters voicing their opinions about what to do. Write it all down without censoring it.
- After five minutes or so, look back at what all these voices had to say. What conflicting positions arose? What values are at stake? Can you state the opposing values in terms of a choice you have to make? What would be the consequences of each option?

(**Internal Software** exercises are active. They invite you to get up and do something—at which point the book itself may become a hindrance. One very easy way to enhance your experience of the Internal Software games is to make an audio recording of the process instructions, using your own voice or a friend's, and play it back whenever you wish to enter the software.)

Dramatic characters are personifications of all these inner voices. They project conflicts out into a world where we can see them, feel them, and reflect on them. In drama as in life, people have to choose between two values, such as freedom versus belonging. The plot is an expression of this conflict of values. Its language is the language of actions that have consequences. By what we see the character do in response to conflict, we see what value he or she upholds. The key relationships in the story reflect the same conflict on another, more intimate level. Dramatic relationships touch the emotional core of what we stand for. Here, too, the same values are at stake. Outer plot conflict and emotional relationship conflict are driven by a conflict of values *within* the hero of the story that can only be called existential. We go back to John Patrick Shanley's "Who am I?" When push comes to shove, do I choose freedom over belonging, or belonging over freedom? Where do I stand? It is on this deepest level where real character change ultimately takes place. *Action, feeling,* and *being* are all involved when we become aware of our process of choice-making. This reflection gives you a taste of how your creative process structures your story. It gives you a more direct sense of what screenwriters spend their days doing.

To write stories with a mythic dimension, we have to take risks, creative risks—and it is exactly at this point, where we must take the plunge into the unknown of the creative process, that we must be ready to leave models and formulas behind. There, at the threshold where we step into the territory of the story, models can at best be sort of loose maps. At their worst—and I have seen this in so many writers with creative blocks—models can actually be false guides, misleading us and neutralizing our own creative impulses. In the creative endeavor, we must never forget that the map is not the territory.

Creative Darkness

It is usually taken for granted that creative breakthrough is the screenwriter's private business. The writer and producer sign a deal contracting the writer to come up with a treatment or screenplay with specific story elements and design by a certain deadline. The producer's main interest is that the work comes back on time and meets the requirements of the project. Just how the writer gets there is her own problem. Unless the producer is aware of both the product and process aspects of screenwriting, and aware of his own potential as a creative collaborator, the subject of process is not discussed. After all, the boundary issues between writer and producer are complex.

Creativity, the creative process, the creative encounter: these are subjects toward which, in our society, we tend to have a split attitude. On one hand, we idealize creativity. We associate it with brightness and light. Creative people are bright people. Screenwriters who pull in seven-figure contracts for their work must be especially bright, having succeeded in a very difficult system. They are the stars. Stars partake of the aura of genius, and we consider genius to be innate. Part of our idealization of creativity is a belief that while technique can be taught, creativity itself cannot be. I contend that this is one of the reasons there is so much emphasis placed on screenplay models being technical and objective. If the screenwriter fails, the fault is not in the model (so this logic goes), but in the screenwriter's execution. There is something reassuring in this for everyone—except the screenwriter who has not lived up to the ideal. By overidealizing creativity, we mystify it and absolve ourselves of responsibility for it.

Considering the gap that exists between the ideal plan and the real process already leads us into the darker side of creativity. Here we encounter the other side of our split attitude toward creating. We are secretly skeptical, even wary, of creativity. It is notoriously unreliable. It doesn't come when you call. In fact, it tends to disappear when you need it most: when you can't solve a story problem, when you are under pressure and a deadline is looming. Creativity can desert you suddenly, leaving you with a creative block, anxiety attacks, and the prospect of some expensive years of therapy ahead. Because this uncertainty in the creative process runs diametrically counter to our general cultural attitude of mechanistic pragmatism, writers who are creatively stuck can feel especially vulnerable and isolated: "It's all my fault; I'm a screw-up," and so on. If we are serious about making screenwriting our profession, this is something we really need to look at. It turns out that our attitude toward creativity, especially our own creativity, helps determine to a large extent how creative we may be and to what ends we will use our creative efforts. Perhaps creativity cannot be taught, but we *can* learn to cultivate a healthy relationship with it. And this begins by accepting the necessity of creative darkness.

We are all created in the dark. The womb of our mother at the moment we were conceived was a Night World. We tend to forget this very simple fact. Much is made of the experience of creative illumination: how the big light bulb flicks on and everything becomes clear in a flash of insight. Much less is spoken about, and known about, the experience of creative *darkness*. We are afraid of the dark; this is a primal instinct. But in order for the light to provide illumination, there must first have been darkness. Most creation myths begin with a state of dark and confusion. Even before the Big Bang, there was creative darkness! As the act of conception tells us, darkness is fertile. Darkness has potential. Darkness sharpens our senses. The symbol of the Tao tells us the truth about this: we see a light half and a dark half intertwined:

The dynamic interaction of the two is what makes the Tao. We must be lost before we can be found. We must be in the dark before we can be illuminated. Clarity, or consciousness, is only conceivable in relation to the unconscious.

We in the West come from a long historical tradition where light and dark are not to be taken as aspects of a dynamic whole, but are rigidly separated. Light is good, sacred, angelic, progressive. Dark is bad, demonic, instinctual, and regressive. These rigid categories still influence us today. And then, in addition, our pragmatic, goal-oriented minds want to say: "Skip the darkness, just give me the light. Stop all this fumbling around and get to the point! Just give me the finished product!" Let it be like magic, for this is how the light-side of the creative process appears. We want to see the screenwriter get up at the Oscars and receive his award. Cut to the chase. But as my partner Tom explained the screenwriter's real challenge most succinctly, compelling screenwriting is predicated on your ability to be with the thoughts and feelings that arise when you are alone with the creative uncertainty of conceiving, developing, and writing your screenplay.

A few years back I was conducting a seminar in Milan and my friend Andrea de Micheli, who was producing the seminar, came up with a metaphor to headline the publicity that at first surprised me. The ads read:

Are you a creative miner?
Come spend a weekend in the mine!

It was a daring, provocative concept, because the image is not immediately appealing. We are so attached to images of getting to the top—who wants to be a miner? It's dirty and dangerous! But Andrea's metaphor was exactly to the point.

Here we are confronted with both the yin and yang of the creative process. Metaphorically we could say that there is one side of the creative process that is like mountain climbing. We climb to the top of the mountain of facts, of data, inputs, conditions. We *surmount* a problem. We rise above it to a higher perspective, an elevated perspective. And because we have gotten to the top and the mountain goes no further—and we can go no further—we conclude that we have "made it." We have won. We have beaten the mountain. This mountain metaphor is loosely identified with the aspect of creativity we call "problem solving." Its virtues are strategy, teamwork, leaving nothing to chance, and "getting in the groove" to execute the plan. For all this to work, it is essential that we see the goal clearly before we begin.

We justly celebrate the problems we have overcome. It is our challenges and problems that force us to become competent and adapted to life. But we overestimate this bright, problem-solving side of creativity if we believe this is all there is to it. Otherwise there would not be so many writers compelled to keep a bottle of Jack Daniels next to the typewriter or do a line of cocaine before sitting down at the computer. There is something that the problem-solving, mountain-climbing attitude does not take into account when it comes to writing a screenplay or making a movie. This is that the goal cannot be *exactly* known before we start. It can only be approximately, tentatively known. Nailing everything down before even writing the screenplay would naturally kill the creative process. The characters would have no room to breathe. Yet when we as screenwriters—or as producers or development executives—approach the screenplay exclusively as a product, we tend to view it as a mountain to be climbed.

The other, darker aspect of creativity, as Andrea suggested, is being a miner. This image is less romantically heroic, less grandiose. It doesn't conjure up visions of fabulously successful screenwriters zooming along the L.A. freeways in their Porsches while making big deals on their cell phones. But thinking of oneself as a miner is much closer to how it feels day after day to get down into the story: suiting up in worn overalls, putting on a hard hat, taking a rattling cage elevator down into the dark—and don't forget to take your canary to tell you when you are running out of oxygen! This is a much more accurate image for the journey into the unknown that we confront each day when we sit down before the blank white page or the blank, scintillating computer screen. We chip away at it, line after line. We clear out the debris. Sometimes the story problems are hard, resistant. We hack at them. We are tempted to use dynamite. And sometimes we are sure we've hit a seam of pure gold.

A movie is made of dazzling light projected through a celluloid curtain. This is what we in the audience read as a movie. But the story starts out in darkness, just as we ourselves were conceived in darkness. To the outer world, the successful screenwriter may appear to be the winner who has climbed the peak of the film industry to wealth and fame. But while he is actually on the job, the writer is someone stumbling around in a darkened room, trying to piece together a jigsaw puzzle which is all over the floor. Writers are like this not because they are strange, under the influence, or romantically tormented, but because this is an unavoidable part of the process.

Actually, it would be fairer and more complete to say we use both mountain-creativity and mine-creativity all the time in complementary phases. They alternate in us like day and night. We dig down into the story, into the act of writing, and each time we do so we risk losing ourselves, getting abducted. We do lose ourselves. In order to enter the territory, we must step off the map. Now the story is taking us. We become for some time unselfconscious vehicles for the story energy. At these moments we are in the flow, but we may not know where we are going. And then there are times we pull back, come up for air, climb out to get a better perspective. We look at how the motifs are building; we wonder if we are headed in the right direction or made a wrong turn back a ways. Is that scene too static? Did we foreshadow the next plot turn? Will anybody like these characters? And so on. Maybe we revise our outline. Then we dive back into the mine again.

This is the rhythm that occupies us, day after day, draft after draft. Anton Ehrenzweig, who researched this aspect of creativity, refers to these two phases as "conscious planning" (mountain) and "unconscious scanning" (mine).[4] The double-tracking of mine and mountain creativity stimulates us and stresses us during every working moment. Creative darkness has been unacknowledged in discussions and books on screenwriting, but in fact it is the "primal scene" of creation, to which the writer must become initiated.

The Entry Point: Uncertainty

This talk about going down into the creative mine and encountering creative darkness is not a mere metaphor. It is not just a pretty figure of speech. It is a way of describing the *actual* experience of screenwriting. The fact that it is subjective does not make it any less real, but because it is subjective we can only talk about it indirectly, by way of analogy. We have said that creative screenwriting has to do with the way we handle fear, the fear and anxiety that surface in the act of writing.

The best way of focusing this broad subject of fear and creativity is through a single word, uncertainty: *uncertainty* in the face of the unknown. Every new screenplay project, every day when we sit down to work, is a brand-new and unprecedented experience, an entire Hero's Journey in miniature. We step off

4. Ehrenzweig, Anton, *The Hidden Order of Art* (Berkeley: University of California Press, 1967).

the map into uncharted regions. Even an actor is not absolutely certain what inflection he will give to a line of dialogue until he actually delivers it—and at that point the dialogue is already codified in the text. How much more uncertainty must the screenwriter carry in relation to lines that have never yet been spoken, heard, or printed? We do not know what the next word, or the next scene, will be until it appears. We do not know how the characters will get out of their conflicts. It is all emerging from creative darkness as we write it. And as it is emerging, we are forced to sit with, tolerate, and ultimately embrace the uncertainty of the process.

Uncertainty seems to bring up experiences of creative chaos and resistance. If you have ever tried to write a full-length script, the following scenario is bound to be familiar to you.

You have announced to all your friends that you are working on a new screenplay. You have spent some months developing the story: working out the plot, creating character sketches, refining a treatment. Maybe you have just inked a contract and have used the first installment of the fee to pay down your credit cards. In any case, today is the big day, the day you promised yourself you would begin the draft. Everything has been arranged: the laundry has been done, the kids are at day care, the dog has been taken for his morning trot and is contentedly gnawing a ham bone. The desk has been ritually laid out. The bills have been removed and hidden on the floor, because everyone knows you can't write a great script while staring at unpaid bills! Your outline is neatly to the left of your computer and two sharpened #2 pencils are to the right to catch inspirational flashes. You have searched through your entire CD collection to find the perfect music: energizing but not distracting. And now you're ready . . . aren't you?

Well, there's just the last detail: a nice mocha latté. Then everything will be perfect. Because how can you write a great screenplay without that warm, supportive rush of caffeine to get you started? In two minutes, java heaven is ready. There you are now, settled down at the computer, latté in hand. That blank screen is staring up at you, virgin territory waiting to be staked out. Really, it takes so little to start a screenplay. All you have to do is type the words FADE IN. That's all. You crack your knuckles once, fingers hovering over the keyboard . . .

. . . and this is when you find yourself suddenly abducted by aliens. My partner Tom did some intensive scientific research on this phenomenon and concluded that that alien abduction is the only hypothesis that accounts for the facts. What happens is that you lose consciousness (which always happens in those alien-abduction stories). Minutes . . . hours . . . days may have passed while you were imprisoned in the spaceship and subjected to terrifying medical experiments—but your memory has been erased. Next thing you know, you come back to consciousness to find yourself standing in the kitchen with an empty bag of Oreos in your hands. An hour has passed and nothing has been written. It's spooky. You rush back to the computer, driven now by guilt.

Every screenwriter has his or her own version of this "alien abduction" story. Some writers are compelled to go out to a café just when it is time to sit down and write, the rationale being that they work better in a lively environment. Then, lo and behold, a friend shows up and forces the writer to talk for an hour and a half. Others feel the itch to check their e-mail, "just to get it out of the way." That may be good for an entire morning's diversion. We identify these distractions as *resistance*. We want to write, we want to succeed, but there are invisible forces holding us back. And how are we taught to handle resistance? Normally, through a combination of shame and bullying. "Pull yourself together! No pain, no gain! If you don't write five pages today, I won't let you smoke your cigar tonight!" Look at the image of Carolyn in *American Beauty*, slapping herself and shouting "Wimp!" and "Crybaby!" because she failed to sell a house. This is a cultural trope we all recognize. This treatment usually succeeds in getting us back to the computer for the time being, but it doesn't quell the resistance. How can we talk about screenwriting without mentioning resistance? It's like talking about conception without mentioning sexual intercourse. Three varieties of resistance can in fact be differentiated, as we will explore further in Chapter Ten. At the moment we are interested in the first of these, resistance as a response to uncertainty.

In effect, resistance persists because it does something for us. It screens from view something *else* we don't want to look at, something harder to handle than the resistance itself. What distracting resistance screens is the sensation of losing control. The situation is very much like those characters typically find themselves in in horror movies. We have the uncanny feeling that we are not alone. We have opened up, unlocked the doors to the imagination, and suddenly we are uncomfortable. There is somebody in the basement of our psychic house. Who's down there? We have no wish to meet whoever it is, and this is what our distracting resistance does for us. It screens our anxiety in the face of the *daemon*. Daemon is not the same as demon, though it may feel like it. Socrates spoke of his daemon. This was the Greek word that in Latin became *genius*. But this "genius" is not a personal possession of the ego. Of all the aspects of creativity, genius is least under our control. Since time immemorial, people have wondered where their bursts of inspiration and creativity "came from." The experience of the creative daemon or genius is the encounter with the *other* spirit in us who appears to send us creative ideas from some zone we can only say is outside our conscious awareness. We cannot call the daemon or genius identical with ourselves. It is the height of naïveté to imagine that "I" thought it all up. In reality, it came into my head. The rest is an interpretation, a cover story. We are confronted with an "other," like Faust was confronted with Mephistopheles. Creativity that takes us beyond problem solving requires us to encounter this other force and to cultivate a relationship with it.

It is ironic that the strategies we use to keep the daemon—our genius or creative intuition—at bay so often involve us in repeating unfortunate patterns we learned as children. As we were shamed and bullied into performing as kids, so we tend to shame and bully the creative child within into performing for us. Part of us identifies with the "boss," the judgmental parent, and this certainly allows us to feel less vulnerable. Such an identification is what we call a "control fantasy." On the positive side, the control fantasy allows us to adapt and function, even to be the "good" boys and girls our parents—and by extension, society—want us to be. On the negative side, the creativity that comes out of the control fantasy is cramped, because we have split ourselves. We identify with the part that remains above, within the control fantasy, while another part we are only dimly aware of feels menaced by the creative daemon, and reacts with fear. We voluntarily limit our creative efforts to what we think will bring us rewards from the control system. Meanwhile, the creative daemon, the real source of potential genius, is kept confined to the basement (the creative unconscious), where it languishes.

Books about how to write screenplays are usually based on the analysis of successfully completed hit movies. This is a position safely within the control fantasy. They often make it appear that writing a screenplay is the easiest thing in the world. Their solutions seem magical because they are presented without the process by means of which the goal was reached. There is just the beautiful product: the baby without the tedious pregnancy or the agony of birth. *Chinatown* is certainly a great story. It may even be the "perfect" script some claim it to be. But it may *not* be an appropriate model for what you have to express. The model for you may not exist yet. You may have to make up the model as you go along. What models could Alan Ball and Sam Mendes draw from in creating *American Beauty*? Clearly, we can sense that David Lynch was guided as much by his daemon as by audience tastes in making *Mulholland Drive*. These are filmmakers forging their own paths. Strong inner (and outer) resistance normally accompanies new and challenging stories because they raise greater fears: fear of rejection, certainly, but also fear of being overwhelmed by the force of the daemon. Stories that take successful risks grow out of writers who, through their courage of encounter, have let the daemon speak what needs to be said in new ways.

The Creative Approach to Resistance

There is another, completely different approach to resistance, distraction, and the shadow of whoever that is in our basement. Fear and repression are not the only way. That completely different approach is simply *not running away* from the experience. When uncomfortable sensations and feelings come up, when you want to run to the kitchen, to the cookie jar, to the telephone or television *contain the impulse. Observe* what is happening. Rather than going unconscious and finding yourself later with chocolate all over your face, simply observe that you have the impulse to escape by eating. Rather than overcompensating by bullying yourself—"Snap out of it!"—simply observe that you have the impulse to bully yourself. Rather than acting it out, contain the conflict of these contrary impulses we call resistance. This may feel uncomfortable at first, but it builds creative "heat" and does not allow it to dissipate. Resistance is actually a symptom of the energy that is in the story. When we fall into one of our escape patterns, the energy dissipates. But when we catch the impulse and feed that energy back into the screenplay, the power of our writing builds up. There are four steps to this process:

1. Catch the moment when an impulse to escape appears.
2. Instead of acting out the impulse, sit with it and feel the emotional qualities it carries: anxiety, fear, excitement, etc.
3. Once you feel the emotion, ask yourself what the connection is between what *you* are feeling right now and what *your character* is feeling right now, at this point in the story or the current scene you are writing.
4. Where would your character like to escape to, and what keeps her from escaping? This takes you toward the heart of the dramatic conflict. Where would *you* like to escape to? What fantasies are awakened by the impulse to escape? Can you consciously make an agreement with yourself to remain present?

This is what we mean by feeding the creative heat back into the screenplay.

Henry Fonda made the shrewd and much-quoted observation that "Acting is the art of doing nothing well." Screenwriting is much the same, in a certain sense. By not reacting to "fix" the anxiety and uncomfortable sensations we experience in the creative process, but rather by simply allowing it all to be present, we invite complexity. We invite the daemon, the creative spirit, by letting it know that we are a strong container. But "doing nothing" is the hardest thing in the world for many of us to do. The only way to know is to try it.

So try it.

Spend two minutes doing *nothing*. No agenda. Do you think you can? Put down the book, and see what happens in two minutes. . . .

Of course, it is not possible to literally do nothing for two minutes. Things start to happen. Your mind wanders. You look at your watch. And you become aware of voices inside. We call these voices "self-talk." The voices start commenting on what you're doing. They say things like:

> "Well, *this* is pretty stupid! It's totally dumb! Whoever heard of writing a screenplay by just sitting and doing nothing?"
>
> "If anyone saw me right now. . . . I must look ridiculous."
>
> "You mean you paid *money* for that book? You loser!"
>
> "You're wasting your time!"
>
> "Just who do you think you are, anyway? Think *you're* gonna write the next *American Beauty*? Who are you trying to kid?"
>
> "Why don't you face reality and get a *real* job!"

Within a minute the self-talk usually comes up full-blast. It gets louder the longer we try to sit with uncertainty. The volume of the self-talk is a gauge of the level of our anxiety. And anxiety is emotional energy that wants to move, but has nowhere to go.

As writers, this is just what we are looking for: to bring these voices out into the open. It's the inner café table again! Here, the cacophony is a little different because the cast of interior characters is not quite the same—or, they are not in the same mood as before. With the "present crisis" exercise there is usually a mix of constructive and critical opinions. In the case of doing nothing, our uncertainty tends to bring out more sharp, frustrated, even hysterical tones of judgment. These particular inner voices are our inner threshold guardians. Every time we want to do something new in life or take a risk, these voices pop up to warn us. The part-selves, or complexes, to which these voices belong believe, in a manner of speaking, that they are doing us a favor. They believe they are protecting us from disaster. The thing about inner threshold guardian voices, however, is that they overreact. They react rigidly and categorically to perceived threats, but they have no common sense, no objectivity. Thus these voices really resist us when we want to move forward with something new. Every screenwriter is faced with this, and learns ways to deal with it.

As we let go of some control in an exercise like doing nothing, and move into the uncertainty and unknown of the present moment, not knowing what is going to happen next, it can feel like we're breaking down. We might even imagine we're going mad as the old ways try to hang on. This is the universal feeling state that arises when fear creates tension in the body. We are confronting the fears, and in the process becoming more aware of them. Every hero's journey is about breaking down in order to break through, and exactly here is the starting point: the energy of awareness straining against an outmoded status quo.

So let's try the exercise again, now with this small foreknowledge of where we are headed.*

This time, as you let go and do nothing, take two deep breaths through your nose, down into your abdomen. Let your belly swell with the inhalation like a big spinnaker.

Exhale smoothly all the way out.

Now take a third inhalation. When you exhale this third time, do it softly through pursed lips. Imagine that if you held a down feather before your pursed lips, your breath would not even stir it. That's good. Continue like that for a moment.

This deep breathing probably makes you feel calmer. It helps bring the mind and body back into accord.

Make the conscious decision to let go.

Of thoughts. Of expectations.

* With this and other real-time exercises, it may be helpful to make an audio recording of the exercise so that you are free to close your eyes and listen to the playback.

You may never have thought about it, but as you relax, more perceptions in fact become available to you. And perceptions are potentially more objective and reliable when not distorted by the fear of losing control. Let your awareness scan your body. See if you are holding tension anywhere. Perhaps the diaphragm. Or the shoulders. Or the throat. Writers, as expressive individuals, often feel their energy caught at the organ of expression in the throat. Allow that tension to dissolve as you breathe deeply and calmly. If thoughts or self-talk come in, just let them drift right out again. Now you are going into openness. There is no right or wrong, no success or failure to this exercise. Allow yourself to be surprised.

How do you feel after two minutes of this? Refreshed? What kind of access to your creativity do you perceive yourself as having right now? When we are relaxed and breathing deeply, it seems to be impossible for the inner monkey-mind voices, the self-talk, to take over. Somehow we really cannot do both at the same time because they are two distinctly different psycho-physiological states. Now we are able to observe the self-talk without buying into it. So this gives us the responsibility that comes with choice. It is not God's command that inner demons should zap our energy. It is something we choose, even if we choose it unconsciously by not knowing better how to manage our creative resource. Exercising conscious, intentional choice is predicated on developing a discipline of awareness in the face of uncertainty. It is a discipline, not to just sit and write blindly, nor to bully ourselves into writing, but to write with this openness and reflective awareness in the body. Yes, it is a responsibility we take on, to build a container and open space where a greater intensity of creative encounter can take place. But once you have experienced it, you won't want to go back.

Even when we try to add reasonable levels of control by writing treatments and outlines and by engaging in story conferences, we sooner or later come to the point where the outline breaks down. Not only does it inevitably break down according to a kind of Murphy's Law for screenwriters—it *must* break down. It is part of the writer's journey that the plan must break down so that it can be superseded by a more authentic vision of the story. There was nothing wrong with the earlier ideas; they were simply what we call "starter ideas," and they are necessary to bring us this far. Without break*down* there can be no break*through*. The story plan grinds to a halt and we are left face to face with the openness of wonderful, perilous possibility. We step off the map into the territory. This is when the writing has a chance to get real. Every step is a step into the unknown. Here we stand at the threshold crossing of our creative adventure.

Screenwriting does make very special formal and technical demands on the writer. New screenwriting software can format the page correctly and effortlessly for us, but it can't tell us what write. All of the important aspects of screenwriting, from plot to character, from the most universal level of the theme to the minutest gesture of an actress's hand, are addressed in the chapters that follow. It is possible, however, to become overwhelmed with all the technical rules and details, as well as with the interpersonal stresses of developing the script. It is easy to forget that we took up screenwriting because we *enjoy* it. We enjoy it because it makes us feel uniquely alive and in the flow. What we essentially want to do when we write is to release the stories we have inside us. We want to unlock the creativity that is there, inside. Techniques are our tools to get where we want to go; they should not draw too much attention to themselves in the process. A logical conclusion from this would be that we get ourselves into trouble when we interfere too much with a process that should flow naturally. Psychologist Mihály Csíkszentmihályi describes the *flow state* as one in which we become unselfconsciously immersed in an activity. We forget about time and experience playful, concentrated delight in what we are doing. We must learn and internalize objective techniques, just as a musician does, so that we can play within the field of our craft. Inner blocking self-talk and distractions, for their part, can become raw material to be fed back into the story we are creating. Moving past the inner threshold guardians to the deeper centeredness we have tasted above prepares us to open up to this flow state.

We call this process moving from self-consciousness to self-awareness. It is part of cultivating screenwriting as a way of life. We must encounter uncertainty but cannot afford to be blocked by it, so by learning to contain it we bring it into the creative flow. "Self-consciousness" means being made painfully aware that in some way we are not "okay": we forgot the producer's name, we accidentally knocked over the bottle of pop on the conference table, we spilled soup on our pants, and so on. "Self-awareness" means being in the flow state while keeping our center. "Keeping our center" means maintaining that certain awareness that we are playing, not allowing ourselves to get abducted, neither by inner voices nor by overidentification with our characters, our story, or the glamour of the movie business. All of these positive strengths derive from the act of facing uncertainty.

When we can write from self-awareness, we can dance with uncertainty. Screenwriting becomes a practice, like the martial arts. There is, as we have suggested, a call and response between something in the depths of the story and something in the depths of ourselves. It can give us a funny, uncanny feeling, like being an animal on the scent of a trail, when we get close to what is calling us. To find words and images to express *that*—the secret thing that calls us through the story and drives us to create—*that* is the excitement of writing. That's what is primal and vital about it. The goal of our work, the production of our screenplay into a movie that will be seen by millions, is in the future. The act of writing has to be in the *now*.

Great Craft: Through Encounter to Authentic Imagination

In this chapter we are developing a more conscious relationship to the creative resource. When we realize that the story we are working on mirrors back to us both known and unknown aspects of our total selves, and when we can accept the challenge of containing uncertainty in the writing process, then we can sustain a more intense level of encounter. Encounter asks us to perceive and respond to the wholeness of a situation with the wholeness of our own integrity. As a result, we are literally able to see more in the story: more plot possibilities, more levels of conflict, more universal themes. I consider this to be the one fundamental skill a writer needs to possess, upon which all other technique is built. We are talking about your instrument, tuning your instrument. The instrument has to be in tune before it can play wonderful music. The instrument, in this case, is you yourself. Or, to use another metaphor, you are a factory—but a factory that cannot be split off from wholeness. This factory has to be producing day after day, churning out scenes and sequences. Those pages don't just write themselves! If the factory goes down, production stops. If we catch a bad flu three weeks into a draft, we may miss a crucial deadline. If we get stalled by a writer's block, we may lose a contract. If we can't retool our factory to incorporate new methods to handle new assignments, to respond to the conditions of the market *now*, we will not succeed. The point is that these are not merely "mechanical" problems. Creative blocks are symptoms that our rapport with the story has suffered a breakdown, that we are "out of tune" with it. Therefore, how we manage ourselves and take conscious responsibility for our own creative process does make a difference.

If we know how to tune our instrument, and keep it in tune, we may then be able to use *technique with insight*. That already distinguishes us from the mass of screenwriters who are mechanically hitting all the plot points, but without insight. The foundation of insight is our intensity of encounter: the courage to be present, to stay present, to stay awake, moment by moment, in the act of creation. Everything that would seem to block us can then be turned around and used to increase our intensity of encounter, as long as we are willing to consciously contain our inner conflict. Turning around negative energy coming at us, from within or without, and using it to our advantage, is a kind of inner Aikido. The four basic energy principles of Aikido fit perfectly well as a guide to practicing screenwriting as a way of life:

1. Keep "one point" in your lower abdomen (stay centered and concentrated).
2. Keep weight underneath (stay grounded and connected to your own gravity).
3. Relax completely.
4. Extend *ki* (intensify the encounter, go to meet whatever is coming—while remaining centered, grounded, and relaxed). *Ki* (*chi* in Chinese) is thought of as the universal energy that animates the universe, the energy of *Tao*.

The founder of Aikido, O-Sensei Ueshiba, was a small man, an elderly man, but these qualities did not pose a limitation to his art. Ueshiba commonly gave public demonstrations where he would be attacked by eight big black belts at once. With a seemingly effortless grace, he would send the attackers spinning off in all directions. He took the attackers' own aggressive energy and turned it onto something he could use.

After one of these demonstrations, the awed students asked, "How can you keep your center in the midst of all the frantic action?" Ueshiba's reply was illuminating: "I don't keep my center. I am constantly being thrown off center. You just can't see how quickly I get back to it again." This makes the basic point about working with the energies that come up while we are writing. We use them the way this master used his partners. We use them to make ourselves into screenwriters capable of great craft: able to use technique with insight because we are able to sustain an intensity of encounter.

Stories, ultimately, are energy. Stories are structures of energy, made up of energy. They are our very nature. Psychologist Jean Houston has quipped that we are "many-storied beings." Each layer of our physical structure comes with its own instructions and tells its own story, down to the story told by our DNA. Carl Jung, who was a physician and psychiatrist as well as a psychologist, conjectured further that one reason the number four and divisions into four are so universally symbolic of wholeness in myths and dreams may be because the carbon atom, central to all organic life, has four valences. When we tell stories, we hook into the story energy that is right there in our bodies. The wisdom of our bodies leads us naturally toward the deep meta-structure of stories we shall be describing in detail in the next chapter, The Mythic Dimension of Screenwriting. As that and the following chapters will show, the more concrete and specific we become in our application of techniques, the more aware we become that we are always working with energy. Every action, every line of dialogue, is orchestrating an energetic feeling experience for the audience.

The dynamic of storytelling brings forth what Joseph Campbell termed the "energy of aspiration," our deepest impulse toward growth and wholeness. It gives that energy a natural channel and expression. This is another aspect of great craft. The drive toward growth and wholeness is universal and innate. In the practice of screenwriting, wholeness expresses itself as a more authentic relationship to our work and ourselves. Authenticity means being true to what we discover as we write. By writing with awareness, we uncover basic parallels between what our characters encounter through dramatic conflict and what we ourselves encounter through the process of writing. We come to see the hook between our characters' backstory wounds and the hidden wounds we ourselves carry. Universal values emerge, and with them a broader, less sentimental empathy that deeply touches the hearts of the audience.

How, concretely, do we use this internal process to make ourselves better screenwriters? First, on an immediate, pragmatic level, we can feed the energy from our distracting inner voices back into the scene we are writing. The dramatic content of every scene is based on characters who have wants that are in conflict;* another character is blocking the hero's movement toward her plot

* Scene structure and the dynamics of conflict within scenes are covered in Chapter Ten.

goal. The specific content of the blocking is different, but if we pay attention we may notice that the tone and "voice" of our own inner threshold guardian has much in common with the antagonist in the scene. There is a dynamic they share. It may be the voice of a father, mother, teacher, boss, or authority figure—the one who says "no" to our aspirations. Or it may be a tempter who tugs at us from below. This is a great opportunity to make our scene better by bringing our own authentic feelings into it.

Then, second, we become aware that the parallel journey we take along with our characters becomes the audience's journey as well. We learn to use our own nature to create the emotional and psychological subtext of the screenplay, that implicit dialogue the audience addresses to the screen. The subtext is what is *not* written on the screenplay page, but is designed to impact the audience subliminally. Part of great craft is knowing how to orchestrate both the text and the subtext for the audience. A screenwriter arrives at this level of communication with the audience, which goes beyond technique, by cultivating empathic awareness.

And third, on a deep, personal level, practicing a discipline of awareness while writing brings us more of the excitement, astonishment, and joy of creation.

Great craft is a confluence of mastery of technique and a heightened capacity for encounter. It is our ability to know both the market and the human heart well enough to reconcile the demands of both. Great craft keeps technique grounded in encounter, that is, the story problems force us to develop greater awareness as human beings, and greater awareness gives us greater capacity to use technique with insight. It helps keep our work grounded in the reality of our shared human experience and helps us get clear about the values at stake in the drama.

In its essence, drama is about *growth through crisis*. The dramatic crisis ultimately involves a tension of opposing values that goes to the very root of what it means to be human. We are almost never aware, when we start working on a script, what it is *really* about, what universal values are really at stake. At the start, we are typically most concerned with making the plot work out. But the universal tension of opposites is not identical to the plot conflict as we first conceive of it or see it presented. It is not:

- Will Lester consummate his infatuation with his daughter's girlfriend Angela? (*American Beauty*)
- Will Loretta marry Johnny? (*Moonstruck*)
- Will John Book bring the killers to justice? (*Witness*)
- Will the wildcat oil drillers save the planet? (*Armageddon*)

These are throughline plot questions. They are vitally important to the success of the screenplay. But the plot itself is the carrier and expression of a deeper and more universal conflict. Through the problems we encounter while writing—the plot won't work out, actions are unmotivated, the characters are flat or badly orchestrated, etc.—we find ourselves in difficulty. Why are we having so much trouble? We suspect that we have blind spots. The work of revision is a process of finding out what we are really trying to say—or what the story is trying to tell us! For most writers, it is this road of trials and frustrations, this repeated firing of raw dramatic events into dramatic steel that ultimately yields gold: the level of truth where writer, hero, and audience are revealed in their deeply shared humanity.

Movie plots concern themselves with local, egoistic, or social values, but underneath there is a universal level, a conflict all human beings must deal with in one way or another. Consider these pairs of opposing values identified in Buddhism as the Eight Worldly Dharmas:

Pleasure	⟷	Pain
Gain	⟷	Loss
Fame	⟷	Disgrace
Praise	⟷	Blame

We are always, in some way, to some extent, being driven by these forces. So are all of our characters. So is our audience. For human beings, there is no escape from the Eight Worldly Dharmas. The wisdom of the Buddhist Middle Way suggests that when we get pulled to one side, to one term of the pair, we inevitably experience suffering. The more we cling to one pole, the more we draw the other to us: attachment to pleasure generates the fear of pain. As individuals, we must learn the lessons over and over again through the crises life presents. The model of the Eight Worldly Dharmas makes the point that dramatic growth through crisis involves overcoming a false, one-sided attitude toward life in favor of one that manifests a deeper balance, vision, and integrity.

The universal value at stake in a drama is a deeper, invisible, and more compelling layer of conflict, yet it is what gives meaning to the plot conflict. It is ultimately what makes a story into a drama. The hero is attached to one side, to one of the opposites, but the universal level embraces both. The hero discovers this level through shattering conflict. We, the writers, have to dig for it. That's why we are willing to put on dirty overalls and go down into the creative mine. That's why Robert Towne, the author of *Chinatown*, had to spend months of agonizing "frenetic passivity" in the belief that he would never succeed with his script. That was his way of digging. And that is why, though it is technically possible to write a screenplay in twenty-one days, it is unlikely that the result will carry significant meaning. It looks like a screenplay and sounds like a screenplay, but it hasn't been through the darkness or the fire. A screenplay demands our own response to a universal dilemma, an authentic vision on our part.

Authentic vision cannot simply be willed, or we would all be doing it. It takes a collaboration of conscious and unconscious forces, as Anton Ehrenzweig's work has shown. Therefore, what we want from screenwriting technique is more than a paint-by-numbers approach to plot points. We want a technique that will carry us to the core, to the essence, of what our screenplay is really about. This approach to our craft of opening up to the unknown is not just a convenience in dealing with distracting resistance and blocking anxiety. It is in fact opening *us* up. If we open up enough, we may experience that the story has a force and a life of its own. We go to our desk in the morning with the conviction that the story has been waiting for us—even impatiently! The characters exist in a world that is very real; they don't cease to exist when we break for lunch. Now they speak for themselves. Authenticity in screenwriting does not mean, "I am in total control!" It means that we allow ourselves to become vehicles for the story energy while remaining aware enough to balance our concern for the process with concern for our end goal: the finished and successfully marketed screenplay.

When we really get into the writing, the story takes on an autonomous life. This can feel glorious—and it can also bring with it some tremendous headaches. We shall address the complexities of this level of writing in Chapter Twelve: The Creative Journey of Story Development. For the moment, we may observe that this "autonomy" of the story is a manifestation of a psychic shift that has taken place. The story is now being projected out of a different part of ourselves. The fact that the story has taken on a life of its own means that it no longer belongs to the ego. It is no longer "mine." The screenplay is now in a twilight zone, the play-flow zone, where it also receives energy, images, and structuring dynamics from the unconscious. We are off the map. The story can now surprise us. It might be a frog who turns into a prince. It might be a prince who turns into an alien. Managing the energies at this level is also part of the great craft of writing a screenplay.

Projection and Reflection as Screenwriting Skills

It is essential for us as writers to know something about projection and how it works. Projection is a natural phenomenon. We all do it. Projection is first of all an automatic way of handling new or unfamiliar situations. We spontaneously project a known context around an unknown in order to grasp it. We do this by constructing comparisons and analogies. An American arrives in Minsk for the first time and the thought keeps running through his head, *This reminds me of Buffalo*. Whenever we grasp the new by means of comparison with the old, we have in effect thrown a mental lasso around it. Now there is a complexity. How do young children learn by projection, since they start off without a base of experience to use for comparisons? It seems that young children compare the new input with those internal form/potential schemata we term "archetypes." The existence of a resource of inborn schemata has been proven by the Nobel Prize-winning research of biologists Konrad Lorenz and Niko Tinbergen. For example, newborn chicks respond with panic when the silhouette of a chicken hawk is drawn on a wire over their coop, but not to silhouettes of gulls or blue jays. The chicks also fail to react when the chicken hawk silhouette is drawn overhead backward. Thus the image is quite specific that releases an equally specific adaptive reaction. There is no possibility that this was learned from experience; rather the image was *released* from a storehouse or file of pattern-potentials that was already on the hard drive, so to speak. Likewise, in very early childhood, our outer experience is driven more by the archetypal/instinctual potentials inside than to memory or to learned behavior. Patterns of archetypal projection are apparent in the first three months of life.[5] But even when we are older, there is always the possibility that archetypes or complexes from inside ourselves will also be cast like lassos around some person or object in our environment. This is what typically happens in projections onto individuals. Our intuition also projects outward from the constellation of known factors in a situation, such as stock market trends, to not yet visible potential consequences. Intuitive story consultants can read the first few pages of a script and their mental maps are already laying out the development potentials and pitfalls.

Some aspects of projection are semiconscious, but more often projection is a completely unconscious act. We go to a party and there is someone in the room that we instantly can't stand. We say they rub us the wrong way, or we call it an "instinctual dislike." This reaction in fact has little to do with instinct. We call it instinct for convenience because we have no rational explanation. Yet if we don't fall for the facile solution, and instead pursue the matter a bit further, we come upon a kind of irrational conviction. We are sure that woman is a schemer. We are sure the guy in the slick, thousand-dollar Italian suit can't be trusted. The one in the old motorcycle jacket is probably a junkie—he can't really be the producer! A BMW convertible jumps into our lane on the freeway, dangerously cutting us off, and we see the quintessential dot.com yuppie at the wheel, yakking on his cell phone. In the instant it takes us to lean on the horn, we have already created a scenario in our heads: we "know" exactly what kind of asshole this is. In reality, we know nothing except the inner movie we have projected for ourselves.

Or we walk into the party, see someone, and instantly fall in love. From the point of view of projection, it's the same difference. In both types of situations we really don't know who that other person is at all. The person is serving as a movie screen onto which we project a movie of our own creating. Yes, there may be a few bits of actual data that evoke the projection, but the unreliability of even these "facts" is attested to by how easily we fall in and out of love. But, since *we* did not make the projection consciously, then neither was it our conscious ego that invented the story, the movie in our heads. So who was it? This is especially intriguing, because when the lasso of our projection whirls around a person or object, it can fit so perfectly and invisibly that we absolutely believe our projection *is reality!* As long as we are in love with someone, we have unshakeable faith

5. Especially the projection of the Self onto the mother. See Neumann, Erich, *The Child* (New York: Harper and Row, 1976), ch. 1–2.

that the person is identical to the image we have of them. But heaven help us when the projection breaks down and no longer fits. We feel we've been tricked, deceived—and then we may replace our idealizing projection with a demonizing projection on the same person we loved five minutes before.

So there are factors at work in our relations with the world that we are unconscious of. They are not under our direct ego control, but can only be known indirectly. Carl Jung identified the unconscious factors in these two kinds of projection as the shadow (carried by the negative projection) and the *anima* or *animus* (the image of the opposite sex that we fall in love with). Of course, these two factors are absolutely central to drama! They become, respectively, the antagonist (shadow) and the love interest (anima/animus) of the screenplay. Drama could not exist without them. The characters we create for these roles in the drama are carrying projections for us. We cannot, no matter how hard we might try, write the characters without projecting onto them—and projection of this kind is by definition unconscious and involuntary. What we *do* sense when these characters come into a scene is that they carry a special energy charge. We know this killer is completely a figment of our imaginations, yet he has the terrible menace of a real person. The love interest character has an irresistible seductive charm. The energy these characters possess can come from nowhere but our own projection.

As a result, we often have the most intimate aspects of our inner lives staring back at us from the computer screen. We project something outward, it takes on a life of its own, and then we are confronted with what is there. For example, we are absolutely determined that these two characters should be in bed together at the end of the story. Where's that "conviction" coming from? We take a certain satisfaction in killing off, on page 75, the banker who was the rigid father of the beautiful girl. We are aware of a secret, sensuous glee in that death. . . . Well, what's *that* all about? These are often moments in which we have made special, though unconscious, investments. These tend to be moments we screenwriters hang on to and defend tooth and nail in development meetings. The projections we make onto our screenplay feel quite compelling. That compulsion is in itself part of the unconscious mechanism. We can always find some rationalization for it, but the emotionality of our defense is a giveaway that a projection has taken place.

In fact, we may be invested in something that does not work for the greater good of the story. Because it is coming out of the unconscious, the projection may not meet the real needs of the screenplay, and our unconscious investment may also blind us to better dramatic possibilities. Many screenplay projects do in fact fall apart this way. So, we are challenged to reflect on our projections. The dual process of projection and reflection is a fundamental psychic activity, and it is exactly what happens in the movies: an unknown story is projected outward onto a screen and then reflected back to us. Afterward, when we walk out of the theater, we reflect on the movie and its meaning. Through that process, we become more conscious. Reflection is the necessary counterpart and complement to projection. Each alone makes but half a person, but together they provide our growth with both intentionality and vitality.

Especially when we (or our characters) are unable to reflect consciously about our situation, we may expect our *life* to act out the dilemma, often in a very dramatic way. This inability to reflect happens exactly because we are over-identified with one point of view. It doesn't matter whether the one-sided view is a deliberately held position or the product of an unconscious projection; in either case, if it is too one-sided it triggers a dynamic process that manifests as conflict, being "out of center." A projection indicates a movement of psychic energy, of interest and vitality, in some direction. The plot goals that motivate our characters and form the throughlines of our screenplays are always such movements of psychic energy. There is a new center of interest in the character, whether this is expressed as a quest, an investigation, or a love story. Some new potential is being born that demands energy, libido, so that it can be lived and made real, often in a way that compensates for the character's one-sidedness. Yet, since the character has a long investment in her one-sided position, we can expect the conflict to bring a destruction of the old that feels painful.

I am indebted to Mme. Catherine Moreau of the International School of Analytical Psychology in Zürich for her insights into this process that goes on within us. She refers to it whimsically as the "Procedure." This is hard to describe, because the Procedure gives words to something of which we are normally deeply unconscious. Trying to talk about it is like trying to grab wisps of smoke. All our resistance buttons get pressed when we do. But since the Procedure pictures what happens when we fall in love, fall out of love, or get seized by a sudden mood or inspiration, it is bound to appear both in our screenplays and in our lives.

What is the Procedure? Let's imagine a love story scenario. Alphonse, happily married, falls madly in love with Esmeralda while on a business trip. He is seized by a burning passion he cannot control. Now, should he leave his wife Mary or shouldn't he? Alphonse is obsessed and effectively crippled by this conflict, so much so that his work suffers and his job and livelihood are threatened. Here is a real conflict people encounter every day.

One conventional morality will say that of course he should go back to his wife, that the new romance can only be an infatuation. The more rigid versions of this conventional morality would tell Alphonse that he has sinned and is in danger of Hellfire. This is conventional because Alphonse's individual experience and feelings are not taken into account. Another conventional morality will say that he must leave his wife because the old relationship must have lost vitality or he would not have fallen for another woman. Why stay in an empty shell of a relationship and play the same bad theater over and over again? All of these conventional responses ignore the specific situation of Alphonse, Mary, and Esmeralda.

This guy is certainly up a creek without a paddle. But if Alphonse can be sincere with himself and keep his head in the midst of the crisis, he will not fall for a conventional solution. He will realize that both conventional choices are inauthentic and are mainly escapes from the terrible conflict. Alphonse may begin to reflect: Mary and Esmeralda mean two very different things to him. We might say they represent two different values in his life that are now constellated in conflict. He might be able to describe the "territory" of each value. "Esmeralda makes me feel so alive. . . . But Mary and I have built so much together; we've created such a deep trust and understanding. . . . But with Esmeralda there is the element of danger; she calls me to a new life. . . ." And on and on, an agony of ambivalence. Each woman has a sovereign claim on him. It seems that to choose one or the other is fatal: it means choosing a destiny.

In fact, the values the two women represent for Alphonse (though not, of course, the women themselves)—are values *within* Alphonse. He talks about what he sees in each woman because he doesn't clearly see what is in himself. Internal values have been projected onto the women in his life, and this has all happened unconsciously, accidentally. Because the unconscious situation within him is unresolved, Alphonse cannot act with authenticity in the outer situation. His only authentic position is to surrender to the conflict, to admit his powerlessness. Alphonse is crucified by this double-bind conflict until something collapses. He arrives at a point where he cannot go on like this any more. The projections collapse, and with them the libido he has invested in both women. The libido, or psychic energy, carried by the images of Mary and Esmeralda, withdraws like a low tide. Alphonse sinks into a depression. Depression means that the libido sinks back within, back into the unconscious. Now Alphonse appears inert and helpless, but in fact things are brewing down below. The sinking back of libido during a crisis is a natural movement: the energy is reflexing (bending back) and re-collecting in the unconscious, so that the wisdom of the unconscious can reshape it. In dramas, the main character spends much of Act II descending into this vulnerable state.

Finally, when the withdrawn energy builds up enough of a charge, it expands again. It produces a symbolic image of a new possibility that may appear as a dream or fantasy, or as a new interest. The symbol may generate a new life-attitude, a comprehensive transformation of all values around a new center.

Alphonse comes to realize that he himself must change. Sides of his personality that have always been hidden may emerge. Feeling himself to be in a "grow or die" situation, he may unexpectedly recover images, desires, and values from childhood that he had renounced on the way to adulthood. Suddenly their meaning in his life returns, and Alphonse recovers a new sense of what he wants his life to be. For instance, he may remember that as a kid he always wanted to build things and dreamed of being an architect, but he became a lawyer because he could not disappoint his father. Through a long process, Alphonse may end up finding a different field of work, a different place to live, a different way to live. From the perspective of the new attitude, the conflict between Mary and Esmeralda ceases to be the center of things. Yes, some sort of resolution does occur: he may stay with one or the other, or both, or neither. He still loves them both, but he has stepped back from obsession and guilt to a new center. The meaning and context of the conflict has completely altered. As Catherine Moreau explains, the conflict had really been *vertical*—between conscious and unconscious, between who Alphonse thought he was and what his life wanted to express through him—but it had been projected onto the horizontal conflict between the two women. You may have noticed that this is precisely the conflict structure Lester faces in *American Beauty*.

Think back to a time when you had such a difficult conflict in your own life, and what the outcome taught you about yourself. Look back at the list you made earlier in the chapter of current crises in your life. Do any of these crises contain unforeseen challenges for growth?

The Procedure describes the absolute core of dramatic character change. It helps us understand what we really mean by the statement that the essence of drama is *growth through crisis*. This cycle of

- projection
- frustration
- withdrawal of libido
- generation of a new symbol
- integration around a new center

is precisely what happens in dramatic conflict. The solution to the outer plot conflict requires a shift in self-perception on the part of the main character. Screenwriting technique allows us to guide the audience through this journey of conflict and growth. The soundness of our dramatic construction, the consistency of our character motivation, our originality with plot twists and surprises, our daring to imagine new dramatic outcomes, all grow out of our capacity for insight. We could put this forward as an axiom:

> Empathic insight is the basis of all technique in screenwriting.

Screenwriting and Empathy

As screenwriters, our field is human nature. If our insights into human nature are strong, the screenplays we write will be compelling. I have found through experience that writers who are capable of increased insight and sustained productivity over time also possess empathy. Empathy is a complex relational skill made up of three aspects. First is the capacity to "feel with"—to feel the experience of someone else as though it were our own, to take it seriously. This includes having empathy for ourselves. Empathy for ourselves is not easy, especially for those parts of ourselves we may be tempted to reject: the part that can't say no to chocolate or vodka, the part that falls for those dumb "Twenty CDs for Free!!!" deals on the Internet, the part that can't get over the terrible broken heart, the part that gets scared and lonely at night. Self-empathy is neither identification with our wounds, nor is it self-pity. Put very simply, it is the capacity to be present to ourselves in an accepting and compassionate way. Self-empathy is the practice and model for all the empathy we have to extend to others.

The second aspect of empathy, which is key for screenwriters, is the capacity to see and construct analogies. We do not need to have the *same* experience as someone in order to empathize with them. We simply need to tap into the place in ourselves where we find something analogous. I may never have been in prison, but I know what it means and feels like to be deprived of my liberty. I may not know the paralyzing terror of facing an extraterrestrial monster, but I do know the paralyzing terror of my own nightmares. I may not have had my corporation stolen out of my hands by my wife and her lover, my trusted vice president, but I have felt betrayed by those close to me. Screenwriters must constantly construct such analogies in order to enter the lives of their characters. This, as we have said, is how our creative intuition utilizes projection as a creative tool. At the same time, we open ourselves and allow the character to come into our feeling life. This may start as a single point of contact. We look for something we have in common with the character, as we so often do when meeting a stranger. But as we write, unexpected connections and depths begin to open up. There is no authenticity to our writing unless something of ourselves goes into it.

There is a third aspect to empathy. It is less widely recognized, yet without it the other two will not work. That is: empathy demands that we keep a sense of our own separateness, our own identity as distinct from the other. As one therapist puts it, "Don't jump in with both feet! You can put one foot in [to share the client's/character's standpoint], but keep one foot back." This therapist would go so far as to wrap one foot around the leg of his chair to remind himself to keep from jumping in with both feet. What would it mean to jump in with both feet? It would mean that we go beyond empathy to a kind of primal identification with our character, a kind of merging of personalities. It may seem innocent enough to start dressing like your main character—the cowboy boots, plaid pants, silk ascot, and beret—but it really doesn't work for our writing. To the extent that we become overidentified with one character, we become dissociated from all the others. We fail to extend the same empathy to those other characters. Then it becomes impossible to write their parts convincingly, and the entire script falls apart.

The necessity to keep a separate sense of identity points out the connection between empathy and play. There is a balance to be found between letting ourselves really go into the encounter and not going so far that we lose consciousness. Part of the play is playing with just where that edge is. We often admire actors who seem to go over the edge and "lose themselves" in the role. Of course, actors have a luxury that screenwriters do not have: they only have to deal with that one character. Still, actors pay a price for being on that edge. That is why they are edgy, and need insulation and protection on the set, their bottle of Evian, their poodle, and so on. Sometimes actors do go too far and overidentify. They may get lost in a role and not know how to get back. Maria

Falconetti, after having been made famous by her transcendently great performance as the suffering Joan of Arc, apparently could not go on. Nor, apparently, could Massimo Troisi after his performance in *Il Postino*. (Both died soon after their signature roles.) The Procedure helps us understand that something is also happening in the depth dimension: the actor may well have an overidentification with a complex or archetype in the unconscious, which may manifest itself as a fatal merging of the actor's personality with his roles. When we try to understand the early, self-destructive ends of gifted actors like Marilyn Monroe and James Dean, we must include the possibility of such "vertical" conflicts as we saw with Alphonse. Screenwriters are not immune to this. They have the advantage that the public does not identify the writer with her characters. But for our own health as artists and as persons, we are wise to learn the ways of creative darkness.

We never know what we are going to discover in a screenplay until we write it. We cannot know what we project into the story beforehand. It is an unconscious side of the creative process. But we cannot for this reason try to hold back or deny our projections. That would kill our creative spirit. We have to let ourselves discover it all as we go along. This is why it becomes necessary to cultivate a conscious practice of writing. Only when we can tolerate seeing ourselves in the mirror of the story can we also use our art to hold up a mirror in which our world can see itself: Shakespeare's great "mirror held up to nature."

Internal Software: Focusing

Every moment we are writing, we receive a symphony of internal subjective feedback. What this book has called "self-talk" is only a small part of this. The ensemble also includes physical sensations, shifts in energy and attention, and an array of intuitive images that may flit in and out of consciousness. Whenever we must make aesthetic choices in a screenplay (which is constantly) this symphony of subjective cues helps orient us. This is an inescapable aspect of the creative process. It is in fact an important creative tool. Think of the way a jazz musician or a basketball player makes use of the flow of instantaneous inner and outer cues to bring more "aliveness" to his performance.

Yet it is possible to gain some objectivity on this very subjective flow so that we can work with it more consciously and intentionally. One of the best ways to do this is through the discipline of Focusing. The **Focusing** technique, developed by psychologist Eugene Gendlin at the University of Chicago,[6] is simultaneously a way of sharpening our senses

Continued

6. Gendlin, Eugene T., *Focusing* (New York: Everest House, 1978).

and sharpening our empathy. It provides the link between sensation and feeling by identifying what Gendlin calls the "felt-sense" of an experience.

Felt-sense is both sensation and feeling, as you shall see. This suggests that the division of feeling from sensation is a somewhat artificial categorizing our minds perform for convenience's sake. But if you have ever had to choose between two shades of wall paint, two shades of carpet, or two shades of nail polish, you know that a very slight difference can in fact have a very forceful impact on you. Focusing picks up this information directly, before it gets split into "sensation" and "feeling," and makes it available to us. The following Focusing exercise is a way to tune up your creative instrument. It is playful and asks to be taken in a playful spirit, though remarkable, even profound, experiences can occur.

Part One

For this Internal Software exercise you will need a nice quiet place, free of distractions. Stand up with your feet about shoulder-width apart, arms hanging easily at your sides. Take a deep breath, relax, and close your eyes. Without trying to do or force anything, turn your perceptions inward and simply attend to whatever is going on. It is as though you have a pair of subtle eyes that are able to look down into your body and see energy. Just notice wherever in your body you feel something. Do not try to label it; simply observe it.

This energy has its own language. Actors work with it all the time. We can use this language in a way that is appropriate for our work as screenwriters. Begin by asking a question that will focus your impression: "What does this feeling *feel like*?" But do not answer with words, let the words go. Let your body answer. You may experience a shift in the energy somewhere in your body. It does not matter if the feeling is vague or tenuous; that is simply a quality of the impression. Just follow the shifts as you might follow the flight of a bird.

Some more questions can help further focus and define the energy. Without resorting to words, let your energy-body respond in its own way:

- Does it feel big or small? ("Big" might mean that the energy seems to expand beyond the physical body; "small" might mean a sense of energy that condenses or takes up a space smaller than the body.)
- Does it feel warm or cool?
- Is it expanding or contracting?
- Is it rising, circulating, or in some other way moving through the body?

Continued

- Are there any colors, sounds, vibrations, pulsations, or other sensory impressions that are part of this experience?

Just let your body answer.

This total constellation or gestalt of impressions is called the "felt-sense." Now, it doesn't matter whether you are excited or calm or depressed when you do this, just as a piece of excited music is not inherently better than a piece of calm or sad music. As a first experience, this may have been something like barely audible music. That's fine. Now just relax for a few moments. You have in fact been listening (if that's the word) to the music of your internal system. Even if it was only a dull buzz, the important thing here is to learn the skill of listening/attending/perceiving. We shall now use the basic skill to perform a couple of inner explorations.

Part Two

With your eyes closed, imagine that one of your very best friends is standing right in front of you, beaming that warm smile you know so well. This is a person you trust completely and unconditionally, someone with whom you feel really open and relaxed. Feel the smile and presence of that person.

Now scan down through your body. Where do you feel something and what does that feel like? Allow your body to answer in its own way, using focusing questions to make your impression more conscious and vivid. Get the felt-sense of this dear friend.

- Does the energy feel big or small?
- Does it feel warm or cool?
- Is it expanding or contracting?
- Is it rising, circulating, or in some other way moving through the body?
- Are there any colors, sounds, vibrations, pulsations, or other sensory impressions that are part of this experience?

You may find that the energy is moving. Just let it go wherever it wants to go, while keeping the image of the dear friend. Soon the felt-sense will become somewhat stable.

Now we shall add a further step in the Focusing process. Once the feeling has found an expression, we shall inquire of the feeling whether there is a word that fits it. Keeping your eyes closed, silently speak a word that seems to best describe the felt-sense. "See" what happens. If the word is not a good match for the feeling, people typically experience a

Continued

disturbance and shifting in the felt-sense. The word is colliding with the feeling in a dissonant way. Let that word go, return to the clear image of the friend and the felt-sense, and then try another word. When we hit upon a word that fits, there can be a virtually physical sense of rightness. Some people experience this as a "glowing" of all the qualities of the felt-sense, others as a "resonance," like the ringing of a bell.

Now, imagine this dear friend coming close and embracing you in a nice, warm hug. How does the felt-sense shift? Observe the changes, using questions to locate the felt-sense more exactly. See if you can find a word that fits this impression.

(Leave a minute or two for this process.)

Part Three

With your eyes closed, imagine yourself standing at the place where you loved to go for holidays as a child. It might be a lake cottage, a seashore, a grandparents' home—wherever you felt really wonderful. What comes to your mind's eye? Really be present at that place and time in your imagination. Take in the quality of the light, the time of day, the sounds and special fragrances of this place. Allow your memory to bring you the full sensory experience.

Now scan through your body. Where do you feel energy and what does that feel like? Work to focus the felt-sense, then see if there is a word that captures for you the essence of this feeling.

(Again, give yourself a few minutes.)

When you have completed this work, slowly and gently open your eyes. Notice with care any changes in your outer perceptions. Does your sense of space seem in any way altered? Are colors softer or more vibrant? Do you have some new sense of how your body occupies this space where you are? While your eyes are open, use your newly developed inner senses to get a felt-sense of now—this place, this moment in time. Simply observe with objectivity the subjective process taking place. How do you feel now compared with how you felt at the beginning of this Internal Software exercise?

Focusing is an important technique for developing your creative potential. More than this, it is an entire world, which is why "software" is an appropriate term. That world has of course always been there, but normally it is below the horizon of consciousness. Small children have the richness of the experience, but lack words for it. Creative individuals keep alive the link between feeling and form, while most of us in our society are taught to believe that without outer stimuli we are "empty." The fact is

Continued

that the energetic form of every experience is recorded vividly in the felt-sense. The felt-sense is the affective component of memory.

What does this have to do with writing? Everything! It is possible that we cannot have a visual image without this affective energy-body component, or that the image would not have meaning for us, would not feel alive. The felt-sense we take in with an experience flows out again when we write about it, giving passion, authenticity, and depth to the expression. When actors or writers want to reach the truth of an experience they themselves have never had, the felt-sense is the real bridge to empathy. It puts the other's experience in the body where we can feel it. As screenwriters, the simple felt-sense operations we made with a dear friend and a favorite spot are precisely the same ones we constantly make with fictional characters and situations.

With Focusing training we are in a position to use our felt-sense feedback more consciously and productively. Dramatic truth, dramatic meaning, necessarily includes a felt-sense, affective dimension. This is what we mean when we say a play or film moves us. That is movement in the energy-body, read by the felt-sense. When we can feel more clearly what moves us, we can write more powerfully.

3

The Mythic Dimension of Screenwriting

> The ultimate value of life depends upon awareness and the power of contemplation rather than upon mere survival.
>
> —*Aristotle*

IN THIS CHAPTER, WE WILL EMBARK on the first of several paradigmatic models that serve us in structuring screenplays. This model, well known in the film business, is derived from mythologist Joseph Campbell[7] and is called the Hero's Journey. The Hero's Journey has sometimes been taken as a model of plot structure. That is a misconception. The Hero's Journey in fact conceptualizes a deep process of psychic growth by projecting it outward into the world as an adventure. In the process depicted in hero myths, an older perspective or life-view is seen to break down and die, giving way to a broader, more inclusive appreciation of life. The Hero's Journey, as a concept, pictures this lived process as a symbolic cycle of Separation, Descent, Initiation, and Return. The model of the Hero's Journey *underlies* all of drama. The hero archetype within us, which impels us toward growth and the encounter with life, makes drama possible, while at the same time it also demands its expression through drama. The Hero's Journey model is the place where the screenwriter's own venture into the unknown intersects with the techniques of story development.

Models can most usefully be thought of as lenses into the story. They help us to better see what we are doing. Each model as a lens reveals the story in a different way, and so the models that follow complement each other. Together they allow tremendous insights into how stories work, and how your own story might work to its fullest potential. One important caveat, however, is that all models work best as lenses when there is something to look *at*, that is, *after* a treatment or screenplay draft has been written. Then models as lenses help us look into

7. Campbell, Joseph, *The Hero with a Thousand Faces* (New Jersey: Princeton/Bollingen, 1949).

what is present in the draft, where narrative links are missing, where characters need further development, and how the three dimensions of the drama* can be integrated and unified into a powerful and authentic whole. Models are misused when they are put *before* the story, before the writer has had a chance to let the story emerge. Models can serve as guides, but they should not become the Ten Commandments. They should not be treated as rigid ideals to which screenplays are made to conform. Such a tendency to use models as abstract "standards" may help everyone in the development process feel in control, but it robs stories of their vitality.

Myth and Drama

The Hero's Journey model requires some special attention for two reasons, first because it is the most fundamental. As we shall see, this model forms the basis, both narratively and psychologically, for the other models that follow. Second, the Hero's Journey demands some special attention because it has in fact been treated like the Ten Commandments in story development. Distorted or oversimplified versions of the Campbell's Hero's Journey paradigm are often considered too literally as the ultimate "story machine," used to both correct errant plots and inject movies with puffed-up fantasies and ready-to-wear universal themes. Myth as an "ingredient" in movies has become as prevalent as sugar in junk food: everyone knows it makes the product taste better. Of course movies, as an important consumer industry, cannot help but reflect the larger society. We are a society continually disoriented by the pace of change, and thus constantly in search of meaning and stability. In our current climate, myth carries the aura of both meaning and stability. For many, that aura is enough, and we may not care to look too closely at whom a myth serves or the consequences of surrendering to it blindly. In this broader perspective, of a society grasping for something to compensate the religious values many have lost, the real challenges to growth and maturity offered by the hero myths are often recast as invitations to a childish grandiosity. The media hypes heroes, only to use them to sell more shampoo and magazines, or to gain rating points. Then some feminists come along and argue that the Hero's Journey is a male invention, a macho fantasy that has degraded women and led to eternal bloodshed. The deeper sense of the Hero's Journey tends to get lost in the postures of the culture wars.

Why is it necessary to go back to myth in order to write original and compelling screenplays? The most important reasons are not those that are the most immediately obvious. Myth takes us into the depth dimension of storytelling, a dimension that is always present, but largely invisible. Myth is the liminal zone of story. It lies between the conscious *story*—the story we are intentionally trying to create—and the *story's unconscious*, what I call the "story field"—the

* See Chapter Five: The Story Molecule.

ensemble of all of the implicit and archetypal elements activated in the writer, in the production, and in the audience, through the story. The conscious story is often identified with the producer's concept. The larger, implicit story is what the writer discovers in the process of developing the material. The ability to work with both dimensions of the story together is one of the real keys to successful story development.

Stories, including screenplays and movies, are patterns of energy. When we are watching and appreciating a movie, we are not merely responding to a string of incidents on the screen. There is something beyond that, beyond the moral dimension of the story, beyond even the waves of tension and release that define a process of growth through crisis. Stories generate energy *fields* that have definite emotional qualities. The story field encompasses both the conscious/intentional and unconscious/implicit dimensions of the story. It is myth that makes this larger story, the story field, accessible to us as writers.

Not long after the release of the original *Star Wars*, it became known in story development circles that George Lucas had closely followed the mythic story pattern described by Joseph Campbell as the Hero's Journey in creating the screenplay. Movies like *Raiders of the Lost Ark* and *E.T.* followed, among the biggest box office hits of all time. It really did appear that Lucas and Spielberg had hit upon the magic formula for box office success, all due to tapping into the mythic points identified by Campbell. The era of the blockbuster mentality was born, and a high-concept, high-stakes approach to story development was initiated. It would no longer be enough to merely return a decent profit on investment in a production. How could that be satisfying when certain movies were hitting the jackpot and grossing hundreds of millions of dollars worldwide? Everyone wanted to tap into this new "universal language" that could play equally well in Peoria and Paris, Caracas and Kuala Lumpur. Joseph Campbell's work ironically came to be closely associated with this "blockbuster" trend. Campbell, who once told me that he didn't go to the movies at all for over twenty years, posthumously became something of a Hollywood celebrity.

Major elements of Campbell's model *can* be identified with some of the key elements in the structure of screenplays. A "mythic grammar" has indeed come into story development. This new grammar has sent many writers on real journeys of self-discovery and has led to new forms of storytelling. One might hopefully see it as part of a broader spiritual renewal. The new mythic grammar has also been applied, in the worst cases, in a kind of paint-by-numbers approach to screenplay development. Ten minutes into the movie, the hero gets his Call to Adventure, supported by a pretentiously heroic anthem. Twenty-eight minutes into the movie, the hero crosses a threshold into a Magical World, and so on. The formula soon became familiar, even shopworn. A curious thing was discovered: the Hero's Journey paradigm was capable of turning out miserably mediocre movies as well as box office smashes. Some thought that the remedy was to make sure all of the mythic buttons in the audience were pushed—*hard*.

Antagonists were made darker and more demonic, as in movies like *Fatal Attraction.* Why settle for a human antagonist when you can bring out the devil himself . . . or *her*self? Dramatic stakes could be pushed to cosmological heights by virtue of new technologies that made the previously unimaginable a cinematic reality. A kind of "mythic inflation"[8] has occurred, both in storytelling rhetoric and in production budgets.

Apart from the obvious facts that models cannot be applied mechanically without loss of authenticity, and that imitations rarely meet with the success of the original, there are some basic flaws in the way Joseph Campbell's insights have been applied wholesale to mainstream screenwriting. First of all, myth and drama are *not* the same thing. They are related, but different, levels of expression. One quote of Campbell's that appears frequently is that dreams are private myths and myths public dreams—but this is not quite the case. It is already something of an overgeneralizing analogy. Myths, like dreams, are closely related to the unconscious in their mode of expression. In dreams, however, the dynamic forces of the unconscious express themselves spontaneously to consciousness with very little filtering on the part of the sleeping ego. Traditional myths and fairy tales, on the other hand, reveal a slow shaping of the dreamlike material through both later re-dreaming and conscious reflection. Mythmaking is a process that goes on over generations, a collective act of creation. The original stimulus for the myth may indeed have been an individual's dream or waking dream, but over time the semiconscious collective wisdom of a society has worked out the personal idiosyncratic or dysfunctional elements in the story. Through this process, myths become deeper and more universal. A myth may nevertheless express the anxiety or neurosis of that particular society in which it was born. Universal elements must be sifted out of the local, parochial context if they are to shine forth in a great myth, work of art, or movie.

This slow evolution of traditional mythmaking is in sharp contrast with both the goals and the process of screenplay development, which is very deliberate and market-oriented. There is, of course, a hazy region where the two meet: the region of art. The effort made by producers and studios to put their fingers on the pulse of society, while serving their own commercial interest, does in fact go beyond the demands of the market. But in this convergence of myth and commerce we are confronted again with the fact that stories by their nature do not come exclusively from our rational minds. The unconscious, intuitively inspired element has to be acknowledged. Mythic structure cannot be directly transferred over to screenplays, as some have tried, without doing damage to both. It is not the inherent "function" of myths to provide a guide to boxoffice success for twenty-first-century moviemakers. Myths have an inherent reality, coherence, and integrity of their own. The sublime structure of the Hero's Journey can be a

8. Mythic inflation is a collective malaise identified by Joseph Campbell in *The Masks of God: Oriental Mythology*.

powerful aid to the creative process, but we must be willing to meet it on its own level, on its own turf, so to speak. If we treat it as a monkey wrench, we will get a monkey wrench.

Myths are the essence of storytelling, and they are also the vehicles through which the wisdom of humanity has been passed from generation to generation. Before there was any such thing as a scientific psychology, a subtle and penetrating understanding of human nature was communicated by means of myth and fairy tale. Myths are symbolic representations. They are not, and were never intended to be, taken literally. Everything in myths and fairy tales, like the "happily ever after" endings, points beyond itself to another level of meaning. In the language of traditional myths, that other level was understood as magical or divine. Today we should consider that symbolic realm in psychological terms. Yet culturally we have trouble making this distinction, because for two thousand years we have taken our own myths literally. For example, because the Garden of Eden was taken as a literal geographic location rather than an *idea* of a state of innocence, Columbus actually hoped he could discover it on his voyages. And, as Joseph Campbell emphasized, if we take our own myth as literally true, then we assume everyone else's myth is literally a lie. A genuine mythic understanding requires us to be playful, penetrating, and shrewd. Myth is not concerned with facts, but with patterns and analogies that reveal our human situation. Black Elk, the Lakota medicine man, reported the center of the universe to be Harney Peak in South Dakota, but—he then added—the center is *wherever you are*. That is an example of a properly mythic understanding.

Myths and fairy tales—like screenplays and movies—are picture-languages. They are made of images, create images in our minds, and ask for images from us in response. We do not know if this picture and symbol-making language came before, or along with, verbal language in our human development. We do know that images have the power to speak directly to the unconscious, bypassing the filters of our conscious minds. This is why filmmakers (and advertising executives, and everyone else with something to sell) are looking for a mythic hook for their stories. They want to get "under the skin" of the audience.

Joseph Campbell's interest in myth was not academic; it was a lifelong passion. He wanted to know what it is that myths possess that compels us to tell the same stories over and over again throughout history. Versions of the Noah and Gilgamesh stories have been continuously told for five thousand years. The myth animating the Ainu bear sacrifice in Hokkaido, Campbell speculated, may ultimately go back to Neanderthal times, sixty thousand years or more, handed down orally through more than a thousand generations. What is this extraordinary power that myths have? Joseph Campbell's book *The Hero with a Thousand Faces* was his first attempt to answer that question. It gives an outline of the archetypal structure of myth. And the archetypal structure Campbell identified does indeed *underlie* screenplay structure. But applying the power of myth to screenwriting is not a question of mythic form alone. It is not merely a question of hitting the right buttons in the right order. That would be a major misunderstanding. These stories would not have survived so long if they were not deeply meaningful, that is to say, they are satisfying to both our conscious understanding and also to the soul. The shape of myth cannot be separated from its meaning. And the meaning cannot be separated from deep psychological movements, the movements of *soul.*

Central to all hero myths, and to the model of the Hero's Journey Campbell derived from them, is of course the figure of the hero. The word "hero" designates both a character and an archetype. It was the Swiss psychiatrist Carl Jung who applied the term "archetype" to describe those deepest structuring potentialities of the human psyche that we as human beings universally share, inborn rather than learned. When Jung first proposed this idea it was highly controversial, because there was a widespread but erroneous assumption at that time that when we are born into this world our brain is like a blank slate. More recent research in evolutionary psychiatry, however, supports Jung's view that we are born with many latent patterns of behavior already present. For example, it appears that we are born with the ability to recognize language structures. Thc structures are present even before we can actually speak. I believe we are also born with the latent ability to respond to dramatic structures. Archetypes, as "dominants" or nodes in the deepest layer of the psyche, also share this characteristic (along with language acquisition) of being latent potentials that are activated by outer stimuli. Archetypes cannot be seen *in themselves* any more than can instincts. They can be seen indirectly through patterns of related behaviors, feeling states, and mental representations: ideas, fantasies, symbols, dreams. They are the stuff movies are made of. We identify the hero archetype through the characteristics hero figures have in common, as well as the inner feelings and fantasies heroes evoke in us.

Nobody invented the myths. Nobody could have invented them. They were *discovered.* True symbols, according to Carl Jung, are not the creations of the conscious mind. They emerge from the unconscious. Symbols are the point where conscious and unconscious meet. Where those two forces meet, an image or symbol precipitates, as in a chemical reaction. We could say the symbol is precipitated by our need to make sense of what we cannot consciously grasp, but symbols are ultimately products of nature, our human nature. Signs, on the other hand, are created by the conscious mind and are relatively conventional (Carl Jung has articulated this distinction). Our lives are surrounded by a wide variety of signs that compress information into representational images. So we have road signs, commercial trademarks, linguistic and arithmetic signs, many codes to operate our many machines and devices, icons on our computer screens. More and more, our daily interactions are with signs rather than with other human beings or the natural world. This can even trick us into the fantasy that we ourselves are signs, or collections of signs, made up, for example, of the brand names on the clothes we wear and the products we buy.

This is because signs and symbols have an ambiguous tendency to shift levels of meaning. The red, white, and blue of the American flag may operate as a simple sign: when we see it flying in front of a building, it may signify that the building belongs to the government; sewn onto a garment label, it may signify that the garment was made by union labor in America. The function of the flag in these cases is completely conventional, and does not arouse much emotion in us. It doesn't involve us emotionally or psychologically. There are other situations, however—the flag-draped coffin of a soldier, or a flag being burned in a street demonstration—which may arouse in us powerful and strangely irrational feelings. Then the flag is functioning more as a symbol, touching the core of some value or center of motivation in the unconscious. A cross may be just a sign on a road map that says, "Here's a church." Or the cross can be a real symbol, if it takes us into the mystery of life and death, the mystery of God and man. Symbols tend to become codified and degenerate into signs. The Hero's Journey is a symbol threatened with losing its mystery. What we will explore later as Aristotle's Plot Curve is also a symbol. When we try to turn them into signs, simple road signs to follow on the highway to success, we are making a fundamental mistake.

Hero images, from Tom Thumb to Hercules, from Joan of Arc to Mahatma Gandhi, from Rick in *Casablanca* to Ripley in *Aliens*, all have some potential to express the hero archetype. But archetypes are not "magic." They are not psychic vitamins with which we can pump up a story. Carl Jung was careful to point out that each archetype has a negative as well as positive pole. A person identified with the hero archetype as warrior might be influenced, under certain circumstances, to become a berserk killer or terrorist. Another identified with the hero as savior could become a Jim Jones, leading hundreds of followers to death. Such "possessed" people have their own rationalization for everything, but they have been to some extent "abducted" by the energy of the hero archetype. They have become vehicles for the archetype, and to that extent have surrendered some level of consciousness. Serious disturbance on the archetypal level, Jung found, can lead to psychosis.

Myths and fairy tales, those stories that perhaps best represent the dynamics at the archetypal level, evolved slowly and carefully as sage, experienced elders observed the effects of the myth on the hearers. Using their intuition and empathy, they weeded out what did not work. Without empathic insight, it is possible to create dysfunctional, damaging myths that disturb people and destroy their adaptation to life. So it is not enough to load mythic elements onto a story in order to lock in box office success. We place ourselves in the position of Mickey Mouse, the Sorcerer's Apprentice in *Fantasia*, when we willfully play with these energies. Jesus's warning about false prophets is also applicable to mythmakers: "By their fruits shall ye know them."

So as we, through the Hero's Journey model, approach the hero archetype, it is equally important to gain some objective distance from it. We want to keep a healthy perspective, because archetypes do generate something like magnetic fields when they are activated. Identifying with the hero makes us feel good, makes us feel bigger than ourselves. But this comes at the price of a loss of consciousness. We get caught up in a mood, in a fantasy. Maybe we are so pumped up, we begin to think we can do anything. Some warriors in the old days so completely identified with the warrior archetype that they ran into battle naked, believing that no weapon could harm them. It sounds so grand, but if you have ever had a friend who, under the influence of cocaine, thought for sure he could fly, and then crashed his motorcycle into a wall, you know how deceptive these energies can be. Myths bring drama into our lives because they generate values, values that come into conflict with the values of others. Myth is not meant for prolonging childhood through fantasy. On the contrary, myth replaces grandiosity with meaning.

The Writer's Encounter with the Hero

It is natural to begin looking at screenplays through the figure of the hero. Not only is the hero the center and driving force of the story, he or she is also the focus of the audience's identification. We ride on the wave of the hero's reactions and moods. Plot events tend to mean for the audience what they mean for the hero. The destiny that the hero makes for herself is transferred over to the audience as the theme of the movie. Consciously or unconsciously, the audience carries this theme out of the theater with them. And the figure of the hero is central because he is the chief vehicle of the writer's projection. The screenwriter projects the story through the main character to the audience. The writer's creative energy tends to be focused in and through the main character the way a lens gathers rays of light. The screenwriter, too, rides on the wave of the hero's experience of breakdown and breakthrough. This projection through the hero makes possible the parallel journeys of writer/hero/audience. The hero is thus the focal point of the transaction that takes place between author and audience. As we move through the model of the Hero's Journey, we are implicitly stepping into the heart of the dynamic we share with our audience in the movie theater.

The essential form of the Hero's Journey is a circle: it describes a cycle of transformational growth. The movement is circular, returning to the place from which it began. The circle is divided into a light half and a dark half, and into four phases: Separation, Descent, Initiation, and Return. The mythic hero starts the journey in the Day World of his life: the familiar, the status quo. He journeys down into the unknown, represented by the Night World. There he has a life-changing, life-renewing experience that amounts to a death and rebirth. Death and rebirth belong to the picture-language of myth. Psychologically, we could say that an old self or an old way of seeing things dies and a new, more comprehensive self is born. In a movie, death and rebirth may be understood psychologically, but they must be expressed cinematically. The power of the drama and the cinematic image create another reality where we experience the hero's destiny as fully our

/ ***The Hero's Journey*** **(based on original by Joseph Campbell, 1949).**

own while our play-sense knows "it's only a movie." In the second half of the journey the hero returns, transformed, to bring to bring the gift of his experience back to the world he left.

Some writers and screenwriting gurus, trying to adapt Campbell's ideas to screenplay structure too literally, have turned the Hero's Journey into a straight line with a linear movement from beginning to end. This is the wrong image, the wrong metaphor. It robs the Hero's Journey of its depth dimension. The circle is a universal symbol of wholeness. The Hero's Journey is a way of looking at our life's journey as a journey to wholeness. What it emphasizes is that wholeness. The image of the Hero's Journey is not the image of the beeline to success. It is not just a straight line from less to more affluence. If the journey could be described in a straight line, as more or less a problem to be solved, then the sacrificial aspect of death and rebirth would be meaningless and to be avoided. Exactly this loss of the depth dimension and loss of meaning describe the cultural and spiritual crisis we find ourselves in at present. The circle, with its light half and dark half, represents the whole journey of life. This division of the circle into Day World and Night World is a basic, intrinsic feature of the Hero's Journey and the mythic understanding, yet it gets completely lost when the cycle is turned into a straight line.

Why are there two worlds? What do they represent? Well, the Day World and Night World express an array of interrelated dichotomies, like the yin-yang of the Tao. In the most general terms, Day World and Night World are simply the known and the unknown. And as we understand from our own experience as screenwriters, the unknown is not neutral: confronting the unknown brings up both fear and fascination, anxiety over loss of control, and irrational responses emerging from the unconscious.

The Day World and the Night World also stand for ego consciousness and the unconscious, respectively. The world as our ego sees it is our known world. The unconscious is by definition unknown, not only in its contents but in its dynamics. Here we also find a split between the head and the body. Many people in Western societies are effectively split at the neck. They equate pragmatic realism with intelligence and imagine this as situated in the head, the "control center." The body then becomes seen as the repository or dumping ground of all the unwanted or uncontrollable impulses involved with the instinctual life. Imagine a television screen or computer monitor above, and below, writhing octopus tentacles reaching out impulsively to grasp at toys, candies, drugs, and so on. Some people experience the split in such drastic terms. It helps us, when developing the screenplay, to know what dichotomy we are expressing through the Day World and the Night World in which the story is set. In fact, it is part of our job to cinematically define the story's Day World and Night World. Movement between the two worlds makes dramatic change visible. This transit is central to both the character development and the theme of the movie. In movies with any character change at all, we are not dealing exclusively with outer obstacles to the hero's goal but with character transformation.

Throughout the length and breadth of the human tradition, as indicated in the myths discussed by Joseph Campbell, it is the Night World that holds the key to the wisdom of the instincts, how to access the instinctual energy in a positive way. Heroes' journeys are always journeys to find lost energy. The main character of the screenplay, no matter what the genre, is on a journey to find or recover lost energy. In one of Ian Fleming's books, James Bond writes a haiku poem:

> You only live twice:
> once when you are born,
> and once when you stare death
> in the face.

In our society, we can spend our lives protected from the raw impact of instinctual energy if we want to. But we seldom get to experience the total aliveness of which this small poem speaks. The aliveness is down there in the Night World, where we "stare death in the face." Yet it is this energy, this aliveness, that we want to communicate to the audience. Usually the screenplay does not "gel" and come together until we, as writers, understand where the character needs to go to recover her lost energy. This understanding grows out of the writer's creative journey.

Finally, the Day World and Night World correlate with mountain-creativity and mine-creativity. As we will see, the Hero's Journey model is equally an image of the structure of creative breakthrough. Thus, the two halves of the circle present us with a very rich context of meaning.

Because it is pictured as a circle, the Hero's Journey implicitly connects us to all of the deep cycles we experience in life, the cycles that connect us to nature. The deep mythic journeys, like the journey of Odysseus, the journey of Jesus, or the journey of the ancient Sumerian goddess Inanna into the Underworld, are symbolic stories about connecting the two halves—head and instincts—connecting us with our deeper nature, finding the deeper nature in ourselves. Thus the cycle of the Hero's Journey also echoes cycles of nature: the cycle of day and night; the cycle of the moon, which dies and is reborn; the menstrual cycle of fertility and cleansing; the cycle of the year; and the life cycle from birth to death. The Hero's Journey expresses in symbolic terms the meaning of a successful human life cycle as one where we have entered the mystery of death and rebirth. All movie stories, whether adventures, tragedies, comedies, thrillers, or melodramas, carry the Hero's Journey in their deep structure and communicate it, largely subliminally, to the audience.

A second aspect to note about the Hero's Journey as a cycle is that it is not static. The hero journeys around the circle. The circle is the shape of experience; this is how he grows. For there are two very different types of growth we experience in life. One kind of growth is linear, incremental growth. Think back to your school days. Every night you would have to read ten pages of the textbook for the following day. You could see your bookmark moving slowly through the book until the book was finished. Then you laid it down and picked up the next book. And when each book was done, you laid it on the stack of books you had read, and watched the stack getting higher and higher and higher. We call this progress, and this is how we mark our progress.

A part of our mind, the mental part of us trained at school in the myth of progress, would like to believe that this is the way that life is. This left-brain attitude has an old mantra: "Every day, in every way, I am getting better and better!" Every year we expect to make more money, take more expensive vacations (this year it may be a week at the folks' place, but next year I'll take a trip to Yellowstone, and in five years—a time-share condo in Bali!). We will trade up our Toyota for a BMW. We fantasize about our lives just going up and up, like the perfect corporate growth curve of Mercedes or Microsoft. There is indeed a part of us that really believes this, or dearly would like to. And then, when life intervenes in some awful way—a messy divorce, cancer, a child drowned in a boating accident, like Bucky in *Ordinary People*—we cannot bear it. We go into denial: "This should not happen! It's not right! It's against the rules!" We desperately want to blame somebody.

Meanwhile, somewhere in the back of our minds, in our body wisdom, we are aware that there is another fundamentally different type of growth that we undergo in life. This other growth is not linear and incremental, but transformational, such as when we pass from one stage of life to another. In transformational growth something old, the old identity or perspective on life—we could call it "who I think I am"—must die if the new is to be born. We can describe this as a process of breakdown and breakthrough, and it is this process that is pictured in the Hero's Journey as the cycle of death and rebirth. How do we break down and break through to something totally new? We must leave the bright world of what we have known and descend into the unknown, really submit to it, if we are to find our new way. Life itself forces us to let go. The passage from childhood to adulthood is one example of a life-passage where breakdown and breakthrough spontaneously occur. The child-ego has in effect to die, and we all know how much we resist this process. Many, many of the fairy tales—the Grimm brothers' tale of the Frog Prince is just one example—are about negotiating this difficult passage. Other examples of life passages include marriage, childbirth, divorce, changing jobs or cities, taking an oath of office, retirement, and death. We may note that all of these events are accompanied by formal or informal rituals. Rituals are ways of summoning and focusing our energies for a leap into the unknown. Such life-passage moments make natural springboards for drama because they place the hero on the cusp of change. In this regard, there is a close connection between ritual, myth, and storytelling. Myths serve the ritual function of showing the reluctant ego the path of transformation. In drama, the cycle of breakdown and breakthrough translates into a curve of growth through crisis.

The Hero's Journey also resonates through the orchestration of characters in the screenplay. We project figures from our own inner lives onto the characters in our story, and this contributes to the feelings we have and judgments we make about them. The audience does likewise. Some of the important projections we make include psychological complexes, such as the persona, the shadow, and the anima.

Persona and Shadow

The Hero's Journey has to do with finding out who we are by being confronted with what we don't know about ourselves. We may identify the Day World with the persona aspect of our conscious ego and the Night World with what Carl Jung termed the shadow. The *persona* is the mask we wear in our social interactions. It's who we want other people to think we are. The word persona is borrowed from the ancient Greek theater and originally meant the colorfully painted wooden masks worn by actors on the stage. The mask simultaneously hid the actor's identity behind the role of the character and amplified the actor's voice so that it would reach the back rows of the theater. Every mask we wear serves the dual role of both disguising and revealing us. In a positive way, our persona allows us to interact with others without feeling too naked or having to reveal too much of our inner feelings. Our social persona is made up largely of what we would like to believe about ourselves.

On the most superficial level, the persona may consist of the brand names we identify with. One person is a Chanel girl, another is a Calvin Klein guy, another an Armani, and so on. Pop divas, TV shows, web sites, sets of hip gestures, and in-group language are all means of persona identification. Persona affiliations through brand names and other consumables have to some extent replaced family and clan structures as means to achieve a sense of belonging. They make up an important part of "who I think I am." Of course, family and upbringing are very important sources of our self-image. They shape our expectations of what our lives will be like, how we will live, and whom we will marry. Since we live our social lives behind this mask, there is always the chance that we ourselves will be taken in by it and come to believe that we are "nothing but" our persona.

The shadow, on the other hand, is an aspect of the unconscious made up partly of all those ways of being and feeling and thinking which do not fit into our social persona. Carl Jung, who identified this complex in the psyche, once said, "The shadow is everything I don't like to admit about myself." It is the opposite or inverse of the ego in general, and especially of the persona attitude. Of course, this definition of shadow may include other things that I *cannot* admit about myself because I am simply unconscious of them. Jung's important clinical observation was that those aspects of our totality do not simply go away because they have disappeared from the screen of consciousness. One way we do experience the contents of the shadow is by unconsciously projecting them onto people who drive us crazy or who we "love to hate." When we begin to scratch the surface of what really burns us up about the guy who cut us off in traffic or the woman acting passive-aggressively in the office, and try to be honest with ourselves, we find a curious, secret relationship to whatever we believe we despise. Sometimes this relationship to the shadow only comes out in our dreams. But an important point in relation to the Hero's Journey is that the shadow has *energy*.

Think of the insatiable, nonstop energy we had when we were two years old. As we progressively dis-identified with behaviors that were considered too infantile, too vulnerable, or too aggressive, we also cut ourselves off from energy. We learned early on that many behaviors are not accepted, and so we dropped them. But in this inevitable process we also lost some of our wholeness. That is why every journey invariably takes us into the region of the shadow to recover lost energy. The old radio show would always begin, "The Shadow knows . . ." and in some important ways, the shadow knows things about us that we ourselves do not.

Internal Software: Projection and Screenwriting

There is an easy way to begin to get a feel for this relationship between the ego, the persona, and the shadow. Take an ordinary sheet of paper and fold it lengthwise, so there is a right half and a left half. Fold the right half under so that only the left half is visible. Now fold the paper vertically, so that you are looking at the upper left quadrant. At the top of this portion of the page, write the words: "How I Want Others to See Me." Now, as quickly as you can, and without thinking about it too much, write a list of words: nouns, adjectives, verbs, whatever, that have something to do with how you want others to see you. The list doesn't have to be exhaustive; the number of words is not important. There is no right or wrong to this, no "correct" or "incorrect" responses. It is what you think it is. The more important thing is to do this spontaneously, without censoring yourself.

Now turn the paper over vertically so that you have the lower left quadrant to work on. Write the heading: "How I See Myself," and quickly write a list of words that pertains to that idea. These may be similar to the words you wrote above, or they may be different. Don't worry about what anyone might think, just let the Buddhist idea of "first thought, best thought" be your guide and be very natural with it.

Now unfold the paper again.

In the upper right-hand quadrant, write, as best you can, words which are the exact opposite or contrary to the words on the left. Then do the same thing with the words on the bottom half of the page, those words that pertained to "How I See Myself."

All of the words on the right-hand side of the page, all the opposites, belong to the shadow. Through a systematic pattern of identifying ourselves with one set, we have also dis-identified with the other. Yet both sets belong to our wholeness, the wholeness of our human nature. It is not easy to admit that the words on the right-hand side also belong to us.

Continued

As we have said, we have a tendency to project our own shadow side onto other people. Where does the shadow go in movies? Who carries the shadow in movies? Normally the shadow is projected onto the antagonist of the story. If that projection is made unconsciously by a screenwriter with no appreciation for his or her own shadow, that antagonist usually comes off as flat, one-dimensional, stereotyped. This flattens out the whole movie, and the drama becomes less compelling. But when a writer dares to confront their own shadow material as he encounters it in the writing process, rather than projecting it blindly, the antagonistic character who emerges is dark and human—and compelling.

Call and Separation

As we move through the phases of the Hero's Journey, we shall focus on those aspects that underlie dramatic structure. Then, in Chapter Eight, we shall make the point-for-point correspondences to drama. The major phases of the Hero's Journey—Separation, Descent, Initiation, and Return—cannot be exactly equated with the three acts that comprise screenplay structure. The situation is more complex than that. There are certain genres, such as fantasy, adventure, sci-fi, and horror, and certain plot structures like the quest and the escape, that do seem to lend themselves to an overtly "mythic" treatment. It is more important, however, to look at how the dynamics of the Hero's Journey paradigm shape the deep structure of all kinds of movie stories, from family melodramas to comedies, from thrillers to movies with alternate, nonlinear dramaturgy.

The Separation phase of the Hero's Journey can indeed be equated with Act I of the plot structure. It is situated in the Day World of the story, the known terrain or status quo of the hero's life. The first point in the anatomy of any story is to establish the status quo world from which the hero's adventure will go forth. This is not merely a setting, not merely "Once upon a time. . . ." The myth or fairy tale takes us into a particular status quo world because there is something wrong there. The first image that opens the myth, fairy tale, or movie establishes the status quo setting of the village, the castle, the hut in the woods, and so on. There we find a king who has three daughters and the youngest is the most beautiful of them all, or an old couple who live alone in the woods, until one day. . . . In a movie, we might be taken into a teenage boy's bedroom, a small town, a police station, or a spaceship coming out of warp drive into another star system.

But the world of the status quo, whether identified as the interior world of one character or the world of small-town America, already contains the seed of its own destruction. This is a universal element of the setup. There is a flaw in this world, which is usually invisible to the characters themselves. When the story opens on a "perfect" kingdom, a "perfect" suburb (as in *American Beauty*), or a "perfect" family, the very perfection is itself the flaw. The wisdom of myth and fairy tale accords with the insights of Taoism, which proposes that creation is always in movement and change, and that status quo situations are by their very nature unstable. Belief in their permanence is illusory. In the opening, we witness the fracture of this world, or we see that it has already lost its vitality, like the American couple and the Japanese and Moroccan families in *Babel*. This is the motif of the Waste Land. In the medieval Parsifal myth, the entire landscape has withered, animals and people as well as the crops. Many screenplays fail in development because the writer is too in love with her characters and their world to see the flaw. But the flaw that is implicitly present is the cornerstone of both the throughline conflict and the theme, so it is wise to give this some attention.

"Once upon a time, there was a king who had three sons. . . ." What's wrong with this picture? This implicit question is activated subliminally in our minds. The answer is left unstated—in the *subtext*—but the question already tells us where the story must go. What is wrong when there is a king with three sons? There is no mother, no daughter, no sister, no queen, no princess. The female element is completely absent. The situation is out of balance. Therefore we already know from the opening sentence that the fairy tale will involve a search for the feminine. The three sons will have to go on a quest to find brides, to integrate the feminine into this kingdom and make it more whole; usually it is the "dumbling" who succeeds. Joseph Campbell underscores the tone of this archetypal moment:

> The familiar life horizon has been outgrown; the old concepts, ideals, and emotional patterns no longer fit; the time for the passing of a threshold is at hand.[9]

The opening situation of the story by its very nature points toward what is missing, and thus forces us to ask questions and become involved. We are orchestrating both the *text* of the story (the plot throughline) and the *subtext* (the theme) in the very opening scenes. The subtext is suggested to the audience *negatively*: through what is missing, incomplete, or unbalanced.

We have an opening situation, but we do not yet have movement. Establishing the status quo of this world sets the stage for the first event of the story, the Call to Adventure. Of all the points of Campbell's model, this is surely the best known. It seems we all love calls to adventure. We love beginnings; we get hung up on them. But as with our new diets or New Year's resolutions, the problem is always in the follow-through. Yet the call in itself is not an invitation only; it is also a destruction. The call simultaneously heralds the "awakening of the self" of the hero and the shattering of the status quo world. These two are aspects of one phenomenon. The call takes us from the world of the ego's hopes and fears to the world of destiny. It is an archetypal moment we have all experienced at some time in our own lives, the call to realize who we already have the potential to be.

9. Campbell, *Hero*, p. 51.

There are actually three ways that the Call to Adventure can come in myths and fairy tales. It can come from three different directions, so to speak. There is the call from within, the call from without, and the blunder or call from below. Each variation on the call adds its own twist or impetus to the direction of the story. Yes, they all serve to get the story moving, but the differences are as important as the commonality they share. We shall differentiate them, because exactly the same three possibilities appear in the setups of movies.

The first way the Call to Adventure may come is as an inner or self-proclaimed call. We might open on a little hut in a tiny hamlet in the woods. Little Hans has grown up to be a big, strapping boy. When he stretches in the morning, his hands break through the roof of the cottage. His pants hardly go down to his knees, and when he flexes his muscles, the seams burst. One day he says to himself: "This hut is too small for me! This village is too small for me! There's a big world out there, and I must find my place in it!" And he sets out into the wide world to make his fortune. In a direct movie parallel, we earlier mentioned the classic film *Midnight Cowboy*, written by Waldo Salt. In that movie, Joe Buck announces his mission right off the bat. He is getting out of this little Texas town and heading up to New York City: "Lotta rich women up there, Al. Beggin' for it. Payin' for it too. And the men're mostly goddamn tutti-fruttis!" Truman Capote, in the opening of *Capote*, declares to the world that he will invent a new form of literature, the non-fiction novel, when he sets out to trace the motives for a seemingly random murder. Rocky Balboa is driven to become a champion, while the captain in *The Perfect Storm* needs to catch fish in order to save his boat and his self esteem. In a movie of a very different tone, *Trainspotting*, Renton's inner call is to try to get himself off junk. T. E. Lawrence, in *Lawrence of Arabia*, has the self-proclaimed Byronesque call to liberate Arabia from the Turkish occupation, while the hero of the Iranian film *Taste of Cherry* simply wants to end his life and is trying to find someone to bury his body decently after he commits suicide.

Though these movies are all quite different in setting and style, the self-proclaimed call in each sets a very definite tone. Of the three ways the Call to Adventure may come into the story, this inner or self-proclaimed call starts the hero off with the strongest impetus and forward momentum. The nature of the individual's call immediately identifies the throughline conflict the character will follow from beginning to end. This inner variation on the call also takes both the character and the audience most quickly into the archetypal realm of the Eternal Child, or the child-hero. The self-proclaimed call sets a tone of hope and optimism. The hero starts off imagining that he is in control of events. These characters are often adolescents, or they are people who have retained a special youthful quality, such as idealism, hope, or innocence, into adulthood. This quality is always going to be tested and transformed by the trials of the journey. In fairy tales, such a call might belong either to a child reaching puberty and ready to break the worn-out horizons of her home, or to a simpleton or fool who is unconscious of danger.

Implicit in the context of the self-proclaimed call is that the hero does not know the trials awaiting him. As we watch Renton, in *Trainspotting*, stack up his tins of mushroom soup, his tubs of orange sherbet, and his pornography magazines in his plan to go cold turkey through heroin withdrawal, we know instinctively that it won't be so easy. When we look at Joe Buck in the opening sequence of *Midnight Cowboy*, we see that he is an accident waiting to happen. We understand that his call is largely empty bravado. It is his defense against the harshness of life. Joe Buck is not really a big cowboy stud, but is emotionally still a child. We realize that he has no idea what he is getting himself into, and that makes us sympathize deeply with him. We are worried for him because we can see, with the eyes of the heart, what is in store. In this way, the opening sequence of *Midnight Cowboy* brings us directly into the archetypal feeling states associated with the Child as Orphan. The foreground tone is bright and cheerful, while the background, or subtext, is full of shadows, anxiety, and feelings of inadequacy. In the foreground, Joe Buck's call is simple: I'm gonna go to New York and be a big hustler. But on a subtextual level, he is being called to get into trouble and to lose himself. What is really going to happen to him during the course of the story is not that he will be paid a lot of money to have sex with rich women, but that he will enter into an edgy relationship with an alter ego, Ratso Rizzo. *Midnight Cowboy* will turn into a different sort of love story than Joe Buck had in mind, one that will begin with betrayal, take Joe Buck deep into an emotional Night World, and end with commitment and devotion. In the development of *Midnight Cowboy*, the orchestration of this opening, with its self-proclaimed call and its immediate connection to the Child archetype, was crucial to establishing Joe Buck as an enduring icon of lost innocence. Joe Buck's journey coincided with a collective loss of innocence that America was forced to endure during those years. This specific setup allowed the deeper meaning of that collective moment to resonate with a vast audience.

The second variation on the Call to Adventure motif is the call that comes from the outside. This may either be an assignment the main character is given, or an event that forcibly destroys the main character's status quo and shakes him into a quest for a new equilibrium. So, for example, a strange magician visits the castle and presents an adventure to the four princes. Or a girl's seven brothers have been enchanted and turned into swans, and she must find them and then return them to their natural form. Or the Loathly Damsel appears in King Arthur's court and challenges one and all to the great quest for the Grail. Or this one: a king has one son, and his single greatest fear is that the son will find the picture of the most beautiful princess in the world, and leave himself and his kingdom unguarded in his quest for this beauty. So the picture is hidden in the thirteenth chamber, where the prince is forbidden to look. And of course one day when the king is out hunting, the prince goes to the old chancellor and orders him to open the door to the thirteenth chamber, exactly because it is the forbidden thing. The chancellor warns the prince, but finally unlocks the door, and as the door swings slowly open the prince sees a radiance he had never imagined before . . . and immediately falls over as though dead.

Stories where the call comes from the outside, either as an assignment or as a sudden disaster, place special emphasis on the nature and the context of the call. What is calling us? *Who* is calling us? In the traditional mythic context, it is ultimately God or the spirit who is calling, even when the call comes in the form of a natural disaster. The direction the story takes then depends largely on the nature of that outer force. For example, a young man named Paris gets the assignment to choose which of three goddesses is the most beautiful, Hera, Athena, or Aphrodite. Each goddess represents a different leading value, so Paris is really being asked which value will lead his life. He is choosing his destiny. The entire drama of Homer's *Iliad* and *Odyssey* grows out of this fateful choice. There are innumerable film examples of the call that comes as an assignment. Entire genres, such as the detective story, are driven by the call as assignment. But we must always ask what is the specific nature of the assignment, because it sets up the throughline for the entire story. John Book, the police captain in *Witness*, gets the assignment to investigate the killing of an undercover officer. It is a call that is part of his job, it is his duty, and is appropriate to his character—to what we will discuss in Chapter Four as the character's *mode*. But because this specific assignment involves him with Rachel and Samuel, the Amish mother and son he must protect, and with Paul, the corrupt police chief who is Book's own father figure, it will take him on a journey that will change his life.

Who is calling, and the context of the call, signifies the nature of the call, and thus the trajectory and tone of the story. By "context," we mean specifically where the hero is and what he is doing when the call comes. Bobby Barnes, the earnest "good CIA soldier" in *Syriana*, is given the assignment to assassinate Prince Nasir, eldest son of an oil-rich Gulf emir. Why Bobby? Because Bobby spoke out too boldly and honestly in an interview for a managerial position at the agency. And why was Bobby, an undercover field operative, being booted upstairs for a role as a CIA station chief to begin with? Because he was too forthcoming about the loss of a Stinger missile that was part of a covert arms deal in Tehran. He sent memos of alarm, and, as his superior tells him, nobody wants to hear about it. The context suggests that the more Bobby tries to keep his integrity and ideals intact, the deeper he is being sucked into a Night World of betrayals.

Archie and Wanda, the two protagonists of *A Fish Called Wanda*, are both responding to exterior calls. The context here is set up in the two contrasting worlds the characters come from. Wanda gives herself the assignment to approach Archie, her jailed boyfriend's barrister, in order to find out where the loot from their bank robbery is hidden, while herself becoming the Call to Adventure for Archie. And one especially strong example of significant context in the outer call is found in Clint Eastwood's *Unforgiven*. What is Will Munney doing when the Kid approaches his homestead? He is futilely chasing pigs around in the dirt. This becomes a metaphor for the entire journey Will Munney will take in the film.

The alternate form in which the outer call can come is through a disastrous or chance event that catalyzes the story. There are events that break into our lives and suddenly change everything. Falling in love, the discovery of an infidelity, getting laid off, or a sudden illness all have the power to overthrow our sense of reality and send us on a quest for meaning. The disaster that catalyzes the tragedy of Oedipus is a sudden plague that strikes the city of Thebes, where he is king. This outer event sets Oedipus on a trajectory to discover the truth about himself; it is intimately bound up with his own fate. It is of course a disaster when the Sword of Destiny is stolen in the opening of *Crouching Tiger, Hidden Dragon*. *The Fugitive* gets a running start with the brutal murder of Dr. Richard Kimbell's wife, yet through the unfolding of the plot we discover that the killing was anything but random. Robert Altman sets up a complex "ensemble of ensembles" in *Short Cuts*, but the catalyzing dramatic element does not come until the waitress hits the news commentator's little boy with her car. The specific context for this disaster is that she had just been harassed by the three fishermen in front of her boyfriend, and was in an emotional, distracted state. *The Sixth Sense* uses an aggressively orchestrated outer call also set up the startling twist at the climax. In each of these cases, a disaster that appears at first as a peripheral or chance event is later revealed to be part of a fabric of destiny. The outer call as disaster in fact asserts that larger patterns of fate impact our lives (the etymology of "disaster" is "unlucky star").

The third major variation on the Call to Adventure is the blunder—and, in a sense, all calls to adventure are blunders, because we don't really know what we are getting ourselves into when we begin. If it is a true call, it always means getting in over our heads. Only getting in over our heads forces us, ultimately, to change. There was a princess (so the Brothers Grimm tell us) who was so dazzlingly beautiful that when the sun shone upon her, he himself was amazed at her beauty. She liked more than anything to go out into the backyard behind the castle where there was a lovely spring—in some versions it's a well—and play with her favorite toy, a golden ball. We all know the story. She throws the ball up and catches it. She is having a wonderful time, and she is relatively unconscious of her surroundings. Without thinking about it, she throws the ball too far. And now she's running, running, like a baseball outfielder, but the ball is going . . . going . . . gone! The ball falls down the well and disappears. Home run.

A blunder is a mistake, but a significant mistake. Of course Freud would say there are no mistakes, and if we let the event resonate a bit so that the psychological story-language of the fairy tale can speak to us, we can begin to see its significance. Here is a girl who is on the verge of puberty. Her old, child way of being is going to die, and that is pictured as the loss of her golden ball. What is a golden ball? It is simple, it is round (complete in itself), it is pure, it is eternal. All of these qualities echo out of the intrinsic qualities of the golden ball—and she has just lost it. It fell down the well. So what is a well? It's a dark, wet hole.

We can guess how that connects to puberty. And yet water is also the source of life. Thus it is appropriate that the ball falls into the well and not a dry hole in the ground or Alice's rabbit hole. The poor girl can only sit down and weep over her lost childhood, as many of us do in adolescence. It is not merely that we can no longer do what we want, but that golden sense of living forever is stolen from us. We fall into time and mortality. Blunders always require us to wake up and become more real, to face life.

Take a moment and recall the last time you made a blunder. Blunders often start as something very small. For example, you are on your way out to go pitch your screenplay idea to a producer, and just as your door is swinging closed, you have the sinking realization that you don't have your keys. It seems to happen in slow motion: you fumble in all your pockets frantically, wildly, and dive for the door just as the lock snaps shut with an echoing boom out of *The Fall of the House of Usher*. You don't have the keys to your car and you can't get back into the apartment. You are supposed to be at this meeting in twenty minutes, and it's all the way across town. For just a moment, your preoccupation with the meeting has knocked you off center, blinded you. And that is perhaps the beginning of a story.

What makes the blunder dramatically significant is not that it seems to happen by chance, but that it reveals an *unsuspected world*. As Joseph Campbell summarizes Freud's judgment, blunders are

> . . . the result of suppressed desires and conflicts. They are ripples on the surface of life, produced by unsuspected springs. And these may be very deep—as deep as the soul itself. The blunder may amount to the opening of a destiny.[10]

A blunder is a challenge to a character to see what has blinded her, to try to turn around and look at the blind side. It is often the character's extreme overdevelopment in one side of life that has led to blindness in another, though when the character is inexperienced, the blunder can come through an inability to understand consequences. The Moroccan boy in *Babel*, an innocent killer, has convinced himself that the hunting rifle is almost useless and could never send a bullet as far as the tourist bus down below. Charlie, the protagonist of Jonathan Demme's *Something Wild*, has just been named vice president of his bank. His blunder is that in spite of his evident affluence, he tries to sneak out of a cheap restaurant without paying the bill—and he gets caught. Again, we could ask who or what in Charlie's own nature is calling to be recognized. Jimmy Stewart's character in Hitchcock's *Vertigo*, Scotty, blunders when he cannot leap across a rooftop while chasing a suspect. As he hangs from the gutter, Scotty witnesses another officer slip and fall to his death, and it is as though Scotty himself also dies. He is a policeman of absolute integrity and unquestioned reputation, yet he cannot bring himself to go back to the police force. Scotty is blind to the fact

10. Campbell, *Hero*, p. 51.

that his very integrity may be used to dupe him. There is something charming—but naïve—in his integrity. The blunder shows us that the hero is out of center as the story opens. As a minor illustration, Lester, in *American Beauty*, drops his briefcase on his way to the car where his wife Carolyn is already infuriated at his being late. This simultaneously reveals his attitude toward work and is a passive-aggressive poke at his wife. In relation to the inner and outer calls, we could consider the blunder as a "call from below," from the shadow or inferior side of our nature.

With the call, the hero is engaged in the first phase of the adventure: the physical, emotional, and psychological separation from an earlier identity and system of sentiments. In the rites of passage of primitive tribes, the child leaves the village and returns an adult, with a new name, a new social rank, and a new interior sense of who he is. This is all accomplished within the tribe's horizon of collective belief. In our own world, separation also means breaking with our tribe to search for a unique identity and purpose. It is incidental whether the tribe is defined as "we who fought the Cold War," or "we who meet at the mall every afternoon," or "we who secretly keep Kurt Cobain pictures under our beds." However it is defined, in the presence of the call the tribe becomes a source of conflict. An entire group can also receive a call, in the case of ensemble movies such as *The Commitments*. And in contemporary movies with interwoven narrative lines, like *Short Cuts, Traffic, L. A. Crash*, and *Syriana*, several characters may receive individual calls, which then bring the separate story strands together.

The Call to Adventure gives forward momentum to the story. But it is exactly here that a detracting element enters. Ambivalence rears its head. As soon as the call comes and the hero starts to respond, a doubter appears on the scene. It may be the heroine's wicked stepmother or the old chancellor. (In fairy tales, every psychological nuance is *expressed*: objectified as a character or event.) The doubter may whisper, but it is always the penetrating voice of secret anxiety: "Forget about that princess, she's not worth it. I mean, first you would have to cross the forest—and no one's ever crossed the forest. And then you would have to cross the desert—and no one's ever. . . . And *if* you did by some miracle finally arrive before the palace of the princess, what would you find? Around this palace is a wall fifty feet high, and on the wall is a row of spikes, and on top of each spike is the head of a prince who came, just like you, seeking the hand of this princess. So forget her. There are plenty of nice girls in our neighborhood. Allow me to call one for you. . . ."

Just that voice of doubt may be enough to nip the adventure in the bud. As soon as desire comes, fear comes: fear of the risks involved, fear that we won't get what we want, fear of what we will have to sacrifice to get what we want, fear of separation. The desire spontaneously constellates the fear. They form a pair of opposites. The outer doubter is merely an externalization of the doubt we already feel inside. Thus there also exists the possibility that the hero will refuse the call. The classic statement on the refusal of the call is: "The gods lead those who will; those who won't, they drag." We all feel ambivalent when we get the call in life because it means change, work. Recall the last time you were approached on the street by a homeless person. How did you respond? If you are like most people, you probably said something like, "Not today, thanks; maybe another time." We want to decide which adventures we are willing to accept. We want to stay in our comfort zone.

Comic characters especially are seen refusing the Call to Adventure. Comic heroes are typically *reluctant* heroes. They reflect what is inferior in all of us: our laziness, our cowardice, our inertia. They do this in ways that help us laugh at those parts of ourselves and accept them. Thus they show us our unvarnished humanness. Comic heroes often spend most of the movie refusing the call. As well as being psychologically valid, this turns out to be a wonderful comic strategy. We can see Charles, in *Four Weddings and a Funeral*, run away from the call to the one relationship that could really shake him up. Only in the climactic scene is he forced to stop evading and stand up for his true value. Loretta, in *Moonstruck*, has a more decisive encounter with her passion, but again it is only at the climax where Loretta can accept her love for Ronnie and her own passionate nature, and act accordingly. Ultimately what is behind the ambivalence the character faces at the beginning of a story is a life-choice between two values, one of which is known, the other being still below the horizon of awareness. The initial refusal of the call by the comic hero leads to a specific variation in Act I of many—if not most—comedies.

Something must intervene to break the deadlock of ambivalence, and this is the entrance of a new personage, called the guide. There has been a major cultural shift, especially in the United States, around the figure of the guide. The first appearance of Obi-Wan Kenobi in *Star Wars* was extremely well orchestrated from a cinematic point of view. But there is also no denying that it also caught hold of and articulated something growing on the edge of the collective consciousness, a collective intuition that a new image was needed. It is also the nature of the guide to appear out of nowhere, as Obi-Wan Kenobi does. When something appears out of nowhere, where is it coming from, in psychological terms? From the non-ego, from the unconscious. The guide is like a personification of the intuition that we *can* dare to take a risk and follow our own path. It is the voice inside which says, "Follow your heart." Of course we all want to have someone tell us to follow our hearts, and the guide is a figure whose function may become banalized. Ever since George Lucas first applied Joseph Campbell's model in *Star Wars*, there has been a continuous stream of typically very benign and shadowless guide figures appearing in movies. In the myths and fairy tales, the situation with the guide is usually much less clear. The guide arrives not to serve *us*, but to serve the process of transformation. Guides may be both shadowy and shifty. They do not play by our rules. An excellent example of the ambiguity of the guide is the wonderful figure of the Khidr in the Koran, who puts Moses through an extraordinary series of tests.

The guide is not an element to be tacked onto a story in a stereotypical way. It is true that the guide is someone who knows much more than the hero. This may be someone who has already taken the journey and has returned to help others, it may be a supernatural helper, or it may well be an outcast of some kind. If we take a broad survey of the fairy tales, we find that guides are most often wise old women or men, helping animals, or grotesque outsiders, even corpses. The boy setting out on his adventure stops by the roadside where there is a gallows. The corpse says, "Will you cut me down? I'm being pecked at by the crows up here!" The boy obliges, and the corpse promises to help the boy if he is in need. What these guide figures have in common is that they are close to the world of nature, which is to say, to the instincts. The old have withdrawn from the social persona; they are of no social use anymore, and are overtaken by the physical decay of the body. They have let go of their social mask. Animals directly represent body wisdom. In the myth of Parsifal, at a key point in the story where Parsifal no longer knows what to do, he just lets go of the reins of his horse. He lets the horse lead him, and the horse takes Parsifal where he needs to go. And corpses could be said to stand for what is dead to the ego: the secret of the "other side." They all have instinctual wisdom rather than ego-based knowledge.

The guide is generally *not* a figure who represents the Day World values of the society. Guides are often shape-shifters because they are essentially non-ego. Joseph Campbell speaks of the hero's guide as the "personification of his destiny," and destiny is by definition outside the sphere of the ego. Sometimes the guide accompanies the hero for part of the journey; sometimes the guide gives the hero an amulet and drops out of the story; sometimes, as in the tales of Moses and Khidr, the guide is a trickster figure who tests the hero. In most all cases, the guide must disappear before the crossing of the return threshold to the Day World.

There are broad limits on the way the guide motif may be used in a film story, depending first of all on the idiom (idioms, genres, and their use for screenplay writing will be discussed in more detail in Chapter Seven). In the idiom of realism, there may not be a guide that we can see. The truth that we so often experience in our own lives is precisely the feeling of being lost and without guidance. That is our existential situation. To bring an Obi-Wan Kenobi into such a context would feel glaringly false. Sometimes the whole point is that the character doesn't have any guide and will have to search inside themselves for a guiding principle. In the expressionist idiom however, where dream or fantasy characters may easily appear on the screen, the guide may be directly characterized. Expressionism as an idiom and stylistic choice in story development is a context where, as in myth and fairy tale, everything on the screen is metaphor; nothing is meant to be taken absolutely literally.

There are many ways to play the guide in movies. The first thing to consider is the impact of the guide on the dramatic unity of the script. How can the guide be made appropriate to the idiom and the genre? How can the guide be orchestrated so as not to steal the hero's thunder or give away too much of the dramatic tension? As we mentioned, there may be no guide. The characters are on their own and must make their own mistakes. Or the guide may be a rather minor character who appears occasionally as a voice of conscience or of balance. The amiable Dr. Dreyfuss, who is C. C. Baxter's neighbor in Billy Wilder's comedy *The Apartment*, functions unobtrusively in this way. His messages are delivered in a teasing, bantering tone that is completely natural to his character.

A guide character may also appear to be antagonistic when we first meet him; he may appear first as a threshold guardian who challenges the protagonist. The antagonism invests this relationship with a lot of energy. This is the way it is commonly handled in love stories. And in the case of love stories where a threshold guardian transforms to become a guide, she normally becomes the hero's *primary relationship* in Act II.[11] In love stories, typically one character takes the active role. This character is the first one to fall in love and see the true potential of the relationship, and may pull the hero over the threshold to intimacy. Ronnie Camerreri plays this role of a threshold guardian who becomes a guide in *Moonstruck*. At first he appears antagonistically to thwart Loretta's goal: not only will he not come to the wedding, he is going to slit his throat right then and there. But the threshold guardian who becomes a guide is not limited to the love story genre. Buddies and mentors may appear this way: Ratso Rizzo in *Midnight Cowboy*, as well as Dubey, the chaotic wedding planner in *Monsoon Wedding* by Mira Nair. These are three films in three different styles. What they have in common is that though the guide figure first appears antagonistically in Act I, he (or she) takes on an "agent of chaos" role in Act II because he embodies a value the hero has to incorporate in order to resolve the conflict.

Much has also been made of the motif of the amulet. Frequently in the myths, the guide gives the hero a magical object as well as good advice and encouragement. Obi-Wan Kenobi gives Luke the light saber, the symbol of the virtues of the Jedi Knight—and a pretty cool weapon. These days, the amulet is popularly called the "power object," and thus it fits into our cultural tendency to make fetishes of our status symbols. It helps us imagine that our "power tie," our "power Chanel outfit," or our "power wheels" are endowed with a magical energy that will make us invulnerable and irresistible. So it would be better to come at this from a slightly different angle and see if we can add some psychological insight to what is there. The power of an amulet does not lie in what it appears to be on the surface, but in the resonance it sends out, its specific symbolism which speaks directly to our unconscious.

Luke Skywalker's light saber, hackneyed as it now seems, is a resonant example. The sword is not merely the *sign* of the old knights. If it were just a sign or reference to this nobler, more genteel earlier era, it would not have much

11. We define the dramatic role of the primary relationship in Chapter Five: The Story Molecule. The primary relationship character often embodies the quality or value that the main character needs to discover in herself. This figure is commonly referred to as the "love interest."

energy. Nor is it exclusively a symbol for "warrior power." Traditionally, in religions around the world, the sword (along with blades in general) is not merely a weapon, but metaphorically a tool of discrimination in the sense of "penetrating insight." When you cut with a sword, one part of the object falls to the left and one part falls to the right. So you distinguish, you differentiate. With a sword, you cut to the heart of a problem, like Alexander cutting the Gordian knot. And this is exactly what Luke Skywalker will be asked to do in the *Star Wars* trilogy, to use penetrating insight to differentiate between the light and dark sides of the Force. This is why the amulet arguably *must* be a sword and nothing else. The fantasy genre of *Star Wars* gives the imagination free reign to utilize mythic material, yet the choice must always serve both the plot and the theme.

Like the guide, the amulet will stand out too much as a story device if it is presented stereotypically. Another way to approach this is to ask the question: what is sacred for my character? What does she carry with her as a power object, and what, on a perhaps unconscious level, does that represent for her? What is that object trying to tell *her*? Jack Walsh, the Robert De Niro character in *Midnight Run*, is always preoccupied with his watch, which doesn't work too well. He has to keep shaking and tapping it, and is never sure if the time is off. The watch's function is obviously not pragmatic, since the watch doesn't work. The watch has another, personal value to Jack. He has an engaged love/hate relationship with his watch. Why hasn't Jack gotten a new watch? Because, he tells us, this watch was a gift from his ex-wife, maybe the first and only gift she ever gave him. He can't let go of the watch, because, even though they've been divorced for years, he hasn't let go of the relationship. This is how the watch is sacred to Jack. A watch is also a "ticker." How's the old ticker?—meaning the heart. So the business with the watch is a nonverbal way of saying Jack has trouble with his feelings, that something's not working in his heart. Jack is tenacious about old wounds he needs to let go of. His interactions with his amulet keep pointing to where his deep wound and his deep value are. In *Midnight Cowboy*, Joe Buck carries his transistor radio around everywhere, while his very problem has to do with communication. "Everybody's talkin' at me. I can't hear a word they're sayin'; only the echoes of my mind." The amulet should have a thematic connection; it is a physical embodiment of a value associated with the theme of the movie.

In these cases, the amulets point to what the character has to learn. But the amulet can also negatively become a fetish that prevents realization. While the amulet is a symbol for a function of the self, the fetish is a concretization of a desire. The fetish has become opaque to its own symbolic dimension. Far in the background, the energies of the psyche are working, but the character is obsessed with the literal object, and the literalism of the attachment turns the fetish into something destructive. By the way Frank, the Dennis Hopper character in *Blue Velvet*, handles his scrap of blue velvet cloth, we can immediately see the very hurt child inside the man clinging hysterically to his security blanket. But Frank is no child. Rather than using the emotions evoked by the blue velvet to heal his own trauma, he literally reenacts his past by terrorizing others. He can only act it out in a very literal way. So when we ask what is a character's amulet, what object is sacred to the character, the way we see the character interact with that object tells us much about the deep structure of his personality.

Crossing the Threshold

After meeting the guide, the next step in the Hero's Journey is crossing the threshold that marks the boundary of the character's known world or comfort zone. This event corresponds to the dramatic crisis that ends Act I of a screenplay. The intervention of the guide and the presence of an amulet really have one function in the Hero's Journey, and that is to prepare the hero for the crossing of the threshold between the Day World and the Night World by activating deeper centers of motivation. A threshold marks the boundary between two properties, two energy states. The warnings of the doubter have been a foreshadowing of the level of anxiety that manifests at this point. Here the sign says: DO NOT ENTER. The threshold we approach now is where the solutions and resources of the conscious ego are no longer enough. We will need other, unknown resources to accomplish the trials that await us. It is natural that we hesitate on the threshold.

Standing at the threshold, and embodying all of the extreme sense of threat and anxiety we experience as we are about to cross into the unknown, is a figure called the *threshold guardian*. We have already met the inner threshold guardians who confront the screenwriter in the form of critical self-talk voices. This intimidating figure restates the implied warnings of the doubter, but at a higher level of risk. The threshold guardian raises the stakes because he poses a real threat to the hero. Mythically an angel or ogre, giant or snake, fairy or monster, it stands, as Campbell tells us, for "the limits of the hero's present sphere, or life horizon."

> Beyond them is darkness, the unknown, and danger; just as beyond the parental watch is danger to the infant and beyond the protection of his society is danger to the member of the tribe. The usual person is more than content, he is even proud, to remain within the indicated bounds. . . .[12]

The threshold guardian, by his monstrous nature, embodies the energies of the Night World. As those energies are magnified by fear, so too the threshold guardian is frequently pictured as a giant, who guards the entrance to the forest: "Fee fie fo fum, I smell the blood of an Englishman!" It does not work to introduce yourself naïvely to the threshold guardian as the hero who is on his way through the forest, across the desert, and over the sea to marry the most beautiful princess in the world. "Oh yeah?" the giant replies. "Know what I do with heroes like you? Well, one is hardly a mouthful. I hang 'em up by their feet

12. Campbell, *Hero*, pp. 77–78.

to season them, then I melt a bit of grease in a pan, add some special herbs, and fry 'em till they're nice and crisp. *Cr-r-rack!* Delicious! *That's* what I do with heroes like *you!*" We have spoken of the Hero's Journey as a journey to recover lost energy, and the ferocity of the threshold guardian is an embodiment of how that energy *looks* to the uninitiated hero in its dissociated, unintegrated state.

Threshold guardians threaten, challenge, seduce, abduct. These challenges might be summarized in the single phrase: "Who do you think you are?" At the threshold to adventure we are challenged on, and *divested of*, our identity. One of the greatest and most instructive tales in this regard comes from the *Odyssey*. Odysseus and his men find themselves on a strange island after having been blown from the "real world" of the Mediterranean Sea into the dreamtime of adventure. They enter a shepherd's cave, where they help themselves to food and drink. Then the owner of the cave enters, the cyclops Polyphemus. He represents the obstacle that Odysseus has to pass through, or pass beyond, and we know from the story that Odysseus tricks him. Polyphemus asks Odysseus, "What's your name, stranger?" And wily Odysseus replies, "My name is No Man." Superficially this answer appears clever, because in this way he gets away from the cyclops after blinding him. But Joseph Campbell points out that Odysseus is prophetically (and unconsciously) announcing his own destiny. Odysseus will indeed become "no man." Step by step he will be divested of everything—his ships, his men, his power—until, naked and alone, he is washed up on a distant shore, a completely "washed-up" man. We ourselves do not set limits on our divestiture when life takes hold of us. This process begins as we cross the threshold and enter the Night World.

Campbell points out that there are two possible outcomes to the hero's encounter with the threshold guardian. The first possibility is that the hero defeats the threshold guardian by force or by trickery. Sometimes it is necessary to throw pieces of meat into the mouths of the three-headed dog and distract it that way. Or sometimes you have to answer riddles. But the other possibility is that the hero is *defeated* by the threshold guardian, is swallowed, and is taken down, like Jonah, into the belly of the whale. "The hero, instead of conquering or conciliating the power of the threshold, is swallowed into the unknown and would appear to have died."[13] As we shall see, both possibilities come into play in structuring film stories, where at the end of Act I we cross from the story's Day World into its Night World.

The question arises: why is there always a threshold guardian, and why does he—or it—always have to be fought? The first response is that it is the threshold guardian's function to push us down, down out of our heads—our attitudes—and into our deeper resources. We have been talking about the Hero's Journey as a journey to find lost energy and as a descent into the instinctual realm. It is

---

13. Campbell, *Hero*, p. 90. The image of the belly of the whale points to how completely we have been overpowered, and at the same time is a womb image pointing toward the new birth. It is a motif found worldwide.

precisely here at the threshold crossing that a specific instinct set gets activated. This is the *fight or flight* instinct. Here is where the adrenaline kicks in, both in the protagonist and in the movie audience as well. The story literally moves to a different energy level. Watch the audience in a theater and you can see it happen. Body postures shift—some lean toward the screen while others are pressed back in their seats. We are no longer detached viewers, but are now viscerally connected to what is happening on the screen. This effect is not limited to action movies by any means. The adrenaline rush really comes from the audience's identification with the hero, which has been established through Act I, combined with a text/subtext sense of what is at stake. When the character is attacked and suffers a loss of control, it is this disorientation and sudden loss of value that provides the sense of danger, even when the threat is not physical. The activation of the fight or flight system brings along with it a demand to be totally present, because now everything is at stake.

The second reason that the encounter with the threshold guardian seems to be necessary in the archetypal dynamic of the Hero's Journey is to pull us down to earth and take us out of a state of grandiosity. Simply setting out on the journey creates a certain euphoria. The first half-hour of climbing the mountain we are full of optimism, but we haven't even broken a sweat yet! Joseph Campbell used to tell a comic anecdote about grandiosity that came out of a seminar he did in California in the 1970s, apparently a more naïve place and time. He was describing the trials of the Hero's Journey when a woman in the audience raised her hand to say that this was all obsolete, that they didn't need the Hero's Journey anymore. Campbell asked her why not. "Because in the New Age we go directly from infancy to enlightenment!" "Then all you miss is *life!*" was Campbell's retort. We have had a little taste, and we think we've got the whole thing. The threshold guardian is there to tell us no, to force us down into the whale's belly where the real work of transformation will begin.

As with so many aspects of myth, the threshold guardian is paradoxical. There is an overt function and then there is a more hidden side. The threshold guardian appears to be trying to keep us out, to prevent our passage. And truly, he does keep out those who are unready. The hero myth has a direct correspondence to the rites of passage of twelve-year-old boys in primitive societies. The men of the tribe have to look carefully at who is ready to endure the initiation and who is not. This is a way of life, after all, where every day, when a man goes out to get food for the table, he is potentially risking his life. A boy too young, too small, or too weak might well be killed by the initiation ordeal. They will have their chance next year.[14] At the same time, the threshold guardian has an

---

14. Primitive or primal peoples, whose social evolution did not take the path of urbanization, have all but disappeared from the earth. Yet they represent the ancestors of us all. We must recall that "civilization" occupies only the most recent one-tenth of one percent of human evolution. The old initiation patterns appear to have been so selected for survival that they persist, and we can expect that they will continue into the future in some form.

occult or hidden function, which is not to keep us out, but in fact to usher us in. When we stand back and look at the whole round of the Hero's Journey from a distance, we see that these adversaries are our secret allies, dancing partners, Aikido opponents. A classic film example is the tough drill sergeant in *An Officer and a Gentleman*. Without the threshold guardian to push against, we could not know our own strength. Without him, our inner growth could never take place. Of course, this is never how it feels at the time. And the initiation elders cannot very well take off their ogre masks and tell a frightened child, "Look here, don't you see it's really Uncle Kwayaso, Uncle Bumba, and the guy next door with the three pigs? There's nothing to cry about!" That would ruin the value of the initiation. In rituals there is always an element of theater, but it is serious theater, acting out and externalizing a real psychological threshold in a context where it does matter whether one crosses over to manhood or remains a little boy.

Dramatically, this entire set or archetypal pattern is constellated by the crisis that ends Act I of the screenplay. This is true even where the crisis sequence in the movie does not press the button of physical danger. The threat can be moral or emotional and touch us just as deeply. Consider, for example, the sense of threat stirred up when Ada, in *The Piano*, crosses the threshold into George's cabin. There she enters into the shadowy contract to buy back her beloved piano, one key at a time, by giving George "piano lessons." Ada is not in physical danger, but her fight or flight instincts are nevertheless aroused. The fact is that the complete pattern of responses already exists within our nervous systems as we sit in the theater, just as it does in Ada. It may feel like a quantum leap in thinking to approach screenplay development in terms of complex patterns in the story meshing with complex patterns in the audience, rather than as a series of impulses that make the audience react. But I believe this is the direction that the art of story development is headed. Every cinema artist works with these complex patterns intuitively, and the sense of pattern grounded in an archetype is already implicit in the Aristotelian concept of *dramatic unity*, as we shall see.

The vice-squad cop, McFee, is John Book's threshold guardian in *Witness*. The moment is the scene in the parking garage where Book is shot. Here, in plot terms, the threshold Book is crossing is into the knowledge of the depth of corruption and betrayal in the police department. Even though John Book is a police captain and thus we may assume he has many years of experience under his belt, this is essentially a crossing over from innocence to experience during the crisis of the plot. Book has just discovered who killed the undercover detective in the train station through Samuel, the Amish boy. It was another cop. Book becomes inflated by his knowledge. When we are inflated, that is exactly when we fall into our blind spots, because the inflation makes us feel invulnerable. Our very successes may dissociate us from ourselves and from our better judgment. Thus, in an unguarded moment, Book tells his old friend and mentor Paul everything he knows. Then he returns home, confident that the case is under control. In a fine detail on the screen, we see that Book has even stopped at the cleaners and picked up his laundry, which is a sure indication that his mind has relaxed. Then he meets the threshold guardian, who says, in effect: "You think you *know* something, man? I'm gonna show you *exactly* what you know!" And—*boom!* The very well crafted sequence of which this scene is a part makes the essential psychological and dramatic insight that while the attack of the threshold guardian appears to come from an outer antagonist, it is equally a product of Book's own blind spot. Book's blind spot is his inability to see the situation the way it truly is. It is a product of Book's *mode*, his "who I think I am." It is exactly this "who I think I am" that will be tested and suffer death in the Night World.

The threshold guardian is an important figure in a movie drama, though usually not the primary antagonist. The threshold guardian may be a member of what we will discuss as the main antagonist's *emotional network*. As in the case of McFee, he may foreshadow the main antagonist. McFee is not the primary antagonist—Paul, the corrupt Chief of Police, is—but he sets the tone of the conflict and establishes what is at stake for John Book as we go into Act II of *Witness*. This is typically the henchman's role. Occasionally the main antagonist does appear to make the challenge at the threshold, but usually under conditions that let us know he is holding back his main power and is in some way "toying" with the protagonist.

Syriana, because it deals with a vast international arena, includes repeated thresholds that the three main protagonists cross. Staying with Bobby Barnes's strand of the story, the tragic CIA agent crosses a deeper threshold into betrayal when he arrives in Beirut in what is structurally the middle of the film. And here we have a significant variation on the threshold guardian motif: this threshold guardian, Mussawi, presents himself as an ally when in fact Bobby is being led into a trap where he will be brutally tortured. (The layers of betrayal here are many, running all the way back to the CIA headquarters.) In this sweep of action we may also note another aspect of orchestrating the threshold guardian and antagonistic characters in general: in order to reach Mussawi, Bobby must encounter a preliminary threshold guardian, the Hezbollah sheikh who runs the south Beirut suburbs. As a rule, whenever a motif—like the threshold crossing or guardian—is repeated, it gains in thematic importance.

Crossing the threshold is already a form of self-annihilation, because we can never go back to being who we were before. It is finished. We become "No Man." When we see Bobby afterward back in Langley, Virginia, at CIA headquarters, just the way he walks, his downcast eyes, everything about his demeanor conveys that something has indeed broken. This shift becomes a key point for the construction of movie stories, because the audience must see the threshold as a point of no return for the hero. If the hero can re-establish the first act status quo, there is no way to successfully build up the dramatic intensity of Act II. In screenplays, trouble with handling the threshold usually results from not establishing clearly what constitutes the Day World and the Night World of this story and coordinating these with opposing forces within the main character.

Essentially, the Day World and Night World stand for two inverse or opposing values. These values must be externalized so that we can see them. We must give them cinematic reality. Thus there is a physical boundary marker as well as a threshold guardian and threshold trauma. The image of Bobby being hooded and hustled into a black car by armed Hezbollah fighters physically marks the threshold to the unknown, as well as signaling his loss of control. Act II of *The Piano* moves into the interior of George's cabin where Ada is confronted with a value opposed to her status quo value. Act II of *The Talented Mr. Ripley* moves the action to Rome, and brings in a threshold guardian, Freddie Miles, whose mode is diametrically opposed to Tom Ripley's.

A physical threshold is utilized to indicate the dramatic shift. Where there is no obvious physical marker, more work must be done to show the audience the emotional or ethical threshold that is being crossed. The mythic resonances of the threshold crossing moment make us see that this is much more than simply an event that hooks into the story and swings it in a different direction. When we look below the surface, we can see that the story is being swung in a specific direction, even though the means that each movie uses will be specific to the story being told.

Because this threshold in the Hero's Journey is so directly connected to a critical aspect of screenplay structure, the Threshold Crisis that ends Act I, let us enumerate the salient points that carry over directly into our screenwriting:

- The threshold marks the boundary between the story's Day World and Night World.
- The threshold is a place of magnified energy: fascination and danger.
- An antagonistic threshold guardian challenges the hero, attacking the hero's sense of self, sense of purpose, or mission.
- Crossing the threshold commences a process of divestiture and breaks down the "who I think I am" (the self-image we shall define as the character's *mode* in the next chapter).
- Crossing the threshold marks a point of no return for the hero, who can never go back to being who she was at the beginning of the story.
- The threshold crossing points forward to an escalating series of trials.

The steps of the Separation phase of the Hero's Journey correspond directly, point for point, with the elements that comprise the setup of the screenplay's Act I. But now that we have crossed the threshold into the Night World, the two systems begin to diverge. The steps of the Hero's Journey that descend into the darkness still reveal on an archetypal level the process that underlies drama, but there is no longer a point-for-point correspondence. Myth has its own necessity and internal consistency, and so does drama. The differences will be seen to increase as we proceed. This is why mythic structure cannot be directly transferred over to plot structure. If we are serious about story development, we naturally want to understand why these differences exist. One of the main reasons has to do with the fact that in myths and fairy tales we are dealing with figures that may be directly archetypal images barely fleshed out with some costuming. They are not individualized human beings. We do not clearly differentiate Cinderella, Rapunzel, and Wassilissa as individuals. They tend to merge together within the "aura" of the heroine. The type takes precedence in fairy tales. Yet we sense an enormous personal difference between Amélie in *Amélie*, Ada in *The Piano*, and the nun protagonist in *Dead Man Walking*. The cinematic image is concrete and specific. All of these women are heroines, and all deal with men in erotically charged relationships. Here, the archetypal aspect speaks to us from the background, from the subtext. We shall see that the Act II screenplay structure is much more articulated and deliberate than the corresponding Descent phase of the Hero's Journey.

Descent

However dramatic the threshold crossing may be, it functions to foreshadow what will happen in the Night World. The hero has just now crossed into the territory where the adventure will really begin. And the tone as we enter the Night World is one of disorientation accompanying the loss of identity. In the world of the unknown, we do not know the rules of the game. We don't know what the game is, or who we are in the context of this game. We are lost, bereft. There are feelings of despair. At this point we would like to run back to safety, but the door has slammed shut behind us. Above the gateway to the Inferno in Dante's *Divine Comedy* is written:

> Through me is the way into the woeful city,
> Through me is the way into eternal woe,
> Through me is the way among the Lost People . . .
> Abandon all hope, ye who enter here.

The first major motif of the Descent phase is called the Road of Trials. We have entered the zone of trials and there is no guarantee that we will come out winners in the end. As they enter Hell, Dante's guide Virgil warns him: "Here you must put by all divisions of spirit and gather your soul against all cowardice." The cycle of the Hero's Journey, looked at from the outside, gives us a general foreknowledge that this way down through darkness leads to initiation, growth, and return. But that is not the way it is subjectively experienced at this point, because we are out of control. We are forced to acknowledge the instinct-based anxieties and distortions of perception that fall under the heading of panic. Mythic Descent feels more like an "elevator to Hell." Extraordinary stresses require a radical integrity, the ability to "keep coming back to center," in Sensei Ueshiba's words.

The hero is now called to undergo a series of trials in a landscape of "curiously fluid, ambiguous forms." Campbell likens the disappearance of the hero across the threshold to the passing of a worshipper into a temple—"where he is to be quickened by the recollection of who and what he is, namely dust and ashes unless immortal."[15] As we suggested earlier, the trials are not merely a series of life lessons or "growth opportunities" in the sense that our ego would like to think of them. On the contrary, the trials serve to strip away all the layers of ego-wrappings until an existential leap is made from an identification with the ego—with its desires, ambitions, feelings, and fantasies—to an identification with the energy that inhabits and carries the ego.

It is with the nature of these trials and the success of the outcome that movies are most concerned. In screenplays, the Road of Trials occupies all of Act II, and is universally considered the most difficult part of the story to construct. It is here that the essential human drama of the "purification of the self"[16] is played out. And it is in the corresponding stretch of the writer's journey that the greatest struggles with resistance crop up. In second acts—and in our own lives—the trials are often amorphous because we are in the middle of them, we have been swallowed by them. But we are all familiar with the hero's Road of Trials from fairy tales and myths. That can help give us a handle on the dynamic, if not the screenwriting techniques, of this part of the journey. In fairy tales, very commonly there are three trials in a sequence of increasing difficulty and risk. The three temptations of Christ or the three tests of the Buddha are variants on this universal motif. A common example the reader may be familiar with comes from the Russian fairy tale called "The Beautiful Wassilissa."

The story has a typical opening where the beautiful Wassilissa's saintly mother has died, leaving her only her maternal blessing and a magic doll. The wicked stepmother, trying to get rid of the girl, sends her to the hut of the Baba Yaga for fire. The Baba Yaga is the great witch of the Russian fairy tales. Around her hut in the heart of the forest is a fence made of human bones. The fence posts are topped with human skulls whose eyes glow at night. The Baba Yaga gives Wassilissa the first task: separating the good grain from the bad grain. Discrimination again, as with Luke Skywalker's light saber. The second day's task is even more difficult, to sow the grain . . . and so on. Always the task must be completed by sundown, or the Baba Yaga will come back and eat Wassilissa. The Baba Yaga in the Russian tales represents Mother Nature, the Great Goddess of Nature, in her dark, devouring aspect. She may be equated with the Hindu goddess Kali, black Time, who swallows all, and also with Maya, the weaver of the illusion of the universe. It is to this figure that Wassilissa has been sent for initiation. The wicked stepmother believes she is going to kill the girl, but has in fact sent her exactly where she needs to go to learn the lessons of survival.

---

15. Campbell, *Hero*, p. 91.
16. Geza Roheim, *The Origin and Function of Culture*, p. 51, quoted in Campbell, *Hero*, p. 101.

Similarly, in the Sumerian myth of Inanna—one of the oldest documents in existence—Inanna, the Queen of Heaven, also undergoes a series of trials, seven in this case. Inanna was a goddess of love, like the Greek goddess Aphrodite. Inanna made one small mistake, however: she fell in love with a mortal man. When her lover Dumuzi is snatched away by death, Inanna goes into the underworld to fetch him back. It is a journey where she must encounter her dark sister, Erishkigal. Here there are seven trials rather than three. Inanna must pass through the seven gates of the underworld, and as she does so, one by one the garments are removed from her body until she stands absolutely naked and exposed before the forces of the world of the dead.[17] This stripping away of garments is the core image of the entire process. Nakedness and vulnerability are seen as the necessary precondition for transformation. As in so many of the myths and fairy tales of transformation, the series of trials leads to a confrontation with and assimilation of opposites. The little girl meets the great witch, the goddess of light meets the goddess of darkness, the ego personality confronts his shadow, the human being faces the nonhuman or the superhuman. The Road of Trials leads to this assimilation of the opposite, of the shadow, by means of a breakdown of the illusion of "who I think I am." A smaller, more limited structure is being broken in favor of a larger, more comprehensive one that incorporates some of the wisdom of the unconscious.

In drama, the process of breakdown takes on a different rhythm and tone than it does in myth and fairy tale. This is because we are looking at it subjectively: how it *feels* to go on the journey, how it *feels* to break down under trials, to have all one's protections torn away. Myth is more emotionally distanced than drama, the better to reveal the essential archetypal structure. Drama, on the other hand, captures every emotional nuance of breakdown, every moment of pain and suffering. The structure of the Road of Trials in movies is more determined by the three levels of conflict we are working with in drama: inner conflict, interpersonal conflict, and plot-level conflict. These three levels, or rings, of what we term the Story Molecule make drama into a three-dimensional stream of meaning that is rooted in myth, but has its own life and dynamics. In movies, these three levels of conflict are catalyzed by three throughline dramatic questions: a plot question, a primary relationship question, and a question that goes to the heart of the inner conflict of values. So, in *Shakespeare in Love*: will Shakespeare successfully write the new play that will tell the truth about love? (outer plot); will Shakespeare be together with his love and muse, Viola? (primary relationship); will Shakespeare become Shakespeare, the greatest playwright of all time? (inner conflict). These three questions are raised at specific points that indicate that the trials are touching ever-deeper layers of

17. The mythic constellation that includes the seven portals and seven garments is especially rich. It connects on one hand with ancient astronomy and cosmology, where the soul descends to earth through the crystalline spheres of the seven planets, and on the other hand with the biblical story of Salome's "Dance of the Seven Veils."

the personality of the hero.* Myth and drama are not the same, but are parallel ways of expressing something universal. Myth does not provide the superficial structure for the screenplay, but is a depth reflection of it, the *meta-structure* of the drama. This is an important distinction.

Initiation: Meeting the Secret Mover

However many trials there are, and whatever twists and turns they may take, there is an end point to the Descent phase of the Hero's Journey. There is a goal, and thus ultimately an experience of meaning rather than absurdity. The series of trials is preparing the necessary conditions for Initiation. The Initiation phase of the journey itself has three important phases. First is an ultimate trial, often referred to as the Night of the Soul. It is the trial that we either cannot overcome, or through the very overcoming of which the leading values we have clung to are destroyed, so that we no longer recognize ourselves. Night of the Soul describes this moment of breakdown where subjectively it feels like we are dying, or have perhaps already died. It feels like a hellish "no exit" situation. We are confronted with "the tragedy that breaks man's face." In fact, the idea of "who I think I am" does die. How many of us can regroup and go on when our love relationship, our brokerage account, our professional standing, our moral superiority, or our physical safety turns out to be radically other than we thought it was? The Night of the Soul is, psychologically and spiritually, a point of "grow or die" for the person. We might also refer to it as the Death of the Ego. It would be more accurate however to think of it as the death of the ego's image of itself, especially to the extent that the ego has been identified with a persona or mask. Dramatically, this moment corresponds to the catastrophe that ends Act II of a screenplay. Contemporary drama does not like to dwell on these moments too long. We must reach back to *King Lear*, the poems of St. John of the Cross, *Job* and *The Lamentations of Jeremiah* in the Old Testament, the Passion of Christ, and the Greek tragedies in order to cultivate a taste for the Night of the Soul. The dramatic story structure that gives most emphasis to the Night of the Soul sufferings of the hero is, not surprisingly, called the "messianic hero." *One Flew Over the Cuckoo's Nest*, with its extended Catastrophe Story Step, and, of course, *The Passion of the Christ* would be examples to view.

A more contemporary metaphor for the Night of the Soul experience comes from the sport of marathon running. Runners talk about an invisible point fifteen or twenty miles out on the course they call the Wall. They say that when you hit it, you literally feel like you have run into a brick wall. Your blood sugar drops suddenly and you start to stagger. Your legs are wobbly, your head is on fire, your guts are hot and churning, you can no longer form saliva in your mouth. Every cell in your body screams out, "I can't go on anymore!" At this point, one

* How this deepening of the three levels of conflict is achieved is detailed in Chapter Eleven: The Sixteen Story Steps.

of two things happens: either you *die*—you fall down and you are out of the race—or you get a second wind and you *grow*.

Now, this idea of a "second wind" is very interesting. We could ask the question, from where is this second wind blowing? It turns out that in many Native American languages, the same word is used for "wind," "breath," and "spirit." A second wind is a second breath is a second spirit. The second spirit is the one you can only find, only access, by hitting the Wall. The second wind doesn't belong to the ego; it belongs to the wisdom of the body, to the instincts. After all, "I" couldn't go on anymore. Who was this "I" that couldn't go on? And who is it, then, who has the second wind and is still running? It is not that same "I." The ego cannot summon that extra resource on a whim; it must first break itself against the Wall. Yet we might also imagine this as something akin to cracking open a shell. What is inside the shell is the organism's deep response to that "grow or die" catastrophe. I am always astonished by demonstrations of karate masters, wondering how they can break those bricks with their hands, their heads, their tongues, or whatever—it seems humanly impossible. Or how could Michael Jordan seem to hang in the air from the three-point line to the basket, twisting and pumping all the way to the reverse slam-dunk? These are pictures of the dimension beyond the Wall. Athletes will say that what is important here is not to be tight, but to let go: surrender to the flow of the game, which is also the flow of yourself. You don't own the flow; the flow carries you. This is a radically different kind of wholeness. Initiation is not the return of the princess's golden ball, the primary unity of childhood. It is the awakening of a new, more complex and dynamic unity that has become one by assimilating its opposite. We are fortunately coming to a better understanding of this trans-rational dimension of performance.

"Grow or die" hinges on how we respond to our own Night of the Soul, to the catastrophic moments in our own lives when we say to ourselves: "If this relationship falls apart, I'll just die," or "If I can't get this movie made, it's the end. It's all over." And then it happens. It is the end. The relationship *does* fall apart. The movie *doesn't* get made. It is the end—and now where are we? Many of us in our own lives, and many movie stories as well, get hung up at this point. The imagination can't go any further. My partner Tom had a critically important insight about this predicament. He noticed that many heroes at this juncture *ventilate* their rage and frustration in a wild outburst of violent emotion. By the standards of polite society this is all wrong, but from the perspective of the instincts it is healthy; another paradox. The ventilation blows away the old inhibitions and gives access to the deeper, life-or-death level of energy. Tom and I connected ventilation back to the idea of second wind. Ventilate comes from the French word *vent*, which means "wind." In this case, the second wind comes blowing through the ego's resistance like an express train. And second wind is second spirit: we are born again. This is a way of describing the connection between death and Initiation, the new birth or new beginning.

If we keep in mind the principle that the character changes something in the way she perceives herself, and that as her self-image changes, her behavior changes, then we can begin to understand how the mythic Initiation transfers into the dramatic context. Initiation means "new birth," and this new birth takes place in the depth of the Night World, in the depth of the psyche. There is a poem that captures the poised and disoriented moment of rebirth with elegant directness:

> I have a feeling that my boat
> has struck, down there in the depths,
> against a great thing.
> And nothing
> happens! Nothing . . . Silence . . . Waves . . .
> —Nothing happens? Or has everything happened,
> and are we standing now, quietly, in the
> new life?[18]

The Road of Trials, in fact the entire journey, is an intuitive pedagogy preparing us for these moments of life passage, preparing us to face them with the right attitude, the right posture. And that "right posture" has to do with submission, the surrender of "who I think I am" (which could also be translated as "what I think my limitations are"). The second wind isn't just something we can order off a menu, or we would all be doing it. There is not a mantra that can do it; there is not a credit card that can do it. It requires the entire journey up to this point to prepare us. The Night of the Soul is thus itself the beginning of the Initiation phase of the Hero's Journey. Death is not followed by rebirth; death *is* rebirth. To the mythic imagination, they are two sides of one coin. Initiation also means the beginning of knowledge, which is to say: meeting the Secret Mover, the Power which, invisible to our eyes, has been propelling the entire adventure forward, leading us inevitably to itself.

> One by one the resistances are broken. [The hero] must put aside his virtue, beauty, and life, and bow or submit to the absolutely intolerable. Then he finds that he and his opposite are not of differing species, but one flesh.[19]

This opposite with whom we are one flesh we may call the Secret Mover of our lives. Who is the Secret Mover of your own life?

I believe that Campbell rightly emphasizes this humbling experience in which the ego experiences itself no longer as the supreme ruler of its world, constantly battling against other egos, but as submitting to a far greater or higher power. Following the archetypal phases of this encounter as they typically appear in

---

18. Jiménez, Juan Ramón, "Oceans," in Bly, Robert, *News of the Universe* (California: Sierra Club Books), p. 105.
19. Campbell, *Hero*, p. 108.

myths, we can shade in degrees of integration or "steps to wholeness." The first "opposite" with whom we are "one flesh" points to the process of integrating what Carl Jung terms the "psychological shadow." As we shall elaborate in the next chapter, the shadow includes that part of our total humanity that was deemed inferior, and was rejected and repressed as we adapted to life: the dark Mr. Hyde to our cherished Dr. Jekyll. This aspect now becomes recognized as "the stone that the builder refused." Next is a reconciliation with the Mother, which, Campbell suggests, means a reconciliation with life, with the basic conditions of life—birth, growth, union, separation, illness, decline, death—to embrace this and say yes to it. The third phase in this triad is reconciling with the Father, that absolute dimension of being beyond all words, all thoughts, all images, all knowing whatsoever. Taken altogether, the Initiation is an encounter with what Jung terms the "Self." The Self may be thought of as the totality of our psychic being, both the center and circumference of our wholeness. As our ego is the center of our consciousness, our conscious sense of "I," the Self is that larger totality inclusive of conscious and unconscious together.

To conclude this process of Initiation there is a third point, what Joseph Campbell calls Receiving the Boon. When we are reborn, we get a boon, a gift. In myths and fairy tales, the *boon* is typically something marvelous, magical, or sacred. The circumstance of its giving in itself makes the boon sacred, even if the object appears to be no more than a feather. As the archaic word boon suggests, this is not an ordinary gift. It is the Ten Commandments or the Holy Grail; not a year's supply of fine chocolates, not a Sony TV, not even a brand new BMW. The boon is not a personal possession at all, but something of universal value. The boon is an embodiment of value, a larger value that replaces the narrow value attached to "who I think I am." This profound shift in values comes directly into play in the character change we witness in the hero at the climax of a movie. Here we have the mythic way of describing it, metaphorically, as a special, divine gift. In terms of the runner who has hit the Wall and found her second wind, the boon manifests as an access to a heretofore-unknown level of energy and endurance. It further manifests as a knowledge, a confidence that one can hit that Wall and discover something beyond it. There is however a task that is given along with the boon: to return with it to the Day World and share it. The Initiation is not the final point of the cycle of the Hero's Journey; it is but the halfway point.

Here dramatic structure departs decidedly from the mythic archetype, because if we can see that the mythic Initiation and the dramatic climax have parallel meanings and functions, we must also note that they come at different points in the story. We think of the dramatic climax as coming just shortly before the end of the movie, not halfway through it. Certain movies created in the fantasy-adventure genre and explicitly following Campbell's model avoid this problem by having a double climax. For example, midway through *Raiders of the Lost Ark*, Indiana Jones finally locates the Ark of the Covenant—but he still has to get away with it. So in the second half of the movie we have a nonstop series of chase and fight sequences, leading to a second climax. This may work in action genre movies with little or no character development, but is not a universal solution applicable to all types of films. There is something more we must understand about the relationship between the inner climax and the outer climax.

The three-pointed Initiation phase of the Hero's Journey marks a profound and complex transformation in the personality. The section of the screenplay structure that corresponds to Initiation includes the catastrophe that ends Act II as well as the dramatic climax in Act III. It is not surprising that this part of the script is the hardest to write with authenticity or make work out satisfactorily. The catastrophe is the dramatic term for the Night of the Soul/Death of the Ego experience. As with the Threshold Crisis/threshold crossing we observed earlier, an entire mythic pattern underlies the catastrophe and resonates through the dramatic situation because we carry all of the mythic associations within us. To put it very simply, the catastrophe is the worst thing that could happen to the character in the context of the story. In fact, a powerful dramatic catastrophe that emotionally prepares the climax involves constructing a dramatic *double bind* that will force the main character to choose between—or better, reconcile—two opposing values. The conflict between two values and perspectives—i.e., man's and God's—is implicit in myth, but in drama it must be rendered as an actual, explicit conflict. It is up to the screenwriter to define the two values and bring them to life through the story. In a screenplay, the conflict of values is expressed on three interconnected levels: internal conflict within the main character, interpersonal conflict in a primary relationship, and the throughline outer conflict that comprises the plot. On the plot level, the conflicting values are carried by the hero and the antagonist.

The mythic-level insight cited by Joseph Campbell above, that the hero and his opposite are of "one flesh," has implications that run all through the structuring of a screenplay, as well as through the writer's experience. For who or what is the hero's opposite in the story? It is of course the antagonist. But the protagonist and antagonist are those opposites who are not of differing species, but one flesh. The antagonist represents what, as we move deeper into the dynamics of character orchestration, we shall call the "dark mirror" of the protagonist. And this "secret" correspondence linking the two, we shall see, has a decisive subliminal influence on the audience. In movies, we too often stereotype the antagonist one-dimensionally as the "bad guy," and get stuck on that. We project our own shadow onto the antagonist and use him as a scapegoat. The psycho killer in *Dirty Harry* is a construct left stereotypically grotesque to prevent our empathizing with him. When he is blown away at the climax ("Go ahead, make my day!") we are not burdened with remorse. But Little Bill, the antagonist in *Unforgiven*, forces himself upon us as a dark mirror of our own virtue, partly through the twist of giving him the same name as the hero, Will Munney. Little Bill is in fact a dark caricature of Dirty Harry himself. This is a much more sophisticated, mature, and honest representation of the antagonist. Drama naturally invites us to take sides. The underlying mythic paradigm, however, emphasizes that hidden unity which must necessarily be represented as a play of opposites.

In myths, the Secret Mover is portrayed as a god or goddess. It is he who has sent the Call to Adventure to the hero in the guise of a treasure to be found or a lover to be wooed. The meeting with the Secret Mover is not so elaborated in movies. Meeting the god or goddess is in the realm of the metaphysical, the invisible, while movies, except in the most overtly mythic fantasies or science fiction, deal with the consensual everyday world, or a romanticized or expressionistic version of it. Movies deal with outer actions and their consequences.

In a screenplay, what stands in the position of the Secret Mover is the discovery of a dramatic truth. Dramatic truth is simultaneously the revelation of character and the solution to the riddle posed by the plot. The dramatic conflict must be of such a nature that the plot *cannot* be resolved unless the hero changes the way she sees things—both herself and the situation. The change in self-perception comes from and leads to a shift in values, meaning that the change is first implicit and then must be tested in action. Loretta Castorini finally has to stand up for the truth of the passionate nature she has kept hidden for years, and tell Ronnie she loves him. C. C. Baxter, in *The Apartment*, finally stands up for himself against his boss and becomes a mensch. John Book, with the help of the Amish witnesses, is finally able to subdue Paul without either killing him or being killed by him. All of these climaxes highlight the character's discovery of a truth and an accompanying change in self-perception. The Secret Mover of a drama is the discovered truth that answers the dramatic questions of the story at the climax. The dramatic climax as a revelation of a truth for character and audience thus corresponds to the Initiation, the meeting with the god. This connection helps lend the climax its aura or halo of justness and finality.

It might be going too far to identify, as certain screenwriting teachers do, the truth that is discovered as a *moral*. In some cases it might be better stated as an existential truth, a psychological truth, or simply the price of survival, as we feel at the end of a film like *Salaam Bombay*. Here we see that life is hard, it is not fair, there is no silver lining—and yet we are alive. Nor does the idea of a Secret Mover exclude ambiguity and deeper shadows, as the discovered truths of such films as *Psycho, Chinatown,* and *Apocalypse Now* can attest. Not all meetings with the gods are propitious in the myths, as the gods are beyond all human categories. A mythic approach to screenwriting has nothing necessarily to do with a conventional happy ending. The dramatic truth discovered at the climax of a screen story may not always be phrased as a moral, but it must touch our hearts. We must feel the truth to emanate from the depth of the story and the protagonist, to be consistent with the entire dramatic development, and also to feel *necessary*. What the meeting with the god *does* suggest for drama is that "The truth shall make you free." Discovery of a truth, even a dark truth or a tragic truth, gives the protagonist—and vicariously ourselves—what Joseph Campbell calls the "freedom to live." In other words, freedom from being neurotically limited by our fear of life and our clinging to small selves that we know shall die. It is freedom to face life, freedom to grow up. Normally at the end of the story we see the character possessing more of this freedom than they did at the beginning. We know how it feels to walk out of a movie theater with our feeling for life expanded. This is a precious gift, which is limited neither by movie genres nor by movie budgets. It is the product of a story's integrity.

Return to the Day World

This "freedom to live" could be another term for the boon of the gods, the gods' gift to the human hero. But the meeting with the god takes place in the Night World, which is to say in the unconscious, the dream or imaginative sphere. At this point it is invisible to outer eyes. For example, it is very common that a person in therapy may have a significant, resolving dream where she can finally tell her father how much his silences hurt her, and the father can hear it and ask for forgiveness. In the dream there is a wonderful emotional reconciliation and release of blocked energy. But it may be years before that person is able to *live* that experience in real life. And she may in fact never have the chance. The real father may have died in the meantime. However, via the dream, something has indeed changed inside. On the level of the psyche the resolution has already occurred, but the realization is still in the underworld, so to speak. The rest of the journey has still to be undertaken: the return with the boon to make visible in the Day World the truth that was discovered in the Night World. This making the truth visible in the Day World is the core of the entire Return phase of the Hero's Journey, whether the process takes years of real time or only seconds of screen time in the climax of a movie.

The first part of the Return phase is still within the underworld. Exiting the underworld with the boon may have its own dangers, because the god may not give the gift willingly. Sometimes, as with Prometheus's theft of fire, the boon must be stolen. The Magic Flight is a well-known and important motif in myth cycles that represents this danger. The prince Gwion Bach in the Welsh tale has gone down into the abyss, where the witch or goddess Caridwen tends the cauldron of poetic inspiration. He daringly manages to steal three drops of the precious liquid. The hag notices something is missing and begins the chase. The boy turns himself into a rabbit and she turns herself into a grayhound; he becomes a fish and she chases him as an otter, and so on. This mercurial sense of transformation or metamorphosis is very common. These motifs all belong to the Magic Flight. Taken together, they describe how very difficult it is to bring the realization—the experience of radical wholeness, of the Secret Mover—back across the threshold of consciousness and into the arena of society. The leading image here is metamorphosis: reality is fluid and shifting. This imagery very aptly captures the actual psychological situation. Magic Flight turns out to be a very important aspect of the creative process. It is a phenomenon all screenwriters and creative people encounter, and we will spend time on it when we discuss the screenwriter's creative journey in Chapter Twelve. However, it is just at this point of the Return that the structure of movies really departs from the circular archetype of the Hero's Journey.

The important departure from the mythic structure is that movie stories tend to skip this quadrant of the Hero's Journey entirely, and cut directly to pick up the hero as he crosses the return threshold back into the Day World, the world of visible action.

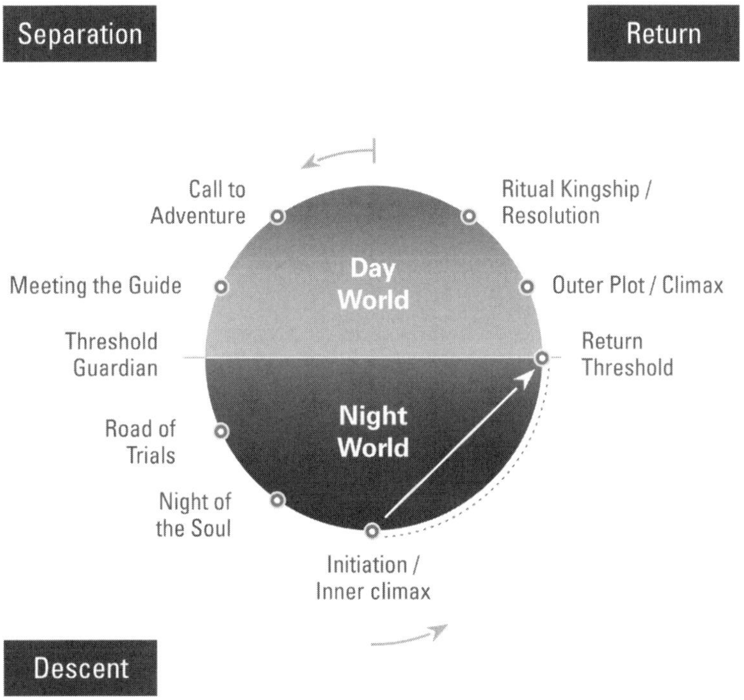

/ Drama leaps directly from inner climax to outer climax.

Normally, the meeting with the god in the Night World corresponds to the inner realization of the main character in a movie, the inner realization of a truth. This is the inner phase of what we will later describe as the ripple climax. The basic insight behind the *ripple climax* is:

> As I change the way I see myself, I change my behavior.
>
> As I change my behavior, I change my relationships.
>
> As I change my relationships, I change my world.

The mythic journey into the Night World is more concerned with the core inner transformation, while movies are more concerned with outer action, with the *consequences* of that change in the outer world.

The road home leads to the Return Threshold, which, like the first threshold, is a place of paradox. Again, it is a boundary between two realities or states of consciousness. And again the hero is to be tested. As the threshold guardian on the way down represented those fearful energies of the Night World, the guardian of the Return Threshold embodies all that is intimidating and resistant to change in the Day World. Campbell called this the "jury of sober eyes," and in effect it is made up of all those who never went on the journey, everyone who never experienced the intoxication of the sublime. They are the "Flatlanders" who know nothing of the heights. Tannhäuser, in Wagner's opera of the same name, returns from his meeting with Venus, the goddess of Love, on the Venusberg, but when he tries to tell people about it, everyone thinks he is crazy. Rip Van Winkle, out hunting one afternoon, encounters the spirits who live under the hills and even engages them in a game of bowls. He drinks with them and then falls asleep for twenty years. When Rip finally wakes up and returns to town, everything has changed and no one recognizes him.

This is a very widespread folk motif, which expresses the pervading sense of strangeness that is encountered at the Return Threshold. The status quo world may be no different, but one's perspective has changed completely, and that makes all the difference. The coffee no longer tastes the same; the laughter of old acquaintances now sounds hideous. The returning person creates dissonance. When one person in a family or other group goes into therapy and starts to change, this immediately constellates resistance in everyone else. The mother who had been counted on to never complain, the daughter who had been counted on to never resist, the employee who had been counted on to follow the company line—they are now causing trouble. Their change puts a pressure for change on the entire group. In fact, the dynamics of the group will have already changed forever. Everyone is shaken out of their comfort zones, and some may be prodded to commence their own journey into the unknown as a result. In *Ordinary People*, we see all of the family relationships begin to shift the moment Conrad crosses the threshold into the psychiatrist's office. The father soon arrives there to talk about himself. The much more neurotically defended mother, under the growing pressure of change, finally flees the family at the climax of the movie, forcibly torn out of her status quo. This is passive resistance on the part of the guardian of the Return Threshold.

There is also another, much more belligerent aspect to the return threshold guardian motif, one which will require of the hero new trials leading to a decisive confrontation. This is the Tyrant King motif, the person at the top of the status quo order who, like a dragon, is hanging on to power for himself. His (or her) entire power structure is threatened by the wind of change brought by the returning hero. Mistakenly identifying the flowing energy of life with his own personal ego and having usurped the symbolism of "divine rule," the Tyrant perceives the hero as a life-threat. Like King Herod in the nativity story, he would murder the new possibility in its infancy. As writers, we know that these figures emerge instantly whenever we finish a screenplay draft: the dismissive producers, agents, competitors and envious friends with whom we must struggle in order to give birth to our creation.

We have said that movie stories leap directly from an inner climax (meeting with the god) to the return threshold and outer climax. In dramas, the main antagonist of the story stands as the return threshold guardian. This will become clear as we move into the model of Aristotle's Plot Curve, and as we explore step by step the dynamics of screenplay construction in Chapter Eleven. But here we can make a useful distinction. At the catastrophe of the drama, which corresponds to the Night of the Soul, the protagonist is forced to confront that opposite or shadow *within himself*, and, immediately at the climax, to confront that same shadow force *in the objective world*, embodied by the antagonist. Act II takes place metaphorically in an underworld, while in Act III we come back to the Day World for the resolution of the outer plot. In a movie we move directly from catastrophe ("grow or die") to climax, and in the subtle moment between them we in the audience must see what has changed in the character. Thus there is between catastrophe and climax a typically brief Story Step we call Calm Before the Storm, where we register this character change in a movie. We see that *inner* change has occurred though the throughline outer plot question has yet to be answered. We are moving quickly toward the climax. Loretta strolling languidly home in her opera dress in *Moonstruck* and John Book finishing the birdhouse and leaning on his shovel are two examples of the Calm Before the Storm.

What the return threshold guardians force us to do, in a positive sense, is to fight for our vision and turn it into something objective in the world—a new philosophy, a new invention, a new political system, a new artwork. We are forced to make visible in the Day World the truth that was discovered in the Night World. Sometimes the character change simply embodies itself in a way of being that implies a "freedom to live." There are among us the "man of Tao" who runs the neighborhood greasy spoon where you always feel peculiarly at ease, the "woman of Tao" who cleans houses as though she were the luckiest person alive.

The circle of the Hero's Journey tells us that it is not enough to go on a trip to achieve our own personal enlightenment or to enter into some sort of ecstatic mood or paradise ourselves. The gift of transformation is not for us alone, but is meant to be shared. This is implied in the picture language of Descent and Return. In many Native American groups, there is a ritual of the sweat lodge. Upon entering the sweat lodge for purification and vision, one utters the small prayer: "All my relations." It is a reminder that I go not for myself alone, but for "all my relations," which is ultimately the entire nexus of life that has brought me forth and given me consciousness.

Sacred Marriage

There is of course no guarantee that the hero returning to the Day World will win acceptance. Many prophets have been driven into the desert, many visionaries taken for crazy. But if the hero is successful in meeting the new trials and establishing something new in the world, some locus where the energies of transformation can enter the human sphere, we arrive at the last point in the cycle of the Hero's Journey: the Ritual Kingship or Sacred Marriage. The motif may take either form, or the two may be combined. The prince and princess marry and establish a new kingdom; Parsifal becomes the new King of the Grail and heals the wasteland, and so on. These motifs express how it feels when we come around the full cycle of the journey, after overcoming the new trials and establishing the truth we have found as a value in our lives.

Marriage as a symbol is the union of woman and man, male and female, and the union of two families and two communities. Male and female form a symbolic as well as biological whole. (In Plato's creation myth, the original human was both male and female, and round like a ball.) The coronation is the union of the king and the nation, of the nation and God; it is the beginning of a new time. Whether pictured as a marriage or a coronation, there is a big party going on, a tremendous celebration. The champagne has been uncorked in our hearts and the bubbles are rising up through our bodies. It is a spontaneous, effervescent release of joyous energy. The Hero's Journey suggests that joy is the natural product of following our path. This release of joy is a natural experience we have all had when we have successfully completed some very arduous task, like climbing a mountain, finishing a screenplay, or seeing a film through all the way to its release. This joy has nothing to do with happiness. Happiness is conditioned by an object—"I got a promotion, so I'm happy," "I bought a new car, so I'm happy," "I'm in love with so-and-so, so I'm happy." But take away the promotion, take away the car, take away the love, and I'm not happy anymore! That happiness was in reality a state of dependence on the object. Joy, on the other hand, is the vital energy that is bubbling up inside. It belongs to life, not to the object. Joy is the energy released by the experience of wholeness, and it is toward wholeness that the symbols of Sacred Marriage and Ritual Kingship point.

Masculine and feminine, left and right, above and below, the light side and the dark side all come together, if only for one poised moment. Forgiveness seems to occur spontaneously in the recognition that all are parts of one whole. This is what happens at the culmination of the parable of the prodigal son. The prodigal son finally comes home from his wanderings and the father exclaims, "Thank God you're back. Let's celebrate!" Many have commented on how often in the parables of Jesus there is a party going on. They run out of wine, so what's he going to do? These celebrations are not merely social events. They are symbols. The party is going on inside; it is a state of consciousness. We are really in the flow of life, and life around us is flowing effortlessly. The flow state is akin to the concentrated play state of children, and in that very intensely pleasurable state, the sense of time disappears. We don't feel time is passing because we are too busy living. I believe this is the true meaning of the phrase that ends so many fairy tales: "And they lived happily ever after." It does not mean an infinite extension of happy moments, affluent, carefree, on a permanent Club Med vacation. No one listening to a fairy tale in the Middle Ages would have been silly enough to take the symbol literally. The time of "happily ever after" is really the eternal now.

The heightened flow state that accompanies the accomplishment of a hero's journey might last an hour, a day, a week, or it may last much longer and become incorporated in the person's way of being. There are cases where people are in the worst imaginable outer circumstances, and yet they dream there is a party going on inside. This does not mean they are deluded. It means that this is the reality their unconscious presents them; it is a picture of their inner state, where there is an experience of celebration. The life of Mother Theresa comes to mind as an example of how the inner reality may create the outer life, rather than the other way around. Confronted by the dying and the lepers of Calcutta, she saw in each of them the face of her Beloved. This is a powerful example of a lived myth. The wonderful book by the psychiatrist Viktor Frankl, *Man's Search for Meaning*, about his own experience in the Auschwitz death camp, is also a treasure in this regard.

While we are in the aura of the Sacred Marriage or the Ritual Kingship, the world feels new. Part of us would love to keep everything just the way it is, to freeze the moment of beauty forever in a kind of living snapshot. But since we are human beings and life is change, we cannot, no matter how beautiful it is, suspend the moment in time. The very attempt to do so already throws us out of the beauty we would grasp; it turns us into the dragon, hoarding life. We must move on to the next cycle. Nature takes us. At every moment in our lives we are somewhere on the journey. Where are you now?

If the king—the legitimate king because he has gone on the journey—tries to freeze-dry his realization and hang onto it, he becomes a tyrant. (To use the word *king* here is not an exercise in sexism. We are speaking symbolically to indicate an element of the psyche—the center or leading attitude of consciousness—which for the most recent few thousand years has been pictured through the metaphor of king.) If the king becomes a tyrant, the resulting world becomes a Waste Land. And then someone else would have to go on the journey down into the Night World, to the abyssal waters of renewal. "The king is dead, long live the king!" This point, to let life keep flowing after one has come round full circle and "become somebody," is considered by many mystics to be the most difficult challenge of the entire journey: the final test. A German mystic of the fourteenth century, Meister Eckhart, said about this: "The final leavetaking is the leaving of God for God." He means, in part, that if you go all the way around the journey and have the great vision of God, you can get trapped by that very image. You become attached to it and stuck with it. No matter how beautiful the image, you are stuck. Meister Eckhart's message then would be to let go even of that, and move on.

All of this is suggested in the dramatic resolution of a screenplay after the climax. Sometimes the motif of the Sacred Marriage is played out literally, as in the big celebrations that end the *Star Wars* films, where all the characters come onscreen and take a bow. One could call this naïvely direct, like a piece of folk art. More often, the human hero's triumph is less than absolute. Sometimes the protagonist has barely escaped to tell the tale, and sometimes, as in noirs, the main character has seen the heart of darkness and returns covered with shadows. *Vertigo*, *Chinatown*, *The Talented Mr. Ripley*, and *Syriana* are examples of dark and troubling endings. Movies must serve both our deep mythological impulses and our reality sense, and these two are not always easy to reconcile.

While screenwriting is highly technical, it is based on dynamics that are deeply part of our nature. It is precisely this nature that we share with our audience. We can trust it. Yet it is not simply a given. Wholeness is something that is lost and must be reacquired on a new level. The very fact of our individual consciousness and our adaptations to the outer world make us split beings. It is the creative power of the stories we tell through screenplays and movies that can make healing bridges.

The Hero's Journey is not a sacred cow, nor is it a cash cow. Its real influence on screenwriting is less direct, but deeper, than some have suggested. As we turn now to the models that directly address the techniques of screenwriting and story development, we have the mythic dimension of the Hero's Journey as a base. It keeps us in touch with the common human essence we share with those fictional persons, the characters in our screenplays who come to live intimately with us for a while, and with all those people we never meet: the audience in the movie theater.

4

Need versus Mode

The Core of Conflict

> When we read the newspaper, we are most moved by the ordinary man or woman forced to act in an extraordinary way. We are moved by heroism. We are not moved by the self-proclaimed emotions of the manipulative, or the famous. We discount to the greatest extent these reports, as we fear, correctly, that they are only advertising themselves. Similarly, at the theater, we are truly and only moved by the ordinary men and women doing their best under extraordinary circumstances, forced to act in an extraordinary way to achieve their goal.
>
> —*David Mamet*

HOW MUCH DOES THE SCREENWRITER NEED TO KNOW about her characters? Some writers get carried away with exactly what shade of lipstick the character wears, what brand of deodorant she uses, and how she looked in her Brownie uniform. This, however, does not answer the question. How much do we *need* to know? The answer is: we need to know enough about a character to convey the dramatic truth of the character and the story to the audience. Another way to put it: enough so that an actor can pick up the script and, without having to concoct anything, play the truth of the character from beginning to end. We must know the character's self-image, that precious "who I think I am," because that is the foundation of his present motivations. We refer to this as the character's *mode*. It is this mode that will suffer conflict and breakdown. And we must also know that which the character *does not yet know* about himself, the new individuality that will be born out of conflict. This latter is termed the character's *unconscious need*. The tension between a character's subjective reality and the steps of growth that the dramatic conflict objectively requires is the core of character. This tension generates both the dramatic throughline and the theme of the movie. It is the source of the heroism David Mamet mentions, that of the ordinary man or woman forced by circumstances to act in an extraordinary way.

The technology of filmmaking has become so compelling in itself that it is easy for the screenwriter to feel overwhelmed by it. It seems that every year the digital envelope is pushed further; the interface between digital and live action images becomes more seamless. Directors, producers, and studio executives come to depend on this new technology for impacts ranging from subtle image enhancement to major story elements, as in movies like *Crouching Tiger, Hidden Dragon*, and *Lord of the Rings*. Sometimes we screenwriters must remind ourselves that the most important part of our craft is always our understanding of characters, of our audience, of our collaborators, and of ourselves.

The study of character is of course inexhaustible. It is certainly possible, and it inevitably happens, that the screenwriter, director, and star can have conflicting interpretations of the same character. We each bring our own personal mythology to the creation of character, with its particular dominants and balances, its hidden symbols, and its blind spots. We are also conditioned in our understanding of character by our society, for it is apparent that every society puts a somewhat different shading on what it means to be a person. A behavior taken for granted in the United States might be considered bad taste in Singapore or Switzerland. Each society has its own map of where the boundaries of the individual meet those of the social collective. Globalization clearly impacts the way stories are told today. More movies are set between or across cultural barriers. Increasingly in story development, we are urged to become aware of the subjective factor in the creation of our characters, the perspective or bias we bring to it. This awareness will become more important as movies become increasingly global. Therefore, working with characters continually begs certain questions:

- Who is this character for *me*?
- What do my characters and their relationships mirror about my own attitudes, beliefs, and assumptions?

Our characters have much to teach us about ourselves. And what we do not know about ourselves usually surfaces at a point where the screenplay gets "stuck." Here the screenplay breaks down, and we may spend some weeks wondering why.

The Need versus Mode model we explore in this chapter is a valuable lens into the human nature of our characters. This model is also a way of identifying the core of conflict in the story. The *core of conflict* is simultaneously a psychological conflict and also a universal conflict of values. The conflict of values is played out via the throughline plot conflict, around which the outer events of the screenplay are constructed. It is also expressed through the theme of the movie, as we see the hero choose one value over another and we witness the consequences of that choice. But for all of the plot and theme conflict to achieve dramatic unity, they must be grounded in the psychology of the character. When action grows out of who a character is, it has integrity and authenticity.

This chapter looks at characters as human persons, with a human nature like our own that we can explore and come to understand. Of course we know that characters are constructs, but we approach them as if they were real for the sake of consistent and believable motivations and behaviors. From this basis we can examine the dynamics of character conflict and character change. Underlying all of this is the mythic dimension of storytelling. Yet while the archetypal, mythic structure may give drama access to deep levels of soul, it is only the humanity of the characters that brings the screenplay fully to life.

The Hero Is a Carrier of Values

Characters as persons ask us to relate to them personally. *The character may be fictional, but the relationship is real.* We have observed that when a story is not working, the root cause is nearly always a breakdown of rapport between the writer and the story—ultimately between the writer and his or her character.

This lack of rapport—lack of feeling—is communicated infallibly to the audience, including studio readers, producers, and actors who will read the screenplay. When the audience loses rapport with the main character, energy drains out of the whole story. This sense of rapport turns out to be a central issue in whether the screenplay gets sold or not. Therefore the first place to go to get the story back on track is into the inner story of the central character. This is where the rapport is either happening or not happening. That inner story is opened up and illuminated by the Need versus Mode paradigm. Because it goes right to the heart of the drama, Need versus Mode may become your structuring tool of first recourse and your key to working with the other models in developing and writing your screenplay.

There was a panel of producers and screenwriters at a film festival some years ago discussing what makes a good screenplay. One of the producers seemed to answer for them all when he said: "Well, it's easy. All you have to do is find the spine of the story, and stay on it. The only problem is that we're not getting good scripts to read!" This unleashed a torrent protest from the writers, those on the panel as well as many in the audience, along the lines of: "You wouldn't know a good story if it was right in front of you! You wouldn't know a good story if it came up and bit you on the nose! I *sent* you a great script two months ago, and I bet you didn't even read it! You sent me back comments and didn't even get the characters' names right!" What was evident from this producer's point of view—that all you have to do is find the spine of the story—was in fact the great mystery and the great challenge from the writers' point of view. Here we find played out the precise difference between mountain-creativity and mine-creativity, between looking at the screenplay from the outside as a product and from the inside as a process. The producer can compare the work in process with successfully completed products and see that something is lacking. From the screenwriter's position, proposing that you simply have to find the spine of the story is like saying all you have to do is find the perfect life-partner, or all you have to do is find the perfect agent. It merely begs the question: what is the spine of the story?

One of the panelists happened to be the great screenwriter Waldo Salt, author of *Midnight Cowboy*, *Serpico*, *The Flame and the Arrow*, and many other outstanding films. With two Academy Awards, he was certainly the "wise old man" of the group. Now, the argument between the producers and the writers was heating up into an Irish Donnybrook when someone happened to notice that Waldo was the only one not saying anything. He was down at the end of the panel gently shaking his head with a bemused smile. The moderator, seeing a chance to regain some control over the mayhem, grabbed the mike, which was about to be used as a club, and pleaded with everyone to settle down so they could hear what Waldo Salt had to say.

Waldo Salt did in fact have the sparkling eyes and elfish humor befitting a mythic guide, and when he started speaking, it was about ourselves—who *we* are. What Waldo Salt recognized, in his own life as well as in his characters, was how our *mode* of living—the way we go about getting things done in the world—is typically in opposition to what we really *need to learn* about life on a universal, human level. We get in our own way and louse ourselves up. This is precisely what interested Waldo about his characters: what does my character need to learn through this story, and how is he getting in his own way? He said further that every day when he sat down to work, with every new scene, he tried to ask a question that went to the heart of the conflict between how the characters behave and what they need to learn. That was how he stayed on the spine of the story. Later my partner Tom spent some days with Waldo Salt discussing just this topic. Our elaboration of Waldo Salt's insights became the basis for the Need versus Mode model.

This is a fundamental tension that goes to the heart of character and the heart of story. The character's mode is basically what we see the character doing as the drama opens: his actions and attitudes. We also refer to this as the character's status quo, his starting position. Underlying these actions and attitudes are the values the character holds, his belief-system or worldview. Different modes reflect different values. The values themselves are universals, and in that sense they are beyond the categories of right or wrong. But what may not be working is the way the main character *identifies* with the mode value. When we identify with one value and believe that is who we are, some other value that is important gets lost.

Let's take as an example Loretta Castorini from *Moonstruck*. What do we see about her actions and attitudes in the first two scenes of the movie? First of all, there is the way she is dressed, all in grays and blacks with tight, high collars. *This is an action that reveals an attitude.* Second, there is her job. What we see is that Loretta is an accountant for an undertaker. What does an accountant do? She works with numbers. It is dry, passionless, emotionally risk-free work. And Loretta does this work for an undertaker, someone who makes dead people look "better than they did when they were alive," as he proudly tells her. So here is an allusion to a false or fake life, what looks alive but is really dead. How do we see Loretta relate to her boss? She treats him like a child, even to the point of pinching his cheek. That is to say, she takes a mothering role. She is certainly the one in control in the scene.

Then, when we come to the second scene, we find Loretta in a flower shop. Carmine, the florist, enters with a dozen red roses he is packing to deliver. He admires the classiness of it: "Ah, the guy who sends these really knows what he's doin'!" Loretta looks up and retorts: "The guy who sends those is spending a lot of money on something that's gonna end up in the garbage." We see that her attitude toward romance is cynical. When we put the evidence of these two scenes together, we get a picture of a woman who is controlling, mothering, cynical about romance, and in all cases not risking her feelings.

These are attitudes. Behind them is a value that both connects and conditions these attitudes. For simplicity's sake, we could call this value *control*. There is nothing wrong with control in itself, yet we can also see that something is missing from Loretta's life, something she cannot get as long as her control mode is in charge. *Moonstruck* nails Loretta's mode in the first five minutes of screen time.

What can we sense is missing from Loretta's life, from her wholeness? This is more subtle: how do you show what is missing? It is a paradox. In fact, what is missing occupies a sort of *negative space*. We cannot see it directly, but we get a felt-sense that something is not right. On a subtextual, subliminal level, we start to ask ourselves, "What's wrong with this picture?" just as we do with fairy tales. "A king has four sons, but no queen. . . ." We sense what the character needs because it is *conspicuously absent*. What the character needs to learn about life turns out to be a value that is the *inverse* of the dominant value that informs her mode. The two values form a pair of opposites: innocence/experience, control/passion, or distrust/friendship, for example. These opposites play themselves out through the Day World/Night World dialectic of the Hero's Journey. This tension between what a character needs to learn about life through the dramatic situation and how he gets in his own way is the tension between these two values. This is the core conflict, the basis of the throughline that holds together plot, character, and theme.

The interplay of the opposing values through all of the dimensions of the story helps us understand the nature of dramatic conflict.

The dramatic conflict must be constructed so that:

1. a conflict of opposing values is constellated both in the hero and in his world
2. the conflict of values is embodied by real objects or characters in the world of the story
3. the hero cannot have both objects/values
4. in order to resolve the conflict, the hero must change the way he sees himself

At the "grow or die" point in the story—the catastrophe that ends Act II—the character will be forced, under great stress, to choose between these two opposing values. At that point, it appears the hero is presented with an impossible set of alternatives. But it is the internal conflict of values set up here at the opening of the movie, and not resolved until the climax, which creates the throughline of the character and the spine of the story. This is the invisible thread that provides the electric current running through the heart of the story. It determines the dramatic necessity of the story events and connects the drama to the hearts of the audience. The Need versus Mode model is tremendously useful while writing and editing our screenplays. Every working day, at the start of each new scene, Waldo Salt would ask a question that went to the heart of the Need versus Mode conflict in the character, and that would keep him on the spine of the story.

You Can't Always Get What You Want—But You Get What You Need

For Waldo Salt, you find the spine of the story not on the level of plot, but on the level of the universal conflict taking place within the main character. Plot grows out of character; it is an expression of the character. The universal need is something we can relate to, at least on a gut level of empathic identification. Universal needs make up a simple hierarchy:

- survival
- human contact and warmth
- stable and secure personal boundaries
- unimpeded development
- recognition, justice, and self-expression
- growth, individuation, and self-actualization

These universal needs, and the road to their attainment, lie at the heart of film stories.

We always have to provide an answer to that large question hovering in the audience's subconscious: why must this character have this specific adventure? If we cannot answer this question, our screenplay will lack dramatic unity. For example, on a plot level, thrillers are driven by the antagonist. Normally in the first act, or even through the first half of the movie, the hero is primarily reacting, he is behind the curve, trying to catch up. Nevertheless, when we look closely at the thriller hero, we see that he has a blind spot or weakness that puts him in jeopardy and at the same time secretly links him to the antagonist. The detective played by Al Pacino in *Sea of Love*, for example, has a blinding emotional neediness connected with his unresolved divorce. Now, undercover, he must get involved with a beautiful woman who he suspects is a serial killer. He must offer himself as the bait, yet we see he is emotionally out of control. His need, indicated by his blind spot for emotional contact, almost gets him killed. In *Seven*, the zeal of young Detective Mills to succeed contains within it the seeds of his destruction. We can see that he lacks a sense of limits, that his approach to his work, to life and death, lacks gravity. He treats the case, naïvely, like a championship to be won. The killer will exploit this latent weakness to destroy Mills. So in a thriller, too, an inner tension in the hero relates to the plot action and holds the two together in a dramatic unity.

To take a different genre, the melodrama is entirely driven by the main character's fantasies of what will make her happy. Her yearning for freedom constellates opposition in the closed world around her, generating the plot conflict. Ada, in *The Piano*, believes that her happiness and sense of self depend on her piano. This belief is at the core of her mode and her outer conflict.

The Need versus Mode model points to a central paradox in human nature that forms the core and premise of drama. Something inside us seems to act against what we believe are our best interests. As St. Paul wrote: "Instead of doing the good things I want to do, I carry out sinful things I do not want."[20] When we are forced to admit to behaviors that are self-destructive, dysfunctional, or merely counterproductive, we become dimly aware of a kind of shadowy nemesis inside ourselves. Yet the same shadowy factor also pushes us into situations where, because of our own failings, we are forced to become more conscious. It creates the state of duality we began to address in Chapter Two. We are of two minds:

> Between the conception
> And the creation
> Between the emotion
> And the response
> Falls the Shadow[21]

---

20. Romans 7:20–26.
21. Eliot, T.S. "The Hollow Men," in *Selected Poems* (New York: Harcourt, Brace, 1964), p. 80.

If we are totally honest about it, we see that this shadowy side of life is intrinsic to who we are, and constitutes the inner dimension of our struggles in life. Carl Jung conceptualized this unconscious aspect of our personality, which seems to work against us, behind our backs, as the psychological shadow.

Exclusion Creates Desire

It is one of the functions of stories to externalize this fundamental inner conflict, this existential split, so that we can see it.

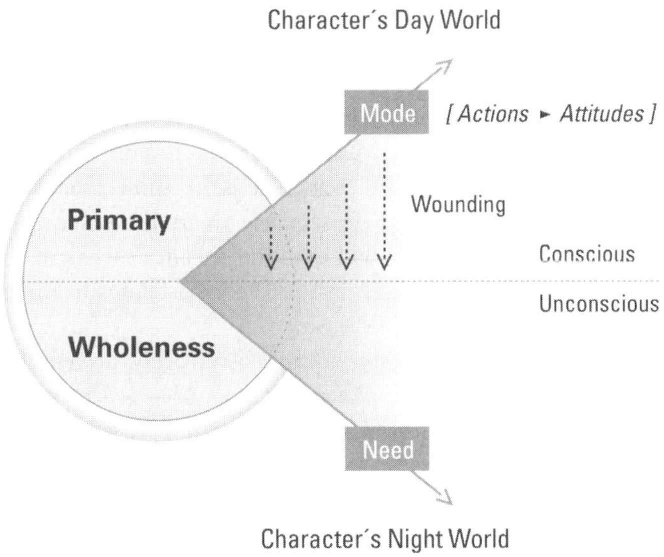

/ ***Need versus Mode:*** **Drama is growth through crisis.** The main character´s Mode (survival mode), how they go about getting things done, is in opposition to what they need to learn on a universal level. The universal Need is in the unconscious (in the subtext).

We use the Need versus Mode model to identify the core conflict of values that will be used to build the throughline, or spine, of the story. What is the spine of your story? The spine is the backbone, the track or path that leads you all the way through the screenplay, from page one to the end. The throughline is what drives and focuses each scene. How do you find it? How do you stay on the spine of your story, and what do you do when you lose it?

In drama, the psychological shadow appears multi-dimensionally: as the flaw in the main character's mode which will cause him to "blunder" into the adventure; as the Night World into which the story takes the character; and as the antagonist of the drama. But where does this shadow come from? And why can't we run away from our shadow, no matter how hard we try? Psychologist Robert Johnson tells us:

Whenever something that belongs to the spirit of wholeness is excluded, it turns against us.

The graphic on the previous page describes the dynamics of the need/mode split, how it develops from our earliest experience and the consequences that follow. It shows us how exclusion creates desire. The striking thing, however, is that we find here a direct analogue to the Hero's Journey. The Need versus Mode model expresses on the level of personal psychological development what the Hero's Journey expresses on the level of mythology. Each model opens up insights into the other.

The circle in the diagram indicates *primary wholeness*. We may hypothesize that at some time in our past we each had some experience of a primary wholeness. Perhaps that time existed only before you were born, in that light and temperature-controlled world of your mother's womb, hooked into the ultimate fast-food restaurant. Between the desire and the fulfillment no shadow fell. There is in fact some sort of proto-consciousness present in the uterus, as we know from research using hypnosis. It is an experience of a unity before the world is split into me and you, mine and yours, before the world of objects exists, and with them, desire and regret. We have an echo of this in Wordsworth's famous lines that "Trailing clouds of glory do we come/from God, who is our Home: Heaven lies about us in our infancy!"

But as soon as we are born, we get a shock. The birth process itself is a trauma. The blissful world beyond time and space starts to convulse and contract. You are pushed out of Eden and squeezed into the writhing tunnel of the birth canal. After a long journey you shoot out into a place that is too cold, too loud, too bright. Then someone picks you up by the feet, holds you upside down, and smacks you on the behind. You start crying. It's a natural reaction. And so life begins.

From that moment on, there commences a succession of further traumas and splits which Old Testament mythology identifies by the term "exile." Kicked out of the Garden, we begin to learn that some behaviors are accepted and others are not. The rising and falling arrows in the graphic represent this succession of splits, whereby, through adaptation, we build up a survival mode while suppressing or repressing other aspects of our wholeness. The split-off and suppressed side is connected to unconscious needs for wholeness. Babies smile spontaneously at their mothers, yet they also learn, long before they have language, that when you smile and say *goo-goo*, mommy smiles back at you. But when you cry, mommy doesn't look at you the same way. The baby learns that the breast does not always present itself whenever it is desired. Now the shadow does begin to fall between the cup and the lip.

Then there is the next big threshold: toilet training, wherein the child learns that it is no longer okay to simply let the bodily processes flow "naturally" and unconsciously—and there are consequences. If you make poo-poo in the right place and the right time, mommy smiles and picks you up, cuddles you and calls you Little Lammikins. But when you make poo-poo in the wrong place and the wrong time—like in the middle of the living room rug during mommy's dinner party—then mommy does *not* smile and does *not* call you Little Lammikins. It is these experiences that we refer to as *woundings* in the graphic. Not only large and small traumas, but all experiences of limitation, create, at the time, a momentary sense of wounding. Woundings lead to constrictions of energy.

At school, children must give up what Freud called their "polymorphous perversity" and mold their behavior to the acceptable limits:

"Sit up straight. Both feet on the floor."

"Stay in your seats until the bell rings."

"Nobody leaves this room till everyone is lined up and *quiet!*"

"Jimmy, don't pull Susie's hair or I'll stand you in the corner."

"Look at me when I'm talking to you!"

These are necessary adaptations, yet we lose something in the process as well. Psychologist Jean Houston has quoted a series of studies which estimated that by the age of twelve—the end of the "wonder years"—90 percent of us have lost 50 percent of our physical flexibility.

Along with the limitation and channeling of our physical behavior comes a whole set of concomitant thoughts and attitudes. An aspect of this, which becomes very important when creating and orchestrating our characters, has to do with the roles we play in our families. Who were you in your family? Were you the rebel who was always getting up in everyone's face and breaking the rules? Were you mommy's little helper, or daddy's little helper? Were you designated the family's arbitrator, who had to keep the peace? Were you the baby? The "balance of power"? Were you the one who just tried to disappear into the TV? We live these roles so completely at the time that we come to believe that's who we are in the rest of our lives as well. The same is of course true of dramatic characters. In the psychology of transactional analysis, all of these roles we take on in life are in fact called *scripts*.

Early splits, social adaptations, and family roles all go into making up a character's survival mode. They have made the character into who she is, or who she thinks she is, as the story opens. They influence to a large extent the opening position the character will take when conflict erupts. The character will react according to her status quo mode, because it is her dominant pattern, selected and reinforced over years. And she will react from a position of constricted energy based on past wounds. The main point of doing character biographies is to identify the character's mode, because this is what is dramatically salient.

Through all of the shaping events of life, some behaviors are positively selected and reinforced. They become introjected, meaning we come to *identify* with those behaviors and roles. And while this is happening, other behaviors are negatively selected, meaning we learn not to do them. We *dis*-identify from those behaviors. For instance, I can recall an old kindergarten game: "Do be a Do-Bee; don't be a Don't-Bee," which was accompanied by cartoons of happy and angry little bees. Of course we all wanted to be good little Do-Bees, and behaved accordingly. Many of us remain Do-Bees all our lives. In the process, it can happen that some of our fundamental needs are pressed down into the "dark continent" of the unconscious. This schism is the price of becoming conscious in the first part of life. We become split into a light half and a dark half, a Day World and a Night World, indicated by the horizontal line in the graphic. This is our status quo, and it is the character's status quo at the beginning of the story. The role or script that the character is playing comprises the illusory "who I think I am" that will undergo trials, death, and rebirth through the Hero's Journey.

At the extreme, some individuals who are very identified with their mode and very much in denial about their wounds may become neurotically obsessed with survival, even though they have outer affluence. We look at such people and remark on their lack of vitality, their lack of flexibility when facing life situations, their almost palpable inner poverty. But we are all of us touched to some extent by a loss of vitality. We begin to feel that there's not enough money, not enough energy, not enough love, not enough hours in a day. . . . We have to grab on to things so we don't lose them. Our lives become full of festering resentments, as was so well expressed by the main character in *Falling Down*. The ultimate teaching of this survival mode is that we can't *live* because we have to survive!

Unresolved wounds hold back our energy. Everyone can recall the universal playground experience of having another kid come up and punch you in the arm just for fun. What is the immediate reaction? You grab your arm and hold it close to you. There is even an instinctual response to bend over and shield the vulnerable parts of the body from further attack. We constrict around the wound as a natural defense. If the blow is a light one, done playfully, we may forget it almost instantly as we chase our friend across the schoolyard, bent on revenge. But if the blow is serious, hard enough to make us cry in front of everybody, it may be a wound we carry for years. If it was dealt by the school bully, we may always avoid contact with that person, or with anyone who reminds us of him. The fact is that we tend to *constrict* around a wound even after it is physically healed. The constriction itself becomes a habit-pattern, part of "who I think I am."

We hold on to a wound until it is released. If we can release it right away, so much the better. If for some reason we cannot process and let go of the wound when it happens—shame is one of the usual reasons for this—we will carry it until it is released. Often this release is a background process, which happens completely unconsciously, and then one day we suddenly realize that we feel better. Sometimes a deliberate process of recall, remembering, and release is needed for us to be able to move on.

The "slings and arrows of outrageous fortune" that life presents us comprise what in Buddhism is called *dukkha*: the afflictions or suffering of life. The original meaning of the word *dukkha*, however, was simply "what comes along in life." In the Buddhist view, *dukkha* comes to everyone, and is nothing to be ashamed of. It is our inability to harness the feelings of fear and desire that come up in the face of what the world hands us that leads us to stay constricted around our wounds and lead small lives. The survival mode can become an adaptation pattern that partly serves to keep us from being more integrated than the norms of the society would seem to allow. Thus the Heroes' Journeys that characters undertake begin by separating the hero from the status quo. The hero is forced to enter the Night World where he never intended to go, but where the split-off energy must be found. This is a journey to recover lost vitality and to integrate back into his life some part of what was split off by a wound. The dynamic of that process is the invisible spine of the story.

Part of the totality is unwanted, and we learn to repress it (the downward arrow), while at the same time we learn a way of adaptation, a survival mode, that will lead us to be adequately nurtured and socially accepted (the rising arrow). In the process we lose our primary sense of wholeness and may spend our entire lives trying to recapture, reconstitute, or compensate for its loss. Movies, storytelling, art, and religious practice all play a role here. Ethnologists have observed that one of the most important functions of ritual is to return the tribe to the "original time" before time, where the feeling of the primal wholeness can be re-experienced through the *participation mystique* of the rite. Vehicles for entering the state of "mystical participation" include music, drumming, trance, ecstasy, and playing.

Theater and cinema are direct extensions of such rituals. We use informal, secular rituals like going to the movies to subconsciously fulfill the same need: to erase the sense of our fragmented smallness and touch again the vitality of wholeness. It is of course not the primary wholeness of infancy this time, but a *symbolic* wholeness created through art. The ritual return to the time of "the beginning" represents mankind's intuition that wholeness is not something that happened once, but is a dimension of our lives, dimly remembered, perhaps accessible, but buried below the floor of our daily existence.

Inappropriate Modes Lead to Conflict

Conflict is inevitable in life. When we look at the world stage, so much of the conflict we see appears to be futile, meaningless, absurd. But conflict in drama differs because drama, as a human creation, is a structure of meaning. In its essence, drama is about *growth through crisis*. Dramatic conflict, while often appearing absurd at first sight, is in reality fateful since it changes the lives and destinies of the characters. Part of what we refer to as dramatic unity involves the secret correspondence between a character (like Ada in *The Piano*) and her destiny, as this is gradually revealed to the audience.

In drama, the crisis* occurs because the main character's mode is inappropriate to the present situation. Dramatic crisis forces growth because it precipitates

* Crisis, as well as catalyst and catastrophe, have specific meanings in dramaturgy. The crisis is a dramatic event analogous to the threshold crossing in the Hero's Journey, as we shall see in Chapter Eight.

a process of breakdown in the inappropriate mode. Yet even before the conflict reaches a crisis stage, the mode is already an accident waiting to happen, because it is one-sided and unbalanced. The mode has become a relatively impermeable attitude toward life, well adapted to stable, status quo conditions, but unprepared for the new reality brought about by the Call to Adventure. In effect, it is the basic tension between the main character's tenacity in hanging onto his mode and its inevitable collapse that structures the conflict in the screenplay, as we shall see in greater detail. The antagonist may frame the context of the conflict, but the hero's actions, her perceived range of choices, are in large part determined by her mode, and the mode values with which she identifies.

Inappropriate mode is another way of speaking about the main character's flaw, which is of course her humanness. But the language of the Need versus Mode model gives us a way of penetrating the character flaw, understanding it, and making its influence permeate both the plot and the theme of the movie. When we see that the main character's mode is one-sided and that whatever has been excluded is always pressing from below to come up and be realized, we need not be surprised that it is the inappropriate mode of the main character that pulls or drives her into the dramatic situation.

In the wake of a successful battle, Macbeth, the ferocious general, encounters three witches. The witches prophesy that Macbeth will become king of Scotland. Yet Macbeth's boundless ambition was already inside him as part of his mode, waiting for a propitious moment to take over. This quality of ambition has been adapted to the conditions of Macbeth's status quo world. It has raised him to the position of King Duncan's favorite general, after all. The three witches, as often noted, merely externalize the notion that has already taken hold of Macbeth's mind. It would seem blithely ironic to suggest that Macbeth is here presented with a "growth opportunity," but this is in fact the case. The Japanese ideogram for "crisis" is a composite, made up of two basic characters: *danger* and *opportunity*. Whether Macbeth grows or dies is a question of how tenaciously he identifies with the mode value of ambition and how long it takes him to see his blind spot.

The way we *see* the character's inappropriate mode pull or drive her into the dramatic situation depends on whether the catalyst/call that gets the plot moving is an inner call, an outer call, or a blunder. The screenwriter makes a choice here.

- Joe Buck, in Waldo Salt's screenplay for *Midnight Cowboy*, proclaims his goal and hops on a bus (inner call). At the same time, this action nails Joe Buck's mode: actions and attitudes clustered around a dominant value.
- When Stewart refuses to take the piano from the beach, this constitutes a Call to Adventure for Ada and catalyzes the plot of *The Piano*. As we see Ada stand on the headland at the end of that sequence, her view zooms in on the lonely piano down below, indicating that the piano is a locus of values identified with Ada's mode (outer call).

- Charlie, in *Something Wild*, blunders into his adventure when he tries to sneak out of a cheap restaurant without paying the bill. This blunder, too, expresses the character's mode.

All three characters are acting out of their mode and the underlying value and way of seeing the world that mode expresses. We in the audience come to see—before the character does—that there is an accident waiting to happen. This is the first big piece of subtext that we give to the audience. The fact is that the character's mode makes fulfillment of a universal need impossible. Its very success as a one-sided adaptation to life implies that the value which is the complementary opposite has been successfully excluded. The dramatic catalyst shakes up the status quo and re-awakens long-buried needs. This is what makes the dramatic conflict inevitable.

We do very often see some irony in the juxtaposition of the main character's unrecognized need with the action that comes out of his mode. Here we can really see what Waldo Salt meant about characters getting in their own way. Tom Ripley's mode in *The Talented Mr. Ripley* is to pretend to be someone he is not, rather than to confront his own inner feelings of worthlessness and emptiness. C. C. Baxter's mode in Billy Wilder's *The Apartment* is to give up his apartment to his superiors for their extramarital affairs, in the hopes that they will like him and promote him in the company. What Baxter really needs to learn is to stand his ground and respect himself. Notice that *both* values of each pair of opposites are presented as the movie begins: the mode in the text and the need in the subtext.

Because the pattern of woundings or conditionings that precipitated the mode is unconscious, crisis becomes the necessary agent of change (we charted this in Chapter Two through Alphonse's marital crisis). The outer plot conflict reflects these inner forces in conflict. It is important in this context to reemphasize that the mode can be inappropriate even when superficially the character is dominant and appears to have it all—in fact, *especially* then. The more sure we are of ourselves, the bigger our blind spot is. We see this, for example, in Dr. Richard Kimbell at the opening of *The Fugitive*, as well as in Dr. Malcolm Crowe, the psychologist in *The Sixth Sense*. Often, in their drive to make their hero likeable and generally wonderful, screenwriters don't want to see that the character's status quo mode coming into the story is *necessarily* inappropriate. It is not merely a question of "bad things happening to nice people." Neither individuals nor societies become more integrated without facing their blind spots. From a process point of view, it is exactly the mode's inappropriateness that makes it a vehicle for growth and change.

The mode is inappropriate because an old way of thinking and responding to the world, which helped the character to survive in some past time, has been carried over into the present, where it no longer fits. This is known as "transference": a pattern, usually originating in childhood, has been transferred into the adulthood. The entire pattern is then projected unconsciously onto current situations. This is naturally most true for those patterns that are most deeply ingrained, those we call the mother and father complexes. When we bring this insight together with the Hero's Journey, we discover that when the hero enters the state of duality caused by the Call to Adventure, caught in the paradox of desire and fear, he tends to regress. The old pattern laid down in childhood takes over as a "default mode." As stress increases on the character, he finds himself looking at the situation through the eyes of the wounded child.

Then, after crossing the threshold into the Night World, the sense of regression becomes ever more intense. The main character's mode breaks down because ultimately it is built on something unsolid left over from childhood. It is for this reason that we refer to the catastrophe that ends Act II of the screenplay (the Night of the Soul) as the "grow or die" moment for the character. The old pattern must die if the person is to grow.

Describing the need/mode split in terms of a dialectic of opposing values makes the model sound simple, perhaps even abstract. But in story development, it is notoriously difficult to keep the main character's mode and need consistent. This goes right to the heart of the problem, because as we define the mode and need of the hero, we are simultaneously contextualizing the theme of the movie, what the audience will take out of the theater with them. In the real world of story development, when we start working on a screenplay we may not even know yet who the main character is. We normally have no idea about the hero's unconscious need. All of this tends to take shape only gradually as the screenplay progresses. With every scene we write, we discover something new about the characters. Our views on them change. The characters themselves revise their thoughts about what is happening in the story. Every day, our sense of the throughline shifts in ways that are often maddening, because we feel out of control. It is through this process that the main character's blind spot, what he cannot see because of his own one-sidedness, hooks into a blind spot of our own as writers. The hero's issue starts to resonate with unresolved conflicts in ourselves.

Nailing the main character's mode is a place where generating questions in story development takes a central role. It is also an essential point to include *yourself*, the screenwriter, in the equation. Some questions that help focus the need/mode conflict include the following. They anchor us in the here-and-now status quo of the hero's life: actions that reveal attitudes, clustered around a core value.

- What forces are already in motion when the story begins? (For example, the disturbed young man in *The Sixth Sense* has already broken into Malcolm Crowe's bedroom.)
- What is out of balance in the world of the story as it begins? (Example: Renton's entire world as a junkie is out of balance as *Trainspotting* opens.)

- How does the protagonist represent or reflect what is out of balance in the world of the story? (Example: C. C. Baxter's compliance with his superiors in the insurance company in *The Apartment* is an illustration of a generalized attitude of opportunism and corruption.)
- How does the main character feel about his place in the social world of the story? Is he the insider, the outsider, the observer, etc.? (Example: Neo, in *The Matrix*, is a dissatisfied, marginal employee in his IT corporation. All his energy goes into his underground life.)
- What, in the simplest terms that we can observe, is the character's mode? What do we see the character *doing* as the story opens? Look for actions that reveal attitudes. (Examples: Ada is peeking out at the world through her fingers; C. C. Baxter is working late at the office because he can't get into his apartment; John Book is taking charge at the murder scene; Lester, in *American Beauty*, is waking up, and then masturbating in the shower ["... the high point of my day"].)
- What is a specific action or behavior of the character at the opening which exhibits *exaggeration* or *inhibition*? About what? (Examples: Lester dropping his briefcase, a passive-aggressive gesture of resistance; Ada's muteness, her "will's" decision not to speak; Tom Ripley's self-deprecating social clumsiness in *The Talented Mr. Ripley*.)
- What is the event that catalyses the story (the hero's Call to Adventure)? How does the catalyst specify the hero's mode and precipitate an outer plot goal? (Examples: Neo receives a call from Morpheus, telling him that the agents have just come into the office to catch him. As a consequence, Neo's mode becomes specified: he is no longer merely a geek with a secret life as a hacker. Now he is specifically the hacker who will encounter Morpheus and learn the secret of the Matrix. Lester encounters his daughter's friend Angela and becomes infatuated with her. Now he is no longer just another frustrated middle-aged loser; he starts to literally act out the fantasy of regaining his youth so that he can fulfill his infatuation.)
- How does the catalyst act as a reawakening of a backstory wound? (Examples: Johnny's marriage proposal in *Moonstruck* opens up relationship issues that have been locked in Loretta since her husband died; the Kid's appeal to Will Munney in *Unforgiven* calls him back to a violent way of life he thought he had left behind.)
- How does the character feel before and after the catalyst/call sequence? What has changed? Use the focusing *felt-sense* exercise to identify the shift.* (Example: With Will Munney, we see a man who at first appears unconscious, chasing his pigs in the dirt. After the Kid leaves, Will has a pang of conscience related to his dead wife, that he is still not the man she wanted

* See the *Internal Software* techniques at the end of Chapter One, p. 49.

him to be. This is a way of telling us that Will's motives in the drama are cluttered by layers of projection and transference.)

- What is the felt-sense of the value animating the mode? Often the best way to approach this is to look at the hero's own mood just after the catalyst/ Call to Adventure. (Examples: When Loretta accepts Johnny's proposal, she is not exactly thrilled; they do not kiss, but she pats him on the cheek. Will Munney accepts his adventure not with the Kid's ambition to build a reputation, but with tones of regret and guilt, like one sliding back into an addiction. This mood here does indeed foreshadow the downward course of the entire movie.)

You may have noticed that some of these questions are *objective*: they help us objectify the hero's mode through specific actions and identify how the dramatic catalyst operates to initiate a process of change. Some of the questions are *subjective*: they focus on our own position as the screenwriter, how we feel about the situation and what it means to us. Still other questions, those dealing with the felt-sense, for example, encourage us to develop an *objective-subjectivity*, to make our own subjective responses objective and use them as a source of feedback and evaluation. This helps bring our creative intuition closer to consciousness and make it more available to us. The range of subjective and objectively subjective questions rarely come up in story development discussions, and that is a pity because an opportunity is lost. These questions bring us into feeling rapport with the main character and the story. After all, it is typically in the inappropriate mode of the main character that the story comes closest to our own lives.

Character and Plot: Need/Mode Tension Structures the Conflict

In drama, a character's unconscious or unacknowledged need is simultaneously masked and pointed to by their mode. Loretta in Moonstruck is a transparent example: we are told explicitly in the third scene that her husband was hit by a bus and killed. As she says this, with the tightly controlled gestures that typify her mode, we subliminally draw conclusions about her need. Loretta has turned herself into a dry widow in gray to protect herself from her wounded and repressed passion. The tension between her survival mode—to protect herself from being hurt again by "unlucky love"—and her universal need to live her true, passionate nature, drives Loretta's character all the way through the story. This is Loretta's throughline. Her need/mode tension *creates* her story. Another character with a different inner dynamic would necessarily live a different story. But we can see that while Loretta's *survival mode* leads her to accept Johnny's marriage proposal, her unconscious desire leads her into a wild affair with Johnny's brother. And this latter event, built on Loretta's underlying conflict between control and passion, constitutes the dramatic crisis/threshold crossing that ends Act I of

Moonstruck. We begin to see how the underlying tension of values structures the outer plot conflict.

What we can observe here is key to setting up a screenplay and making it work. The Need versus Mode model identifies the underlying tension that drives the story from within. But this tension in itself is not visible to the audience. It must be *externalized* before it can become real.

There are three steps in this process of externalizing the underlying thematic tensions in story development. The first step is to identify a value with the mode—in Loretta's case, the value of *control*—and portray that value by way of actions that reveal attitudes. The need value—the inverse or opposite of the mode value—is implicitly laid in the subtext because it is *conspicuously absent*.

The second step in externalizing the need/mode tension is to find the significant object in Loretta's world that embodies or stands for the mode value of control, and another object that embodies or stands for the unconscious need that is the opposite of control: passion. What are these two objects in *Moonstruck*? They are, respectively, Johnny—the mama's boy who wants to marry Loretta—and Johnny's brother Ronnie, who is passion personified. We see that Loretta can wrap Johnny around her little finger. If she marries Johnny she will become even more controlling, more locked into her survival mode, and more estranged from her vitality. Ronnie immediately takes Loretta out of control, and as a result, she begins to recover her passion.

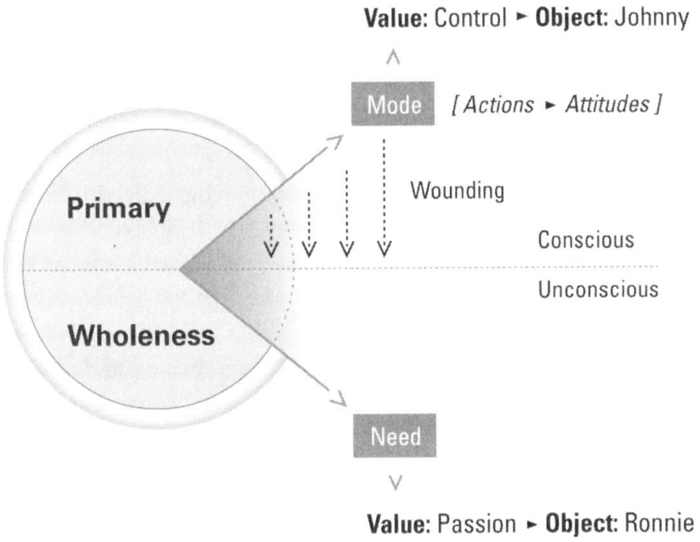

/ ***Need versus Mode:*** **Loretta Castorini in *Moonstruck*.**

The third step in the process is to put the hero in a double bind where she must choose one of the objects, but cannot have both. At the climax of *Moonstruck* we will see Loretta forced to choose between Johnny and Ronnie. As she does so, she is in fact choosing between the two values. In this way, she is also choosing whether she will cling to her mode or will realize her unconscious need. To summarize:

- Identify a value with the mode and portray that value by way of actions that reveal attitudes.
- Find the significant "object" (a person, situation, or physical object connected with the plot goal) that embodies or stands for the mode value, and another "object" (the primary relationship or love interest) that embodies or stands for the unconscious need.
- Put the hero in a double bind where she must choose one of the desired objects, but cannot have both.

We don't need to be taken inside Loretta's head in order to get the point. It is all directly externalized through the dramatic action.

By the end of Act I of the screenplay, the opposition between the mode value and the need value has been constellated in the outer plot conflict. From this point onward, the entire construction of Act II will force the main character into a corner where she must choose between the object embodying the mode value and the one embodying the need value. By the choice she makes, she is choosing a life-path, a destiny. Try to imagine Loretta's destiny if she had married Johnny. It's not a pretty picture. Yet she was headed in that direction! At the climax, we will see Loretta stand up for her passion. Her dramatic journey leads to an increase in wholeness. This is a very broad outline of how the need/mode tension structures the dramatic conflict. Loretta is a simple, obvious example because *Moonstruck* is a very broad comedy. But we could equally take Ada from *The Piano*, Tom Ripley, or the trio of bratty yuppies from the Scottish thriller *Shallow Grave*, about all of whose backstories we are told virtually nothing. In every case there is of course an outer plot, but the *meaning* of the plot—what it means to the hero and thus to the audience—is charted by the shift in the main character's allegiance between the mode and need values.

As we have already suggested, the Need versus Mode model is central to establishing the audience's *subtext*. In a sense, the subtext is the "real" story for the audience, because it is the source of the audience's active involvement in the movie. The subtext is the subliminal inner dialogue the audience directs at the screen. Without this inner involvement, watching a movie would be reduced to a dull, passive series of reactions. The audience is more than willing to collaborate in this underground relationship with the movie. The point is to orchestrate and lead the audience so that, through the interaction of subtext and text (the events happening on the screen), the audience receives the dramatic and thematic riches you have to offer. The subtext of what is missing or lacking is established at the opening of the movie by clearly establishing the hero's one-sided mode.

It is standard wisdom for screenwriters that we must nail the main character the first time she comes on screen. The entrance of Rick in *Casablanca* is cited as the textbook example. But what does this phrase really mean, to "nail" the character? It means that when we introduce the character, we focus on actions that reveal attitudes, the attitudes that define the core mode value. What is the first dramatic action we see in *Shallow Grave*? We see the three central characters aggressively brow-beating and humiliating people who have answered their ad for a flat mate. Their attitude seems to be that the three of them exist on some higher plane than the rest of humanity. They are tougher, smarter, and have better taste. The core value around which these actions and attitudes cluster is ruthlessly egocentric (though the trio may believe that their sibling relationship is somehow different and precious). The movie has not wasted any time on background exposition, but has gone directly to the heart of the matter. Without this ruthless egoism there would be neither drama nor theme in *Shallow Grave*.

It is not enough to merely tell the audience about the character and expect them to get it. It really is necessary to focus the opening action so that the mode is clearly defined. If, in writing the draft, there appear to be two or three modes that are each half-clear, more is not in this case better. That invariably leads to two or three partial throughlines and a weak, diffuse story that cannot be satisfactorily paid off at the climax. More work is required to find the core mode value that embraces all of this character's behavior in a definitive way.

Meanwhile, how do we handle the need? By definition, the protagonist's need is unconscious at the beginning of the story. It is a value that has been repressed or suppressed at an earlier time of life, as part of the splitting process that created the survival mode. If we hear a character *tell* us what they need in Act I, we can be sure they are fooling themselves—or it is bad writing. As we said, by nailing the main character's mode we are already laying the universal need in the subtext by its conspicuous absence. In this way, the need is *virtually* present, implicitly present. It is present in the hero's unconscious, and is represented to the audience via the subtext.

We want to keep the hero's need in the subtext until the time is ripe to bring it forward, at the moment when it is a question of "grow or die," at the end of Act II. So the hero's universal need remains unconscious (in the subtext) all through Act I and Act II. Only as the survival mode breaks down and collapses under conflict is its hold loosened enough that the "stone that the builder refused" (the unconscious need) is allowed to return home and find a place of honor.

Modes Lead to Plot Goals

The need/mode dynamics bring up a crucial point for story development: establishing the main character's *plot goal*. There is in fact a general confusion about the nature of plot goals that tends to lead either toward superficial stories or toward development hell. It is very common to meet screenwriters or development people who voice some version of the following: "My hero's plot goal is to be the champion. That's what he wants, and that's what he needs: to be the champ!" Here the plot goal is identified with the main character's *need*. So let us be very clear about it. The plot goal grows out of the character's *mode*, their "who I think I am." The plot goal is a specification of the mode. It focuses the attitudes and core values of the mode onto a throughline action directed toward an object. Ada, already almost autistically withdrawn into her artificial world comprised of her piano, her daughter, and herself, is on a quest to get her piano back after Stewart has left it on the beach. This is her plot goal. Lester Burnham, already escaping from the realities of his failing career and marriage into daydream, becomes infatuated with his sixteen-year-old daughter's schoolmate, Angela. In all these cases, the achievement of the plot goal in its original form would simply reinforce and solidify the core mode value that is already dominant. The character might "get" something, but he would not grow.

Since the need value is the complementary opposite of the mode value, the plot goal as originally perceived by the character cannot by definition be what she really needs to learn about life. The character does not *know* what she really needs. It is unconscious. It is in the Night World. This does not imply that the plot goal is necessarily *wrong*, or that the character should not want to be champion. Of course Ada should have her piano. Of course Lester should fight against his lethargy and sense of humiliation. This is simply the perspective the character has before they have started on the journey. But the meaning that comes out of it, the initiation, will be the product of the journey itself. The plot goal, as the hero perceives it in Act I, is really the *pretext* for the journey, the catalyst, strictly speaking. Along the way, the plot goal may itself be transformed, along with the hero, by deepening conflict. This leads in the end to a new relationship to the plot goal.

In fact, if we consider that the plot goal is not something objective and fixed, but is a subjective product of the hero's value system, we realize that the plot goal is co-evolving with the character. Characters and plot goals tend to develop in one of three directions:

1. It may be that the hero gets what he wants, but in a different way then he had planned. John Book does bring the killers to justice—but in fact, no he does not. The tough, lone, super-competent police captain is powerless when Paul has a gun to Rachel's head. It is really the nonviolent Amish who ultimately bring the killers to justice. That is a lesson in humility for the action hero who thought he had all the answers. In other cases, the hero must sacrifice himself to achieve the plot goal, as the Terminator does to save John in *Terminator 2*. This is certainly a case of getting what we want, but in a different way than planned.
2. It may also turn out that the hero must *renounce* the original goal as the deeper unconscious need surfaces. In these cases the actual decision or choice

between the two objects is the central action at the climax. Loretta must renounce Johnny, and with him security and control—which is quite clear by the way the climax scene is played. Ada must renounce her piano if she is to accept a life of real embodiment and incarnation in the world, personified by George. C. C. Baxter must renounce his career at the insurance company if he is to regain his self-respect and become a mensch.

A further possibility is that realization of the inner need renders the original plot goal *incidental*, devalued in relation to a new value. This may be a transitional step toward ultimately renouncing the exclusive control of the mode value that propelled the goal. In *Midnight Run*, Jack Walsh *does* get the Duke to L.A. before midnight, but in the act of doing so he seems to realize how petty and self-centered his motive has been. As a consequence, he renounces the $250,000 reward in favor of giving the Duke his freedom. In Act I, the plot goal is an external object of desire. By the climax, the value projected onto that object has been placed in a new context: the context of deep character change.

3. The character may attain the original plot goal, and in the way imagined according to the mode, but the result is tragic. Tom Ripley's Call to Adventure is an invitation to join the golden circle of the wealthy and carefree. More than this, it is specifically to emulate and even to merge with a "perfect" man, Dickie Greenleaf. As Tom watches Dickie through binoculars while preparing for their first meeting, he says to himself: "*Questa è la mia faccia*" ("This is *my* face")—he is reading an Italian phrase book. At the end of the story, Tom has attained a place in this elite society and has in fact "become" Dickie Greenleaf. But rather than being liberated, Tom himself tells us that he is locked in a dark basement with his demons. The tragedy is in clinging to the mode rather than opening to a larger and truer sense of self. Contemporary tragedy is not about the death of kings. It charts the psychological and ethical death that accompanies attachment to a fixed concept of "who I think I am."

There are some story-forms and genres where the hero does not change appreciably, and yet they are not classed as tragedies. The thriller genre, for example, is plot-driven rather than character-driven. This means that the plot is determined first according to genre conventions. Character is then a function of plot rather than plot being a function of character.

In thrillers, the character serves the plot, and the character change must also serve the plot. The need/mode tension is de-emphasized or is handled in a special way.* What is important to the thriller audience is the plot question: whodunit? Will they get out alive? Will Clarice Starling in *Silence of the Lambs* catch Buffalo Bill before he murders the girl? Will Neo destroy the Matrix before the last

* Other aspects of creating and orchestrating genre stories are addressed in the next chapter, and in Chapter Seven: Orchestrating Character and Style.

hope for humanity is wiped out? In this context, the inner need/mode tension in the main character is expressed as a tension between the character's *core virtue* and her *blind spot*. What the hero needs to learn about life is focused specifically on what she needs to discover to solve the case and not get killed. Usually the two are related: seeing the blind spot will require some degree of character change. It drives the plot from within, because the hero must see her own blind spot or weakness that either prevents her from getting the key clue or makes her fatally too weak to confront the antagonist. Starling must face her deep fear and guilt about the slaughter of the lambs. Dr. Richard Kimbell must realize that his best friend is his worst enemy, and that he has been betrayed by his own naïve faith in human nature.

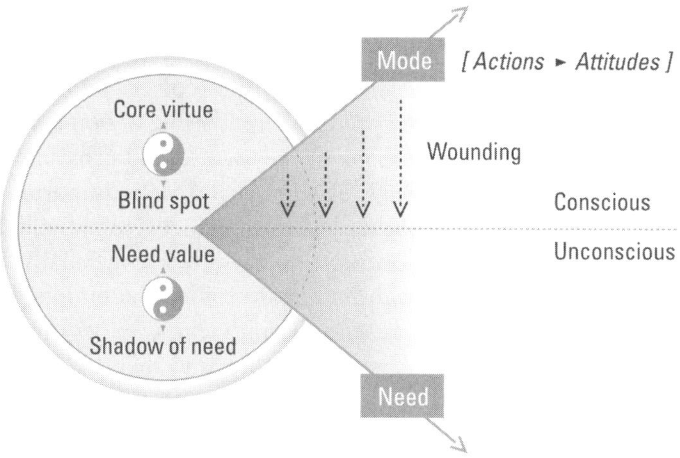

/ Core Virtue versus Blind Spot.

In orchestrating the thriller, we set the hero's core virtue against her blind spot. As the hero goes deeper into the night world and enters into lethal danger, the tension grows. Which will prevail? If the core virtue prevails and the hero sees her blind spot, she comes through, like Starling. If the blind spot is stronger than the core virtue, the hero loses, like Detective Mills in *Seven*.

Pure action fantasies such as James Bond movies and Jackie Chan vehicles are built on two-dimensional characters and predictable plot structures; the characters are fundamentally invulnerable to change. In a sense, the whole point is that the character is *not* going to change. This involves the audience in a greater suspension of disbelief. The setup of the world of the story forbids our asking whether James Bond ever has to go to the bathroom or brush his teeth. Such heroes are closer to the pure hero archetype than they are to recognizable human beings, though even the Jackie Chan characters have their foibles.

All movies invite the audience to project themselves onto the hero. In character drama, that projective identification takes the audience into transformation: the breakdown of the mode and the breakthrough of a need that leads to greater integrity. In stereotypical action stories, the projective identification of the audience is used to create a bond of *participation mystique* with the hero. We are meant to identify directly with the hero in the primitive way we identify with sports heroes and movie stars, which is to say that we unconsciously live through such larger-than-life figures. This kind of idealizing identification lowers the level of consciousness in the audience. The distance required for objectivity and reflection—and thus empathy—is removed. Many people experience this temporary lowering of consciousness as pleasurable, because it is a state of grandiosity. It is what is meant by the term "escapism."

On the pragmatic plot-construction level, the plots in pure action movies are often thought of as settings, or pretexts, for the big action sequences. The heroes themselves tend to become icons (if they work, and provoke our unconscious identifications) or *stereotypes* (if they don't). It is important to point out that where the need/mode conflict has not been developed and defined so that it pulls the hero deeper and deeper into the story, continually raising the emotional and ethical stakes of the drama, real problems in building the second act invariably come up. Why? Because the script lacks an inner dimension. It is difficult to endow these characters with inner life, and their dialogue with subtext. Lacking inner drama and subtext, the only way then to keep the dramatic intensity rising in Act II is to literally make the size of the action bigger: bigger car chases, bigger explosions, more blood. Each new combat gives us chance to wonder at the hero's virtuoso fighting skills. Usually comic elements are added to keep the critical left-brain from objecting too loudly and spoiling the fun. In Jackie Chan's movies, the farce-comedy tone may even swallow the action.

A concomitant strategy is to use the action to continually reinforce the iconic action hero's "legend," and thus the audience's projective identification. The shadow side of this is that the one-dimensional villains in such movies become an easy means for demonizing other races, religions, or political groups, as the furor over the movie *300*—with its depiction of the Persians as a subhuman and perverted enemy, just as threats by the U.S. government to attack Iran were escalating—illustrates. Along with pure action movies, broad farces, spoofs, and satires may also, for their different reasons, feature main characters who show minimal change. These are heroes who are both more and less human. And for all their action and frantic pace, the movies are often surprisingly flat, because the subtext, that subliminal dialogue between the audience and the screen, is missing.

The Universal Need Is the Throughline Subtext of the Movie

Establishing the throughline subtext is equally as important to the screenplay as establishing the outer plot throughline. Only together, through their mutual influence, is a dramatic whole, a dramatic unity, created.

The universal need is laid in the subtext. Here we get into the complexity of how meaning is conveyed through stories. We want the audience to get hints of the hero's universal need, which they normally perceive subliminally. The character cannot speak of it directly, thus there are several places to look for the indirect expression of this unconscious need. One of the most important is body language, or *dissonance* between what a character says and how he behaves. Another is comprised of the character's mental lapses, slips of the tongue, and other small blunders. Taken together, we could say that these are places where we can feel an *energy charge* in the character that manifests itself through tension or inhibition. These behaviors point indirectly to stuck places, constrictions around old wounds. They hint at what has been excluded. Drawing the character is not complete if we have neglected this aspect.

As a screenwriter, you are not trying to micromanage the movie or dictate to the actor how to move and gesture, but you do want to portray the character so that the actor can feel what is inside the character and, in collaboration with the director, find the behavior to bring it to life. We want the *quality* of the character's actions to present a subtle marker for the audience, so that they engage in the subliminal dialogue: "What's wrong with this picture? Where's Loretta's *passion*?" Verbal slips and "stuck places" are very natural means for making the character more three-dimensional and alive, and pointing to the unconscious need at the same time.

MODE =	TEXT →	DIALOGUE *(EXPRESSES TEXT)*
Need	Subtext	Body Language
		Freudian Slips (*express subtext*)
		Dissonance

Mode is to need as the text of the scene is to the subtext. The mode creates the text of the scene, what the scene is about on the surface, what the characters say they want, and what they do to get what they want. The unconscious need is what the characters don't know they want. Therefore they cannot act on it consciously or find words for it. The need/mode conflict gives a character three-dimensionality because it sets up a *foreground* and a *background* to the character. It creates a sense of perspective that has a dynamic impact on the audience. The mode is the foreground; the need is the background. Even though the need is unconscious for the character and invisible to the audience, it is still driving the action. The audience feels it in their belly like the subterranean rumble of an express train, still around the bend but coming fast. When the universal need is revealed to the audience in Act III, and is either embraced by the hero who has gone through a transformation or is rejected by a tragic hero unable to change, the audience gets an "Aha!" experience. If the mode and need are set up as a true pair of dialectical opposites, the revelation of the need conveys a sense of inevitability that can touch an audience very deeply.

Character Development and Character Arcs

Abraham Lincoln, speaking on the question of whether the United States would ultimately become all-slave or all-free, made an observation so simple and universal that it pertains to our work with characters as well:

> If we could first know where we are, and whither we are tending, we could then better judge what to do and how to do it.

Who is the character when he comes into the story, whither is he tending, and what has changed by the end? How much character change in a movie is motivated, necessary, or realistic? The answers to these questions have very much to do with the degree of tension between mode and need, as well as the idiom and genre of the storytelling. While genre conventions govern to a large extent the stylization of characters within the genre, character transformation is always one of the great challenges in screenwriting. No change or too little change in the character and she can appear flat, static, and boring. Worse, the character defies nature, which is constant change. Even the structure of individual scenes pushes through conflict toward incremental character change within the scene. On the other hand, trying to force character transformation too far results in unrealistic and unmotivated "jumps" in the character that are hard to hide from the audience in the movie theater. Actors tear their hair out trying to somehow fill the unmotivated gaps in such character development.

We can chart the change in the main character by means of a simple *character arc*. The shape of the character arc follows that of Aristotle's Plot Curve* of tension and release. This it is not surprising, since it carries the same dynamic of tension and release. A *relationship arc* is also constructed for the primary relationship in the movie. Here we are using the character arc to graphically chart the inner need/mode conflict of the main character.

When writing a screenplay, we can visualize where the character is at the opening by the way we use actions to define the status quo mode. We may also have an image of where she is at or after the climax. For example, at the opening of *The Piano*, discussed in detail in Chapter Nine, Ada is like a little girl, peeking out at the world from between her fingers; she tends to escape from banal reality

* The dynamics of the outer plot are covered in Chapters Eight and Nine.

into her music while trying her best not to deal with the world around her. At the climax, she is reborn out of the ocean after having faced death.

Similarly, at the opening of *The Matrix*, Neo is a computer geek searching for secret meaning; he tends to passively resist the odious corporate world in which he works to explore an alternate reality. At the end he is a fully realized god-like savior who has overcome death. At the opening of *Witness*, John Book is a he-man taking charge; at the climax he is saved by the nonviolent Amish, and at the end he returns to his duties with a more humbled attitude. The opening and closing images of a script should tell us how much transformation the writer has asserted. We can then ask if this degree of change will work with the type of story (idiom and genre) we are telling. Obviously it would not work to have Book turn into a fully realized god-like savior at the end of *Witness*, because it would be inconsistent with the tone and world of the rest of the story. Nor is "maximum" change necessarily better. Many movies, like the comedies of Woody Allen and Eric Rohmer, work very well by observing small changes (chains of actions and consequences) closely and faithfully.

Character growth is not merely the order in which the hero learns things. The potential for growth always meets the character's own resistance. The mode represents how the hero has learned to adapt and survive. When that mode is threatened, it feels like life itself is threatened because the character has identified with the mode. The mode hangs on for dear life! So, beneath the simple curve of the character arc there is a deeper dynamic going on: the Call to Adventure catalyses the need/mode tension by awakening desire and fear. Then the Threshold Crisis that ends Act I reveals the flaw in the mode and starts it breaking down. The mode now begins to have negative consequences for the hero. But we can expect the hero to use every means possible to defend the mode and keep it going. It is one of the paradoxes of psychological growth that the tenacity of our resistance actually pushes the conflict to deeper and deeper levels. Thus, when the collapse of the mode does come, it is all the more complete and final. Outer plot conflict is of course pushing this process, but, as we have said, it is the nature of dramatic conflict that the outer situation cannot be resolved unless the character changes the way he sees things.

There are in fact four more or less distinct phases to the deepening conflict:

1. From the dramatic catalyst to the end of Act I, the conflict appears to be external, about an issue *external* to the hero. The hero has a fantasy of being able to overcome the conflict without being himself changed by it. Tom Ripley hopes that by playing on his charming, ingratiating persona he can be accepted by Dickie into a world of carefree luxury.
2. Crossing the threshold into Act II, the Night World, up to the core crisis at the middle of Act II, deeper conflicts become implicated. These are first of all *emotional* conflicts of allegiance. Tom finds himself an outsider and increasingly has to fight for Dickie's attention and affection.

3. From the core crisis, termed the "midpoint" by some writers, to the end of Act II, the deepest, *existential* level of the conflict begins to emerge. This is the core conflict of values attached to the mode and need. It is the fundamental question of "Who am I?" in the context of the hero's character. Is Ada the woman who will always fly away on the wings of her art? Or is Ada the woman who will answer the call of the man who loves her—and whom she loves—for commitment, commitment to *this* world? Tom Ripley, at this point, finally rejected and humiliated by Dickie, kills him—and then he becomes Dickie. He takes on a dual identity. Who is he really? Is he Tom or is he Dickie? This existential crisis, impossible for Tom to resolve, becomes increasingly tragic for him.
4. The internal tension between the mode and need finally breaks as the hero is *forced to choose* between the object connected to the mode and the object connected to the need. Significantly, the character in *The Talented Mr. Ripley* who most embodies what Tom has to learn is Marge, Dickie's girlfriend. As Tom becomes tragically caught in his own net of lies, Marge takes on the role of the antagonist, pushing to bring the truth about Dickie's death to light. Tom's attachment to his mode makes it impossible for Marge to take on the role of a guide for him toward a simple and truthful self-acceptance. This means that the end can only be tragic.

The added levels of conflict as the problem burrows deeper into the personality go far toward explaining that great mystery for screenwriters: what keeps the dramatic intensity rising throughout Act II? The outer plot development by itself is often not enough to bring the hero to a point of "grow or die." The new paradigm of the Sixteen Story Steps (Chapter Eleven) will show how, on virtually a sequence-by-sequence basis, outer plot conflict and need/mode conflict work together to raise the dramatic stakes in the phases described above. This deepening conflict corresponds precisely to the Descent in the Hero's Journey—and the stripping away of Inanna's seven veils is exactly how the character feels in this process.

Projection and the Archetypal Identity of Character

Character change in a screenplay feels mysterious. In spite of our meticulous planning via treatments, scene outlines, and discussions, our characters always manage to wriggle out of the prearranged program and behave in ways that surprise us. They slip out of our grasp in a way that is can only be described as *shadowy*.

As we write, it is inevitable that we project our own unconscious "stuff" onto the story. There is especially a tendency to identify ourselves with the hero. Here we face another paradox, because we cannot write this character effectively and authentically unless we do "fall" for the character. Only by falling do we make such an intimate bond with the character that we experience her feelings as our own. But we also cannot do this without at the same time losing our objectivity. The character becomes our phantom double, our "secret sharer," to use Joseph Conrad's phrase. He or she comes to share our lives for weeks, months, years—perhaps forever. It is a real, intimate relationship, because the character seems to know *us* as well as we know her—especially what will make us mad, frustrated, or inspired.

This is such a fundamental point about the creative process of writing that it deserves to be stressed:

> The character is fictional, but the relationship is real! All those hours sitting at the computer constitute a similar psychological/emotional investment to that of any interpersonal relationship.

Our own ideas, feelings, perspectives, and unconscious convictions about life, growth, freedom, good and evil—in short, our basic level of consciousness—all impact how we structure our characters and set them free to live their story. Certainly we marvel at and respect Shakespeare's capacity to bring to life such a range of characters, temperaments, and consciousnesses. It suggests an awareness of nearly cosmic proportions to be able to embrace all this life. Dramatic writing can indeed broaden our perspectives and understanding of human nature, but there is always the hazard that we will sink to a lower level of consciousness through identifying with our hero. Everyone who has ever attended a screenwriting workshop or writer's group has encountered fledgling screenwriters whose main characters are transparent idealizations of themselves: younger, slimmer, hipper, smarter, full of social graces, and ultimately more successful. There is of course the inverse possibility as well: the writer makes a *negative* identification with the character, and projects on to him all of the shame, maladroit weaknesses, and victim mentality he does not want to carry himself. These tangles of identification get in our way as writers. It is helpful to us to have some concepts whereby we can objectify the character enough so that we can keep a personal boundary with the character.

A good place to start is to look at universal needs in relationship to life stages. Our sense of what we need is subjectively colored, can shift from moment to moment, and has everything in the world to do with our mythology. Here we speak of mythology not merely as a set of beliefs, but, even more, as the highly charged images we carry within us: images of value that can often carry a decisive weight when we are in crisis. A symbol can motivate us even to the extent of overriding our instinctual drives. The subjectively perceived hierarchy of needs may then become inverted. Joseph Campbell told a story about an incident that took place in Hawaii, where he retired at the end of his career. There was a spot where a highway ran along a sheer cliff above the sea, often chosen by suicides because of its dramatic windswept location. One night a police patrol came upon a young man ready to jump. An officer leapt out of the squad car and rushed to grab him. The boy was about to pull the officer off the cliff with him when the second officer came up, and together the two dragged the boy from the edge. The newspapers of course wanted to interview the first officer. They asked: why he didn't let go when it appeared he would be pulled to his own death? The officer replied that he would not have been able to live with himself he had let that boy jump. The image/value of compassion overrode this officer's most basic instinct, that of survival. This is a vivid example of the surprising fluidity of our values, as well as the heroism to which David Mamet referred.

Our characters, the ones we tend to identify with, also tend to twist around our sense of values as writers. This is because when the hero is identified with her mode, like Loretta Castorini in *Moonstruck*, she is usually involved in confusing a less essential need as more essential. Subjectively, she believes that her mode *is* her need. She is driven to keep her mode going, even when it becomes clear to the audience that the mode no longer works. It is not immediately obvious to Loretta that "playing it safe" is a lesser need than "living her passion," because her backstory wound has distorted her perception of her needs.

Need is a question of perception. When the character is in the comfort zone of his status quo, he has one perception of himself and his needs. When he arrives at the Night of the Soul and everything has been stripped away, then everything appears different. We know of persons who have given their lives for a principle. On the other hand, we have heard of people killing each other over a parking space or because somebody dissed their dog. We know that perception of need is also subject to external manipulation. When a friend says to you: "You really *need* to hear the new Madonna CD," or another says: "I really *need* to find a skirt that matches this sweater," how is the word *need* being used? What does it do to your own perception of yourself to talk in this way? We live in a highly charged media environment filled with messages designed to get under our skin and influence our motivations. The entire thrust of modern advertising is not to sell a product, but to sell a universal value. The product is simply identified with the value. When we see an ad where a Jeep Cherokee is perched on the rim of the Grand Canyon, what we are really being sold is *freedom*. Who can say no to freedom? Freedom and the Jeep Cherokee are made to symbolize and stand for each other. This can be very confusing to our sense of needs and values.

Finding the single compelling dialectical pair of opposing values identifies the inner split and creates compelling character change. Seeing this further in the context of life stages helps us gain some objectivity about our hero and step back from our projective identifications with him. There are identifiable levels of human development, and a person's entire sense of reality is transformed at each level. Each level carries its own perspective and life issue to be dealt with.

The chakra system of Hinduism, with its symbolism of seven energy centers rising up the spine, is an example of such a multileveled psychology. It is not necessary to believe in the literal reality of energy centers in the body to appreciate the value of the metaphor. The lower four chakras are to be thought of as representing the energies of, respectively, the sheer brute will to live, pleasure and eros, power and domination, and the opening of the heart to compassion. Joseph Campbell identified these four with Behaviorism, the Freudian pleasure-principle, Adlerian "Will to Power," and Jungian psychology. Each would be a different, increasingly potent or coherent lens with which to look at the world. In the view of the chakra system, someone at the higher level could comprehend and have empathy for those at lower levels of development, while someone at the lower level has absolutely no idea about the higher. That person on the lower level has no capacity to "read" the greater complexity.

Each of these chakra centers represents a nexus of attitudes toward life, sets of values, and thus modes. Each chakra suggests "personas" that might inhabit the world of that chakra level: the couch potatoes and apathetic creeps of chakra one, the seductive sirens and Viagra junkies of chakra two, the hard-charging captains of industry and bullying parents of chakra three, and so on. We can see from film stories that some characters are clearly at a higher level of internal growth and complexity than others; they are more *mature*. John Book is capable of genuine self-sacrifice. We can imagine that there is a certain level of human value that he would never give up, no matter what pressures are brought to bear. We might see him in *Witness* as moving between the third and fourth chakra levels. His consciousness, values, and hierarchy of needs would be unimaginable to the characters in *Trainspotting*, *Shallow Grave*, or *Blue Velvet*. Conrad in *Ordinary People* is relatively more conscious than his mother; Edna May in *Resurrection* relatively more than her father.

Carol S. Pearson, in her book *Awakening the Heroes Within*, has developed a useful model of personal transformation which can serve the screenwriter well as a conceptual approach to character development.[22]

Pearson manages to bring together a number of vectors relevant to understanding how people grow: the idea that there is an innate evolutionary drive toward self-actualization and wholeness as suggested by paradigms like Abraham Maslow's hierarchy of needs and the chakra system, the sense that we pass through life-stages which have their unique challenges, and the *archetypal* perspective that individuals tend to relate more closely to one archetype and thus can be associated with a particular archetypal identity.

Pearson's model is constructed around twelve archetypes,* which are paired according to six life-stages, starting with childhood and ending with maturity and old age. Each developmental pair of archetypal identities shows a contrasting response toward a fundamental problem or universal need.

22. Pearson, Carol S., *Awakening the Heroes Within* (New York: Harper-Collins, 1991).

* Pearson conceptualizes archetypal images into a typology. The archetypes themselves, as we have said, occupy a deep level of the unconscious and cannot be seen *in themselves*. Archetypal images are the representations of these deep psychic factors as they appear in the field of consciousness.

Security:	Innocent versus Orphan
Identity:	Seeker versus Lover
Responsibility:	Warrior versus Caregiver
Authenticity:	Destroyer versus Creator
Power:	Magician versus Ruler
Freedom:	Sage versus Fool

We carry all of these archetypes inside us in potential, but at different points in life or under changing circumstances we may identify more with one or with another. Each archetype, according to Pearson, has its own shadow-side, its own *dragon*, and its own virtue. The fundamental problems of security, identity, responsibility, and so on are universals we struggle with all our lives. Nevertheless, there is a definite sense of stages which emerges. In Pearson's analysis, our childhood experience tends to constellate one of two archetypal responses around the issue of security. We could typify them as either "Life is fun and can be trusted" (Innocent) or "Life is dangerous and I am abandoned" (Orphan). In adolescence, we may tend to define our identity either in relation *to* others (Lover) or as distinct *from* others (Seeker). Our way of taking responsibility may emphasize *overcoming* (Warrior: John Book, Jack Walsh, Ada) or *cooperating and harmonizing* (Caregiver: Rachel, Loretta, The Duke, C. C. Baxter).

These archetypal pairings help us step outside our own personal system and look at character development more objectively. Most writers, like most people, tend to believe that their own archetypal identifications constitute an absolute truth: *my childhood was like this, ergo, reality is like this! I'm on my own and you really can't trust anybody*. Pearson's model of archetypal development helps us step outside our collective bubble as well. We tend to collectively value the Innocent, Lover, Warrior, Creator, Ruler, and Fool more highly than we do the Orphan, Seeker, Caregiver, Destroyer, Magician, and Sage. According to our public images—the types of people who appear in ads, on television, and in movies—we would seem to identify more with the first set of archetypal identities. They carry qualities we value highly; they are carefree, sensual, decisive, creative, in control, irreverent. We tend to believe in them unreflectively. Collectively, the first set seems to many somehow more *true*. It comprises a special lens through which we look at reality. However, if we went to Poland, Peru, or Indonesia, we would likely find another set of preferred archetypal identities. How we relate to our characters, whether we like them or not, whether we overidentify with them or disidentify from them, has a lot to do with how each character's archetypal identity interacts with our own archetypal identifications.

When we are trying to get a handle on our main character, one of these archetypal tags may immediately seem to fit. *Awakening the Heroes Within* outlines the pattern of behavior we can, in general, expect to see from the character: the typical goal (plot goal), fear (backstory wound), dragon (response to the threshold guardian), response to task (what the character needs to learn), and gift/virtue (boon at the end of the journey). For example, if our character is an Innocent (a person who is unconsciously identified with the Innocent archetype), the goal tends to be in the area of remaining playfully innocent; the fear, a fear of abandonment; the reaction at the crisis, to deny the problem or to seek rescue; what must be learned, perseverance and discernment in conflict; and the boon at the end of the story would be trust and optimism.[23] These represent the major steps of a self-consistent character development that would avoid the impression of character jumps.

A character's archetypal identity is not necessarily the same as her personality or the role she plays on a plot level. For example, Robert Kincaid, the *National Geographic* photographer in *The Bridges of Madison County*, is the lover who comes into Francesca's life, but Lover is not his archetypal identity. Deep down, he is a Seeker. When we understand this, we know that he can neither stay with Francesca nor take her with him. The closing image of Kincaid standing alone in the rain is powerful because it cuts to the archetypal identity of Kincaid's character,* and the choices determined by it.

In genre-based stories, most comedies, and other stories where the main character goes through a minor degree of change, the hero's action may remain within the same archetypal identity. In stories with greater character change, we may see the hero undergo an important life-passage from one stage to another, such as from Seeker to Warrior.

After the climax, we may see the hero enter the problem-field that belongs to the new stage, or change attitudes as a result of going on a hero's quest. But unless a movie story has an epic time frame, it would be hard to justify, dramatically or psychologically, a character moving more than one developmental level. Just imagine the time required to take a character from Innocent to Sage. It rarely happens, even in a long lifetime.

Iconic Heroes and Shadow Projection

The relationship between the hero and the antagonist, which develops over the course of the story, cannot help but mirror our hero's attitudes, our own attitudes, and the dominant cultural attitudes we have inherited. That relationship also mirrors the relationship between the ego's social mask and the psychological

23. Based on Pearson, *Awakening the Archetypes Within*, pp. 10–11.

* The shot shows us in one powerfully condensed moment Kincaid's fundamental *posture* toward life (and links him iconically to the restless wanderer, played by John Wayne, at the end of *The Searchers*).

shadow. To the extent that we identify ourselves and our ego-values with the hero, we tend to project the inverse of those values onto the antagonist.

The antagonist, the adversary who sets himself against the hero and blocks the path of her desire and goals, inevitably introduces the element of evil into the story—and without evil there could hardly be a drama. It is the antagonist who brings about the conflict that leads to the destruction of the protagonist's status quo mode and forces her to change. The Night World into which the hero must venture indicates that part of the Hero's Journey has to do with confronting the experience of evil and coming to some understanding of the nature of evil and its place in the larger wholeness. As Episcopal priest and Jungian analyst John A. Sanford has said in his book *Evil, the Shadow Side of Reality*, ". . . the proper function of the ego includes becoming conscious, that is, psychologically enlightened and aware." But the ego does not usually take this initiative on its own.

> Few people become conscious without having to become conscious, without being driven to it by necessity. And this is where evil comes in. For the most part, it is only when people encounter evil in some form—as pain, loss of meaning, or something that appears to be threatening or destructive to them—that they begin to find their way to consciousness. And only when people are tested in the fire of life, so that what is weak within them is purged away and only the strong elements remain, does individuation take place in the context of certain amount of suffering and struggle.[24]

A potent hero who touches us deeply, whose struggles resonate with our own, and who is capable of capturing the imagination of the public, has a personal encounter with evil that reflects the larger evils society itself must confront. His encounter with evil leads to greater consciousness for the character and the audience. The protagonist stands at the cutting edge between society's mask of righteousness and the world of the shadow. While this is especially evident in the setup of thrillers, it is true of drama in general. A hero whose journey does not take her out of the pale of the status quo will not have much energy or charisma for the audience. This confrontation with the shadow side of life leads to discovering that evil does not reside in the antagonist alone, but within us as well.

John Sanford points out that we usually think of the shadow as the personification of our tendency to act in anger, or out of lust or greed. But in a larger sense "the shadow personality can be thought of as *unlived life*."[25] Each of us develops a survival mode in life, which excludes what we have repressed as being intolerable or unacceptable. The excluded comprises our unlived life. Those traits and ways of being which are rejected from our social persona fall out of conscious awareness, but they do not go away. They make up our shadow. And because we have an innate drive toward fulfillment and wholeness, there is a drive on the

24. Sanford, John A., *Evil, the Shadow Side of Reality* (New York: Crossroad, 1984), p. 40.
25. Ibid, p. 51 (italics mine).

part of the unlived life to express itself. To this point Sanford recounts the setup of Goethe's *Faust*. An eminently successful researcher has reached the end of his rope. His life has dried up and he even contemplates suicide.

> Enter Mephistopheles on the scene, and the two of them make a bargain: If Mephistopheles will do Faust's bidding in this life and see to it that Faust experiences all the deep emotions and experiences of human life, when Faust dies he will give his soul to the devil. . . . Faust casts off his role as a professor and lives out his unlived life of feeling, eros, power, and sex.

Faust had been such a super-intellectual that he had missed life! Mephistopheles offers Faust a connection to his unlived life. Mephistopheles can offer this because it was projected onto him to begin with. Projection refers to the judgments and impressions we make about other people that come from unconscious aspects of ourselves we have unintentionally superimposed on them. What I can't admit about myself, I discover in someone else. Over the course of human history, evil has been projected onto the enemy: the neighboring tribe, the other nation, the other race, the people who are not like us. In our struggles with them, *we* are doing God's bidding, while *they* are the servants of the devil or the pawns of an evil empire. As the antagonist carries our shadow projections, he becomes a *dark mirror* reflecting back to us what we have trouble admitting in ourselves. That is exactly the challenge. Through the hero-antagonist encounter, the hero may recover his unlived life. Faust, in order to recover his unlived life, must tolerate Mephistopheles, even make a pact with him. This is the catalyst for Faust's drama of redemption, as Goethe saw it. In the Hero's Journey, death is specifically the death of the character's identification with his mask/mode.

When I first started recording my dreams, the shadow appeared as exactly that: an indistinct, shadowy figure of menace stalking me through the fetid streets of a strange city, breathing down my neck, dressed in a heavy overcoat. His face was always obscured, but I could feel his *weight*. I had an instinctive animal reaction of dread: these were real nightmares. Gradually, as I paid more attention to the dreams, the figures became more defined, though still generic, still very close to the unconscious. They were Nazis, Mafiosi, drug lords, and the scheming heads of international conglomerates.

Then, among these antagonists, there began to appear in my dreams very individualized and differentiated shadow figures, like the handsome young SS officer in riding boots surveying from a high platform all the people in the checkout lines at the supermarket. I could feel his hawklike stare penetrating me as I tried to move undetected with the herd of people. Later, I grudgingly had to admit that this ferocious character had some positive traits I wished I had more of myself. I had to admire his total confidence and control, which had made me quail and try to hide. I had to ask myself: were there situations in my life where I myself needed more hawklike mastery, but was instead just trying to get by without making waves, to be "one of the crowd" because I didn't want other people to think I was being too aggressive? It turned out that there were. I was being advised to remove the moral compulsion to niceness and generosity, to disidentify from an attitude of modesty I had taken for granted as correct—without actually becoming an SS officer. This describes a personal process, through successive dream-dramas, of assimilating some of the energy of the shadow.

The Antagonist as Dark Mirror

In movies, the antagonist is a dark mirror for the protagonist. He reflects back the shadow side or the unlived life. In a well-orchestrated drama we feel a strong resonance between protagonist and antagonist. The antagonist mirrors the protagonist because he embodies the protagonist's shadow, projected outward and coming back now from the outer world. The hero's own character flaw appears magnified in the antagonist. The evil of the antagonist is normally present in the hero in seed form, like an incubating virus. John Book and Paul Schaeffer exemplify this. The evil of Paul and his accomplices grows directly out of the corrupt abuse of their power as police officers. They have taken advantage of a successful drug raid to steal hundreds of gallons of PCP and sell it themselves for a profit of $22 million. But is John Book entirely free of the arrogant abuse of power, or is he himself infected? In a small but crucial scene in Act I of *Witness*, we see Book shove a black suspect roughly up against the squad car. When it is obvious that this is the wrong man, Book's "Hey, honest mistake . . ." comment sounds glib. He is so sure of his purpose that a charge of police brutality would be absolutely unimaginable to him. However, from the point of view of the black man and his friends in the bar, this was unquestionably an abuse of authority by an arrogant white cop.

Book's unquestioned arrogation of virtue to himself is a symptom. It is the first step on a slippery slope of corruption that would lead to . . . Paul Schaeffer, the police chief who is the main antagonist. This is the mirroring effect. The antagonist in drama may force the hero on the path of growth through crisis, but he also embodies who the hero might become if he does not change. Hero and antagonist often have the same proficiencies, equal cunning, and equal determination, but with opposite moral accents. We understand that they are two halves of one whole, and are thus necessary to each other. When we can identify the Need versus Mode tension in the main character and see that the antagonist is an embodiment of the hero's shadow side, we have something both deeper and more precise to work with than the trite idea that the hero and the antagonist "want the same thing."

In the new wave of TV series, like *Lost*, *24*, *Prison Break, Six Feet Under*, and *Nip/Tuck*, where character and action lines are drawn out over much longer time frames, stories are exploring the many ways characters mirror each other or stand in each other's shadows. Each character is used as a foil for the others and makes the many facets of another character stand out in fascinating ways. For example, in *Lost*, Jack's father plays a clear shadow role for him, challenging Jack as not being good enough, tempting him to take a corrupt path that would lead him to betray his medical calling. But Sawyer is also a shadow figure for Jack: savvy, saucy, the opposite of the responsible Boy Scout that Jack sometimes appears to be. Sometimes we wish Jack would not be so scrupulous around Kate and just kiss her. Hurley and Charlie, for all their limitations, also reveal virtues that Jack lacks when placed next to him. Sophisticated TV drama, because of its length and multiple time frames (episode throughlines, pod-groupings of several consecutive episodes in which a major dramatic development takes place, season and series throughlines), is able to extend this dark mirror function out through the entire character web.

We can follow the antagonist as dark mirror longitudinally through the dramatic structure. Even before the antagonist appears onscreen, the flaw in the main character's mode, the split off and unlived life in the character, creates a sort of vacuum that draws conflict to them. The antagonist is going to fit that vacuum perfectly. Even before Ronnie Camerreri appears, we anticipate, we know subliminally, that the dam of Loretta's repression cannot hold back her passions forever. Ada, who seems to have held herself aloof from relationships in the magic world of her own creativity, will draw to herself, by her very nature, a man who will become obsessed with her and ultimately force her out of her silence.* C. C. Baxter has developed, as part of his mode, the thesis that by ingratiating himself and letting his apartment be used for illicit affairs, he is going to rise up the ladder of success. Instead, he is inevitably going to meet the man who will push him to the absolute limit of his passivity. Baxter himself has set up the conditions for this by inviting abuse of his generosity. The blithely criminal trio in *Shallow Grave*, through what they consider an innocent brutality, magnetically draw real brutality to themselves and out of themselves. In each case, the weakness or blind spot in the hero's old mode has been exploited by an antagonistic force and produced negative consequences.

Because of this inner correspondence, the reaction from the antagonist at the Threshold Crisis (end of Act I) breaks the status quo of the main character. This helps us understand how the crisis can be at once an outer and an inner event, and how the protagonist's mode breaks down under the stresses of the outer dramatic conflict while it is unraveling from within. The antagonist is strong exactly where the protagonist is weak, and seems able to exploit that weakness as we go into Act II. Truman Capote, in *Capote*, has always been able to count on his engaging persona to charm and disarm people while he gets what he wants. But in Act II, Truman finds himself confronted by people who see beyond his mask and ask the truth from him—not the literary truth of a story-spinner, but the truth of his personal integrity. Sometimes, especially in thrillers (as in *Seven*), the antagonist

* It is typical in love stories that the love interest first appears antagonistically in Act I. To the extent that the love relationship challenges or breaks down the hero's mode, it is natural that the hero will react as though threatened. In fact, he *is* threatened—by change.

is lent an air of superiority and invincibility ("... the Shadow knows ..."). He knows exactly what the hero is thinking and anticipates his every move. He takes away the hero's freedom of action by forcing him to be on the defensive. The epitome of the antagonist as dark mirror is the arch-nemesis or arch-competitor. The wily captain of the French frigate *Acheron*, who shadows Jack Aubrey's every move in *Master and Commander*, is a fine example. The hero becomes chained to the cause-and-effect momentum of the antagonist and normally has to change the way he sees things. This mirroring effect is characteristic of the shadow and its influence on our lives. The shadow, as an element of the unconscious, knows our hidden impulses and desires before we become conscious of them ourselves.

The antagonist as dark mirror is the tester and initiator of the protagonist in Act II. He sets the limits of the conflict, how far the tension can rise, and thus where the catastrophe that ends Act II will occur. One of the necessary elements in the dramatic setup is the moment where we see the antagonist establish the plot stakes of the drama. What is the antagonist willing to do to get what he wants? Lie? Falsify documents? Blackmail? Murder someone? Murder masses of people? Kill indiscriminately and for the sheer cruelty of it? By setting the outer limits of the conflict, the antagonist also sets the tone of the movie in terms of how dark the drama, or the comedy, will become. When the hero and the antagonist are not in the same tonal range, we have an uneasy sense that they don't belong in the same movie. Then they fail to act as mirrors. As a result, the story may seem to be caught uncomfortably between two genres and lose its dramatic unity. For example, Charlie in *Something Wild* is a comic character, and the movie at first establishes the tone of a screwball comedy. But the antagonist belongs to the world of dark melodrama. He is deadly serious and raises dramatic stakes that Charlie appears unprepared to match. The movie tries to cover this problem by turning Charlie's attempts to rescue Lulu into comic beats. This strategy avoids the issue and leads to a jarring shift of tones at the climax. *Midnight Run* is more successful in this regard, because the Jimmy Serrano character played by Dennis Farina has just enough comic exaggeration in his threats, and is surrounded by such buffoonish henchmen, that he does not destroy the comic tone of the movie. He and Jack are much better matched, both dramatically and thematically.

In Act III, from the catastrophe to the climax, we say that the successful hero *breaks the mirror*. This is central to the hero's Initiation. When the Night of the Soul moment finally breaks down the main character's mode, he has a chance to realize the pattern of transference that has conditioned and limited his behavior. As the unconscious need becomes realized, there is a union of opposites within the character. Through this combination of effects he is able to see the outer situation more clearly. Ada realizes that she has to let go of the piano. C. C. Baxter realizes that, whatever comes, he is ready to be a mensch. He will no longer let his life and his self-worth be defined by Mr. Sheldrake. Sheldrake, as the antagonist, has mirrored the conflict in the depth of Baxter, between his persona and his authentic feeling. By forcing Baxter to choose between these two values,

Sheldrake forces Baxter to break the mirror he holds up to him. By throwing the job right in Sheldrake's face, Baxter does break through to a new perspective. He assimilates some of the negative shadow energy, the positive egoism and willpower, into himself and takes responsibility for it. He steals Sheldrake's thunder and reduces him literally to silence. Baxter loses his job, but regains his self-respect. As he goes home and packs his things to leave the apartment, he is in greater possession of himself: outer problems (the persona world of the insurance company) are no longer taken as a reflection of his self-worth. This is what it means to break the mirror.

Returning to what John Sanford has said, it is "only when people are tested in the fire of life, so that what is weak within them is purged away and only the strong elements remain," that individuation takes place. Our mode can ultimately be said to be our identification with something that is weak in ourselves, that which holds us back from life and wholeness. If that is true, then our very mode—our comfort zone, our complacency and false security, our concern not to have our views or our schedules upset—is the seed of an evil we carry within ourselves. If we choose to remain unconscious of it, it may ultimately manifest itself as an antagonist that bedevils our outer lives. To the extent that our survival mode, whatever it might be, has become a reflex, a habit pattern, a defense against growth, the best training, as Montaigne observed, would be to "unlearn our evil."

Reconciling Mode and Need: The Dramatic Synthesis

We have seen that a play of opposites acts itself out on multiple levels through the drama. It is this play of opposing values, whether defined as mode and need or personified through the hero and the antagonist, that pulls all the events of the screenplay together to achieve a dramatic and thematic whole. Working with the Need versus Mode model as a development tool, we begin to get a feeling for the way the dramatic conflict ultimately forces the hero to choose between the two values. Yet we must always recall that there is a Hero's Journey process of deeper character change involved as well. The character who makes a choice at the climax is no longer the same character we met in the opening scenes. So this is not a simple lateral choice. It is not like having a glass of red wine and a glass of white wine presented on a table and you reach for the one you prefer. No, it is not a lateral choice but a dynamic choice, based on the structure of the dialectic: thesis → antithesis → synthesis. In fact, the three acts of the screenplay can be identified with the three phases of this dialectic:

Act I: Establishing/Day World/Mode Established = *Thesis*

Act II: Rising Action/Night World/Mode Breaks Down = *Antithesis*

Act III: Resolution/Return/Need-Mode Reconciliation = *Synthesis*

What we expect to see at the climax and resolution of a story in which the character goes through some transformation is not only that the hero comes to realize and act on the unconscious need. It is equally that this choice at the climax is being made at a more conscious and integrated level. Synthesis of the opposites leads to greater wholeness. This means that, ideally, the hero is not just flipping from one side to the other. Such flipping between the opposites can appear dramatic, but it is not growth. It is more like the rhythm of bulimia, of binge and purge, and is a highly unstable state. The real evidence of character growth is in how far the character is able to reconcile the opposites. That is, to recognize and stand up for the value of the universal need that had previously been unconscious, while not disowning the mode value. Through Act I of *Moonstruck*, to follow that example, Loretta is identified with her status quo mode of control. At the crisis, she totally loses control in a wild affair. In Act II she struggles unsuccessfully to regain control, until she finally accepts her passion on a somewhat more conscious level at the end of the second act. There, she takes Ronnie's hand and deliberately goes up to his place with him, though she still believes her life is ruined. Yet even here at the end of Act II, Loretta has still not been forced to make the final choice of values. At the climax, we see Loretta choose to marry Ronnie. She chooses to live her passion ("Do you love him, Loretta?" "Ma, I love him awful!" "That's too bad."), but not in a way that is totally out of control. Loretta has come to see that control is not an absolute good in itself, nor is it even humanly possible. However, marriage gives the vitality of passion a structure and container. We can imagine, or at least hope, that the marriage between Loretta and Ronnie will remain edgy and alive, a place where the opposites of control and passion will remain at play. This is a much more integrated position than marriage as a mere comfort zone. Loretta has to some extent achieved a reconciliation of these opposites.

How we see the main character move to a new place where a reconciling choice is possible is one of the central ways in which we deliver the theme of the movie to the audience. The hero goes on the journey and experiences an initiation, a new birth. What is born in the hero, the boon, we could rightly term a symbol. Something new is alive in the person, and it is this new thing that permits the synthesis or reconciliation of the opposites on a higher level. But now, we as screenwriters and storytellers must comprehend that, on another level, *the movie itself* is acting as such a uniting symbol *for the audience*. This is the power of drama and the movies as an art form. Carl Jung states, "As opposites never unite at their own level, a supraordinate 'third' is always required, in which the two parts can come together."[26] The movie itself is the "third" that resolves the need/mode tension of opposites for those watching the movie. This is why a tragedy can be a completely fulfilling experience for the audience, even when the hero dies and appears to have failed completely. This is why both our skills and our sensitivity as screenwriters are needed. In all the labor of our craft, it is this elusive "third," the power to reconcile opposites, that we are seeking.

26. Jung, Carl, *Aion* (New York: Bollingen Foundation; New Jersey: Princeton University Press, 1959), p. 180.

Internal Software: Memory Banks

Here is a project for you to do—not just think about.

I have learned a great deal about the creative process from psychologist Jean Houston. The first part of the following exercise was adapted from one of her innovative learning games.

EXERCISE ONE

Invite a friend to join you for an exercise in memory. Memory is closely associated with creativity, and it all has to do with patterns, "patterns that connect," as Gregory Bateson said. One thing Jean Houston discovered is that people with phenomenal memory power rehearse their memories and keep them present and vivid. They fit memories into patterns, categories, and mental maps. New experience is seen in the rich context of these larger patterns. A related aspect in people with extraordinary memories is that they remember with multiple senses. Memories are not only factual or visual; they can include sounds, smells, tastes, and textures. It is well known that learning goes deeper and is more efficient when more than one sense mode is engaged. Learning the ABCs through a melody is neurologically quite sophisticated. The memory experts seem to have a spontaneous (or sometimes learned) knack for multimodal remembering.

Triggering one memory, it turns out, also triggers a bank of associated memories. The object of this game is to activate large banks of memories with a few triggers.

The game works like this: sit with your partner in a secluded and calm place. Remember when you used to go with your best friend into a field, a vacant lot, or up on the roof of the neighbor's garage to tell unbelievable stories? You would go to these places to insulate yourselves from distraction and to draw kind of "magic circle" around the two of you. Try to create something like that.

In this game each person has a role. One will be remembering, while the other facilitates the memories by asking questions in a few target areas. The facilitator says: "Tell me about . . ." and then listens actively to the response. Try to develop many different memories around the same topic. This seems to activate larger banks of background memories.

Storytelling is a kind of transaction in which both parties are necessary, the listener as much as the teller. *Active listening* is a skill closely related to empathy. It means consciously giving your full attention, focus, and feeling presence to the speaker. The quality of the listening does impact the quality of the storytelling; we know this from our own experience. Of

Continued

course, while you're listening, your own memories and images are bound to come up. Just let that go and come back to listening. This is why I say it is a discipline. It is in fact a key discipline for story development meetings, where typically everyone comes in with their own agendas. I find that these meetings work out better if people can set aside their egos for the moment and agree to simply do what serves the story.

There will be four subjects for the rememberer, then you may stop and change roles. Take about three minutes for each topic.

Facilitator 1

"Tell me about . . ."

- favorite foods from your childhood
- animals you knew as a child
- old women you knew as a child
- tricks you played on someone or that someone played on you as a child

Facilitator 2

"Tell me about . . ."

- holidays or trips you took as a child
- someone weird, strange, or funny you knew as a child
- old men you knew as a child
- secret hiding places you had as a child

After you finish with the exercise, stand up and walk around for a moment. Be aware of all the sensations and impressions in your body and mind. Does the room look any different to you now than it did before the exercise? Do you feel heavy or light? Drowsy or awake? How does this feel as a place from which to do your creative work?

You can extend this exercise by doing a "wild" writing or drawing of whatever comes to mind that is brought up by your memories. Or you can put on some good music that reflects the energy you are feeling and ***dance!***

EXERCISE TWO

Tell your partner a story from your childhood. It doesn't have to be the biggest event in your life, just something that happened. It helps if this is a story you have told other people before, and it should be a true story.

Continued

One special aspect in telling this story is to speak in the *present tense*, even if the event happened long ago. Why would we do this? First of all, it makes the experience more present, taking away some of the filter of years to bring out the immediacy. And second, *movies are always in the present tense*. The entire screenplay, including flashbacks and love scenes between Caesar and Cleopatra set two thousand years ago, is written in the present tense.

Take about ten minutes with your story. Then listen to your partner's story, always trying to be an active listener, and giving the concentration and eye contact which helps the speaker bring out the best energy in the story.

When you have both told your stories, you may ask questions of each other to help deepen or clarify the story. Sample clarifying questions include:

- Where did the story begin?
- Where did the story end?
- What changed from the beginning to the end?

That's good. But resist the temptation to analyze the story. For now, let the story be just what it is. We shall return to these stories later.

In our society today, memory threatens to become a dying art as we rely on technological means to store information. Writers, however, cannot afford to let their memories fail. As you may have experienced from these exercises, memories are anything but mere "data." Memories, even simple ones, are complexes of associations, not all of which can possibly be made conscious. For example, you might focus on a moment of distinct feeling in the story, a feeling associated with the taste of your grandmother's lipstick. The feeling is related to the memory, but is not *identical* to it. If you ask yourself, "Where does this feeling *come from*?" you may find yourself facing a kind of dark tangle of further associations that might go on forever.

For screenwriters, the importance of keeping our memory function sharp lies not in memories as individual "facts" or "snapshots," but in the patterns of meaning into which our creative intuition has *already* woven them. When you bring your grandmother's ring or Thanksgiving turkey recipe into a story you are writing, you are not transferring a single piece of data but an entire constellation of associations into a new context.

5

The Story Molecule

> If you were to represent the self by drawing a series of five (or ten) concentric circles, like a bullseye, with the center representing that which is most essentially "you," how would you label the circles? What would you put in the middle one?—a value? a quality? a possession? a relationship?
>
> —*Mihaly Csikszentmihalyi*

Character Webs

WITH THESE MODELS, we are trying to open a new approach to screenwriting, one that includes the screenwriter and her process of writing. We are moving away from the traditional approach—which is linear, deductive, and left-brained—toward one that is more visual, psychological, inductive, and engages both sides of the writer's brain. (These two aspects of brain function are analogous to the problem-solving mountain-creativity and intuitive mine-creativity.) As we make this shift, we discover a new way of looking at the characters in the story. The old left-brain way of developing the cast of characters was to define the roles according to a model, and then to create characters to fill in the blanks.

- Who is the hero?
- Who is the antagonist?
- Who is the love interest?
- Who is the guide? (Ya gotta have a guide these days!)

It feels like we're making quick progress when we can fill in the blanks, but at the end of the day that's exactly what we've accomplished. We have a list of names and functions. We can collide them together through cause and effect to make conflict. But we do not yet have a living social network that contains all of these characters and makes a vivid fictional universe of their lives. We don't see how each character relates to all the others. We don't see how each character's actions are going to ripple out through the social fabric. We don't see the hidden relationship between the love interest and the antagonist. The deductive approach of

"There has to be a love interest, so who is it going to be?" doesn't invite us to *see* at all. It is not visual thinking.

And there is something else we are missing, something of key importance in the screenwriting process. How, when writing our screenplay, do we modulate the balance between plot and character? If we have created our characters around plot functions, then the balance is already tilted in favor of plot. We as writers are already biased against our characters as fictional persons who have their own interiority, who can come alive on the page and surprise us.

We commonly talk about movies as being either plot-driven or character-driven. There is a tendency to associate "high-concept" with the former and "soft and fuzzy" with the latter. Examples given of the two categories are usually polar and obvious, like James Bond versus *Driving Miss Daisy*. But most movies fall somewhere in between, and it is absurd to think of a plot without characters. The question is really: how do we as writers move between plot action and character exposition in ways that enhance the dramatic whole? How do we reveal character dramatically without slowing down the action? It is not enough for an expert to tell us: "Exposition scenes should be dramatic!" Of course we want the whole screenplay to be dramatic, from start to finish. What will be precisely useful is a lens that allows us to look specifically into this aspect of character orchestration. We already have a sophisticated paradigm to look at the universal, archetypal dimension of the story in the Hero's Journey, and we can look into the depths of character change with the Need versus Mode model. Now the Story Molecule will show us how to move the story energy between the plot dimension and the character dimension. The Story Molecule brings plot and character together into a dramatic unity.

From Character Web to Story Molecule

Director and screenwriter John Sayles, in an interview with my seminar partner Tom Schlesinger, made a comment about working with characters that became the touchstone for the Story Molecule. (He took the idea from Allan Dwan, who had started directing back in the silent era.) Sayles said that when he is developing his story, he lays out all of his characters on a piece of paper, with the main character in the center, and then he draws lines of connection out from the main character. Who is the main character connected to in this world, and what kind of connection is it? Sayles does not stop there, but draws all the lines of connection among the other characters as well: the antagonist, the primary relationship or love interest, the secondary characters, and so on. This gives us a *character web* for the world of this story.

What makes this so different than listing characters according to their plot function? We immediately see relationships via the lines of connection. Some characters are deeply embedded, surrounded by connections, and so woven into the fabric of the story's life that everything that happens will impact them. Other characters are on the outside, semi-isolated. Their existence in this world may be precarious. We are invited to see the situation from each character's point of view. Some character webs are thick and complex; some are thin. But each one is unique. It is a picture of a social context, and already suggests the interpersonal dynamics that will play out through the drama—and why. The main character is the center of this nexus, with more—and more highly charged—bonds of connection radiating to other characters. We can imagine that this character's actions are going to have great impact on the entire web.

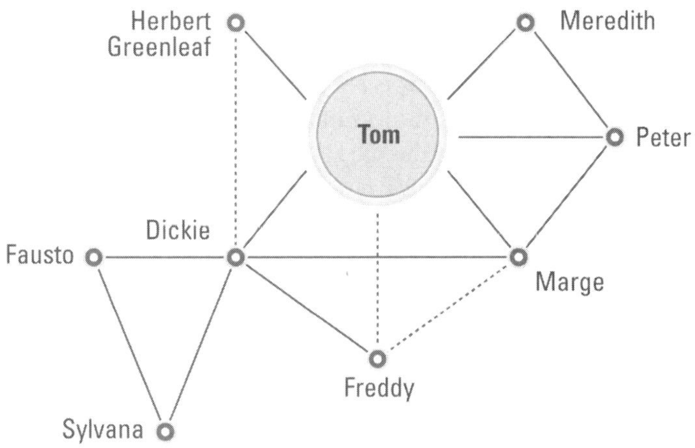

Looking at the character web of *The Talented Mr. Ripley* above, we can see that Tom Ripley is the hub of this entire fictional world, even though the connections among the other characters are also important. Tom is the only person we see with all of the other major characters. We never see Dickie in a scene with his father, for example. We never see Freddie with Meredith or Peter. This reveals one of the central strategies to *Ripley*: to make Tom, the outsider, the interloper, the center of this social world. This strategy, growing out of the character web, starts to suggest dramatic complications that will become individual scenes. How will Tom hide the fact that he doesn't belong in this society? How will he make himself necessary to everyone? How will he defeat competitors for the space in the center? How will he cover his original lie with other lies? What will happen when the truth finally comes out? All of these rich dramatic complications grow out of placing Tom at the center of the character web.

Just for a comparison, let's place Dickie at the center of the web and see what happens. After all, Dickie is the charismatic focus of his circle of friends and becomes an obsession for Tom. As soon as we remove Tom from the center, there is less energy. With Dickie in the center, the energy is flat because the social situation is no more than we would expect. But Tom's position at the center is

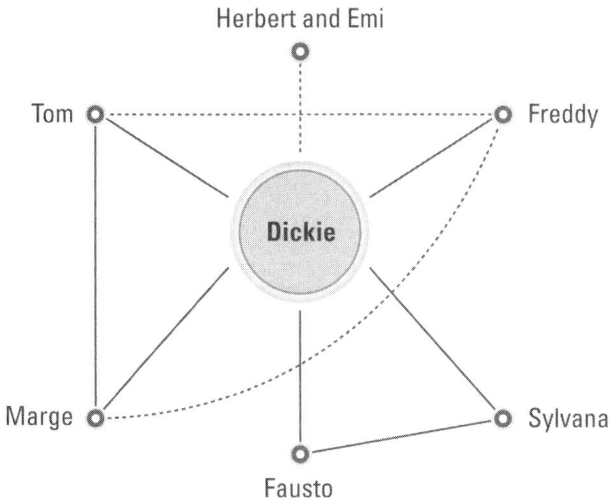

inherently unstable because he doesn't belong there. Tom is not merely an outsider, he is an imposter. This is the core of the entire drama.

As a sidelight, the character web suggests that the character of Freddie has to be played as someone with equal power to Dickie, Dickie's equal. Why? Because if he were too subordinated to Dickie, like Marge, it would threaten to thrust Dickie into the center of the character web and displace Tom. This might have thrown the drama out of focus and made it impossible to successfully tell the story. The character web, a component of the Story Molecule, is a tool that can give you immediate results.

This is *visual thinking*. It is qualitatively more complex than making lists of character functions and assigning roles. It begins to give us a feel for the *texture* of the story. It is imaginative and playfully engaging. But Sayles's character web is not yet the Story Molecule. It was when the idea of the character web came together with the storytelling perspective and Need versus Mode that a larger model began to appear. With the hero's inner need/mode tension in the center of the character web, we could see three levels of dramatic conflict appear. Dramatic storytelling became *three-dimensional*.

From the storytelling perspective, stories are energy, patterned energy. The story moves energy from the storyteller to the audience through a dynamic wave of tension and release. Since Tom and I began developing the Story Molecule model in the 1980s, we have seen other versions of a model showing three rings of conflict. This is to be expected, since these three levels exist objectively in the story. But what struck us from the beginning was that these rings are not *static*; they are not *objects*. They are conduits of energy, ultimately between the movie and the audience. This is why the image of the molecule seemed appropriate. If we change our lens and look at a story as energy rather than as a *thing*, what does that suggest? What it suggested to us was that, through action and reaction, opposing motives and desires, cause and effect, energy is constantly circulating within and through the story. This is what is termed a "paradigm shift."

When the main character acts, the impact radiates out through the world of the story. It is like throwing a stone into a pond. The wave radiates out in all directions. Who does the wave of the hero's action touch first? Those closest to him. When the antagonist reacts, that reaction radiates back in on the hero. The character web is the medium through which this energy has to pass. We came to refer to the character web as the *emotional network*, because it is really the emotional stakes present in those relationships that are dramatically important for us. We must always bear in mind that these are not chess pieces! Every important relationship carries feelings, projections, and values. Each character in the drama, as a person, has invested in relationships, and *what* he or she has invested tells us what is at the core of his or her motivations. It is the relationships in that emotional network which make the inner life and inner conflicts of the main character visible to us. The emotional network moves the energy from the outer plot level in to impact the inner life of the hero, and from the inner back to the outer plot again. Thus the Story Molecule model is pictured as a molecule with three zones, like the rings of Saturn: the *inner conflict* of the main character, the *emotional network* of the character web, and the *outer plot*.

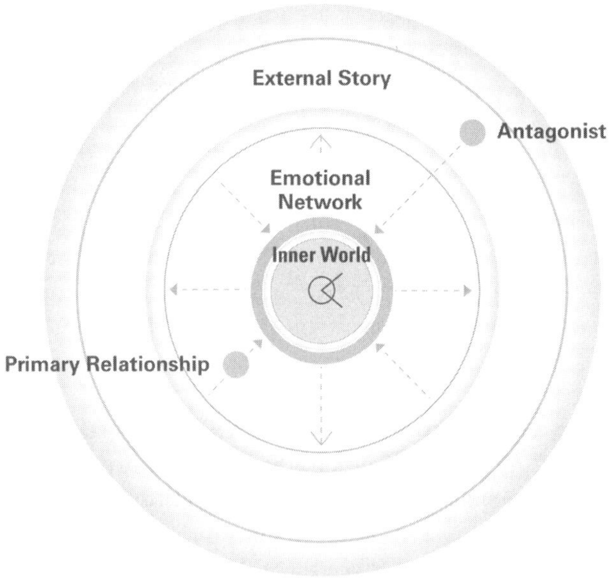

/ ***The Story Molecule:*** **The Three dimension of drama.**
Transformation is marked by an inner change in self-perception which goes out through the emotional network to the external story. Response comes from the antagonist, builds dramatic intensity. Energy circulates throughout the molecule via cause and effect. The primary relationship (love interest) pushes the hero toward a deep change of values.

The inner ring is the nucleus of the Story Molecule. And we can be even more precise than this. Because the need/mode tension is the driving force within the main character, it forms the core of this nucleus. The need/mode tension is the core of the entire drama, and we shall recall that the Need versus Mode model restates in terms of individual character psychology the archetypal insights of the Hero's Journey. The middle ring, the emotional network, is the social context in which conflicts are played out. It is the place where values are reflected in personal and emotional terms. The outer ring signifies the outer plot level of the story. It is where motives and values in conflict are expressed as *action toward a plot goal*. The outer ring could also be pictured as the larger objective world of the story beyond the immediate network of the characters, be it New York, the CIA, a dusty Georgia town, or outer space. It is the relevant world as defined by the story: the world of *meaning*.

Thus, each of these story development models is implicated in the others; they form a whole larger than the sum of its parts. Conflict—dramatic energy—is constantly moving through the Story Molecule. The Story Molecule itself moves through time: the time of the narrative. We use the Story Molecule model as a lens to view this movement in three dimensions. It allows us to open up any moment in the screenplay and understand what is going on at each level. As we shall see in the later chapter on scene structure, the energy, the power, is shifting moment by moment in the scene, yet these shifts within a single scene have implications for the larger story. The decisions characters make—large or small, conscious or unconscious—will resonate on each level of the Story Molecule.

Theoreticians may argue about whether character is plot or plot is character. The everyday problem facing screenwriters is the dual challenge of giving life to the characters while keeping the story momentum building. The answer is not an abstract or categorical answer, reassuring as that might appear to be. The answer is found in our own process as writers, and it has to do with our ability to write with these three levels of story in mind. It is a constant weaving together of the consequences of these three dramatic levels, using the conflicts in each to enhance the others. The Story Molecule model is a powerful tool we use to look into and adjust the balance between plot and character, as well as between text and subtext.

The Story Molecule demonstrates that a story is not a line, it is a three-dimensional whole moving through time. And it is *alive*. The question of plot *versus* character is a false question to begin with. There is not a plotline first, and then some characters to shade it in (though a story development may of course *begin* with a plot idea or premise). Actually, there are *three* throughlines of dramatic development, one for each level of the Story Molecule. There are thus three throughline dramatic questions: an outer plot question, an emotional network question, and an inner need/mode question. All three questions reflect the theme of the movie as well as each other. As these three throughline questions are answered at the climax, and a theme emerges which is rich and complex, not merely a simplistic "moral." This is because the three rings of the Story Molecule are interacting, interweaving like strands of rope, and are bound together in one destiny.

The Story Molecule paradigm shows us how the transformational energy of the drama moves out through the world of the story. This harks back to one of those very simple core ideas: *energy radiates outward*. In the process of personal transformation, a change in the way I see myself leads to a change in my behavior, and a change in my behavior leads to a change in my relationships. The partners in those relationships incorporate the change, and the impulse flows outward from there. We observe this transformational energy happening on all three levels of the story at once: the inner Need versus Mode conflict of the main character, the primary and secondary relationships of the story, and the outer plot.

These three lines of development comprise what we call the three *substories* of the screenplay. Sub*story* is not to be confused with sub*plot*. Substory refers to the dramatic throughline of each level of the Story Molecule, while subplots are secondary plots or plots connected to secondary characters. For example, in the comedy *Moonstruck*, there are three sub*stories*, most easily identified by the throughline questions they generate:

- "Will Loretta marry Johnny?" (outer plot)

This line is set up as Loretta's Call to Adventure in Act I. It provides a loose outer context for the farce.

- "Will Loretta fall in love with Johnny's brother Ronnie?" (emotional network)

Ronnie is the primary relationship in the story. He forces Loretta to change. This relationship becomes the vehicle for Loretta's inner transformation.

- "Will Loretta recover her passion?" (inner conflict)

The inner line will determine the answer to the other two questions. All three questions are "paid off" at the climax.

In *Moonstruck*, the outer plot question grows out of Loretta's *mode*. The emotional network question points toward her unconscious *need*. The conflict between the two lines externalizes Loretta's deep inner conflict so that we can see it. This turns out to be the typical way the dynamic works. You will notice that the outer plot here is not the substory with the most juice, since we do not expect Loretta to marry Johnny, and Johnny is furthermore in Sicily for most of the movie. This is a common farce strategy. Among other things, it prevents us from empathizing with Johnny and feeling bad about the infidelity.

There are also two sub*plots* in *Moonstruck*. First is the father's affair with Mona, and second is the mother's mild flirtation with the naughty professor. Both subplots directly reflect aspects of the romantic theme. Both subplots ultimately intersect with the main plot.* Subplots contribute secondarily to the screenplay; the three substories form the *core* of the screenplay. As the three substories

* Subplots will be explored further in the next chapter.

interweave, they form the *spine* of the story. Together they ensure the *dramatic unity* of the movie.

The Story Molecule can be used to look into the plot/character balance at any point in the screenplay, like a cursor moving through a page of text on a computer screen. Scene by scene, it helps us build the rhythm of advancing plot and revealing character that makes exposition "invisible" and does not slow down the plot momentum. We shall look at each of the rings more closely.

The Inner Ring of Character

The Need versus Mode model forms the core nucleus of the Story Molecule. While every character's actions ripple out into the world of the story, ultimately it is the need/mode tension in the hero that becomes externalized as the driving tension of the plot. (Genre stories, such as thrillers, work with a split in the main character in an analogous way, a variation on need/mode. The thriller hero's blind spot drives the subtext of the drama.) As writers, we need to know our central character well enough to know what is happening on this inner ring of the Story Molecule if we are going to successfully balance character and plot. Plot events are breaking down the character's mode, and the character's increased vulnerability is raising dramatic stakes on the plot level. Finding the right balancing point for your particular story is crucial. A rich story can be dragged down by flat characters, while a stereotypical story that fails to generate a compelling subtext can turn potentially convincing characters into caricatures. A number of factors impact the plot/character balance, but the most important is the degree of transformation or dramatic change in your main character.

But who *is* that person at the center of your story? Every character you create will carry a need/mode conflict; that is, simply a universal human condition. And, as we noted in the last chapter, when writers begin a project, they may not know who the main character is. Some writers begin with a plot premise. Others feel a need to sketch out the world of the story and the character web first in order to get a feeling for who is in the center (this is a common practice of John Sayles and other screenwriters who are attracted to working with ensembles). Sometimes the main character shifts during development for a variety of reasons—some story-based, some for reasons which may have little to do with story logic but rather have to do with the production or marketing of the movie.

A story-based reason for changing the main character while developing the story might be the realization that the dramatic throughline questions raised by who we *thought* was the main character are in fact less compelling, less juicy, than the dramatic questions implicit in another character. From the point of view of this other character, the story has just got more energy—and the writer feels more energy working on the screenplay. Feedback from how the story makes us feel while writing cannot be ignored; it is the voice of our creative intuition. There is no guarantee that everyone in the development process will see the story the same way, however. Sometimes the result is some sort of compromise where the audience's attention ends up split between two characters.

The comedy *A Fish Called Wanda* presents this situation. Wanda is clearly driving the action, and she is at the center of the web of characters. But she is set up as a rather flat character to be the protagonist. There is no need/mode tension developed for her, and as a result there is not a complete set of throughline questions around her character, nor are the stakes for her clear and compelling. Wanda is played as emotionally impervious; she seems to have nothing to lose. It is hard to empathize with someone who has nothing to lose. As a result, she is more active than compelling; she does not need our sympathies, so she tends not to get them. It is Archie, the klutz, who comes to be the character we identify with. Archie is more complex, with a conflict of values that raises real stakes for him. As a result, Archie is the most active character at the climax, while Wanda rather disappears dramatically. This may have been a necessary compromise, but is it completely satisfying? *Wanda* certainly has very funny scenes and bits, and the involvement of top comic talent. But is it everything it could have been? Can this movie stand up next to, say, *Some Like It Hot*? Here let us simply note that there are cases where a script doctor has made an emergency "house call" to a set where it has been discovered in midshoot that they have the wrong hero.

There must be ways to test out how well a chosen main character fits the dramatic development of the story. The choice of main character determines some major aspects of the entire story. These include:

- The dramatic trajectory of the story
- The point of view (POV) of the storytelling
- The idiom, genre, and tone of the movie

For the screenplay to really work, not only does the plot have to work in its own right, but the plot, the characters, and the above dramatic elements must all work together. Therefore, if we have the wrong main character or have not orchestrated our main character correctly, not only will the plot have problems, but we will expect to see problems in these aspects as well. Conversely, these aspects of the story's concept largely determine how well character and plot will fit together. They raise questions that should be addressed at the very earliest stages of the project's development.

It should be noted that the Story Molecule parameters for a TV series are different than those for a feature film. In a feature film, the main character is the locus where dramatic unity originates, the unity of character, plot, and theme. The hero of the film has to be strong enough to hold the audience's attention and complex enough, with enough internal tension, to generate the three throughline questions. Those questions build one overarching wave of tension rising to a climax—and release. This is all because the story must be told and resolved in one hundred minutes. In the new, complex TV series there is much more liberty to develop several ongoing subplots connected to other members of the emotional network. Episode throughlines fit within pod (a sequence of several episodes with a narrative link) throughlines, and those fit within season throughlines. In a TV series the concept still makes plot and character fit together, but in a different timeline and with a different trajectory.

Dramatic Trajectory

The main character is the character whose actions determine the trajectory of the story. Dramatic *trajectory* means both where the story goes and how steeply the dramatic intensity of the plot rises. Where the story goes—what kind of Night World it enters and how deeply into that Night World it travels—is connected to the main character's unconscious need, or her blind spot in the case of a thriller. In character-driven stories, the Night World is directly expressive of the hero's unlived life. The hero, like Loretta Castorini, is drawn into it magnetically. Or, we could say, she draws it to herself. In thriller, horror, and some action subgenres, the Night World expresses more the *audience's* collective anxiety and shadow. The genre hero faces the evil as the audience's proxy. Therefore the emphasis is not so much on discovering a disowned part of the self, but on finding the inner courage and virtue to overcome evil. But the thriller hero is typically someone who straddles the worlds of innocence and crime. She also has one foot in the Night World through a past trauma, like Clarice Starling in *Silence of the Lambs*, or through a personal weakness, like the loneliness of Frank, the Al Pacino character, in *Sea of Love*. In both variations the dramatic stakes include probing into a region of inner character weakness that corresponds with the story's Night World. So, in thrillers and other plot-driven genres there is nevertheless an unconscious factor within the main character that determines where the story goes.

How fast the plot develops depends on the main character as well: his temperament, training, challenges, and motivation. Comedies often have a relatively long setup and slow plot development in Act I because comic heroes are usually reluctant heroes. When the Call to Adventure comes they would rather stay in bed, and must be called again. This gives a special rhythm to the setup of comedies. Loretta literally has to be telephoned from Sicily and prodded into the comic complication. Charles, in *Four Weddings and a Funeral*, is defined by his reticence and avoidance. Thriller heroes are usually unprepared at the opening for the antagonist's attack, since one of the defining characteristics of the thriller is that the antagonist drives the action. The hero is placed in lethal danger and experiences a loss of control. This adds extreme emotional vulnerability to the thriller tone of overwhelming evil. Thus the thriller trajectory may be low in Act I and brooding and ominous even to the middle of Act II. Then the pace accelerates quickly and the trajectory rises steeply, along with the level of danger.

Heroes who are ready to react quickly and move into action quickly can support a high dramatic trajectory, a fast pace from the opening. The action is already present in the character's temperament. Bruce Willis in the *Die Hard* series comes to mind. At the other end of the spectrum, characters who are capable of little overt physical action, or who need time for reflection, lead to movies with flatter trajectories, like Woody Allen's *Hannah and Her Sisters* or the comedies of Eric Rohmer, as well as many melodramas. Revenge stories are typically structured around a reluctant hero who is finally prodded into action, resulting in a sudden shift of dramatic trajectory in Act II.

The main character also determines the dramatic trajectory through her impact on other characters in the emotional network. The main character is normally at the center of the emotional network of the story. More than this, because the main character participates in both the Day World and the Night World of the story, he becomes the pivot around which this world turns, the bridge between the two worlds. This puts added strain on the main character. Look at the character web of *Witness*:

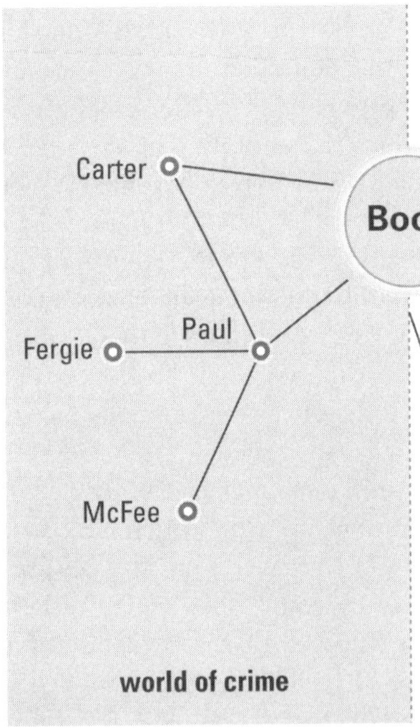

We can immediately see that John Book is the conduit between the world of the Amish and the world of the corrupt police because he participates in both worlds. The killers have to go through him to eliminate Samuel. Similarly, when Renton moves to London in Act II of *Trainspotting*, he becomes the pivot between the straight working world and that of the down-and-out friends who invade his apartment. Ultimately this will force Renton to make a choice.

The strategy of the narrator/witness as main character, which is so common in literature, does not tend to work well in movies. There is a well-known story about the development of the screenplay for *One Flew Over the Cuckoo's Nest*. Ken Kesey, who had written the novel, was given the job of adapting it into a screenplay. After long labors, Kesey came back with a three hundred and fifty page draft that was structured, like the novel, with the Chief as main character. The Chief had worked well as a narrator/witness in the novel, but for the film production he posed a couple of problems. The first was that the Chief was pretending to be deaf and dumb as a way to survive in the insane asylum, which severely limited the dramatic impact he could have. Second, there were no bankable roles for seven-foot Native Americans in those days, and Jack Nicholson had already been cast in the role of McMurphy. But the most compelling *story-based* reason for changing the protagonist was that it is McMurphy who, through the impact of his actions on the other inmates, has the greatest influence on the trajectory of the story. Effective dramatic questions could not be built around the Chief. As a contrasting example, Captain Willard in *Apocalypse Now* does spend most of the journey upriver in the role of a narrator and witness to the madness of war, but he is the main character because it is his assignment to kill Col. Kurtz that drives the whole movie forward. Positioning the main character to have this decisive impact on the dramatic trajectory via the secondary characters is important in setting up your story.

By determining the trajectory of the story and generating the major dramatic questions, the main character dictates the theme, the dramatic situation, the POV, the genre, the idiom, the pace, and the tone of the film. Loretta determines the theme of *Moonstruck*, which is the recovery of passion. The dramatic situation: she is going to marry a nice mama's boy because it's safe. Loretta sets the farcical tone of the movie the moment she makes Johnny get down on his knees and formally propose to her in the middle of the restaurant. This also establishes the genre of *Moonstruck* as a farce, which brings other elements of farce along with it, including the improbable deus ex machina ending where all the characters come onstage for the grand comic dénouement. As Loretta changes, the emotional tone of the story changes. If it were Ronnie's story, however, all of these elements would have to be radically different. Or try to imagine how the elements of a story like *Midnight Run*—tone, pace, dramatic situation, and theme—would have altered if it had been built around the Duke as the main character. It probably would not have been a comedy, because from the Duke's point of view the stakes are too serious: he risks getting killed. This is not an irrelevant exercise. As script doctor Linda Seger reminds us, even some great films like *Witness*, which may appear "perfect" in their finished form, went through long and tortuous development processes.

Still another important story element related to the dramatic trajectory is determined by the choice of main character. This is the *point of attack*[27] for the

27. The concept of the *point of attack* has been well elaborated by Lajos Egri in his book *The Art of Dramatic Writing* (New York: Simon and Schuster, 1946), Chapter 3.

story. The point of attack refers directly back to the Hero's Journey. A movie story begins when the main character is ready to receive a Call to Adventure. This does not mean that we see the call in the first scene. We rarely do. But, remembering that the call can come as a self-proclaimed inner call, an outer assignment, or a blunder, we want to come into the story when the character is ready for change. We are looking at this change from a deep, soul level. The character himself, meaning the conscious personality, is neither prepared for nor agreeing to the change that is about to happen. As we open the story, we are ahead of the character because we know that change is about to erupt and destroy the old status quo. Part of our job as writers is to foreshadow this for the audience by the way we set the opening tone.

The movie sets the stage for the call, which appears as the dramatic catalyst of the drama. The setup that precedes the call to change may be brief and shocking or slow and lingering. There is no ideal page count for this, and I believe it is counterproductive to think rigidly that an event must happen on a specific page. *The Fugitive* begins with a running start, a violent hook where we see Dr. Richard Kimbell's wife murdered, and Kimbell himself arrested, tried, and convicted for her murder. During this opening, we are also shown Kimbell as a man who has reached a plateau of success, affluence, and security. He appears to be a man who has it all, who should not have a care in the world. Countless myths and fairy tales tell us this is a perilous place to be. As the Chinese wisdom of the Tao suggests, it is when the light is reaching its maximum that the darkness is already creeping in. In his self-satisfaction, Kimbell is unsuspecting, and thus vulnerable. This opening hook instantly destroys the status quo of Kimbell's life, though the actual catalyst of the plot comes later. In fact, the point of attack shows us that his world is already destroyed, but he does not yet realize it. Kimbell's character is orchestrated to work with such a violent opening: we are shown that this is a supremely competent man able to respond actively to emergencies.

The opening of *The Piano* superficially appears to be completely different, but the underlying dynamic structure is surprisingly similar to *The Fugitive*. Again the process of change is already moving as we come into the movie. Ada's father has betrothed her to a man in New Zealand she has never seen. As with the hook in *The Fugitive*, this event serves an establishing function whose purpose is to set up the world and the conditions of the drama. The point of attack is where Ada's belongings are already packed; her world is already dislocated. We still have the sea voyage and the long establishing sequence on the beach before we arrive at the catalyst of the drama. This catalyst will come when Stewart refuses to bring Ada's piano from the beach. Yet the impact of the change has been underway from the moment Ada was betrothed. Her old status quo world is gone. The moment of departure provides a natural starting point for the journey into the unknown.

Selecting the point of attack is simultaneously a question of determining the relationship of the present-time story to the *backstory*. The backstory is all that has happened to the main character before the movie opens. The time frame of the story as it appears on the screen inevitably makes reference to a larger time frame of events. Everything that happens prior to the point of attack is compressed into the backstory. Though *Last Tango in Paris* tries hard to isolate the two main characters in a romantic present with no reference to the past, the very fact that the suicide of the Brando character's wife forms the point of attack foreshadows the tragic impossibility of the existential freedom he imagines. Orchestrating the backstory is one of the biggest challenges in writing Act I of a screenplay. Naturally it has a major impact on the dramatic trajectory.

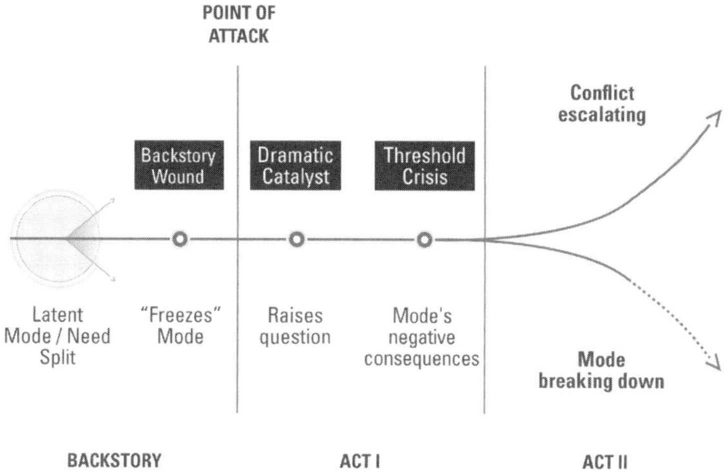

Back in the character's past is the formative pattern of his need/mode split. And in his more recent past is typically an event, a trauma, which has in effect "frozen" the split so that it cannot be resolved without some new journey of breakdown and breakthrough. This more recent trauma is called the backstory wound. Sometimes the *backstory wound* has happened just prior to the point of attack; sometimes it happened some years earlier. The key question is whether a specific backstory wound has a determining influence on the main character's status quo attitude, on his mode, as we come into the story. During a period when moviemaking was very influenced by Freudian psychoanalysis, great "revelation scenes" of these backstory wounds became fashionable. Set against this psychoanalytic trend were two camps, those of the pragmatists who felt that these revelation scenes needlessly dragged down the plot momentum, and those who felt that human motivations are at root unknowable or absurd and for whom the revelation seemed too pat and easy.

It is not always necessary to have a specific backstory wound, and the backstory wound does not necessarily need to be exposed in a "revelation" scene. We need rather to ask how best to handle the backstory wound and point of attack in *our* screenplay. Jack Walsh in *Midnight Run* has a specific backstory wound which is laboriously revealed. John Book does not. Nor does Tom Ripley in *The*

Talented Mr. Ripley. Loretta has a specific and obvious backstory wound, as does Ronnie. But Charles in *Four Weddings and a Funeral* does not. We could conclude that a specific backstory wound is not *necessary* in setting up your character, but may help in determining the point of attack, because either the story's establishing incident or catalyst will raise the specter of the old wound. We want at the very least to have a subtextual feeling that the character has another side we have not seen. What is necessary is to nail the main character's need/mode split, and the paradox that that entails, the first time we see her. Further, it is important that the split in the character points *beyond itself* to a flaw in the status quo of the world defined by the story. Otherwise the wound will lack thematic relevance and may appear trivial. Loss of passion is not only Loretta's problem: her parents' marriage has lost its spark, Ronnie's life is stuck because of romantic disappointment, and we see a world where passion for life has been dulled by daily routine. Not only is John Book personally betrayed by his father figure, the world of *Witness* is threatened by men in a position of authority and confidence: the corrupt police.

As writing is a process, we don't always know the point of attack for the story when we begin writing, just as we don't always know who the main character is. It tends to shift as our understanding of the character's mode and universal need deepen. Sometimes we must write an entire draft, a "throwaway draft," describing the character and her family and her world until we feel we know her, just to get a handle on exactly where the story should begin. We may be a hundred pages into such an exploration before we find the point of attack where the character is ready to act. That's fine. It's part of the process. Here we definitely want to lift from our shoulders the moral compulsion to get it right on the first draft. But when we arrive at that point on page 100, where the hero is finally ready to change, we take that long, long setup and compress it into the backstory. Then we find ways to bring out the backstory exposition as we go along. There is a certain rhythm to delivering this backstory exposition. It comes best at specific points in a scene or sequence.

Character and Point of View

Point of view (POV) grows naturally out of the Story Molecule, and it is one of the most critical aspects of the way a story is told. A screenplay can have engaging characters, sparkling dialogue, and a great story, but if it is told from the wrong point of view, it will fail. What does point of view have to do with screenwriting? Point of view ultimately has to do with how you orchestrate the audience's relationship to what is happening on the screen. Specifically, POV establishes the psychological and emotional distance between the audience and the main character. How closely will we experience and share the main character's dramatic journey? The possibilities range from deep empathic identification through degrees of romanticized idealization to an iconic distance, with many shades in between. This is not to be confused with what POV means to the cinematographer, where a "POV shot" is a shot seen literally through the eyes of a character, but we shall see that the two concepts are connected.

The fundamental idea is that POV is predicated by the degree of change or transformation taking place in your main character. If the change is profound, we want to be closer to the character in order to have a more direct experience of that process of change. If the character is more flatly iconic and will not change, such as a broad action hero, or if the character *cannot* change, in the case of a tragedy, then we want to look at the story from a more removed emotional perspective. Of course this is a question of interpretation, which makes it all the more important to outline the rationale behind these choices in the early stages of developing the screenplay. The screenwriter is not going to specify every shot. The interpretation of the screenplay—its breakdown into the concrete levels of production design, locations, and selection of shots—is the work of the director. But it *is* part of the screenwriter's job to use language to bring us close to the characters or to put us in a superior position to the characters. Hopefully the writer and director come to a shared vision of the project that includes agreement on the POV.

In the cinema, there are many possible shadings of the audience's point of view, depending on where the camera is placed, camera movements, and so on. By the way the scene is broken down into shots, and by the framing of each shot, the director includes or excludes information which helps determine POV. But we borrow terms from literature—*first person*, *second person*, and *third person*—to use as a shorthand to describe three basically different emotional postures for the audience vis-à-vis the movie. They are also three ways of structuring the information you will give the audience. This has to do, among other things, with whether the story will be linear, following one character, or will interweave different storylines. POV governs how crosscutting between actions is used. And choice of POV determines what the audience knows in relation to what the character knows. Knowing more than the character puts us in a superior position and breaks our exclusive identification with her. Point of view is suggested in the very first images of the movie's—or screenplay's—opening, and underscores their importance in guiding the audience.

First-Person Point of View

In literature, first-person address means that the narration is from the point of view of an "I." We are within the subjectivity of one single character, and that character's view of all the other characters necessarily colors our own experience of them. In movies, we use first-person when we want to emphasize the inner ring of the Story Molecule, the inner conflict of the main character. The extreme of first-person POV storytelling in the cinema would in fact be continuous use of the "POV shot" or "camera-eye," where the camera literally becomes the eyes of one character. This is not a practical possibility for the length of an entire feature movie, but it emphasizes the main feature of first-person POV, that in first-person POV we see the story figuratively through the main character's eyes. We see what she sees and know what she knows. And it follows from this that we do *not* know what she does not know. The restriction of our view may be accompanied by the main character's voice-over interior monologue, further taking us (the audience) into that character's subjectivity.

One of the advantages of this first-person narrative strategy is that we are brought very close to the character. Think of it as telling the story in close-up, by way of analogy, as the close-up (CU) seems to have the power to take us through the character's eyes and reveal her soul. Consider the first-person opening images of *The Piano*. The very first image is so subjective we cannot even tell what it is. In a few seconds we come to understand that we are looking through fingers, peeking out at the world from behind someone's hands. Ada's interior monologue begins, then we cut to the reverse close-up of Ada herself peeping out through her fingers. This sets up a very strong identification with Ada, with her inner life and inner mystery. We could say the story itself is "framed" by these opening images. By subliminally identifying us so strongly with Ada, the movie is already influencing how we will see all of the other characters, as well as the plot events.

The practical extreme of first-person storytelling includes movies where we follow one person constantly and ride through the arc of the story emphatically with her. The main character is thus onscreen *all the time*, in every scene, and we discover plot-related information only as the hero herself discovers it. This is also to say that we never break away to a scene where the main character is not present. This is one possible narrative strategy. As a result, our POV in the audience is very strongly identified with the hero and very much emotionally immersed in that person's dramatic journey. Of course, this puts extraordinary demands on an actor, to be in every scene of the film. The whole movie is riding on his shoulders, like Matt Damon in *The Talented Mr. Ripley*. Other successful examples of extreme first-person POV are *Rosetta* by the D'Ardennes brothers and the very good French melodrama *À Nos Amours*. In *À Nos Amours*, a talented teenage actress, Sandrine Bonnaire, is in every scene of the movie, and we live a very intimate experience with her. Here the selection of POV works together with the genre: this is a family melodrama, which requires defining the dramatic world of the story in terms of "family." Obviously this strategy has risks. To keep this technique from becoming monotonous, scenes in *À Nos Amours* often open on other characters, the mother and brother, for example. A dramatic situation is established, and then the main character enters the scene. Thus she is not literally present at every instant, but her presence on the whole defines our experience. The other characters have an existence, but do not take on dramatic significance independent of the main character.

Movies like *The Piano* and *Trainspotting* are still predominantly in the first-person voice, though the technique is not so rigorous. Both movies have a few scenes where the main character is not present. Sometimes this is necessary in order to give the audience some important expositional information, or for a burst of humor. This raises a question that often troubles many screenwriters: when, how, and why do I break away from my main character? Some writers have a general problem cutting from the main character to other action. They may be overidentified with the main character, and then they have some work to do on their own perspective. Yet there remains the strategic question of how to set up a first-person POV while still opening out the story. The answer is to set up the first-person POV *first*, at least through the catalyst, before breaking away to scenes with the antagonist or to subplots.

What are the first scenes in *The Piano* where Ada is not present? At 8:10 into the movie we have a short scene where Stewart, George, and the Maori porters are in the forest on the way to greet Ada at the shore. Stewart, tense, stops to take out a small photo of her. Thus, the scene refers directly to Ada and their impending meeting in the next scene. The next significant scene after that is at 27:30 into the film, already late in Act I. Stewart tells some neighboring women that Ada has carved a piano keyboard into the tabletop. He wonders aloud if she might be mad. George is in the shadows, overhearing. In the next scene, George will offer Stewart eighty acres of land in exchange for the piano, which had been left on the beach. From this point the story will begin to open out, but Ada as the central consciousness of the story has already been firmly established.

When and under what conditions would you want to try first-person storytelling in a screenplay? Understand that the movie is going to live or die based on whether or not the audience takes the main character to heart, because you really are not giving them other alternatives. Be confident that, for whatever reasons, your audience is going to find your character compelling. Joe Buck in *Midnight Cowboy* and Renton in *Trainspotting* are both set up to define a certain time and a certain generation. They are established as icons of the zeitgeist. Both movies took the audience into "walk on the wild side" experiences that projected cultural futures. Both were successful in getting a specific segment of the audience to identify with them, which then built bridges to a larger audience.

Second-Person Point of View

Second-person narration emphasizes the emotional network of the Story Molecule: the key relationships that carry the dramatic momentum of the story. Second-person address, which in literature would be a "you" narrative voice, implies a dialectic rather than an identification. The way second-person is used in movies is not identical to literary usage, because the language of cinema, made up of images, differs from verbal language. We could say that cinematic second-person keeps us close, keeps us connected, to the point of view of one character while breaking our exclusive identification with them. The audience's identification with the main character may predominate, but it is not exclusive. Our point of view is able to move away from the hero to see what is happening to other characters at the same time. With second-person POV, *parallel storytelling* becomes possible, and the possibilities inherent in parallel storytelling have, on the whole, proven more compelling for movies than the extreme intimacy of an exclusively first-person POV. Now we may know what is going on in the story before the hero does. This is not only important for suspense, but it engages the audience in a different way, forcing us to entertain equally the feelings, motives, and perspectives of several characters. If the analogy to first-person storytelling is the close-up, the analogy to second-person is the two-shot, also called medium shot (MS) or *plan américain* by the French because it was so typical of classic Hollywood movies. The two-shot can be described as a shot from the knee or midthigh up which usually encompasses two or three characters. The beauty of the two-shot is that it is close enough to allow us to read facial expressions while at the same time being loose enough to put the characters in a spatial relation to each other. Thus it focuses our attention on the *relationship*. While first-person close-up storytelling isolates and emphasizes the interiority of one character, second-person two-shot storytelling emphasizes personal relationships.

This is a very different way of experiencing a story. Most mainstream Hollywood movies are primarily in a second-person POV, but will shift for stretches into a first-person mode for greater emotional emphasis. A movie sets up *either* first-person or second-person as the *dominant* posture for the audience within the first two minutes or so of screen time. Then it shifts our attention between the two as the dramatic situation demands. *Midnight Run* opens with a "hook" in what seems like first-person on Jack Walsh. We are alone with him, and visually very close to him, as he tries to pick the lock to an apartment door. At the same time there are also elements that create distance: the action genre situation, the tone of the music, and the lack of intimacy or interiority in the situation. By lack of interiority, I mean that during this brief moment we are always aware of *looking* at Jack Walsh. We are not invited into his mind or his feelings as we watch him. So this is more of an establishing moment to show us the character than a real first-person opening. Then we cut to inside the apartment where a fugitive reacts to the noise. Now we know that first-person will not be the posture of this story. Rather, there will be first-person *moments* where we will get closer to the character. Because *Midnight Run* is a genre action movie, Jack's character must first of all serve the plot. We will not be placing Jack's inner change in the foreground.

It was also necessary to open out the POV for the sake of narrative exposition. Thus the movie uses broad second-person POV to advance the plot. We have many short cutaway scenes to tell us how the antagonists are reacting to Jack's moves. But on the other hand, we never have a full sequence with other characters where Jack is not present. More importantly, however, in terms of adjusting the audience's point of view, is the character of the Duke. The Duke takes the dramatic focus away from Jack and creates another perspective on him. The questions the Duke poses to Jack, the ways he prods Jack to open up and change, model the audience's attitude toward Jack. Yet even the Duke can hardly be said to have a dramatic existence independent of Jack's perception of him. For example, the Duke has only a few short expositional scenes very late in Act II where Jack is not present. This actually enhances the Duke's quality of being a "traveling angel," to be taken as a projection of Jack's "wise self." Genre dictates the overall POV of *Midnight Run* as second-person, but it is used flexibly.

There are many kinds of stories where our point of view *must* go beyond the main character in order for the meaning of the story unfold. As we have noted, action and suspense genre movies have special narrative needs. They must broaden the POV to fit the scope of the action, and by their nature they tend to focus on outer plot more than on interiority of character. Thrillers can be structured to keep us very close to the main character, but must be predominantly second-person to allow us to see the actions of the antagonist. Love stories require that we see both lovers separately in order to appreciate them as people, and not merely as projections seen through the eyes of the other. Trying to tell a love story in strictly first-person would not work; the beloved would have no independent existence outside the lover's infatuation. Family dramas and melodramas, where the perspective of each member on their common experience is central, also are typically in second-person. And wherever there is a collective protagonist, whether that be a "milieu" drama such as *E. R.* or a collective hero going on a journey (like the Dublin soul band in *The Commitments* or the group of men in *The Full Monty*), we need a broader narration that can encompass the social world.

It could be broadly stated that when we have several interesting characters, we will identify more with the character who gets more screen time (more pages in the screenplay), and who we see more often in close-up. This tendency poses dangers that had better be addressed in the story development process. We cannot always tell while writing the screenplay which character will have the most allure for the audience. If this turns out not to be the main character, a confusing situation can be created for the audience. We need then to go back to make sure our reasons for picking the main character are persuasive. Opening out the POV creates many new narrative possibilities. It is a challenge for the screenwriter to open to all this complexity while keeping a sharp dramatic focus.

Third-Person Point of View

By analogy, the third-person POV is like experiencing the action through long shot (LS). In LS, we see the characters full-figure in the distance, like a caravan crossing the desert. We cannot see their facial expressions from this distance, so characters are identified by their broad physical gestures and other markers. To that extent, the characters are relatively de-personalized. The emphasis is on the relation of man to the larger social or natural environment. The individual tends to be seen as a representative of a type, or an *icon*. Third-person storytelling, then, is like looking in on the Story Molecule through the outer world, more distant, omniscient, or God-like. The massive scale of epic action may force us to pull back in order to see its scope. Or a tragic or satirical tone may emotionally distance us from the characters. We are pulling back even further from identification with the subjective life of one character. The impossible extreme would be to see the entire movie in LS, or as though appearing on a stage. Of course no one would want to do this; it would be too emotionally flat. So what we are talking about in third-person from a storytelling point of view are *distancing devices* that set up a third-person perspective, as though from an omniscient or elevated perspective. As with all POV, it must be set and established in the opening images and minutes of the movie.

Distancing devices are used to set up a third-person narrative tone in epics, tragedies, black comedies, and satires. One such device is to open with a "God's-eye POV" establishing shot, literally from a great distance or from high overhead. Do you recall the opening of *Psycho*, that modern counterpart to ancient Greek theater? Most people cannot visualize the opening images. Some people think the movie opens in a hotel room, with the main character and her boyfriend in a banal conflict about when he will leave his wife. But this is not how *Psycho* opens. The first image is an extreme LS of a city, with the title: PHOENIX, ARIZONA.

This is followed by a closer shot, a medium shot (MS) of the city, but still extreme LS of individual buildings.

Then a group of buildings.

Then a *single* building, MS, which is now LS of the individual windows.

Closer view. Now we have picked out a single window. Finally we go in through the window to the scene in the hotel room.

Hitchcock, through this series of images, is subtly redefining what the subject is. A God-like intelligence, through chance or destiny, is guiding our gaze to just this window at just this moment. This creates a framing around the story and conveys a strong subliminal message: do not get too emotionally close to Marian, the main character. The opening message is not to identify, but *observe*. It is a precise visual counterpart to the opening chorus in Greek tragedy, and it anchors us subliminally in third-person, even after the movie moves into a "normal" narrative flow. This prepares us to detach from Marion when she is killed at what structurally should be her mythic threshold crossing.

Another third-person distancing strategy is to show us the end at the beginning—opening with the narrative resolution that is normally reserved for Act III, and then flashing back to the inciting incident of Act I, as in *Amadeus* and Agnes Varda's *Vagabond* (*Sans Toit Ni Loi*). This is very typically done to open tragedies. We are shown the death or moral destruction of the hero as a prologue. The use of voice-over narration is also an important distancing device.

Normally it reduces our sense of risk and identification by assuring us that the narrating character is still alive at the end of the story in order to tell it. The opening of *Apocalypse Now* creates a paradoxical effect by combining a phantasmagoria of subjective images with the distancing of a narrator. Distancing and character-identification strategies can be interwoven for a wide range of specific dramatic effects.

In epics like *Lawrence of Arabia*, *Reds*, and *Gandhi*, there are literally more long shots: crowds of people, figures in immense landscapes, and panoramic action sequences. They are needed to take in the scope of the action, the vast crowds of people, and to suggest the scale of the stakes involved in the story: the freeing of Arabia from Turkish rule, the Bolshevik Revolution, the nonviolent liberation of India. Epics have their own storytelling style, determined partly by the language and the rhythm of the long shot in alternation with scenes where we establish smaller social groups. The smaller groupings allow us to approach the central characters in a more human way. These groupings of central characters are key to the success of an epic because it is through them that we shift our focus from outer actions viewed from a distance to inner motivations and values. Thus epics set up a third-person point of view as the dominant posture, but then move into second-person or, more rarely, first-person POV. One of the great challenges of structuring an epic is how to embrace both the large scale of the action and an intimacy that will make the characters' feelings and inner lives real for us.

A specific strategy for handling the paradoxes of third-person POV in epic storytelling is the *point-of-view character*. Point-of-view characters are secondary characters who stand in directly for the audience in order to make the epic more accessible to us. With them we come close to the literary third-person: "he" or "she." But the point-of-view character as used in movies is still not the same as a narrator in literature. The point-of-view character's role in movies is usually more limited and has a very special function to play: to give us the right "lens" into the main character. Historic forces and heroic sentiments that are not in our own direct experience often drive the protagonists and antagonists of epics. Forty years after Martin Luther King Jr.'s "I have a dream" speech, forty years after he said that he knew each time he went out to speak or demonstrate he was "tempting death," the heroic force which propelled him and visibly animated his features has become incomprehensible to many Americans. By definition, epic heroes are not people like us. The epic hero needs to be mediated by POV characters both as a way to humanize him and as a way to expand and externalize the hero's charismatic or social impact on others. The surrounding secondary characters represent and magnify a wider social network.

So the POV character "interprets" the great man or woman for us. The POV character is always more "normal," more like us, and a representative of our attitudes. Through the way we see the POV character react, and through what we hear him say to other characters about the hero, what is foreign to us becomes more digestible. Thus Gandhi is surrounded by a series of American and English followers and journalists, with Western mindsets, who are meant to make Gandhi accessible to a modern mass audience. A certain amount of authenticity is lost as a result. Our potential confrontation with Gandhi is softened, but at the same time he becomes accessible to millions of people as an immediate, living presence. Framing a story with a POV character may be as much a marketing consideration as it is a story necessity, but its basic function is always to give us the right "lens" into the story.

Point of View and Character Growth

We have described how first-, second-, and third-person POVs work. But how we orchestrate them into the story is dependent on what is happening in the inner ring of the Story Molecule. The Need versus Mode tension in the hero determines the point of view of the storytelling. The POV is dictated by *the degree of transformation in your main character*. The greater the change in the character, the closer we want to live the story vicariously along with her. A major degree of change means really going into the need/mode problem of the hero and seeing a change of self-perception lead to a change of behavior. It means seeing the character go on the Hero's Journey of breakdown and breakthrough, of growth through crisis, and being vicariously right there with her. In first-person storytelling it is the character's immediate experiences, reactions, feelings, and reflections which communicate to us the essence of the Hero's Journey, and it is on a direct feeling level that we receive it.

There is a natural relationship here: because the change is taking place deep within the character, we want to be close enough to see what is happening inside. As writers, we want to create the dramatic situations that give us access to that inner life. Very often these are delicate, silent moments in the movie where nothing more can be said. We just have to look into the character: the moment John Book, having finished putting the birdhouse back in place, leans on his shovel; the moment Ada, riding in the Maori canoe, dangles her fingers in the water. In each case the character is not performing an overt action, but catching such moments makes the story complete and three-dimensional. Ada watches the coiled rope playing out like lightning from the bottom of the boat, and then puts her booted foot in the midst of that wild coil. She looks up, and we *know* what she is thinking and what is about to happen. In first-person we are close enough to experience the hero's emotional catharsis as our own. Examples of movies where the main character undergoes a major change and where first-person storytelling is used extensively include *Midnight Cowboy*, *The Piano*, *Frida*, *Trainspotting*, *Almost Famous*, and *The Talented Mr. Ripley*.

When there is a lesser degree of change in the main character, where that inner change is not at the center of the story, or where genre conventions interpose themselves as a filter between the hero and the audience, we are focusing more on the emotional network of relationships. This means we are basically in second-person POV.

One of the most common situations for second-person storytelling is where the main character is not going through great change himself, but is primarily causing change in others. Variations of this include "messianic character" stories and "traveling angel" stories. A messianic character transforms others through self-sacrifice. *One Flew Over the Cuckoo's Nest* is the classic example. McMurphy himself does change; he goes from being completely egocentric to fighting Nurse Ratched in order to instill a sense of liberty in the other inmates, and ultimately to save/avenge Billy. In the end, McMurphy sacrifices himself for the men. But the thrust of the story is about how McMurphy awakens the other men from torpor to rebellion. Throughout Act II, the energy is gradually shifting from McMurphy to the other inmates. This aspect needed work during the script development. It was noticed in a middle draft that McMurphy had all the funny, rebellious lines, and in a sense wasn't sharing the energy. So the writers, Bo Goldman and Lawrence Hauben, reportedly wrote another draft, taking some of those funny lines and putting them in the mouths of the other inmates, resulting in a dramatic proof of McMurphy's impact.

Because McMurphy is a messianic, sacrificial character who meets a tragic end, we do not want to go through to the end of the story being directly identified with him. So we remove our identification with McMurphy by removing the point of view. There is an important moment at the end of the chaotic party the inmates stage to express their liberty, where we see McMurphy watching the inmates like a satisfied father. Then he looks toward the open window. In a long, ruminative close-up, we can see him considering that he could escape now through the window—and we see him decide not to. Then we cut to the Chief, watching McMurphy, perhaps guessing his thoughts. If we continued the story from this point on in a direct identification with McMurphy into the next sequence, it would be as though we were going through the shock treatment along with him. While we do have the scene of his shock treatment as punishment, the fact that we have created another "center of consciousness" to identify with, the Chief, subtly and effectively gives us enough room to breathe at the tragic climax. The important point here is that this shift must be set up at the opening and through Act I if it is going to be consistent for the audience when it comes at the end of Act II.

"Traveling angels" come into a troubled status quo world of characters who are stuck in their survival modes. The traveling angel effects change on this world without herself going through a major change, and leaves again at the end of the story. Because these characters come from "another world" and somehow know more than the characters they influence, they seem to be angels. Perhaps the most famous traveling angel in the movies is E.T.

Traveling angel stories are usually comic. The "angel" may have a plot conflict—how will E.T. get home?—but normally does not have an inner conflict.

The traveling angel is a lighter, more comic version of the messianic character, who only leaves through death. Sometimes the character is literally an angel, as in Wim Wenders's *Wings of Desire*, or is figuratively an angel, like Jasmine in Percy Adlon's *Bagdad Cafe*. Sometimes the traveling angel is a picaresque comic character who bounces from adventure to adventure, leaving a fecundating chaos in his wake, like Tati's Monsieur Hulot or Chaplin's Tramp.

The traveling angel character may bring a unique character orchestration or a subplot into a movie that is not explicitly a traveling angel story. The Duke in *Midnight Run* is really a traveling angel/guide figure for Jack. Orchestrated in contrast to De Niro's character, the Duke shifts the tone and the theme of the story. The Duke speaks as the voice of Jack's conscience, though he does this so cleverly and comically that we don't feel he is giving away the subtext. In another context, *Tootsie*, while Michael Dorsey is confused about his own identity ("Why can't Michael Dorsey just be Michael Dorsey?"), Dorothy Michaels is acting as a traveling angel on the set of the soap opera, and ultimately in the homes of millions of TV viewers. And sometimes the message the traveling angel has to bring is so rude or dark that we hesitate to use the word angel at all. Clint Eastwood's *Pale Rider* is an angel of vengeance and apocalypse, and Boudou, in Renoir's anarchic comedy *Boudou Saved from Drowning*, so upsets the bourgeois household that takes him in that they are all ready to call him a monster.

Love stories and buddy stories also work best in second-person POV, and for similar reasons. The structure of these stories, like those of messianic and traveling angel stories, involves a pair. We need to pay attention to both halves of the pair, sharing identification with both and following each of them through the story. In fact, most often one of the pair is in the role of a guide. Couples in love stories usually appear constellated as a *lover*—who seems to know from the beginning that this relationship is special and who takes the active guiding role—and a *beloved*, who needs to be wooed or convinced, and who holds out until the climax. This orchestration may be obvious, as with Ronnie and Loretta, but even in a movie such as *Four Weddings and a Funeral*, where the trumpets of romantic destiny do not blow loud, Carrie seems to have a better grip on what's going on than Charles does. We have the feeling that she has completely masterminded their first affair at the country inn, even though Charles thinks he is taking the active role. The lover as guide can also be a *negative initiator*. Alvie Singer plays this role in *Annie Hall*. His controlling, neurotic love ultimately pushes Annie to realize a talent within herself. What should be noted in the orchestration of love stories is that the main character, whether active lover or receptive beloved, is normally the one going through the *greatest change*.

The scale of the story may also help determine POV. The famous prologue opening of *Apocalypse Now* begins in a feverish first-person voice, but we could not go through the entire story in such a subjective "purple haze." And it would be far too confining and too much at odds with the epic scale of the adventure.

We are not going to see Willard go through major character transformation; he is going to be primarily a Dante-esque witness to collective madness. It is difficult to carry themes that embrace society as a whole, such as the American experience of Vietnam, from a first-person POV. So it was necessary to establish more removed point of view. The moment we shift from first-person to second-person POV in *Apocalypse Now* is handled very economically and successfully. As the first-person prologue closes, we cut to two officers coming up the stairs to take Capt. Willard to his new assignment. They are the "straight men," people like us. In the moment, they serve as functional POV characters to help the audience over a threshold into a world of madness, while on the mythic level they come to announce the Call to Adventure. They knock on the door—two, three times. They chuckle self-consciously over some private joke. Finally the door opens and Willard appears wrapped in a bloodstained bed sheet. We see Willard now from their POV, as a psychic wreck, framed in the doorway. The doorway separates us from Willard. Now we are no longer inside his head; we are *looking at* him. That is the shift to second-person POV. Now we have shifted to a point of view that will allow us to take in what is about to happen without going crazy, like Willard himself. It is typical to use a prologue in this way, to set up either a first-person or third-person POV, which is subsequently placed in the subtext (in the viewer's subconscious) while the story moves into a more standard second-person storytelling.

We have already suggested, in describing how third-person POV works, that it has some connection to tragedy. How is this set up by what is happening in the need/mode core of the Story Molecule? When the main character is *not* changing—cannot change or refuses to change—then we want to have a more distant perspective on him. This is not a judgment on the character or the character's values. What it means is that when the tragic-fated character meets his destiny, we don't want to be riding along in a complete projective identification with him. Otherwise we would end up lobotomized like McMurphy, killed in an auto wreck like Karen Silkwood (*Silkwood*), or banging our heads against a wall like Jake LaMotta in *Raging Bull*. Our natural, visceral reaction at such moments is to recoil physically, emotionally, and psychically, balanced by a fascination and pity that wants to witness the horror.

The cinematic device of pulling back to a broader, more distant point of view corresponds to our body's reaction. So in tragedies where characters are not changing, this shift is made usually going into the catastrophe or immediately after the catastrophe, at the end of Act II. But in order for the shift to work, it must, as mentioned earlier, be prepared by establishing the third-person POV at the opening and using some of the distancing devices to give the audience another point of view to fall back on. Tragedy is not merely a "downer" ending. Tragedy strikes primal chords of awe and dread deep in our souls. One of the ancient playwrights said that tragedy "breaks man's face." We need a perspective on tragedy that provides three things: gives us the power to continue to watch and experience catharsis, allows us to feel adequately safe, and puts us in a position of insight into the hero's tragic nature.

Psycho is an especially bold example of handling tragedy, and Hitchcock plans his shifts of POV masterfully. A more recent and simpler example is *The Perfect Storm*. As with the ancient tragedies, the outcome here is already generally known to the audience. The opening sequence engages us on a broader third-person level. A tone of heroic romanticism is set with the two fishing boats motoring home from the limitless expense of ocean. Then we establish the larger life of the Gloucester harbor community as the boats arrive: long-separated loved ones embrace and the docks come alive with the activity of unloading and weighing the catch of swordfish. Only gradually are the central characters identified in this welter of action, each with his or her own personal melodrama of hard times.

This is an iconic opening in the manner of the classic John Ford Westerns. The Western town or homestead has been transferred to New England, but the baseline message is the same: this is how it is, this is how it's always been, and this is how it will always be. The faces change, but the roles remain the same. The life of the community comes before the life of the individual. Swordfish boat captain Tyne and his crew are tragic-fated characters, driven by money, by survival, driven to maintain their place in the order of things—and ultimately, through Captain Tyne, driven by hubristic pride. They are *tougher* than the storm: after all, they are Gloucestermen! Embracing the subplot of the sailing yacht, there is a theme being developed here about the consequences of masculine pride and stubbornness. The yachtsman is saved by his more pragmatic female companions; Tyne and his crew have gone too far to be saved. As they move toward catastrophe, we cut increasingly back to the community on land, the survivors. This strategy gives us in the audience another place to stand. At the tragic climax, we see the men meet their fate, but we do not go down with them. Finally, only the Ishmael-like Bobby is left when the boat goes down. Bobby finds a reconciled attitude, sending his undying love to his girlfriend a thousand miles away—and now we pull way back and above in a God's-eye POV to see Bobby as a tiny speck under the shadow of a towering wave. For the resolution of the story, we return to the iconic community of Gloucester, which will go on, grieving, but with its core values intact. This gives an outline for a characteristic strategy of shifting POV in tragedy: setting up the third-person perspective at the opening and returning to it at the end.

Whenever "rules" are set up, such as these correlations between the degree of change in the main character and the POV, there are immediately those who want to break the rule or find exceptions. Screenwriters and directors have their Faustian pride, after all. It turns out, however, that you can't really force an audience. If you try to push the audience's face into something from which they would naturally and instinctively recoil—like too much graphic violence, or the death of the main character without another perspective to fall back on—what happens? Well, the audience simply checks out. They may not physically get up and leave the theater, but they go numb. They go into that deer-caught-in-the-headlights place in the psyche. The audience becomes like a traumatized subject in a Pavlovian conditioning experiment. They may be captivated by a violent spectacle, but they are no longer in a state to appreciate the drama or be receptive to the theme of the movie. Using the focusing techniques we have developed in the earlier chapters, try to imagine how you would feel if *The Perfect Storm* had ended with the sinking of the boat—the struggles of the crew trapped below deck, Captain Tyne disappearing into the green depth, Bobby about to be crushed by the huge wave. How would that feel in your body? How would it feel to put on your coat and go out of the theater, fumbling for the car keys in your pocket? Isn't it important to know that life can somehow continue? Stories are energy, and as such they have the power to chill our will to live as well as to enhance it. How we choose to handle that energy does matter.

There was at one point a taste for shocking "blackout" endings, such as in *Looking for Mr. Goodbar*. That movie ended with the sudden, graphic, and absurd murder of the main character, played by Diane Keaton. She picks up a guy on New Year's Eve to have some pleasant, if compulsive, casual sex. What she does not realize is that the fellow has a sizable chip on his shoulder, having been beaten up earlier by a bunch of gay-bashers. Exactly at the point of orgasm, he grabs a kitchen knife and guts the helpless woman before our eyes—ROLL CREDITS! Such blackout endings may have come from a conviction that it all is truly meaningless and, as Paul Schrader once said in an interview, "Why should I give resolution in my stories if I don't have resolution in my life?" Probably another motivation, however, was purely commercial: the supposition was that the shocked audiences, unable to contain their shaken-up feelings, would generate buzz for the movie. That might be a cynical extreme. In most cases, however, the dramatic resolution is structured to offer us a doorway out of the theater in possession of ourselves, carrying with us the theme of the movie. This is the idea of dramatic catharsis.

Producers and studio executives, as well as people who write and teach seminars on screenwriting, are fond of saying that a great script "just leaps off the page at you!" This is one of those set phrases that can mean pretty much whatever you want it to mean. It is a convenient response in an interview. When pressed, it is not hard to name an obviously successful recent movie whose script, in retrospect, seems to have leapt off the page. But this dodges the real question about what makes a screenplay dramatically exciting. Many screenplays today, especially those written by beginners with studios and the mainstream market in view, are written expressly *to* leap off the page. They are so tricked out with hooks, "elements," and special effects that they leap right into outer space. But the dramatic substance is not there. Meanwhile, if you look at a middle draft of an Oscar-winning screenplay like *Witness* or *Ordinary People*, you will see serious problems that still need to be resolved: entire subplots which need to be taken out, dialogue that gives away the subtext, and so on. This is all part of writing and refining the screenplay. What is evident even in the middle drafts of these screenplays are dramatic concepts that are both compelling and complex, manifested in the need/mode conflicts of engaging main characters, and articulated through all levels of the Story Molecule. The dramatic viability of solid stories can be tested and confirmed while the screenplays are being refined.

A screenplay *must* clearly establish its point of view in order to achieve dramatic coherence. This should be decided upon early in the story development process. Without a clear POV, it is impossible to set a consistent dramatic tone. The wrong POV may make the story impossible to tell or impossible to resolve dramatically. And since a wrong POV cannot be pinpointed as easily as a wrong plot element or a static relationship, it is often harder to fix in development. In choosing the right perspective to tell your story, the key things to keep in mind are that POV is determined by the degree of transformation in your main character, and how closely the audience is meant to identify with him or her.

The Emotional Network: Where Drama Becomes Visible

A screenplay may have an exciting premise, a compelling hero going through great change, and a fast-paced plot, but it is through the relationships of the story that the drama becomes visible. Relationships define value, and value is what the emotional network addresses: how each character sees and values what is happening in the story. The emotional network is the matrix of the key relationships in the movie. The emotional network is where *value* is expressed through *relationship*, and relationship is expressed in how characters react to one another. Some movies, as we have suggested, play primarily in the emotional network. The juice of the movie is in the relationships, and the plot grows directly out of this nexus. Farce comedies and melodramas are two genres where the energy is mainly in the emotional network. As in all stories, the world of the characters has to be circumscribed and set apart from the rest of the universe in order to create a dramatic unity. In movie genres that play in the emotional network, the protagonistic and antagonistic forces are going to be found within the microcosm of the social group.

The context of the characters' reactions to events suggests value to the audience. It has often been said that the cinema is "the art of the reaction shot." This is very true. The action itself may tell us what is happening, but not how to feel about it or value it. We may be watching a gun battle or a car chase or a love scene, but unless we see someone react to what is happening—with surprise, with horror, with laughter—we ourselves may not know how to respond, how to *value* it. Our response draws us into *relationship*; it implicates us, the viewers, in a larger emotional network together with what is happening onscreen. In *Independence Day*, our sense of horror at the alien attack is magnified and given human significance through the horror we see on the faces on the screen. And comedy in particular, because it is built on a serious subtext, relies on reaction shots to establish the comic tone. At the end of the Act I crisis in *Moonstruck*, Ronnie hurls the kitchen table out of the way, grabs Loretta roughly in his arms, and kisses her. We catch the alarmed look on Loretta's face as she shouts, "Wait a minute! Wait a minute!" Her reaction makes us feel—and participate in—the value which is at stake. It also gets a laugh a moment later when she kisses Ronnie, because her sudden shift has set up a release of tension.

The emotional network of the story extends this basic idea of the reaction shot into a principle of story structuring. Each character in the emotional network brings his own set of values to the dramatic situation, and as he reacts and interacts, we see the collision and interplay of these values. The opposition of values in the story is carried by the two characters whose relationships with the main character are most important: the antagonist and the primary relationship. We will look at how these two figures create force fields in the emotional network. They are force fields of values. At the same time, the antagonist and the primary relationship dimensionalize the main character and establish the theme of the movie through how they are orchestrated around him. Secondary characters and subplots, when seen through the lens of the Story Molecule, also reveal rich layers of significance.

The Two Key Relationships within the Emotional Network

It takes many writers some time and experience to realize that a movie cannot be constructed like a novel (though, increasingly, novels are being constructed like movies). A novel has an open format; it can be any length. The more or less set length of theatrical feature films (one and a half to two hours) limits the amount of story that can be told, which limits the number of characters that can be fully developed. The general consensus is that, apart from the main character, two other characters can and must be developed in a dramatic feature film. Naturally we want to protest at this limitation: *Oh yeah? Who sez so?!* There is no scientific measurement for this. So let's look at it another way. Our time to tell the story *is* limited. In this context, which are the *most* important relationships in terms of the interaction of plot and character, and who in the story carries these relationships? The characters who carry the key relationships in terms of storytelling functions are the most essential to develop in a limited time.

Dramatically, the two most important relationships are the relationship of *opposition*, which produces the throughline conflict, and the relationship of *transformation*, which pushes the hero toward deeper change. The character of opposition is the antagonist, and the character of transformation is the primary relationship. The primary relationship may appear as a love interest, like Carrie in *Four Weddings and a Funeral* and George in *The Piano*, or he may appear as a guide figure like the Duke. We do not want to be stuck semantically on these terms, though. The narrowly erotic associations with the term "love interest" are too confining for our current time. We have seen that the lover often has a guiding function as well, and guiding may be an aspect of caring, a quality of love. Many movies are structured to have both a love interest *and* a guide. *An Officer and a Gentleman* is a good example. Therefore, we want to go beyond the labels and determine which character has the greatest impact on the hero's *inner* conflict. To be more precise: who seems to embody and externalize the main character's unconscious need, what the hero needs to learn about life? That is the role of the primary relationship.

These two characters, the antagonist and the primary relationship, have valences that go deep into the psyche. They connect to the complex of the shadow and the archetype of the anima/animus. We shall explore the interaction between them in the next chapter. Here, the important point is that these two characters dimensionalize the Story Molecule by drawing out the different levels of the main character. It is fundamental for us as writers to work with them, get to know them, and feel the quality of their impact on the main character. Often this means allowing ourselves to feel their impact on *us* as well, whatever particular allure, fascination, obsession, or dread they evoke in us.

And when we suggest that only two characters apart from the hero can be fully developed, what does the phrase "fully developed" mean, anyway? This question brings a basic point about the emotional network to the foreground: characters are developed and revealed through relationships, through interaction and conflict. The fact that these two characters have the most intensive and sustained interactions with the hero makes it almost automatic that they will be the most developed. This is true even when the antagonist spends much of the story offscreen, or with motives so disguised that we in the audience do not see who they really are until Act III. The relationship is based on engagement. The *quality* of the antagonist's actions is always present in how they force the hero to respond and in how they make us in the audience feel, emotionally and intuitively. In that way the antagonist is always revealing who he is dramatically. The hero and the audience have the challenge of interpreting those actions to get to the truth. Character is revealed in a relationship expressed through dramatic action. By contrast, "talking about"—having characters talk about themselves or each other onscreen, about their likes and dislikes, their current problems or backstory wounds—is *not* a good vehicle for character development because it is essentially discursive and undramatic. It does not carry consequences or provoke change. To fully develop two or three characters in a feature film means to put them on a dramatic curve of growth through crisis.

Character development implies character change, and character change is the result of dramatic conflict. Dramatic conflict comes from two or more characters who have opposing *beats* (a beat = a motive + an action) and who are each acting *right now*, in the dramatic present, to get what they want. Characters with diverging motives and well-differentiated beats will be well orchestrated. Each will stand out distinctly against the other like two contrasting colors set side by side. Over the dramatic time charted by the Plot Curve model, we shall see the progress of this conflict, and how the characters are changed by it. While working on a screenplay, character development can be isolated and pictured by means of character arcs and relationship arcs. The progress and conflicts of the primary relationship express the transformational impact of the primary relationship character on the hero. The conflict arises because the hero's mode value is challenged by this other character, who embodies a complementary opposite value. The relationship arc for Ada and George in *The Piano* is a dramatic curve with its own catalyst, crisis, catastrophe, and climax *in the relationship*. Who are Ada and George to each other when they meet and who are they at the end? These relationship arcs are as important to the success of the screenplay as the outer plot.

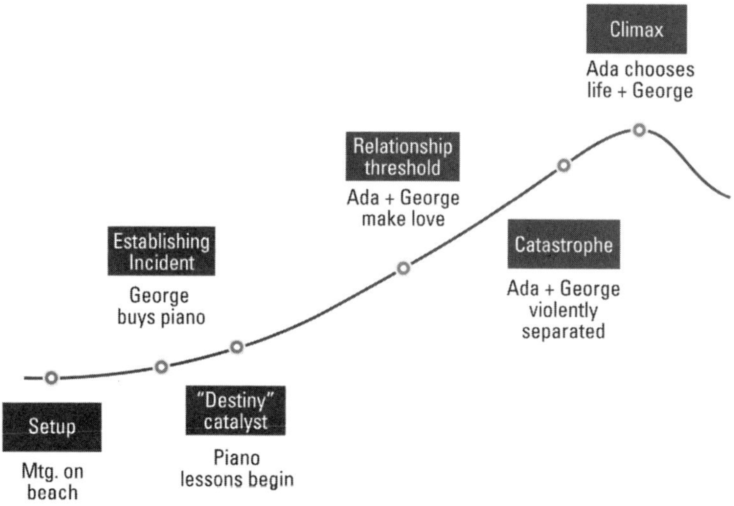

It is also understood when working with the emotional network of your screenplay that each important character has his own web of social contacts. These will be secondary characters, but they will also be impacted by the central conflict. These secondary characters can be used to record the rising dramatic tension through their reactions. No character exists in isolation. Note how George is portrayed with sympathetic Maori women friends. It is not made explicit that they have sexual relations, but early in the story, we hear them tell George he should get married. At the end of Act II, when George finds the traumatized daughter carrying Ada's finger, the women are present to support both him and the child. This is in deliberate contrast to the rigid, repressed, gossiping women in Stewart's circle. And then compare the example of *The Piano* with *Four Weddings and a Funeral*. Carrie floats in and out of the story without any apparent web of social contacts. We never know what she is doing at the first wedding to begin with. We never see her with her own circle of friends or social contacts. The only characters around her are other men who desire her, men peripheral to the story at best. Carrie is an idealized *image* of a woman, an iconic woman. This is a problem with Carrie's character and adds to the escapist feeling of the movie. Lacking any real social context, Carrie is a figure who is not quite dramatically real. She may be lovely, but we never know what motivates her. Carrie's lack of grounding in a social world or emotional network gives an arbitrary, deus ex machina flavor to her appearance at Charles's wedding. The effect is charming, but not richly satisfying. The heavy atmospherics at the climax of their relationship arc ("Is it raining? I didn't notice.") were probably needed to carry the audience past the lack of more concrete feelings and motives. Giving Carrie an emotional network would have given her, and the movie, more reality.

Character Orchestration in the Emotional Network

In the context of the Story Molecule, the emotional network acts as the conduit between character and plot, between mode and need, between the dramatic and thematic throughlines. Dramatic energy is constantly moving from one ring to the next of the Story Molecule, in and out. Tom Schlesinger likes to say that if we could pull the emotional network out of this context like a skeleton and look at it by itself, it would appear as the "soap opera" of the story. It reveals who is sleeping with whom, who is disinheriting whom, who is jealous, who is depressed. By itself, without deeper inner character motivation and development, and without an outer plot that compresses the action into rising peaks of tension and release that demand a final resolution, the emotional network could in fact become an endless soap opera. In the more dynamic arena of feature films, however, the emotional network is charged and polarized by the conflict between protagonist and antagonist. The antagonist is willing to push the conflict to a decisive, climactic confrontation. The outer plot stakes must be both clear and concrete, and the plot conflict must have consequences for the entire emotional network. Every character must have a different point of view, a different judgment on, and a different stake in, the dramatic situation in every scene: a different *beat*. This is the essence of *character orchestration* in the emotional network.

Until a character's *dramatic position* is orchestrated, he may make a vivid impression and yet be somehow "floating." Look, for example, at the role of the nameless daughter in *The Piano*. She is neither the antagonist nor the primary relationship. At the beginning of the story, her point of view on the dramatic situations seems to be merely an appendage or extension of Ada. This is very well captured in the scene where the two ask George to take them to the beach to see the piano. George tells them no, then comes out to saddle his horse. As they watch him, mother and daughter are given identical gestures and tilts of the head. The daughter does not have a distinct dramatic beat of her own. But later, when Ada's relationship with George has negative consequences for her, the daughter's point of view becomes differentiated and distinct. Once Ada starts excluding her from her visits to George, the daughter feels betrayed and enraged. Her perspective about these visits becomes completely different from Ada's. What they mean to *her* is not love, but abandonment. The daughter, too, has something at stake. This leads to her eventual betrayal of Ada. Here is one example of how, in the context of the entire Story Molecule, the emotional network acts as a conduit between character and plot, between mode and need.

The main character provides the central vehicle for the audience's identification. This identification is the audience's primary window into the story. Now the emotional network opens out another dimension of the story, confronting the audience with opposing viewpoints, convictions, and motivations. Dynamics are created that place the audience in the middle of conflict and paradox. The conflicting voices on the screen, each with its own take on the dramatic situation, mirror the voices so often at war within us when we ourselves face conflict. The emotional network functions to externalize and reflect the attitudes, beliefs, and values of the main character as they change through the drama.

There are many additional ways of looking at character orchestration in the screenplay: physically, according to plot function, through how they serve to shade in the protagonist, in terms of how they can play in triangles in individual scenes, and so on. But in all of these cases the guiding principle is to find difference and create *contrast*. This is a basic aesthetic idea, which is the same in music. Orchestration in music creates tonal coloration, but the orchestration only works if it allows us to hear each voice or combination of voices distinctly. If you have ever heard a bad performance of a Mahler symphony, you know what a torture muddy orchestration can be. So it is with character orchestration. Thus, when approaching the task of orchestrating the characters in your emotional network, the key question to always have in mind is: what is the difference—especially of *value*—between my characters, in this scene, *right now*? All of the secondary factors of character orchestration—clothing, gesture, social class, and so on—should be seen as means to achieve this. Lajos Egri makes a strong statement that cuts to the heart of dramatic difference in character orchestration:

> Orchestration demands well-defined and uncompromising characters in opposition, moving from one pole [of emotion, conviction, or behavior] toward another through conflict.[28]

While many contemporary characters, such as Renton in *Trainspotting*, will not make the complete classical movement from pole to pole that he suggests, Egri's emphasis on opposition and difference is justified.

28. Egri, *Dramatic Writing*, p. 115.

In orchestrating the characters in the emotional network, we want to find expressions of difference that are not merely superficial, but which reflect the most significant levels of dramatic and thematic conflict the story contains. Difference can be shown physically, so that we feel the characters' different positions and perspectives even before a word is spoken in the scene. Difference also comes through in dialogue, body language, and the whole sense of style a character has or is given: the car they drive, the way they light a cigarette or handle chopsticks while eating sushi. In fact, there are so many ways to indicate difference that we can end up creating difference for its own sake rather than for the sake of the drama. Many independent movies that try to stand out because of their "quirky" characters get in trouble here. The quirkiness can create a level of difference that is specious and trivial, and which distracts the audience from dramatically significant difference. It is important not to confuse secondary characteristics with the primary aim. Variations of costume and speech are dramatically irrelevant unless they reveal the characters' modes—their attitudes, perspectives, and values—in *contrast* to those of the main character.

It is true that, especially in comedies, some secondary characters may appear to be in the script primarily to create personality or style contrast with the main character. One such example is the comical sidekick, whose main function is to make the hero look nobler by contrast. Farces often take this further, creating contrasting but parallel high-comedy/low-comedy storylines. The lead characters play the high-comedy romantic line while the secondary characters play exactly parallel scenes for low comedy or slapstick. An excellent example of this is found in the parallel Tony Curtis/Marilyn Monroe and Jack Lemmon/Joey Brown romances in *Some Like It Hot*. Loretta's father and Mona play the parallel low-comedy line in *Moonstruck*. The technique goes back at least as far as the commedia dell'arte. Thus what may begin as a simple comic device can also take on major thematic importance.

The principle of contrast really applies to all of the relationships in the story. We build it into the Story Molecule early in the story development process. The contrast may not become apparent until the middle of the second act, as characters are forced to take sides in the conflict. But only when we arrive at the cutting edge of difference between two characters does their dramatic potential come to life.

The Story Molecule suggests some of the ways that the emotional network externalizes the conflict of values within the main character by engaging the main character in conflict, conflict which reflects aspects of that character and of the theme. The emotional network also tells us how thick the texture of the character orchestration is. We return to John Sayles's technique of placing his main character in the middle of a page surrounded by the other characters and drawing lines of emotional connection between them. Emotional networks with many lines of connection will tend to be character-driven movies, relationship movies, or ensemble movies. The way a story like *Do the Right Thing* must be told is determined to a large extent by the number of very rich characters. Though there are many forces in opposition to each other, we are ultimately looking more at the journey of this neighborhood than at the journey of any one individual. The love story in *Four Weddings* takes on a different feeling by being placed in a milieu of friendships that constitute a loose extended family, rather than being placed in a rarified romantic atmosphere of two lovers in their own world. *The Commitments* gives us the ensemble of the band very deeply embedded in their working-class neighborhood. *Short Cuts* shows an "ensemble of ensembles" that is so broad it ultimately seems to encompass the entire society. These are examples of very dense emotional networks.

On the other hand, sparse emotional networks with few lines of connection yield movies with a different texture, probably more linear and plot-driven, or more intimate and possibly in first-person POV. These movies start by delimiting in development the scope of the world we will look at. Though *The Crying Game* deals with the Irish Republican Army and could be called a political thriller, our view is basically limited to five characters. This makes sense for the dramatic situation, because the terrorists are members of an isolated cell on a mission. We would expect Dil to have more friends and social contacts, but these are deliberately kept out of the story. A line is drawn around the dramatic core. The thriller *Seven* effectively limits its dramatic world to four characters, as does *Terminator 2*, even though there the entire human race is at stake.

To be well integrated into the story, according to Sayles, each character should have at least two lines of connection to other characters. It is then possible to write on the lines of connection what the relationship is, and to specify whether it is the antagonist who carries the plot, the primary relationship who acts as the vehicle for the protagonist's character transformation, a secondary character, or a functional/incidental character. Sayles emphasizes that if there is only one line of connection to a character, there had better be a good reason for it.[29] For example, it might be the very point of the character that they are socially isolated, "hanging on by their fingernails." *Breaking the Waves*, by Lars von Trier, socially isolates the main character in this way. The strategy builds up a sense of doom and tragedy around the heroine. Otherwise, a character who has only one strong line of connection to the story, or a few weak lines, tends to become incidental by their very nature: they have few ways of impacting the rest of the emotional network.

If a sketch of the character web reveals a character who is disconnected, a decision can be made. Either give that character more, and more juicy, connections to other characters, or eliminate that character altogether and consolidate the function carried by that character into someone who is more integrated in the emotional network.

29. Sayles, John, "Putting People Together," interview with Thomas Schlesinger in *Film Quarterly* (1980): p. 5.

Internal Software: Character Webs

Practice making character webs from a variety of sources. Start with some simpler webs such as the ones in *The Full Monty* or *American Beauty*. Move on to some more extended webs: *Shakespeare in Love*, *Hannah and Her Sisters*, or *Monsoon Wedding*. Notice that now it becomes much more important to label all of the connections. Where are the highest stakes in these extended networks?

For a challenge, try this with one season of the TV series *24*. In such an action series, key characters may be kept offscreen for several episodes at a time. But they are still active behind the scenes; their impact on the world of the story is not a factor of their screen time. Of course, this is all planned as the season is laid out in development.

Movies like *Babel* and *Syriana*, with parallel plot strands happening simultaneously in different continents, involving characters who never meet, present something special. The connections may be two or three degrees removed. In *Babel*, how is the Japanese girl connected to the Mexican housemaid?

6

Character Webs and Story Worlds

In animals the pattern of eye contact often establishes dominance. A stare is often interpreted as an aggressive act—hence the dangers of looking at gorillas through binoculars. Visitors to zoos feel dominant when they can outstare animals. I suggest you try the opposite with zoo animals: break eye contact and then glance back for a moment. Polar bears may suddenly see you as "food." Owls cheer up perceptibly.

—*Keith Johnstone*

Dramatic Unity and Dramatic Stakes

WHY IS IT IMPORTANT TO HAVE YOUR CHARACTERS embedded in the matrix of the emotional network? The first reason is that it is necessary to maintain Aristotle's dramatic unity (of time, place, and action) to make us feel that this is one dramatic world. Second, relationships full of emotional consequence do more to raise the dramatic stakes.

Say you run a small company, and you discover that your accountant is really not keeping up with things. After a period of time and many discussions, you come to the conclusion that you have to fire the accountant and get someone else. Try to feel this situation. How much charge does it have? Put this simply, the emotional charge may not be so great. It is merely an objective, functional business decision. But now, say the accountant is your father-in-law. . . . How does that change the feeling-tone of the situation? What is at stake now? Who else is going to get involved? What might happen at your breakfast table? What might happen in your bedroom? This is a situation with a much higher charge. Not only are the stakes in this particular relationship raised, but the stakes are raised in other relationships as well. When conflict occurs in a relationship that is deeply embedded in the matrix of the emotional network, it impacts the entire network.

Deeply implicated relationships are channels into the mythic dimension. Our most important relationships are those where we have put the most psychic energy, the most projection. These relationships carry our transferences of the emotional patterns of our childhood. These are the people who can wound us the most deeply because they are part of the very fabric of who we are. Through them we are re-wounded: patterns of wounding from our past are dragged into the present. Disappointments and betrayals are magnified by this psychic background of transference and are more likely to send us into liminal realms of regression, depression, and anxiety, shifting tectonics down in the soul. Our status quo becomes threatened, and our whole messy Need versus Mode conflict may rise to the surface. When the protagonist is re-wounded by such a relationship, the audience is engaged on a deep level of feeling and empathic identification. Paul Schaeffer, in *Witness*, is John Book's personal mentor and father figure as well as being the police chief. Book has made a father-transference onto Paul, as we can see from Book's behavior toward him. Because of his need to impress Paul, Book is not careful and puts himself in jeopardy. The special nature of that relationship has implications that follow through all the way to the climax of the movie. Ronnie Camerreri is not only Loretta's lover, but also her future brother-in-law. Jack Walsh is put in the dramatic double bind that he must/must not deliver the Duke to L.A. because of Jimmy Serrano. The Duke is not just a job, but becomes a friend, while Jimmy Serrano is not just a Mafia boss, but the person who ruined Jack's life in the backstory. High-stakes relationships like these tend to raise double-bind situations with many dramatic obstacles for the hero. We need such double binds in order to bring the hero to the "grow or die" point at the end of Act II, as we shall explore in the chapters on Aristotle's Plot Curve. Sometimes in movie stories these high-stakes relationships have already been established by the backstory; sometimes, as is typical in love stories, they are new relationships that are set up in the first act.

If we say a story world has a "tight" character web, it means that most of the relationships we shall see on the screen are deeply implicated, deeply embedded in an emotional nexus. All other characters and relationships are streamlined or eliminated. The importance of secondary characters beyond the core group is much reduced. If the characters in the core group are well orchestrated, there will be a strong and intimate emotional subtext running through every scene. This is a strategy one may choose and points to a storytelling decision to be made early in the development process. A tight character web is not the only possibility, however. Some movies, by the very nature of the stories they tell, require a broader stage, with more secondary and incidental characters. Epics and action dramas may not generate the same intensely intimate subtext; that is not their strategy. These stories will generate stakes for the audience by showing us the escalating consequences of the plot conflict, making us anticipate what will come next. Farce comedies like *Monsoon Wedding* utilize many colorful secondary characters to keep the action bubbling. The secondary characters in this movie are significant; there is hardly a clear demarcation between them and the primary core of characters. Dubey's helpers often comment on his romantic foibles, another device of farce. Altogether, *Monsoon Wedding* gives us a fuller community, much as John Sayles described his approach to the character web.

American Beauty is an example of a tight character web. You will notice that the world of the story is already delimited in Lester's opening voice-over: this is *his* town, *his* street, *his* life. And although Lester does seem fully alive as a character, we are only involved in selected aspects of his life. What we come to know about Lester is very tightly clustered around his need/mode tension: his attitude about getting his youthful spirit back again and his goal of attracting Angela. Lester's first job is dispensed with in two brief sequences; only Brad, the efficiency expert, is at all individualized. Although Lester says the Pontiac Firebird is the car he always wanted, we do not see him buy it. The story is kept to essentials, and so is the character web. *American Beauty* is told with seven characters: Lester, Caroline, Janie, Ricky, Angela, Col. Fitts, and Buddy Kane. Each one of these has at least two deeply implicated relationships that at one time or another generate hot conflict that is placed center stage. The exception is Buddy Kane, who is left monotone, a comic type. Buddy Kane, along with Ricky's mother, are the secondary characters in the story. All other characters are strictly incidental.

Sketching out the emotional network for your story is a form of visual thinking, or "clustering." It is a time to give your right brain a chance to open up your imagination about the story. There are universal principles to dramatic development, but individual writers start from different places because of their individual creative temperaments. Some writers, like John Sayles, begin by sketching out the emotional network until they feel they know all the characters, and then develop the story from there, out of the dramatic potential inherent in those characters. What is your way of exploring the emotional network? Your inclination might be to start biographically with the main character. Who already exists in her emotional network before the plot begins? Who carries the vestiges of her backstory wound? Who is she invested in trying to control?

You may prefer to sketch in the emotional network chronologically from the protagonist's point of view: whom does she meet first as the movie begins, and how do the relationships build up as the story goes along? Or it may make the most sense for you to start with the main character, the antagonist, and the primary relationship, and to build the character web outward from there, keeping the main character as the pivot between the two worlds. Each story is unique and makes its own demands. Notice, for example, how in *Four Weddings*, an ensemble movie with no outer plot antagonist as such, the screenwriter still must draw a character out of the social group to act as a situational antagonist at the comic climax. Duckface, as a character, does not have our sympathies, so she is not a strong or effective antagonist. But without her presence, there could have been no climax. This was a way of giving more dramatic shape to the story, as well as raising the stakes for Charles.

The Lady and the Tiger

We have said that in most cases there is only enough screen time to fully develop two major relationships, that is, to build complete relationship arcs for them. One of these, the antagonist, carries the outer plot conflict of the story. The protagonist's plot goal (also called the "desire line") and main throughline motive are set up in relation to this character, and the plot climax involves the resolution of this relationship. The second major relationship, the *primary relationship*, is the one that most impacts the hero's inner life and where the inner changes in the main character are manifested. With the core triangle of hero, primary relationship, and antagonist, there enters a powerful constellation of archetypal elements. The two forces confronting the hero could be variously called Love and Death (or Beauty and Death), desire and fear, being and nonbeing, the shadow and the anima (or animus). These are *soul* elements, and they subliminally speak the language of dreams to the viewer, even when the movie is in a realistic idiom.

In "The Lady or the Tiger?," a well-known short story by Frank Stockton, a barbarous king administers justice by means of a trial. The accused must choose between two doors. Behind one is a beautiful maiden who will marry him; behind the other, a ravening tiger who will eat him. To choose is to choose one's fate, love or death. But, behind the scenes, the lady and the tiger, via the king, are in a hidden contact with one another. Love and death are part of the same game of life. They are present in every drama.

As archetypal figures, Love and Death push the "bottom" of the story out of the range of the ego and its uses, into the trans-ego, the mythic dimension of the psyche. A drama cannot be reduced to a pragmatic formula to improve your self esteem or your love life. Why not? This is largely because these two figures, who manifest the energies of love and death, cannot be reduced to mere human beings with human motives. There remains something elusive attached to them—call it an aura, allure, fascination, or awe. Existentially, we are always facing those two perilous doors.

Every love interest partakes of this larger, semisubliminal archetypal background. She is not just a beautiful woman as a human individual; she is also Beauty. Of course, the connection to the archetype in the movies is less direct than it is in fairy tales. The photographic movie image contains so much specific detail, while fairy tale descriptions are kept deliberately nonspecific. In fairy tales, she is simply "Beauty," "the girl more beautiful than the sun," and so on. A deep level of the listener's imagination fills in and completes the nonspecific image. Classic Hollywood movies worked very hard to endow the first onscreen entrance of the love interest with an electrifying allure and charisma. At that moment, she is meant to be the most beautiful girl in the world for every man in the theater. While the classic glamour techniques of old Hollywood may belong to another time, there are a number of actresses who project the nonspecific Beauty archetype along with—or even beyond—the personality of the character they are portraying. Sandra Bullock, Gwyneth Paltrow, Julia Roberts, and Gong Li come to mind. A writer or production team may choose to diminish, deconstruct, or satirize the Beauty archetype, but a writer cannot afford to be ignorant of its power.

Dramatically, we record the power of the primary relationship character's allure through her impact on the main character. First, there is her power to *call* the main character, to make him stop in his tracks and hold his breath, to destroy his status quo and peace of mind. In fairy tales, it is not uncommon for the hero to fall into a coma "as though dead" at the first sight of the Beauty. Folklorist Max Lüthi refers to this as Beauty's "shock-effect." And here we also get a first hint of the Night World connection between Beauty and Death. The shock of Beauty kills life-as-normal. There is something more than human about Beauty. She touches the absolute. She is *absolutely* beautiful. And so there is inevitably something uncanny and dangerous about her as well. Most often in fairy tales, the Beauty is the daughter of a monster, is secretly married to a monster, or is bewitched. The man who falls for her must pass through mortal danger, soul danger, to win her. This is all part of the archetypal background that accompanies the primary relationship played as love interest.

Beyond Beauty's ability to call, shock, and take the main character beyond himself is her power to become the *animatrice* of his inner life. At her best, she animates and brings to life a drive for wholeness—for recognition and integration of the split-off unconscious need. Wholeness becomes pictured as union with herself. It is not enough for this character to be iconically beautiful. What counts, what makes the character dramatically viable, are two factors. First is how we see the hero project paradoxical qualities of his Night World onto her: danger and fascination, trust and doubt. She generates an emotional riptide that carries him out into deep water. This makes the hero vulnerable, and contributes to both the breakdown of the mode and the breakthrough of the need. Second, this all functions to integrate the three levels of the Story Molecule *only if* the primary relationship character embodies the value counter to the hero's mode value. There are an infinite number of ways of playing this out, as many as there are love stories. The anima figure may *engage* with the main character and become humanized through contact, or she may remain iconic and idealized. (This will also be true with same-sex love.) But we can expect some degree of idealizing projection to remain attached to the Beauty. The strength of the underlying archetypal pattern is so great that usually both the main character and the audience forget to do a reality check. This is Beauty's role as creator of illusions.

The immediate impact of a masculine Beauty can be quite similar for a female protagonist, though the dynamics of the animus differ from those of the anima. There are many tales of the masculine Beauty around the world, but normally the undercurrent of danger is stronger. The shock-effect of Ronnie Camerreri on Loretta is a movie example that attempts self-consciously to evoke the ambiance of fairy tale. But while he is broadly contrived and played for laughs, Ronnie is more dramatically specific than simply being a beautiful hunk. He embodies Loretta's unconscious need and becomes the animator of her inner life. George, the neighbor in *The Piano*, does not immediately appear to Ada as a Beauty. To her, he is little more than a savage who cannot read. He becomes a threatening figure when he buys the piano and then offers Ada a manipulative deal to buy it back. Yet because George's character is very well orchestrated to embody the earthy groundedness that Ada needs to integrate into her life, we feel another dimension to him, even while it is still in the subtext. The relationship between Ada and George will be charted in detail in Chapter Eleven.

Male actors who project the Beauty-animus, like their female counterparts, often have trouble with finely shaded character roles because they tend to overwhelm the part with their allure and charisma. They cannot stop being beautiful. This can work to their advantage, however, in genre roles that are designed to project an iconic quality. Errol Flynn and Steve McQueen projected this quality, as do George Clooney, Brad Pitt, Sean Penn, and Hugh Grant in their own ways. One look at how carefully Nicholas Cage's first appearance in *Moonstruck* is orchestrated, how he is surrounded by symbolic objects and spaces that magnify the iconic aura, will quickly make the basic point. While the screenwriter is not going to venture into set design and does not know who will be cast in the role, she *can* work with the awareness that there is both a foreground personality and a background archetype, the alluring Beauty, to the primary relationship character. There is a creative tension we have to seek and maintain between building an iconic aura and establishing a believable character.

"Love interest" is of course not the only form the primary relationship can take. There are many kinds of love, after all. So there are buddies, mentors, and guides of both genders. The point, again, is not the label on the character but the character's impact on the hero. As with every relationship in the emotional network, we want to ask what the *difference* is between this character and the main character. What is the specific way this person animates the inner life of the hero? How is this impact tied to the hero's need/mode split? How does she evoke or force a revision of values in the hero? What relationship grows out of this, and what is its consequence? The first time Lester meets Ricky Fitts, for example, the issue of freedom, and the meaning of freedom, comes up. Their attitudes about freedom are different, just as their attitudes about marijuana are different. Lester becomes very attached to marijuana. Ricky sells it in order to save for the day he will leave his family, but he is not attached to the drug. The transactions, the sharing, that make Ricky into a guide for Lester have many layers. Such other primary relationship figures partake of other archetypal backgrounds, archetypes of the Guide, the Twin, the Doppelgänger, the Totem Animal or Helping Animal (such as R2D2 in *Star Wars*), and so on. These archetypes also deserve the screenwriter's consideration so that she can understand who this character is (existential foreground and mythic background), not only for the hero, but for the audience as well.

The antagonist also comes with these layers of a foreground personality and a background archetype. The antagonist appears as an embodiment or condensation of the Night World of the story: the unknown or unacknowledged, the horrible or frightening. Depending on how dark the Night World of the story is, and how far away it is, in moral terms, from the story's Day World, the antagonist may also appear as an embodiment of evil. A Night World is not *in itself* evil. It is a world of shadow. As we discussed in the last chapter, the Night World of a movie is primarily a projection of the unlived life of the main character. The degree to which the Night World is identified with evil is (or should be) a deliberate story development decision based on the idiom and genre of the story, the market, and the convictions of the creative team. There is of course a wide range of antagonistic opposition possible. The antagonist may be a simple opponent or competitor who is also fully human and whose motives we understand and may even empathize with. Or she may be nonhuman: a devil or someone possessed by absolute evil. These are degrees of shadow. Yet even when the shadow element is mild—as in an arch-competitor, such as the captain of the French frigate *Acheron* in *Master and Commander*, or the two parents battling for child custody in *Kramer vs. Kramer*—we must always record the *difference* between the antagonist and protagonist. What is it? It is always a difference of values. It is a moral difference. Naturally we want the audience to know what makes the hero the hero, but exaggerating the moral difference for the sake of heightening the drama does risk unfairly demonizing not just the antagonist, but an entire people, group, nation, or religion.

Let us recall from the Need versus Mode model that the value the hero is acting on for most of the story is a value growing out of that character's mode, not out of her wholeness. In character-driven movies we will see that mode break down. Either the main character will break through to a new attitude that is more whole, or he will have a tragic destiny. In action and thriller genres, where character must serve the plot, the hero may stand in for the society's dominant values and thus be more of an icon than a human individual. In that case the hero's inner conflict will not be central to the resolution of the outer plot. The hero's journey then is in the outer plot dimension—and this also impacts how the antagonist must be played. Hero and antagonist mirror each other, even though they may not play in many scenes together. They must have an equal strength of will. They are equal halves of a dialectic. We intuitively perceive them as balanced, if not secretly linked, because they are constantly being compared with one another.

Take the captain of the *Acheron*. What salient difference is established between him and Captain Jack Aubrey? Jack is frank and bluff, and his strategy tends to be likewise. He states his preference to "go straight at 'em" when he encounters the enemy. He believes in playing fair. At the beginning of *Master and Commander*, Aubrey lacks the wiles of his adversary and is repeatedly caught off guard. Added to the wiliness of the Acheron's tactics is the secret technical edge the French warship has. This raises the stakes for Aubrey, because he literally cannot get his *Surprise* close enough for a fair fight on his terms. Aubrey must change the way he sees things, but he cannot accomplish this change on his own. Only by putting friendship above ambition and returning to the Galapagos so that Stephen can collect wildlife samples does Aubrey discover the trick that will win the climactic battle. Finally he is able to outmatch the captain of the *Acheron* in wiles. Aubrey adapts wiliness because he must, while maintaining his core virtues of frankness and fairness. The French captain is sneaky to the end, an arch-competitor, but is not vilified or demonized.

An old proverb says that if there were no dragon to fight, the hero would be unnecessary. Beyond this, the limits of the antagonist's characterization automatically place limits on the protagonist as well. This may sound surprising, but it is an important consideration when orchestrating characters. A flat, one-dimensional antagonist will automatically flatten the hero into a cartoon, even if this is not what the screenwriter intended. Here we enter into the deeper dimension of stories revealed by the Story Molecule.

The main character's plot goal has an underlying flaw because it grows out of a flawed mode, an outgrown manner of looking at the self, others, and the world. There is something the character needs to learn. The Need versus Mode model suggests that what the character needs to learn is carried by the primary relationship. What, then, is the antagonist's inner connection to the hero, beyond the simple necessities of the plot? This can be described in two ways, using two metaphors that highlight related aspects. First, we could say that the antagonist is, or carries, a nightmare version of the hero's flaw. In character-driven stories, this flaw is specifically the shadow side of the main character's mode. Every mode value—whether it is control, authority, generosity, or sincerity—has a shadow side that comes out the more the mode is one-sided.

That part, usually the egoistic or instinctual aspect of control, authority, generosity, or sincerity, etc., is unconscious and unacknowledged, so it is down in the Night World along with the unconscious universal need. Loretta would never imagine herself as rigid, controlling, and humorless. She would have a hard time seeing or admitting to that side of herself. It is the antagonist who in effect acts this out. It is Ronnie, appearing in Act I as a threshold guardian, who comes off as rigidly self-pitying, controlling, and humorless when Loretta goes to see him. He wallows in his backstory wound in such an exaggerated way that we laugh. But notice that it is an exaggeration of Loretta's own tendency to control. The antagonist's action is a nightmare version of the flaw. In this case, we say the antagonist is who the hero could become if they don't wake up and change. The antagonist is a dark mirror of the hero.

In Act I of *Witness*, we see that John Book himself is mildly infected with the abuse of power. Grabbing a black man out of a bar seemingly at random and smashing him violently against the squad car is an abuse. If we could take Book aside and question him about it, he would certainly defend his action as justified under the circumstances. After all, a fellow officer has been murdered. This is the shadow side of Book's laudable zeal for justice. Paul Schaeffer presents the nightmare version of the abuse of power, ready to murder even a child to retain his position. In Act I of *Sea of Love*, we see the Al Pacino character possessively telephone his ex-wife in the middle of the night. The antagonist of the movie is a possessively jealous husband pushed into a nightmare, murdering men he thinks have had sex with his ex-wife. Clearly, we are not able to set up this correspondence as screenwriters unless we really nail the main character's mode—including its shadow side—in Act I.

In thrillers, the antagonist carries the hero's secret fear or is connected to the hero's blind spot. This is the second metaphor that is useful in orchestrating the antagonist. The hero must confront the blind spot in order to resolve the plot. There is a direct cause-and-effect relationship here. Buffalo Bill, in *Silence of the Lambs*, is not a nightmare version of who Starling could become. As is typical in thrillers and other action genres, Starling does not have to change her entire mode; she has to overcome an old fear in order to catch the psychopath. Buffalo Bill carries a nightmare version of Starling's childhood trauma. He forces her to face her hidden dread. Unlike a character-driven movie, in *Silence of the Lambs* the emphasis is not on whether the hero will reintegrate a split-off part of herself and become qualitatively more whole. The emphasis is on whether she will get Buffalo Bill and save the girl. Starling's vulnerability must serve the plot. She will overcome the fear that has limited her up to now by facing the dark slaughter pen inside Buffalo Bill's house. Her success will allow her to become the agent she wants to be.

We say that the antagonist holds up a dark mirror to the hero. This is already suggested when we say that the antagonist acts out the nightmare version of the flawed mode, who the hero could become if he doesn't wake up. But the "dark mirror" metaphor highlights the ways the main character may see himself reflected in his antagonist and be confronted with that reflection. How can you kill the monster when you are forced to realize that this monster is your own unlived and secretly longed-for life? The antagonist may also carry something the hero needs to incorporate into himself: energy, vitality, power, control, vision, daring, fearlessness, deception, eros, divinity. The hero may have to assimilate some of the antagonist's power without "falling into the shadow" if he is going to meet the antagonist's challenge. Jack Aubrey must abandon Admiral Nelson's "straight at 'em" mode and become more like the antagonist. When this situation pertains—that the antagonist has qualities the hero needs in order to succeed—then the conflict between them often becomes tinged with a powerful erotic subtext. From the midpoint to the climax of *Seven*, there is a growing sense of a bond that can only be called erotic which develops between Mills and John Doe. There is a secret covenant between them that leads to a tryst, and finally to a Romantic "union in death." This contributes to the peculiar dark tone with which the movie ends.

The dark mirror, as an element of the Story Molecule, can be handled in many ways and degrees. The audience may see the mirror while the hero does not, or hero and audience may see the reflection together. This revelation may carry a strong emotional charge like pity or compassion, or it may not. Even the monsters in the *Aliens* series or *Independence Day* are only trying to survive via the best strategies they can manage, as are the astronauts and the earthlings in those movies. Of course the monsters rarely elicit our compassion. But where there is in fact a feeling-toned revelation of the antagonist as dark mirror, this is a major moment in a story. It may foreshadow the outcome of the plot. It may lead to the main character breaking through to a new understanding of herself. Or it may come as an unmasking of the antagonist at the climax. It will be built into one of the major plot events—the Core Crisis, the catastrophe, or the climax—often as the climactic point of the sequence, or Story Step, where it appears. Consider how carefully the figure of Darth Vader was developed as a dark mirror through the three episodes of *Star Wars* in order to set up his dramatic unmasking and re-conversion to the light side of the Force at the end.

So, as a result of the catastrophe in *Apocalypse Now*, Captain Willard is pushed beyond himself and must in a sense *become* Col. Kurtz in order to kill him. He must absorb the primitive shadow-spirit that caught Col. Kurtz without "falling into the shadow" himself. The killing is by this point no longer a strategic military order but a ritual sacrifice, a sacrifice to which the victim himself has assented. At the climax of *Seven*, Detective Mills is himself swallowed by his dark mirror when he shoots John Doe in a rage of retribution. And at the midpoint of *The Talented Mr. Ripley*, Tom Ripley murders the friend and nemesis whom he himself longs to be. In that act, Ripley murders Ripley. Ripley, as an integrated consciousness, is no longer. The alter ego becomes dominant. Ripley has been drawn into the mirror. This represents a kind of tragic soul death, as his opening and closing voice-over also tells us.

We think of this dark mirror aspect of the antagonist in relation to *self-limiting* beliefs. The hero's self-limiting beliefs shape the character's perceived reality in ways that keep her from thriving, from reaching her goals or being completely alive. We can recognize our own self-limiting beliefs in the critical self-talk of our inner threshold guardians and saboteurs, with such statements as:

- "There's not enough [jobs, land, money, food, love, oxygen] to go around."
- "There're those that take, and those that get took."
- "I'd rather be the hammer than the anvil!"
- "We're just dogs, scrappin' in a bone yard."
- "You're nothing special."
- "You're so special that no one can understand you!"
- "Winning isn't everything, it's the *only* thing."

We know these voices come out when we are under stress. Beliefs of this kind underlie the flaw in the main character's mode and drive him into conflict.

The inner connection we want to bring out when working with the Story Molecule is that the antagonist is acting out of his own version of the same self-limiting beliefs. Both characters are essentially unfree. And in this relationship of opposition the hero's reactions are being conditioned, from the crisis that ends Act I all the way through Act II, by the actions of the antagonist. On the surface level of the plot these two are against each other. But on a deeper level, they are performing a duet to the tune of their self-limiting beliefs. The antagonist is so locked in to the melody that he cannot escape from it, but the hero still has a chance to change. The change, which is the Initiation via the Hero's Journey, is specifically for the hero to realize that she is *not* identical with her mode, that she is *not* a reflection of those around her, is *not* bound by what happened to her in the past, is *not* constrained to believe what everyone else believes, and is *not* who she thought she was. When that moment of change comes, the hero breaks the mirror that holds her in conflict with the antagonist. At the climax she is able to be in the present, unconditioned by the past, and thus can find a new way out of conflict and toward resolution. As a dark mirror, the antagonist has been the secret partner who has made it possible for her to make this realization.

In order to bring the story powerfully together as one dramatic whole, it is important to go a step further with the primary relationship and the antagonist. We have to find the hidden line of connection between these two characters, between the character who leads the inner transformation and the character who drives the plot conflict—the lady and the tiger. This link closes and concentrates the energy. A triangle is formed. Love triangles are the obvious example, but we are looking at something even more fundamental. The triangle is an archetypal figure. In Freudian psychological terms, every such triangle re-constellates the Oedipal triangle of mother, child, and father. One might also see in the triangle the archetypal constellation of ego, anima, and shadow. This triangle brings a powerful background of subconscious, subtextual energy to the story.

But a screenplay is more than this dream dimension. The specific qualities of the lines of connection among these core characters are very important. They will shape the actual story. The line of connection between Paul Schaeffer and Rachel Lapp is strong: Paul and his cohorts need to find Rachel and eliminate Samuel, the witness. Paul would kill Rachel; Book would protect her. This is the throughline plot conflict of *Witness*. By contrast, in *The Fugitive* there is a different sort of triangle. First of all, there is no anima figure, and so there is an absence of feminine energy in the story; the feminine has been "killed" as the story begins. This is a masculine dramatic triangle. And it is an open triangle: there is no direct connection between Detective Gerrard and the one-armed man or the primary antagonist. Only at the end of Act II will the one-armed man become real for Gerrard. As a result, all of the story energy has to pass through the conduit of Richard Kimbell, which puts a special focus on this character. And yet a different constellation, in a more enmeshed set of relationships, is represented by Tom Ripley, Dickie, and Marge. As Tom murders his love object at the Core Crisis of the story, he becomes an antihero. He keeps the love relationship going by *becoming* Dickie, in a schizoid way. Marge, the moral center of the story who might have been a guide for Tom, is ultimately the antagonist, the one who senses the truth about the murders. But the relationship between Dickie and Marge is equally important. They become for Tom a set of idealized parents from whom he must win approval and acceptance. Tom's fundamental sense of insufficiency drives him to "act out" for these others on whom he is dependent, even to the point of violence. In each of these film examples, the emotional network triangle gives us the essential character/plot/theme dynamics in a visual shorthand.

Background archetypes, basic patterns, will be constellated by this core triangle. They may become visible to our intuition in the process of laying out the Story Molecule, if we open ourselves up to the right-brain process.

The Emotional Network as the Barometer of Change

Each of the three central characters in the drama has his or her own personal character web or emotional network of friends and relations. These secondary characters can be laid out on the larger character web. We have seen in the character web of *Witness* how both Book and Paul have their own cluster of relationships. What happens to a central character in effect happens to that character's entire emotional network. It is not only characters who collide in conflict; *entire emotional networks collide.* The dramatic collision starts change moving throughout the whole world of the story, destroying some relationships and building new ones. Book is not shot by the primary antagonist, Paul, but by McFee, who is part of Paul's character web. Book is not the only one threatened; his entire emotional network, including Rachel and Samuel, is threatened. It is in fact this threat which catalyzes the bond between Book and Rachel. It draws the three levels of the story together. The character arcs of Rachel and Samuel are now wrapping around that of John Book. The cluster of John/Rachel/Samuel becomes a sort of collective protagonist, because their destinies are so intertwined. When we look at the values the protagonistic cluster represents, we see what values the film is upholding: innocence, family/community, feeling bonds, duty, compassion, and sacrifice. Looking at the antagonistic cluster, we might not see Paul himself as a cold-blooded killer, but we have seen that McFee and Fergie are. Together they dimensionalize the evil that Book faces: powerful position, cunning, brutality, betrayal disguised as friendliness, depersonalization—in short, ruthless egocentrism. Together they create an embodiment, like a three-headed monster, of the powers and the emotional tone of this movie's Night World.

One of our objectives as screenwriters in working the secondary characters into the emotional network is to use them to dramatically and thematically "shade in" what we represent through the central characters. The hero's emotional network is a barometer of his inner change. Barometers measure atmospheric pressure, and by looking at the "atmospheric pressure" in the emotional network, we can see the hero's process of breakdown and breakthrough reflected there, most especially in the primary relationship. We can chart the changes in pressure starting with the Catalyst Story Step or sequence (more on this in Chapter Eleven), where the separate emotional networks of protagonist and antagonist touch each other for the first time and begin to overlap. These two sides of the story world whose pivot is the main character begin to have consequences for each other and to become dramatically necessary to each other. At the crisis, the threshold crossing at the end of Act I, the emotional networks of the protagonist and the antagonist become locked together in conflict. They will not be disentangled again until the climax. The fact that two clusters are colliding, rather than merely protagonist and antagonist as two individuals, gives the conflict scope and dimension as we go into Act II.

Relationships go on a journey as well. They go through a complete arc of development. They are transformed by crisis. This is especially true of the central "transformational" relationship—Book and Rachel, Jack Walsh and the Duke, Ada and George, C. C. Baxter and Miss Kubelik (in *The Apartment*). Because this primary relationship touches the main character's unconscious need, it is the most accurate barometer of his breakdown and breakthrough, a window into his soul. We chart the shape of that journey as the *relationship arc*. The primary relationship will have its own catalyst, crisis, catastrophe, and climax, which will be causally connected to the major outer plot points and intertwined with the outer plot consequences. As we will see in the context of Aristotle's Plot Curve, the outer plot crisis/threshold crossing also acts as the catalyst of the primary relationship. The relationship suddenly becomes necessary rather than incidental. As Rachel sits beside Book's bed through the night, wondering if he will die, she realizes she loves him. When the Duke turns the tables on Jack aboard the airplane, we see that we are in for a duel of wits and wills. George buys the piano from Stewart, who then suggests that Ada give him lessons, thus drawing Ada against her will into dangerous emotional territory. The relationship arc is intersecting with the outer Plot Curve, tying all three rings of the Story Molecule together. The main character is pulled out of control, deeper into the story. This is the inner dimension that makes the Threshold Crisis not only a plot turn, but a major shift in the drama.

The relationship arc of the primary relationship, now catalyzed, also has its own emotional threshold crossing. This is a key moment in constructing a screenplay. The two characters in the primary relationship somehow transcend their ego-boundaries and cross an emotional threshold of vulnerability to a kind of sharing which has many names: true intimacy, falling in love, empathy, friendship. This means that at a certain point the two characters must go beyond their plot functions and become "real" to each other—even though this character movement beyond the plot dimension is paradoxically crucial to the outcome of the plot. These moments are found at the Core Crisis Story Step. At this Core Crisis/midpoint, Book and Rachel cross the threshold in their relationship when they dance together in the barn. Now they have exposed their feelings to each other, and there will be consequences. They cannot go back to being who they were before. Jack Walsh is compelled to expose to the Duke the old wound of his failed marriage when he must go to borrow money from his ex-wife. During the scene, the Duke's presence does take on the quality of a guardian angel. Afterward, as the two take to the road again, a bond of friendship begins grudgingly to grow between them. This will have consequences for Jack, and ultimately place him in a double bind that will force a choice of values. At the core crisis of *The Piano*, Ada, for the first time of her own free will, goes to George and gives herself to him, tying fast the knot of the fateful erotic triangle and of her own internal conflict.

In each of these films, the Core Crisis deepens the feeling-tone and raises the dramatic stakes to forge the protagonist's *inner being* and *outer goal* into one true dramatic unity. Heart and soul, everything is now at stake. During story development, a plot-oriented approach of "Let's work out the plot first and *then* go back and shade in the characters" can easily miss this moment. In itself this emotional threshold crossing in the primary relationship is often a "nonplot" moment—Jack's visit to his ex-wife comes in the falling action of a big shoot-up scene—yet it is crucial to the plot. These are scenes where we may go into "real time," or where time may seem to stand still. If we are thinking of plot as a series of cause-and-effect events, this character threshold is often an irrational, transcendental scene, catalyzed by the plot events but ultimately caused by the inner necessity of the characters. This may partly explain why these Core Crisis scenes are often among the most memorable scenes in movies.

Plot and character are co-evolving through development, and the relationships of the emotional network are the conduits between the two. The primary relationship must not only have consequences for the outer plot, it must also be our window into the soul of the hero. When working out this relationship, we often ask questions like "Will these two fall in love/become friends?" even though we already know the answer is yes. Perhaps a more revealing question would be: "What does each character in the relationship stand for in the soul of the other? What part of their inner necessity do they see mirrored in the face of the other?"

How we handle this arc of the primary relationship goes far to determining whether plot or character will be the focus of the audience's attention. The closer it is linked to plot events, as with the buddy detectives in a thriller, the more plot is emphasized. The more that relationship leads away from plot into other dramatic territory, the more character is emphasized. It is primarily through building this relationship arc that we adjust the balance between plot and character throughout the story.

Emotional Network: Orchestrating Subplots

The Story Molecule is moving through time. The three substories that express the concentric rings of the Story Molecule can thus be visualized as three strands of a rope. They wrap around each other so that when one "plot strand" is in the foreground, the other two are in the background. As the story rotates the emotional network into the foreground at the beginning of Act II, the outer plot strand moves into the background. The dramatic questions addressed to each substory of the Story Molecule are sometimes in the text of the drama (overt subject matter), sometimes in the subtext. Yet even when a strand of the Story Molecule is in the background—in the subtext—the dramatic tension is continually rising. Our examination of Act II will show in detail how this works. The onscreen action of the present scene, a love scene for example, touches both the text and the subtext. The present action has both onscreen and offscreen consequences. In a later scene we must pick up those offscreen consequences, and the later action must be "seeded" earlier in the story. The scenes and beats are always circulating the dramatic energy through the three rings of the Story Molecule.

The character arcs of the subordinate characters wrap themselves around the main character, like nerves radiating from the spine of the story. And likewise, the movie's subplots wrap themselves around the main plot. As the subordinate characters serve to bring out different aspects of the central characters, the subplots reflect different aspects of the movie's theme. Sometimes the need for subplots only surfaces at a later stage during story development, when it appears that the story feels too thin or too linear. Subplots bring color and scope to a story that would otherwise be flat and, especially in the current moviemaking environment, they deserve major attention. For it is often the subplots which distinguish a film or a screenplay from a hundred others with basically the same bare plotline. What is going to make your road movie or your heist-gone-bad movie special? The major plot elements of genre movies are so familiar that they often serve as a mere framework for exploring quirky characters, unusual tones, and new dimensions of relationships. The main outer plot throughline may always be what goes on the poster and brings the audience into the theater, but it is often what happens in the relationships and related subplots that keeps the audience there and gives a movie its "legs."

Subplots can be made of anything, any dramatic material, as Linda Seger suggests. But there is one thing they should *not* be, and that is irrelevant to the theme of the movie. Subplots usually, though not always, connect causally with the main plot. But subplots that do not contribute to our awareness of the theme break the basic dramatic unity. The audience walks out of the theater with a confused impression.

There are three main categories into which subplots fall: *intersecting* subplots, *parallel* subplots, and *brief* subplots. Intersecting subplots crisscross the main plot, and have a material impact on its outcome. There may be an additional emotional valence, but the plot connection must be there. A good example is Stephen's Galapagos excursion in *Master and Commander*. This subplot begins with the plot level and the relationship level already conjoined: the fact that the *Acheron* is chasing the English whaling fleet to the Galapagos will give Stephen a chance to explore the islands' biological marvels. Conflict develops between Aubrey and Stephen when the captain breaks his promise in order to chase the *Acheron*. The Galapagos subplot feeds into the Core Crisis when Stephen is accidentally shot, and Aubrey must choose between chasing his prey and saving his friend. Returning to the islands to perform the surgery to remove Stephen's bullet on dry land, Aubrey let's go of the chase. But during Stephen's explorations of the island, he spies the *Acheron* in a cove. This discovery sets up the final confrontation. Here the subplot works as both the critical test in the relationship and a challenge to Aubrey to see things in a different way, and it advances the plot at the same time. Movies like *Sense and Sensibility* work with many subplots, some of them even occurring completely offscreen, because the character web is so tightly interlaced.

Parallel subplots are often subplots happening to secondary characters that share a thematic focus with the main plot. *Traffic* has a number of interwoven plot strands, and an important subplot. This subplot, given much screen time, involves the drug czar and his daughter. The daughter becomes addicted to drugs but is not involved in smuggling. So her story runs as a thematic parallel, showing a different aspect of the drug scourge. *Moonstruck* has two parallel subplots. Both revolve around the subjects of passion and infidelity, and serve to open up dimensions of the theme about the nature of true, enduring love. The father is having his affair with a woman named Mona, which is intercut with Loretta and Ronnie's towering passion. The mother has a brief little flirtation with a narcissistically childish and unfulfilled professor. Both of these subplots are played for their broader comic possibilities. The mother's brief subplot never intersects with the main story. The subplot of dad and Mona reappears, each time implicitly reinforcing the parallel. Loretta encounters her father and Mona at the opera during Story Step #12: Breaking Point, which sets up the catastrophe sequence. The encounter leads to farcical confusions and accusations—and to the "grow or die" point for Loretta. This subplot interweaves with Loretta and Ronnie's romantic line. The moment when the two lines intersect is carefully chosen for its dramatic impact on Loretta. As a consequence, she is no longer able to contain the conflict of values inside her. This is the high-romance/low-comedy parallel plot structure common to farce, found also in *Some Like It Hot*, for example.

The brief subplot usually runs its course within a single sequence or a few consecutive story steps, where we will see it set up, developed, and paid off. A brief subplot may intersect the main plot. That is, it may be an action that impacts the direction of the main plot. It may act as a brief parallel plot attached to a secondary character. It may be linked to character exposition of the main character. Or several brief subplots might be woven into an unstructured, episodic narrative style, as we might find in a picaresque comedy or a road story. We have mentioned the mother's brief subplot in *Moonstruck*, which is woven into the fabric of the emotional network, and thus remains relevant because it forces the mother to come to grips with what she had been avoiding: her husband's infidelity. It makes her ask the question: what makes men chase after women? And her brief subplot is further tied back into the movie's social fabric because the person she asks this question of is Johnny Camerreri, suddenly returned from Sicily.

The Fugitive illustrates a brief subplot that causally intersects with the main plot. Dr. Richard Kimbell, concealing his identity while working as a janitor at a hospital, is given the task of wheeling a critically ill little boy up to a ward. Taking a furtive look at the boy's chart, he can see immediately that the diagnosis is wrong. The boy's life is in danger. Will Kimbell risk giving himself away to save the life of this boy? There is an entire Plot Curve to this episode: catalyst, crisis, development, catastrophe, climax, all played out within the same sequence. It does impact on the main plot because he is discovered. A doctor confronts Kimbell as Lt. Gerrard is also closing in on the hospital, and the hero has to make a desperate escape.

The shape of the emotional network may already suggest how subplots can be used. In *The Talented Mr. Ripley*, we are shown that the extroverted Dickie has made many friends in the village, while Marge has not. A look at the character web shows that Dickie and Marge have two separate circles of acquaintances. The only bond we see them share, until Tom arrives, is with each other (a shared social circle is mentioned, but is kept offscreen; Freddie is Dickie's friend, but Marge doesn't go for him). So a secret love affair between Dickie and Silvana, a local woman, is rendered plausible by the shape of the emotional network. This becomes an intersecting subplot. In *Moonstruck*, the father/mother/Mona triangle makes a natural mirror for the Loretta/Johnny/Ronnie triangle. The conflict in both triangles deals with loss and recovery of the passion that leads to commitment. In Clint Eastwood's *Unforgiven*, the subplot of Sheriff "Little Bill" Daggett brutalizing English Bob both parallels and foreshadows the later conflict between Little Bill and the main character, Will Munny. The potential for this effective foreshadowing may have been visible in a sketch of the Story Molecule. At the extreme end, it takes the many subplots of the intersecting characters in *Syriana*, *Crash*, *Do the Right Thing*, and *Short Cuts* to bring out the thematic lines of those films. But the eventual uses of these subplots are already implicit in the structure of the Story Molecule in each case.

Short or long, intersecting or parallel, subplots must always have plot dynamics in themselves. They must go somewhere. The scenes carrying the subplot may be scattered throughout the movie, but the essential form of Aristotle's Plot Curve will be there. Not only will there be a dramatic shape we can pull out of the script and look at by itself, with a catalyst, threshold crossing, and climax—but there should also be *consequences* to the subplot which will resonate with the theme of the movie. The subplot will either directly impact on the plot or give us a parallel conflict we can compare with the main conflict. It is the consequences of the subplot resonating with the theme of the movie which can give even a minor subplot a different effect than other kinds of motifs that may run through a story, such as a running gag. A running gag may reappear at several points in the story, and it may be used to reveal character, like C. C. Baxter's cold in *The Apartment*, or Charles's lateness and general social clumsiness in *Four Weddings and a Funeral*. By revealing character and setting a comic tone, the running gag may indirectly contribute to the way we feel about the theme, but it does not help define the theme. It is not because of C. C. Baxter's cold that he ultimately chooses to become a mensch.

Orchestrating subplots so that they enhance rather than interfere with the main plot is not always easy. Major Story Steps, like the catalyst, Threshold Crisis, Core Crisis, catastrophe, and climax are so complex in themselves, and carry so much plot momentum, that we would not want them bogged down by the presence of subplots. Subplots are begun after the main plot catalyst and are paid off before the main plot climax.

In addition, the juiciest throughline question of the Story Molecule is paid off *last*. If the outer plot is the most important substory, it is the last and highest peak of the climax. But the order really depends on which substory has the most dramatic energy for the audience. Which subtextual question is the most tantalizing in the audience's mind? Often it is the question linked to the love relationship. In some unusual films it may even be the inner ring of the main character that has the highest peak, though the inner conflict must always be externalized cinematically, as in the climax of *The Piano*. Ada decides the piano must be thrown into the ocean, then sticks her foot into the coil of rope and is dragged into the water. Her inner conflict is only decided when she frees herself and struggles to the surface.

In *Tootsie*, where the outer plot is more of a framework or pretext for the farcical complications in the relationships, the question of whether Michael will produce and star in his roommate's play is answered in a throwaway image of a theater marquee. But the last scene of the movie resolves the primary relationship substory between Michael and Julie. In the climax of *Moonstruck*, all the minor subplots are resolved first, then the plot question of whether Loretta will marry Johnny, and finally the emotional network substory question of Loretta's and Ronnie's love. After the question of who is marrying whom is settled, we finally have the kiss. The erotic triangle in *The Piano* works itself out in a kind of anticlimax confrontation between the two men, leaving a foreboding energy for the climax of the relationship arc of Ada and her piano. When the emotional network substory has the last and highest peak of the ripple climax, we will need a final beat of plot resolution in the falling action at the end of the movie. In *Moonstruck* we have the celebration of Loretta's engagement. Ada has a new home, is in some way balancing her inner and outer worlds, and she has regained her voice.

Laying out the emotional network on paper is something to do early in the development process. We can formulate new questions for both the plot and the theme out of the patterns of connection that appear on the "palette" of characters. It helps us judge when we need to have an expository scene with a subordinate character and when we don't. For example, the family setting of *Moonstruck*, with its many close bonds, already suggests that there will be intertwining subplots. The emotional network ultimately helps us determine how many characters and how many scenes we will need in the screenplay. We need enough characters to move the story forward; we need enough to differentiate the dramatic and thematic perspectives; we need enough to dimensionalize the main character either through supporting characters or contrasting characters. Through the lines of connection we draw between them, we can see how best to economize our characters while raising the dramatic stakes and compressing the action.

Ensemble Movies

Ensemble movies play primarily in the emotional network of the story's characters. That is to say, the outer plot is de-emphasized, loosely or episodically structured, or it forms a thin pretext for the emotional network conflicts. This distinguishes ensemble movies from collective-hero action genres, such as heist movies, *Mission: Impossible*-type adventures, and disaster flicks. These latter are plot-driven movies, while ensemble stories are really driven by the character and relationship dynamics within the emotional network itself. This is a difference of approach to storytelling, and often a basic difference in attitude toward life on the part of the screenwriter and director. Ensemble stories focus on the social milieu. Ask yourself, for example: are you more interested in obstacles and challenges that come from the external, objective world or those that come from the social context? While the narrative goals of the collective-hero story and the ensemble story are different, both genres focus on the emotional network to tell the story.

In collective-hero stories, an external threat or challenge creates an opportunity to examine the variety of human reactions under stress. Individuals with varying temperaments and skills, weaknesses and strengths, must put aside their egoism for the sake of collective survival or for the success of a collective enterprise, as in *Master and Commander*. The emotional network becomes a microcosm of society, allowing us to explore how society survives crises. These stories always involve sacrifice of some kind. Sacrifice can lead to maturity, while those unable to sacrifice threaten the team and themselves. Usually the outer plot stakes in collective-hero movies are high: lives are at stake, perhaps all of humanity. These action movies tend to be very clear about which actions are viable and which are nonviable. The stories by their very nature tend to be in a larger-than-life romantic idiom. And, as they are larger than life, they are also iconic: the team comes to symbolize society as a whole. When a shift does occur in the iconic presentation—such as when the bellicose and obsessed sea-dog captain is eaten by the shark in *Jaws*, while the "soft male" intellectual manages to destroy the monster—this signals or reflects a shift of attitude in the society as a whole. When developing a collective-hero screenplay, we want to ask what social icons we are evoking and how we want to handle them. This demands creative intuition on the part of the development team.

In ensemble movies, we have the inverse emphasis. The ensemble is not primarily threatened by a force outside itself. Thus the focus of the storytelling is not on analyzing which behaviors or attitudes lead to success and which do not, though this may play a secondary role. More likely, in the ensemble film, human actions in relationships and in society are regarded for their complexity, their ambivalence, their irrationality, even the unknowability of their motives, and not for the pragmatic productivity of their outcomes. People are seen as being fundamentally interesting in themselves. The character web in an ensemble movie also comes to stand in for society at large, but in a different way from collective-hero stories. Ensemble stories represent a slice of life, rather than a sampling of characteristic "types" that make up a team. Ensemble movies tend to play in a more realistic idiom than collective-hero adventures. These are everyday people whom we come to know. Jean Renoir was one of the early masters of the ensemble structure. Usually in Renoir's movies there is no ethical antagonist, no villain. Dramatic conflict arises out of ordinary human egoism, misunderstanding, stupidity, and compulsion. This approach does not generate an ethical dualism by making the antagonist "evil." Renoir once said that if you don't love your characters, you have no business writing about them. This attitude of embracing the social world still colors ensemble movies today, even if it may be at times a chilly and ironic embrace.

While ensemble movies, unlike the collective-hero genre, do not always have a strong, driving plot that unites the characters in the emotional network, there must still be some outer form imposed on the story. A perimeter is needed to mark the boundary of the dramatic world as distinct from the rest of society. For ensemble movies, defining the group is one of the first and most important tasks in developing the story. There are three ways of making this definition: geographically, through a central plot, or thematically. Ultimately two or all three of these factors are combined to set off the world of the drama.

Geographical definition for an ensemble movie is a milieu, typically a neighborhood or a focal hangout for the characters, such as a bar, diner, beauty parlor, or clubhouse. The setting needs to be localized enough that we can encompass it cinematographically in one establishing shot or scene. The action will be more or less confined to this milieu location—the *focal hub*—and to the individual spaces radiating from it. The rhythm of the storytelling is created by the rhythm of the gatherings at the hub, where often the characters are engaged in telling each other their own stories. Sal's pizza parlor in *Do The Right Thing* and the waterfront bar in *The Perfect Storm* are two examples of focal hubs. Every time we come back to these focal locations we are also brought back to the central themes of the story. The locations themselves take on the quality of a leitmotif.

The definition by central plot involves the throughline action that brings and holds all the characters together. Here we may find a core of characters within the ensemble engaged in an external plot and acting as a collective hero in relation to the larger group. The working-class hopefuls who form *The Commitments*, in the Irish movie about a group of down and out young people in north Dublin coming together to form a "soul music" band, act on behalf of themselves and also their entire north Dublin neighborhood. The fishermen of *The Perfect Storm* embody the values and stakes of the larger Gloucester fishing community. Just where the line is between an ensemble story and a collective-hero story is not clear-cut. Largely it depends on how the story opens and is set up—does it open on the larger social world or on a core task-group? In addition, as we build Act II, the two genres will make different use of cutaways. In a collective-hero story, all the dramatically important characters—with the exceptions of a Chief Commander or a love interest to be defended—are in the core task-group and onscreen most of the time. In an ensemble film with a core group involved in a central action, dramatically important characters in the ensemble will be in both places, the point of small-group action and the social hub. The cutaways to "home" will be more extended and will not merely function for the plot. They will have dramatic beats and dramatic life in themselves. The lives of the lovers and friends of the fishermen in *The Perfect Storm* keep us connected to the central plot, but remove our perspective to temper the tragedy.

Finally, movies like *Crash*, *Do the Right Thing*, and *Short Cuts* define their worlds thematically as well as geographically. They use what could be called an "art movie" strategy. The theme is foregrounded and announced to the audience right in the opening. *Do The Right Thing* does not even wait for the beginning of the movie. The theme is asserted in the title music: "Fight the power!" The neighborhood is defined geographically as we meet the characters waking up and beginning to interact. Then a "Greek chorus" character, speaking directly to camera, shows us photos of Martin Luther King and Malcolm X and ends with the line: "And we still have to fight against *apart-hate*!" The dramatic plot could be considered an enactment or an acting-out of this thematic text. In *Short Cuts*, a much more diffusely structured movie, the geography is broad and there is no one central plot that involves all the characters directly. Thus we may well ask what they all have in common. The answer is thematic. The characters in the many subplots are linked by themes of alienation and contamination, pictured via pesticide-spraying helicopters that crisscross the city. *Short Cuts* is an "ensemble of ensembles," yet as we are introduced to each subgroup we notice breakdowns of psychic and social boundaries so that each setting is contaminated with inappropriate or impulsive behaviors. People make dates while listening to a concert; a husband watches his wife have phone sex while she changes the baby; a helicopter pilot, back from his nightly pesticide patrol, urinates in a plastic cup in a phone booth while he wakes up his ex-wife to wish her a happy birthday. Underlying this modern absurdism is the "pain of disconnection." Here in Short Cuts it is the theme that defines the geography as much as the reverse. Because we can all recognize something of ourselves in the malaise of these characters, the theme transcends geography to imply or assert a universal contamination.

A story development issue that comes up in ensemble stories, and wherever the emotional network is emphasized, is the question of how to handle subplots. Where the outer plot is loose or kept in the background, and there are also many characters, there is a potential for subplots to bubble out of control. They may become an end in themselves and diffuse the effect of the movie so that it leaves only a vague impression on the audience. One can see this as at least a potential danger in *Magnolia*, *Syriana*, and *City of God*. Whenever there are so many characters or story strands that the audience has to stop to figure out who is who, the audience is no longer completely in the story. We have lost them, to some degree. Here is where it is crucial for everyone on the development team to be very clear about the concept behind the movie—the theme, the values carried by the theme, and the necessary story structure required to put that theme across. The many subplots in *Monsoon Wedding* are firmly held in place by the event of the wedding and all that means for the family, the extended family of guests, and Dubey the wedding planner, extending out even to the most secondary characters.

It would not be too much to say that the looser and more "random" or "chaotic" the story superficially appears, the tighter and more controlled the concept has to be. *Short Cuts* is a successful example, where the thematic and emotional subtext elements are strong enough to unify the movie in the absence of a central throughline plot. The audience is being asked to do some work to connect the dots; there is no overwhelming plotline in this sort of movie that allows the audience to simply ride through it. Therefore, the thematic connections must be apparent enough and important enough to reward the audience's extra effort.

And, regarding subplots, it will be necessary for subplots in the ensemble movie to be both clearly subordinated to the main action and thematically linked to it. Take the example of the quarrel between the two crewmen on the swordfish boat in *The Perfect Storm*. This is kept as a brief subplot, occupying a couple of continuous sequences where we see the subplot catalyzed, developed, and resolved. The quarrel threatens to become violent, but the conflict is already extinguished by the time the big storm sets in. At the same time, the resolution of the crewmen's quarrel focuses on the themes of the inherent boundlessness of men's heroic posturing, as well as the need for individual egos to be tamed for the sake of the group. It is a classic strategy to put the group through such a preliminary test to iron out the group dynamics before entering the main trial.

Ensemble movies encompass many styles and subjects. The genre could make an entire study in itself. An instructive example to look at is *The Commitments*. The organization of the three levels of the Story Molecule shows how an emotional network movie reconciles the potential competition for our interest between an individual main character and the ensemble. The opening montage first establishes a social context for the story; the settings at street markets and public housing sites present us first of all with the life of this community. The lead character, Jimmy Rabbit, hunting members for the new soul band he wants to build (in an Irish parody of Christ calling the disciples), is always pictured in the midst of this vibrant working-class activity. Jimmy Rabbit's individual line is simply that he has the drive to create the band. His plot goal is kept from becoming too serious as we hear him comically fantasize the talk-show interviews he will give when he is famous. Thus we downplay his personal ambition as a dramatic focus. The character is not given personal complications or a love interest that would force us to concentrate too much energy on him. And yet, he is the driving force of the story, the reason the band exists at all. So there is a balance established: Jimmy Rabbit is made interesting enough to hold our attention through Act I as the band forms, but he is kept too small to carry the entire story by himself.

As the band assembles and starts to rehearse, the musicians are individualized to varying degrees, but none is given a compelling throughline that takes us away from the story of the band. We do not go deeply into any one character and do not expect to see great character change. The outer plot question is likewise kept diffuse: will the Commitments be successful as a soul band? There is in fact not one highly defined outer plot goal toward which all of the central action moves. There are instead minor goals: to make their first performance, to get a small recording contract, to have Wilson Pickett come to their concert. These outer goals are kept modest, so as not to draw too much energy away from the relationships. The story development keeps pointing us right back to the emotional network because the question of the band's success or failure hinges on whether they can get along. The evident strategy is not to let anything compete dramatically with the emotional network. Thus *The Commitments* does not fall into the collective-hero genre. It is really the dynamics of the group itself, how they come together and how they tear themselves apart, which is at the center of our interest.

Plot in the Context of the Story Molecule

In these two chapters, we have seen that there are in fact three levels of dramatic interest in constant motion. The core of the dramatic conflict is expressed outward into visible plot action through the emotional network of characters. We have gone, in some depth, into how the story energy moves from ring to ring and have given some examples of how an understanding of the Story Molecule can help your story development process.

Along the way we have defined the outer plot as the outer ring of the Story Molecule. This means that the structure of the outer plot itself contains and shapes what happens within the inner two rings. The outer plot, and the outer world it defines, generates both limits and potentials for character development. The trajectory of the primary relationship is likewise limited and potentiated by twists of fate that make up the plot. We might simply recall that if an undercover cop had not been killed in a train station toilet, Book and Rachel would never have met. Their potential love only exists within a fragile window, bounded on one side by Samuel's discovery of the killer's identity (which ends Act I) and on the other side by the killers' discovery of Book's hiding place (which ends Act II). The outer plot as the outer ring of the Story Molecule actually encompasses everything we normally mean by "story structure," shaping both what we see on the screen and what is orchestrated in the subtext. Part Two of this book is devoted to the dynamics of plot. In the present context, we shall just summarize some of the points that relate the outer plot to the Story Molecule.

- The Story Molecule opens up the "invisible" dimensions behind the plot and allows us to see the drama as a three-dimensional stream of meaning. The inner soul-journey of the main character, represented by the round of the Hero's Journey, is reflected in the outer plot through the dynamics the two share. The external plot expresses the inner conflict of the main character. The process of transformation within the main character moves out through and changes the emotional network, forcing a response from the antagonist, building dramatic intensity and structuring the plot.
- The external story grounds the drama in observable action and consequences. When the action is fine-tuned through the Story Molecule, it does more than just make the audience react. The audience is engaged on a deeper emotional level and resonates sympathetically with the universal level of the conflict.
- Locations, settings, and descriptive passages in the screenplay (referred to as "body copy") work to advance the plot. They should also resonate with the subtext and make it hum in the audience's subconscious. Ultimately, it is the work of the director, camera, lighting, and set design to bring in all the subtle emotional colors, but the screenplay has to establish the palette.
- As we shall see, each major Story Step sends ripples through all the levels of the Story Molecule. We expect to see some dramatic shift in the outer situation, in the emotional network, and in the main character afterward. The first scenes following the catalyst, Threshold Crisis, Core Crisis, catastrophe, and climax tend to show us what has changed on each level.
- The arc of the primary relationship weaves a fugue with the plot as the dramatic momentum is passed between them.
- Foreshadowing later developments is a basic strategy to build interest and keep a story from becoming too linear. Foreshadowing is often more interesting and subtle if it is not delivered in dialogue by a central character. The

character web of the emotional network can suggest other characters through whom to foreshadow future plot turns. Plot events radiate in all directions and have direct or indirect consequences throughout the world of the story. Secondary and incidental characters are affected through the emotional networks of the central characters. Foreshadowing may be done through these secondary characters.

- In genre/action films where the main character does not go through an inner Hero's Journey and show a decisive change, the rising dramatic intensity can only come through escalating the outer action. But where a potent dramatic subtext is lacking, it is hard to engage the audience on the feeling level.
- Each film finds its own way of balancing the Story Molecule. Some movies lay the stress on the inner story, others concentrate on the emotional network, and a large number of movies are plot-driven, like *Terminator 2*. Balancing the story energy in the three rings of the Story Molecule is a central task of story development, just as much as deciding the genre and the idiom, or working out the plot. It is part of the screenwriter's journey, along with that of the entire development team. Balance is achieved partly by finding the deep themes that unite the three rings of the Story Molecule, so that each level of conflict causes the others to resonate. On each level of the Story Molecule there is a compelling conflict and, because the three levels of conflict are intersecting and reinforcing, we have in the end a story that is much greater than the sum of its parts.

Internal Software: Childhood Story/Reverse Perspective

This is definitely for you to do—not just think about! Plan to do this with the same partner you used for the *Memory Banks/Childhood Story* exercise at the end of Chapter Four.

We have placed some emphasis in the preceding chapter on the function of the antagonist. We have seen him as a dark mirror of the hero. Many writers have a blind spot in relation to the antagonist in their story and do not empathize with him. As a result, the antagonist is not developed as a character and the whole script suffers for it. My partner Tom and I created this exercise to give you a direct experience of leaving your comfort zone to enter empathically the world of the antagonist.

Taking turns as you did before, you will tell the same childhood story again, but with a slight variation. This time, tell the same event from the point of view of the antagonist in the story, that person or force that seemed to be most against you at the time. It might be a parent, another child, an angry dog, a storm, a bumblebee . . . tell the story from that perspective.

Continued

This means that now you are that character, speaking in first person and present tense from that character's point of view. For example:

> "It's four o'clock in the afternoon and I'm only now getting around to washing the lunch dishes, and then I've got to start dinner right away. It never ends!"

And so on.

If for some reason there is no antagonist in the story, find the person whose point of view on what was happening was furthest away from your own. And if you told a story where you were alone, walking in a meadow, etc., then simply take the point of view of a passing cloud or bird. Let your imagination suggest something.

It may take a little work to enter this other point of view. A good way to start is to imagine what that person is seeing right now—where am I, what time of day is it, what sounds do I hear, are there special smells in this place? The idea is to let yourself be inhabited by that perspective. If that person is taller, imagine looking at the world from that greater height. Take the time you need for this before starting to tell the story. Generating the right mood is part of the art of storytelling.

You may also find that from the other character's perspective, the story/scene has a different point of attack. That person may come into the scene earlier or later than you did. The story may have a different ending point as well. In fact, it is a different story from the other person's point of view! It has a different theme, a different meaning.

When you have finished this storytelling, you may have some strong feelings about it. Often the story told from the reverse perspective is actually a better story. Even the storyteller enjoys it more, much to her surprise. Discuss together the differences in the energy of the two stories. Where was the juice in each version, and which one felt juicier? What were the structural differences in each version?

- Where did each version begin?
- What was the Call to Adventure in each case?
- Was there a threshold crossing to a greater level of conflict or risk?
- What was at stake in each case?
- What was the climax or endpoint of each story?
- What changed as a result?

Then there is the question: "What's the story all about?" It's surprising, but there are so many people who feel that their daily actions do not really mean anything! Many others think their lives would be significant if they

Continued

were discovered by MTV. But powerful and authentic screenwriting starts from the art or discipline of seeing the meaning in everything we encounter, down to the smallest gesture. The great thing is that when we tell our stories out loud and see the instantaneous response in the face and body language of our listener, then we know the meaning.

But we may still need some reflection before we can connect the felt experience of meaning with a theme we can articulate verbally. This is where the above questions can help. Conflict results in change. The nature of the change often reveals what the conflict was about. But both the conflict and the change were probably different for each version of the event. In one of my seminars, a man told a story in reverse perspective that had very rich lessons in this regard.

As a boy, he would play soccer in a field after school. The field lay between two neighborhoods, and the boys from the different neighborhoods would make up teams. In his own childhood story, he related that one day a bigger boy from the other neighborhood accused him of a foul and started chasing him, saying he was going to beat him up. This angry boy challenged him to come the next day and they would settle the score alone. That night the boy was frightened; he didn't want to fight because the other boy was much bigger. But he didn't want to be ashamed. That night he happened to see an episode of *Kung Fu* on TV, and the hero tricked a bad guy by pretending to run away, then ducked down suddenly and made his pursuer stumble over him. Somehow the boy felt fortified by this. The next day he went to the field and the bigger boy ran straight at him. He did just what he'd seen in *Kung Fu* and suddenly ducked. And it worked! His adversary stumbled over him and fell heavily. At this point the boy froze, expecting the bully to really beat him up in revenge, but instead, the other boy got up and just walked away. He never bothered him again. The moral of the story from his own point of view was: "Even if you are smaller, you can still win if you know what to do."

Now, what about from the other boy's point of view? When the seminar participant started speaking as the other boy, the tone of his voice was immediately different. And so was the setting: the park didn't just divide two neighborhoods, but specifically a wealthier neighborhood and a working-class one. So immediately an element of class conflict came in that had been absent from the first version. This bigger boy was from the working class, and whenever he went to the field, he could see that the wealthy boys had nicer shoes, nicer clothes—they owned the ball. And there was this weaselly little rich kid who was fouling everybody and thought he could get away with it. That's why he had to get him. [Notice

Continued

that the motivation here is class justice, while from the first POV the story was about an intimidating bully.] So he challenged the little punk to come the next day and fight like a man. And the climax, the *Kung Fu* trick, from the bigger boy's perspective? Here the storyteller was totally in this boy's character when he said, "That's it! You can never beat these rich kids. They *always* have something else, something you don't have." That was why the bigger boy walked away.

When the storyteller finished with that line, there was a deep silence in the room. He had made it all up, but in doing so he had discovered a truth, not only about the other boy, but about himself as seen through other eyes. There was one part still missing for the story to be complete. I asked the man, "Now tell the truth, did you commit that foul?" The seconds before he answered appeared to be real soul-searching time for him. Finally he said, very quietly, "Yeah, I fouled him." A kind of gasp went through the room. There was something awesome in this confession, not because the "crime" was so great but because he was so naked.

I relate that incident because this screenwriter was honest enough with himself to let a cherished David-and-Goliath personal myth get demolished for the sake of looking a larger truth in the eye. The victory of the little guy is still of course there. But the antagonist has regained his humanity as well, while the layers of moral ambiguity and survival imperative have become much richer. There is suddenly a complex and mature story revealed in this simple incident.

This is the kind of work we as screenwriters perform with all of our major characters. Either we plan for it in the earlier stages of developing the story, or we are forced into it later when we encounter middle act problems or creative blocks. In any case, we can expect the process to change us.

As a final step, if you wanted to make your childhood story into a short film, you now have a variety of POVs to choose from. You could tell the entire story from the original POV or you could tell it entirely from the antagonist's POV. Or you could orchestrate a more distant, second-person POV that would allow you to cut back and forth or shift the audience's focus and sympathies from character to character. This is a very concrete story development choice that screenwriters make and then hand on to directors. Try out some different solutions in your own story. See what orchestration of POV best expresses the story you want to tell.

7

Orchestrating Character and Style

> Why are we concerned with art? To cross our frontiers, exceed our limitations, fill our emptiness—fulfill ourselves. This is not a condition but a process in which what is dark in us slowly becomes transparent. In this struggle with one's own truth, this effort to peel off the life-mask, the theater . . . has always seemed to me a place of provocation. . . . This defiance of taboo, this transgression, provides the shock which rips off the mask, enabling us to give ourselves to something which is impossible to define but which contains Eros and Caritas.
>
> —*Jerzy Grotowski*

Designing Stories

THE STORY MOLECULE IS A BEAUTIFUL, complex, living pattern. It makes the point that a story is more than a story *line*. This means that we can never grasp story by thinking about it in a linear, left-brain way. It is ultimately not productive to plan a story *line* first, and then turn it into a movie. We want to see a movie from the beginning! Obviously a movie is more than plotline *plus* characters *plus* setting, etc. A movie is more than the sum of its parts, it is the *expressive pattern* of its parts. As the Story Molecule suggests, we have to start thinking in terms of significant patterns, not just lines. The line itself is an element of the pattern, and pattern-thinking is qualitatively different than linear thinking. We *design* stories as much as we write them. Thinking cinematically is left- *and* right-brain thinking.

Thus there is a world of important story development considerations and decisions that are not part of the plot structure at all. Nevertheless, they are part of the larger story pattern. Here we are talking about the qualities of the movie's universe: the idiom and the genre; the iconic qualities projected by characters, events, and objects; visual motifs and metaphors; and the sensuous, seductive power of the images in relation to the audience. Decisions about idiom and genre are among the first and most important ones made in the story development process because of their impact on both budget and market. However, beyond this, the meta-structural aspects of the larger story pattern set up an entire subtext of communication with the audience. They constellate what we have called the "story field" for the audience. Whether a movie succeeds or not has as much to do with how the story field maps over onto the audience's field, and how it catches the spirit of the times, as it does with how solid the plot is. This "field map-over" in turn impacts how the audience "recognizes" the movie, embraces it, finds it somehow necessary. We know that, notwithstanding a studio's "p & a" (publicity and advertising) budget, it is the audience taking the movie to heart that builds the market. These factors of the larger story pattern are so basic that the screenwriter must learn how to work with them.

My Big Fat Greek Wedding, for example, presents an interesting case. The movie appears as a modest, low-budget, regional, or independent feature. From the nature of the concept, the plotline, and the story structure, there is no obvious reason to expect the movie to be more than a made-for-TV feel-good romantic comedy. The major hit *MBFGW* became seems to have been a surprise to everyone involved. This in itself is a sign that the movie's story field touched something in the zeitgeist. Cultural trends are so vast and diffuse that they tend to elude our left-brain nets like smoke, and may only show up peripherally in instruments like opinion polls. But we are looking at two interlocking or resonating patterns—one in the movie and one in the audience—that have produced a massive reaction.

One conspicuous aspect of *MBFGW*'s story universe is that the tone of the comedy is a throwback to the 1960s. We have two simple, sincere, chaste adults who fall in love. There are none of the major hang-ups, obstacles, or ambivalences that we associate with contemporary relationships. The movie's world and tone are pre–gender confusion, pre-AIDS, prefeminism, even pre–sexual revolution. Apart from the cars, there is nothing to reference the movie to 2002, or any other specific time. One might question whether the movie would have been a hit had it been made and released three years earlier. Likely not. Same movie, but a different relationship to the audience. But in 2002, with the world poised for a war of uncertain consequences and trying to cope with economic stagnation and the constant anxiety of terrorist threats, the innocent charm of this romantic comedy may well have taken on an additional iconic dimension. It became, in effect, a collective compensatory fantasy of safety and the reconciliation of ethnic and religious differences in one big, happy family. It is this impact that cannot be deduced from story structure alone.

Of course, here we are involved once again with the dual nature—conscious planning and unconscious scanning—of creation itself. It is typically our unconscious scanning, our creative intuition, that picks out the wisps or filaments of connection with what is brewing in the collective consciousness. We need to develop some new tools to help us access this other side of the creative resource. This, too, is part of our professional competence. Pattern recognition is an index of creativity, and of intelligence in general. It is in fact one of the universal distinguishing features of all life forms, from viruses on up the ladder of evolution. We incorporate many levels of pattern recognition into intelligence, and it is probable that the pattern/field dimensions of information go in at a deeper level than does verbal/linear information. For this reason, the graphic representations of our story development models are not simply "visual aids" to reinforce the verbal message. The images are *themselves* the message. Our ability to work with complex patterns comes directly into play when, for example, we try to understand how the iconic dimension of our hero may impact on the audience.

When we first start working on a screenplay concept, we may not have much of a pattern to build on. In fact, this is not quite correct; the pattern may be present, but it is not yet within our field of consciousness. Ingmar Bergman, who as a director was especially articulate in describing his process, used the image of a "bright thread sticking out of the dark sack of the unconscious" to picture his starting point. If he teased out and wound up the thread carefully enough, Bergman believed, he would end up with a movie. The pattern gradually emerges as we work on it with our creative intuition. When a director begins to collaborate on a project with a cinematographer, they will both typically bring a few "bright threads" to their first meeting: photos, paintings, color swatches, toys, comic books, and so on. Then they start "dreaming" images together. It is exactly the paucity and disconnectedness of this information that stimulates the intuition and puts it to work. From the one bright thread, the intuition "sees" into the dark sack. Overstructuring the development process at the beginning buries the creative intuition under data, renders it inoperable, and robs us of its contribution.

Designing stories is not exactly drawing pictures, but is more about creating the conditions where images, motifs, metaphors, and the patterns that connect them are invited to emerge from the dark sack of the unconscious.

A versatile approach that utilizes both the right-brain and left-brain grows out of the well-known practice of mental mapping. Mental maps lay out information in field relationships rather than in logical sequences. Connections take on visual characteristics such as proximity or distance, clustering, triangulation, and paths of approach. The character web we introduced in the previous chapters is an example of a mental map, one laid out exclusively in terms of the characters. Mental maps are also commonly used to explore the territory of the main character's mode value. Take for example Melvin in *As Good as It Gets*:

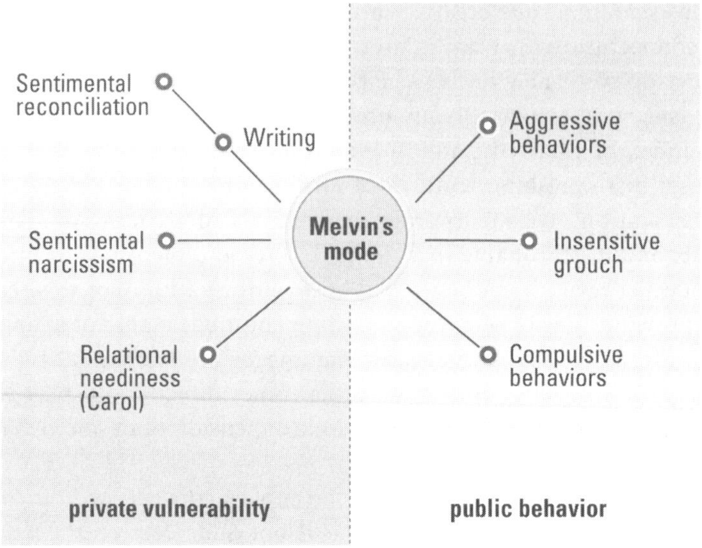

/ **Melvin's mode.**

What associates to the core value? What clusters around it? This helps us find the actions that reveal attitudes, and so nail the character's mode. But it is equally possible to place a character in the middle of the page and create a different mental cluster: of objects, gestures, images, colors, and sounds related to the character. This reveals another dimension of the field around the character. It tends to make the character immediately "visible," unique and cinematic, while also bringing out the iconic or archetypal background. Here is Viola de Lesseps from *Shakespeare in Love*:

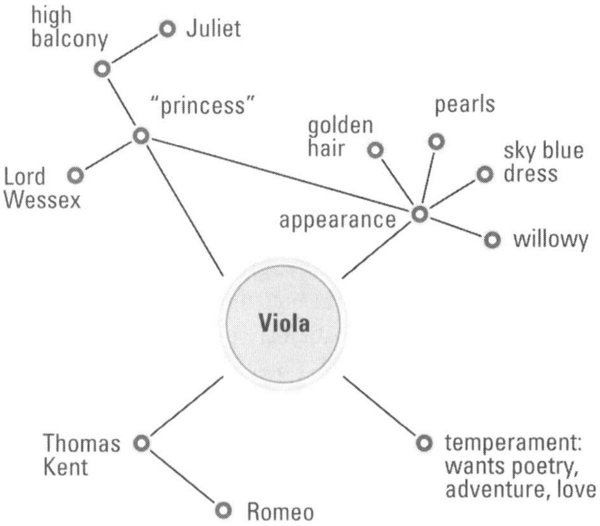

/ **Mental mapping: Viola.**

Individual elements of the map may be further probed by putting *them* in the center of a new map. Say, for example, that while doing a map of one of your characters, the color *beige* comes up in association. You see the character wearing or being attracted to that color. Why beige? Beige is specific; it is not brown or gray or any other color. Perhaps you cannot explain the connection any more than you can explain your own favorite color. But the intuition has its own reasons, which may lie in a part of the field out of our awareness. Try building a cluster around beige as an exercise. Let the associations arise without directing or censoring them. So, why beige? Beige is going to suggest certain things about the character. If a character dresses predominantly in beige and other mild tones, the entire web of associations is transferred subliminally to the audience. This web is much richer and more complex than the color cues given in fashion magazines. This is especially true because any object placed within the movie frame is already magnified in its effect, even before it is projected on the movie screen.

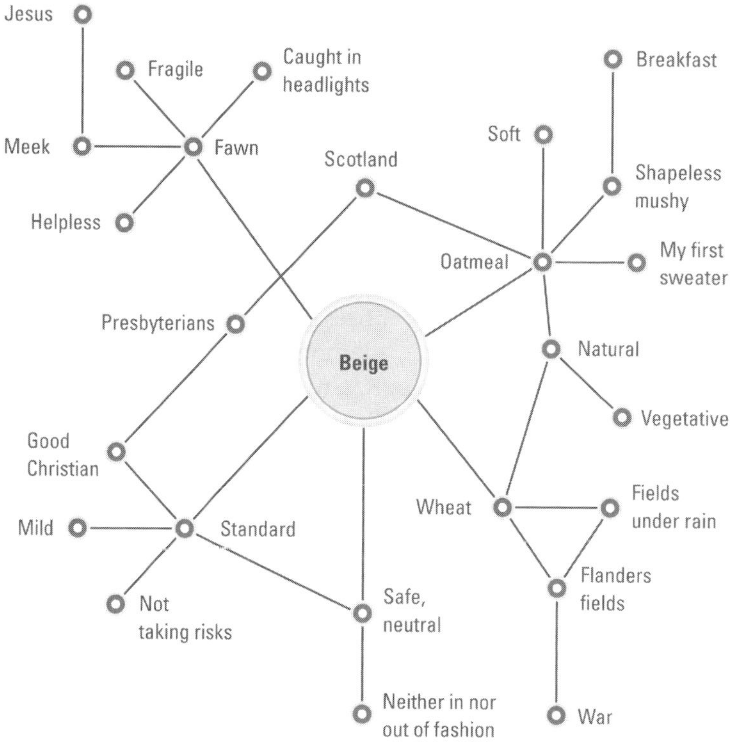

How do these considerations actually make a difference in the story we have to tell? Let us take the visual presentations of Tom and Dickie in *The Talented Mr. Ripley*. In this movie, clothing and personal style are central to both plot and theme. What is the difference between the way Tom dresses and the way Dickie dresses? This difference should mean something. Difference is always necessary to character orchestration, and in a movie we want to telegraph the salient difference to the audience visually, before a word of dialogue is spoken. And let's take it further: what is the difference between the way Tom wears *Dickie's* clothes and the way Dickie wears his *own* clothes? On one level, the differences serve to *tell* us about the characters, their social classes and attitudes. On another level, they communicate subtle *feelings* about them, which the audience will perceive as their *own* feelings.

In the opening scene, we see Tom in the borrowed Princeton blazer, a tie with conservative brown stripes, and cheap plastic glasses. In the next scene with Dickie's father, Tom wears the beige corduroy jacket and a dark brown tie. His shirts always have button-down collars. In Mangiobello, we see him either in the same corduroys or a dark suit. Just as Tom's hair flops boyishly in his face, his sense of taste also appears naïve and undeveloped, marks of his general immaturity and unconsciousness. His puce bathing suit exaggerates how pasty white his skin is. Dickie, on the other hand, always wears his shirts open a few buttons. His colors are brighter and more varied, simultaneously more comfortable and more assertive. Seeing them together on the screen, Dickie literally stands out while Tom recedes.

Significantly, when they go to the nightclub in Naples together the color scheme is reversed. There, Dickie has a tan/khaki jacket while Tom wears a dark brown, almost black plaid. Dickie does have a tie, yet his collar is open. The reversal of the color scheme foreshadows on a subliminal level that, at least in Tom's fantasy, the two personalities will become reversed or fused. Differences in taste show us the contrast in background and exposure, and between an introvert and an extrovert. Yet they constantly establish Dickie as an ideal, a supernormal erotic-identification object, and thus a carrier of Tom's projections. The audience, too, is meant to find Dickie dazzlingly alluring, aligning them with Tom's point of view. Tom's own drabness keeps pointing to his lack of identity. This presentation helps to successfully position Tom Ripley as an Everyman for today: vapid, devoid of self-esteem, seeking cues from the environment about how to be.

Colors actually make rather easy examples because they are thickly coded with social meanings. The colors we wear are what we show the world. But when doing a mental map around a character, other, less easily grasped terms may also crop up, like shapes. A character may be described as spiky, willowy, blockish, or egg-shaped. In literature, we have the option of using such words in descriptive passages to help conjure an image in the mind of the reader. In a screenplay, however, we must give the reader, or viewer, an impression without being so explicit or "literary." What do we mean by "egg-shaped," anyway?

Let's say that "egg-shaped" popped up in a mental map as a key word to a larger field of characterization. Our option as screenwriters is to develop some or all of these motifs that reference "egg" and indirectly point to it. Ultimately these motifs will come into a movie via props and set design as well as gesture and other nuances of performance. The actor or actress will make his or her own discovery of connections while preparing the role. These motifs add to the richness of the theme the audience takes away with them. Janet Frame, the main character in *An Angel at My Table*, carries the fragile, delicate, rounded, nesting aspects of the egg. But surprisingly, Melvin in *As Good as It Gets* has some of the egg characteristics as well. Melvin emphasizes the shell, the rigidity, and egocentrism. Yet we come to see that, behind the shell, Melvin is also fragile and easily broken. What both characters have in common is that they are self-contained introverts, which makes sense since both are writers.

Mental maps are half visual, half linguistic. Direct or fantasy images, like colors and shapes, take us deeper into the nonrational, right-brain resources when we draw or paint them. Then they may elicit strong and definite visceral reactions, which comprise yet another level of information for us as writers. The key thing, again, is not to try to be too explicit or literal. Much later in the development process, storyboarding gives us a very different access to visual thinking. At that point, however, the script is already out of the screenwriter's hands. The storyboard is a tool of preproduction after the writing stage is completed, and is more technical than intuitive, moving toward specific camera angles and compositions. The use of visual, right-brain techniques in the early stages of development is always to open the story up—or rather, to open us to the story on multiple levels.

What follows is an exercise where you can begin to work directly with images. I would not call it "art" because its purpose is not to be "artful," but to discover the spontaneous *form of feeling*. I am once again indebted to Catherine Moreau for my first exposure to this technique, because it is a process that can yield strong insights into the forms of feeling. Most of us are not used to handling art materials, and most of us are not used to letting completely spontaneous expression emerge in any form. It takes a little letting go and a conscious decision to surrender to the process.

Internal Software: The Forms of Feeling

For this exercise, it's a good idea to prepare some materials in advance. You will need some large sketch paper (11" x 14" or bigger), eight 3" x 5" index cards, and some colored drawing materials. Oil pastels are perhaps ideal for this; crayons, dry pastels, or markers are also good; colored pencils and pens may be too fine for this purpose. Have a variety of shades to choose from.

First is a warm-up exercise, but in fact the warm-up contains the essence of the whole thing. Here we will explore the essential forms of eight basic feeling states:

- anger
- hope

Continued

- loss
- happiness
- joy
- despair
- sadness
- peace

Write these eight words on the eight index cards, shuffle the cards well, and lay them face down on a table. Then divide your paper into eight rectangles of equal size.

Place the paper next to the cards and arrange the pastels or crayons so that you can see and reach them easily.

Each of the spaces on the paper will be for one of these basic feelings. But the trick is to be spontaneous—don't think about it, just do it. This is why the cards are face down on the table. The process is to turn a card over and give yourself thirty seconds to pick a color or colors and make your mark. Take a couple of deep breaths to clear your mind, and then dive in. When you have completed one, don't stop to think about it. Just take another deep breath, turn over the next card, and go for broke. Don't worry about what it looks like or whether it's "right" or "wrong." Trust your own innate capacity to respond to basic feelings through color and gesture. Go on till you have done all eight, then sit back and reflect on them for a minute or two.

You may very likely find yourself to be in a slightly altered state of consciousness than normal, perhaps hyperalert or strangely excited. It is like part of your brain is waking up. Now look at your work. You may notice similarities, for example, between the expressions of happiness and joy. Note also the differences. There may be some basic shapes, like circles, ascending or descending lines, triangles, boxes, etc. There may also be areas that look chaotic, fiery, flowing, or broken. This is all a very direct form of feedback, often striking in its ability to convey the truth of feelings. In fact, this is an exact parallel to the Focusing techniques introduced earlier. There we generated a felt-sense, then tried to find a word that matched. Here, we use a trigger-word to generate a felt-sense that is then projected out through a medium where we can see it. As with the felt-sense, the images are beyond judgment. They are what they are. Yet they tend to be universal enough that cinematographers build the same or analogous forms into their compositions to convey precisely the same feelings.

Once you are in this image-space, stay there. The warm-up serves to open our instrument. Now we can approach feelings in contexts. Try these two "energy portraits" using the same technique:

Continued

- you, how you feel at this point in your life right now

This time, give yourself five minutes for this exploration. Don't try to figure it out; let the image show it to you.

And then:

- an image of where your life is going

Again, give yourself five minutes. You may not know where you are going, yet some image will appear. This image may be clumsy and tentative, or it may be very strong. The image itself is beyond judgment. It is true in the sense that it is the way the intuition sees and expresses itself on the question.

You may conclude this internal software exercise by writing about what you have drawn: thoughts, feelings, further associations. If possible, just suspend judgment about whether this is right or wrong, and certainly about whether it is "art."

Because we are unused to accessing feeling and intuition consciously, it is often hard to accept it just as it is. We want to "fix" it according to some conscious model. We want so much to pull it into the territory of the ego so that we can feel in control. But it is the intrinsic nature of the intuition that it works in the background. Once we start thinking about it, it is no longer intuition but something else. This is why the time frame must be so brief. With the intuition, less is (paradoxically) more. I once heard the great physician Ashley Montagu state that he had a high accuracy rate with intuitive diagnoses by simply looking at a patient for three to five seconds. Later examination would confirm his intuitive hunch. After five seconds, however, the longer he continued to observe the patient, the less accurate the hunch became.

When we look at the sketches or scribbles we made in response to a current feeling or situation, we see that something inside us responded by automatically picking certain colors and not others, certain forms and gestures that simply poured out through the hand. The result is not a picture of an object, but of a feeling state. Here we are reaching into the level not of what will appear on the screen, but of feelings that will arise inside the audience.

A further step in exploring this would be to perform the same exercise with a scene from a movie. Pick a scene with a strong and lingering feeling-tone. The opening sequence in *The Sixth Sense*, where the psychologist played by Bruce Willis is shot in his bedroom, is an example. Play the scene for yourself, having prepared the materials, then immediately cut the video

Continued

and draw for five minutes.* While this may be easier with scenes that contain strong or violent emotions, you can really explore any kind of scene that has dramatic content (i.e., is not merely expositional or transitional). A scene that "works" yields a definite impression that will come through on the paper. Scenes that are not fully achieved leave a muddy or unsettled impression. They are harder to draw because our energy literally does not know where to go.

When you have worked with this technique of intuitive visual response to the point that it feels somewhat natural, it's time to try it on screenplay scenes, written either by you or by colleagues. Sometimes we get so focused on what we are trying to say conceptually that we lose touch with the energy that in fact shapes the scene. The visual brings home to us the truth that stories are energy. Sometimes we discover that what we wrote was completely logical—but where's the energy, where's the feeling? This is of course the same question an actor reading the script is going to ask. The mechanical approach to writing says: "If you want your writing to be more colorful, use more color words." The creativity-centered approach replies: "If you want your writing to be more colorful, live it more intensely, increase the intensity of encounter!" Consider these techniques to make intuitive visualization more conscious as tools to heighten the intensity of encounter. At the same time, entering this design dimension helps us make a bridge between story and style.

Story Universes: Idiom, Genre, and Style

Decisions about idiom and genre are among the first and most important in the development of a film story. Idiom and genre are *controlling ideas*, in that so many aspects of the movie's total expressiveness depend on these core choices. Like many controlling ideas, they are often not made explicit because they are taken for granted. They are part of an "understanding"—which is fine until there is a misunderstanding. When this happens, the project can be headed toward development hell. This is because different idioms describe different story universes with different premises and different cinematic means to convey them. They are apprehended by the audience in very different ways. So defaulting on the task of consciously orchestrating idiom and genre is like not knowing in which universe you are. The audience will experience this indecision as well.

* An alternate method would be to let your hand move spontaneously with the crayon while the scene is playing. This works especially well with the nondominant hand.

We may ask, upon what are style choices based such that they enhance rather than detract from dramatic unity? This is a hard but necessary question to pose, because whenever the audience has to confront shifts of tone or style, they tend to momentarily fall out sync with the story. It is also a difficult question because the variety of contracts possible between filmmakers and audience is without theoretical limit. Irony, kitsch, aggression, seduction, snobbery, and voyeurism can all form the basis of a meta-communication contract as long as there is a market for it. Yet we cannot escape the fact that movies with dramatic unity, with force and authenticity, succeed more often than movies lacking those qualities. Dramatic unity is not an add-on. It is a product of *vision*. The idiom is one of the primary ways vision expresses itself.

Idioms

My approach to idioms and genres is not that of a film critic or sociologist. There are endless ways of picking apart a movie's "discourse" from various theoretical, political, and semiological standpoints. But here we are interested in just one goal: how to tell our stories most effectively. My experience with screenwriters and filmmakers is that theoretical baggage tends to take one out of center and up into the head. The story becomes didactic, which kills much of its real power. So I want to limit myself to those aspects of idiom that are so intrinsic to screenwriting that we cannot avoid discussing them, and then to conceptualize these as simply as possible.

Idioms are conventions of film style. They are conventions in the positive sense of that word: by customary use and tradition. Conventional does not mean arbitrary. Many conventions are based on dominant tropes in our experience, and this turns out to be the case with film idioms. Idioms are based on modes of human perception. In order to talk about them, we borrow aesthetic terms that were established to describe styles in painting: realism, romanticism, and expressionism. For many, many years people have thrown these terms around, usually advocating one -ism over others. But when we look beyond intellectual fashions and ask what realism, romanticism, and expressionism represent, taken altogether, we see that in fact they stand for the spectrum of consciousness. The spectrum runs from objective waking reality through daydream to dream and nightmare. So the idioms actually represent divergent ways of seeing, and thus very different contracts with the audience.

And it *is* a full spectrum. There are seemingly unlimited degrees of shading between the major positions where each movie can establish its own unique sense of style. It is also true that, since film idioms mimic modes of perception, certain experiences and types of storytelling lend themselves to one idiom and not another. Each idiom has its strengths. Thus it is significant that a movie can find a niche like poetic realism where it can garner advantages of realism and romanticism alike. For a development team, what really counts is knowing

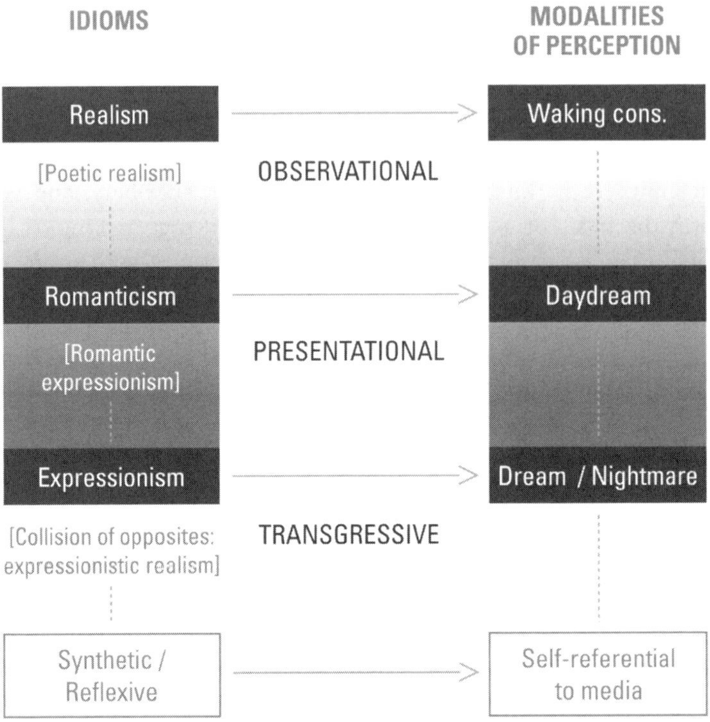

/ Cinematic Idioms.

what you are doing and being consistent with your choice. We are talking about universes after all.

The idiom controls these storytelling and stylistic elements:

- world and scope of the story
- moral quality of that world
- the audience's relation to the events on the screen
- plot structure and storytelling strategies
- dramatic stakes
- pace and tone
- nature of hero and antagonist
- internal consistency and suspension of disbelief
- dialogue
- mise-en-scène
- sound design
- production budget

Along with the hero's journey and the core need/mode conflict, choice of the idiom is probably one of the most important aspects of designing the story.

Realism

Realism is of course not reality. It is a style whose elements work together to create an impression of reality. That is, it invites the audience to accept the events on the screen as part of the real external world rather than belonging to an invented fictional world or an inner subjective reality. One could say this is its reason for being: to refer us back to the "real world." Realism's mode of storytelling is *observational*: real life is observed with care and then rendered into drama. Realism cares about reality, gives primacy to the objective world—especially that of social and political forces—and attempts to be faithful to life.

By analogy, it is as if the movie screen were an enormous window open on the world, just as it is.* What we see through the window may not be familiar to us, the viewers, because it is a different social milieu. But if we could go across town, or to a Mexico City barrio, or to the fringes of Teheran, we could find a reality that matches the movie. This is realism's prime function as a stylistic approach. Realism attempts to bring us into reality, not to escape from it. There is not an attempt to make characters or events bigger than life, but to bring excitement to the audience through an intensity of reality-feeling. Certainly this presents a filmmaker with voluntarily chosen limits: no super digital effects to make it all grandiose and superhuman; no perfect studio lighting to make everyone look gorgeous. Every aspect of the filmmaker's craft comes into play in a highly disciplined way. But it is in the service of a very special idea: the respect for reality as it is, for the passions and sufferings of real people.

This basic premise leads to a cascade of consequences for the creative team. For the screenwriter, the most important of these is that we are looking at a world and at characters who are *morally ambivalent*. There is no character who embodies GOOD, and none who embodies EVIL. Instead, all the characters have some good, some bad, some strengths, some weaknesses—just like ourselves. They are people who inhabit an everyday world, where they are subjected to real-world forces. They have work pressures, time and money concerns. They have in-laws who nag. They must go to the dentist and put gas in the car. They don't know how to handle crises. They stutter and scratch their heads.

In this moral ambivalence we are meant to identify empathically with all the characters and see them all as human. This is surely one of the strengths of the realistic idiom: the emphasis on an empathic understanding of human motives in a complex world. Realism is closely linked to the important movement of global humanism that flourished between the end of World War II and the end of the Cold War. It was a time when people around the world were seriously trying to grapple with how we had made such a hellish mess of things. The observational impulse at the heart of realism goes back to the first days of the movies, to the Lumière brothers' documentary shorts of 1893. But it was another French

* I owe the simile of the window to my colleague Chap Freeman.

filmmaker, Jean Renoir, who laid the foundations for realism as a dramatic idiom. We mentioned Renoir's saying that if you don't love your character you have no business writing about him. Renoir's movies demonstrate that he extended this sense of universal sympathy or charity through the entire world of the story. Thus, in this idiom there will be a dramatic antagonist, but not necessarily a *villain*. The antagonist is not defined as *evil*, but is in the end just another person trying to get along.

As we have said, realism has implications for every aspect of the craft. For example, it becomes a prime task of the cinematography to be prototypical (corresponding to the original). The camera style is often "invisible"; it does not call attention to itself. Lighting is designed to render an image on the film emulsion the way the real setting would look to our eye if we were "really" present, not to make it look pretty or dramatic. An office with bland fluorescent lights should look like one. A factory interior should look like a factory, a supermarket like a supermarket. These places are not beautiful in reality.

Wherever you are right at this moment, put the book down and look around you. Look at objects, people, faces. Simply observe the quality of the light. Is it:

bright ———————— dim?

sharp ———————— diffuse?

single source ———————— multiple source?

warm ———— white ———— cool?

deep shadows ———————— pale shadows?

You may have never tried this before, but it can teach you something about reality, because the quality of light tells a lot about a place. Now, in the idiom of realism the cinematographer and gaffer must simultaneously meet the demands of reality and the demands of art. This is not easy, since neither film nor video record light the way our eye does. The cinematographer must still achieve dramatic effects, but motivated by the prototypical qualities of the setting. Otherwise it will not feel real.

For the screenwriter, it will mean researching the script by going to real locations, observing people, and listening carefully to the texture of their language. Many movies in this idiom have a regional flavor. There are local dialects and accents, whether you're in Tennessee, Yorkshire, or Ardèche. There are local customs that become part of the dramatic fabric. The society may be diverse, like the London of *My Beautiful Launderette*, or insular, like the small village in Périgord in Claude Chabrol's *Le Boucher*. "Local color" in realism is not put there as eye candy; it is an authentic reality in which the story is based. Characters in the story may be trying to hide their shadows and make themselves pretty, but the movie simply records this as behavior. The rawness of life is left intact, neither hidden nor glorified, as we can see in *Kids*, *Rosetta*, *Amores Perros*, the Iranian film *Taste of Cherry*, and the Brazilian *City of God*. As with visual images, so too with the screenwriting: we want to see events as motivated by real, observable forces in the world of the movie.

The premise of realism lends itself to a special storytelling texture. There also tends to be a different relationship between script, director, and actors. In accordance with the observational mode of perception, there is an emphasis on finding the dramatic truth in the performance and using the camera to record it. Jean Renoir would set the camera farther back in order to keep the action within its context. Then he would move the camera to reframe and select the point of dramatic interest. The idea was that the action had an integrity of its own. John Cassavetes improvised in collaboration with the actors while developing the script, and continued this into the shooting as well. With improvisation, the screenplay remains something loose and provisional, while the visual plan is also in ongoing evolution. A further approach related to realism is to tell part or all of the story in "real time." Abbas Kiarostami's *Taste of Cherry*, set in one afternoon in Teheran, uses time to convey immediacy and urgency. There is a tendency in realism to use new faces and nonprofessional actors. Big stars tend to break the "window" effect. Their faces and gestures are so well known that we look *at* them rather than *through* them into the "real" world of the story. (It is almost impossible, in *Babel*, not to see Brad Pitt as Brad Pitt.) With so many story and visual elements conditioned by the idiom, the screenwriter has to take an approach appropriate to the material.

Realism has evolved along with the technology of movies. The style found in early neo-realist movies like *Open City* and *The Bicycle Thief* was made possible because smaller cameras and more sensitive film provided the opportunity to shoot in real locations without elaborate studio lighting. This opened up new worlds of storytelling that had not been available before. One could say that realism emerged from a confluence of needs and opportunities. Waves of interest in realism come along with advances in technology that favor decentralization and allow realism to compete for visibility in the marketplace. Recently, digital video with enough memory to support transfer to 35mm release prints has made it possible to shoot "at home" with a minimal infrastructure and cost.

There is a documentary urge at the heart of realism, a desire to tell the truth about the suffering and heroism of ordinary people in the face of injustice, pettiness, and self-delusion. The intrusion of "movie magic" would diminish rather than heighten the effect—yet the drama must still work on its own terms as defined by the idiom. An intense passion for reality comes through in *Open City*, which was shot on the streets of Rome in the weeks immediately following Rome's liberation in 1944. It dramatizes events that had just happened, shot in the locations where they occurred, with a cast of primarily nonprofessional actors.

In the end, realism is an attitude, a dedication to face life not as we wish it to be, but as we find it. That said, realism may potentially be used for any kind or genre of story. For comedies, one could take as models *Hannah and Her Sisters* and certain other Woody Allen films, as well as the French comedies of Eric Rohmer and the ensemble comedy *Monsoon Wedding* by Mira Nair. Claude Chabrol has made a long career of thrillers in the realist idiom. One of the consequences the choice of realism has on the thriller, as we can see from Chabrol's masterpiece *Le Boucher*, is that a sense of intimacy and emotional charge is generated that Hitchcock would never have attempted. The result is a more intimate relation to evil and a more empathic understanding of it. Much of this power comes from the fact that the movie as such becomes more or less transparent, a window on reality.

Romanticism

The central point to romanticism is that it presents a world that is larger than life. This, as Hitchcock suggested, is life with all the boring parts taken out, where the women are beautiful, the men virile, and the stakes high. The drive is not to directly reflect or mimic external reality, but to use the tools of cinema to create a compressed and emotionally heightened reality. Again, every aspect of the filmmaker's craft is brought to bear, now with the end in mind of creating a special world of movie magic.

Because romanticism shows us a world that is bigger than life, it is intimately connected with daydreams. In daydreams, we commonly fantasize wish-fulfillment or disaster scenarios: what if I suddenly became a billionaire? What if I met the Hollywood star of my dreams at a party? What if terrorists suddenly took over my plane? Like daydreams, the idiom of romanticism has inherent tendencies toward grandiosity and regression. It puts us in a childlike wish-fulfillment state of psyche where the Disney theme "When you wish upon a star . . ." is always playing subliminally in the background. It was long ago noted that when a man sitting in a movie theater gazes up at a twenty-foot-tall close-up of Greta Garbo, his physical relationship to that image is precisely that of a baby at the breast gazing up at mama. This regression effect is one of the particular pleasures of romanticism, one that makes it a very different way of seeing than realism. This is, not surprisingly, the idiom of mainstream commercial filmmaking.

One thing the screenwriter should know in order to construct the special world of romanticism is that the story is not about ordinary people like you and me. The very fact that the characters are larger than life transforms the nature of characterization itself. While observation is used to ground the characters in an external reality and make them plausible, the characters must first of all satisfy the demands of the idiom, of idiom-linked genres, and of the market. They must be fascinating, alluring, charismatic. They must have unforgettable lines and prepared moments where the star will deliver that dazzling smile or sizzling-hot sexy look. Above all, the characters themselves must be ample enough, "great" enough, to carry the supernormal dramatic stakes of the romantic plotline. Not everyone can handle the ruthless criminals who have hijacked nuclear missiles and are threatening to blow up San Francisco unless their demands are met in forty-eight hours!

In the process of fashioning a more high-profile character for the romantic comedy or action-adventure, a certain streamlining takes place. Salient features central to the genre, the character type, and the role (embodied by the actor) are reinforced. Charles, in *Four Weddings*, is shy, gorgeous, and covers his social awkwardness with deft, self-mocking humor. There is much we don't know about him—and are not supposed to ask. The streamlining of a character's complexities goes along with the general suspension of disbelief generic to the romantic idiom. Melvin, in *As Good as It Gets*, displays a snarling social mask that hides a sensitive, emotionally underdeveloped interior. He is obsessive-compulsive, but also talented and productive in his work. Thus he is more complex and finely drawn than Charles, yet he is still squarely a romantic-idiom figure. At the extreme of this streamlining process, the character may become a caricature, reduced to a few iconic gestures, virtually a living cartoon. The Man With No Name in *A Fistful of Dollars* is sketched in with just a few broad strokes: the steely gaze, the cigar, the poncho.

While features that speak an iconic meta-language to the audience are foregrounded and heightened, whatever is mundane or accidental in the character is toned down or suppressed. Does James Bond ever have to brush his teeth or go to the toilet? It is hard to even ask such a question. Banal, everyday behaviors are only included in the romantic idiom specifically to either serve the plot (if Bond is in the bathroom, it is because he will be attacked there) or because they are needed to make the character plausible or likeable. The process is to simplify the characterization around the need/mode core conflict and the nature of the plot goal and genre, and then add flavor as needed. The characters are "purified" of much of their humanness, and this is a large part of what makes them appear larger than life. They are, in fact, explicitly *characters* rather than *people*. They could exist nowhere but in the movies. This makes them both more and less than human. They are more than human in that they are passion, ambition, and vitality writ large. Romantic idiom characters live heroic lives, privileged because they have destinies that lift them above the anonymous masses. They are surrounded by the extras: the rubes who are clueless and can merely scream as raptors crunch them, or who move through the background of a scene, following their banal private agendas. But the romantic idiom heroes are also less than human because, to the extent that they are larger than life, they are not *fully* human. In the same way, we too are both more and less than our fantasies and wishes.

The romantic idiom typically takes us out of our own social worlds into worlds to which we do not have access in our daily lives: the ambience of the wealthy and elite, fashion models, detectives, astronauts, mafiosi. Commonly, the Day and Night Worlds of the story show us a "little" person forced by circumstances to encounter one of these special worlds and cope with it, as when an ordinary citizen stumbles on a murder and must run for her life. In order to survive, she must learn the code of this Night World. For the special worlds of the romantic idiom, in addition to being larger than life, are *coded* worlds. There are codes of behavior, special trainings or initiations, in-language, in-gestures, and ways of dressing. These codes emphasize the special nature of the romantic world because they close out the ordinary. These codes are elaborately *displayed* to the audience. Displaying in this context also implies participation, what anthropologists term *participation mystique*. We are sucked into the movie. We lose a certain level of consciousness, and at the same time flow into a more intense identification with the hero who displays such control of the code. Every major star has the capacity to embody codes and model behavior, or they would not be where they are.

When we go to the movies, we consume codes and modelings as much as we consume a dramatic story. In the romantic idiom, these two become one and the same. The gangsters, fashion models, and billionaires present and model in-behavior that takes on grandeur and magnetism because it is shown as bigger than life. There is evidently a feedback-loop effect in this modeling which is further involved with the mechanisms of consumerism. Even Hannibal Lecter is implicitly presented as a role model. He is such an embodiment of absolute control and cool superiority that impressionable or susceptible individuals might be tempted to imitate his mannerisms in order to absorb some of his "manna" (charisma, which in primitive societies was thought to be a spiritual essence, like the nectar of a flower, that could be transmitted from the leader to his followers). It was reported that on the Port Ranier naval base after the shooting of *An Officer and a Gentleman*, young officer candidates could be seen doing the "Richard Gere strut." Romantic characters are eminently assimilable and consumable.

Just as people are simplified and clarified into characters, behavior is simplified into coded gestures and speech is clarified into lines. The challenge with dialogue in this idiom is to retain a relatively naturalistic sound while compressing the lines so they are more concise and powerful.

- Go ahead, make my day!
- Just *do* it!
- Is that a pickle in your pocket or are you just happy to see me?

There are many degrees of shading between realism and romanticism, and limitless stylistic possibilities. We can learn something about these shadings by comparing the two Jack Nicholson roles in *As Good as It Gets* and *About Schmidt*. The Nicholson figure dominates both movies, and we can recognize in both the familiar Nicholson repertoire of postures, gestures, and facial expressions. This in itself belongs to the romantic idiom because it subliminally reminds us that we are watching a movie. Yet we may also notice that Melvin is the more broadly drawn and played of the two. Nicholson's scornful grin when playing Melvin is a bit tighter, and held a bit longer, than it is when portraying Schmidt; the nervous finger movements are displayed more. Both of these performances are appropriate for the subjects and styles of the two films, but *About Schmidt* is played closer to realism. A common strategy in handling the Story Molecule in romanticism is to orchestrate the central roles, played by the stars, "larger" than the secondary roles, and those slightly larger than the minor roles and extras. (It is striking that this scaling according to importance in a hierarchical scheme is exactly the visual strategy found in the tombs of the Egyptian pharaohs.) There will also be hierarchical differences in the use of dialogue: the bigger roles will get the juicier lines. And, of course, the principals will be lit and photographed with greater attention and dimensionality. They will subtly appear larger and more alive to the audience.

While the core visual strategy of realism is to reproduce the visual qualities of real environments, the core visual strategy of romanticism is to make everything look attractive and dynamic. Let's face it, the flat fluorescent lighting of an office or classroom is ugly! Who wants to look at that? While we might adhere to the general qualities of the original—the softness and diffuse shadows—we would first of all ask what dramatic mood we wish to achieve with the scene. The mood would be defined as high-key or low-key, and this would be translated into a key to fill light ratio.* To create dimensionality and visual separation, back lights and hair lights would be used. The result is an image that is subtly *hyper*-real. It seems to pop off the screen at us.

These are standard visual strategies of the romantic idiom. They are intended to express and reinforce the story by decisively funneling the audience's attention toward the focal point of dramatic action. The lower level of stylization of the secondary characters provides a "bed" of apparent reality grounding. The main characters rise above this bed like soloists above an orchestra. Look at the way group scenes are handled, for example those in *Groundhog Day*. The background characters are treated as visual masses rather than individuals. Their anonymity generates both plausibility and normalcy. It also creates a contrast: they are only alive by virtue of their participation in the collective and its rituals, while Phil is singled out as an individual. He is *more* alive; the others are *less* alive. Phil becomes increasingly charismatic by contrast, which, repeated throughout the movie, confers upon him an iconic, mythic identity as a picaresque victim of chaos in the tradition of Buster Keaton.

Working with the romantic idiom would seem to present the challenging task of bridging fantasy and reality. Here we are greatly helped by the long tradition of movie magic. Romanticism, as the mainstream entertainment idiom, is a convention upon which filmmakers and audience are in complete tacit agreement.

* The key light is the brightest light on a character, normally motivated by an apparent light source in the scene: a lamp, a window, etc. Because film and video "see" more light/dark contrast than our eyes, additional lights are needed to fill in the dark shadows and make them appear natural.

On the whole, we prefer not to peek behind the curtain and discover the Wizard of Oz to be a cheap con. Yet what ultimately holds reality and fantasy together is the power and integrity of the drama itself. As long as the drama presents a real conflict that resonates with the audience, and is willing to develop that conflict to the "grow or die" point for the main character, it will have vitality. Suspension of disbelief will not then be a major problem; the audience will be too absorbed. Fantasy does not necessarily mean escapism; it is simply a facet of human life. Some kinds of stories can only be told in a heightened world above that of the daily grind. The great virtue of the romantic idiom is that this heightened, heroic story language allows us very compressed experiences of life in an aesthetically saturated environment. It utilizes the power of cinema to convey a dramatic truth that enters us deeply, touching levels of fairy tale, myth, and the archetypal depths of soul. Realism puts the audience in the position of an engaged and empathic observer of the drama. Its literalizing tendency posits psyche primarily as a product of external forces. The seductive strategies of the romantic idiom, on the other hand—a larger than life, coded world; a controlling, presentational style; projective identification; and participation mystique—all provoke the audience to become more caught up in the drama. In so doing, the potentially transformational energies of drama may be evoked as well.

Expressionism

Expressionism, like romanticism, uses all the powers of the medium to create a special world of movie magic, but takes it in another direction, toward dreamlike or nightmarish worlds, which typically requires an even greater suspension of disbelief on the part of the audience. Expressionism has its basis in what psychologist Erich Neumann has termed the "transgressive" nature of archetypal energies. That is, it is the nature of the human psyche that information from deeper levels of the unconscious erupts into consciousness in the forms of dreams, fantasies, and affect-disturbances associated with complexes. Expressionism endeavors to capture this world of the irrational and put it directly on the movie screen. In the process, expressionism emphasizes the limits of the power of the ego, and especially of rationality, in life as it is actually lived and experienced.

The special power of expressionist filmmaking is that movies can make the images of dreams and nightmares look as solid and convincing as "reality." A paradox is created for the audience: what is irreal and irrational is presented as "objective" (external to ourselves because it is on the screen), and thus "rational." As the old TV ads for the midnight "creature features" would exclaim: "You'll be screaming, 'It's *only* a movie!!!'" While realism takes the empathic observation of the world as a starting point and romanticism creates a larger than life experience, expressionism's aim is to take the audience directly into irrational feeling states.

We could make a list of strategies the expressionist filmmaker utilizes to achieve the goal of suspending or overturning our rational presumptions about the world, but this would be rather misstating the issue. Because normally the irrational perspective is already present in the author (screenwriter or director) himself. As a result, the expressionist story concept takes a different route through development. The concept is irrational to begin with, therefore it is not so easy to calculate the movie's effect on the mainstream audience. Expressionist stories often have a sense of obsession about them. This goes back to the author. If the filmmaker's obsession can translate into the conviction needed to successfully pitch the idea, and if the producers believe that it will resonate with something in the minds of the audience, then the project may defy the risks and become a movie. This idiom is the most difficult to evaluate in terms of public response because it goes against the culture's view of reality. Expressionist projects are also harder to fit into objective development criteria of working/not-working. Basing a risky expressionist piece on a successful novel or well-known figure (like Steven Soderberg's *Kafka*) is a common strategy to reduce risk. But in the end, one must have enough faith in the project to roll the dice.

Within this context that includes a level of uncertainty, we can identify elements that appear again and again in expressionist films, and which could be considered tools or strategies:

- The premise is impossible or defies logic (i.e., the same day repeats itself or time flows backward)
- The world of the story is unreal because it is:
    - dreamlike or nightmarish
    - disconnected or nonlinear
    - fantastic or monstrous
- The action may take us between a "normal" or logical Day World and a transgressive, dreamlike Night World
- Time may be distorted, reversed, or suspended
- There are often transformations or metamorphoses of objects
- The story features or includes characters who are nonhuman:
    - ghosts, the dead, or otherwise nonliving
    - monsters
    - angels
    - symbolic figures
- The visual style emphasizes the irrational or uncanny:
    - unexplained events
    - POV shots not connected to any character
    - flying or floating camera movements
    - disorienting cuts

- altered camera speeds (fast/slow motion)
- lighting with unnatural colors or from unnatural/unmotivated directions (especially from below)

One observation that emerges from this outline is that many of the traditional strategies of expressionism have entered mainstream commercial filmmaking as stylistic devices. There appears to be some confluence between the aims and means of expressionism and those of romanticism. One reason is that society has progressively lost its exclusive faith in rationalism and has accepted the exploration of nonrational states of consciousness. Probably the main reason, however, is that commercial filmmakers are always looking for new and more powerful ways to impact or control the audience. This takes them naturally into the territory of expressionism. What holds all of the above tools of expressionism together and gives them their power to generate vivid magical worlds are primal emotions and feeling states. These are the irrational feeling states that drive the author to begin with: desire and loathing, fascination and fear, supernal delight and unmitigated disgust. The audience is pulled out of their comfort zone into extreme psychic spaces, and the potential regression effect is correspondingly greater. Unconsciously, the audience becomes even more dependent on the filmmaker as their guide through the labyrinth. In a saturated media environment where competition for the audience's attention is constantly escalating, it was inevitable that expressionist strategies would be picked up by mainstream filmmakers.

As realism has its cinematic roots in the first Lumière shorts, and romanticism was already nascent in *The Great Train Robbery* (1907) and has characterized American cinema from the beginning, we can trace expressionism back to early German movies. The expressionist palette was already articulated in silent features like *Nosferatu*, *Vampyr*, *The Cabinet of Dr. Caligari*, and *Metropolis*. In films like these we find dream sequences, characters going in and out of consciousness, grotesque set design with skewed angles and false perspectives, and the tones of dread and fascination we associate with expressionism today. It is perhaps not surprising that expressionism grew out of the same cultural milieu as psychoanalysis. There were parallel movements in literature and painting. In an early Willem de Kooning painting, for example, the painter renders a woman's mouth with a red gash on the canvas. Obviously, this is not a "real" mouth or a "beautiful," ideal mouth or a visual impression of a mouth. It is a direct response to a strong emotion that must be said to belong more to the painter than to the subject of the portrait, or to be part of a transaction between them. Expressionist directors seek to bring similar nonrational feeling states onto the set. German director Werner Herzog cast a schizophrenic street person in the lead role of one film; in another, the entire cast reportedly performed under hypnosis.

Expressionism used to have outlets in the B-horror, gothic, and low-budget sci-fi genres. As these genres folded into the mainstream of big-budget filmmaking, the expressionist style has mainstreamed as well. *The Fall of the House of Usher* has become *Seven*, *Silence of the Lambs*, and *The Sixth Sense*; *Invasion of the Body Snatchers* has become *Independence Day* and *The Matrix*. *Groundhog Day* recycles an idea used by the surrealist Luis Buñuel in *The Exterminating Angel* and *The Discreet Charm of the Bourgeoisie* of people trapped in a purgatorial time from which they cannot escape. Expressionism as a pure idiom is not often to be found, but its devices have become part of the mainstream repertoire. Of course, the same effects in the context of a different idiom have a different meaning. Transferred to the romantic context, expressionistic devices add the edginess of the irrational to enhance the entertainment value.

For example, *A Beautiful Mind* uses many expressionistic strategies to take us inside the mind of the main character. But this movie is not an expressionistic exploration of madness; it stops short of sinking us in the direct experience of madness. Rather, it is a romantic image of a Hollywood view of madness. We are protected from madness by the romantic style itself. The schizophrenic hero's fantasies are presented as perfectly logical and coherent—only they are not real. The insane fantasies, in fact, turn out to be an exciting Hollywood thriller! This gives us the illusion that we understand something. In the romantic setting, the story design function of the paranoid spy plot in *A Beautiful Mind* is really to make the character, the love story, and the movie more compelling to the audience.

When developing a screenplay that has elements of both expressionism and romanticism, important stylistic decisions need to be made about how to integrate it all into one story design. The question to ask is: which is the main idiom of the movie? Is expressionism to be in the service of romanticism or visa versa? The answer to this question will undoubtedly impact the theme of the movie. When expressionistic devices are used to give juiciness and edginess to a romantic movie, Act II may venture into bizarre or nightmarish worlds, but the resolution in Act III will bring a neat closure. The audience will be brought back to their comfort zone. We see this in the climax of *The Sixth Sense* and the afterlife resolution of *American Beauty*, both securely in the romantic idiom. But when the ending is left unresolved or aggressively jagged, we are more in the territory of expressionism. The unresolved ending is itself an expressionistic device when it is coupled with anxiety. The psychic energy invested in the film by the audience is left hanging in midair. This helps us differentiate *The Sixth Sense* from *Mulholland Drive* or *Jacob's Ladder*.

Between romanticism and expressionism there are also many degrees of shading. This is an area where the larger than life world of romance becomes saturated with metaphor and symbol. Depending on how the author approaches it, we in the audience may be made consciously aware that the action on the screen stands for something else beyond what is presented—or we may not. Andrei Tarkovski's *The Sacrifice* is so explicitly referenced to cultural icons—Shakespeare, Dostoevsky, Bergman, Russian Orthodox mysticism, Zen, etc.—that the movie itself takes on the quality of a cinematic cultural icon. It is as though a Russian icon has come to life, unfolding the saint's struggle with faith and doubt and yielding the perfectly iconic ending where the dead tree bursts into blossom. David Lynch's *Mulholland Drive*, on the other hand, does not at first sight give us such a reassuring container. While both the screenplay and the directing are impeccably crafted, *Mulholland Drive* leaves us with an uneasy grip on reality. Something continues to feel threatening long after the movie is over. We may blame the movie, but in fact the disturbance is nowhere but in ourselves. This disturbance is the expressionist effect. The seductively romantic style of *Mulholland Drive* serves to lure us into a seemingly irrational Night World and leave us there.

Expressionist touches can also appear in realism, where the injection of a note of irreality can lift the story to another level. There are specific Story Steps where such shifts of level tend to happen. A striking moment appears in the second half of Abbas Kiarostami's austere masterpiece, *Taste of Cherry*, where expressionism intrudes in a realist context without breaking it. The plot goal of the main character (whose name is never given) is to find a helper. He seeks someone charitable enough to cover his body with dirt after he commits suicide. As suicide is illegal in Iran, this is a potentially dangerous mission. Thus the hero haunts the fringes of Teheran, hoping to find a day-laborer desperate enough for cash to agree to the job. Suggesting that he has work, he picks up a series of men and takes them to a hillside where he has already dug the grave. The men invariably run away. After one of these encounters, the hero is alone on the hill where enormous bulldozers and earthmovers are carving the hillside for future development. Falling toward despair, he stops to watch. At this point there is a long take of his shadow on a constant cascade of falling dirt. The shot is held so long, in fact, that the shadow appears to take on a life of its own. In effect, the entire movie is compressed into this one image. The effect is expressionistic, dreamlike, though the cinematic means remain within the idiom of realism. The moment does not break the movie's stylistic integrity, but enhances it. This is an example of masterful directing and storytelling.

Expressionism highlights the fact that nothing on the screen has only a single level of meaning. The audience *dreams* the movie as they watch it, just as the screenwriter dreams the movie unconsciously while constructing it consciously. Our awareness of metaphor, heightened by expressionism, is important in opening up our writing from boxlike predictability into fresher and more risky creative spaces.

Metafiction: The Synthetic/Reflexive Idiom

Realism, romanticism, and expressionism portray a spectrum of consciousness and modes of perception. In that sense, they have always been with us. We can see these idioms emerge in the early days of the movies. Since that time, however, there has been a new development. More and more of our experience is prepackaged—*mediated*—for us. People in industrial societies probably spend more time looking at media products than they do looking either at nature or at other human beings. If movies are to reflect our lives, they must reflect this aspect as well. A new idiom is visible that looks directly at our existence in this media envelope. It is called the *synthetic/reflexive idiom*. It is synthetic because it freely mixes together the other idioms, along with genres, old TV series, kitschy pop culture—in fact, anything it finds appealing or provocative. It has a universal appetite. It is reflexive in that its subject is ultimately itself. This idiom is self-conscious and self-referential. Here, the three other idioms make their appearances, no longer as modes of perception but as media products. In the new context, realism, romanticism, and expressionism lose their transparency. They become opaque and suffused with irony. We look *at* them rather than *through* them. Thus the synthetic idiom constantly reminds us that we are looking at a media product, one that has the power to make us look at it.

How are we to approach the design of a movie like *Traffic*? Here we have a mix of two idioms. The Mexican scenes are shot in a realistic, pseudo-documentary style, with unknown faces, probably some nonprofessional actors, and hand-held camera movements that have a spontaneous, improvised feel. The American scenes have most of the features of romanticism: an elite and powerful level of society, very well-known stars, and genre elements such as the buddy relationship of the two DEA agents and the melodramatic father-daughter conflict. Yet this stylistic mix is made even more complex as the realism of the Mexican scenes is rendered slightly irreal or hyper-real through the use of an amber filter. Likewise, in the American scenes, the fictional world of romanticism has reality intrude upon it as real public figures appear in cameo roles playing themselves. The result is neither realism nor romanticism, but something synthetic. Whenever the movie shifts from one style to the other we are subtly reminded of this. In the end, it is the audience that synthesizes the movie into a dramatic and stylistic unity.

The mix in *Traffic* is still relatively straightforward because the story, though woven of several strands, is generally linear and the tone is consistent. But the synthetic idiom also goes along with alternate strategies like nonlinear storytelling and an aggressive use of distancing devices, such as irony and pop-culture references, as in *Pulp Fiction* and *Lola Rennt* (*Run Lola Run*). This is a growing edge in contemporary filmmaking, as people look for fresh ways to tell stories. The synthetic idiom really does present the audience with a different kind of universe. It also creates a different relationship between the audience and the movie, one that is less simple because of this reflexive quality. How can we describe the complex nature of this relationship?

Far more than romanticism, the synthetic idiom makes us deliberately aware that this is a movie, an element of an omnipresent pop culture, that it has the power to manipulate our feelings—and that we like that. The self-conscious pleasure of being entertained by a movie refers back, through the synergy of cross-marketing and product placement, to the pleasure of consuming in general. This idiom is intrinsically ironic and distancing, while at the same time it uses every device to draw us in. This complexity is not without its subtle double binds, however. How do you empathize with a character you are constantly being reminded is not real? There is also typically a metacommunication common to advertising that is simultaneously ingratiating to the consumer (look how hip you are, part of the in-group that *gets* it!) and condescending (we've got you eating out of the palm of our hand, and you love every minute of it).

The synthetic idiom is also much more self-conscious about the power we have given the media to model and validate our own experience. The blind spot of an extremely extroverted society like our own is its lack of inwardness. Lacking inwardness and the reflection that links us back (*to link back* = re-ligare, the etymological root of religion) to unshakeable depth in ourselves, we become easily blown about by winds of fashion and change, winds controlled to a very large extent by those who operate the media. Many people rely on the media to tell them what's hot and what's not, what colors to wear, how to eat, sleep, and make love—in short, how to *live*. With increasing dependence on the media comes increasing valuation of the media as reality. Polls suggest that there are people who believe the characters in *Sex and the City* are more real than they themselves are. "Sex and the City" clubs and techno-parties are organized in various countries to help people act out their projective fantasies. The synthetic idiom plays with this trend while reinforcing it in a feedback loop. This is part of a double bind. It is a double bind because our choices would appear to be either to step back and respond with ironic distancing of our own or to be drawn into an increasingly codependent relationship with the mass media. The boundary issues here are complex. We may be modeling a society that is on the whole more ironic, skeptical, and defended, and less able to trust and make commitments. The trend appears to be toward what psychologists have termed a "narcissistic society."

Of course, there are positive aspects to the synthetic idiom or it would not have caught on with filmmakers and the audience. It is beneficial to take a step back and become aware of the media as media, as the synthetic idiom insists, and not be naïvely swallowed up by the image as romanticism invites us to do. Ambivalence toward media products is a step of differentiated growth, if not a comfortable one. Ambivalence, that "luxury of consciousness," might lead further, to a playful interaction.

Synthetism, anyway, is here to stay. It is part of the post-modern landscape. Use of the synthetic/reflexive idiom is growing, and as it does it presents new opportunities to screenwriters. The important ingredient for the writer in working with this idiom seems to have a playful attitude. It requires a willingness to take idioms, genres, and conventions, as well as plot and character, as playthings. Nothing is sacred, but everything is surprising. The Hero's Journey is a plaything; "growth through crisis" is a plaything. However, even play does not relieve us, the storytellers, of the demands drama places on us, since that structures the audience's experience. The real art of working with the synthetic idiom is to create a story that is playful, distanced, and self-referential, while at the same time conveying dramatic integrity and authenticity. This is a path of special challenges and delights.

Genres

We have outlined idioms as conventions of film style, broad style categories to consider in the early stages of developing the project. Genres, on the other hand, can be thought of as conventions of film content. That is, genres are significant sets or constellations of story elements that are found together: typical settings, characters, objects, conflicts, plot structures, Day and Night Worlds, etc. Genres thus present concrete story worlds that are based both on a society's common experience and mythology. This already separates genre stories from the idiom of realism in most cases. The worlds of realism may also be based on society's common experience, but the genre does not try to look at this "objectively." A genre is a lens through which society looks at itself, a lens that simplifies and codifies experience according to dominant traditions and beliefs. Genres go back at least to ancient Egyptian art, where we can see the sense of *type* dominate over the portrayal of individual uniqueness. It is the typical aspect that accretes into tradition and perpetuates itself. In some circles, genre filmmaking was considered second-rate "hack" work. But genre places no limitation on quality whatsoever. We might simply remind ourselves that Rembrandt, Monet, Cézanne, and, yes, Picasso were all genre painters. Any story can conceivably be told in any idiom, but in practice the vast majority of genre films are in the romantic idiom.

In his discussion of genre, Robert McKee points out that there have been many systems of genre classification, with no final consensus among them.[30] He then goes on to present his own breakdown of twenty-five major genres with numerous subgenres. Some members of this list strike me as true genres, others as standard plot structures that may be used in a variety of settings. Genre will always be imprecise, though everyone tells us that genres have very specific codes that must be addressed by the screenwriter. Genre remains imprecise because any story elements that are successful for a time, that are used over and over again, tend to become generic. They no longer represent original creative innovations for the writer, but are part of established patterns. They become coded elements of the culture: a reference to the name of the class ("thriller," "Hollywood ending") stands for and evokes the entire class of experience. Genres and generic elements even have life cycles, as fashions of all kinds do. The Western genre has been virtually dead for some time. What do we mean by "dead"? It is no longer a world in which we invest our imagination and libido. It no longer compels our psychic energy or reflects our concerns. The libido has found more compelling containers.

30. McKee, Robert, *Story* (New York: Harper Collins, 1997), pp. 79–99.

As the pace of life quickens and the level of restlessness and ambient anxiety in society increases, it appears that the cycle-time of generic elements, like that of fashions, is growing shorter. The insatiable hunger for the new replaces whatever is on center stage with something else, the latest, the ultimate. This social trend, coupled with an accelerating image technology, is changing the look and meaning of genre. It is harder than ever to successfully write and market a "standard" genre piece, one that would have worked according to the development criteria of a few years ago. Increasingly, innovation is demanded of the screenwriter either to blur genre boundaries, to mix two or more genres, to inject genres with new characters and relationship patterns, or to give the genre story a very contemporary look. Competition and the inflation of storytelling rhetoric have also figured into this. Every movie that can possibly support it is loaded with thriller twists and shocks, such as the transformation of a biopic into an action-adventure in *A Beautiful Mind*. As these changes are certain to continue, it seems better to take a more fundamental, stripped-down approach to genre. The useful differentiation is between the core level of genre that remains relatively stable through these changes and the level that changes very quickly as it responds to cultural fashions. We shall focus on the former, for this is where we will find a core of meaning.

Genres simplify personality and behavior into dominant types. Genre types work only if they are recognized by the audience/society. So there is a sort of feedback loop between the dominant types already recognized by the audience and those presented by a new movie. If there is not enough overlap, there will not be recognition, and the audience will likely not embrace the new presentation. However, if the overlap is too complete, there will not be enough of a spark for the new product to stand out and attract. This process of "matching" pertains to perception in general, but it is especially relevant to genre films, which make self-reference part of the show. Genre, as a controlling idea in story development, embraces plot, setting, character, and tone. By doing so, genre suggests style possibilities: the audience's expectations of shocks, twists, and a confrontation with evil in a thriller condition the way space, camera, lighting, sound, and music are used, as well as the way the screenplay is structured. Genres are loosely defined story worlds, locations in the atlas of story possibilities, each with their own ecology of forms.

The fact that genres are possible at all again is due to the parallel, foreground, and background nature of psychic processes. New information is constantly compared to internal schemata. This is a process that goes on largely unconsciously. It has a double root: schemata develop on one hand from learning and direct experience, but on the other from archetypal dominants deep in the unconscious. On one hand is the *stereotype*, on the other is the *archetype*. We give stereotype a pejorative connotation, but it is simply a step in the learning process of comparing new data with the internalized information base. E. H. Gombrich has shown this very well in his book *Art and Illusion*. For example, early printed books used the same woodcut illustration of a generic city to portray Paris, Rome, Mantua, and Constantinople. The reader's own imagination created different cities out of the same image; we could say he actually *saw* different cities. The stereotype sufficed as a starting point, a rough idea. Its very lack of specificity gave it a power of suggestion.

The only problems with the stereotype are when we get stuck with it and fail to proceed to a more differentiated view or when we use it to support a prejudice. An archetypal image, on the other hand, comes from another source, the archetypal level of the psyche. While an image that carries an archetype is concrete in itself, it carries an undertow of numinosity. That fascinating, awesome numinosity tends to draw us toward the unconscious and a less distinct layer of the psyche. This is very subjective, though Jung suggests that an eruption of archetypal imagery is central to revolutions and other mass movements. As images, stereotype and archetype easily flow into each other. The result is that genre movies feel close to myth. The mythic/archetypal level resonates in the background or subtext of the genre story. To the extent that a character or situation evokes a type, it also represents something beyond itself.

Genre movies reflect cultural dominants and myths. This is why they are truly *popular*, "belonging to the people." They act as conduits, bringing deeper collective energies into cultural expression. Because we have the mythic level involved, we can expect it to give shape to the different story worlds we recognize as genres. It turns out that the main genres work with all of the story models we have presented, starting with the Hero's Journey. While there is always a Day World and a Night World, each genre puts its own inflection on the Day/Night dialectic, investing them with special values or emphases. Thus the story world of each genre has an identifiable quality or energy. This specific constellation of Day/Night forces in turn conditions the nature of the main character's journey, the landscape, tone, conflict, and initiation. The durable aspect of the genre conventions comes from this mythic level, while the concrete details keep shifting with passing social trends.

What we call character-driven drama depicts a universal level of human nature by taking the audience deeply into the conflict of a more or less unique individual. Conflict strips away the superficial mode adaptation of the character (as we saw in Chapter Four), revealing a more universal and authentic personal experience at the "grow or die" point, leading to initiation and climax. Initiation is both universal and uniquely personal, like the experience of love. As we journey with the hero through the Night World, we empathize deeply. In effect, we come to love the character. Genre movies take a different tack, via collective structures in the society.

Genre movies are about society. They reflect society to itself. The conflict structure looks at society's weaknesses and shadow side. The heroes of character-driven dramas of course inhabit social worlds. But the genre hero represents society as a whole and its collective values. The genre hero is identified by his social role rather than his idiosyncratic personality. Every detective in a thriller, despite his individual differences, is first of all *The Detective* as a type. He is the one charged by society to plunge into the Night World of evil on our behalf and as our proxy.

Through their quality of being part stereotype, part archetype, genre heroes become carriers of collective projections from the audience. They are invested with tremendous value. There is something keenly ritualistic about this: it is only a few short steps backward from Bruce Willis in *Die Hard* to Gary Cooper in *High Noon*, and only a few steps more to the matador facing the *toro* in the bull-ring. And suddenly we find ourselves deep in the context of myth and ritual. As with all rituals, while participating with a collective in a movie theater watching a thriller, melodrama, or romantic comedy, a lowering of consciousness tends to occur. We temporarily lose some of our individualized ego-consciousness and flow into the collective. Look at people in the movie theater and you see them moving and responding in unison, cells of a macro-being that has for a brief time become manifest. We touch here on something primitive that is deeply satisfying. In this way, genre movies are not only about society, they actually *reconstitute* society, renewing people in their sense of shared values through a collective "passion" experience.

Each of the main genres would be worthy of full-length study, though books tend to be written about genres after the libido has gone out of them. There are entire shelves of books on film noir and the Western, but surprisingly little on the contemporary thriller. In the present context, we shall look at two of the genres as story worlds to see how we can use development models to guide us to the core level of the genre conventions. A twenty-point comparison of thriller and melodrama will give us a foundation.

Thriller

1. It is common to talk about thrillers as being plot-driven. In fact, they are ultimately *audience-driven*. From beginning to end, thrillers are constructed with the audience's every response in mind. The rhythm of thrills, twists, suspense, and revelations pre-exists the screenplay. That's what *generic* means. Characters, too, serve the plot. Thriller characters are constructs, though as stated before, thrillers can be made in any idiom. Yet even in a realist thriller, like Chabrol's *Le Boucher*, the necessary lethal stakes must be set early in Act I, or we do not have a thriller. All character action in the thriller is under the imminent threat of attack. This fact conditions all decisions in character development.

   Thrillers have a long audience tradition. People watch thrillers because they have enjoyed other thrillers. They want a spectacular roller-coaster ride. The orchestration of the plot and all the other story elements in thriller development is designed to satisfy the audience's expectations.

2. Thrillers explore the shadow side of society as it manifests itself in deadly crime. Society is pictured as split between a naïve status quo side, which takes social masks at face value, and a dark, hidden side where the violent shadow is acted out. It is a fundamental strategy of thrillers to take us into taboo zones: transgressive behaviors, contracts, and milieus we prefer not to look at. As a subtextual theme, thrillers probe society's wounds through the question: *where does evil come from*?
3. The iconic role of the main character in a thriller is that of the detective. Either the hero's social role makes him officially a detective, or the hero is an ordinary person forced by circumstances into becoming one in order to survive. As mentioned, the role of the detective has a special mythology. This is a hero who is part scapegoat. The detective enters the shadow world on our behalf, confronts evil, and as a result returns contaminated with knowledge of the dark side. Even the successful thriller hero is forever set apart from the status quo society by this knowledge, and typically becomes something of a loner and outsider. This positions the audience in a special way as they ride through the movie in identification with this figure.

   But the thriller differs from the whodunit because the hero herself comes into lethal danger. The *endangered hero* is one of the core conventions of the thriller genre, for without this condition it is impossible to generate the thriller tone.
4. The universal issue common to thrillers in general is that of *faith vs. doubt*. On the thematic level, this is faith vs. doubt in the basic values of society. Since the killer antagonist acts out a split-off shadow side of society, he holds up a mirror to something about which we are in denial. Some thrillers question fundamental tenets of the way we live: capitalism, patriarchy, corporate codes, repression, and order. Others question human nature itself by exposing the heart of human darkness.

   This split of faith vs. doubt comes into the plotting of the thriller by putting the hero in a relationship with a character, often the love interest, who might be the killer. Two contradictory sets of evidence are created that point to either innocence or guilt. The audience is put in a position of paralyzing uncertainty along with the hero. This positioning of the audience is integral to how the thriller genre works. John Truby has well emphasized this aspect of thriller development.
5. The tone of the thriller is of course based on the *thrill*. Thrill is where fear and pleasure flow together and are given a kinetic release. Underlying the plot-level fear is a primitive sense of *dread*, which contains elements of helplessness, disgust, betrayal, taboo, and regression. The audience is pulled forcibly by the shock of crime out of their comfort zone and into a pervasive irrational state. Dread is highly regressive.

The thriller evolved out of combining earlier crime and horror genres, which dealt with violation and dehumanization, respectively. Put these two together and you have an intoxicating cocktail of emotions.

6. The stakes of the thriller are always lethal. More and more, thrillers get a running start by showing a murder in a hook opening.* The pattern of victims must come to potentially include the hero herself.
7. We have mentioned the phenomenon of *regression* repeatedly. Thrillers play on regressing the audience as another central strategy. Fear starts the flow of adrenaline, which in itself starts to carry us out of our rational state of consciousness. Adrenaline urges us to an unreflected physical response. In the movie theater, this is only possible via projective identification with the hero, who himself is victimized by imminent threat. When the tone of fear and dread is combined with the loss of control of the endangered hero, the audience is in effect regressed back to the state of a terrified child.
8. Working with the Hero's Journey model, the Day and Night Worlds of a thriller take on a special inflection:

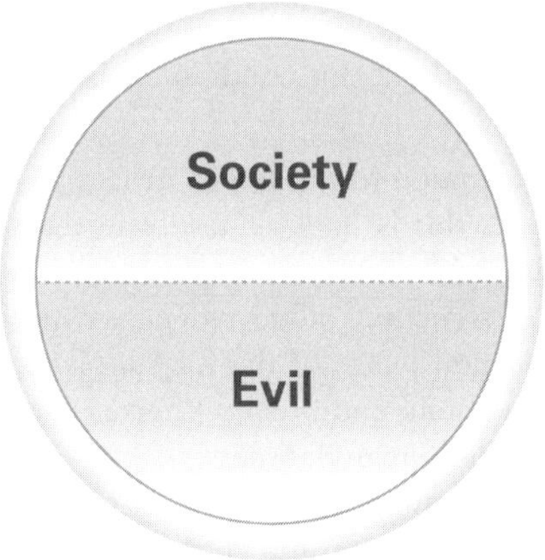

The social status quo of relative innocence is established in Act I. Into this world evil irrupts as a violent transgression. Even when the hero is a professional detective, the nature of the crimes must still have a transgressive and shocking power.

It is a convention of the thriller that the antagonist is already moving in the backstory and has the beat as the movie opens. The antagonist leads the action at least through the Core Crisis/midpoint of Act II. The hero must venture into the antagonist's world and force field to meet the menace.

---

* See Chapter Nine for more on openings.

9. In the thriller, evil may come from one of three directions:

   - from *within* society, i.e., *The Fugitive*, *Shallow Grave*, Jerry Lundegard in *Fargo*. These antagonists are respectable members of the status quo Day World.
   - from *beneath* the Day World of society, from a sinister underworld or subculture, as in *Silence of the Lambs*, *Blue Velvet*, and *The Crying Game*.
   - from *outside* the human world, as in sci-fi, supernatural, and medical subgenres: *Terminator 2*, *Armageddon*, etc.

   Tom Schlesinger did some important work in conceptualizing these vectors of evil in the thriller. Clearly, in dramatic terms, it has a correspondence to the three levels of the Story Molecule. The antagonist is either positioned as "like us," as a related shadow aspect of that macro emotional network which is society, or as a completely outer and alien phenomenon.

10. Working with the Need versus Mode model, we orchestrate the main character as being split herself. She has one foot in the Day World and one in the Night World. This is accomplished by giving the character a *core virtue* that relates to the social role and a *blind spot* that connects to the specific nature of the crimes being committed. The blind spot is a weakness that puts the hero more at risk.

    When working with buddy-heroes, it is typical to give the core virtue to one and the blind spot to the other, as in *Seven*.

11. The inner conflict of the main character revolves not around deep character change, but specifically: which will prove to be stronger under stress, the virtue or the blind spot? The blind spot is a character weakness that is an obstacle to figuring out the crimes because it is in some way connected to the nature of the crimes. It makes this hero especially vulnerable in this specific situation. On a plot level, will the hero see his blind spot before the killer gets him?

12. The Call to Adventure in thrillers is an outer call to investigate a crime, either as a professional duty or after having been victimized (*The Fugitive*, *Hand That Rocks the Cradle*).

13. Laying out the emotional network of a thriller's Story Molecule, there are some special aspects. First, the relationship with the antagonist is predicated on two facts: the antagonist is in control and the antagonist is unknown. The unknown antagonist may be offscreen most of the story or may be present but hiding behind a mask of innocence. This means that it is not always necessary—or the most effective drama—to portry scenes of direct and open confrontation between hero and killer. It may take the first half of the movie or longer for the hero to discover the identity of the antagonist. As a consequence, antagonism is also secondarily developed around obstructing characters in the emotional network in order to keep the tension level up. These may be conniving superiors or competitive colleagues. The "good

guys" in a double-chase structure also fulfill this function (the FBI in *North by Northwest*, Marshal Gerard in *The Fugitive*). Meanwhile, the hero-killer line develops as a battle of wits and wills expressed through an escalating series of killings. This battle of wits defines a relationship even when the antagonist is offscreen. The sense of relationship underlies the plot events and holds them together. For this to work, it is necessary for the stakes to be clear to the audience.

The primary relationship or love interest is often, though not always, played for ambiguity and potential betrayal. This is especially true in erotic thrillers (*Sea of Love*).

14. The more ambiguous or conflicted the primary relationship is, the more important it is to introduce another character for tonal balance. As the love interest in *Sea of Love* is especially ambiguous (she might be the serial killer), she is balanced in the story design by giving Frank, the main character, a lighter, more comical buddy, played by John Goodman. In *Seven*, Gwyneth Paltrow plays an important role as Detective Mills's wife by bringing warmth and relatedness into the detectives' contentious relationship. This of course serves the plot level by allowing the buddy detectives to make a deeper commitment to each other and the case, and it also serves the design of the story by providing tonal balance.
15. The crisis/threshold crossing that ends Act I suggests, through the pattern of crimes, that evil may be out of control and the hero powerless to stop it. The crimes reveal an irrational depravity, obsession, or cold-bloodedness that takes the audience into unknown territory.
16. As the main character moves into the Night World of Act II, the mode starts to collapse under stress. Unlike in character-driven dramas, here the emphasis may be entirely on the outer plot consequences. Inner mode breakdown leaves the character less confident and more vulnerable to the antagonist. This puts greater urgency on the question of whether the hero will put the puzzle together before it's too late. *The Hand That Rocks the Cradle* plays strongly on this.
17. The Act II mechanics of the thriller almost always involve twists and reversals. These typically come at specific Story Steps, like Story Step #12: Breaking Point. Here, what looked like the big break in the case actually lands the hero in greater jeopardy. The twists and reversals may, in erotic and psychological thrillers, focus on whether the primary relationship means love or death. But in action thrillers, the chess match between protagonist and antagonist will be foregrounded.
18. Obligatory scenes, beyond those already mentioned, include a revelation scene—placed normally in Story Steps #12, 13, or 15—of how dark the evil really is. The full plan or depth of violation and dehumanization are shown to both hero and audience, as in Buffalo Bill's flaying house in *Silence of the Lambs*.

19. At the catastrophe ending Act II, it appears that evil wins. The hero may have put the puzzle together only to learn that it is apparently too late to stop the big disaster. There is a desperate feeling of too little, too late.

    This sets up a reversal at the climax, Story Step #15. It is part of the thriller code to take the hero all the way to the edge, to a seemingly impossible situation, before resolving the plot.
20. The resolution of the thriller normally shows us order restored. Not only has this traditionally been the case, but contemporary levels of graphic violence on the screen almost *demand* decent closures in compensation. The widening split between graphic violence and secure closure (happy ending) must certainly have a stunning and dissociating impact on the audience. Thrillers make us react, but they can, if they so choose, also make us think and reflect. You may notice that *Fargo* delivered graphic violence in a very measured dose. By not causing the audience to freeze in shock at its climax, more energy was available to take in the complex theme of the movie.

    Resolution also includes a final beat in the primary relationship to help suggest closure, as is true with movies in general. However, this is very often followed in the very last shots by a shocking stinger. The stinger may be played to show us that the monster isn't really dead, or it may be played for a joke or humorous curtain line that breaks the tense atmosphere, as in *The Fugitive* and *North by Northwest*.

Of course, such a brief summary cannot hit all of the points and variations that appear in the thriller and its subgenres. The function of this overview has been to show how the thriller as a genre creates a special kind of world with its own ethos and rules. The twenty points listed are genre elements that tend to be stable over time and across the range of subgenres. How thriller works with the Sixteen Story Steps in detail must be left to a fuller study.

Melodrama

1. Melodramas arc *audience-driven*. While plot is always central to reaching and engaging the audience, the melodrama tone is often its most striking feature. Ads and posters for melodramas feature relationships more than plot excitement. The melodrama tone is one of breathless claustrophobia because the story premise places the main character in a weak, confined situation from which there seems no way out. More often the stakes are not lethal, as they are in the thriller. But this does not stop melodramas from generating intense dramatics through empathy with the trapped hero.

    That empathy begins by defining a socioeconomic context recognized by the audience as the world of the story. The melodrama world is a *closed* world, under constant internal pressure. Constructing a closed dramatic pressure cooker is a necessary element of the melodrama setup. Because the hero is in a weak position in a closed system, melodramas often have tragic or "down" endings (*Dangerous Liaisons*, *Raise the Red Lanterns*). The hero either breaks free from confinement or is tragically, pathetically crushed by the restraining force. This is also part of the melodrama convention. It is not what the character learns in the end (since the character may fail), but what the *audience* learns about how to live.

Melodrama as we know it today has naturally evolved from different sources than the thriller. Formerly, melodrama (or "dark drama") was principally about women and children, because society's rules made legal, financial, moral, and psychological independence almost impossible for them. The confining setting was usually the home, the antagonist most often a domineering man, landlord, or other agent of heavy-handed power. As women gained the power to vote and gradual parity, melodramas have shifted their focus to explore the tension between freedom and belonging more broadly. In the process, melodramas have generally become more universal in their themes.

2. Melodramas also probe the shadow side of society, not through violent crime, but through the dynamics of family. Melodramas are about family; they define the status quo world of the story as a family. It may be a natural, biological family, or it may be a substitute or transitory family. Any group that can be circumscribed as a family can be used for melodrama: an office, a team or military unit, a scientific expedition, a beauty contest. Within this world, melodramas pose a fundamental tension between freedom and belonging. The antagonist plays a special role in melodrama, for this character embodies the "family's" dominant values. So the melodrama world is like a small laboratory reflecting the larger dynamics in society.
3. The iconic role of the main character in melodrama could be described as the "problem child." The hero is established as the member of the group who does not fit and who yearns to break away to a more authentic life or to a fantasy of freedom. There is something fundamentally childlike about this character, relative to the dominant figure in the family. He is shown to still retain some impulse toward healthy growth, despite the dysfunctional family bonds constraining him. Certainly Valmont in *Dangerous Liaisons* is not innocent in terms of conventional morality. But all of his lying protestations of reform become truth through his experience of love. The antagonist in this case, the Marquise de Merteuil, may long for love but can only act out control and destruction. This relative innocence of the melodrama hero gives him an iconic link to the sacrificial lamb, sacrificed by the family/society to its own destructive impulses (*Breaking the Waves*).
4. In melodrama, the universal issue centers around freedom vs. belonging. In order for this conflict to be dramatically sustainable, the values of both freedom and belonging must be contextualized and shaded in for the audience. That is, we must be shown the negative consequences of not belonging and the challenge of responsibility and solitude that freedom entails.

The melodrama hero at the beginning of the story is not prepared for either the negative consequences or the responsibilities of freedom. As a result, she tends to dream about a fantasy freedom: freedom from constraint and limitation. Ada in *The Piano* simply wants to get lost in her music and otherwise be left alone. We never see her take an active part in the life around her. We in the audience want her to have her freedom, though at the same time we know it would be impossible, even destructive. Not only is belonging questioned in the melodrama, but the nature of freedom as well.

The outer plot, emotional network conflicts, and inner need/mode conflict all present variations on this universal issue.

5. The tone of the melodrama is very different from that of the thriller, even when the hero's life is in danger. The thriller is built on a rhythm of shocks and surprises, while the melodrama is built on confinement, compression, and a crushing sense of inevitability. Instead of the thriller's subtextual dread, there is subtextual *hysteria*. Thrillers have something cerebral about them because there is a puzzle for the audience and a battle of wits. It is kinetic because the hero has a path of action. Melodrama is predicated on the *impossibility* of effective action, or else on a crippling ambivalence in the hero. There is a tremendous emotional charge built up because emotion is suppressed by the family code.

   A melodramatic tone, pushed to exaggeration, can also be used to set up comedy, as witness the deadpan prologues to *Amélie* and *My Big Fat Greek Wedding*. The opening situation is one of confinement and helplessness in a drab life. But immediately we can see that there is no serious antagonist in the family, so we begin to expect a comedy.

6. The main character is threatened by the family code, which creates a double bind between entrapment and rejection. Normally, one of these two poles is in the text while the other is laid in the subtext. In *Breaking the Waves*, it is emphasized that rejection (freedom) by the rigid religious community would kill Bess, while on a gut level (subtext) we can feel that remaining there (belonging) is already killing her. In *Raise the Red Lanterns*, it is the pole of entrapment that occupies the text of the story, the overt content of the scenes. The penalty accompanying rejection only surfaces late in Act II, bringing with it a tragic dénouement.

   The stakes in a melodrama are really set by the antagonist: how far is he willing to go to maintain the family order? For the patriarch husband in *Red Lanterns*, freedom for Song Lian is out of the question.

   Stakes may also come into the melodrama through the fantasy love relationship. Often this relationship appears to offer freedom and bliss to the entrapped hero, but the reality may be far different. The hero may succeed in separating from the family, only to be betrayed, abandoned, or mistreated by the lover. Part of the lesson of the melodrama is that the fantasy love object in itself is never the solution. The solution lies in the hero's own journey of separation from the family.

7. The melodrama also regresses the audience, in this case to the stage of early adolescence. This is the period when the libido starts to leave the sphere of the family, but we are not yet ready to take on responsibility. Freedom vs. belonging takes on special urgency at this age.
8. In the melodrama inflection of the Hero's Journey, the Day and Night Worlds mark the boundary between the family and the outer world:

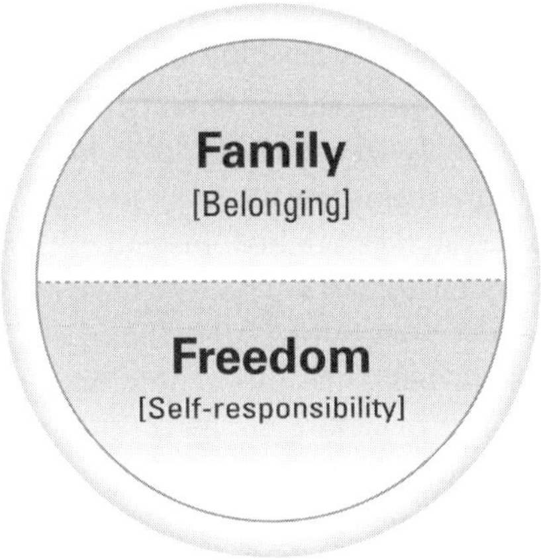

The family and its dysfunctional code must be established in the opening. The hero's mode is identified with her position in the family. If the hero's "weakness" and nonconformity are not established immediately, then they appear as a consequence of the Call to Adventure. The call comes from the outer world as a fantasy or desire, but it is predicated on a state of readiness within the character. It represents the Night World because it is unknown or taboo within the family.

Because the universal issue in melodramas, freedom vs. belonging, is expressed primarily as tension within the main character, the melodrama tone is generally more interior and reflective than that of the thriller.

9. Thrillers necessarily deal with evil. But in melodramas, the antagonistic forces take the form of resistance to the main character's desire. Resistance is not necessarily evil. Resistance, too, comes from the three levels of the Story Molecule:

   - introjected family codes that cause the main character to feel "bad" inside, or limited
   - family members, especially the antagonist
   - codes and rules governing the community, as in *Breaking the Waves*, or the entire society, as in *Dangerous Liaisons*

It is one of the melodrama conventions that we are shown the antagonist up front, prominently part of the family. Melodrama is not a puzzle, it is a double bind.

10. The split within the melodrama character that helps us build the need/mode conflict expresses itself as ambivalence about escaping the family, provided this is even possible. The family, no matter how violent or dysfunctional, is after all the known, the comfort zone. It is thus a shield against the unknown. Renton, in *Trainspotting*, comes off heroin in the movie's introduction. But because he remains enmeshed in the "family," he falls back into it at the end of Act I. This ambivalence is equivalent to having one foot in each world in the thriller. The family is not viable, but the plan for escape is not realistic.
11. The inner dimension of the ambivalence focuses on the conflict between the main character's *weakness* (in the eyes of the family) and his saving grace. Usually these are two aspects of the same trait or potential. The weakness is attached to the character's mode, while the *saving grace* must be discovered and accepted in a context outside the family. Ada's saving grace in *The Piano* is that her will to live, at the crucial moment, is stronger than her impulse to fly out of life (with Ada, one is tempted to say: "her wounded-child impulse to escape from life"). But Ada is a creative person, and the creative daemon that drives her through her music cannot be reduced exclusively to a painful childhood or any other personal factor. The creative drive is a factor on another level. Likewise, her saving grace, which appears at the moment she has abandoned herself to going down with the piano, cannot be equated to willpower as we commonly think of it from the ego standpoint. She says, "My will chose life." She does not say *she herself* chose life, but makes her will a separate factor, like destiny. Saving grace, like a universal need, is not in the melodrama character's awareness at the opening of the story. One could also say that Ada's saving grace worked behind her back to bring her together with George.

    Because the main character is in a truly weak position, he does not always have the power to save himself, but may have some positive quality that attracts help from the outside, as in *My Left Foot* and *My Life as a Dog*.
12. The Call to Adventure may be either an outer or inner call, or a blunder. It is the blunder of setting an accidental fire that gets young Ingmar in *My Life as a Dog* sent away from his mother to his relatives in the country. At that moment it seems to be a disaster for the boy, but it turns out to be a new beginning for his life. We know that the fire was precipitated by an awful family situation. The Call to Adventure breaks the circle of the family's closed horizon. In a melodrama, the call constellates a romantic interest or an escape plan.
13. Melodramas play primarily in the emotional network. The outer plot may be little more than a thin container to contextualize the relationship conflicts.

The emotional network of the melodrama is built heavily on triangles. The antagonist, who is the dominant family member, and the primary relationship character, who comes from outside the family, represent forces pulling in opposite directions. We want to see the main character graphically pulled by these forces. So we want to create scenes where we see these characters together. What does each one want? How do these influences impact the main character? How do they raise the dramatic stakes? Who is strongest and who is weakest in this triangle?

There may be further secondary triangles formed, within the family, competing love interests, outer world repetitions of the family antagonist, etc. The dynamics of the triangles take precedence over the individuality of the characters in the triangles. Melodrama characters may start out as pure stereotypes. They tend to be coded for the audience as either good or bad. However, once this coding has been broadly established, it is possible to bring as much shading and surprise to the characterizations as we wish. Stewart, in *The Piano*, shows us something fresh and surprising just before the climax of that movie when he suddenly lets go of Ada instead of continuing to possess and control her.

Melodrama is highly emotional and subjective. The audience is positioned to experience the characters and relationships through the hero's eyes, while the subtext warns us we are headed for trouble.

14. The primary relationship character, or love interest, may be a true guide for the hero, but is usually experienced as ambiguous. Orchestrating this relationship is key because the movie really hangs on it. Here there is important room for the screenwriter to play with point of view, how much she decides to reveal to the audience. The audience may be in a very close first-person POV with the hero and go through all the ups and downs of infatuation and disillusionment with the hero. Or we may see more of the love interest's true intentions before the hero does. George, in *The Piano*, is presented very sympathetically at first. Then there appears to be a reversal at the end of Act I when he forces Ada into a deal to buy her piano back. Suddenly he appears antagonistic. This is why it is important to look beyond the plot function level of the characters. Because through it all, George embodies what Ada needs to learn on a universal level. He is a man through whom Ada can discover that her will chooses life. This is the inner consistency of George's character, laid in the subtext from the first time we see him.

A single primary relationship figure is the easiest way to orchestrate the melodrama, but it is not the only possibility. Sometimes there is not one figure in this dramatic function, but a series of them. Some road movies are melodramas at heart. Or there may be a conspicuous lack of a guiding relationship, as in *Trainspotting*. Alternately, there may be someone who receives the hero's fantasy projection—"If I just could have *him*, then everything would be perfect"—but who does not embody what she needs to learn. In these latter two cases, the movie will usually end in a tone of disillusionment, if not tragedy.

A marked difference between melodrama and straight drama is that the melodrama hero, defined as somehow childlike, needs outside help in order to grow toward autonomy. This is, anyway, the hero's belief, which is at the core of the conflict.

15. At the end of Act I, the family status quo is shattered. This impacts not only the hero, but the entire system. In some melodramas this is a small, local system (*Raise the Red Lanterns*, *The Piano*). In *Dangerous Liaisons* it is a much more complex—though still limited—network of relationships.

    Here, we typically see the main character betray a core value. This is a delicate dramatic point, because we are talking at once about a character value and an audience value. The audience has a visceral reaction: "Oh no, don't do *that!*" Their feelings and expectations are challenged. This makes the moment a threshold crossing. Yet the violation must not be so great that the audience rejects the hero outright. The audience must be placed in a position where their own allegiances are torn. There is no way to tell how it will work out, but from this point on the hero is in the grip of opposing forces.
16. These opposing forces characterize the Night World throughout Act II. The hero must find her way between the confinement of the family and a not-yet-mature impulse to fly off into a fantasy solution of romance, wealth, escape to Rio, etc. This entails discovering and facing the skeleton in the family closet, the reason for the family's restrictive code. Usually the skeleton, secret, or lie is a family shame—as in the rooftop chamber where disobedient wives are hung in *Raise the Red Lantern*—or a family prejudice, such as the code of masculinity in *Billy Elliot*. This is really an initiation process of breaking through to one's own center by transgressing a limit imposed by the family. What makes this a productive rather than merely a hysterical resistance is that it is based on discovering and accepting a truth that had been hidden by collective shame. The melodrama hero potentially brings liberation to the rest of the family as well, as does Conrad in *Ordinary People*. In the process, the hero's old mode of "problem child" will collapse.
17. The Act II mechanics are determined largely by the antagonist, the dominant family member. The Marquise de Merteuil keeps pushing Valmont further. Just when Renton has gone through a painful heroin withdrawal and set up a new life in London, Begby arrives and crashes in on him. How far can the antagonist raise the stakes? Whose strength of will is ultimately greater? In *The Piano*, Ada is stronger than Stewart, as we have sensed from the beginning. But in *Trainspotting*, Renton has no alternative but to run away, and in *Red Lantern* Song Lian is ultimately crushed. Her will to resist is not as strong as the opposing system.
18. One very important obligatory scene in a melodrama is to show us the core triangle of hero/antagonist/love interest. This is of course utilized for its plot

potential. But the melodrama plays primarily in the emotional network; the outer plot grows out of those dynamics. Many melodramas, like *The Talented Mr. Ripley*, *Trainspotting*, *Jenseits der Stille* (*Beyond Silence*), *American Beauty*, and *The Piano*, set up this triangle early in Act I, the first time we are introduced to the characters. Others place it late in Act I but before the crisis/threshold crossing. Up to that time, we may have seen the hero with each of the others in separate scenes. *Dangerous Liaisons* places this triangle scene rather late, though the screenplay has carefully built up our expectation of an inevitable collision. The scene in which the Marquise de Merteuil sees Mme. de Tourvel for the first time—and how Valmont looks at her—comes just before, and sets up, the dramatic Core Crisis of the movie. When it does happen, it immediately sends the story into a deeper level of conflict.

A second obligatory scene comes at or just before the catastrophe that ends Act II. This is the revelation of the family's wound or secret, the skeleton in the family closet. We are not talking about a murder here; normally the family secret involves an unhealthy pattern about which the family is in denial. The denial is aided by a cover story: the *family myth*. This is powerfully done in *Trainspotting* at the catastrophe itself. Begby beats a man in a pub half to death for spilling beer on his suit. The family myth that they are all "good mates" collapses, and the truth that each is desperately out for himself comes out in the open.

19. At the catastrophe ending Act II, it appears that the negative power of the family triumphs over the drive for separation and autonomy of the main character and/or that the romantic "rescuer" is a fraud. As in all drama, the melodrama catastrophe is multileveled. The hero may have to endure a moment of complete rejection and isolation. At the same time the family's wound, which has hovered over the entire story like a ghost, is now finally out in the open. The disillusionment can be so great in a melodrama catastrophe that a truly helpless feeling is generated. The hero wonders if life is worth living, and so do we in the audience, when we see the hero apparently lose both the original family bond and the fantasy of romance and escape. Here all values seem to be lost, or the antagonist is in control, as in *My Life as a Dog*, *Trainspotting*, *Dangerous Liaisons*, and *The Piano*.

    The "grow or die" question is whether the hero has let go of her saving grace or held onto it through the conflict. This largely determines whether the climax moves up toward freedom or down toward final disaster. We see Valmont and Song Lian lose their saving grace. Ingmar, in *My Life as a Dog*, keeps his. And we see Lester in *American Beauty* regain his sense of value at the crucial moment.

20. Resolution of the melodrama means either independence or tragedy. In the tradition that evolved into the contemporary melodrama, there was often a deus ex machina reversal that led to a last-minute happy ending—the

faithful lover arrives at the last moment to pay the mortgage and save the farm, etc. In that older tradition, characters normally got what they deserved from the point of view of Victorian morality. The good were rewarded and the bad punished. This gave melodrama itself a low repute. But for a contemporary culture unable to embrace true tragedy, melodrama provides models for facing personal pain and limitation. As it has evolved today, melodrama pictures the growth process of moving from dependence on outer authority to relative independence and authenticity.

The very wide stylistic variety of films sharing the melodrama structure and world is an indication of the great potential of this genre.

Genre Blending

The entire notion of genre is changing with the accelerating transformation of the media environment. Genre traditions are undergoing warp and breakdown under the pressure of competition, not only between traditional players such as studios versus independents but between old versus new media: the cinema versus the iPod. More and more, genre traditions form the raw materials to be transformed by the synthetic/reflexive idiom.

Genres continually evolve within their traditions, and outworn forms are discarded along the way. The dime novel became the comic book; the superhero comic book is giving way to superhero interactive games. MTV and new media, including the Internet, have an increasing impact on the way movies look because of their growing place in our visual environment. This is not a temporary impact, nor has it reached a plateau of stability. On the contrary, turbulent instability appears to be a reasonable expectation. Genres as such have been and will be shaken up. Genres are built on tradition, and normally tradition takes time, time for the audience to respond and form attachments, not only to individual movies, but to patterns of repeated generic elements. One consequence of this is the attempt through promotion and advertising to beat the wave by creating ersatz traditions. New products are announced as "instant classics" or instant collectors' items, like the Cabbage Patch doll craze. These are designed to provoke instant attachments. The marketing strategy seems to work on most people, because it is a way of combating the anxiety of instant obsolescence, instant irrelevance, through a mental trick we play on ourselves. A programmed nostalgia appears regularly in the promotion of more standard genre movies. The genre tradition is deliberately evoked to raise the value of the present movie by making us connect it in our fantasies with "classics."

But the creative direction appears to be along the lines of the synthetic idiom, using genres as playthings that can be broken, bent, or blended into new forms. The successful new movies usually retain enough genre elements to give them an easily identifiable marketing slant, plus enough crossover elements to make the product "new, daring . . . a breakthrough!" The imperative of newness is so great that a more traditional genre piece has a hard time getting recognized on its actual dramatic merits. A very brief look at the ways four successful films have blended genres will give some indication of the new landscape. They are presented in an order of increasing complexity.

- *Trainspotting* is clearly structured as a melodrama. Renton's Call to Adventure is self-proclaimed: to get off the skag. This puts him immediately at odds with his "family," and by the end of Act I he has fallen back into heroin. It becomes clear to the audience, long before it does to Renton, that he must separate from his family. The Act II development pushes the conflict to a harrowing catastrophe/climax.

  The fresh thing is that the tone of the movie is in shades of dark—from sarcastic to black—comedy. But when we look more closely, the key dramatic moments—the Threshold Crisis, the Core Crisis/midpoint, and from the "polarization of opposites" through the climax*—drop the comedy and are played straight. The comedy has been used to carry the exposition, disarm the audience, and set up those moments where the stakes are real.

  Trainspotting uses a relatively simple design which basically involves de-coupling the melodrama structure from the expected genre tone. The structure itself remains consistent.
- *The Crying Game* presents a much greater departure from genre norms. The movie begins as a political thriller with the kidnapping of a British soldier by an IRA cell. But immediately, melodrama elements come into play: the IRA cell clearly has the dynamics of a family, in which Fergus is the "problem child." In addition, a fantasy/erotic bond is formed between Fergus and the prisoner, Jodie. This involves the paradox that the prisoner offers the guard a freedom, recognition, and belonging that Fergus does not experience within the "family." This bond has added taboo elements because Jodie is a black man (homosexual attraction is foreshadowed not only through the interactions, but by the name Jodie itself, more commonly a woman's name). So the standard melodrama dynamics of the main character caught between allegiance to the family and attraction to a new life possibility are strongly established in Act I.

  This clever setup allows the surprising shift in the first half of Act II, where the world of the thriller completely disappears into the subtext. Thriller and melodrama worlds collide at the core crisis when the survivors of the terrorist cell track Fergus down in London, where he has established a new life. From that point on, the challenge is to craft a catastrophe/climax that resolves both the thriller and the melodrama. In fact, this is done with great facility, showing how fluidly these genres can be brought together.
- *American Beauty* has additional levels of complexity because there are multiple throughlines along with a mix of genre elements. A comic tone is laid

* These terms refer to the Story Steps, which are described fully in Chapter Eleven.

over an opening that contains equally comic and melodramatic potential by means of a voice-over (also utilized in *Trainspotting*). There are two great challenges here. One is to orchestrate the audience's POV, and the other is to lay out a palette of dramatic tones that is very broad, but strong enough to hang together as a dramatic unity. This is another level of accomplishment relative to *Trainspotting*, where a consistent structure was countered by an opposing tone. *American Beauty* uses elements of comedy, drama, and melodrama without being securely in any one genre.

Part of the solution is to link different tonalities to the different protagonists. Lester is orchestrated as the most comic, Ricky's line is the darkest, and Janie is aligned between them. Of the antagonists, Carolyn plays the comedy line and Col. Pitts plays the dark line. Angela, who acts as the melodrama fantasy vehicle for Lester, is also a threshold guardian for Janie. Her tone is aligned between those of Carolyn and Pitts. Looking at it from a design point of view, we could say that the symmetry of this design helps give the complexity of *American Beauty* a container.

- *Fargo* manages to juggle even more complexity. The three interwoven throughlines of *American Beauty* are acted out in one melodramatic closed space, the Burnhams' immediate neighborhood. Fargo has three lines with three tones, enacted in essentially three spaces that only occasionally intersect. One could certainly call this risky.

  A crime thriller is immediately set up as Jerry hires the kidnappers. Here in the opening minutes there are already two complex aspects: first, the audience is caused to identify with Jerry as a sympathetic criminal, and second, there are so many touches of satire and dark humor that it seems hard to take the contracted crime seriously. When the comical kidnapping becomes serious murder, the floor seems to drop out from under us. The comedy has been an effective deception to render the audience unsuspecting and vulnerable. To pull this off requires masterful control of tone through every aspect of the craft.

  Another great risk is bringing in Marge, the pregnant police chief, to investigate the killings at the opening of Act II. It's stretching it just about to the limit to introduce a principal character so late in the movie. Now, we have Jerry as simultaneously the antagonist of the crime thriller and the protagonist of the tragedy. Marge becomes the protagonist of the crime thriller, counter to all genre expectations, while Carl plays the kidnappers' subplot as black comedy. The result is a unique creative accomplishment that could nevertheless attract a large segment of the thriller genre audience.

The conventional wisdom would say that innovation carries risk, the risk of something untested in the marketplace. But we may have arrived at a point relative to idioms and genres where some positive risk-taking is indeed necessary for a distinguished product. At the same time, the risks of trying to play it safe may be growing, at least in the field of feature filmmaking. Knowing how story worlds communicate with the audience and how they interact with plot and character are important tools for those who want their risk-taking to be well grounded in the principles of story design.

Icons and Images

Story and image come together in the figures on the screen. Sometimes these figures can take on a magnetic charm and charisma for the audience. This is a mysterious happening when it does occur; there is something involuntary about it, something out of our control. It is not simply a product of the larger than life visual rhetoric of the romantic idiom. Of course, star images are intensely crafted and hyped, like soft drinks or mobile phones. But out of all of these, relatively few become what we identify as *icons*. Many are called, but few are chosen. Iconic figures receive a collective projection from the audience because they carry something for the collective, something the collective is unaware of or unable to carry consciously for itself.

But while we tend to get fixated on who's hot and who's not, or whether it is the actor, the director, or the role that provides the magic, the truth is that we are dealing with a mysterious quality of the image itself. Icons can to some extent be manufactured, but this is only possible because *everything* we put on the screen has another dimension added to it. Art has everything to do with context. When we place a frame around any object, be it an old pair of shoes, a kitchen chair, or a bottle of perfume, we imply that our relationship to the object has taken on a special character. We elevate it above the surrounding reality. Whether we are willing to call the result "art" or not, we are forced to view the object in a different context. Think of the immensity of meaning conveyed by Van Gogh's painting of a pair of old, worn shoes. Immensity of meaning is not the same as quantity of information: they are simply two old shoes. The shoes become iconic through what they say—as witnesses—about the nature of human labor and human suffering. And there is an additional mystery dimension because in fact they are empty. The inhabiting spirit that shaped them has departed, leaving the shoes as evidence. This capacity of all images to open outward, so to speak, into mystery is the dimension of the iconic. The screenwriter works on this edge, between the seen and the unseen. It is beyond story mechanics, but is part of the story field. While we do not know who will be cast in the parts we write, an appreciation of the iconic dimension will give our writing richness and inner life.

Standing for Something: Characters, Icons, and Archetypes

Icons stand for, symbolize, or evoke a world beyond themselves. They are carriers of numinous energy. As such, they act as conduits for the energy of a field, energy we experience as fascinating, uncanny, awesome, or sacred. The phrases "mythic dimension" and "archetypal dimension" relate to this territory of the psyche that impinges on, but cannot be encompassed by, our consciousness. The icon is a kind of personified symbol. It provides an opening, or an "eye," that lets something pass into awareness from a zone outside the ego. The charismatic figure opens out backward, like throwing open a window. In the near background it merges into the *type*, that fluid space where stereotype and archetypal image coexist in less differentiated layers of the psyche—and then further, into the psychic matrix that is the mother of all images. The source of imagination, the "uncreated creative," can be itself imagined but cannot be objectively seen. Yet something of the quality of this ultimate background of consciousness comes through the opening which is the icon. Its capacity to bring a hint of *that* dimension into *this* here and now dimension is responsible for the attribution of divine power to the icon.

In our secular society, we have to remind ourselves that the original significance of the word *icon* was religious. A religious icon is not primarily a picture or representation in objective terms. It is a locus where divine energy itself is present. The saint, for example, is present in the icon and is seen by the faithful—and has the active power to see them as well. In Greece, not only churches and homes, but shops and offices contain icons so that what is done is done in the presence of the saint. Icons, in order to possess this power, must be created in prescribed ways. The goal is not *likeness*, but *essence*. And essence is not achieved by making the figure approachable, with a sweet, reassuring smile. That is to say, the iconic image is not brought completely into the banal human realm. It is positioned on the boundary between the human and the divine. The gaze of the icon is not directed toward our personality, but directly to the soul.

In the West, sacred images were gradually officially divested, through *iconoclasm*, of their iconic power. In the Protestant Reformation, saints' images were often destroyed or defaced. The rational Western mind has tended to refuse to attribute to the image powers it has not put there itself. But that does not mean that this dimension of our relation to images has ceased to exist. It was merely driven into the unconscious. This points to one central difference between religious icons and cultural or media icons: the impact of the former is conscious while the impact of the latter is largely unconscious. The religious person before the religious icon is aware that she is confronting another dimension. A secular man staring at a secular iconic image of Marilyn Monroe may only be aware of a peculiar enthusiasm and the stirring of certain appetitive impulses.

So, for the most part, we are unaware of how cultural icons work on us. There are both similarities and differences to religious icons. There is a *presentational style* to icons as well as an iconography. Iconography describes ensembles, complexes of associated objects and attributes, that amplify the essential identity of the iconic figure—like St. Peter's keys, but also like Marilyn Monroe's dress billowing up in *The Seven Year Itch*. That moment becomes an essential part of the Marilyn iconography, a captured moment that seems to stand outside of time, on the edge of nontime or eternity.

In terms of presentational style, we may first observe that traditional icons tend to present the subject frontally, symmetrically, centered, and in a posture that feels fixed and stable rather than transitory. These qualities set the icon off from surrounding space, mundane space, and place it in a highly charged, limited visual field. The eyes of the icon create a very different interiority than those of a portrait. We see there not a personal interior, but an infinitely distant yet absolutely present energy. This gives the icon the transparency of a window. The style may be flatly two-dimensional, but the intention is to project the viewer *through*. It is only when icons cease to be such and become "art objects," collectors' items, that we look *at* them. I believe this "window to another world" effect, at least in aesthetic terms, is a large part of the magnetic charisma of religious icons. The icon implies a mystery dimension beyond the board on which it is painted, a world self-contained yet present, as in the sayings: "Split the stick, and I am there," or, "The fire is in the firewood."*

Now we come to cultural and cinematic icons. We are interested in how they manifest in movies, but it is not possible to keep movies artificially separate from the milieu in which we see them. Obviously the presentational style of *dynamic stasis* we have described in painted religious icons does not apply to moving images. We must understand dynamic stasis in a looser, more figurative way.

First of all, we could say that movie icons are "intensely regarded." This phrase comes from James Joyce's *Ulysses*: "Any object, intensely regarded, can be a doorway opening to the eon of the gods." Joyce, through his character, did mean literally *any* object, the object in question at that moment being a bottle of Bass Ale. "Intensely regarded" means the movie focuses and concentrates both the viewer's conscious attention and his unconscious on an image to endow it with iconic grandeur. How? Part of this is the framing and visual composition, which isolates the important element. Equally important is the dramatic context, which sets up and underscores the visual presentation. Frank McConnell illustrates this with a still of Henry Fonda as Marshal Wyatt Earp from John Ford's *My Darling Clementine*, which he describes as a classic iconic image:

> [Earp] strikes an archetypal *pose* upon a rooftop, against the big sky, balanced at the left by gigantic cactuses. The elements of nature and culture—the monstrous plants on one hand and the rough-hewn building upon which he stands—are poised in as graphic a counterpoint as one could wish.[31]

This is an example of concentrating an image toward an "iconic regard" in a long shot. It is not rigidly frontal and centered, but the classical balance of the composition suggests weight, gravity, stasis. The eye literally becomes calm, not roaming around the frame seeking a focus. Also note that Earp/Fonda is *posed* there on the roof. He is being shown or revealed to us in this posture in

* From the Gospel of Thomas.

31. McConnell, Frank, *Storytelling*, p. 272. Italics mine.

order to communicate subtextually to the audience that which McConnell has translated into words: the man who tames nature, and the savagery of human nature, so that civilization may flourish. Significant close-ups can also be used in this way, and have been since the beginning of the movies the primary vehicle for "iconizing" an actor or actress and turning them into a star. From Mary Pickford through Garbo, Gable, and Marilyn to George Clooney and J-Lo, the attempt to create icons through the beauty close-up has been a central strategy. The organization of the framing is matched by a temporal organization: as the image is posed, it is likewise suspended in time. Holding the pose subliminally takes the moment out of time into nontime. By holding that pose on the rooftop, another dimension comes into Fonda's characterization of Wyatt Earp. Even Marilyn's billowing dress is cleverly suspended for a beat. The image outside of time travels to a deeper level of the unconscious without our being aware of it.

Performance by the actor in an iconic role is also concentrated and/or suspended, allowing the other dimension to enter. Actors learn to focus their inner energy, in ways exactly parallel to the martial arts, in order to create *magnetism*. That inner intensity and vitality can reveal itself best when an actor is, in Fonda's words, "doing nothing." Helen Mirren's portrayal of Queen Elizabeth in *The Queen* plays heavily on doing nothing. The role is largely reduced to iconic presence/stasis, concentrated to its essence. But Helen Mirren is so adept in this concentration, and is so magnetic, that the queen merely needs to enter the scene to capture our attention.

In addition, the iconizing practice focuses performance on the character's dominant qualities or tropes. This is rendered through the repetition of certain actions, gestures, looks, and dialogue lines. The expression of ecstatic suffering on the face of actress Maria Falconetti, repeated over and over again in the silent masterpiece *The Passion of Joan of Arc*, created one of the greatest iconic performances in the history of the cinema. German actress Hannah Schygulla found a similar expression for her character in Andrzej Wajda's *Love in Germany*. Schygulla's look of dreamlike ecstasy in the midst of suffering added a transcendent dimension to a drama nevertheless in the realist idiom. It is as though the character sees something the rest of us cannot see. The repetition of a gesture or look comes to *typify* the role, to focus and magnify the trait it expresses. Other behaviors of the character slip relatively into the background, providing a context or frame for the iconic moment.

A great deal of trouble is taken to orchestrate these impressions for the audience. What, ultimately, do these looks, gestures, and precious, held poses signify—or to what do they point? They do form a system of iconography, suggesting that they open out into another dimension and invite the energies of that other world to enter via the window of the icon. Since we are dealing with cultural rather than religious icons, the background dimension does not present itself as divine or sacred. But icons do reflect what people "hold sacred" in the secularized sense of "holding dear." For most people in a society, the core values are tacit, inherited with mother's milk, and not consciously reflected upon. These values form part of the dimension made half-visible through the icon. Jack Nicholson has played on the same tropes, the same gestures and grimaces and transgressive, abusive verbal humor in role after role. It is a fixed repertoire, and yet it always seems to work. Whatever this is about has some iconic value for the audience, meaning that this repertoire hooks into the audience on a collective, largely unconscious level. It is as though we have designated Nicholson to carry a certain kind of shadow for all of us. In role after role, he gets away with racial slurs, anti-Jew jokes, endless lechery, unbounded egoism, and an insistence on hogging the scene. What's it all pointing to? In Martin Scorsese's *Departed*, the mafia boss Nicholson plays is explicitly equated with the devil, especially through two "iconic" scenes that are completely gratuitous to the plot of the movie. Answering the question of why we as a society need someone to act out our devilishly egoistic impulses onscreen would take us very far into understanding how cultural icons work.

We can identify three levels of collective value that are projected through icons in movies. They blend into each other, but may be distinguished. Closest to the traditional religious sense of icon, a role—or the actor playing it—embodies a mythic/archetypal figure. This may be the most universal level the icon carries. Naturally, it will be inflected in the local style specified by the associated iconography. The archetypal hero battling against evil in a Bollywood epic is going to have different specific costumes (many!) and gestures than Wyatt Earp, or Neo in *The Matrix*. Yet beyond the cultural specifics there will be another level of indicators that also carries the mythic level. Through its evocation of the mythic dimension, the icon models wholeness in some way.

On a lower level, the iconic figure may act out a psychological complex. Psychological complexes are relatively universal patterns of behavior between the individual and the archetypal. Like the Oedipus complex or the power complex, when they possess us and we act them out literally, our behavior has a compulsive, driven—or inhibited—neurotic flavor. Behavior through a complex is less conscious and is basically unfree. Yet this driven quality of the complex characterizes some of the most memorable movie roles, including Melvin in *As Good as It Gets*. The same tactics that create emphasis to form a hero icon can also be used to create icons of pain and lack of freedom. These figures model our fragmented condition. Nearly all characters in soap operas are examples of this.

Finally, on a third, still lower and less archetypal level, what are popularly called icons are carriers of stereotypical status values. They model wealth, power, sexiness, in-your-face chutzpah, and so on. Those beautiful people that fill magazine and TV ads are icons of this type. In every conscious attempt to create icons similar strategies are utilized, though to different ends. The visual and rhetorical organization of the image is designed to give the figure prestige and an aura of specialness that lifts it to another sphere above its mundane surroundings. As a result, these levels of iconic address become confused: it becomes easy to equate sexiness, the Chanel outfit, or the Rolex watch with wholeness. Using the strategies of iconization to position the product as the route to wholeness is in fact the core premise of contemporary advertising. We can see how easily cinematic icons subtly blend the "sacred" into the mercantile.

The icons that carry a strong archetypal charge seem to stand involuntarily above their time. They receive such an enormous collective projection that they are lifted up. It may never be possible to trace exactly how this process works, because we ourselves are part of it. The projection comes from the public, but there has to be something in the figure to make the projection stick and grow. It is, further, impossible to discern how much of the "hook" for the projection derives from the way the role is written, how much comes from the actor, and how much from the directing, set design, costuming, etc. It is more than the sum of its parts. Biographies of Marilyn Monroe and James Dean suggest that much of themselves went into their performances, yet those roles were also selected and tailored specifically for those actors. There is a reinforcing feedback loop. Beyond this, we may hypothesize that an actor consciously or unconsciously embodies a mythic/archetypal figure. Marilyn became publicly identified with Aphrodite, the goddess of love; Mick Jagger with Dionysus, the god of intoxication and orgiastic ecstasy. Yet projection obviously happens even when people do not know what is being projected. And though Aphrodite and Dionysus are pagan deities, seemingly incarnating themselves in pop culture idols, archetypal iconization cannot escape altogether from our civilization's collective religious basis. How many times have we read that Marilyn or Elvis "died for our sins"? How often have we heard that they are still alive somewhere? These are the spontaneous operations of a collective folk-mind that is still very much with us.

"Living icons," like saints perhaps, are compelled to carry some complex or archetype for society. They are given every inducement to remain on the pedestal where we have placed them. Sounds like a "divine" job, but for the carrier—the actor—it is perilous to come down and perilous to stay, because archetypal energies are indeed collective and overwhelming. That is, unconscious energies do not have the qualities of individual consciousness. They lack a sense of limits and provoke psychic inflations that often enough lead to trouble and tragedy. Rare actors that are able to step outside of and manage their iconic image can bring a gift of mature reflection to society. One example that comes to mind is Clint Eastwood the director managing Clint Eastwood the icon. Over a long series of films, Eastwood has succeeded in deconstructing and transforming the lone cowboy/Dirty Harry image, yet without killing it. In the process, he has given himself room to breathe as an actor. His roles have included creative countericonography: the Marine sergeant who reads women's magazines so he can learn how to talk to his wife; the globetrotting photographer, his loneliness exposed, standing in the rain; and the cat burglar who periodically sneaks into his daughter's flat to stock her refrigerator. Eastwood's star power gives these fresh images much greater cultural reach than they might otherwise have.

How is the screenwriter to work creatively with this elusive power of icons? There is a general answer and a technical answer. The general answer is to become aware of myths and archetypes evoked by the story you are telling. Make myths and fairy tales your bedtime reading. Wonder about what they mean and why they are constructed the way they are. Another way is to pay attention to your dreams and the inner worlds as they unfold at night. And a third is to use fantasy and associative methods like those in the first section of this chapter and in the other *Internal Software* exercises in this book. You noticed, for example, that the color beige, through its quality of mildness, leads through a chain of associations to Jesus.* It seems that the unconscious is constantly computing more such chains of association that we could ever possibly handle consciously.

All characters carry something iconic, however faintly. All stories have a background dimension that speaks directly to the unconscious. This is inherent in the richness of stories themselves. But we cannot afford to forget that our first job is to make sure the screenplay itself is dramatically sound. If the screenplay is not strong, it will not be able to carry the iconic level in its subtext, where it should be. If the audience is glued to the story, the iconic/mythic aspect will pass via the subtext to touch the heart. If not, attempts at iconization will stand out as clumsy, pretentious symbolism that further weakens the movie. The audience will be distracted trying to figure out what the symbol means. Or the attempt at iconization will merely lead to eye candy: another beautiful face riding in a beautiful car toward a beautiful yacht in a picturesque little harbor on the Riviera. There might be an icon of luxury in there somewhere, but it may as well be a Diesel Jeans ad.

The technical answer about working with iconic presence in the screenplay has to do with texture in screenwriting. Texture means creating spaces with pace and tone. Characters who are active all the time leave us no chance to look into them, to be with them and feel them on a deeper level. It is a mistake to think the main character must be *active-active-active!* Likewise we shouldn't expect there to be conflict going on at every moment. That approach lacks texture and will stupefy an audience. As writers, we must make silence as eloquent as dialogue, stillness as eloquent as movement. This is where parentheticals and other devices in the screenplay format are used to control pace and tone, to create spaces. Wyatt Earp's pause on the rooftop makes his action complete. You can and should be free to write such a moment, as well as to bring motivated silent beats into a dialogue, where the director can hold on a soulful close-up. But when is the right moment? When will it be significant?

The answer to this lies in the story development models. Those beats in the story that cry out to us to hold on to a significant iconic pose or penetrating

* See the graphic on p. 212.

close-up are not moments of simple rest. They are moments of *poise*, like the poise of a diver on the highest platform, about to launch himself into a difficult triple twist. Or, the same diver, towel poised halfway to his face as the scores are read out. There is inner tension and intensity. The Need versus Mode model is a guide for us, because, in terms of the dramatic throughline, we are talking about the poised tension between mode and need. That dynamic goes through many stages of dis-equilibrium and tension of opposites. The following chapters connect this inner process to the plot/story structure that makes up the outer ring of the Story Molecule. And of course, the Hero's Journey is always resonating behind and through those models. Taken together, they will allow us to match the significant moment of inner character shift with the right moment in the plot structure, the moment of *dynamic stasis*. If we as screenwriters, having found such a moment in our story, can enter it and let it open out its timeless dimension to us, dreaming with it (via mental maps, for example), images and associations will come up. These, if we follow them like Bergman following his colored thread, will point us toward the essence or archetypal background of our character, what he or she stands for on that more implicit, universal level. It is this quality that we want to concentrate into that look or gesture which, when delivered by the actor, will open out the iconic dimension for the audience.

Part II

PLOT AND THE DYNAMICS OF CREATION

8

The Soul of Drama

You don't f___ the ineffable.

—Alan Watts

STORY AND PLOT ARE *NOT* IDENTICAL. A story is a sequence of events with a beginning, a middle, and an end. Jokes, anecdotes, and news reports are all stories. A plot, on the other hand, is a dialectical structure of growth through crisis. It is the dynamic of the plot that transforms the cycle of the Hero's Journey into something specifically dramatic. Why make a distinction between story and plot? Because the total story we want to convey to the audience, as we have seen, is more than the plot.

A movie is a three-dimensional stream of meaning. It was important to establish this perspective before entering into the structure and dynamics of the outer plot, exactly because in story development there is a strong tendency to focus on the plot dimension alone. Part of this tendency is because the outer plot events are easier to see, easier to discuss, easier to manipulate. In addition, it is taken for granted that it is the *action* that is the best hook for getting the audience into the movie theater. Action is considered low-risk because it appeals to the "lowest common denominator" of the public (*everyone* reacts to exciting explosions and chases), and because the "elements" are stable. That is to say, the elements of action movies are not only generic; they are iconic. The characters and situations are only roughly individualized. They remain largely embedded in a collective matrix, a more primitive "group mind." These factors reinforce this tendency to reduce the three-dimensionality of a screenplay to the outer plot.

It is only when you have to get suited up in overalls and go down into the creative mine—when you must actually write the screenplay and not just talk about the concept—that the shortcomings of the plot-driven approach to story development really stand out. Everyone who actually writes, develops, or consults on a screenplay quickly comes to appreciate that a screenplay is a gestalt: a whole made up not of the *sum* of its parts, but of the *expressive pattern* of its parts. Every part affects and conditions the whole. It is no more possible to change one element without changing the entire story than it is to change your nose without changing the expressiveness of your entire face. And this is true not only on the level of the outer plot, but throughout the whole fabric of the Story Molecule. Whether a Story Step works and fulfils its dramatic function or not may hinge on a single line of dialogue or prolonged look. It is all interconnected and resonating together. This helps us put our consideration of the plot into the proper context. Plot, like character, is an entire world in itself, yet it must work together with all the other aspects of the writing if the final screenplay is to convey a powerful dramatic unity.

The Basic Pulse of Drama

If the Need versus Mode model identifies the core conflict of values that is the engine for the drama, and if the Story Molecule shows us how the dramatic energy flows between the three dimensions of the screenplay, it is the outer story structure that forms the expressive container for the whole thing. We are purposely using the phrase "outer story structure" rather than "outer plot structure" because it is here that we orchestrate everything happening on all three levels of conflict in the Story Molecule—text and subtext together—into a unified experience for the audience. The outer story is what the audience is going to see, and is also the container for what we *don't* see. But as a container, dramatic structure is not just a box. It contributes its own inherent dynamic that brings the material to expressive life.

It would be fairer to say that drama is not a structure in the fixed sense. It is a *pulse*, an electric current running between the story and the audience. The simplest way to describe this is as a pulse of *tension and release*. The essence of drama is "growth through crisis," and this is expressed through pulsations of tension and release. The dynamic of this pulse marks the fundamental difference between what we call the Plot Curve model and the Hero's Journey.

This curve is the dynamic shape of growth through crisis. It is a great wave of rising dramatic intensity that carries the audience through the movie. There are a number of models of dramatic structure currently competing in Hollywood. Every screenwriting guru wants to put his proprietary twist on it or trademark her own terms for age-old processes. But the fact is that all current models of dramatic structure owe their origin to the observations made by Aristotle in the fourth century B.C. Aristotle studied the plays being performed in the Athens of his time and asked himself what they had in common that made them work. He could see that the structure created its own special way of arriving at a dramatic truth. Aristotle did not *invent* the observations in his *Poetics*, but what he identified about the structure and dynamics of drama—the basic pulse—has

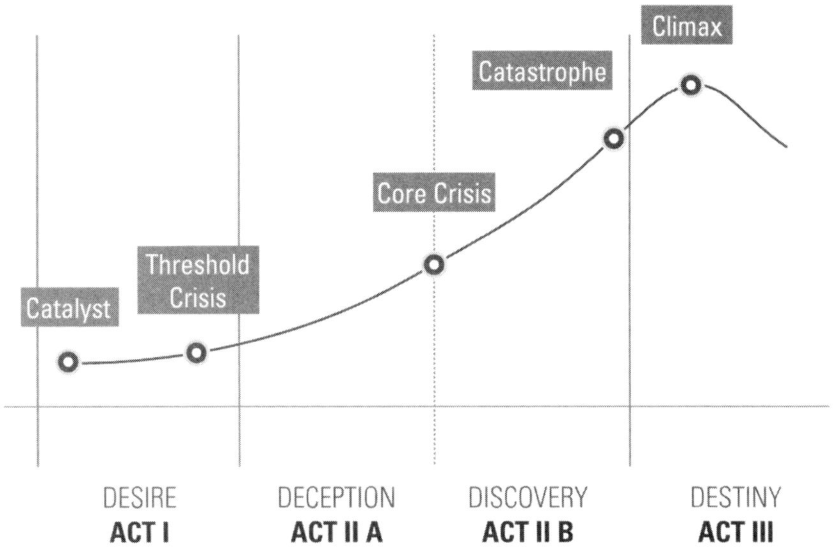

proven valid ever since. His inductive method of looking at common elements in many plays to identify universal principles is similar to Joseph Campbell's inductive approach to myth. There is of course a close connection between myth and drama. Drama grew directly out of myth, as it continues to do today. Both living myth and living drama are rooted in deep body wisdom and the archetypal layers of the psyche. The pulse of drama is where we see body wisdom, dream wisdom, and the collaboration of a shaping conscious awareness all come together.

The Plot Curve model helps us picture this energy. In that way, it is superior to straight-line plot representations. It helps us bring the sense of story energy back into our bodies. On the horizontal axis is *time*, the running time of the play or movie, which today we are also able to relate to the length of REM sleep cycles. As screenwriters, we want to be aware that the dramatic curve starts moving with the very first images onscreen, and continues through to the end credits and music. This all constitutes what some like to call the "roller-coaster" that the audience is going to ride. The vertical axis in the graphic represents *dramatic intensity*: the level of conflict, risk, and emotional intensity for the characters that translates into excitement for the audience. Because normally the audience is allied and identified with the main character, peaks of intensity for the hero are peaks for the audience as well. We shall look at this general curve in increasingly greater detail, but the point here is that ultimately we are orchestrating the *audience's* experience through the vehicles of the hero and the plot. What we see in the Plot Curve is the level of dramatic intensity rising toward the climax like a surging wave, which breaks and subsides rapidly as the story is resolved. The shape of the Plot Curve paradigm, like that of the Hero's Journey, is archetypal. It already exists in each of us, screenwriter and audience member alike.

It is with an appreciation bordering on awe that I view the achievement of those very first dramatists whose plays formed the basis of Aristotle's observations on dramatic form. By Aristotle's time there was already a dramatic tradition of a hundred and fifty years or so. Dramatic practice already had codes and conventions, competing factions and revolutionaries. Yet there was still a vital sense of being close to the roots of drama, and that imparted a tremendous excitement. It is hard for us to imagine, over twenty-three hundred years later, that there could have been a time when drama simply did not exist. And then, suddenly—within two generations—there it was! We do not see a period of futzing around with models that did not work. They seem to have gotten it right the first time out. The plays of Aeschylus, who belonged to that first generation, are still performed today because they still have vitality today. The dynamics that propel Aeschylus's *Agamemnon* continue to propel movie stories today.

Of course, drama didn't appear out of nowhere. Prior to the dramatic revolution there were religious festivals where a myth story would be sung and enacted. There might be a dialogue between a hero, or a chorus standing for human society, and a god. We might picture these religious pageants as analogous to a Christmas or Easter pageant. Someone portrays Mary, others Joseph, the shepherds, the three kings, and so on. Onstage they act out, in the sense of *embodying*, a story we already know. The embodiment, the performance, makes the story alive for us. Still, this is not drama. Drama, and the special engagement that drama brings for the audience, only enters with dramatic conflict, which is a conflict of essential values and allegiances. The religious pageant is rather a feedback loop of certainty—that which was established as true at the time of Creation, in the mythic past, or as part of the unfolding of a divine plan, is repeated, renewed, and affirmed in the present. We support the pattern with our energy, our libido, and thus renew the certainty of our relationship to the faith in ourselves. Drama, by contrast, is founded on, and thrives on, doubt and ambivalence. How can there be a powerful resolution unless there is first an awareness of division?

As soon as we have characters with motives and life-impulses that are in conflict with each other, whether they are gods or mortals, we enter into the energy field of the dramatic curve, commonly called Aristotle's Plot Curve. The Plot Curve reveals the pulse of drama. It is the specific shape of growth through crisis, and, in Aristotle's time, it really did constitute a revolutionary new way of looking at the world. It was a revolution because the earliest dramas always involved conflict between man and god, and that conflict revolved around urgent central questions: does man have free will or does he not—and is that a good thing or isn't it?

Imagine: an audience of god-fearing persons was asked to seriously contemplate the possibility that the gods where wrong! Of course, this challenge was left primarily in the subtext, but it was implicit in the structure of the conflict. The audience was placed in the middle, between two opposing forces, and their loyalties were pulled in both directions. One part of us knows that Oedipus has committed mortal sins: he has murdered his father and lives in incest with his mother. And yet we are *for* Oedipus; he has our allegiance and sympathy. As he himself pushes the dramatic actions that will ultimately reveal himself to himself as the source of the evil, we see Oedipus as equally victim and perpetrator, innocent as well as guilty. And we realize that this poor king has been set up: he is, as he tells us, the "fool of the gods." One can hardly obey the gods if one has been tricked by them. There is a legitimate ambivalence instilled between obedience and disobedience to the divine will. Until drama, neither the structure nor the presentation invited the audience to live the characters' motives and feelings from the inside, to enter the ethical crisis and double bind along with them. It is this tension, engendered by the audience's ambivalence in relation to the hero, that generates the pulse, the wave of the dramatic curve.

With this pulse, this wave of drama, it is as though the pace of human transformation quickens. Now everything can be questioned—*if* we have a way of articulating and containing the conflict of opposites within ourselves through dramatic performance. The gods can be questioned, as Socrates (Sophocles's contemporary) was questioning them, and as, not far away, Job was questioning his God. Contemporaneously in India, Vedantic Brahmins were coming to the conclusion that even the gods are less powerful than the awakened human consciousness. The boundaries of tribal allegiance can also be questioned, and found too narrow for the compassionate heart. For example, Aeschylus, in that very first generation of dramatists, who had himself fought against the Persian invasion at Marathon, could write a tragedy with the Persian tyrant Xerxes as not the enemy but the tragic hero! (Compare this attitude with that of the movie *300*.)

Drama emerges at exactly the same time and out of the same forces as the earliest democracy. It could be argued that democracy fundamentally owes a great debt to drama for two reasons. First, the capacity of drama to contain warring opposites and channel conflict toward resolution modeled new relations based on equality and dialogue, rather than strict social hierarchy alone. And second, the theme of free will, as it evolved from Aeschylus through Sophocles to Euripides, embodied the philosophical development leading from divinely sanctioned laws to laws rationally and democratically determined by men for their own common weal, and subject to democratic change and review. It was one very large step toward what we understand as modern human consciousness.

The Plot Curve Structures Energy

Aristotle was taking the pulse of this revolution in feeling. He did not specifically refer to a plot "curve" in his *Poetics*. The curve is a modern interpretation. But from the way Aristotle describes the build up of the drama from beginning to climax, it is clear that the dynamics he saw are those that still apply today. Here we may also clarify parallels and differences between Aristotle's Plot Curve and the Hero's Journey model. There are many specific correspondences between them, but the shapes are obviously different.

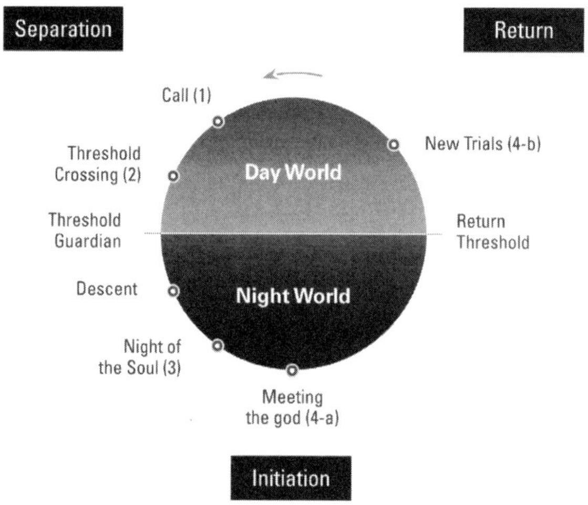

/ *The Hero's Journey:* **Underlies plot structure.**

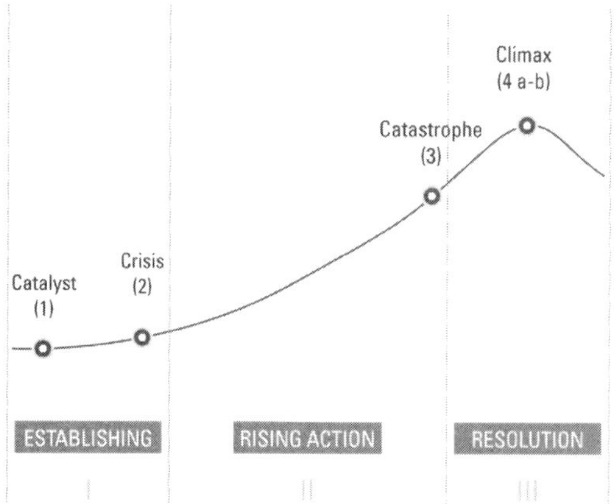

/ Aristotle's Plot Curve.
The classical plot curve, following Aristotle, 4th century B.C.
Key points in the plot curve correspond to the Hero's Journey.

The difference in shape comes from the difference in perspective between myth and drama that we have alluded to. Myth looks at the human adventure from, we could say, a detached or "divine" perspective. The Hero's Journey as a *cycle* is a shape without beginning or end, intimating eternity. And, like the Christmas pageant, myths present themselves as being "just so." The language of myths is narrative, but does not try to force us to take sides or feel grief, pity, or anger. Fairy tales are similar. A fairy tale may describe that Hansel and Gretel felt frightened when they realized they had lost their way, but the description is not colored to control our feelings. We naturally react with empathy for the lost children, but we are not induced to live their fear. A certain distance is kept between the story and the hearer. With Homer and the Old Testament, a more vivid narrative language starts to break down this distance, and with drama it collapses altogether.

Aristotle identified the large sections or phases of the dramatic structure. Each comprises a major function that takes up its own portion of the curve and thus has its own special energy. The relatively flat opening portion of the curve is termed the "establishing scene." Its function is to establish the world of the story, the characters, and to start the plot moving. We consider it equivalent to what we now call Act I of the screenplay. In the ancient theater, it did not take much to set up the story, because it was already known to the audience. Like with the Christmas pageant or the medieval *Everyman* plays, everyone already knew what would happen to Oedipus, Electra, or Orestes. It was enough for the leader of the Chorus to set the scene, describing how the people were dying like flies from the plague, and how Oedipus the king must intervene. Immediately we are ready to launch into the plot. But a modern movie is a brand new experience for the audience. Starting with the opening images, we are not only establishing a story and a plot, we are teaching the audience how to "read" the movie.

This has to do both with idiom and genre and with the POV of the storytelling. In addition, we could say that the establishing, Act I, takes place in the story's Day World and establishes the values of the Day World, which are the dominant values of the main character's mode. After setting up the world and the conditions of the story, the first dramatic event, the *catalyst*, starts the plot, and with it the dynamic of growth through crisis, moving forward. The catalyst gives the plot a trajectory toward a distant outcome, the *plot goal*. Then we see what action the hero initiates to achieve that goal. The hero's steps toward accomplishing her goal bring her into inevitable conflict with an antagonist who has a countermotive. So, in a movie, the establishing function comprising Act I is already quite complex. Four Story Steps articulate Act I.

As the graphic indicates, there is a direct correlation between Act I and the first quadrant of the Hero's Journey model. Both have an establishing scene that shows us a status quo situation with its flaw. The dramatic catalyst is identical to the hero's Call to Adventure, and the catalyst may likewise come either as an inner call, an outer call, or a blunder. Following this catalyst, we expect to see the hero's first steps toward their plot goal. This corresponds to Little Hans stepping out of his little hut into the wide world or the beautiful Wassilissa being sent to get fire from the Baba Yaga. Then, when the hero meets a major obstacle in the form of the antagonist, we have the equivalent of the mythic meeting with the threshold guardian, played in another key. This encounter is the Threshold Crisis that ends Act I. It is here that myth and drama begin to differ appreciably, because the dramatic intensity of the story starts rising precipitously.

Where the wave starts to swell and surge, we have a new quality of energy. The modern translations of Aristotle term this the "rising action"; in screenplay structure it is identified with Act II. It is also equated with the Night World journey of the hero. Graphically, it is as though the circle of the Hero's Journey has been detached and stretched out in time. The Night World, which *underlies* the Day World in that model, here appears sequentially. Act I takes place in the Day World, Act II in the Night World, and Act III shows us a return to the Day World or brings the two worlds colliding together at the climax. The Threshold Crisis ending Act I, which works as the encounter with the threshold guardian, simultaneously propels the hero out of her comfort zone and into the Night World.

The crisis establishes the dramatic stakes for all of Act II; it sets a rising *dramatic trajectory*. This dramatic trajectory is aimed at a distant point that is laid in the audience's subtext. The endpoint of this rising conflict will be the catastrophe that ends Act II. The *catastrophe* point is determined by two factors: how high the antagonist can raise the stakes, and at what point the hero's mode breaks down. To take two simple examples: in *The Piano*, from the moment Ada makes the deal to buy her piano back from George, we know that inevitably the erotic triangle that is forming will one day explode. And in *The Talented Mr. Ripley*, from the moment we see Tom propose to get into the bathtub with Dickie, we realize that his erotic—we could say existential—longing is out of control. Tom's lack of boundaries will *inevitably* cause some kind of disaster. The catastrophe that ends Act II could be thought of as the *worst thing* that can happen to the hero in the context of the story.

It is clear that the catastrophe at the end of Act II coincides with the Night of the Soul: the point of breakdown in the Hero's Journey. Yet here the graphic shapes differ increasingly. What the Hero's Journey sees as a descent into the Night World, the Plot Curve sees as a rising wave of tension. This is the key to the difference in the two perspectives. We also notice that Act II is by far the longest; it may take up an hour or more of screen time and routinely is the most difficult to write. From this we can judge that drama puts a special emphasis on the Road of Trials. We have a battle of wits and wills between hero and antagonist. In drama we are also taken into the hero's subjective state, and thus into the psychology of growth through crisis. All of this takes time, screen time, to articulate. Nine Story Steps build the intensity of Act II.

The "resolution" of the Plot Curve model, also called the dénouement, the "untying of the knot" of destiny, occupies Act III of contemporary screenplay structure. The resolution includes both the climax, the highest point of dramatic intensity where the wave crests and breaks, and the *falling action* that brings the movie to a close. While the resolution is structurally the shortest act, it is the most momentous, encompassing the greatest change and having a decisive impact on the audience. Within a short time frame of perhaps ten to fifteen minutes onscreen, the resolution compresses the initiation and entire return portions of the Hero's Journey. The climax is the dramatic payoff for the whole script. While it is quite often the biggest scene—the big fight, chase, or confrontation—it is not the scale of the action that makes a powerful climax. The climax is decisive and final because it answers the throughline questions we began to identify in Chapters Three and Four, starting with the Need versus Mode model. A big action that fails to answer the throughline questions will not satisfy. It fails to untie the knot of tension in which the audience has been bound.

In Act III, the structural variance between Plot Curve and Hero's Journey becomes even more striking. Here, the dramatic climax precipitously comes just before the end of the movie. It cannot therefore correspond exactly to the mythic initiation, which takes place midway through the Night World journey in Campbell's scheme. Here is where we will come to appreciate the Story Molecule model. Because only when we work with all three levels together can we fully understand how the climax is orchestrated and how to craft powerful climaxes for our own screenplays.

The Power of Dramatic Questions

What makes the dramatic intensity rise toward the climax? What keeps it from fizzling out? Since there are in fact many, many movies where the story energy does fizzle in Act II, the answer to this question is by no means easy in practice. This is why the producer's response, that writing a good script is just as simple as identifying the throughline and staying on it, brought such a storm of protest from the screenwriters. Aristotle himself was occupied with this question. His way of answering it was to point to what he called a chain of cause and effect. Because Stewart refuses to bring the piano from the beach, Ada goes to see George to persuade him to take her to the piano. Because George finally agrees to this, he witnesses the quasi-erotic rapture Ada enters when she plays. And, as a consequence, George approaches Stewart and buys the piano in exchange for a piece of land. This is a very clear chain of cause and effect, action and consequence.

Aristotle's stress in these observations was more logical than psychological. The chain of events leads to an inevitable collision. The Hero's Journey model, for its part, emphasizes the symmetry between the nature of the hero's Call to Adventure and the nature of the trials he must undergo. There, the emphasis is less on logic and more on the subtle guiding power of that which calls us: the god, the daemon, the Self. Both of these approaches have their own internal consistency and validity. However, the most directly useful way of defining the throughline takes us back to Waldo Salt, to his idea that with every new scene he writes he tries to ask a question that goes to the heart of the drama. Aristotle's chain of cause and effect and Waldo Salt's chain of dramatic questions are two ways of describing the same thing. The rhythm of questions has the advantage, however, that it reveals how the pulse of drama operates on the micro-level within scenes.*

* We shall pursue this on the micro-level of dramatic beats with a scene in Chapter Ten.

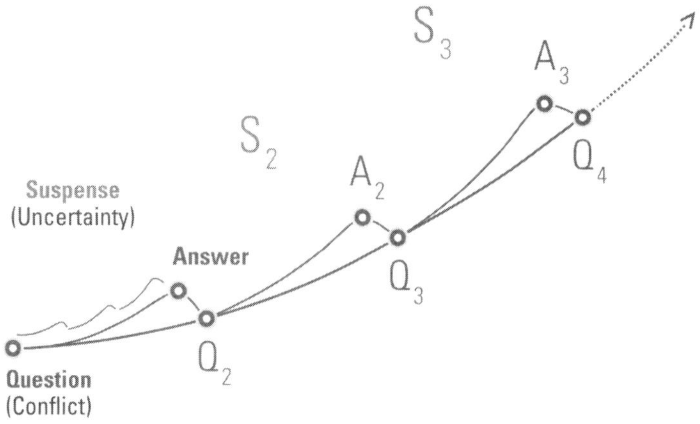

/ Dramatic chain of rising intensity.

We start by asking a question that engages the audience. For example, in Act I of Billy Wilder's *The Apartment*, C. C. Baxter gets the literal call (a phone call) saying he is wanted in Mr. Sheldrake's office on the twenty-seventh floor. The man at the next desk asks: "Hey Baxter, what gives? You getting promoted—or fired?" Baxter's comeback is to bet a dollar that he'll be promoted. The question starts to establish the stakes for the encounter and engages us in the outcome. It is a useful strategy to have a character in the scene ask the question out loud. This is more often done in comedies. In serious drama, the question is normally left in the subtext; it is the audience who subliminally poses the question to themselves. In either case, the effect is to engage the audience both mentally and emotionally, to make the audience *invest* in what is at stake.

So you raise a question that engages the audience. And then you deliberately *do not* answer the question. You *suspend* the answer. You leave it hanging. Suspending the answer creates *suspense*. Suspense means you create *tension* in the audience, because they want the answer but are not getting it. The longer the answer remains suspended, the higher the tension rises. We can see this phenomenon clearly with stand-up comedians. Comedians learn how to build up a joke to just before the punch line—then they hold it . . . and hold it . . . and hold it, building the suspense. Finally, the audience starts shouting and pleading, they want that punch line so badly. Whether in comedy or serious drama, thriller or melodrama, this question → suspense → answer → question unit is the basic mechanism of rising dramatic intensity.

When the answer, the punch line, comes, there is a release of tension. The audience heaves a collective sigh of relief. This, too, is an automatic psycho-physical mechanism: answering the question spontaneously releases the tension. The buildup of the tension is slow and gradual; the release is almost instantaneous. Here, on the micro-level of a joke, we see the pulse of tension and release.

The psychophysiological mechanics that make the joke work are the same as those that make the Plot Curve as a whole work. The larger Plot Curve is made up of smaller pulses of tension and release that build progressively. This is because in drama, like in science, the answer to one question always leads to a new question. In this case, the new question is at a higher level of energy because the stakes have gone up. Will Baxter be promoted or fired? What happens in the scene in Sheldrake's office is that first Baxter is threatened with the loss of his job. Then he is promised a promotion—*if* he lets Sheldrake use his apartment for an illicit love affair. Baxter is only too eager to comply; this is the way his mode has scripted his life for him. But we can see that instead of gaining more freedom and respect, Baxter has only indentured himself to a more odious master. Baxter goes out happy as a lark, but because we can see that Baxter's blind spot now has consequences, we know the stakes are rising. And the following scenes of the sequence confirm this: Baxter has just made a deal for Sheldrake to take the very woman Baxter loves to Baxter's own apartment and screw her in Baxter's own bed.

As the Story Molecule model has shown us, there is not just one single chain of questions and answers we are working with. There is in fact a nexus or braid of such chains, reinforcing one another as they move through the story. We need a more complex metaphor than a simple chain, because the totality is more like the spiraling double helix of a DNA strand. Each level of the Story Molecule generates its own questions, and this, we shall see, is the real key to developing Act II. There is one overarching throughline plot question. This question is "set" at the dramatic catalyst early in Act I, either stated overtly or laid in the subtext. The catalyst corresponds precisely to the Call to Adventure in the Hero's Journey model and sets up the main character's plot goal. The answer to this throughline question is going to be suspended and held all the way to the climax, and only answered at the climax.

Since this degree of suspension asks a lot from an audience, the throughline plot question is broken down into smaller plot questions that take us step by step along the way. There will be a question that frames the action for Act I. The answer to that question will raise a new question at a higher level of risk, which will frame the action in Act II, up to the catastrophe that ends the act. And the answer to that question will propel us directly into Act III and the dramatic climax, where the overarching throughline question is answered. These major act-framing questions will be further broken down into smaller and smaller structures.

Using questions to frame the action within each act is important. We want to realize that the powerful questions we generate while developing the screenplay correspond to the subliminal questions that the audience generates in the theater. The audience engages in their own "unconscious scanning"* of the story, where

* See footnote 3. "Unconscious scanning" for the audience in the movie theater is a process similar to the writer's unconscious scanning (right-brain process) while writing. In both cases a subliminal flow of associated imagery is activated that complements what our conscious attention tells us.

the story *might go*. The chain of inner subliminal questions generates an invisible track for the audience through the story. The audience has a gut feeling of being "with it." So the consistency of the questions we use to frame each act constitutes a special communication with the audience. Take the familiar example of *Shakespeare in Love*:

- In the opening it is announced that Will Shakespeare is writing a new comedy, but we quickly see that he has writer's block. So there is immediately a question: how will Shakespeare successfully complete the play if he has writer's block?
- The preliminary answer is that he must find his muse.
- New question: who will be Shakespeare's muse?
- He gives the bracelet to Rosalind, but she is neither available nor right for him. Meanwhile, out in the palace audience of *Two Gentlemen of Verona* is Viola, enraptured with the poetry, which she seems already to have learned by heart.
- New question: is she the one, the muse?
- The questions build through Act I to the Threshold Crisis, where Shakespeare has discovered that Thomas Kent, the actor, is in fact Viola, dressed as a man—but he has at the same moment discovered that Viola belongs to a different world than he, the world of the noble and wealthy. So he has found his muse, but there are obstacles. How can he be together with her, he, Will Shakespeare, a lowly player?
- They dance, and their eyes say that the attraction is mutual.
- Just then, the jealous Lord Wessex has a knife to Will's throat, and promises to slit it.

We have answered the Act I framing question: will Shakespeare find his muse so that he can write his play? The answer is yes. But we have a new question to frame Act II, which is at a higher level of dramatic intensity, with higher stakes: will Lord Wessex kill Shakespeare? Obviously, Will cannot successfully write the play if he is murdered, so this new question is still on the overall throughline. It adds a new layer of interest as we go into Act II.

A strong and clear throughline plot question is a necessity if the audience is not going to walk out of the theater feeling vague and confused. It is a concrete and simple yes or no question, answered by the resolution of the movie, that is, by how the audience is presented with the consequences of the climax. The nature of the throughline plot question suggests the nature of the action because it defines the plot goal. The question can be small, as long as it is clearly set up and clearly paid off. The charming small comedy from Norway, *Elling*, is propelled by a very simple question: will Elling, who has spent his life literally tied to his mother's skirts, find a place for himself in the world after his mother dies?

In *In the Mood for Love*, from Hong Kong, the question is whether the man and the woman will ever consummate their love. The question in the Iranian movie *Taste of Cherry* is put explicitly right out front at the opening: will the main character find someone to give him a decent burial after he commits suicide? And the throughline question of *The Full Monty* is given with the title.

It is rather typical during the story development process, as we alluded to before, that the Act I throughline question and the Act III answer get out of alignment. After writing a draft, we discover that the climax does not answer the specific question posed in Act I. The story is demonstrably not working at this point because it lacks dramatic unity and closure. Unless the writer or development team have access to tools like the Need versus Mode and Story Molecule models, there is usually just a vague sense that something is missing. This event throws the writer deeper into the creative Night World. He will go over the screenplay again and again, trying to discover why it doesn't add up. There is a great temptation to fix things superficially, for example, to make the plot climax bigger. This follows from the notion that if I talk loud enough, I can make you understand me. But if the bigger event still does not convincingly answer the throughline questions, it will not be a superior achievement. Perceptive critics and audience members are going to notice, to the detriment of the movie's potential success.

With all models and all generalizations, it is important to test whether this in fact improves your screenwriting and story development. It is of course always a delicate thing to refer to projects that are in process and not yet released, but concrete examples are sometimes the only way to check a model against your own experience. I was recently consulting on a project whose premise was that a young woman is invited by the man of her dreams to join him in a distant land, to marry and build a home together. The throughline question the development team had been working with had been some variant of the following: "Will Mary find happiness and fulfillment with her true love?" The emphasis of the throughline question was always on the love story. But this was not borne out by the action in the screenplay. First of all, when the heroine arrives, she finds that her new husband is madly obsessed with a native woman. Second, there is another man who becomes interested in Mary. And third, there is a war going on that directly involves both men. It was proving impossible to find a climax that satisfactorily resolved the desired love story because in fact the screenplay was investing its energy elsewhere.

The development team, the screenwriter, and the producer were all aware that it wasn't adding up. Their first instinct was to re-orchestrate the character web, trying to make the relationship between Mary and her husband Bill juicier, in spite of the fact that the two would not be together at the end of the movie. The one thing they could *not* achieve was to force Bill to fall in love with Mary—not without destroying his character—because Bill's core motive for inviting Mary to come and join him was for the sake of appearances, not love. The throughline question started to shift: "How will Mary cope with the loss of her dream?" Jealousy? Rage? Withdrawal? Revenge? Exploring this avenue led to developing Mary as a stronger and more passionate character, yet it did not lead to a single, definitive climax. There was a diffuse, unconvincing climax with three different events happening simultaneously to the various characters. Ultimately, the writer decided that it was not her intention to write a story on the theme of jealousy. That was not the story she wanted to tell. The story development problem lay in a basic and very common confusion: the love story is the setup, but it is not the throughline. A useful comparison was made to *The Piano*, where a melodrama structure and an important emotional network triangle provide the setup, but the throughline ultimately has to do with Ada's relationship to her piano. This is proven by the fact that, at the climax, Ada is not choosing between Stewart and George, but between the piano and George—which becomes simultaneously a choice between death and life.

My experience in counseling writers through this process is that you can help them find the right questions, but they have to make their own discovery. The right question does not resonate until one is ready to hear it. And yet, having the right question is already a great help! Focusing on the need/mode question at the core of the character can typically save a couple of screenplay drafts that might wander and explore and still not find the solution. Every attempt to solve the problem of this screenplay left Mary alone at the end, but standing on her own feet. Finally it became clear that the answer had to dictate the question: "How will Mary find her place in a strange new world?" The answer that suggested itself was in fact bolder than the screenwriter had previously considered: by having her romantic illusion shattered, but learning to take responsibility for herself. This clicked for the writer. It was in fact the story she herself was living. And even against her conscious design, it was the story she had written. This was the throughline question that best framed the totality of the action.

The Flow and the Act Breaks

When we are discussing or working with the Plot Curve model, the main thing to keep in mind is the fundamental dynamic shape of it, because the dynamic of tension and release reproduces itself on every level of the screenplay structure and in every scene. In fact, where you really want to keep the curve is in your body. It is a rhythm, like a golf swing. Natural-born dramatists are people with a sense of rhythm, a sense of swing. When you are in the middle of the draft, with a deadline looming, you are normally too busy to cognitively process all the theory. That is when the sense of rhythm, your internal connection to the breaking wave of tension and release, is your most reliable guide. Trying to arbitrarily micromanage your screenwriting with fixed page counts for the act breaks tends to get in the way of the creative flow.

There is much discussion in Hollywood as to whether the Plot Curve naturally falls into three acts, or four, or five. One screenwriting teacher sees it as a marketing advantage to call the three-act structure old-fashioned and obsolete. Another wants to call all designation of acts completely arbitrary. The reality is that the Plot Curve can be broken down in a number of relevant ways. Each manner of subdividing the curve will highlight certain features while throwing others into the background. None of these systems has an absolute validity, but at the same time they are not merely arbitrary. Each act-break model does identify necessary features of the dramatic structure. We may properly call these designations *conventional* in the positive sense of that word: generally agreed upon through customary usage. Conventions are helpful as long as we recall that the map is not the territory. If we forget that, any convention can trap us in conventionality.

Today three acts is the most commonly accepted feature film screenplay structure. It is the dominant convention. Most producers, agents, studio readers, and others in the business will automatically think of a script in three acts. They will look for the act breaks where they expect to find them. It is good for this convention to be challenged, not because it is wrong, but to keep us all from becoming lazy. One hears egregious stories about studio readers, who get paid by the number of scripts they read and write coverage notes for, opening a screenplay directly to page 28. If they don't find the "plot point" that so-and-so told them they should find on page 28, they toss the script. The screenwriter gets the standard form rejection letter, but the screenplay was prejudged before it was read. Nevertheless, the three-act structure does make common sense. Each act occupies a part of the curve that is quite characteristic: setup, rising action, and resolution. Three acts captures both the musical aspect—theme, development, recapitulation/resolution—and the dialectical aspect: thesis, antithesis, and synthesis. For these reasons we can expect the three-act breakdown to remain dominant.

But Howard Suber, from the screenwriting program at UCLA, rightly pointed out (in interactions with my colleague Tom Schlesinger) that Act II may be thought of as having two separate *movements*. The length of the second act and the difficulties of its construction have bothered screenwriters for a long time. It can feel like such a vast and featureless terrain! As a matter of fact, with the new Sixteen Story Steps paradigm, the terrain of Act II becomes visible as it never has before. Suber's hint about Act II being made of two musical movements, along with the Story Molecule, was one of the keys without which the new model would not have come into being. Howard Suber rightly saw the two sections of Act II as each having its own feeling-tone, as well as its own distinct *arena of action*. His way of analyzing dramatic structure would fall into four acts or symphonic movements, designated by a key word that identifies the essence of that movement: Desire, Deception, Discovery, and Destiny. They are indicated on the graphic of the Plot Curve model. Think of these four words as generally describing the action and feeling tone at that stage of the drama, like four key signatures in music, moving from the major key to the minor, the dominant, and so on. Because cinema is a constant flow in which a complex emotional experience is orchestrated for the viewers, it has at least as much in common with symphonic music as it does with theater. You can see that this is also in complete accord with the four phases of the Hero's Journey: Separation = Desire, Descent = Deception, Initiation = Discovery, and Return = Destiny. Suber's contribution has been highly perceptive and has spurred new insights.

And what about five acts? If we let our dramatic sensibility be dominated by the crucial Story Step sequences that mark significant dramatic turns, we will see the story in five acts:

1. Catalyst/Call
2. Threshold Crisis/Threshold Crossing
3. Core Crisis (or "Crucible of Character")
4. Catastrophe/Night of the Soul
5. Climax/Initiation

After the catalyst, which raises the throughline dramatic questions, these four major story steps each mark both a peak of tension and a distinct shift in the story's energy/tone. In the five-act structure, each one of these major dramatic moments has its own act. The action within each of the five acts is tightly constructed to lead to one of these high moments. The five-act structure was the convention for Shakespeare. One thing that can be said about five acts in relation to three: it suggests a different organization of dramatic time. If you look at Shakespeare's plays, you see that while the action *within* each act tends to occur in a compact time frame, the time lapses *between* acts are longer and often vague. That is theater, and is not constructed with the ongoing forward momentum of physical action we have come to expect from movies. Undoubtedly there were those early on in the movie business who felt that five acts went too counter to the sense of flow that is basic to the cinema, and another convention was developed. These different ways of breaking down the dramatic curve—which is itself continuous—have nothing to do with right and wrong. Shifting lenses to one of these other models, as an exercise during story development, might in fact reveal something you have missed.

The whole idea of act breaks has more to do with how we talk about stories than with the stories themselves. Keeping this in mind, we can look at how the story material is structured, especially in Act II. Some second acts are structured with a linear feel and a continuous buildup of momentum. That is to say, there is an emphasis on one line of plot action from crisis to catastrophe. This will be most apparent in quest and chase plots, road movies, and whenever the end goal at the climax is already known to both the characters and the audience, and the action is driving toward that goal. In this case, the shifts within Act II from Deception to Discovery, and the importance of the Core Crisis (midway through

Act II), may be de-emphasized. They may be relatively subordinated to the sense of a continuous rising action.

An action movie like *Terminator 2* would appear to fit this linear Act II scheme pretty well; it appears to be composed of one exciting action sequence after another. But a closer look shows that this is not the case. At the end of Act I, the Terminator has helped John rescue his mother, and they have escaped the bad Terminator. Now, going into Act II, the pace slows down. The first movement of Act II focuses primarily on the emotional network, the potential new family the three might comprise. They get away to the desert to Sarah's extended family, we see John start to teach the Terminator how to be human, and Sarah says to herself that she has finally found the perfect father for her son. This leads to the subclimax of this movement, where Sarah goes off to assassinate the computer engineer, and John and the Terminator make a deeper bond to prevent her from committing the crime. There is a major shift into the Core Crisis of values: must human ethics be maintained even in the face of a dire threat? The second movement in Act II finds the pace accelerating as the heroes make their first proactive move. The attempt to destroy the files, chips, and material from the future leaves them vulnerable to discovery. Soon the chase is on again, relentlessly, until the heroes can go no farther and are cornered in the steel mill. Each of these movements in fact has its own distinct arena, pace, and tone. This is because each of these movements has its own narrative function to fulfill.

Most successful screenplays exhibit two distinct movements within the flow of Act II, each characterized by its own arena, action, and dramatic development. The Sixteen Story Steps model reveals why this is the case. In a fully articulated screenplay, one in which a throughline of consequence is built for each level of the Story Molecule, the interactions of these levels result in qualitative changes in the nature of the conflict. The whole story goes deeper. What had appeared as an outer-world/plot problem in Act I becomes, in addition, an intimate emotional and relationship conflict of allegiances in the first half of Act II. An entirely new level of conflict has been added. Then, after the Core Crisis, the problem goes deeper still, becoming an existential/identity crisis. Here we put into question the core values upon which a life has been built and prepare the final breakdown of the mode.

After considering Howard Suber's insight along with the other paradigms, we have evolved more precise ways of characterizing the two movements of Act II. The first movement (Suber's "Deception") we now term "Wounding and Recovery." This first phase of Act II picks up the falling action after the hero has been wounded at the Threshold Crisis by the threshold guardian. There is a shift to the primary relationship (emotional network), which prepares the hero for a new effort toward her plot goal. The second movement of Act II (Suber's "Discovery") is termed "Setting the Double Bind." It leads us from the Core Crisis to the catastrophe that ends Act II. As we begin to unfold the inner workings of Act II, we will discover it to be less mystifying, yet far move elegant, than we had imagined.

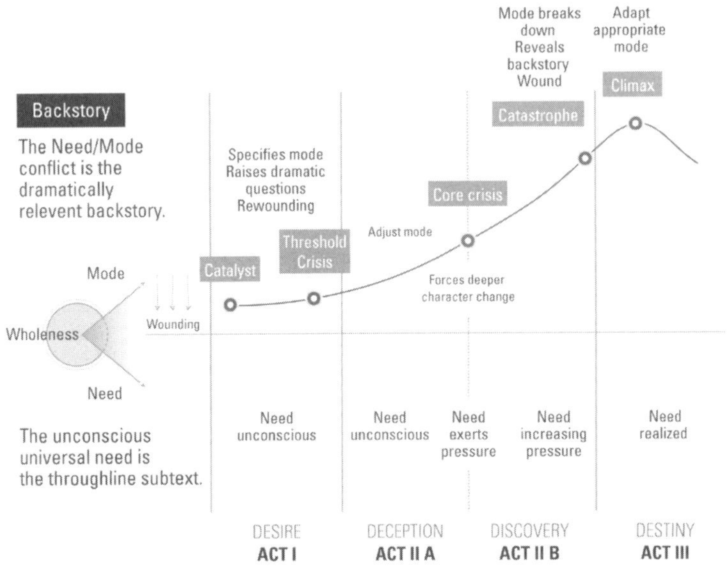

In movies that convey a feeling of five acts, with the action compacted around the major Story Steps—catalyst, crisis, midpoint, catastrophe, and climax—the storytelling strategy is also more episodic. Each episode may have its own time frame, with gaps of time—days to years—between episodes. The time gaps naturally function as act breaks. This strategy is found most typically in adaptations from stage plays and novels. For example, let us look at the organization of dramatic time in *The Apartment*, itself an adaptation of a stage play. The setup of the story through the dramatic catalyst takes place in autumn, as we can tell from the rainy weather and falling leaves. There is then a time gap, bringing us to Christmas Eve, when the crisis/threshold crossing event takes place: Miss Kubelik attempts suicide in Baxter's apartment. A few days later, we have the comical spaghetti dinner at Core Crisis the midpoint. Then we jump to New Year's Eve for the catastrophe and climax. This strategy is not necessarily less dramatic than a linear development of Act II. It is not a question of this at all. Success with Act II has far more to do with the dramatic basics: is the throughline question clear and compelling? Does it reflect the core need/mode conflict of values in the main character? Does it resonate through all three levels of the Story Molecule? Is the throughline question well broken down into subquestions that frame the action in each act?

Beneath the Waves

Dramatic storytelling, whether genre or character-driven, serious or comic, is predicated on character change. The root of great stories is growth through crisis: "We are moved by heroism of the ordinary person acting in an extraordinary way," as David Mamet has said. The hero is faced with a crisis that can only be resolved by inner change, change in the way she sees the situation and herself. Even the darkest, most tragic movies, such as Andrzej Wajda's *Kanal*, about resistance fighters trying to escape the collapse of the Warsaw uprising through the underground sewer system, turn on the characters' belief—and our own belief—in the power to change our circumstances. Look at all those characters in *Titanic*, struggling for life even as the ship goes down. Otherwise, there would be no buildup of dramatic tension; the characters would merely be victims of fate, pathetic yet not tragic. Faith in our ability to take our fate in our own hands reveals something beyond the survival instinct. We could call it an instinct toward growth. This is distinctly human, closely connected to our spirituality. When we surrender this faith, we quickly lose other aspects of our humanity as well. But while we may have abstract faith in change, we may not be ready for the changes we must make in ourselves.

The dramatic conflict must be of such a nature that—here is a variant on our earlier axiom—the characters cannot resolve the conflict at the same level of awareness that created the conflict. They must change their level of awareness. And that is their Hero's Journey: to find the strength, the insight, the heart that they do not possess at the opening of the story. Thus there always comes a crucial moment in action movies where the hero's super-car breaks down, or the super-weapon malfunctions, or the guide and protector is unavailable, and the hero is thrown back on his inner resources. At the moment of truth in *Silence of the Lambs*, Starling must hunt Buffalo Bill alone through the pitch-black cellar of his flaying-house, confronting her own deepest memories of helplessness and fear. Her long years of FBI training will come down to one instant of instinctual response. Whether Starling sees clearly in this darkness, and has the penetrating insight to survive, will be dependent on whether or not she is still identified with the frightened, helpless child in herself.

Resolving the dramatic conflict is a question of change at the level of fundamental core attitudes and beliefs, the attitudes and beliefs that are so deep we must live them out. These are the attitudes we are not even aware we have until life puts us to the test. There is a limit to what willpower and discipline can achieve; that limit is the field of what is already conscious. When we say the character *changes*, we make the process sound more consciously willed than it is in reality. We could equally say that life, providence, divine will, or grace changes the person. There is a Buddhist saying to this effect:

> Truth is conveyed
> Not by action and
> Not by words
> But by life itself.

Change is like a stone thrown into a pond. The ripples of change radiate outward from the core of the person, through her behavior, and out into her world, the world of the film story. As we in the audience perceive these waves of change, we intuitively sense the truth of it. It is this moment of truth, and the sense of sharing that accompanies it, that we attempt to disclose, paradoxically, through the art of our storytelling craft.

The process of character change suggests that there is more to Aristotle's Plot Curve than meets the eye. If we take it simply as a graph upon which to hang plot points, we miss the living dimension of it. What we really want from a story structure model is a lens to look deeper into the nature of growth through crisis. When we get in sync with *that*, then the outer structure of the screenplay largely takes care of itself. At least our storytelling choices will be in line with our gut feeling. In the next chapter, we shall look more deeply at each of the four movements—Desire, Deception, Discovery, and Destiny—that comprise the three acts of a screenplay. However, as we prepare to do so, it is worth spending a few minutes to reflect on how drama and character growth intersect with mythic wisdom in tragedy.

Drama asserts that it is our human nature to seek to know the truth and act on the truth. Further, drama asserts that the truth is so precious, we may choose it even over our personal survival. Of course, we are not speaking here of an absolute or metaphysical truth. We are speaking about the truth of the situations we find ourselves in, the truth about others' motives and our own, the truth about our projections, self-betrayals, and limiting identifications. Here, truth means seeing through some of the mist of illusions within which we lead our daily lives. It means seeing things as they are. Not just "who I think I am," but the larger wholeness. Not just what I want, but what wants to be lived through me. In this way, dramatic truth is a route to the sublime, the divine. When Oedipus realizes he has been the fool of the gods, he not only gets to the truth about himself, but also glimpses a truth about the gods themselves. Oedipus arrives at the truth by following his path all the way to the bitter end. This desire to uncover the truth is the essence of what Joseph Campbell called "the way of tragic affirmation."

The word *tragedy* has become so overused in our society that it has lost its original affirmative sense. Whenever someone dies in an accident, a glamorous celebrity has a miscarriage, or a cousin fails their school exams, we call it a tragedy. The word evokes feelings of sadness, pity, and sympathy. The sad feelings may be inflated by media coverage of an event to the point where we may feel flooded with overwhelming sentiment. But these sentiments are not in themselves tragic, or, better put, they express only half of the tragic emotion. It was not the intention of tragedies to make the audience feel sad and pitying. Sadness and pity are not what we feel at the end of *Oedipus*, *Macbeth*, *Fargo*, *Mulholland Drive*, or *Raise the Red Lanterns*. Pity is but one of the two tragic emotions identified by Aristotle. The other is terror. This terror is a cousin of the terror in thrillers. James Joyce, elaborating on Aristotle, defined pity as the tragic emotion that connects us to "whatsoever is grave and constant in human suffering," and links us to the human sufferer. Terror is the tragic emotion that connects us to "whatsoever is grave and constant in human suffering," and links us to the secret cause of the suffering.

Secret cause! What might "secret cause" mean? Most of us draw a blank at this point. There is a hole in our collective sensibility, which says something about why so many sentimental and inauthentic screenplays deluge studios and producers every year. We have repressed the secret cause in the same way we don't want to meet whoever or whatever is down there making noises in the basement of our psychic house. Joseph Campbell felt that, as we commonly use the word tragic, we in fact *invert* its original meaning. In this regard, Campbell was fond of sharing two anecdotes to illustrate.

The first is the ancient Greek myth of Actaeon the hunter. As the tale goes, Actaeon was the greatest hunter of his time, and he had to go farther and farther afield to find challenging game. Finally he found himself in an unknown landscape (i.e., the Night World) and, following a stream to its source, he discovered a hidden spring. There, peering through the bushes, he witnessed the goddess Artemis and her nymphs bathing in the waters. But the goddess chanced to see him and grew wrathful. Splashing water in Actaeon's face, she challenged him: "Go now and tell everyone, if you can, that you have seen the Great Goddess!" Terrified, Actaeon turned to flee, but his arms were already turning to forelegs, and stag antlers were sprouting from his head. Before he could get away, Actaeon was caught and torn apart by his own hunting dogs.

Now, the conventional-morality interpretation of this story, Campbell commented, would be that Actaeon went too far, broke a taboo, and was punished. As a man, he responded to the revelation of the divine feminine not with awe and humility, but with lust. He behaved like an animal, became an animal, and died the death of an animal. Actaeon was literally torn apart by his appetites. This conventional view agrees with our sense of morality and order.

Not contradicting but complementing this view is the tragic perspective. The tragic sense is neither moralistic nor pitying—"Poor lad, how was he to know?" The tragic sense is simply to *affirm*, to say yes to the circumstances of life. "Yes, he went too far. Yes, he was torn apart. But he did it! He saw the goddess!" Such was Campbell's statement on the properly tragic view of the story. Actaeon is in that sense someone who completely achieved his life, "following the stream all the way to its source." If this sounds alien to you, it may be helpful to recall traditional Church doctrine of the "felix culpa," the "fortunate sin" of Adam and Eve that would ultimately necessitate the incarnation of the Redeemer. The paradoxical intertwining of our faults and virtues is an untidy nuisance we tend to push into the background. We pragmatists have little taste for paradox.

This leads to Campbell's second example of the powerful affirmation of life in tragedy. Campbell was a passionate admirer of Martin Luther King Jr. He noted that in the weeks leading up to his assassination, King more than once admitted that he knew every time he went out to lead a rally that he was tempting death. Now, Campbell asked, what is the "secret cause" of Martin

Luther King's death that makes it a properly tragic death? If you point to the bullet that killed him, you point to the *instrumental* cause, not the *secret* cause. You could do a paper on ballistics, but it wouldn't be a tragedy. If you say that racism in America killed Martin Luther King, you could write a book on sociology, but it wouldn't be a tragedy. What is the *secret* cause? It is there that tragic terror lies—and it lies within Martin Luther King himself. The secret cause was that vital force in King, the force of his truth, which made him actively pursue his destiny rather than choose safety. King had already accomplished so much. He might have "quit while he was ahead," but no. He chose—or was compelled by his daemon—to live his truth to the bitter end.

The terror of tragedy bursts in upon us like a clap of thunder. There is an old spiritual that goes: "Last night I heard my Lord callin' / he said you sure better quit your stallin'. . . ." It terrifies us simultaneously with what we could be—and what we are, nestled in our comfort zones. A life like King's holds up a mirror to us and challenges us. The terror has not to do with how great the outer forces constraining us are, but how vast the living force *inside* us is, what it might do if it got free—and what it might demand of *us*. Tragic heroes, properly speaking, are not victims, neither of outer circumstances nor of their own impulses. They are people for whom a radical integrity, being at one with one's destiny, has inverted the usual hierarchy of values. Princess Diana was a high tragic figure. She seemed to embody the "princess type" in a measure beyond her personal will or choice. So many people around the world identified with her because she carried—or was carried by and touched by—some larger force. But how much can the tragic emotion be diluted before the sense of it is lost? How, when it is our pettiness rather than our grandeur that drives us into catastrophe? Could a tragedy be built around, for example, the negligent Greek ferryboat captain who was watching a soccer match on TV as his ship went aground, killing eighty people on board? We all, in one way or another, move toward a destiny, be it tragic, pathetic, comic, or ironic.

Drama shows us characters presented with alternate paths, paths not entirely of their own choosing but in accord with something in their own nature, the inner tension between their status quo mode and a universal need. The choice at the climax is the choice of a destiny. When the character chooses in favor of the repressed need, she is picking a more conscious destiny that will continue to unfold into the future. At the end of Act II, Ada chooses to break the piano in order to send George a love token. She pays for this with the loss of her finger, yet it also sets up the greater choice she will make at the climax: to let go of the piano altogether. Whether the destiny is as grandly tragic as Martin Luther King's or as simple as Loretta Castorini choosing passion, the endpoint is less the issue than the process of growth through crisis that leads to greater risk and authenticity.

Catharsis and Resolution

The case of tragedy illustrates, even better than action adventure movies can, the deeply visceral and transrational nature of drama. It is to be expected that an audience will react to life-threatening situations and to the mechanics of the action genre. There, the relation between stimulus and response is simple, direct, and clear. To a large extent the reaction is predictable, and thus controllable. But the hair standing on end, the strange mixtures of dread, grief, and exaltation that belong to tragedy, that is harder to program—and yet that, too, is rooted in the body. Over the past few centuries, during which time the Western world embraced the ideology of rationalism, and nonrational experience was suppressed along with witches and folk ritual, those powerful sensations elicited by tragedy have drifted further from ego-awareness and into the shadow. Nevertheless, the dramatic curve itself is a testimony to the enduring force of a more primal level of psyche. The curve exists in the body, in the nervous system where body and mind meet. This is why drama cannot be adequately described as an argument, theorem, or proof.

Climax is the point of catharsis in drama. Yes, the throughline questions are answered, and this is greatly satisfying. There is a release of tension. But here is where a dramatic climax differs from the punch line to a joke: in the quality of that release. Though the ritual function of catharsis has been forgotten, the physical experience is as alive in our bodies as it was in those of ancient peoples. The psychic energy that has been dammed up over the course of the drama is released at the climax, and it flows down and out of the body when the throughline dramatic questions are answered. We calm *down*. This, too, seems to be part of an instinctual response pattern, or rather, an archetypal pattern that encompasses both an instinctual and a psychological aspect. It is impossible to separate the one from the other, as they irrupt together into our awareness. The experience of catharsis belongs to rituals of death and renewal found all over the world. Joseph Campbell took pains to re-establish this background context on which drama and the movies are founded:

> As Gilbert Murray has pointed out in his preface to the *Poetics* of Aristotle, tragic katharsis [*sic*] (i.e. the "purification" or "purgation" of the emotions of the spectator of the tragedy though his experience of pity and terror) corresponds to an earlier ritual katharsis ("a purification of the community from the taints and poisons of the past year, the old contagion of sin and death"), which was the function of the festival and the mystery play. . . . The meditating mind is united, in the mystery play, not with the body that is shown to die, but with the principle of continuous life that for a time inhabited it. . . .[32]

To return this to the language of contemporary dramaturgy in movies, the viewer's awareness is directed from the character's mode—their precious "who

32. Gilbert Murray quoted in Campbell, *Hero*, p. 26.

I think I am," which is shown to die—toward a larger, evolving self. The mode is shown to be illusory in the sense of relative, not fixed, and final. It is a stage in the evolution of the self, a costume it has momentarily put on and grown attached to. Once the attachment has become concretized, the journey of death and renewal becomes necessary in order to free the deeper movement to proceed. The mode itself is not wrong; it is perhaps only outmoded. It is the "stuck" quality of the attachment that becomes "wrong" in terms of being against one's own best interests, against one's own instinct toward growth and fulfillment. Joseph Campbell goes on to define sin and death in relation to this dynamic of unfolding that is at the heart of drama:

> [Tragedy and comedy] are the terms of a single mythological theme and experience which includes them both and which they bound: the down-going an the up-coming (kathodos and anodos), which together constitute the revelation that is life, and which the individual is to know and love if he is to be purged (katharsis = purgatorio) of the contagion of sin (disobedience to the divine will) and death (identification with the mortal form).[33]

Resolution is directly connected to catharsis. When the great dramatic tension is released at the climax, we literally fall away from the screen. Look around the movie theater and you can watch this happen. This is the precise point where the energy shifts from one level to another. The cathartic release is a moment where we are open to receive a new pattern, and at precisely this moment we are most intimately bonded to the hero. Dramatic growth through crisis brings the hero's universal need to consciousness via a "grow or die" situation, "so that what is weak within him is purged away and only the strong elements remain," thus releasing the universal level of his personality into play in the world. We witness a union of opposites in the character. As it happens in the hero, it is modeled *in potential* for the audience. This is part of what is meant by catharsis, and why we feel cleansed and purged of violent affect through the drama. In the resolution, the hero exhibits a *freedom to be* (freedom from the old attitudes limited by overidentification with the mode). This freedom is not so much an indication of ego-mastery as it is a suggestion of the nonduality of hero and world, and thus, by extension, of audience and world.

The Dramatic Curve Is You

My first introduction to the Plot Curve came years ago through my colleague Chap Freeman (who had himself picked it up through the Iowa Writers' Workshop, I believe). After putting the curve up on the blackboard, he would lean out toward a theater full of young, first-year film production students and leer suggestively: "What does this remind you of . . . *hmmmm*?" The students would

33. Ibid, p. 28.

glance uneasily at the floor. A few would open their notebooks to see if they had missed something. Then some would chuckle. That would get others riled up: what are they laughing at? The punch line was that the Plot Curve is the same as the curve of sexual response found by Masters and Johnson.

And it's true. Names of parts of the curve are even the same. Fortunately, reading a book is a private act, unlike an online chat room. You are free to recall some recent (or less recent) amorous encounter that sent you riding Aristotle's roller-coaster. Do that now.

What was the establishing scene? A club? A party? A museum? What was the catalyst? As troubadours have been telling us since the Middle Ages, love stories are catalyzed by a meeting of the eyes that signals mutual interest, and an opening of the heart. This is what makes a catalyst different from an infatuation with a pretty face or designer jeans. There is a deeper spark there. You gonna rise to the challenge or not? Because, ready or not, here comes that dynamic duo: desire . . . and anxiety. Suddenly you feel so vulnerable. If you answer that call, it will lead to a crisis and a threshold crossing. Otherwise it all remains on the level of a fantasy. Someone has to cross that crowded room, laying themselves open to possible rejection. It is a naked moment, and naturally the self-talk comes up full-blast: *What do I say? "What's a nice girl like you . . . ?" No, I tried that last time. It's useless, pointless. I'm making a damn fool of myself . . .* (etc., etc.).

Let's set this story in a bar. With the hawklike eyes that belong to writers, we have just observed two people cross that first awkward threshold together. Now they have started an exchange of corny lines: "Do you come here often?" and so on. Okay, we'll go get a drink and come back in a bit to see how they're doing. Half an hour later they've moved on to their jobs. "My day job is steel welding, but my real love is ballet." "I'm not really an IT geek, one day I'll have an organic farm in Tuscany." "Oh yeah, I see what you mean . . ." and all that. Confessing some truth about themselves. Fine. We return an hour later, and they have both taken their wallets out and are showing each other photos of themselves at the age of four, at their high school graduations, on the rugby team, or stoned with friends on Bourbon St. "You were so cute back then! Same little nose!" This is rising action. But as we know, all rising action has a limit where it can rise no more. Old Fred is wiping down the bar now: "Okay you guys, it's two a.m. Gotta close up!"

Catastrophe. Grow or die. There is another threshold here: this is the point where one invites the other to come over and see some original Picasso etchings or to have a nice herbal tea. ("Really, I can't let you drive home in the state you're in!") Here is a much higher threshold: a challenge to open up, not just your charming personality but your real person, to being emotionally penetrated by another. And so a new sequence begins, with its own establishing moment as the door opens on a dark apartment, its own rising action as items of clothing land on the floor, on the lamp, on the dog. Then finally, to the climax. . . . And, of course, the falling action, with its disengagement rituals, which in Europe and many parts of the world seem always to involve the ritual sharing of a cigarette in bed.

Now, we have no evidence that Aristotle was conducting sex research. So what accounts for the similarity of these two curves of sex and drama? Were the ancient dramatists, like the founders of disco, inserting subliminal sexual cues in their plays in order to hook the audience and make them spend more drachmas at the bar? Unlikely. It seems more likely that there exists a deeper center in the nervous system that accounts for our sexual response as well as for the dramatic curve. It has to do with how our nervous system structures emotional experience in time into waves of tension and release. After all, every art that works with time—movies, theater, music, dance—is built around these rhythms of tension and release. And, if we extend this spatially rather than temporally, the same would be found true of painting, sculpture, even architecture. Psychology and aesthetics meet here. A successful movie, song, or building finds a balance of tension and harmony through form. When the form fits, we have an experience of rightness and of meaning. We seem to have an innate need to articulate the flux of tension and release within ourselves into dynamic patterns, or gestalts, of meaning.

Nor are the connections limited to the world of the arts. As we suggested in an earlier chapter, the creative process itself utilizes the same Hero's Journey/Plot Curve complex of dynamisms. Even when we believe we are engaged in a purely rational problem-solving process, the invisible engine that gives us energy to hunt for the logical solution derives from this same deep, form-giving center that Jung has termed the "transcendent function." This is all linked to language and language-formation. As language researchers like Noam Chomsky demonstrated some decades ago, we are not born into this world with a blank slate in our heads. We are born with neural templates that allow us to recognize and respond to language structures and other significant patterns. We carry within us a "virtual grammar" which is actualized in the context of our early language environment. That is to say, we recognize that words not only have different sounds and meanings, but also different *functions*, and that those functions occupy special places in a grammar. We learn to tell a word's function by its place in a sentence. And now, when we come to look at storytelling for movies (through the lens of the Sixteen Story Steps model), we perceive that a movie drama is also structured as a language in itself. Within the Plot Curve of tension and release, there is a grammar of storytelling. Each step has its specific function in the grammar of the whole, all of it carried by waves of tension and release.

Drama turns out to be the place where sex and language intersect—which, if you know anything about sex and anything about language, is saying quite a lot.

9

The Journey in Four Movements

There is a kind of character in thy life,
That to the observer doth thy history
Fully unfold. Thyself and thy belongings
Are not thine own so proper as to waste
Thyself upon thy virtues, they upon thee.
Heaven doth with us as we with torches do,
Not light them for themselves; for if our virtues
Did not go forth from us, 'twere all alike
As if we had them not . . .

—*Shakespeare, "Measure for Measure"*

THE GOAL OF THIS SUMMARY OF THE FOUR DRAMATIC MOVEMENTS noted by Howard Suber is to show how the models we have developed dynamically interact within the screenplay structure. This itself is a preparation for the more detailed articulation of the dynamics of storytelling in Chapter Eleven: The Sixteen Story Steps. We are moving from the broad outline toward greater detail and specificity. Here we start to look at what makes each act work, while supporting our understanding of the broader premises of drama.

We have noted that the operative convention concerning feature films is to speak of three acts. Therefore, the three-act structure coordinates with four "musical" movements as follows:

- The first movement, in the "key signature" of *Desire*, begins with the opening of the film, seeds the throughline dramatic questions at the catalyst/Call to Adventure, and ends with the Threshold Crisis/threshold crossing from the Day World into the Night World that ends Act I.
- The second movement, *Deception*, begins with the immediate consequences of the Threshold Crisis, includes a relatively inward-turning period of wounding and recovery in which the primary relationship (or love interest)

takes on greater importance, and climaxes with the Core Crisis in the middle of Act II.

- *Discovery*, the key signature of the third movement, finds the conflict deepening as the hero journeys toward a catastrophic "grow or die" point. Here, in the second half of Act II, the hero discovers the limits of his mode and watches it fail, as the pressure to see and respond in a new way grows. The catastrophe that ends Act II climaxes this movement.
- The fourth movement, *Destiny*, corresponds to Act III of the screenplay structure as commonly conceived, and gives the audience both the peak climax that answers the throughline dramatic questions and the resolution that communicates the theme of the movie to the audience.

The new TV series—such as *The Sopranos*, *Lost*, *Prison Break*, *24*, *Six Feet Under*, and *Rome*—work explicitly from a dynamic plot development model laid out in four acts. In television, the subclimax at the end of the second narrative movement takes on greater weight and importance because it comes just before a major commercial break. As a consequence, a cliffhanger or intense moment

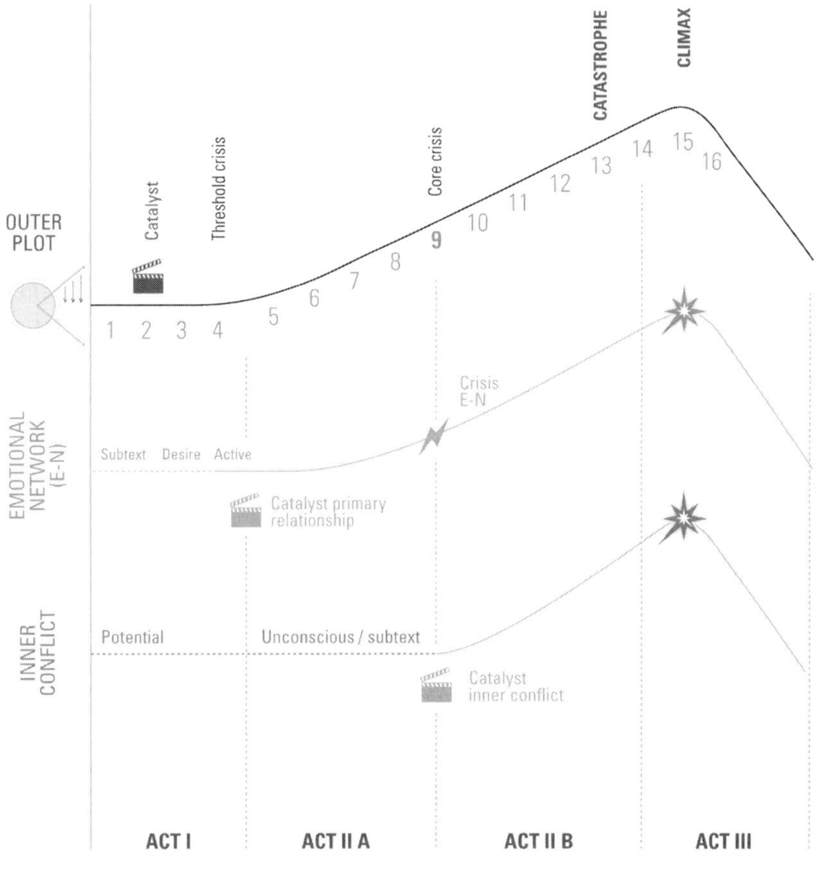

is planned for the end of the second movement in order to keep the audience glued to the show. This emphasis on the end of the second movement gives the dramatic development of these series a distinctly different feel than a feature film. Narrative techniques spurred by the success of this new TV dramaturgy are now influencing story development in feature films. What distinguishes the feature film structure are the balance of the three levels of the Story Molecule and the way the action drives toward a definitive climax that answers the three throughline questions.

The First Dramatic Movement: Setting the Stakes

First Image, First Impact

Act I of the screenplay structure comprises the first movement, in musical terms, played in the key of Desire. We pointed out earlier that Act I of the screenplay structure matches the first quadrant of the Hero's Journey quite closely. Like the opening line of a fairy tale, the first images of a movie give the viewer specific information in a very compressed way. The opening images, the first two or three minutes of the movie, contain the most compressed and concentrated visual storytelling. "Concentrated" here does not necessarily mean fast or violent; rather, the images must be very well chosen and suggestive. The opening has to carry us over a threshold out of our everyday world. And it also is an *induction*, which teaches the audience how to look at *this* movie. We are already establishing a style and a subtext, a subliminal relationship with the audience. Current movies do this more and more assertively, using the most aggressive visual rhetoric possible to grab the audience. There is an almost palpable anxiety on the part of some filmmakers to control the audience from the instant the movie begins.

From the screenwriter's perspective, there is quite a list of specific things that must happen under the simple term "establishing." What we must establish in these first minutes, narratively and stylistically, includes:

- Idiom
- Genre
- Pace
- Tone
- Scale
- Point of view
- Day World of the story
- Flaw in the status quo of this world

In these first minutes we may also introduce the main character, in which case we must nail the character's mode, as we saw done with Loretta Castorini. Sometimes the opening is shot as written. Very commonly though, the opening is one of the last pieces of the movie cut together in the editing room. The screenwriter is normally not responsible for writing an image-by-image opening montage. What the writer is responsible for is establishing the above elements by a choice of opening scenes and how they are handled, including the use of hooks and prologues. The audience is not ready to absorb the impact of the dramatic catalyst and move with the story until these above stylistic elements are in place.

In general, all of these stylistic elements are connected to the journey the main character will take, and thus to the need/mode split, the Day World/Night World split, and the theme of the movie. Here we may remark on some qualitative differences between character-driven stories and genre stories. These are two storytelling modes with different emphases. In genre movies, since character is a function of plot and plot is a function of the genre, the genre elements are normally established and emphasized first. A second reason for this is because the genre elements comprise a quick, shorthand language to take us into the world of the thriller or melodrama. The tone and pace almost instantly set up a set of genre expectations into which the other story elements (like plot and character) will fit. But the setup of a character-driven story must be more individualized to fit the protagonist and her journey. The Brooklyn neighborhood of *Do the Right Thing*, the alienated family in *American Beauty*, and the very secret inner world of Ada's will not to speak in *The Piano* are three unique story universes set up immediately at the opening. Likewise, an ensemble story requires its own specific approach. We must always determine what the audience needs to know in order to orient themselves to a specific story before the plot begins.

Catalyst as Call

Status quo worlds each carry their own flaw, the seed of their own dissolution. They do this by the very fact they are status quo: there is something defensively static and counter to the flowing nature of life. The stability of a world, whether it be of an individual, a relationship, a family, or a society, is bought at the price of the splitting off and suppression of disharmonious elements. The security we create is always a false security, a false comfort, if it takes us out of the flow of life in favor of a rigidly defended comfort zone. Usually at the opening the flaw is already present, but hidden. It may be hiding under a mask (*Shakespeare in Love*, *The Talented Mr. Ripley*, *Tootsie*), a false truce (*City of God*, *Do the Right Thing*), denial and irony (*American Beauty*, *Groundhog Day*), behind-the-scenes betrayal (*Syriana*, *Crouching Tiger, Hidden Dragon*, *Chinatown*, *Witness*, *Silkwood)*, or the simple self-betrayal of our personal illusions and naïveté (*Capote*, *Fargo*, *Mulholland Drive*, *Trainspotting*, *To Die For*, *Moonstruck*, *The Apartment*). In most cases, the main character is "between two worlds," and is already something of an outsider. Or he is waking up, like Lester Burnham in *American Beauty*, to the realization that life is out of sync. This situation causes the hidden flaw to resonate out of the subtext. What's wrong with this picture? Why does Lester hate his life? Why can't Ada speak? Why is Shakespeare creatively blocked? If Michael Dorsey is the greatest actor around, how come he can't get any work? That first subliminal question (which is not yet the throughline plot question) already presents the theme of the movie in seed form.

The dramatic catalyst that gets the plot moving is the Call to Adventure for the main character. This one event unifies the outer and inner dimensions of the story. If there is only a *plot* catalyst, or if the hero gets a call that fails to touch him personally in some way, then an important dimension has dropped out of the story. So here we may run through a short checklist:

- Does the catalyst event raise the throughline plot question?
- Does it generate a plot goal appropriate to the hero and the nature of the movie?
- How does the hero's plot goal specify his mode? (For example, the moment Lester lays eyes on Angela, he is no longer just a disgruntled, passive-aggressive middle-aged guy, he is *specifically* the disgruntled middle-aged guy with the fantasy of literally recapturing his youth.)
- How does the catalyst help to bring together the emotional network? Who else is involved?
- How does the Call to Adventure foreshadow the Night World of Act II?
- What stakes are established or implied on the plot and need/mode levels?

We mentioned that the Call to Adventure may come from any of three directions: outer call, inner call, or blunder (call from below). The nature of the call does suggest something about the nature of the Hero's Journey. The audience, after all, accepts every piece of information on faith as part of a meaningful pattern. Because of this, we want to pay some special attention to the blunder-dimension of the call: how is the hero getting in over her head? That dimension of the call is always going to be present in the subtext. As subtext, it has a foreshadowing function that involves the audience more deeply. In a serious drama, melodrama, or thriller, the blunder-dimension of the call generates dread, a sense of terror, doom, or difficulty. The moment Bobby Barnes in *Syriana* sees one of the Stinger missiles he has just sold taken away by unknown Arabs, the tone is set for more dark betrayal to come. In a comedy, the blunder-dimension foreshadows comic chaos and laughter. When we see young William Miller in *Almost Famous* get his first assignment to interview Black Sabbath, then get dropped off at the concert by his mother because he is too young to drive, we know delicious trouble is ahead. That setup perfectly establishes the tone of a light coming-of-age story.

The nature of the call sets up the hero's relationship to the flaw in the status quo world, which in turn reflects a seismic fault line within themselves. We make this need/mode fault line active in the story through the blind spot in the mode. The *blind spot* is one of the key elements to identify in the main character. Neo (*The Matrix*) flees into fantasy virtual realities because he has no real faith in himself and his ability to be in the world. Joe Buck (*Midnight Cowboy*) proclaims an inflated call contrary to who he really is, because he is running away from his past. Loretta (*Moonstruck*) believes she is just running an errand, asking Johnny's brother to come to the wedding, but she is about to encounter her own suppressed passion. That is Loretta's blind spot. Detective Mills (*Seven*) is blind to the shadow of his own naïve zeal. Through the blind spot, we begin to get a feeling for the character's relationship to the shadow, which signals subtextually the nature of the Night World they will enter and the trials they will endure.

Call as *encounter* points to what is happening in the Story Molecule at the catalyst. The dramatic event that catalyzes the outer plot acts as an establishing incident for the emotional network, especially the primary relationship. Normally we will have seen some or all of the central characters in the establishing scenes. But as the dramatic catalyst "ties the knot" of destiny that binds hero and antagonist together, which will not be untied until the resolution, we also have the primary relationship implicated as well. The primary relationship character (or love interest) is pulled into the conflict through alliances that form at this point. This will constellate dramatic triangles. It is very good to bring the triangle together visually, so the audience can compare the three characters and the bonds between them. In *The Piano*, we have the one triangle constellated on which the melodrama will turn: Ada, Stewart, and George. In *American Beauty*, we begin to set up the first of what will be a whole array of dramatic triangles. In the scene in the parking lot after the basketball game there are four potential triangles, three of which will become active: Lester/Angela/Carolyn, Lester/Angela/Janie, and Lester/Carolyn/Janie.

Using triangles at the catalyst is an important tool for orchestrating your characters. The general rules for character orchestration are heightened here, because we are witnessing the characters just at the moment when the throughline dramatic stakes are being set. What we really want to focus on is: what is the difference between the way each character views what is happening *right now*, in the dramatic present, and how does that nail each character's mode? On that windy New Zealand beach, Stewart's take is that Ada is "small," which is not what he expected. George recognizes empathically that Ada is tired. Ada herself is primarily concerned about her piano. All the relationship dynamics to be developed through the story are rather effortlessly laid down for the audience in less than a minute of screen time. This is powerful, concise storytelling. Using the emotional network at the catalyst to orchestrate the characters, and using the character orchestration to foreshadow the dramatic development, is an opportunity we as screenwriters don't want to miss.

Consequences: The First Stone Thrown into the Pond

Actions have consequences. It would be fair to say that the entire dramatic curve is ultimately the consequence of the catalyst/call. But in the scenes of Act I just following the catalyst, we have the *immediate* consequences to look at. The most important of these are to define a clear and concrete plot goal and to show the first step the hero makes toward that goal. These two crucial bits of exposition will define the throughline action of the movie. Referring back to the screenplay-in-process example of our last chapter, we can note that we don't want to define the main character's action too narrowly, or it may throw the audience in the wrong direction. Mary, the young woman who crossed the ocean to be with the man she loved, spends this part of Act I preoccupied with her husband's strangely aloof behavior. Yet we also see her establishing her position on the farm, with the servants, and in the local society. It turns out that the question about building a wonderful home with her true love is really the subsidiary part-question that frames Act I. At the end of the Act I crisis, that possibility is pretty much destroyed. It may seem that the movie has just destroyed its own premise, but in reality the audience has been placed in exactly the same position as Mary herself—with the rug pulled out from under her. There is a new, urgent question now: how will Mary find her way in this new world? This will only work if her other activities, suggesting her streak of self-reliance, have been established in the portion of Act I immediately following the catalyst. This is a perfectly legitimate sleight-of-hand to play on the audience, as long as the actions following the catalyst are legitimate consequences of it.

Does there have to be a doubter and a guide? Here is where that character would come in, according to the Hero's Journey model. But here is where we must not take Campbell with knee-jerk literalism, but rather respect the integrity of our own story. It will depend on the idiom and the genre, and, frankly, how buffed-out with commercial elements the movie is intended to be. The old wisdom would say not to add elements unless they are necessary to tell the story, because they will in fact detract from the clarity and concentration of the throughline. However, the stretch of Act I between catalyst and crisis is the place where subplots are initiated, especially those long-term subplots with thematic value: parallel subplots and intersecting subplots. There is a natural opportunity for this here because, as the hero responds to the catalyst and makes first steps toward his plot goal, the impact of his action is rippling out into the world of the story. It is here, after the catalyst, that we will sketch in the other members of the emotional network, including those characters carrying the subplots. Along with subplots that will run through the story, thematic images, leitmotifs, running gags, red herrings, and other secondary elements that enrich the fabric of the story are "sown" at this point, to be "harvested" later in Act II. Normally, subplots must be initiated after the catalyst, once the plot throughline question has been set in the audience's mind. Why is this so? To prevent any confusion in the mind of the audience as to which line is the plot throughline. This is also why subplots are paid off before the main plot at the climax.

It is important to see the consequences of the catalyst. Consequences ground the story in reality, even if it is the fictional reality of the movie's world. In fact, it is the consequence of the catalyst that makes a world out of the virtual space established on the screen. That house, city, planet, etc. doesn't become dramatically real until there are consequences. This is the meaning of the word catalyst. A stone is thrown into a pond. Ripples start to spread, breaking the peaceful surface. The ripples hit rocks or other objects and bounce back. The resulting wave-pattern tells us much about the thrown stone—and much about the pond as well.

Threshold Crisis and Threshold Crossing

The Threshold Crisis is the major event that ends Act I. Everything in the story thus far has been leading up to this crisis. We could justifiably call the Threshold Crisis the "climax of the setup." So the crisis is not merely an event that hooks into the story and spins it in another direction. General formulations like this miss what makes the crisis *dramatic* rather than merely potentially exciting. The dramatic element is that the crisis is an *inevitable consequence* of the main character's desire. Because of desire, the hero starts moving toward a goal that will fulfill the desire. That movement in itself creates conflict: it sets up a collision course with the antagonist. Superficially, the crisis may appear to come from the outside, yet its ultimate source is deep within the hero, calling a destiny upon himself. If we forget this, we will end up with a weak, dramatically ineffective crisis that fails to set the trajectory, the stakes, and the subtext for Act II. The outer plot and the need/mode conflict are not two separate things; they are two faces of the same process.

We have summarized the dramatic elements of the crisis elsewhere, in the contexts of the other models. We will also come to it again in the Sixteen Story Steps. Here we will take time to shade in or integrate aspects that belong specifically to the Plot Curve. When we are writing and developing a screenplay, we typically have some sense or intuition about the "bad thing" that happens here at the crisis. But what do we really mean by "crisis"? What defines a crisis differentially from other sorts of bad things that could happen? We have to be able to recognize a crisis when we see one, or we will not know if ours really works.

The crisis is fundamentally the intersection of two lines. The outer plotline is that the hero's forward momentum carries him to the threshold guardian, who blocks his passage. The result is an antagonistic reaction by the threshold guardian against either the hero's goal, the hero himself, or both. The inner line that intersects with this is that the crisis is the point where the blind spot, presumption, or inflation in the hero's mode has concrete negative consequences. We have spoken enough about the element of self-betrayal in the crisis that is caused by the main character's misapprehension of the reality of the situation.

Normally it is this inner self-betrayal that actually occurs first and precipitates the outer plot crisis, but is only recognized as such by the audience in hindsight. And frequently the main character remains oblivious to his or her own part in the events until the end of Act II. This typical way of intersecting the two lines is exemplified by Tom Ripley, Will Shakespeare, Ada, Mills, C. C. Baxter, and most other heroes of character-driven movies.

The unrecognized self-betrayal puts the audience ahead of the character: we know more than the hero does, even if this is a subtextual, subliminal knowing. This situation tends to generate greater empathy for the hero. In some very light comedies and stereotypical action-adventures, the crisis may be played as a purely outer event, which of course reinforces the superficiality of the story line. By the nature of the plotline, the crisis in *The Fugitive* is necessarily an outer event, a long complex of events in fact, that climaxes with Richard Kimbell leaping from the dam. But notice how the authors slip the self-betrayal into the following story step: Kimbell naïvely contacts his colleague, the real killer, and, simultaneously, makes a phone call that reveals his location to Lt. Gerrard after he had successfully gotten away.

Typically, a Threshold Crisis Story Step leads with either the attack aspect or the threshold crossing aspect in the foreground. A more complete handling of the crisis may articulate and make us aware of both aspects. Working with both together, we can create a complex and satisfying end to Act I. For example, the Threshold Crisis Story Step sequence in *Moonstruck* is structured around three literal threshold crossings. The three doorways are visual symbols that subliminally contextualize and frame the action in the sequence. Framed within these three doorways we have first an attack by the threshold guardian and then the crossing of a threshold. At the establishing moment of the Threshold Crisis Story Step, Loretta crosses the first physical threshold. Where does she go, specifically? *Down* into the basement of the bakery. And what's down there? The bread of life, the fire of life, and—Nicholas Cage in a sweaty undershirt! (Not to mention the phallic baguettes!) Loretta announces her plot goal—to marry Johnny—and we have the response from Ronnie as threshold guardian: hell no, he won't go the wedding. He'll cut his throat instead. Ronnie walks away, and notice that it is *Loretta* who pushes to keep the contact going, following Ronnie to the far corner of the basement, saying, "Can't we just talk?" Ronnie opens a door, sunlight floods upon them, and they *ascend* into the light, the second threshold. This moment visually foreshadows their love story, supported by the swelling music. The audience takes all this in subliminally. The third threshold crossing is when Ronnie picks Loretta up and carries her to the bed. What is *that* all about? As wedding symbolism, it foreshadows the climax and resolution. Framed by the three thresholds, we have the whole story in miniature, but played in a different key, as it were, one of Desire turning to Deception. Loretta is losing control and entering the Night World. The Story Step charts Loretta's loss of control in her encounter with passion. As Act I ends, Loretta's mode is starting to break down.

We mentioned how important it is first of all to differentiate between a movie's Day World and Night World, and then to externalize the threshold between them so that the audience can have a direct experience of it. The simplest and most visual way to do this is by shifting to a new location, one which is dramatically, thematically, and visually significant as a Night World place. It does not literally have to be the Death Star or Buffalo Bill's torture chamber; the Night World is relative to the hero's (and audience's) experience. See the location through the character's eyes. What does it mean to her? In *The Piano*, we move to the interior of George's shack, which, at that moment, Ada might well construe as a torture chamber. But if there is no physical change in location to indicate that we are moving into the Night World, then we must see some other change in the situation of the hero. Renton, in *Trainspotting*, falls back into his heroin habit. The location is the same Glasgow neighborhood, but we are back in the nightmare of addiction. The threshold crossing into the Night World often figures in movie titles. At the end of Act I, Richard Kimbell has *become* the fugitive, Michael Dorsey has *become* Tootsie. As that mob of unemployed north Dublin youngsters crosses the proscenium of a local church meeting hall to make their fist public performance, they become The Commitments. And it is the shift to the second Veronique, occurring at this point just after the death of the first (a unique threshold crossing), that propels us into *The Double Life of Veronique*.

We also want to address what is happening at the crisis/threshold crossing in the emotional network of the Story Molecule. It turns out that the outer plot crisis acts as the catalyst for the primary relationship or love interest in the emotional network, and often for a nexus of relationships. The crisis turns the primary relationship from an *incidental* relationship into a *necessary* relationship. The two characters in that relationship are now bound together in one common destiny. The incidental relationship in Act I is on a level of social roles: George is merely Stewart's neighbor; Rachel is *merely* the witness's mother; the Duke is *merely* the guy Jack has got to get to L.A. (*Midnight Run*); Carrie is merely a beautiful, unknown woman who shows up at the wedding with an impressive hat (*Four Weddings and a Funeral*). The relationship is catalyzed at the end of Act I because the outer crisis creates a necessary alliance or emotional bond between the two characters. Usually the bond has already been implied, even if we see the future lovers or partners of Act II fighting like cats and dogs in Act I.

This starts a new line of dramatic development going, the dramatic throughline of the emotional network level. The primary relationship line will have its own catalyst, crisis, catastrophe, and climax. The rising conflict in this line will raise stakes in the outer plotline. Its resolution will contribute to the overall theme of the movie. These two lines will continue to interweave and intersect at key points through Act II, most notably at the Core Crisis Story Step.

Catalyzing this relationship also means that the two characters enter a shared energy field, which may be defined as love, friendly rivalry, competition, mutual antagonism, or aspects of all of these. The three key aspects to pay attention to in development are: the characters are bound together by outer and inner forces, they cross over into the Night World together with no way back to the status quo, and they make or recognize a commitment to one another. When Detectives Somerset and Mills in *Seven* cross the threshold that takes them deeper into the dreadful mind of the serial killer, they make a deeper and more complex bond, despite their ambivalent feelings for each other. This E-N line is also called the "relationship arc" of the primary relationship.

The falling action of the Threshold Crisis Story Step carries us into the territory of Act II. The scenes that follow really belong to Act II, but let's keep in mind that this is one flow of action. John Book arrives at Rachel's farm. It is the location for Act II, but we are still in the falling action of the Threshold Crisis, Act I. This blend makes for a smooth bridge between acts. When Book loses consciousness, there is a cut to black and an indeterminate time lapse. This functions as an act-break curtain. Furthermore, as Act I ends with the hero attacked and wounded, losing control, mode starting to crack, it should be clear to the audience that the hero is now *further away* from the plot goal than he was before the crisis event. It should also be clear that this is a *point of no return*, as decisive a marker as the Doorway to Hell in Dante's *Divine Comedy*. Because if the hero could escape at this point back to the status quo comfort zone, in all likelihood he would. This is also part of the dramatic construction of the crisis: it smashes the status quo ante. There is no return; there is only movement forward into the unknown.

It is natural that the character would want to go back. This is where the fight-or-flight instinct comes in. There is a feeling-tone of dread, a sinking sensation in the stomach. Of course, this has to be motivated by what happens in the Threshold Crisis Story Step. This is why the Threshold Crisis warrants careful thought and construction. When it works, the instinct set of fight-or-flight, with its sudden release of adrenaline, is awakened in the audience as well, in empathic identification with the hero. There is a mind-heart-body bond between them, which is where you want the audience to be.

Crisis and Value

The dramatic crisis touches us not only because the protagonist hits an obstacle or threat. There is also a *value* at stake which the character holds dear, and which has its own feeling-tone. By using the tools of *focusing* we have introduced to explore this complex—made up of a crisis event, a threatened value, and a feeling-tone associated with it—we learn how to approach the crises of our characters on a more comprehensive level. The threatened core value is embedded in a way of looking at the world—a mode—and the entire mode, the "who I think I am," is threatened by the crisis. Whether or not the character's core value is one we personally identify with, we can all relate to crisis moments when we feel our core, our identity, called into question. Through the universal feeling state of the crisis, the audience feels connection with the hero's mode value. This is why a screenplay must be clear about the values attached to the protagonist's mode and need. These deep audience identifications with the hero's mode form the ultimate dramatic engine at this point. The tension of mode and need values need not be voiced aloud, but they need to be set up as a dialectic of opposites in order for the entire story line to come across powerfully.

Some screenwriting experts emphasize that the hero and the antagonist want the same thing, and that this is the source of confrontation. This may appear to be true in plot structures that feature competition, rivalry, chases, or treasure hunts. These elements have been staples of the action movie genre since the silent film days. Competition has an energetic curve *like* drama, because there is an end goal known both to the players and fans: the two outs at the bottom of the ninth, the three-point jump-shot at the buzzer. There are heroes, stakes, and projective identifications. But here is where the analogy ends, for in most dramas, competition is not the central issue or the direct cause of conflict. There is an old studio witticism directed at screenwriters: "If you wanna send a message, call Western Union." But one could also say, "If you want competition, watch the Super Bowl." It is much more to the point dramatically to ask what *differentiates* the hero and antagonist from each other. Character orchestration is built on differences. Yes, C. C. Baxter and Sheldrake both want Miss Kubelik. But it is their *way* of wanting, and what they each want the desired object *for*, that makes *The Apartment* a comic drama with three dimensions. In short, it is *motive*. As we go into Act II, we want the difference in the values motivating the hero and the antagonist to be clearly defined for the audience.

It is exactly here, at the crisis, that the first real challenge often appears for the screenwriter. It is here that so many screenplays get stuck or fall apart. Part of this has to do with the fact that Act I is by far the easiest to construct. Act I is really the screenwriter's comfort zone. Arriving at the end of Act I, the superhighway suddenly ends, and there is only a primitive dirt track pointing ahead—into Death Valley. Another aspect has to do with what we as writers have projected unconsciously onto our main character. As the main character's mode starts to break down, it often has a contagious "undertow" effect on the writer. When we try to think about the Threshold Crisis Story Step and everything that is involved in it, the complexity can feel quite daunting. The situation becomes even more convoluted in story development meetings where everyone has competing solutions to offer. Each idea is clever, but they just don't convince on a gut level. Much frustration ensues, but little progress. These are all signs that the writer has to take the story to a deeper level. The problems we face when trying to work out a vivid, satisfying crisis act like a threshold crossing for *us* as writers. We are forced to come down out of our heads and really encounter the story.

The Second Dramatic Movement: Wounding and Recovery

Up to the present time, writers and teachers have contented themselves with generalizations about Act II. Phrases like "dramatic complications," "more conflict," and "relationship conflict" are repeated, and when asked for more precision the experts will say they do not want to inhibit the writer's creativity. This is an indication of how our understanding of the anatomy of screenplays is evolving. The Sixteen Story Steps paradigm identifies *why* the dramatic conflict keeps rising and how the dramatic complications orchestrate themselves as the story energy passes through the rings of the Story Molecule. Aristotle himself was not very specific about how we get from crisis to catastrophe, but adding the reflections of other minds, like Campbell's and Howard Suber's, and taking the dramatic structure as a symbolic representation of real processes of growth through crisis, we can understand much more.

Suber's insight about the two movements of Act II has really been quite important. His term "Deception" is suggestive, because deception can mean both betrayal and, if we borrow from the meaning in French, disappointment. Together they capture the flavor of the moment we find ourselves in after the falling action of the crisis, a combination of self-betrayal, woundedness, and depression. This is where we are after we have crossed into the Night World, and the road slopes down from here. A subliminal anxiety animates every scene of Act II, because we have set the stakes through the Threshold Crisis and threshold crossing. What we see as we enter Act II are the *consequences* of that crisis. An action is only real for us if we see it to have consequences. How is the hero wounded, and how gravely? The first movement of Act II takes us from this experience of wounding and having the hero's trajectory toward his plot goal blocked, through a natural inward turn of the hero's libido, development of the primary relationship, and, finally, recovery and new steps toward the plot goal.

If we chart the flow of the hero's libido, or psychic energy, through this stage of the story, we will see a sharp dip, even a nosedive, at the point of wounding, and then a gradual recovery. The hero's mode has been challenged, but he has not been pushed far enough to force the deep character change that is needed.

Rising Action, Rising Tension

The first point—a double point—necessary for Act II to work will already have been set at the end of Act I. This is to subtextually project the inevitable endpoint to Act II, the catastrophe. Doing so simultaneously sets both the trajectory and the stakes for Act II. As we have said, the *trajectory* and *stakes* are set by the antagonist. The antagonist's determination, resources, and, we can say, level of evil tell us what he is capable of, how high he can raise the stakes in Act II. But typically there is also a structural, logical point that is established by the throughline. Sooner or later, either Somerset and Mills *will* or *will not* catch

John Doe—and we know they will. Sooner or later the bad Terminator will catch John and his protector. Sooner or later Loretta will have to face Johnny Camerreri. In *Tootsie*, the moment Michael Dorsey puts on his disguise he crosses one threshold, and when he takes it off he will cross another threshold and face the consequences of his charade. The very nature of the action makes the end point of Act II inevitable; without it there would be no story. Yet it is so easy to forget this while we are writing the script. It takes the maturation of the story through several script drafts, typically, for the throughline plot question and the end of Act II catastrophe point to come into focus together.

By the way we show the audience the consequence of the Threshold Crisis as we go into Act II, through dwelling a moment on the hero's wound and letting that sink in, we are reinforcing the plot impact of the Threshold Crisis Story Step on a more intimate, emotional level. This touches the audience in a more personal way. The moment need not be long, but if it is missing, the audience will not connect strongly with the main character.

This connection with the audience needs to be stressed, because the first half of Act II is the part of the plot curve where it is easiest to lose the audience. We have already looked at the chain of question → suspense → answer → question. It is important that the audience's subtextual question going into Act II carries more risk than the question posed at the catalyst: "How will Ada get her beloved piano back, now that Stewart has sold it to George?" The difficulty for the screenwriter comes because, for the moment, the hero is *wounded* and powerless. There is no effective step she can take toward her goal. Yet the audience has been led by the Threshold Crisis to expect immediately rising dramatic intensity. This is a paradox that can only be resolved by shifting the story to another level and generating new stakes on that level.

Here is where the model of the Story Molecule is invaluable. If we try to develop the first half of Act II by considering the outer plot alone, we are rather stuck. We may tend to take the paranoid/manic position that we dare not slow down the plot for an instant or the audience will leave the theater, surf to another channel, or whatever. This may come from an inability to establish, or lack of confidence in, the throughline subtext, which is the main character's unconscious need. Or we may make the alternate mistake of building up the love interest because we've been told by gurus this is what we're supposed to do, without linking it to the hero's wound and the outer plot stakes, in which case we *do* lose the audience.

We have to understand two things at this point: *subtext* and *libido*. For a dramatic beat or two, the focus and drive of the story has to be carried by the subtext, and we must have faith in that, just as visually we need moments when the character is "doing nothing." Recall that Henry Fonda described acting as the art of "doing nothing well." These moments allow us to look inside the character. And what do we "see" there? The root subtext, the basis of both the outer plot conflict and the love interest relationship, is the need/mode tension within the main character. We need to see the point where the hero has been blocked by the threshold guardian not as an *absence* of action, but, in a positive sense, as a necessary point where the conflict is driven to a deeper level. This is why it was necessary to spend time on the Hero's Journey's paradigm to appreciate the value of deepening conflict.

An illumination in regard to conflict and libido came to me from something that Jung wrote on the subject. His metaphor for libido was flowing water, a river. It is natural for the libido to flow toward objects of interest or desire (i.e., the plot goal). But when we cannot reach our object of desire, the flow of libido is blocked. This is like damming up a river. A reservoir of libido then forms and builds up under pressure, until it finds another outlet. The outer movement is blocked, but the *inner tension is rising*. When it finds a new outlet, the libido moves in a new direction. This new direction is into the emotional network, into the primary relationship, which has been catalyzed at the end of Act I. The flux of libido in the main character, based on the fact that the mode is starting to disintegrate, is the inner necessity that motivates the shift of the story at this point in Act II.

Meanwhile, the outer plot tension is put into the background as we turn to the audience's attention to the emotional network. The outer plot question is not dropped; it is *suspended*. What's the difference? We are in effect rotating the Story Molecule at this point. Through Act I, the outer plot events have been in the foreground; they constituted the text of Act I. The primary relationship has simultaneously been established in the background, in the *subtext*. We know from their first encounter that there is some kind of energy, or chemistry, between Ada and George, partly because they are such obvious opposites and opposites attract, and also because George can see Ada as a real person while Stewart cannot. But as we watch those scenes in the movie theatre, this remains subliminal knowledge. George is simply the obliging neighbor. Now, in Act II, we shift the primary relationship to the foreground *because* the plot movement is suspended. Now the outer plot—specifically that Act II endpoint—is put into the subtext, where it must continue to build tension. Often at this point the hero has escaped temporarily to a safe haven, but we know the antagonist is hunting. In *Terminator 2*, they escape to the desert. In *Tootsie*, Michael Dorsey has temporarily escaped into Dorothy Michaels. In *Witness*, Book is temporarily safe at Rachel's farm.

In order to keep the outer plot tension rising, we need to be reminded of the outer plot stakes, and that it is the antagonist at this point who has the advantage. These reminders can take different forms. At four separate points in the first half of Act II of *Witness*, we have short cutaway scenes to show Paul and McFee hunting for Book. In *Terminator 2*, we have the mother's premonitory nightmare of the world catastrophe. In *The Piano*, we have the shadow play. In *Trainspotting*, we have Renton's arrest and the death of the baby. How many reminders are needed? This is a very individual question whose answer will be different for every story. But we need to see that this pressure from the plot conflict also has an impact on how the primary relationship develops. At this stage in *Seven*, there are more killings, which force the two antipathetic detectives to bond more tightly. The outer plot pressure is part of what pushes this relationship toward a threshold.

The emotional content of the love interest scenes is underpinned by the Night World feelings that are welling up in the main character. The dramatic intensity is also rising because the hero is descending, breaking down, losing control. Often the primary relationship is unusual, out of the ordinary. Under normal circumstances, Book and Rachel would never have met, much less become romantically involved. Nor would Jack Walsh and the Duke ever have spoken to one another, much less become reluctant allies. Loretta and Ronnie, or Ada and George, would normally have avoided each other. But the extraordinary conditions of the Night World change everything. This primary relationship is under extraordinary stresses because of the pressure from both the outer situation and the hero's inner breakdown. Of course, that serves to make the new bond all the more intense, edgy, and erotically charged.

Descent = Breakdown = Abduction = Regression

The journey into the Night World that occupies Act II is always a symbolic journey. That is not to say that it is not "really happening" in the world of the story, but we want to point out that the dimensions of this journey are communicated directly to the audience's unconscious. This is perhaps most obvious in thrillers, where the sense of dread can almost act like an invisible, but palpable, character. But this "Night World effect" is implicit, even when the idiom of the movie is realism. Realism is the style, the medium, but the Night World effect comes directly from the archetypal level of story, the archetypal structure of the Road of Trials. We contemplate death and morality through a wounding, and this opens the soul. As the fourteenth-century German mystic Meister Eckhart said: "Suffering is the fastest horse that takes man to perfection." Even if the hero has escaped to a safe haven, there has indeed been a death: of a status quo way of life, a relationship, an innocence, a comfort zone. This loss is a universal experience. What do we do when we lose that which has sustained us? Like the hero, we journey down into the wound.

This is most fundamentally a descent into fear and uncertainty. The hero must meet a heightened outer danger while at the same time feeling inwardly wounded, disempowered, disoriented, and regressed. Fight-or-flight instincts are unleashed, swamping the capacity of the ego to make coolheaded judgments, as we see happen to young Detective Mills in *Seven*. The destruction of the status quo leaves the protagonist without a viable life-role, a rider without a horse. Like Odysseus after meeting the cyclops, the hero has become "No Man" in a spiritual labyrinth.

Typically, at the beginning of Act II we see the hero constrict around the wound and try in some way to re-establish the old status quo. This defensive gesture actually drives the problem to a deeper level. From the perspective of mythic wisdom, this is just where the problem needs to go. As we recall, the function of the Road of Trials is to strip away all the ego-wrappings until the character "hits the wall" and the old mode—or the hero's overidentification with it—dies. Constriction may paradoxically lead to opening. The experience of death has been called "the great opener." Facing death, one has nothing left to lose. In this way, the death of the mode may open the possibility of Initiation, a new start. The Night World in the first half of Act II gives a tone and a context to facing death: physical (*Terminator 2*, *Silence of the Lambs*, *Midnight Run*), moral (*Seven*, *Shallow Grave*, *The Apartment*, *Trainspotting*, *Dead Man Walking*), or emotional (*Four Weddings and a Funeral*, *The Piano*). But it takes the entire second act for the hero to undergo the process of breakdown.

Core Crisis: The Crucible of Character

The first movement of Act II establishes a new center of interest and a new level of conflict. What had been a purely external conflict now takes on a more personal, feeling-toned dimension—without resolving the outer problem. These two levels of conflict are linked both causally and thematically, so they reinforce one another. The rising dramatic intensity is not only quantitatively greater, it has more color, nuance, and immediacy. This primary relationship has its own dramatic curve, thus it must have its own crisis and threshold crossing. This brings us to the important story step called the Core Crisis.*

The Core Crisis is not merely a "plot point" that appears around page 60 in the screenplay. It is the pivot between the two movements of Act II. It also draws together the three levels of the Story Molecule in a very special way. After the Core Crisis, we will have added another, deeper level of conflict which will send the wave of rising tension mounting ever higher. We call the Core Crisis the "crucible of character," because the midpoint very often foreshadows whether the hero will ultimately grow or die. The full contours of the Core Crisis were brought out by the Story Molecule paradigm and point to the power of the Story Molecule as a story development tool. The act of asking the simple question: "What is happening *right now* on each level of the molecule?" gives us so much focused insight about our screenplay.

---

* Other writers and people in the business commonly refer to this as the story's "midpoint." We used this terminology at first, but recently our ideas on what is happening at this stage in the dramatic development have evolved. Midpoint is a misnomer first of all because there is no such thing as a "point" in a movie. A movie is in constant movement! The Core Crisis Story Step typically occupies five to eight minutes into a movie. It has its own dramatic development and acts as the climax of the second movement. The reader will find a more complete exposition of these new ideas in Chapter Eleven.

I first became interested in midpoints when I saw a great movie by Terrence Malick called *Days of Heaven*. The story line is at once simple and elusive. The opening is set in Chicago, around 1915. An impetuous young man, Bill, who may have killed his factory foreman in a fight, runs away West with his lover, Cassie, and his little sister. Because they are not married, he passes Cassie off as another sister, and they sign on as migrant farm hands to harvest wheat. The wealthy farmer thinks Cassie is free and asks her to marry him. Cassie is against the deception, but Bill pushes her into it; this farmer has a terminal disease and the lovers believe he will die soon, leaving them the money. So Cassie agrees to the sham marriage. But after the wedding, the tensions in the triangle are too great. The farmer shows no immediate signs of dying, so the frustrated Bill leaves.

The sham wedding is a threshold crossing for the runaways, a threshold from innocent deception to criminal intent, and, for Cassie, a threshold into a dream world of comfort and security. We are approaching the midpoint when, some months later, Bill returns. He finds Cassie not merely "playing house" with the farmer. She seems to have accepted her place as this man's wife. The dynamics within the group have shifted, and there is a strained atmosphere. Appearing superficially reconciled to Cassie's marriage, Bill has to sleep in the bunkhouse where the hired help stays. Then comes a sequence that has haunted me since the moment I saw it. It was a piece of movie magic and I couldn't get it out of my mind. I knew nothing about midpoints at the time (this was before screenwriting books), but I knew that something special was happening on the screen, that I was being told something crucial here. *Days of Heaven* does not give its secrets away easily, however.

A few nights later, Bill cannot take it anymore. He enters the house, creeps into the couple's bedroom, shakes Cassie awake, and steals away with her into the night. It is a beautiful, enigmatic moment as they walk out through the moonlit wheat fields. They play, they laugh: it is like old times. We see them taken by, and at one with, the mysterious forces of night. Bill is warm and seductive. Then, on an impulse, he holds up the bottle of sherry they brought with them. "See this bottle? I'm gonna break it!" He hurls the bottle into the night. We hear it break on a rock in the tall grass. They laugh. But from this moment the tone of their escapade subtly and decisively changes. The night now takes on feelings of solitude, loneliness, shadow. A coyote yips and dashes away in the moonlight. The sense of impenetrable mystery deepens. The lovers are at a juncture. The fact is that there is now a great distance between them, and this makes Bill even more insistent. He can't stop telling her how she drives him crazy. What are they going to do? As dawn comes, Cassie manages to sneak in the kitchen door as her husband goes out the front door looking for her. Is he suspicious our just worried? It is hard to tell.

When I reflected on how this sequence worked, and what gave such a small sequence with so little overt conflict so much dramatic power, I discovered the pivotal role of the Core Crisis/midpoint.* The dramatic situation took me back to the opening of the movie and reconnected me to Bill's prime motivation: to get away with his girlfriend to someplace where they won't have any problems or worries. Here we see the lovers together again, and again they are running away. Only this time the stakes are much higher, because Cassie is married to another man she has come to respect, if not love. And the sequence also foreshadows the ending, the climax and resolution. By wantonly smashing the bottle, Bill is impulsively declaring, "There are no limits!" He will break the bottle, the vessel of the spirit. He will break the boundary of Cassie's marriage. He will break the vessel of his own life. It's not even that he *wants* to do it, but we see that he has it in him; he won't be able to control himself. From this moment, we know the story is destined to be a tragedy; the end is foreshadowed right here. The resolution of the primary relationship line of the Story Molecule is also foreshadowed. Commonly, the characters we see together at the midpoint are those we will see together at the end of the movie, with an emotional tone that is the fulfillment of the one suggested here. The climax of *Days of Heaven* bears out the foreshadowing, displaying the tragic consequences of Bill's impulsiveness. In the last image we see of Bill, Cassie is cradling his dead body after the two of them have been hunted down by the police.

One of the keys to great screenwriting is knowing how to "seed" or foreshadow events and how to "harvest" images and moments from earlier in the story, thus bringing the entire drama into the present for the viewer. The Core Crisis, the pivot between the first half of the drama and the second half, is the most important point in the screenplay where this happens, and a good place to demonstrate how it works.

On the outer plot level, the Core Crisis acts as a pivot because it points both backward and forward. Pointing backward, it evokes the Call to Adventure and reminds us of the hero's plot goal. How does the Core Crisis accomplish this? Because this is when, after a wounding and period of recovery, the hero is once again ready to reassert himself and take active steps toward either the original plot goal or toward a somewhat revised plot goal still in keeping with the character's mode. By getting back on track toward the plot goal, we are also reminded of where the outer plot was headed. Loretta reasserts her intention to marry Johnny; Book reasserts his intention to bring the killers to justice; Jack Walsh,

---

* Some might find it embarrassing, but live and learn: way back then, I thought I had really unlocked a secret through *Days of Heaven* . . . and maybe I had. Before we developed the Sixteen Story Steps model, I assumed this sequence to be the midpoint of the movie. But returning to it with the tool of that new model in hand, I realized that the sequence referred to here is in fact what we would call Story Step Seven: Reminder That the Outer Plot Stakes Are Rising. What I see now as the Core Crisis in *Days of Heaven* is the later sequence when the flying circus comes to the farm: the farmer witnesses Bill and Cassie kissing, Bill then realizes that Cassie loves the farmer and he flies away with the circus. Linda, the narrator, concludes with the words: "I think the Devil was on the farm." This is more clearly a threshold in the relationship triangle, and a direct foreshadowing of the hellish prairie fire that leads to the movie's catastrophe.

after nearly being caught by the FBI and killed by the mob in Chicago, reasserts his determination to somehow get the Duke to L.A.; Renton reasserts his desire to get off heroin.

But this determination to get back on track is in an entirely new context—that of a highly charged primary relationship.* That relationship now makes its own demands and arrives at an emotional crisis and threshold crossing, a point of no return. The crisis/threshold crossing in the primary relationship happens on the E-N level of the Story Molecule at the same time that the outer plot pivot is happening on that level. Each simultaneously causes and is caused by the other. The crisis/threshold crossing in the relationship is when that relationship has *consequences*. For example, Book and Rachel spend the first half of Act II with Book adapting to life on the farm. We know that Rachel has fallen in love with Book. The feelings are bubbling below the surface, but both characters are suppressing and containing them. In fact, Rachel and Book can love each other to death, but as long as they do not reveal their love to one another, there are no consequences. Book can go back to the city; Rachel can continue her life on the farm. But the moment they can no longer contain their feelings and open their hearts, that's when there are consequences. This moment comes when they are in the barn together at night. Why are they in the barn? Because Book is trying to fix the car. Why? So he can go back to the city and finish his job (restating the plot goal). This forces Rachel to say something to assert *her* goal: Book can stay for Sid's barn raising. Then the music starts, and they can no longer hide their feelings. This is how outer plot and emotional network levels collide at the Core Crisis: the emotional crisis in the relationship is sparked by the immediate plot situation.

The Threshold Crisis at the end of Act I ties the two characters together in a knot of shared destiny. The present relationship threshold makes them necessary to each other emotionally and spiritually. Every true relationship opens us to being changed by the other, changed at the level of our core feelings and values. This is the key to how the primary relationship takes the story deeper from this point on, and why we also call it the "transformational relationship." It is via this relationship that the deepest level of change will be constellated in the hero. This is true even if it does not lead to a love relationship in any conventional sense. At the point where Jack Walsh has to accept, in spite of himself, that the Duke is his friend, at the point where Ada returns to George's cabin, not for the piano but for *him* (the Core Crises in *Midnight Run* and *The Piano*), the implications for the stories are suddenly much deeper.

The actual scene content of the Core Crisis is much less predictable than at the catalyst, Threshold Crisis, catastrophe, or climax. There is nothing in the

* There is a significant lack of a primary relationship in *Trainspotting*. Any character who might embody what Renton needs to learn is conspicuously—and, one must think, deliberately—absent from the emotional network of the story.

Hero's Journey model that corresponds to this point. The Core Crisis grows specifically out of the dynamics of drama, but it is much more definite than simply "more complications." This may be the first time in the story when we see the main character, if only for a moment, lower his mask and reveal his true self. An example is when Ada, frustrated at her inability to communicate herself to George, starts hitting him wildly. It seems that only through this act could she discover what she really wanted. In many other cases, this is a point where the character's backstory wound awakens; it may be revealed or indirectly pointed to. In *Midnight Run*, this is the scene where Jack, with the Duke in tow, must try to borrow money from his ex-wife. In a series of subtly but effectively framed shots, we are shown the vulnerable side of Jack's feelings. As the Duke has foretold, this relationship crisis is "very good" for Jack, because his vulnerability breaks down his defenses and opens him up to the possibility of friendship.

Thus, through the emotional network level crisis, an even deeper level of conflict is activated. This is the core existential conflict: who am I? The outer plot midpoint also acts as the catalyst for the core inner conflict of the main character. We know this conflict has always been there, running beneath the surface in the subtext. But at this point it becomes an *actual*, active conflict. We can specify that this core question that becomes an identity crisis, "Who am I?," in this context really means, "Am I identical with my *mode*?" Friendship does not figure into Jack Walsh's mode. The possibility of friendship specifically *threatens* Walsh's mode, because it is founded on distrust. Distrust is essential to the world Walsh operates in as a bounty hunter. But why is Walsh a bounty hunter chasing the scum of the earth around Hell's half-acre to begin with? Because, we discover, Jack Walsh was once such a good cop, with such high integrity, that he refused to take kickbacks from the mob. As a result, the mob boss contrived with Walsh's crooked colleagues to smear him and ruin his career. So distrust is Walsh's survival adaptation to a severe backstory wound. At the Core Crisis, this is all challenged: is Walsh the guy who can't trust anybody, the tough loner who just wants his cash, or is he the guy who will risk being hurt again for the sake of friendship? This inner, existential question cannot really be asked until Walsh and the Duke have crossed that emotional threshold into a relationship with acknowledged consequences.

Now we have *three* active lines of conflict, following each other like a musical fugue. The Threshold Crisis of the outer plot catalyzes the primary relationship. Then the plot midpoint/pivot acts as a crisis in the emotional network, and this emotional crisis catalyzes the core need/mode conflict of values. We have a new dramatic question at this point: will Walsh choose the money (mode) or the friendship (need)? If he chooses friendship, he has to let the Duke go, and in consequence forfeit the quarter of a million dollars.

It becomes evident that the Core Crisis, beyond its role as a horizontal pivot in the outer plot, is also a vertical pivot in the depth dimension of the story.

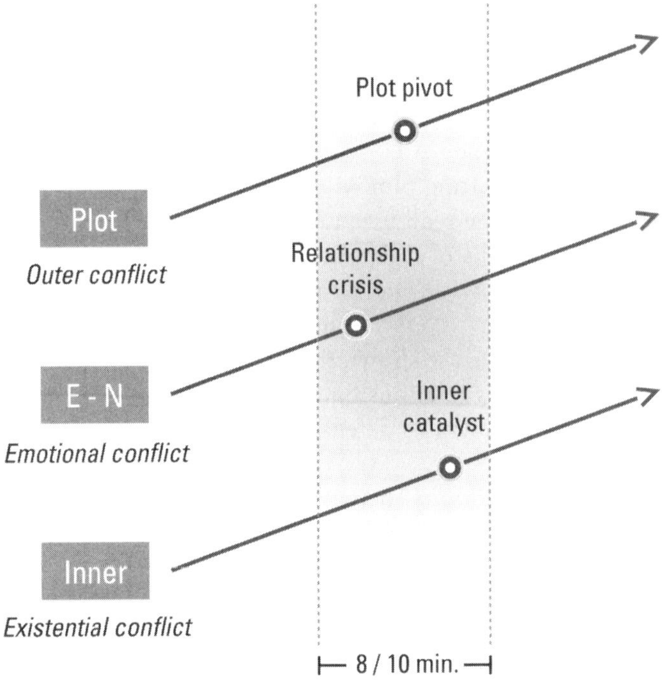

/ The Core crisis.

The balance is beginning to tip in favor of the unconscious need. The mode has already broken down to such a point that a countervalue can assert itself. Up to the Core Crisis, though the mode has shown its flaws and has started breaking down, there has been no question of the main character's allegiance to it. The hero has not been able to imagine an alternative; that would imply being another person. Now, while the universal need is in itself still unconscious, the primary relationship takes its part and champions it indirectly. This is why the primary relationship or love interest character, in orchestrating the emotional network, is not merely attractive in a generic sense, but is attractive specifically because that person embodies the need value. This embodiment makes the need concrete for the audience while keeping it in the subtext. The Duke embodies trust and friendship for Jack; George embodies a healthy earthiness and instinctuality for Ada; Ronnie embodies passion for Loretta. At the Core Crisis we are setting up the two competing—yet secretly complementary—values between which the hero must choose at the climax. The horizontal and vertical pivots turn on each other.

The Third Dramatic Movement: Setting the Double Bind

While the first half of Act II takes the main character and the audience on something of an inward turn leading to the engagement of deeper levels of conflict, the second half of Act II now focuses all of this conflict with building momentum toward the catastrophe. The catastrophe will end the act and send us directly into the climax. The story picks up momentum because the hero is ready again to take steps toward the plot goal, often with a somewhat adjusted strategy. It is quite common in the construction of thrillers that the main character is only able to take a first proactive step at the Core Crisis. All through the first half of Act II he has been reacting, behind the curve. At the Core Crisis/midpoint he gets a key clue to the puzzle, and in the second half of Act II we see him act on that new knowledge. Whereas at the Threshold Crisis ending Act I the antagonist has taken the dramatic beat or momentum in the story, at the Core Crisis the hero takes the beat back. Yet we must not forget that we are in the Night World, and every step forward is also a step closer to the antagonist. From the Core Crisis onward, every decision the hero makes is moving toward the catastrophe, the "grow or die" moment where he must finally face the imperative to let go of the old way of seeing.

Thus the second movement of Act II falls under the signs of Discovery and Reversal. The hero may feel that he is moving forward, may think that now he really knows what's going on, and imagine seeing light at the end of the tunnel. But since he has not yet faced the most difficult trials, this optimism can be a self-delusion. Moving deeper into the Night World, the hero is moving deeper into the "aura" of the antagonist's power. Think of the Core Crisis and the following Story Step from *Seven*. Somerset and Mills, who have succeeded in tracking down the address of John Doe, enter the dark, decaying building, and arrive at the apartment door. John Doe shoots at them and flees. Mills chases him wildly through the building, across a street, and into an alley. There, the antagonist turns the tables on him and has a gun to Mills's head when Somerset arrives. They return to the apartment and, without a warrant, Mills impulsively smashes in the door. Now we are taken deeper into the killer's world, into the macabre labyrinthine space where all of the crimes have been meticulously documented. This sequence climaxes with Mills's discovery that John Doe has taken a photo of *him*. We get an ominous, sinking feeling. *Seven*, as an expressionistic thriller, has used every cinematic means to portray this archetypal sense of sinking to a deeper level of the Night World. Not all movies, depending on their idiom, will use such explicit means, but this is the feeling-tone in the subtext. The confrontation, the moment of truth, has been deferred, and meanwhile the conflict is driven still deeper.

Up to this point in Act II, the main character may have made some minor adjustments to his mode, strategic adjustments. But he has still pursued the same goal, with basically the same attitude—the same *motive*. Exactly *because* of the proactive success at the Core Crisis, we often see the hero try to repress the weakness of his earlier wound and revert back to the original motivation and attitude. Or he may believe that the superficial change has "done the trick." So there is often a moment of premature elation, a psychic inflation. Jack Walsh in *Midnight Run* has traded the Greyhound bus for his ex-wife's station wagon, and now he thinks he's got it all under control. Superficial change is a subtle, backhanded way of trying to retain the old status quo and shows that the process of breakdown is only half done. The essence of the dramatic conflict is still unresolved. But the Core Crisis on the level of the emotional network touches the hero's longings for love, trust, understanding, acceptance: for healing and the positive bonding we are capable of at our best. The universal, unconscious need is stirring, though still unrecognized by the hero. The call now is not only to win on the outer level—but *to become someone new*.

Because the main character is moving actively toward her plot goal once again, it is natural at this point in the story to define and set the stakes for the audience via a framing question for this third dramatic movement. While the hero's end plot goal will remain consistent, the immediate stakes, and the path to get there, may have become both more specific and more perilous. For example, in *Terminator 2*, John, his mother, and their protector have spent the first half of the story running away from death. At the Core Crisis the tactic shifts: will they be able to alter the future? They go on the attack, with the help of Dyson, to destroy all the research and development that could lead to the future creation of Skynet, including pieces of the first Terminator sent back from the future. They are trying to change the future, but of course they need to go deeper into danger in order to do so. In a lighter, comic vein, once Loretta goes to the beauty parlor and sees herself in the new gown, the power of her unrecognized passion to overthrow her status quo becomes so much greater. As she looks at herself reflectively in the mirror, glass of wine in hand, her plot goal (to marry Johnny) is in greater jeopardy than ever before, even though she *thinks* she is doing this all as part of a deal to make Ronnie leave her alone forever. The stakes, tone, and screen time of these sequences from *Terminator 2* and *Moonstruck* are completely different, but *structurally* they are directly analogous. Once we learn to see these analogies and apply them to the screenplay we are writing, the entire process of story development suddenly becomes much clearer.

As the two sides, protagonist and antagonist, converge in the second half of Act II, we have a comparison of the two values behind their motives. This is to say that we as screenwriters want to find the opportunity to provide this comparison for the audience. It becomes, in fact, one of the most important pieces of exposition in this part of Act II because it "seeds" a key subtext for the climax. On the level of core values, the audience will have a subliminal sense of what is at stake, giving a depth dimension to the climactic showdown. An example of this comparison of the two values comes from *Dances with Wolves*. Lt. Dunbar and his Lakota comrades, hunting the buffalo the tribe needs desperately for food, come upon a plain full of slaughtered and skinned bison that have been left to rot. The food/community value is directly contrasted with the greed/mercantile value where they both naturally intersect: the buffalo. Another very clever comparison comes from *Terminator 2*, during the same sequence of the battle at the high-tech headquarters. The Schwarzenegger character has a huge machine gun, which he sprays continuously at the attacking security forces. But he has promised John that he won't hurt anybody, and as the smoke clears we get a cut to the cyborg's internal computer screen that confirms: "0.0 CASUALTIES." To make sure that the contrast of values is explicit, the ice-cold bad Terminator arrives on the scene just at that moment. The essential life value of human sympathy is set against the death value of the autonomous machine.

The comparison of values in the second half of Act II foreshadows the choice of values the hero is normally forced to make at the climax, and thus is an essential underpinning for the theme. Lt. Dunbar will have to choose between his allegiance to his new world or to the white world he has left. Jack Walsh will have to choose between money and professional pride on the one hand, or friendship and trust on the other. Ada will have to choose between love and her piano. During this phase of the story following the Core Crisis, the resistance/delusion on the part of the main character is typically the fantasy that somehow she can have *both*. At the catastrophe that will end Act II however, it will appear certain that she shall have *neither*. Discovery will lead to reversal. This is the essence of this second movement of Act II.

Steps to a Double Bind

We defined the dramatic catastrophe starting from the mythic point of view by equating it with the Night of the Soul, the point of breakdown and, hopefully, breakthrough. It is the point where the main character's mode breaks down. But we cannot expect this mode, with which the main character is identified, to break down as long as there is any way out. So the catastrophe must be, by definition, a point where there is no way out. How do we know, as we are developing the story, where that point must be? In action movies, it is possible to paint the picture in purely physical terms: the hero is cornered at the edge of the parapet, or the end of the broken bridge over the abyss, and the most dreadful monster imaginable is stalking closer, or the enemy is ready to attack again but now we're out of ammo. One knows one can wrench a gut reaction from the audience with this predicament, but it obviously will not work with all kinds of stories. There must be a more systematic way to approach this climactic point of the entire Act II trajectory—and there is.

On a structural level, all of the Story Steps from the Core Crisis to the catastrophe serve to build the double bind into which the main character falls, as into a trap. And the double bind is indeed the trap from which there is no way out.

No contrivance is needed on the screenwriter's part; the story doesn't need to be pumped up with rubber (or digital) monsters. All the material needed is already present in a well-developed story. What is needed is an understanding of the relationship between the need/mode conflict and the Story Molecule. There are three easy steps to set the double bind, but wait—what *is* a double bind, anyway? This is another phrase we tend to toss around casually, without much precision. We need to know both the structure and the impact of the double bind if we want to use it skillfully in our screenwriting.

Biologist, anthropologist, and cyberneticist Gregory Bateson is credited as the father of the double-bind theory, at least in its application to human behavior. His double-bind theory of the origin of schizophrenia revolutionized our understanding of how we look at interaction and relationship. A double bind, most simply put, is a situation where there is no possible correct action—and at the same time, you *must* act. It is analogous to a checkmate, with the difference being that one is not even permitted to abdicate the game. To make the double bind less abstract, here is an old double-bind joke:

> The scene opens in a romantic little restaurant. The camera moves with a waiter carrying a bottle of champagne on a silver tray. Over there, in a candlelit corner, is a couple holding hands across the table and gazing deeply into each other's eyes. They hardly notice the waiter as he pours their champagne. There is a musical plink of their glasses. We can just—*mmmm*—feel the energy flowing between them.
>
> Then there is a disturbance in the Force. A tall man stands at their table.
>
> "Tom!"
>
> "Er . . . Rick! Nice to see you." Tom turns away, hoping Rick will disappear, but he just stands there with a friendly grin.
>
> "Aren't you going to, uh—" Rick nods toward the beautiful woman in the candlelight "—introduce me?"
>
> "Uh . . . oh, yeah. Marybeth, this is my old friend Rick. We go back a long way. Rick: Marybeth."
>
> Social duties done, Tom expects that now Rick will leave them alone. But Rick just nods and beams his unwavering smile upon them, for just a beat too long.
>
> "So, Tom," Rick says with an innocent tone. "Tell me, have you stopped beating your wife yet?"

What can Tom say? If he says *yes*, then he admits that he used to beat his wife. If he says *no*, he implies that he hasn't stopped yet. Either way, his evening is ruined.

Here is another double bind—not a joke this time. It is said that so-called "psychology experiments" of this kind were performed an animals in the dark days before someone cooked up the notion of animal rights.

- *Step 1: Take a dog.* (Picture a specific dog if you can—but not your own. Is he large or small, spotted, floppy-eared?)
- *Step 2: Put the dog in a cage.* (Now we have a dog in a cage. Picture that. The dog is not happy.)
- *Step 3: Do not feed the dog for three days.* (Picture a famished dog.)
- *Step 4: Place a dish of food in front of the cage.* (The dog is going crazy, barking and banging at the cage.)
- *Step 5: Open the cage. The dog leaps at the dish—but every time the dog approaches the dish, it receives a very painful electric shock.* (Fear and desire again!)

This is the very picture of the double bind. The dog simultaneously *must* eat and *must not* eat. If he goes for the food, he loses; if he doesn't go for the food, he loses. What happens to the dog in this situation? There is an activation of an instinct set that an animal goes into when cornered: head down, teeth bared, snarling, hair standing up on the back of the neck. But even this emergency behavior cannot resolve the double bind. So what does the dog do? The dog dies. It was said that an animal caught in this double bind may die in a matter of hours, not from starvation but from simply giving up the will to live. This is where we are taking the character at the catastrophe. And this is what we mean by "grow or die."

What is the cage in which your character is locked? It is made up of the contradictory yet sovereign claims of mode and need which are now rising up into consciousness. The hero is confronted with what she cannot have as long as she clings to the old mode, while at the same time the old pattern makes a desperate attempt to hang on. Through the double bind, the stakes on each level of the Story Molecule flow together and tower over the character's head. As long as Michael Dorsey (*Tootsie*) remains dressed up as a woman, he can never get close to Julie, who he loves. But if he takes off his masquerade, he will lose the wonderful job and the role that has become almost more real than himself. If Loretta takes Ronnie's hand and goes up the steps into his bed a second time, she fears to lose forever her self-image as a decent woman. If she doesn't, she loses the passionate love she craves and deserves. If Jack gets the Duke to L.A. before midnight, the Duke will be murdered by the mob before he has a chance to testify and Jack will lose the golden chance to redeem his life. If he doesn't get the Duke to L.A. on time, he loses a quarter of a million bucks and (he believes) the golden chance to redeem his life. Because the materials that go into constructing the double bind are inherent in the story itself, once we learn to look at the story as three-dimensional, they should always fit the idiom, genre, and style.

The first step toward the double bind is in fact the fantasy the hero creates for himself at the Core Crisis. Unable yet to face the contrary demands of the mode (represented by the plot goal), and the need (represented by the primary relationship), the character goes into a state of denial. This denial can take a variety of forms: wishing the problem will go away, procrastinating on a key ethical decision, maintaining a belief that it will be clear sailing from here on, or adopting a willful blindness to the facts at hand. Jack Walsh, for example, engages in the fantasy that he and the Duke can be pals on the road, and he can *still* turn him in and get his dough. It is a bubble of wishing. The bubble can last one scene or several sequences before it is popped, but popped it will inevitably be.

John Book's bubble endures rather long onscreen, the length of the barn-raising sequence, which is the longest single sequence in the film. The dramatic function of that sequence, apart from the serene feel-good imagery, is to establish Book's bubble. This is the fantasy that Book could really be accepted and integrated into this peaceful community, with Rachel as his partner. We are given repeated shots of the Amish men looking up admiringly at Book as he saws manfully away at the barn's ridgepole. Then we have a scene at the lunch break where Rachel implicitly declares Book to be her man by serving him, rather than her father, the iced tea first. We see how the entire community reacts. Unless this fantasy is established as a potential reality, Book cannot be placed in the position of being forced to choose whether to stay or go. By contrast, Ada's bubble is popped almost immediately. Her fantasy is that she can maintain her sham domestic situation *and* have George as a lover. But the first time she tries to sneak off, Stewart traps her and locks her in the house. C. C. Baxter has the fantasy that he will take Miss Kubelik "off Sheldrake's hands," and everyone will thank him.

All of these fantasies share a quality of wishful thinking.

When the bubble pops, the hero is left staring at the conflict of opposites in all its naked glory and dread. It becomes suddenly clear that he cannot have both, and the character has no response to this predicament. He is simply crucified between the opposites, which are now polarized and tearing the hero apart. This is the second step of the double bind. Rachel takes her bath, pushing Book into a decision he is not ready to make. Loretta runs into her dad and his mistress Mona at the opera, destroying her fantasy of a noble, heart-rending goodbye with Ronnie and precipitating all her guilt feelings. Sheldrake announces that he is getting a divorce and will marry Miss Kubelik. Very often, this is where a late second-act reversal occurs: what looked like the best thing that could happen turns out to be the worst thing that could happen. In *Seven*, John Doe walks into the police station and appears to give himself up. Song Lian, in *Raise the Red Lanterns*, betrays her sister-wife, believing that she will be rewarded and move up in the pecking order. Instead, she loses her best friend while she herself is also punished.

This overwhelming conflict pushes the hero to a breaking point, a last, desperate attempt to keep the old mode going. This third step ties the knot of the double bind and is the immediate setup for the catastrophe. The outburst itself proves the hero's impotence and sends her into the Night of the Soul in a raw, weakened, vulnerable position. The ego-wrappings have indeed been pulled away. A simultaneously poignant and comic example of this breaking point comes in *Midnight Run*. The Duke has popped Jack's bubble in the previous sequence as they rode across Arizona in a boxcar. Now Jack steals a Jeep to get them to L.A., further losing his integrity to the point of becoming a criminal himself. Soon they are cornered by literally dozens of police cars, but Jack refuses to give up. He takes off wildly across the desert, completely out of control. He no longer has a plan, just the headstrong determination to go on. At this point one could say that he is possessed by his mode. The upshot is that he loses the Duke to Marvin, who will sell him to the mob, while Jack himself is caught by the FBI. Jack's desperate gamble to control his fate has itself precipitated this catastrophe. Ada's breaking point comes when Stewart tells her that George will move away to another island and she will never see him again. Her outburst is to break her piano in order to send George a love-token. This act, too, precipitates catastrophe.

Catastrophe: The "Worst Thing"

The origin of the word *catastrophe* comes from the ancient Greek. Its meaning is literally "downward stroke." This describes in a nutshell what happens in a classical tragedy. The classical tragedies, such as Sophocles's *Oedipus*, were preoccupied with the conflict between man's free spirit and will to disobey, and the overwhelming power of the gods. From the beginning, there were conflicting opinions as to whether disobedience and guilt were synonymous, or whether man is forced to disobey by the very immorality of the gods. The theological interpretations of this conflict evolved, but one element of the dramas remained constant: the gods are obviously more powerful and man must ultimately submit. The catastrophe in the classical tragedy was that point where, after some success in resisting or evading the will of the gods, the human hero's fortunes turn against him. For a while he has been rising, inflated by hubris (immoderate pride or psychic excess), but now he is about to "hit the wall." The gods are about to descend and crush the hero. The catastrophe is like the breath of the gods sending a chill down our spines.

In a well-done tragedy, the catastrophe has a power to touch us viscerally in a very peculiar way. In *Oedipus*, to compress the play egregiously, there is a plague on the city of Thebes. It is Oedipus the king's responsibility to find the cause. The blind seer Tiresias, who knows the secret will of the gods, is brought into court and Oedipus demands that Tiresias tell him what he knows. Tiresias's answer, in short, amounts to: "Don't ask me. You really don't want to know." But Oedipus presses him. He is the king, he must know; Tiresias must tell him now! Even before Tiresias speaks the words that will condemn Oedipus, we get a sinking feeling in the pit of our stomachs, goose bumps on our arms, and our hair stands on end. We know that the awful truth is going to come out now and *nothing* can stop it.

In Macbeth there is a parallel moment. Cornered like a bear in his castle in Dunsinane, *Macbeth* heartens himself with the witches' prophesy: "I will not be afraid of death and bane / Till Birnam forest come to Dunsinane." *Cut* to Birnam Wood: Malcolm orders his army to cut down the boughs for camouflage as they advance toward the attack. A moment later the watch on the parapet reports that Birnam forest is indeed moving to the castle. The prophecy is coming true! For four hundred years, this moment in *Macbeth* has given audiences the shivers. It makes us reflexively gasp and hold our breath.

What is going on with these involuntary physical reactions that come at the catastrophe of a well-performed tragedy? What's with the goose bumps, sinking stomach, and hair standing on end? Think back to the dog in the experiment. These are *instinctual* responses, the exact same set. The cornered dog's hair stands up on the back of the neck. It is the instinctual set that is activated when we face imminent death. At the same time it is archetypal; instinct and archetype are two faces of the same deep patterns. There is a psycho-physiological component to the archetype of the plot curve. Tragedy has the power to constellate this reaction—the goose bumps, the hair standing up, the sinking stomach—in such an acute way that we are able to isolate and identify it. Yet, because it is part of a general instinctual/archetypal pattern, it is *always* implicit in the catastrophe that ends Act II. It lies in the story's archetypal subtext, from whence it resonates directly into the subconscious of the viewer. This will be true even in a comedy.

We are approaching the secret of the power of drama, which cannot be understood without reference back to the Hero's Journey. We have described the journey of breakdown and breakthrough as a journey to recover lost energy. It is a spontaneous movement to overcome dissociation by coming down out of the head and reconnecting with the instincts, with the primal wisdom in the body. This reconnection is not a mere regression. It is not a question of going unconscious and melting into the mob, but of re-forming and renewing the relationship between the ego and the unconscious matrix in a way that yields greater wholeness and conscious integration. In a movie or on the stage, this process is not only acted out for the audience in the sense that one might demonstrate an argument or mathematical proof. We can see that a sequence of instinctual responses—the desire/fear duality, the fight-or-flight instinct, and now a "grow or die" imperative—is released *in the audience itself*. Drama does put us directly in touch with life energies that for most of us have been seriously weakened through repression and being "civilized" in the wrong way. Here, at the end of Act II, the coordinated appearance of this transrational feeling state in both the hero onscreen and the audience in the theater creates a bond of tremendous intimacy between them.

On a psychological/mythic level, this is the Night of the Soul, leading to symbolic death, the annihilation of the ego's identification with a mode or life-role. In designing the actual catastrophe sequence, it can help to ask ourselves: What is the *worst thing*, in the context of the story, that could happen to my character?

Of course, the character could get hit by a bus, or caught in a meteor shower, or eaten by a raptor, but these may not be in the context of the story. Especially in comedy, the "worst" may not be lethal, and we in the audience may not take the threat so seriously. But the *character* takes it seriously. The worst that could happen to Loretta, in her mind, would be to mess up her life by falling in love with her fiancé's brother, thus ruining her chance to be a bride. The worst thing that could happen to Charles in *Four Weddings* would be for him to marry the wrong woman for the wrong reason, never being true to his own heart. The worst that could happen to C. C. Baxter would be for Sheldrake to get a divorce and marry Miss Kubelik. The worst that could happen to Lt. Dunbar in *Dances with Wolves* would be to be captured by his own insane army, who will court-martial and hang him for becoming sane and joining a community of noble, resourceful, caring human beings. The "worst thing" must always be a real story event that can be put on the screen with the emotional and archetypal impact of catastrophe, because this is the event toward which all of the action of Act II is moving.

The catastrophe is not merely "hitting the wall" in the outer plot. There is catastrophe on every level of the Story Molecule. Three catastrophes coincide and reinforce each other in one sequence. This gives us the feeling that everything is being stripped away from the hero until he is as naked as the goddess Inanna entering the Underworld.* Thus the catastrophe is the point of greatest dramatic intensity so far in the story. *Dances with Wolves* presents an especially elaborate and articulated catastrophe. Its rhetoric of victimization is spread over fifteen minutes of screen time and generates tremendous pathos for the hero. But the same elements will be found orchestrated into the catastrophe sequences of most movies.

The Lakota tribe is set to move on, away from the proximity of Dunbar's defunct fort. Dunbar has made the decision to go with his new family, but he has committed a blunder: he has left his journal at the fort and is afraid the Army will use it to track the Lakota down. He must go back alone to retrieve it, and then catch up to the tribe. When he arrives at the fort, soldiers are there. Seeing a lone "Injun," the soldiers become hysterical and start firing. Dunbar's "animal helper," his devoted, miraculous steed, who had carried him through the war, is killed in the volley. Dunbar is brutally beaten and put in chains to be interrogated by a merciless, rigid colonel, while his cherished journal is used as toilet paper by illiterate, infantile soldiers. When Dunbar won't cooperate by taking the Army to his family, he is shipped by wagon back to Fort Hayes to be hung. In the last beat of this catastrophe, even Dunbar's wolf companion is shot wantonly by the demonic soldiers. At that moment we feel that Dunbar has been stripped absolutely bare, he is alone and helpless—until the next cut reveals the Lakota war party concealed behind the rise.

At the catastrophe, the hero appears to die—physically, emotionally, and morally. All three are implicated in the catastrophe, even in comedy, because comedy,

* See Chapter Three, where we discuss Inanna passing through the seven gates of the Underworld.

as mentioned, always plays off a serious premise. The emotions unleashed by the utter breakdown of the character's mode—while his universal need is still unconscious—are globally irrational. The ego function of the conscious mind has gone into eclipse. The catastrophe is the point where the backstory wound crashes into the present and the subtext crashes into the text: the character lives the catastrophe through the eyes of a frightened, wounded child.

To emphasize the moral death of the character's core motivating value, the antagonist often offers him a last chance to sell out, as is handled forcefully in the drama *Silkwood*. And it is at this point, absolutely pushed to the wall, that something decisively new may flip in the character: a breakthrough much like Kierkegaard's "existential leap."

The Initiation, or inner climax, of the character sometimes appears right in the midst of this Night of the Soul. The knot of C. C. Baxter's double bind tightens with Sheldrake's announcement of divorce (the worst thing that could happen to Baxter on the emotional network level). Baxter, still hanging on to his "buddy-boy" mode, congratulates Miss Kubelik while trying to make it sound as though he has cleverly used Sheldrake to advance his own career. We feel Baxter has lost his chance to choose a better value for his life. As the breaking point, the final straw, Sheldrake demands the key to Baxter's apartment so that he can take Miss Kubelik there. It is New Year's Eve, and Sheldrake expects Baxter to be compliant. It looks like we are seeing his final cave-in, when suddenly Baxter resists, throwing away his job, not to restore his fake persona but to recover a long-lost human dignity (reversal: what appeared to be the worst thing turns out to be the best thing). In this case, catastrophe and inner climax have an immediate cause/effect relationship. Something has flipped in Baxter: losing everything has paradoxically freed him to be himself at last.

Loss of Control and Ventilation

What is going on here? It has something to do with the paradox of losing control and regaining vitality. When we are driven to the breaking point and lose control like this, our gut response is primal rage, rage that is *ventilated* in a spontaneous outburst. The rage may have a moral component, but more deeply, and more accurately, it is the naked will to live: physically, emotionally, ethically. The dammed-up primal life energy is finally released. This is what we often see in a catastrophe sequence, whether it be the physical outburst of John Book beating up a couple of punks who are tormenting an Amish family, or the more modest outburst of C. C. Baxter declaring that he is going to "be a mensch." Look at the word *ventilation*. It comes from the French root word *vent*, which means "wind": the second wind of the runner. And wind = breath = spirit. Yet ventilation is always morally paradoxical. The paradox runs deeply through our society, which simultaneously forbids and exalts raw expressions of rage. The growing problems of road rage, haphazard cruelty, schoolyard shootings, and violence in the media are indications that we are indeed a society in a state of double bind when it comes to this level of rage.

You can't solve your problem at the same level of consciousness that created the problem. Ventilation of anger takes us into an altered state of consciousness where we may spontaneously jump to a new awareness. The transformational energies are moving. Ventilation comes out of the gut, out of the unqualified life-energy, just like the karate master's shout before he smashes the stack of bricks. The outburst cuts right through the contradictory emotions of the double bind. It takes the character beyond the ego in a way that is instinctively "right" in terms of supporting survival through breaking down an inappropriate attitude and releasing energy. John Book's outburst here at the catastrophe is not to be compared with the abuse of power he exercised earlier in the movie when he roughed up a suspect; this is coming from a much deeper necessity. Right and wrong at such moments melt down into a single *is*. Grow or die. A saying is attributed to Homer that captures the primal satisfaction of this release: "Anger burns the eyes like smoke—but it tastes in the mouth like honey." We are not speaking about absolute good and evil, but of relative ideas of right and wrong that are based on the limited view of the status quo mode. God's order to Abraham to sacrifice his son Isaac and Moses's encounter with the angel Al-Khidr in the Koran are demonstrations that actions appearing morally repugnant from the limited human (ego) view may nevertheless be part of a larger divine plan.

One thing that happens through the ventilation is that the character leaps into the *absolute present*. Past and future disappear, and with them anticipation and regret. In fact, it is potentially a state beyond all mental dualities. Breakthrough is a break through duality to a new unity. It is beyond the character's old mode, her old way of seeing herself and the world. This is the reason that the ventilation appearing as a character's last desperate outburst can paradoxically clear the way for a new imprinting, a new possibility or potential, and a new "birth." It could be considered a moment of existential truth, such as Camus was always trying to express. Specifically in the screenplay, it is the character's potential to see the dramatic conflict from a fresh point of view. It is said that the point of power in life is in the present. By cutting through the carcass of the dead mode, ventilation makes the resolution of the character's inner need/mode conflict possible. She is freed to find a new solution to the plot conflict.

With this ventilation, the deepest truth of the character* is coming out, just when she seems to have lost everything. This process of breakdown may appear like torture from the materialistic-pragmatistic view of our culture that only the body and the pleasure-principle are real. But when we look back at the Hero's

* We must sometimes remind ourselves that dramatic characters are not real people. They are constructed with one dominant dimension of conflict. Change in a dramatic character is condensed and more decisive, which enhances its ability to model the process.

Journey model, we see the symbolic wisdom that there cannot be a birth unless there is a death. This is not a circular logic, but a penetration beneath the surface. The horror of the catastrophe makes present the power of the archetype of the dying and resurrected god. (In the spirit of St. Paul, "It is no longer I who live, but He who liveth in me.") This is apparently one of the oldest pieces of our collective human heritage. Hunting tribes all over the globe, in offering animal sacrifices or the ritual sacrifice of prisoners captured in war, would characteristically torture and torment their victims before killing them. The point of this was to make the animal totally present by putting it in a rage, so that when it was sent into the Other World, its power—its *spirit*—would be at a maximum, and that energy would be transferred to the tribe. This practice has been recorded by many ethnologists and noted by Joseph Campbell, who sees possible parallels going all the way back to the Neanderthal bear cult. The mythic idea that links catastrophe and ventilation to rebirth may be a hundred thousand years old, yet it is still fresh in each of us.

The Fourth Dramatic Movement: Grow or Die, Destiny

In the dialectical structure of thesis → antithesis → synthesis, all of Act II has been taken up with the antithetical force, specifically the breakdown of the mode under pressure and the emergence of its antithesis, the unconscious need. The catastrophe has taken that process of breakdown as far as it can go. We arrive at the moment of truth. Will the hero grow or die? If the ventilation has successfully carried away the old mode, we have already had a discovery of a more comprehensive personality. But still to be enacted is how that discovery becomes lived as Destiny in the outer world. The destiny the character makes for himself as a consequence of inner change, or of a tragic inability to change, comprises the climax that dominates Act III. This is where all of the throughline questions must be answered, one for each level of the Story Molecule. The dialectic model suggests yet another aspect or dimension to Act III: *synthesis*, some integration of the two opposing sides. Or, to follow the musical analogy: in Act III, as part of the synthesis we are in effect returning to the "home key" as we here resolve the questions that were posed way back in Act I. In the context of the Hero's Journey, we are returning to the Day World—carrying the boon of the Night World journey with us. This may also take the form of a violent collision between the Day World and the Night World at the climax.

I have summarized these aspects underlying and orchestrated through the climactic action because, as with the other crucial steps in the Plot Curve, at the climax there is a lot happening at once. The climax is where much that had been resonating in the subtext is brought out in the open, yet because the action is compressed into a few minutes of screen time, a lot of it must still be expressed indirectly. As always, a fully articulated screenplay is more than just a story *line*;

it is a living, three-dimensional stream of meaning. This is still true at the climax, no matter how much the requirements of the plot force us to focus our attention as writers on the climactic action. That plot climax, we can now see, is a product of the entire process of Act II. The very fact that we have arrived at a point of "grow or die" without a resolution means that we are still dealing with indeterminate factors deep within the character. Does the hero grow or die, and if the answer is no longer in the eclipsed ego's determination, then what power is it that shall lead him to his destiny?

Moving into Act III, we find the most decisive difference between the Hero's Journey and the Plot Curve models. The Initiation that follows the Night of the Soul is an inner climax—yet victory in the new trials the hero faces upon returning to the Day World is also a climax. Which of these is the "real" climax? People have been arguing over this question ever since *Oedipus*. Is the climax of *Oedipus* when Oedipus puts his eyes out? Or is it the moment just before, when Oedipus realizes the truth: that he has been the fool of the gods? To my mind, the only productive answer to this question is that both aspects are necessary to articulate the meaning of the climax. From these observations my colleague Tom and I developed the concept of the "ripple climax": *as I change the way I see things, I change my behavior; as I change my behavior, I change my relationships; as I change my relationships, I change my world.* This rippling effect as the climax moves through the levels of the Story Molecule can be observed in every movie where all three dimensions are active.

In a movie, as opposed to the mythic model, these waves of climax come *boom-boom-boom*, one right after the other. The mythic Initiation corresponds to the inner climax; the new trials corresponds to the outer plot climax. Yet in the Hero's Journey model, these two climaxes are separated by the long return journey. Here the rhythm of drama is very clearly different from that of myth, because it is operating via the release of physical energies that belong to the curve of sexual response. The mythic wisdom is reshaped by the wave of tension and release.

In effect, the entire third quadrant of the Hero's Journey model taking place in the Night World is cut out. Instead, in movies we move directly from inner realization to outer action. Depending as always upon the genre and idiom of the movie we are making, we may choose to externalize and portray some or all of the steps in that third quadrant which expresses the part of the return still in the Night World. We may choose this either because of the action potential of the Magic Flight motif, or because return from the underworld to the light is central to the movie's theme. Normally it is enough, and more economic storytelling, to record a hint or moment of inner shift in the main character, then cut to pick up the character as they are crossing back into the Day World, or as the two worlds are about to collide. As with every aspect of screenwriting, however, when it comes to the specifics there are no standard answers. Inner and outer sides of the climax will be there, but their exact timing and orchestration must fit the requirements of the story being told.

Calm Before the Storm

Catastrophe is the point where the dramatic conflict can rise no further without finding a resolution. It is the scene with the highest stakes—the highest arc of conflict and suspense—thus far in the entire drama. But in the case of the catastrophe, the high suspense generated is not resolved within the sequence. The suspense is left hanging, and with it, the audience is left hanging on the edge of their seats. Catastrophe leads directly into the climax, where the dramatic questions will be answered and the dramatic tension will be released.

Some kind of small bridge sequence is often needed following the catastrophe to prepare the climax. We need a moment to breathe. When the catastrophe falls, we gasp and hold our breath. Now we need to let it out. This small breathing space that comes after the catastrophe is also the point when its consequences, its ramifications, sink in for us, while at the same time we know that the final confrontation is just ahead. We call this small story step the "Calm Before the Storm." This sequence was not specifically indicated by Aristotle, but in the classical drama a chorus on the empty stage would serve the same effect. The Calm Before the Storm functions to put one last brake on the action before the headlong rush into the climax. But its real significance is not only structural.

The sequence between the catastrophe and the climax is where we see, in a hero who is capable of change, that the character's *mode* has died—but the character's *self* has not. And in a character who is not changing, we see whether he has now realized the truth about himself and is prepared to meet his destiny in a properly tragic sense, or is doomed to be a pathetic victim. In *Midnight Run*, there is at this point a quickly paced sequence where we see that Jack is able to drop his old "loner" mode and elicit the cooperation of the FBI in order to save the Duke from Jimmy Serrano. As we see Loretta strolling home in the morning after the opera in the structurally parallel moment, we can see from the way she walks that, whatever happens, she can't hide the radiantly romantic and sensual person she truly is. Loretta is crossing a threshold back to the Day World. She has yet to face her fiancé Johnny, but she is certainly no longer the Loretta we saw at the beginning of the story. Her old mode of playing it safe has died, freeing Loretta to live. When we see John Book finishing the birdhouse in *Witness*, we know that he has the will and strength of character to see his job through to the end, and we feel hope born out of hopelessness. Karen Silkwood, in *Silkwood*, for whom there is no hope, is determined to keep on fighting. She is a tragic heroine for whom the primacy of survival-based motivation has been transcended by a larger principle of truth. And the unnamed protagonist of *Taste of Cherry*, who has finally found someone understanding enough to bury him after he commits suicide, returns home for the last time, to put his place in order, take his fatal overdose, and turn out the lights. He prepares to face his own truth in his own way.

There are motifs in these Calm Before the Storm sequences that bridge to the outer plot climax which do in fact echo the motifs of Magic Flight and Return

Threshold Crossing from the Hero's Journey. If we keep in mind the principle that the character changes something in the way she perceive herself, and that as her self-image changes, her behavior changes, then we can begin to understand how the mythic Initiation transfers into the dramatic context. Initiation means "new birth," and this new birth takes place in the depth of the Night World—in the depth of the psyche. There needs to be some inner process, lasting months or a fraction of a second, before a character is ready to translate new self-image into changed behavior that we can see. If we as screenwriters are aware of this, then we can create a resonant, living moment out of it, such as the moment Renton, in the Calm Before the Storm in *Trainspotting*, pours out the old wine and drinks a glass of cold water instead. This is a rhythmic beat that prepares us for the climax, but the small, very concrete gesture reveals an inner change in Renton that makes the scene dramatically complete.

The Return Threshold

At the moment of the character's breakthrough, the new life has only an embryonic existence. It is an embryonic energy, like a screenwriter's creative breakthrough in the middle of the night, which might make it across the threshold to find its own objective life in the outer world—or might dissipate like a mist and be forgotten by morning. At this moment the character could scarcely articulate the change that has come over him: it is still too close. The character has in effect to wean himself from the mesmerizing impact of the sublime or horrific experience of death and rebirth he has just had. But change is beginning to ripple outward. In the Calm Before the Storm sequence, we suggest or imply this sort of "embryonic journey" from the point of realization to the point of action: from inner climax to outer climax. It is a journey back to the threshold of the Day World, which must all be suggested in no more than one or two minutes of screen time.

We are crossing from Discovery to Destiny. As we have suggested, the return threshold is the boundary of the Day World, of the status quo the hero has left at the end of Act I and which will now have to be decisively confronted. The main conflict here will be the outer plot climax, but there is sometimes a minor threshold guardian, representing the status quo value, who challenges the hero. This secondary character serves the function of dramatically externalizing the main character's internal change. *Moonstruck* presents an excellent example of this as Loretta dances into her kitchen to the internalized melody from *La Bohème*, only to be confronted by her mother. Mother isn't amused:

M: Where've you been?

L: It's a long story.

M: [pointing an accusing finger]: Your hair's different!

L: Ma, everything's different.

At this point Mom drops the bombshell that Johnny Camerreri showed up last night, looking for Loretta. Loretta can't believe that he is back from Sicily, and quickly starts wiping off her lipstick and pinning up her hair, the badge of her romantic feeling. Just then the doorbell rings—it must be Johnny! Loretta jumps up to hide in a closet as her mother exclaims:

> **M:** You've got a love-bite on your neck, cover up that damn thing. What's the matter with you? Your life's going down the toilet!!

Here is the voice of the guardian of the return threshold.

This kind of a minor threshold guardian externalizes exactly what the hero feels at this moment: alienated from the worldview she left behind long ago, unsure of who she is now, and tempted to be anxious about whether she will be permitted back into the world. The threshold guardian acts in much the same way as the doubter of Act I: clarifying what is at stake at this moment as well as announcing the coming of the main antagonist. Sometimes it is this minor figure who instrumentally brings the protagonist and antagonist crashing together for the climax. The old busybody in the catastrophe of *Witness* who shouts after Eli Lapp's carriage: "This ain't good for the tourist trade, you know!" is next seen telling the local police about the fight. We get a sinking sensation in our guts: we know now that Book has betrayed his hiding place, and Paul and McFee will immediately close in to kill him. It is this old man's strictly mercantile concern that thematically links him to the antagonists. Paul and his accomplices have inverted the core police value—"to serve and protect"—for the sake of the cold cash. In both cases the feeling-related human value has been subverted.

Sometimes the return threshold is marked for the audience less by an individual guardian character and more by the situation as a whole. This may be supported by evoking and repeating a motif from the setup in Act I. We mentioned briefly the Calm Before the Storm in *Trainspotting*. The scene is worth looking at in greater detail because of the way it brings setting, situation, and character together to create a striking threshold moment. We see the four lads passed out in their hotel room. Then we notice that Renton is awake, biting his nails. He gets up and goes to the sink, then looks back at the sleeping Begby, who is cradling the duffle bag with the money. The threshold here is implicit: if Renton wants the money, he'll have to take it out of Begby's arms. And we know what Begby is capable of, after seeing him beat a man half to death for spilling beer on his suit. Renton opens the faucet, dumps last night's booze down the drain, and drinks a glass of cold water instead. Sobering. He looks in the mirror, steeling himself. Now, this action builds suspense, and it also mirrors exactly the look Renton gave himself in Act I, the first time he resolved to get off heroin. If you can imagine this scene exactly as it is, but minus that look in the mirror, you can understand that something would feel subtly incomplete. That one moment's glance marks the return threshold and evokes Renton's whole journey, making it subtextually present for the audience. This is effective storytelling.

Notice that each of these three examples handles this return threshold motif in a somewhat different way. In *Witness*, the return threshold guardian is inserted in the falling action of the Catastrophe Story Step. *Moonstruck* uses the Calm Before the Storm Story Step to bring in the mother to confront Loretta. *Trainspotting* finds a moment within the climax itself to show us a threshold, while using that threshold to build rising tension within the scene. What can we learn from this? That once we understand how the dramatic elements of story structure function, we have to be flexible in the way we apply them to the story we are writing. There is no one way it always works. What we *can* say is that the Calm Before the Storm and return threshold motifs are orchestrated between catastrophe and climax. Your specific solution must grow out of your own story. These three examples all work because the screenwriters have found appropriate moments within the flow of the action. While one could question the "realism" of the old man's line in *Witness* or why the police do not immediately arrest Book, there is nothing artificial imposed on the stories in these three cases. By contrast, a need to *contrive* an obvious threshold here is usually an indication that Act I has not quite done its job.

This limpid space between catastrophe and climax is also where we resolve any subplots that have not yet been paid off. This, too, we must handle with flexibility. Depending on how much juice the subplot has and which characters are involved, we will develop a strategy for staging the subplot resolution. The important thing to have in mind here is that we want to use the subplot to build up the climax, but want to avoid by all means letting the subplot upstage the main plot or the most important throughline. This means that if a subplot or secondary relationship has great inherent tension or high stakes, we typically perform two operations on it. First, we find a way to hold it back a bit, not play it fortissimo. Second, we leave it with a hanging resolution that is open-ended enough for the free energy to feed into the climax. The climax of the love story in *Witness* is handled with a passionate kiss, then the scene is immediately cut. It has been trimmed to its essence so it will not intrude on the outer plot climax. In *The Piano*, the adultery subplot is paid off as an edgy, ambiguous anti climax. When the two teenage lovers in *American Beauty* decide to run away to New York, the shots on them are simple, suspending them and the threshold they are about to cross. Their decision is not allowed to generate new conflict in the family that would detract from the climax of Lester's line. *Moonstruck* chooses to pay off its numerous farcical subplots within the climax scene in order to generate the maximum comic chaos out of the scanty material. This is also in the long tradition of classical farce. Similarly, in *Tootsie*, several romantic subplots are resolved simultaneously—to virtuoso effect—the moment Dorothy pulls her wig off and reveals her true identity. All of these are paid off with reaction shots, and all of them before the highest beat of the climax when Michael confronts Julie.

The Ripple Climax

Crossing the return threshold, we are already in the energy field of the *ripple climax*. While the entire plot curve has an archetypal basis, the moment of climax has a very special place in both body and psyche. If we look back at the graphic of the Plot Curve model, we may note that not only is the climax the highest point, but—here we can imagine a wave that is now cresting and breaking—it is also the point that has the greatest depth beneath it. The climax is where all of the opposites come together, not only those opposites directly constellated in the story as mode and need, persona and shadow, but, implicitly, all opposites *as such*. Not consciously, of course, but in layers of subtext: good and evil, love and death, the eight worldly Dharmas. It is as though the climax energy field creates a vertical vortex in reality, sucking into itself hopes and fears, primal memories in the body, interpersonal boundaries, me and you, all in a Chagall-esque whirl. The matador draws his sword from beneath the cape. The bloodied, trembling bull readies his last charge. Reality goes into a spasm of emotion. And then it's all over, and at the same moment a new reality, a new day, has incomprehensibly appeared. We are somehow both destroyed and renewed. This is an inkling of the depth implicit in the climax.

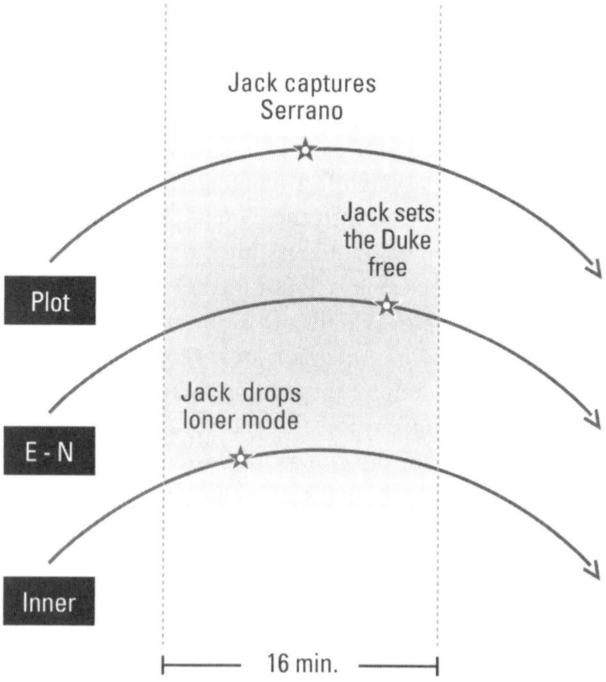

/ **The Ripple Climax: *Midnight Run.***

At the ripple climax the big stone lands in the pond, warping the entire surface. These are waves of *consequences.* As there is a central dramatic question that goes to the heart of each substory of the Story Molecule, there must also be a climax on each level where that question is answered. These peak moments cannot all happen at once, but must occur successively as the energies of change ripple out from the main character into the world of the story. It becomes our task as screenwriters to find the most effective orchestration of the three climaxes that will occur when all three levels are developed. It is necessary to know what climactic event will answer the dramatic plot throughline question set up in Act I, but it is equally important to know which level of the story has the most juice for ourselves and for the audience. The most important dramatic question is the one that must be paid off *last.* This choice will also ultimately determine what kind of movie we are going to be looking at: the POV, the tone, the style, and where the scenes are going to be spending their time. Is a movie an action-adventure or a buddy film? This is not always an easy question to answer. In fact, it may be tortuously hard. It is common for the writer—and the producer—to say, "Of course, I want both! I want it all!" We want to have excitement happening all the time. But until we have clearly decided which of the two possibilities must dominate—that is, which level of the story carries the theme—the story development will always be out of focus. Perhaps the open-ended question: "Is this an action movie or a buddy film?" is the wrong question to begin with. The better question may be: "What is the most dramatic orchestration of the ripple climax?" Which question needs to get paid off last? The answer to that question should determine the tone of the second-act development.

Midnight Run is an example of an action comedy that has significant change in the main character, Jack Walsh, and a compelling relationship between Jack and the Duke, as well as a big action line. The action line features expensive production set-pieces, location shooting across the country, high-speed chases, gun battles—in short, a lot of "production value." But is this where the real juice of the story is? Well, when we ask the dramatic throughline questions—"Will Jack get the Duke to L.A. safely and on time?" (outer plot), "Will Jack get his $250,000 bounty and be able to buy his coffee shop?" (Jack's stated plot goal), and "Will Jack learn to let trust and friendship back into his life?" (inner/relationship throughline)—which question is the most fresh and the most interesting? In the hands of lesser talents, the emphasis might have gone to the outer plot and the result might have been a well-crafted but mediocre movie without staying power, without resonance. In any case, it would have been a different movie.

At the catastrophe of Midnight Run, we see Jack completely lose control. Marvin takes the Duke away from him and Jack can only rail impotently at the desert. He wanders by foot into a diner, his dream of owning his own coffee shop destroyed. He doesn't even have money left for coffee . . . and at that moment Alonzo Mosely walks in with a phalanx of FBI men and busts him. Here Alonzo

Mosely acts as the return threshold guardian, but the scene is *played* as a continuation of the catastrophe because things are still getting worse. This is confirmed when, a scene later, we witness Marvin make a deal with Jimmy Serrano's goons to turn the Duke over to them. The absolute worst we could imagine has come to pass. But Jack is resourceful, and comes up with a plan to trap Jimmy Serrano and rescue the Duke. As we go into the climax we are carrying many high-energy plot questions. How will Jack get the Duke out of Serrano's hands? Will Serrano fall for the bait of the fake computer discs? Will Mosely's men move in fast enough to keep Jack and the Duke from being killed by the goons? Every player has his own motive and strategy in the scene, including the wild card Marvin, which ensures a down-to-the-wire action climax where the antagonist is captured and the Duke saved. So the answer to the outer plot question animating this action climax scene is *yes*: Jack will successfully overcome his obstacles.

Jack does finally get the Duke to Los Angeles before midnight, but we can feel that the story is not over. The tension has not been released yet. We can see this from Jack's face and body language as he rides down the escalator at the L.A. airport. He could be triumphant, he could be relaxing, but he is agitated. There is a question we have not answered yet, and because it is still unanswered it reveals itself to be the most important dramatic question. We have needed to clear away the outer plot questions in order to focus on it clearly: is Jack going to allow trust and friendship into his life, or is he going to go on as an embittered loner? Is Jack going to *act* out of a value of friendship or out of a value of the most narrowly defined self-interest? Is he going to turn the Duke in or let him go? In this particular case the answer to the most interesting question has been held for the falling action after the plot climax. When we see Jack uncuff the Duke, we can finally breathe a sigh of relief. Here is evidence that there is no one formulaic way that the ripple climax always unfurls. It is a question of knowing which of the substories carries the greatest dramatic and thematic interest.

The climax as a confrontation between protagonist and antagonist, already discussed in the contexts of other models, can of course also be played as the final test for the hero. In that way it is a symbolic threshold crossing. In effect, the antagonist is a test of whether the hero has learned his life-lesson. This is equally true of *Silence of the Lambs* and *Four Weddings and a Funeral*. It is the action of the climax that grabs us, but it is the *meaning* of the climax that makes it function in the entire story. How are the three interrelated throughline questions answered? What complex theme emerges from them? The antagonist is most closely connected to the plot goal, while also embodying a shadow aspect of the hero's mode. Therefore, it is not just question of who is the winner. Because the climax has got so much depth beneath it, and so many layers are activated, it is inevitable that at that moment, as at a moment of sexual climax, the characters lose some of their individuality and become carriers of life-energy and values. Yes, we appreciate that C. C. Baxter has won. He has succeeded even though he has lost his career with the insurance company. On one level we relate to him as a likeable person, so we are happy for him. On a second level, he is a carrier of the value of integrity—hard won, genuine integrity. And on yet another, more primitive and mythic level, he is the matador, the one who faces the bull of darkness on our behalf.

Any value whatsoever can be promoted via drama, be it realistic or fatalistic, romantic or pragmatic, optimistic or pessimistic, idealistic or cynical. A value is projected through the structure of climax, whatever it is the hero ends up standing for through the orchestration of the climax and how we in the audience are made to feel about it. It is not simply about winning or losing. He won the race, or the girl . . . so what? It is the motive, what it *meant* to the character, that stays with us most deeply after the climax. Is Baxter a winner or a loser? Depends how you evaluate his values. Is John Book a winner, or are the Amish the real winners? Is Ada a winner, as she is pulled into the boat by the Maori men? About Ada, we can only say so far so good. The climax itself often provides only rough hints about how it should be evaluated. The task of bestowing judgments is left to the movie's resolution.

Resolution: To See More Clearly

The climax answers the throughline dramatic questions, so what else is left? The action at the climax should answer the throughline questions definitively, to such an extent that new questions with higher stakes in the same story line would be unimaginable. If new questions arise, then the climax was incomplete and was not set up properly. As we noted, the climax is the greatest point of tension and release. As the questions are answered, the audience experiences catharsis, a purging of the tension they have carried. It is literally a new psycho-physiological state for the audience, what we have termed "falling away from the screen." This does not mean that the audience is now totally disengaged, but it is extremely difficult, even perverse, to try to get them excited again. So there are no new plot points possible, though ever since Darth Vader hurtled into space at the end of the first *Star Wars* episode, presumed but not confirmed dead, it has become a common commercial practice to use a *stinger*, a reversal of feeling-tone at the very end of the movie. A stinger is a part of the resolution that leaves wiggle-room for the sequel. It follows the main business of the resolution, which is about consequences.

The resolution is the "reaction shot" for the whole movie. This is why it should not be disposed of as an afterthought. Every part of the dramatic curve is equally important, because without each part the integrity of the whole is destroyed. In this case, the prime function of the resolution is to transfer the theme of the movie to the audience. This can only be done by showing us the *consequences* of the climax, and giving those consequences an emotional tone and value. We want to see who's alive and who's dead, who's standing and who's fallen, who's together and who's apart—and what that means for them, and for the audience. The climax will have impacted on the entire world of the story, thus in the resolution we want to cycle through that world again to see how it has changed. It is equally important to show us how the characters feel about their new situation. If you have seen *Dangerous Liaisons*, you will recall the last images of Glenn Close as the Marquise de Merteuil. According to her own standards, she is a winner. She has beaten everyone. But the devastated, mask-like face tells us in the language of movies what her victory really means.

There is no such thing as a "value-free" movie. Drama by its very nature is an assertion of value. One of the old proverbs of the movies, handed down from the days of D. W. Griffith, is: "Cinema is the art of the reaction shot." What this means is that an action on the screen, whether a killing or a kiss, tends not to take on meaning until we see someone react to it. If there is a violent event onscreen and nobody in the story reacts, it has a strange, dissociative effect. It becomes disconnected from the other actions around it and from the entire dramatic context. Naturally, this is especially true of the climax, which is why we need the resolution as the reaction shot for the whole movie. We have been on the edge of our seats with our adrenaline pumped up, and now we fall away. As we take a step back, we gain enough objectivity and perspective to ask: what *difference* did it make? The lone cowboy, after cleaning up the Western town, rides away into the sunset. Do we see that the townspeople have learned something and can now manage their own affairs? Or do we see the next gang of crooked land barons riding in on the other side of town to begin the cycle all over again? It does make a difference. In the resolution, we have some moments after the dust has cleared to see a new status quo created or implied (ritual kingship, sacred marriage).

Because the primary relationship has been both the vehicle of transformation for the main character and a symbol of the newly emerging possibility connected with the universal need, it is most important to show a moment, a final beat in that relationship. Where are the friends or lovers at this point? Ada and George are together—new house, new finger, new piano. Jack and the Duke, having learned from each other, are ready to part as friends and each go his own way. Yes, there is something conventional about this. In the old days, there would be the predictable curtain-kiss, the witty one-liner, or the noir detective stalking away into the foggy San Francisco night. But again, this convention is founded on the natural energy curve of falling action that is in both the characters and the audience. We have to finish the relationship arc, as we do the plot. After the shooting is over, Book must say his goodbye to Rachel. There is a brief, wordless scene between them, he outside on the porch, she framed in the dark doorway of the house. The ambivalent feelings of the moment communicate themselves to us through eye contact and hesitation, and through the orchestration of light and dark on the screen. The last scene in *Midnight Run* still had a major dramatic question to answer, so it was still part of the climax. The scene with Book and Rachel is clearly falling action. It does not raise or answer new questions, but resolves the relationship and the energy we have invested in it.

The function of resolution is integral to the story. How we handle it is up to us. It is thus the last place where we as screenwriters can check in on our own rapport with the story before we let it go. What does the story mean to *us* after the long journey of writing it? One way to approach this is to review the screenplay using our felt-sense training, to be as aware as possible of the potential feeling impact of each scene on the future audience. We may also pick up where we have invested our own attitudes or complexes in and through the story. This, too, has consequences. In an earlier chapter, for example, we talked about the "blackout" ending after the eroticized murder that climaxes *Looking for Mr. Goodbar*. A consequence was that, though most of the movie was in the idiom of realism, the absurd ending turned the main character into an opaque, pathetic victim-figure. To that extent, she lost her humanity, which would seem to be counter to the movie's objective. It was a sudden, unprepared shift, not only in tone, but also in idiom; we were thrown into a different universe. The real disappointment in *Mr. Goodbar* is that the movie raises issues about its own dramatic tactics that it avoids answering. In the case of most films, however, the resolution is structured to offer us a doorway out of the theater in possession of ourselves, carrying the theme of the movie with us. As screenwriters, our rapport with the audience is implicated in how we deliver the resolution. These are some of the aspects we would want to review in relation to our intention for the screenplay. This is, after all, the resolution phase of our writing process as well.

As it relates to the last step of the Hero's Journey, the resolution brings us symbolically full circle, either back to the beginning or to some other image of completeness and wholeness. Bringing us back to a physical setting from the opening, or to a significant image motif, is a visual way to state completion. In addition, taking us back to familiar territory highlights what has changed in the hero and the world. In *The Piano*, Ada is finally leaving the wild New Zealand coast where she arrived in Act I. The falling action of the climax of *Fargo* shows us the same snowy road and an identical atmosphere to the opening shot, only now Marge (and the values she stands for) is in the "driver's seat." At the end of *Terminator 2*, it is not possible to return to earlier locations. Instead, we have an evocative POV shot of a highway at night, rolling forward into the unknown future. But we do pick up the mother's voiceover narration from the opening prologue. The effect is both appropriately edgy and satisfying. Even more edgy is the ending of *Mulholland Drive*. The final minutes take us back to images from the opening, which have lain deep in the subtext through the entire movie.

The story development questions for the end of Act III focus on how we have answered the throughline questions and what impact we expect that to have on the audience. What is the *final taste* we want the audience to walk out of the theater with? And what is our own investment in that? Is there some compulsion to make the audience feel good? Do you want to teach them a lesson, or even punish the audience? It is not easy to gain objectivity about our own attitude toward a screenplay we have worked on feverishly for months or years. This is one of the advantages of collaboration and shared vision in the development team: there are multiple perspectives.

Resolution does not necessarily mean "happy ending." Nor does it mean that all plot strands are tied up without a trace of ambiguity. *Trainspotting* ends with Renton walking relentlessly toward us, his face becoming a grotesque, out-of-focus mask, while in voice-over he goes through the same litany of banalities he recited at the opening. He tells us he is going straight, choosing life, but the feeling tone is darkly ironic. This ending is assertively ambiguous. *The Piano* has, in effect, three endings whose tones are in conflict with each other, leaving a sense of an unfathomable mystery in the human spirit. *Taste of Cherry* has a sudden reversal after the climax: shifting to handheld video imagery, we see the character we thought had died smoking a cigarette with the camera crew. The entire paraphernalia of location shooting is exposed to us with blunt frankness after a climax of exquisite poetry and intimate feeling. The effect is a powerful stinger.

What resolution *does* mean is that we see more clearly what the issue was. We use the same word in reference to how a lens works: resolution is the power to present a clear image. Having traveled full circle, we turn and look back at the place where we began. It is in this often-subliminal act of reflexion/reflection that we take the theme, the most universal level of the story, into ourselves. The last images, like the first, are the most compressed visual storytelling in the movie because of their potential impact on the audience. The screenwriter may be tempted to rush ahead toward those words that spell relief: THE END. But the ending, like the opening, is usually cut and re-cut and re-cut in the editing room. Directors and editors lose a lot of sleep over it in order to get that final taste just perfect. The last step of the journey asks as much from us as the first.

10

Act, Sequence, Scene, Beat

The Dramatic Present

> I make a proposition to an actor's imagination such as, "She is leaving you." At this moment deep in him a subtle movement occurs. Not only in actors. The movement occurs in anyone . . . [but] the actor is a more sensitive instrument and in him the tremor is detected. In the cinema the great magnifier, the lens, describes this to the film that notes it down, so for the cinema the first flicker is all.
>
> *—Peter Brook*

WE HAVE JOURNEYED THROUGH FOUR INTERLOCKING MODELS that address the shapes and dynamics that power screenplays. We have seen how the structure of a screenplay grows organically out of the process of writing it, starting with the act of facing the unknown. While we have yet to take up the screenwriter's creative journey in detail, the outlines of the parallel journey that we take along with our characters begins to emerge. You may already have a gut sense of how we are linked to our characters by the dark umbilicus of our shared anxieties and universal needs. You have come to understand conceptually the basic principle that story energy radiates outward, both from our characters and ourselves, shapes itself into waves of tension and release, and moves toward an Initiation, a growth through crisis. Both in dramatic terms and psychological terms, this Initiation means that the character is forced to "see through" an old, unconscious pattern that has ruled her life. As her old way of seeing herself dies, she has to find a new way to be in the world. The combined lenses of these four models have brought us to a point where we can work with the dramatic structure in greater detail and with greater appreciation.

The next chapter will introduce the Sixteen Story Steps model. The Story Steps are the "vertebrae" in the "spine" of the story, and through them we shall have virtually a sequence-by-sequence structural guide through the writing of the entire screenplay. As with the vertebrae of our own spines, the Story Steps have a necessary order through which they articulate the structure of the screenplay. As with our bodies, the spine is the core structure that frees the individual parts to act for our benefit. Working with this new and comprehensive model, the long stretches of Act II will no longer feel like alien territory.

But the fact is that when we sit down to write, day after day, we are not writing Plot Curves and Heroes' Journeys. Nor are we writing Act I or Act II. We are not even writing one of the Sixteen Story Steps. What we are writing, day after day, are *scenes*. It is the scene that carries the absolute present tense of a movie: *what is happening right now*. The larger structures remain in the background and rather abstract as we write. Perhaps they guide us intuitively (while their impact on the audience is subliminal but decisive). Yet the scene is where we live or die as writers. Live *and* die. As writers, we live by constantly letting our fixed notions of what the scene is about die. The scene is the ideal place to learn the craft of screenwriting. It is brief enough that we are able to see and feel its dramatic structure and the dynamic forces at work. If we can write a good scene, we can write a good sequence. If we can write a good sequence, we can write a good act. And if we can write a good act . . . you get the picture.

The Layers of Dramatic Structure

The scene is absolutely present, happening right now, but that does not mean it is devoid of structure. It turns out that the dynamics of a scene are a miniature of the dynamics of the screenplay. It turns out, in fact, that a screenplay is a *hologram*. You have certainly seen holograms, like those holographic necklace pendants that always seem to show the Eye of Horus, the mystical Masonic Pyramid from the back of a one dollar bill, or . . . a portrait of Elvis. So imagine one of these glass pendants. Allow yourself to feel the size and mass of it in the palm of your hand. Do you know what would happen if you took that pendent, say the one with Elvis looking up dewy-eyed at you, and smacked it with a hammer? Go ahead. Imagine yourself hitting the hologram with a hammer. Now there are fragments of glass all over the place, but something very special has happened. Pick up one of the pieces and take a look. What do you see? With a normal image, each piece of glass would show a fragment of the whole. One bit would show part of Elvis's right eye, another would show his lips, chin, or part of his sideburns. But this was not a normal image; this was a hologram. In this case, what you see before you are *dozens of little Elvises*, each one essentially complete, each staring up at you with that same soulful gaze. Each glass fragment would contain the whole image. That is the unique thing about a hologram, what in fact makes it *holistic*: the whole is contained in each of the parts. And so it turns out to be with a screenplay as well: the entire dramatic curve is present in each of the dramatic subunits.

Each act has its own curve, each sequence and scene have their own curve, until we come down to the very smallest unit of dramatic construction, the beat. It is in the *beat* that the entire Aristotelian plot dynamic of is anchored. The presence

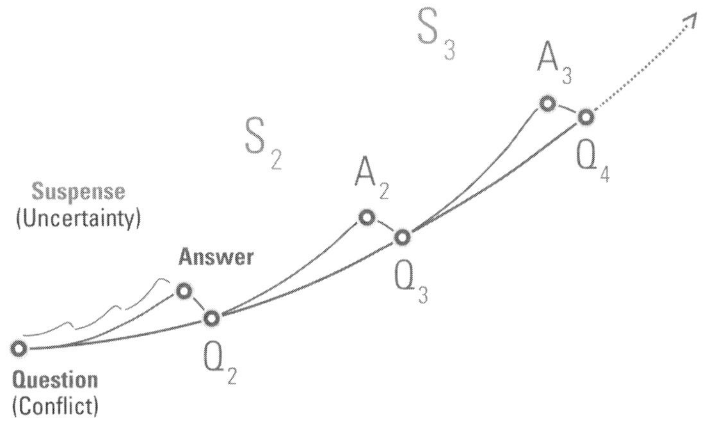

/ **Dramatic chain of rising intensity.**

of the entire dynamic in the smallest unit gives the beat its own curve of tension and release. If the beat works, the next beat grows naturally out of it. The beats shape the scene. But where the beats do not work, the scene dies dramatically, it becomes contrived or must rely on flat (nondramatic) exposition to get its point across. Thus the larger waves of tension and release that make up the overall movement of Aristotle's Plot Curve are themselves made up of smaller and smaller wave-forms of the same essential shape. This "nesting" of waves of tension and release is happening, as we have seen, on all three levels of the Story Molecule.

So before going into the dynamics of scenes and the beats that comprise them, we should take some time to define these substructures of drama we just mentioned, terms we tend to use casually and imprecisely, adding this smallest structural element, this "atom" of drama, the beat.

ACT
SEQUENCE
SCENE
BEAT

Acts are made up of sequences; sequences are composed of scenes; and scenes take their shapes from the beats within them.

The Act

We can review quickly that the acts are the largest structures of meaning in a screenplay. In a traditional three-act screenplay, as we saw in Chapter Nine, each act has an overall function that contributes to the movement and meaning of the screenplay:

Act I—The *setup* of the conflict through to the crisis and threshold crossing

Act II—the *development* of the conflict in the Night World, where the hero's mode is put under stress and finally breaks down at the catastrophe

Act III—the *resolution* of the conflict at the climax, and the falling action where we see the dramatic and thematic consequences of the climax.

We understand that a screenplay, like a movie, is a continuous flow of dramatic action. Nevertheless, each act has an organic function in the overall dramatic curve that is not merely arbitrary. Defining the acts clearly as we structure and write our screenplay allows us to articulate the dramatic energy more powerfully when it gets down to writing the individual scenes. Because each act has an overall function to fulfill, it must be shaped to perform its function. As we write, there is an organic shape that emerges. We want to foster a cooperation between our story sense and our market sense. We must trust our creative intuition to let the innate shape of the story we have to tell come through in the early stages of writing. Starting with the most defined and dramatically charged events—the catalyst, Threshold Crisis, Core Crisis, catastrophe, and climax—we begin to shape each act. In many cases, it is from these major Story Steps that we pick up the dominant feeling-tone and central action of each of the four movements of the screenplay. Then, as we rewrite and revise, we see how the exact function of each act is articulated by the Story Steps which comprise it.

The Sequence

Acts are made up of sequences. Here we must anticipate the next chapter and observe that the way the word "sequence," as commonly used, is variable and imprecise. Sequences can be thought of as the major episodes, or chapters, in the story. A sequence is a block of action that tells one part of the story. Usually it is composed of several scenes. As mentioned in an earlier chapter, each of the major plot points in a screenplay is in fact a sequence or a set of sequences that needs time to be articulated onscreen. But the word "sequence" is also used in preproduction and production to designate the scenes occurring at or around a given location where dramatic action is set: e.g., "the restaurant sequence." Sequence can be used to describe a major event or a continuous block of action—"party sequence," "chase sequence"—without defining its structural function in the screenplay.

We can see that the word "sequence" is used so loosely that it is ultimately unsatisfactory as a way to define story structure. The word itself does not tell us whether the action is part of the main plot or a subplot, whether it is playing on the outer plot level or the emotional network, whether it is a transition or a major plot event, or whether it is fulfilling any real dramatic function at all. And the term "plot point" is itself a misnomer and is more misleading to the screenwriter than it is helpful. It takes *time* for an event onscreen to unfold its meaning, which is why we have found it necessary to introduce the new concept of Story Steps. Story Steps identify not blocks of action but structures of meaning that are necessary for the story to come across to the audience. The major "plot point sequences," or Story Steps—catalyst, Threshold Crisis, Core Crisis, catastrophe, and climax—have their own complete dramatic structures. Each in itself presents a wave of dramatic movement and meaning. The key difference between these smaller curves and the overall dramatic curve is that the conflict is not resolved at the end of the sequence, but is carried over, unresolved, into the next wave of rising dramatic tension.

Thus we can look at the Threshold Crisis Story Step of a movie like *Witness* and break it down to see how that crisis expresses itself as a wave of dramatic structure. There is a catalyzing moment in the Story Step when Samuel finds the photo of McFee and realizes he is the killer. There is a crisis/threshold moment when Book naïvely tells Paul everything he has discovered. We move immediately to the catastrophe of the sequence where McFee shoots Book. Then the climax of the Story Step: as a consequence, Book has to flee the city with Rachel and Samuel. And the resolution/falling action finds us already over the threshold and now in the arena of Act II as they arrive at Rachel's farm. It requires *twelve* scenes to articulate this action:

1. The police station: Samuel identifies McFee.
2. Book arrives at Paul Schaeffer's house, greets the family. This establishes the "familial" quality of the relationship between Book and Paul.
3. Paul's den: Book tells Paul what he has discovered. The setting, a masculine space where male bonds are formed and male secrets are shared, is significant here. Paul suggests that they keep the investigation secret and asks where Samuel is hidden.
4. Book returns home, is shot by McFee in the garage of his building.
5. Book, badly wounded, rushes to his sister Elaine's to rescue Rachel and Samuel and get them out of danger.
6. Driving Elaine's car, they flee the city. We see that Book is out of control, betrayed, and that the rock his life has been founded upon (his mode) has been shattered.
7. Book stops at a phone booth and calls his partner Carter (there is a cross-cut scene of Carter awakened in the middle of the night): they are in danger and must hide the paperwork from Samuel's testimony.
8. Carter goes to the police station, removes the documents, and leaves.
9. Early morning: Paul, McFee, and Fergie arrive at Elaine's. They find Book's car in the garage and evidence of blood. McFee gloats: "I knew I hit him!"
10. Elaine's: Paul goes to the door and questions Elaine, insinuating that Book may have committed a crime.
11. Book, Rachel, and Samuel arrive at the Lapp farm in Lancaster County. Samuel greets Eli while Rachel offers Book coffee. Book says he cannot stay and drives off. But he loses control of the car and crashes into the birdhouse. Rachel and Samuel run to the scene, see the loss of blood. Book warns them not to contact a doctor or hospital—their lives depend on it.

12. Minutes later, Eli has hitched up the wagon and pulls up next to the car. Book is weak and pale from loss of blood. As the others transfer Book to the wagon, he passes out. *Cut to black*.

Beginning with Samuel, each character commits actions that ripple out through the world of the story. A tightly braided rope of cause and effect leads us from point to point through the sequence, articulating its meaning on all of the levels of the Story Molecule. The story energy moves from the outer plot to the primary relationship of John and Rachel to Book's own inner conflict: his old mode doesn't work anymore. Now, as we cross over into Act II, Book is in the Night World. Place and time define each scene, but how many sequences do they comprise? This can vary depending on how we choose to define the action. We could argue that these twelve scenes together make up one sequence, the "crisis sequence." This one sequence would then be equivalent to what we mean by the Crisis Story Step (to be defined in the next chapter), which has a specific place as a vertebra in the spine of the story. But some might argue that the opening action at the police station is a separate sequence, likewise the nighttime action around the shooting of Book and the flight from the city, and likewise the "farm sequence" the next morning. There is in fact no standard, industry-wide definition of "sequence." Yet whether seen as one sequence or more, the narrative *functions* that make up the Crisis Story Step, and which must be present in it in order for it to work in the spine of the story, *can* be clearly identified.

It takes time and a number of events for an important sequence to unfold. Sequences in their turn are made up of, and articulated by, scenes. It is possible to have a sequence that is played all in one scene, but normally a sequence is made up of a number of scenes. There is no set number of scenes that is "right" for a sequence. That is entirely up to the rhythm of your storytelling. In general, movies with many sequences and numerous scene changes within sequences feel very active for the viewer. This may be right for an action movie. But if there is not also a throughline strong enough to unify the action, it may merely feel "busy." *Terminator 2*, as a counterexample, is structured around a smaller number of sequences, each of which carry more weight and are fully developed in terms of their action potential.

The Sixteen Story Steps, those necessary vertebrae that must be in the spine of the story, are closely associated with sequences. But the Story Steps are not identical to sequences themselves. Not all sequences fill a major plot point function. Some sequences are minor, though they are still necessary to tell the story. They may shade in the emotional network, show us the primary relationship, or take us into the inner world of the character. A small sequence may be used simply as a transition between acts. This is why we speak about sequences very loosely: the "party sequence" or the "restaurant sequence," for example. Especially once we move to the shooting script and organize the shooting schedule, the word "sequence" tends to become associated with the action taking place at a given location, organized into interior and exterior scenes that cover the action. Dramatically speaking however, the action at that setting may make up only a portion of the larger movement of a Crisis or Catastrophe Story Step. It is important for us as writers, especially when we move past the first screenplay draft into revisions, to question the function each sequence has in the screenplay. A sequence is a major dramatic episode, a link in the telling of a story. Are we using this sequence primarily to construct the outer plot throughline? Do we need it to radiate from the main throughline into a subplot? Is it a flashback, flash-forward, or dream sequence? The story step is the essential key around which the action at this specific point in the story needs to be organized. The requirements of the story step will suggest how we may tie the action of a sequence back into the fabric of the narrative in powerful and authentic ways.

The Scene

The word "scene" at first appears to be more precise than sequence. From the screenwriter's point of view, we define a scene as the action happening in one place over one continuous period of time. If we have action happening outside a theater and then the characters move into the theater where something else happens, these are two separate scenes because they take place in two separate spaces. If there is a time-gap, even of only minutes, again there are two scenes. The scene is dramatic unity: one space and one continuous time. And fundamentally, it's that simple. But in practice there are three sets of definitions for scenes—or, to put it another way, there are three sets of scenes to a movie. John Sayles has remarked that a movie is made three times: when it is written, when it is shot, and when it is edited. Correspondingly, the screenwriter, the director, and the editor interpret the same dramatic material differently. The point of attack and the point of exit for the scene normally undergo changes as the movie evolves. But the common goal of writer, director, and editor is always to shape the scene into something dramatically potent. Each is, in his or her own way, a miner, digging into the scene to reveal layers of character and conflict; each is working to get to the heart of it.

The scene is where we find that basic Aristotelian dramatic unity, unity of place and unity of time, where we can see the cause-and-effect interconnectedness of human motives and actions demonstrated most clearly. But what exactly do we mean by space and time? In movies, space and time are variable: the characters are busy moving from place to place, and the camera may also be moving. The camera might follow the characters right through the doors of the theater or, as in the famous opening of Orson Welles's *A Touch of Evil*, across a border from one country to another in one continuous shot. How then do we define the scene's unity of place? A scene may also include a character's flashback memory or fantasy, embracing more than one "time." So on one hand we as writers must have a fluid and flexible conception of what the scene can be, while because of this, on the other hand, we need to be more focused on the unity of dramatic action taking place within the space/time flow of a scene.

In today's filmmaking, the relationship between scenes and their dramatic content has become more and more varied, fragmented, and complex. The old theatrical tradition would say that there is one major dramatic point to be made in each scene, which gives the scene its reason for being. The action and conflict in the scene develop to this point, and when the point is reached, the scene is over. In the theater this makes sense because each scene change involves an interruption for the audience. But in movies the scene change is instantaneous and the audience is conditioned to take it in effortlessly, even subliminally, as part of the flow. Thus, a single dramatic point can easily be carried over a series of quick, fragmentary scenes, like a conversation we only hear bits and pieces of. How this congruence or *dis*-congruence of scene structure and dramatic content is handled has a lot to do with the tastes and attitudes of the writer, director, and editor. Some directors are more dramatists (to whom the essence of drama is performance) while others are more cinéastes (to whom the essence of movies is montage—putting images together). This is a spectrum: is dramatic meaning found *within* or *between* scenes/images? Do you get to the point of a scene by conjunction, adding the dramatic beats one after the other, like evidence in a legal argument, until a conclusion is reached? Or do you prefer disjunction: colliding meanings together incongruously from shot to shot and scene to scene, forcing the audience to create a dramatic unity out of the pieces? Think of the stunning, frantic opening of the Mexican film *Amores Perros*. The writer or director who is more of a dramatist will tend to create scenes where the wave of tension and release coincides with the structure of the scene. These movies tend to feel more "classic." At the other end of the spectrum, the writer/director who is more of a cinéaste will tend to create scenes where much is left hanging, where the scenes themselves are fragmentary, and the meaning of the sequence is completed through the montage/editing.

I refer to these scenes as fragmentary because, while they show us events happening at one place and time, it may be an incomplete dramatic action. The scene in itself may not have a complete dramatic arc. This creates a more complex syncopation between meaning and structure. One small scene may provide a catalyzing moment of a Story Step or major plot turn. Then we cut, and in another quick scene we get a crisis moment within the same dramatic development, and so on. Such scenes may be quite brief, and often go along with cross-cutting (cutting between two separate actions happening simultaneously), jump-cutting, or fast-paced or truncated visual styles. There is indeed a dramatic development taking place, but it has been decomposed or deconstructed into "bits." In this case, we have to think of the dramatic entity as being stretched over several cinematic scenes.

In Waldo Salt's *Midnight Cowboy*, for example, Ratso Rizzo (played by Dustin Hoffman) sets up his con on Joe Buck, telling Joe that he can introduce him to an expert "handler." Joe Buck assumes this will be for his business as a stud. The setup of the con and Joe Buck naïvely swallowing it together constitute one arc of dramatic action/reaction culminating in Joe's encounter with this "handler." This arc of tension and release could have been staged in one scene, up to the point where Ratso takes Joe to the handler and asks for a commission. The single scene could have been played on the street or in a café, but the single-scene approach would have been rather static. Such a one-scene treatment would have made good theater, but bad cinema. Instead, Ratso's pitch is begun on the sidewalk, is interrupted frequently, and finishes in a bar. The interruptions and the jump-cutting style help to build anticipation and also bring an edgy urban pace to the story. Pace and immediacy of tone are most often the determinants behind the choice to break an arc of dramatic action into fragmentary scenes. With the increasing influence of MTV-style fast-cutting, the fragmentation of scenes has become even more radical, to the extent that dramatic meaning may become diffused into the kind of kinetic impressionism that seems to dominate movies like *Amores Perros*, *Syriana*, *21 Grams*, and *Babel*.

In fact, it's possible to play with changing and shifting the scenes and the dramatic content within the scenes almost endlessly. For example, many screenwriters like to work with scene cards, 3" x 5" cards with a brief summary of the scene written on them. The cards can then be laid out on a table or on a big paste-up board. (There is now also software that imitates the use of scene cards.) By rearranging the cards, the order of the scenes can be manipulated to try different effects or bring out unseen possibilities. On the positive side, this process can give the screenwriter a sense of power and control while opening up the story, but on the downside, it becomes easy for a writer to start to second-guess herself and completely lose focus and confidence in the writing itself. Shifting scenes around can become a form of escapism for screenwriters: thinking *about* rather than going deeper. Then the order of the scenes can begin to feel arbitrary. When the scene order comes to feel arbitrary or relative, that is a symptom that we are out of rapport with the story. This is one of the pitfalls of the screenwriter's journey, a kind of mythic writer's labyrinth.

On a pragmatic level, finding the way out of the labyrinth usually means for the writer to go back to the basics, the Need versus Mode and Story Molecule models, to refocus on where the main character's conflict is at this point in the story. This conflict is moved forward by each Story Step; the Story Steps govern the organization of the action. It is also important for the screenwriter to be clear about the idiom of the story he or she is telling, as well as genre codes that may impact the style possibilities of the storytelling. On a deeper level of the screenwriter's journey, the labyrinth is a kind of test of whether we have allowed ourselves to get inflated with the sense of infinite possibility the movies seem to offer. Finding the way out requires the writer to remain focused on his intentions and goals for the screenplay, to keep a cool head, and not let himself be abducted by distracting fantasies. We shall go deeper into this in Chapter Twelve.

To summarize, the scene is the pivot between the instantaneous micro-actions of the characters—a word, a glance, a shrug, a grimace, a choice from a menu, the lighting of a cigarette—and the larger structures of dramatic meaning. The scene is where, in the most immediate sense, each character's desire is heated in the crucible of conflict.

The Beat

The beat is the smallest, atomic unit of dramatic action. It contains the essence of drama. It is a specific, concrete action within a scene driven by a specific motivation. As the name implies, the beat gives pulse and rhythm to the scene, and ultimately to the entire screenplay. It is the drumbeat, the heartbeat, the syncopation. A beat can be defined as follows:

Beat = Want + Action

As the above indicates, a beat is a want plus an action. I want something and I act to get it, right now, in the immediate present of this scene.

- I want to know who killed my partner, so I search through his papers for clues.
- I see a cute woman across the room at a party, so I pick up my plate of celery hors d'oeuvres and go closer.
- I want to impress my new boss, so I come to work early.
- I don't want to jeopardize my divorce settlement, so I keep my affair under wraps.
- I'm angry at my friend so I'm really going to whip his ass in our weekly squash game.

All dramatic potential comes from two characters with conflicting beats. That is, two characters whose wants are contradictory, who are both willing to act to get what they want, and who cannot both succeed.

Actors know all about beats. An actor will commonly say to their director, "What am I doing here? What's my *beat*?" An actor playing even a secondary character sees the scene through the eyes of that character; he too needs a clear beat to play. Say we were to drop in on the set of a movie in production and interview the young actor dressed in the hotel bellboy's outfit. "Excuse me, but what's this story about?"

> Well, I'm working at this hotel, see. But it's just so I can put myself through acting school. Right now I'm pissed off. I shoulda been off work fifteen minutes ago, but I've gotta take an order of champagne and duck pâté to some rich farts

in Room 508. Then I can punch out and tear off this sick uniform. I got another job across town, as a DJ. Way cooler than this.

The actor has to see the scene through his own character's beat or he has nothing to "play" with. The bellboy has his own want in the immediate context of the scene, and an action that grows out of it. It may simply be to get his job done and collect his paycheck. Behind that he has other wants, other desires. These may surface in the scene through how he does his job: his attitude. Recall that we look to a character's attitudes and actions to reveal her mode. If the screenwriter hasn't written the character a beat that includes both a want and an action—what I want *right now*, and what I will do to get it *right now*—then the actor has to invent it from scratch. Yet it is surprising how many screenwriters lack both the concepts and vocabulary to work with beats.

Part of the problem is that "want" and "action," like "sequence" and "scene," are words we think we know the meaning of, but which we in fact use in imprecise, ad hoc ways. Action, in the dramatic context, is not simply what the characters *do*; action is the vehicle for revealing character. Unlike novels and other forms of narrative literature, in movies we cannot go inside the head of the main character to reveal who she is independently from what she does. Unlike theater, which communicates primarily through words and only secondarily through nonverbal gestures, movies are driven by physical character actions. In movies, we think of dialogue as another form of action: verbal action. As action, one character uses words where another might use a gun and a third might use a kiss: to get something he wants. *Action*, in the dramatic context, is specifically this: *what I do to get what I want, to achieve a goal or objective*. Of course, there are degrees and forms of wants. We have spoken about the main character's throughline want, or *desire line*. It is motivated by her plot goal, which in turn grows out of her Call to Adventure. All of this is connected to her mode. Then there are more obscure wants, whose sources may be in the unconscious and may be connected to the unconscious need. Human beings have both conscious and unconscious motives, and there are many shades of semiconsciousness in between. The *character* may act unconsciously, but we, the authors, need to know even what our character keeps hidden from herself.

It is the beats, the specific individual actions a character takes to get what she consciously or unconsciously wants, that lead the character into dramatic conflict and shape the direction the drama takes in the scene.

Action Is Not Activity

Beat = Want + Action

The beat, the smallest unit of dramatic tension and release, is defined as a want plus an action. In turn, the beat helps define what we mean by *action*, specifically dramatic action. Action means what we do to get what we want. As writers, we want to distinguish *action* from *activity*. *Activity* is nonbeat behavior that is not driven by a character's want. It is not directed toward a goal or on a dramatic throughline. Activity thus includes all the nondramatic business or shtick that the characters are performing in a scene: they are having breakfast, playing golf, driving in a car, piloting an intergalactic probe through outer space. Activity is dramatically passive, neutral behavior that may have an expositional value but is not integral to the process of dramatic conflict. A certain amount of activity is necessary and inevitable in a screenplay. It is used to tell us about a location, to establish the authenticity of time and place, and to reveal character. But as activity is not driven by a dramatic want, there is always the potential that activity will take us away from the dramatic throughline by distracting us. In that case, unnecessary activity harms a screenplay.

This is a question of balance. The way nondramatic activity is used will vary greatly depending on the idiom and genre of the story. If a character's behavior is too narrowly defined by his plot goal, the character will lack dimension and realism and will fail to draw our empathy and identification. This is common with one-dimensional villains, but will happen whenever the writer has not gotten sufficiently into a character. At the opposite extreme, characters with too much activity behavior will come off as unfocused, frivolous, and dramatically inconsequential. Here is one key area where a screenplay differs greatly from the narrative fiction of a novel. There is not the time in a screenplay, and it is not the purpose of the screenplay, to include the wealth of passive detail that makes the world of a novel real for the reader. In addition, the narrative rhythm of novels is completely different. When a screenwriter identifies too much with a character or the character's milieu, or tries too hard to *make* the characters quirky or endearing, the result is usually too much nonthroughline activity. By distracting us from the character's dramatic motives and diffusing the character's focus and intensity, the screenwriter can unwittingly hurt the character—and the screenplay.

Dramatic characters are constructed to serve the drama. So the general rule is to *reduce* the amount of nondramatic activity in a scene and to concentrate on the dramatic action. As noted, this dictum is relative to the genre, idiom, and style of the film. A heavily plot-driven action movie like *Die Hard* leaves much less room for character-shading activity than a slower, character-driven drama or a loosely episodic milieu-comedy. In these latter types of storytelling, part of the pleasure of the movie is in entering the characters' world and living their daily lives with them. Realism as an idiom requires a different approach to character construction than a broader romanticism. In realism, where the characters ask to be taken as individuals rather than as types or icons, there is typically more shading required to exactly place the character within what we might imagine as a real world. In romanticism, on the other hand, the whole effort of characterization goes in another direction, that of heightening the impact of the character according to genre and plot requirements. In the course of this, some features of the character are emphasized while much nonplot character detail is streamlined.

There are two ways to reduce the activity in a scene: eliminate it or turn the activity into action. Eliminating activity usually means simply cutting it out, cutting it out of the script so that it doesn't have to be cut out of the edit later. Virtually every screenplay has too much expositional detail in the early drafts. Often we put extra description in the first draft because we are trying to make the scene visible to ourselves. Typically we are blind to these excesses as we write, and, like all creators, we become attached to our creation. Only later, when we go back to proof the draft, do we realize the scene is full of passive activity.

Let us take an absurdly broad example of unnecessary activity in scene exposition. Say we enter a scene on a businessman getting ready to leave his home for work. We come in on the character adjusting his tie, giving himself one last "power look" in the mirror, grabbing his briefcase, and heading to the door. Then next shot picks him up as he comes out the front door and double-locks it. He takes the newspaper from the step as he walks to his BMW parked in the driveway. The car makes a cheerful chirp as he presses the remote to unlock the door. We see him sit down, buckle his seatbelt, turn on the ignition, check the rearview mirror, and pull away from the curb. If I see a sequence like this in a movie, my audience subtext runs along the lines of: "If that damn BMW doesn't explode I'm gonna be mad—why am I watching all this?" As an audience, we expect something to *happen*. Unless we suspect the car is wired with a bomb, this is dead time on the screen. It seems like this should be an obvious example, but I have seen such scenes in countless screenplays. Overwriting the early drafts is all part of the process. Yet the same criticism is also true of some of those character moments that a writer inserts to make the character "lovable," but which are not on a beat or do not significantly reveal the character's mode. We may need to sacrifice these moments as well for the sake of the script.

The other way to work with activity is to turn it into action. This means finding a beat, a *want plus an action*, within the activity—or *imposing* a beat on the activity. Looking for the beat in "innocent" activity calls upon our insightful understanding of human nature, of unconscious as well as deliberate human motives. Look into the activity until you find where it resonates psychologically. Where does it carry subtext for you? That is to say, where are you curious and forced to ask interior questions or make interior comments about what's going on? Why does the character act like this? Why does this behavior surface exactly now, in the present context? Here, when we want to look into our characters and really concentrate the dramatic power of our scenes, the Need versus Mode model is most helpful. Identifying a character's mode lets us look both at the character's conscious beat action and at unconscious impulses pushing for expression.

Text and Subtext

We are confronted with the fact that our characters have very different levels of want that all contribute to their behavior, and this takes us immediately into the important subject of dramatic text and subtext. Subtext is the voice of our intuition, which, led by subtle cues in the movie, is several steps ahead of our conscious awareness. Subtext is what we don't know—*yet*. Or, more precisely, it is what we know but are not yet *aware* of knowing. As screenwriters, we are orchestrating both the text and the subtext for the audience. But, again, our understanding of the text and subtext evolves as we work on the screenplay.

Very simply, we could define the text as what the characters say in the scene. The subtext is what the characters do *not* say, but which is either implied indirectly by the characters or is communicated to us in the audience by the energy level of the scene, the chemistry between the characters. In fact, there are two complementary aspects to subtext and we must address both of them. We refer to these two aspects as the *character's subtext* and the *audience's subtext*. Let's look at the audience's subtext first. We know that when we are sitting in the movie theater our bodies and our psyches are constantly responding to what is happening on the screen. There is a stream of questions and comments that we direct toward the screen, just as though we were having a conversation with the movie. These questions and comments are mostly subliminal, that is, we are only rarely aware of them. But sometimes we catch ourselves almost speaking out loud:

- Look out, that guy's crooked!
- How did they get out of there alive?
- When is he going to kiss her already?
- Oh no, not him! He's completely wrong for her!
- Wait, aren't they going the wrong way?

In some theaters people do in fact talk back to the screen. Here we have the cute babysitter heading to the bedroom to get a sweater out of the closet. We've got a bad feeling about it, we just *know* the slasher maniac is hiding in there. The tension is unbearable. Then someone near us shouts out, "Don't go in there!"

This is a variation of what we call "speaking the subtext." When the audience does it, it is a way of dispelling an overwhelming level of tension. But those comments we hear are only the tip of the iceberg. This inner conversation is going on all the time, below the threshold of our awareness. Really, when you think about it, the subtext is just as important for the audience as the text of what overtly happens on the screen. It is the subtext that makes viewing a movie an active experience. Take that away, and you take away the audience's active participation. The audience would be reduced to the position of dogs in a Pavlovian experiment, salivating every time the bell rings. Fortunately, it is impossible to create a movie without subtext for the audience because if the audience doesn't find a subtext, they will literally make one up. They will project meaning into what they see.

How else could an audience sit through Michael Snow's *Wavelength* and other experimental works? Giving us only minimal cues, this movie nevertheless plays with our expectation that something *must* happen. Perhaps the deepest level of audience subtext, buried very deep indeed, is the Hero's Journey itself. Behind the Hero's Journey are the archetypes in the unconscious, which may become activated by the dramatic material. We may never be aware of this level of subtext, yet we must assume some potential for the unconscious to be activated.

The audience's subtext is always there. But does it come from the movie, the audience, or from somewhere in between? Clearly, it takes the form of a relationship. The audience behaves *as though* the movie were alive and responding back to them. So we have the responsibility to orchestrate that subtext as well, even though we cannot be sure how the audience is going to respond. It turns out that knowing when to keep something in the subtext is just as important to good screenwriting as knowing when to reveal it. What is present in the subtext of the scene has a different impact on the audience than what is made explicit. The subtext speaks directly to the subconscious, bypassing the audience's conscious filters. It creates a subliminal dream-level to the movie that has a peculiarly powerful effect on the audience. Therefore, we want to plan very carefully when we choose to bring something important out of the subtext into the text of the scene. There is an inevitable de-potentiation that occurs whenever we drag a secret into the light of day.

Interlocking with the audience's subtext are the characters' subtexts. Character subtext is the undercurrent of communication between the characters in the scene. It exists as an unspoken mood, tension, or chemistry between them. We can distinguish two levels of character subtext. The first includes what a character is conscious of but cannot—or chooses not to—express to another character. Very often this is connected to the plotline, as in the obvious cases where the lover doesn't want to tell her partner that she has been unfaithful, or where the detective has to question a suspect we know is lying. The subtext allows us to give the audience subliminal information which they then piece together later. When John Book tells Paul he has found the identity of one of the killers, the fact that Paul himself is the leader of the killers stays in the subtext.

But then there is a second level of character subtext: what the character herself is honestly unconscious of, but which is nevertheless somehow present in her behavior. It is this second level of subtext that connects the audience to the hero's unconscious need. As we have noted, we sometimes read this subtext through a kind of negative space, through what is conspicuously *missing* in the character. It is because we, the audience, also read meaning into what is missing that the characters' subtexts in a scene can appear to permeate or hover over the atmosphere of the scene, semi-independently of the characters themselves. The audience's subtext includes the audience's subliminal reading of the characters' subtexts, along with symbols, motifs, and other kinds of cues that are part of the total experience of a movie.

Our characters act from both conscious and unconscious motivations and impulses, like we do ourselves. By definition they are only aware of the former. Unconscious, need-based action is *unintentional*. Intentional, plot goal-oriented action flows from the character's mode, plot goal, and desire line. This conscious level of motive forms the text of the scene, what it appears to be about on the surface. George, in Act I of *The Piano*, casually offers Stewart eighty acres of land for the piano that was left on the beach. That is the text of the exchange of dialogue between the two men. And it is apparently only on this text level that Stewart hears the offer, because he counters that Ada might give George piano lessons. He doesn't hear the *sub*text of George's offer.

We look for the text of the scene first of all in what we call the character's "scene beat." The scene beat is the largest throughline want the character has right now going into the scene: he wants a piece of information or evidence, sympathy, seduction, protection. What does each character *consciously* expect out of the encounter? How are the conscious wants of the characters in conflict? The scene beat is then played out through smaller beats—individual actions—leading to that objective. We expect to find the characters' conscious wants expressed through their dialogue. They will ask, state, demand, argue, or coax, depending largely on their mode. This is dialogue *on a beat*, verbal action to move the character toward what he wants in the immediate present of the dramatic context.

But as screenwriters, before we even get into the dialogue of a scene we want to ask ourselves why these characters are in the scene to begin with. What has brought them together at just this place and at just this time? When we write a scene without considering the scene beats of each character, the scene usually turns out unfocused. The characters start talking about trivial things because they don't know what else to do. We have to then go back and refine the scene by rewriting it. But much of that rewriting can be spared if we bring a sharp focus to the scene before writing it, during the treatment or scene outline phase of story development, by defining the scene beats of each character. One way to go deeper into this aspect between drafts is to visualize: where was each character *just before they entered the scene*? Where are they coming from, what happened there, and what mood are they in right now as a result? And also, what is significant about the setting of the present scene? These are not academic questions in any way. This has to do with the real day-to-day craft of writing. It turns out, and countless writers can testify to this, that if we choose the wrong setting for a scene, the characters simply will not speak. During the writing, the scene will feel flat, constrained, or contrived. Ultimately this goes back to lack of attention to the characters' scene beats, which provide the raison d'être for the scene.

Where do we look for the subtext in a scene? In the character's unconscious or unintended behavior, out at the edges. Mode-based action toward a goal is on the beat. Unintended, unconscious, need-based action can come into a scene through a character's slips and mistakes, through what he *doesn't* say, and, always, through his body language. We also look for subtext in *dissonance*:

incongruities between what a character says and the tone of her voice, between what she says and what she does, between what she does and how she seems to feel about it. The subtext comes into the scene by slipping in *under the beat*, between the cracks, through the back door.

Action: Conscious (Mode) →	Text →	Dialogue Beat Action
Unconscious (Need) →	Subtext →	Body Language Dissonance

It would be too much micromanagement on the part of the screenwriter to try and spell all this out on the page. You have to trust the actor to come to the part and discover the subtext in his or her own way. You have to trust the director, cinematographer, gaffer, and everyone else on the production team to bring the right mood to the scene that will enable the audience to pick up your subtext. That is their work. If you have set up the need/mode conflict clearly and let that tension propel the character from within, and if you give the character a clear beat coming into the scene, then you can trust the actor to find it. If not, the actor may have to invent his own subtext.

The Need Is the Throughline Subtext

The most important subtext is the main character's unconscious universal need, the initiation toward which his journey is moving. This is naturally in the subtext because the main character is unconscious of it. Action coming out of a character's unconscious need cannot be the text of the scene for the very reason that it is unconscious. Loretta Castorini in *Moonstruck* is completely unaware of her unconscious motivations, but they are nonetheless present. Why, after all, did she ask for that glass of whiskey in Ronnie's apartment? The universal need hovers below the surface of the scene as a mood or tension, but especially in the splits we perceive between what a character does and how she seems to feel about it. Love stories always contain this unconscious behavior. We see the characters respond to each other viscerally, we see all the signs of attraction, but the characters appear to be oblivious. They may be quarreling all the way through Act I, all the way through the movie, but we can feel their chemistry.

This truly unconscious behavior makes up the other important part of the subtext of the scene. As the common example of the lovers suggests, the unconscious level of the character's need-based action and the subtext it generates occupies a somewhat different place in the storytelling than does the subtext of what a character is deliberately holding back. We noticed that when a character deliberately holds something back, this is usually functioning on the outer plot level, to build suspense or create a twist by concealing a character's motives from another character. The genuinely unconscious level of character subtext behavior connects more to relationships, especially the primary relationship. The primary relationship is the most emotionally charged, carries the greatest stakes, and is the relationship that propels the main character toward inner change. So it is natural that this relationship pushes the main character's buttons and brings out unconscious or involuntary behavior.

Can the main character's unconscious behavior be used to advance the plot? Absolutely it can. In fact, it must. We return to the fundamental idea that the hero cannot resolve the dramatic conflict unless he changes the way he sees things. In a character-driven story, this means the hero discovering and integrating this need. In a genre-driven story like a thriller, it may mean that the hero must discover the blind spot that either prevents him from seeing the important clue or that keeps him hooked in some symbiotic way to the antagonist. Therefore, we must see how what the character does not know impacts on him negatively.

To summarize: the universal need is the *throughline* subtext. In a character-driven story, the outer plot goal may be made explicit, but in terms of energy and subtextual audience engagement, the greater energy is attached to the unconscious need. The unconscious need, as we have said, is the hidden force driving the character into dramatic conflict, and the eventual uncovering of that subtextual force in the character is key to the resolution of the outer drama. We want to keep the need actively in the subtext and not reveal it too soon. That would spoil its effect. If you have worked out the need/mode conflict in the character during development, then from the moment in Act I that you nail that character's mode, the throughline subtext is already established, as the audience senses intuitively what is missing in the character's life.

Beats, Conflict, and Character Orchestration

As we have established, beat is a want plus an action. Drama happens when we bring together two (or more) characters with opposing beats, that is, two characters whose wants are in conflict *right now*, and who are both willing to act to get what they want. All the dramatic potential in the scene starts from this point.

/ Opposing beats

This graphic is a simple way of visualizing the situation. Character A wants one thing, which is contradicted by the want of Character B. The difference between the wants may be small—I'm determined to drag you out with me for pizza, but Italian food gives you hives. Or it can be great—the bad Terminator in *Terminator 2* wants to kill John, while the good Terminator wants to protect him. It is up to the writer to know the difference between the two characters' wants and the stakes involved for each, as well as the energy charge of that difference. These tell us the dramatic potential of the scene. Setting up the characters' opposing beats clearly as we go into the scene is the key to actualizing the dramatic potential. But in addition, these opposing beats are also the key to effective character orchestration. Opposing beats—wants which are in conflict and which lead to action—make each character's position stand out clearly and distinctively. We see the difference between what each character wants, and also the difference between what each character is willing to do to get what they want: their tools, weapons, tactics, limitations, blind spots. Behind each character's actions and attitudes, we can feel the deeper values that are in conflict.

As you begin each new scene, ask yourself what the difference is between your two characters, both in terms of their goal—right now, in this scene—and also in their way of going about it. Both the goal and the means are expressive of the character's mode. There is an important scene in Act II of *American Beauty* where Lester acts out against Carolyn, hurling a plate of asparagus against the wall. Both Carolyn and Janie are shocked into silence as the scene ends. The next scene picks up Janie in her room. Carolyn is knocking on the door. Now, the fact that they have both just been subjected to Lester's new assertive temper does not mean they are in the same place. Janie responds to the knock with a strong "Go away!" What does Carolyn want at this moment? What is her beat? What is Janie's beat? How do we get from Carolyn wanting to apologize for Lester's behavior to her slapping Janie? What motivates each step for each character? One thing you should notice is that while their opening beats immediately bring them into conflict, the terms of the conflict keep shifting as they react in the immediate present to each other.

Using opposing beats to orchestrate the protagonist and the antagonist, or the protagonist and the primary relationship, is pretty common knowledge. The key thing, however, is that this should be applied to *all* characters and *all* scenes. At every moment in the story we should be able to feel what the difference is between the characters. But we want to avoid being dogmatic about the other extreme as well. Some producers tell their writers that they want to see conflict immediately when the scene opens. As a dogmatic rule, this is a mistake. The writers end up creating spurious, insignificant, and distracting conflicts, and characters who come off as thoughtlessly mean and passive-aggressive. The point is not to see *conflict* the moment we come into a scene, but to see *difference*. The difference will generate conflict, but the trajectory the conflict takes should grow naturally out of the dramatic situation. Again, we want to remember the power of what is left in the subtext.

Wants in conflict and contrasting styles of action, growing out of each character's mode—how each character has adapted to what life has presented to him—are the common dramatic tools of character orchestration. But movies are first of all a visual medium, and therefore we also want to orchestrate the characters visually so that the moment we come into the scene, before the characters have said a word, we already *see* and *feel* the difference between them. The visual setup for the opposing beats includes everything you know about the characters—the way they dress, differences in age, size, sex, race, social and economic backgrounds, attitudes and expectations—the whole character biography, compressed into a sense of where the character is right at this moment. It especially includes the state of tension each character carries into this scene from what just happened in the scene immediately preceding. A very good exercise to follow when revising a screenplay draft is to ask some focusing questions at the beginning of each scene.

- Where was the character immediately before this scene opens? (Here we refer to the movie's "real time," not to the previous scene. Hours or days may have passed since the previous scene with this character, but we want to know where she was five minutes ago.)
- What is each character's mood at this moment? How does this color her present beat?
- How does the character feel at the end of the present scene? How has the character changed? How does the audience see this change?

How broadly the visual orchestration is drawn, based on biographical and immediate dynamic differences, should fit how broadly characters themselves are drawn. This is a function of the idiom and the genre of the storytelling. Are the characters to be taken as real people, romantic icons, or completely synthetic constructs? American movies are generally very aware of the need for visual character orchestration. Come in on any scene between Jack Walsh and the Duke in *Midnight Run*, and you can instantly feel the many differences between them. They are so well orchestrated visually that, without words, we can sense the dramatic potential between them: Jack's hunted, nervous gestures and body language is in sharp contrast with the Duke's stoic firmness and humor. The exaggeration and incongruity of their appearances makes us expect something comic to happen. If anything, movies today are perhaps hyperaware of, and driven by, a need to instantly telegraph the visual orchestration to the audience. It is as though there is an unstated anxiety that if you fail to grab the audience with that first shot, you will never engage them. This can lead to characters that are overly quirky, overly cute, overly demonic, and somewhat dehumanized. A character too broadly drawn cannot be subtly shaded. Beyond the requirements of idiom and genre, the visual orchestration must be grounded in the characters' modes first of all, not genre caricatures.

For the sake of illustration, let us look at the opposite extreme: a scene that lacks adequate visual orchestration. This illustration is hypothetical, but refers to a very real problem. Let's say we come into a theater, settle in with our popcorn, put up with a half-dozen trailers, and now the feature movie begins with a panoramic aerial shot of lower Manhattan, Wall Street. The camera swoops down to street level. It's lunchtime and the streets are crowded. Ahead is the window of a chic restaurant that's popular with the brokers. We pass magically through the window, past a number of groups animatedly talking and eating, to a table where a couple of young stock brokers have just ordered lunch. They both have that scrubbed "fresh out of Wharton" look. They have the same sort of Armani suit, the latest style ties. They both have their hair spiked up a little, to let everybody know that they may be brokers—but they *party*. Now they've both ordered martinis because it's an old drink that is hip again, a drink that tells people: "I make my own rules." And they have ordered the same Cozumel shrimp salad with ceviche sauce. Their grins tell us it was a good morning on the Exchange.

If you are the writer, you have really put yourself in a hole by setting up a scene like this, haven't you? Now you have a lot of work to do to show us the *difference* between these two characters, because with this setup you have already prejudiced us in the other direction. And how are we going to be shown this difference? The main tool left at your disposal now is dialogue. Yes, there is always body language, though now the audience must see past the clothing to get at it, and if the ties are too bright that will take some effort. Of course, you might want to make the point that men who dress the same and apparently belong to the same milieu cannot be judged by appearance; their souls may be very different, as in *In the Company of Men*. But it is worth noting that this setup, by its very nature, tends to commit you as a writer to subtler shadings and more lengthy exposition. Thus it is already predicating something about the pace and later dramatic development of the scene.

The dramatic function of visual orchestration is to give us a quick way into the characters, to help us access them. This could also be put the other way around: to give the characters a quick way into *us*. The visual orchestration is there to support the dramatic beats that will develop and express the conflict in the scene. The opening beat of the scene acts like the catalyst of the larger screenplay. It sets a tone and a trajectory for the scene by showing us who comes into the scene with power and who does not, thus signaling a fault line or zone of conflict between them.

Building Conflict in the Scene

When you ask yourself what the difference is between two characters as they come into a new scene, one thing you'll notice is that they rarely come in with the same power or dramatic momentum. Power may take the form of urgency, the driving force of a motive, or status: social, political, or financial clout, physical brute force, sexual power, or charisma. Every character is somewhere on the power scale of the world described by the movie. Characters on the Hero's Journey typically experience themselves as losing power as they go down into the Night World. By "dramatic momentum," we mean the energy or zeal the character has *right now* to move toward a goal. We may call it a mood, but it acts as a force field. Dramatic momentum is highly colored by what has just happened. Sometimes one character's dramatic momentum is sufficient to overcome another's social power. The character in charge as the scene opens, the one with the opening beat, may actually be in control of the social situation—or she may simply have greater urgency or charge around her want at this moment. We say this character who comes into the scene with more momentum, the one more actively pursuing her want, *has the beat* in the scene. In terms of the dramatic potential of where the scene will build, this is the most important difference between the characters. One character has the beat and the other doesn't. We add this power differential to our picture of two characters with opposing beats:

- their wants are in conflict
- both will act to get what they want
- it is not possible for both to succeed
- one comes into the scene with more power

Each character comes into the scene wanting something: his major *scene beat*. But they are not blind, nor are they mechanically driven in a single direction. They are constantly reacting to each other and the evolving situation. Sometimes they are not aware of what they *really* want until something happens in the scene to shift the ground, such as a new piece of information comes to light or another facet of the other character is seen. Then we may see a character's want change in the middle of a scene. If it's a new want, it's a new beat. And catching exactly those moments when a character's want transforms itself are real opportunities for revealing the deeper layers of her underlying attitudes, feelings, and beliefs.

One character comes into the scene actively wanting something. He has the beat, and as he moves toward what he wants, this brings him into conflict with the other character. Now we want to see how the other character will respond, how she will come back to assert her want or defend her territory. If we don't see her reaction immediately, we may wonder *if* and *when* she will come back. And so we are engaged. There is tension: a dramatic question has been asked, but the answer has been suspended. Right here in the beat structure we have the entire dramatic curve. The individual actions each character takes in pursuit of their scene beat will comprise smaller beats within the scene. We expect that the other character will assert herself. She will not abandon her own want, but will try to take control in the situation. When she does turn the tables and take control, we say she *steals the beat* from the first character: she takes the momentum in the scene and controls its trajectory. She controls where the action is headed. Until the first character steals the beat back again, that is.

And so we begin a seesaw of power as the stakes rise with each beat. Finally, in what could be called the *climax* of the scene, we see which character—if any—gets what she wants.

A scene that shows how this tug of war between two characters may be played for comedy comes at the crisis/threshold crossing in *Hannah and Her Sisters*. The escalating series of beats raises the dramatic stakes in comically incongruous ways. We shall look at the entire scene as it appears in the screenplay. It would also be valuable to watch the scene to see how the staging and body language help express the beats.

Elliot has become infatuated with his wife Hannah's sister, Lee. In an earlier scene, we saw them run into each other at a bookshop. Elliot offered Lee a book of E. E. Cummings's poetry. Now he brings a rock star, Dusty, to see the artwork of Lee's lover, Frederick. It is Elliot's pretext to have some time with Lee. Elliot's text want in the scene is to help Dusty find some artwork for his living room, but what he really wants is to find out if Lee shows a spark of interest in him. The energy is in the subtext, because Elliot can't tell Lee his real reason for being there. Lee, sensing this subtext, acts out the want of keeping the situation under control. The dance of approach and avoidance between Lee and Elliot, powered by what is in the subtext, takes the form of innocuous small talk. This small talk makes for a consistent series of text beats, as they try to avoid the issue or change the subject. But the real engine of the scene is the subtext. Every time Elliot moves physically closer—and closer to his real motive, his unstated beat—Lee moves away and puts some space between them. Even Lee's sudden, out of context comments about rubber gloves and dental anesthesia make sense if we understand her want of keeping some emotional distance. These behaviors are the individual beats in the scene that lead toward a larger goal.

What results is a complex dance where the text beats (the small talk) are riding on the subtext beats (what the characters cannot tell each other). The dance is fully supported by the simple staging of the scene where, for example, in the opening of the scene Elliot and Lee are placed at opposite extremes of the frame. This creates tension and anticipation in the audience by creating graphic compositional tension in the shot. The forces keeping them apart—specifically Lee's lover Frederick, acting in the mythic role of the threshold guardian—here occupy the center of the frame. As a final note about this scene, using Elliot's inner monologue to *speak the subtext* to the audience is a specific comic device. The scene still makes perfect sense without it. This is a strategy that would only be used in comedy. Here, it exaggerates the absurdity of the situation, that both Lee and Elliot appear to be perfectly aware of the secret that they are trying so discreetly to keep under wraps. Elliot speaking the subtext in such an earnest tone adds another layer of absurdity. In addition, a further layer of audience subtext is added: we say to ourselves, "These so-sophisticated grown-ups are acting like children!" This is a running subtext of all farce comedy. Otherwise, the rule about not revealing the subtext generally holds true.

Normally, in orchestrating the characters' scene beats, not only are the wants different, but the tactics are different as well. A setup where the characters have the same weapons/tactics risks looking and sounding like a collective bargaining session. We know from countless martial arts and gladiator movies that the fight is more interesting when one character has a big mace and the other a trident. But if it is handled well, and the dialogue (as weapon of choice) is sparkling, surprising, and creative, a scene with such well-matched characters can feel as breathless as a championship tennis match or the climactic Errol Flynn–Basil Rathbone swordfight in *Robin Hood*. The beats really fly back and forth.

An outstanding example of such a verbal battle of wits comes in *Tootsie* when Michael Dorsey bursts into his agent George's office in Act I. This scene occurs as part of a large Catalyst Story Step that runs directly into the crisis/threshold crossing. Michael has just discovered that George hadn't sent him up for a part in a big production of *The Iceman Cometh*. For the first time in the movie, we see Michael galvanized into decisive action. He rushes across town to the agency, dodges past the secretary, and barges in on him.

GEORGE: Hang on. Will you wait outside? I'm talking to the Coast.

MICHAEL: This is a coast. New York is a coast too.

GEORGE: Oh, boy. Sy, are you—God—Look what you—Margaret? Get him back. I cut myself off. What is it, Michael?

MICHAEL: Terry Bishop's doing *Iceman*. You promised to send me up for that. You told me I'd get a reading for that. Aren't you my agent?

GEORGE: Stuart Pressman wants a name.

MICHAEL: Terry Bishop is a name?

GEORGE: Michael Dorsey is a name, when you want to send a steak back. Wait, wait, wait! You always do this to me. It was a rotten thing to say. Let me start again. Terry Bishop is on a soap. Millions watch him every day.

MICHAEL: That qualifies him to ruin *Iceman*? I can act circles around him. I played that part in Minneapolis.

GEORGE: If he wants a name, that's his affair. People are in this business to make money.

MICHAEL: I'm in it to make money too.

GEORGE: Really? The Harlem Theatre for the Blind? The People's Workshop at Syracuse?

MICHAEL: Wait a minute. I did nine plays up at Syracuse. I got great reviews from the critics. Not that that's why I did it.

GEORGE: God forbid you should lose your standing as a cult failure.

MICHAEL: You think I'm a failure?

GEORGE: I will not get sucked into this conversation. I will not.

MICHAEL: I sent you my roommate's play to read. It had a great part in it for me.

GEORGE: Where do you come off sending me a play for you to star in? I'm not your mother. I don't find plays for you to star in. I field offers. That's what I do.

MICHAEL: Who told you that? The agent fairy? I could be terrific in that part.

GEORGE: Nobody's going to do that play.

MICHAEL: Why?

GEORGE: It's a downer about a couple that move back to Love Canal.

MICHAEL: But that actually happened.

GEORGE: Nobody wants to watch people living next to chemical waste! They can see that in New Jersey.

MICHAEL: I don't want to argue about it. I'll raise $8000 and produce his play. Send me up for anything. I don't care. I'll do dog commercials. I'll do radio voice-overs.

GEORGE: I can't put you up for that.

MICHAEL: Why not?

GEORGE: Because no one will hire you.

MICHAEL: I bust my ass to get a part right!

GEORGE: And you bust everybody else's ass too! Who wants to argue about whether Tolstoy can walk when he's dying or walk when he's talking—?

MICHAEL: That was two years ago, and that guy's an idiot!

GEORGE: They can't all be idiots. You argue with everybody! You've got one of the worst reputations in this town. Nobody will hire you.

MICHAEL: Are you saying that nobody in New York will work with me?

GEORGE: Nobody in Hollywood will either. I can't even get you a commercial. You played a tomato, and they went over schedule because you wouldn't sit.

MICHAEL: Yes, it wasn't logical.

GEORGE: You were a tomato! A tomato doesn't have logic. It can't move!

MICHAEL: So if he can't move, how's he going to sit down? I was a stand-up tomato. A juicy, sexy, beefsteak tomato! Nobody does vegetables like me! I did vegetables off-Broadway! I did the best tomato, the best cucumber! I did an endive salad that knocked the critics on their ass!

GEORGE: I'm trying to stay calm here. You are a wonderful actor.

MICHAEL: Thank you.

GEORGE: But you're too much trouble. Get some therapy.

MICHAEL: Okay, thanks. I'm gonna raise $8000 to do Jeff's play.

GEORGE: Michael, you're not gonna raise five cents. No one will hire you.

MICHAEL: Oh, yeah?

So we see Michael come in with what he believes is a strong want; he definitely has the beat. But George is ready to match Michael's energy immediately, even go him one better. He steals the beat. Michael is not ready to be put down without a fight by this classic threshold guardian figure, and so we're off to the races.

This duel of wits sparkles and engages us, but a very different scene structure emerges when the power between the characters is *unequal*, where the characters do not appear to be well matched. Here the beat structure develops in a different way. One character coming into the scene with the power may retain the beat most of the way through the scene, so much so that we can feel the other character pushed into a corner, up against the wall. If there are real dramatic stakes in the scene, a great subtextual urgency develops around the thought: "This can't go on! When is she going to fight back?" While engaged in a movie, it is hard for us to imagine that the character will remain passive and thus become a victim. We have to imagine that sooner or later she *will* react, and the deeper she is pushed into the hole, the more violent the reaction will ultimately be. At some point her survival instinct will overcome whatever is holding her back, and she will lash out. This unequal setup does not rely on the back-and-forth "tennis match" dynamic, but on an ineluctable buildup of suspense until the dam breaks. It is thus perhaps capable of more intense dramatic effects.

At the Core Crisis of *The Talented Mr. Ripley*, Tom and Dickie have gone off together to San Remo. The subtext for each character around what this escapade means is very different. Tom is looking for an opportunity to more openly express his desire to Dickie, while Dickie wants a "nice" way of getting rid of Tom. The pressure in Tom has built up to an emotional breaking point where it can no longer be contained. This Story Step climaxes in the scene where the two have taken a small launch so that Dickie can look for a new waterfront villa. The development of the story has cleverly kept one key fact in the audience's subtext: not even once has Tom had the beat thus far in the movie! As the scene plays, it gradually dawns upon us that this nice, overly dependent young man is a walking time bomb. Dickie, of course, figures it out too late.*

Between these two extremes, the "tennis match" dynamic and the "pushed to the wall" dynamic, there are many shadings and opportunities for dramatic surprise. The establishing incident of *Moonstruck* opens with the character of Johnny apparently coming in with a strong beat. His want is to marry Loretta, and his action is to propose to her in their favorite restaurant. In reality, however, Loretta dominates the entire scene, even to the point of telling Johnny what to have for dinner. Even though Johnny tries to assert himself and take some initiative in the scene, he is never quite able to steal the beat. The moment he proposes, Loretta demands that he kneel on the floor. No sooner is he kneeling than Loretta asks where the ring is. By showing us how Loretta dominates Johnny, we confirm our

---

* The entire second movement of *The Piano* (first half of Act II), comprised of George's escalating sexual encroachment on Ada, works on this same dynamic.

sense of her mode—control—while quickly nailing their relationship. The structure of the beats, and thus of the scene, tell us on a gut level how unsuited for each other these two are (even if some might consider a control-freak woman and a mama's boy to be a perfect neurotic match). The beats fully support the dramatic function of the scene and communicate that to the audience on a rhythmic level. Looking back at the quoted scene from *Tootsie*, you'll notice that the structure of the beats suggest, without being overt, that Michael and his agent are perfect mirrors of each other, and for all their fiery tempers, they share a deep affinity.

This tells us something of great importance about beats: the beats are the *deep music* of the scene. The structure of the beats conveys an inner level of meaning to the audience. This inner level of meaning bypasses the rational mind altogether and speaks directly to the *feelings* of the audience.

Deep Music

With this in mind—that the structure of the beats forms a deep music that communicates the meaning of the scene on a nonverbal level—we can have a new appreciation of the very compressed and concentrated power movies can have to touch us. A scene with all the right beats can be elegant and mesmerizing. We could say this music speaks to us on a soul level, because the beats, like all the mechanics of the movie, normally touch us subliminally. But the elegant scene still has to contribute to the larger dramatic throughline. Therefore, we want to build the beats, and the scene's conflict, on the cutting edges of the characters: their deep need/mode conflicts, where they are on their journey in life, what is dying and what is struggling to be born in them.

A scene that finds just its right place in the overall dramatic structure, advancing the plot or revealing character, and whose beat structure makes that moment resonate on all levels of the Story Molecule, has a special charm. It represents a superior achievement in screenwriting, a place where storytelling and music become indistinguishable. Such a scene conveys simplicity and inevitability.

As an illustration for this, I could choose from any number of showy, Oscar-caliber scenes. Instead, I prefer a scene that is so simple it appears to be dramatically insignificant, in order to show how much can be done in a very small package. I believe that if you can see how the beats effortlessly take us into the core of the relationship between the characters while providing a dramatic pivot, all in a very few minutes of screen time, then you are well on your way toward understanding in both mind and body (feeling the deep music of the beats) how to write a screenplay.

The scene we are going to look at is the hot dog scene from *Witness*. The hot dog scene? You probably don't even remember it. That's alright. It's not a scene that is trying to get itself noticed. It is just quietly doing its job—but what a job it's doing! The hot dog scene comes in Act I, where it is a small bridge between Story Step #3: Forward Movement and Story Step #4: Threshold

Crisis. In the preceding Story Step, John Book has begun his investigation, towing Samuel and Rachel around town looking for suspects. The Story Step climaxes with fruitlessness and frustration as Samuel is unable to identify any suspects from a police lineup. In the present scene, the hot dog scene, Book, Samuel, and Rachel take a break for lunch. Immediately after this short bridge, they go back to the station for the first scene of the Threshold Crisis Story Step, where Samuel discovers the photo of McFee and recognizes him as the killer. So this hot dog scene comes in the falling action of the investigation sequence and sets up the discovery/crisis sequence. (It would be helpful to review this scene on video.)

This scene is a fine example of the holographic aspect of drama. Though brief, it has a complete dramatic curve, made up of individual beats. If we take some time and care with these beats, they will reveal their elegance to us. To put the scene in context, this is virtually the only place in the script where we get backstory exposition about John Book. John Book is ultimately a genre-hero. He stands before us more as an iconic sheriff figure than as an individual like ourselves. We identify him by his role and by his values. These are signs that we are working in the romantic idiom. We are never taken into Book's personal living space. We are never told about his childhood or his backstory wound. This is deliberate. So here, in the hot dog scene, we are getting some facts about John Book, getting into the deeper character dimension of his mode, his attitudes and values, and his blind spot. Yet this exposition passes effortlessly because it is riding on the much more interesting subtext created by the beats between Book and Rachel. Second, this small scene sets up the entire love story development of Act II. Without this scene, Act II of *Witness* simply would not work. It's a nice trick if you can do all this while eating hot dogs.

The scene begins with an establishing moment. We come in on a little neighborhood greasy spoon. Book and Samuel take their hot dogs to the table and join Rachel, who is already seated. Samuel removes his hat while Book puts mustard on his dog. We have simply and economically set up the scene. If we ask what John Book wants right now, the answer is simply to eat. This is his beat. The beat that opens a scene does not have to be spectacular or tricky. Think of it as making a platform to work from.

But the next thing that happens is that while Book bites into his hot dog, Rachel leads Samuel, heads bowed and eyes closed, in a silent grace. What can we imagine to be Rachel's beat here? Let us recall that from the opening of the movie, and especially since Samuel witnessed the murder, Rachel's life has been completely out of control. Rachel has wants, but she is largely unable to realize them. She wants to go on her way with Samuel to her sister's house in Baltimore. But instead, she is kept in Philadelphia against her will, lodged with someone she doesn't know, and subjected, along with her son, to a world she finds shocking and degrading. And the animus of all her troubles is John Book, who determines what she can and cannot do. In a larger sense, Rachel lost the beat in her life before the opening of the story, through the death of her husband. That is Rachel's backstory wound. But Book is the one who has the beat coming into the scene. It is Book's will that directs the trajectory of Rachel's life at the moment.

In this context, the simple act of saying grace means something different than it might have meant day after day in her own home. This pause with eyes closed, this moment of quiet, is a way of reaffirming her own values. She can't leave Philadelphia; she doesn't have the liberty of her person. But no one can stop her from praying in her own manner. Her inner life is still her own.

But this simple assertion has an unintended consequence: it makes Book uncomfortable. Book pauses, unable to swallow. He appears undecided as to whether to continue eating, join them, or at least give some gesture of respect. This is the first time in the story that we have seen doubt on Book's face, the passing shadow of anxiety. And at that moment, the power in the scene subtly shifts. Rachel has stolen the beat.

What does this hesitation on Book's part say about him? We perceive a small crack in the armor of Book's personality, but where is it, specifically? This is the economy of the storytelling in *Witness*, which in its final realization onscreen we must credit director Peter Weir, Harrison Ford, and the cinematographer as well as the writers. Book chokes on his hot dog. Why? This moment is pointing to where Book's wound is. It has something to do with family, the family bond and togetherness, maybe the way religion was handled in his family. We cannot be more specific than that, nor do we need to be. Book's mode, the social persona he has adapted to meet life, is that of a tough, in-control cop. A loner. He has to be, because his job is to investigate other cops. He has adapted a hypermasculine persona, appropriate to a dangerous man's world. A corpse he can handle without blinking an eye, but a woman praying is something else.

Rachel praying takes Book out of his comfort zone. For a moment we get a small glimpse into John Book's particular Day World and Night World. Book's Day World has body bags. His Night World has a woman praying. This very simple gesture of choking quietly on his hot dog makes Book human and three-dimensional. And now we get a small subtextual foreshadowing about where Book will go in Act II. He will go into a Night World where he will be confronted by what he is not adapted to: family, community, and femininity. This small revelation of John Book's vulnerability here comes to touch us. It establishes a deeper connection between Book and Rachel, and saves their relationship from improbability and banality.

Now, as Rachel sees Book's discomposure, she appears to take on new courage. She looks up at him brightly:

—Your sister told me about you. . . .

Rachel has taken the beat. She has a new beat, a new want leading to an action. What does Rachel want right now? This is intriguing, because Rachel's want here seems to be only semiconscious. She didn't come into the scene with this beat; she is discovering it herself as she goes along. But she sees Book's vulnerability and exploits it. And here she begins a series of needling remarks based on information she has gleaned from Book's sister.

—Your sister told me about you. . . .

Book is so surprised he can't even react. Rachel can press her beat now. Book doesn't have a family. He has to swallow that one. Elaine, the sister, says he ought to get a family of his own instead of trying to act like a father to hers—except that she thinks he's afraid of the responsibility. Rachel launches these lines as a series of little zingers, small, invisible needles she delivers with a smile that doesn't betray the slightest conscious irony. Thus it is perfectly in keeping with Rachel's character, which is to say nonviolent, sort of.

Rachel's beat—her want and her action—must both be consistent with her mode. Rachel is an Amish woman out of her element in the city, but in her element at the family table. She doesn't have some of the options for action open to John Book. Book, as we have seen, can smash a suspect up against the squad car window. His wants are big and important, involving large-scale issues of justice. He doesn't imagine, *can't* imagine, that his own motives or values could be called into question. Yet Rachel too wants justice, after her own fashion. Would it be too much to say she wants revenge? Certainly as the scene goes on and she keeps pushing, we could say she's getting back at this man who is controlling her life. Book's lack of riposte implies that it all must be true. In his heart even he has to admit it.

This rising action is shown to us in a series of reverse close-ups, where we can feel Book getting more tense with each zinger. Rachel is pushing her beat further and further, pushing Book into a corner. But we know that Book is not a passive character. We know he will react sooner or later. We know he is capable of violence. All this is bubbling in the subtext. We don't need anyone to tell us.

So we have a dramatic curve of rising tension built on these beats:

Establishing moment: They sit down to eat, pray

Catalyst: Rachel sees that Book is off-balance

Crisis: Rachel's first zinger

Rising Beats: Rachel's subsequent attacks, Book's nonreaction

This dramatic curve in the scene is rising toward a catastrophe and climax, but we do not know what they will be. When Rachel turns her attack toward Book's arrogance as a policeman, she is further raising the stakes, treading into much more sensitive territory. What will Book do? Will he have a witty comeback? Doesn't look like it. He has been caught off-guard, blind-sided, and now he is in the hole. Will he suddenly burst out, "Mind your own business, bitch!" or something like that? Maybe. We'll never know, because at this moment a third force comes into the scene.

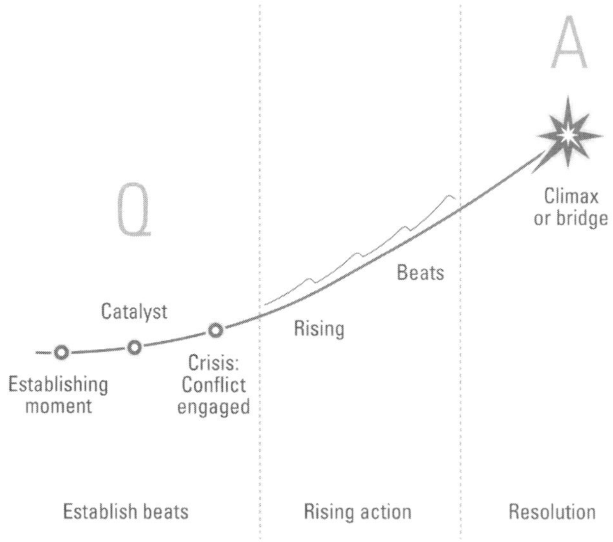

/ Scene Structure.

Samuel belches. Rachel says to him, "Good appetite!" and then turns back to Book with a smile that could only be called the magnanimity of a conqueror. Book laughs, the tension is broken by the unexpected, and the scene ends.

Right here, when Samuel burps, the scene actually uses a device from comedy. The scene becomes a comic scene. Beat structure in comedy is a bit different from that in serious drama. Comedy always begins with a serious premise ("Comedy is tragedy that's happening to the other guy," said W. C. Fields), but leads to an absurd, incongruous, or irreverent consequence. Thus the comic scene may appear to start off with the setup and development of a serious conflict. At least, the characters believe it's serious—think of Loretta! The tension rises as the beats go back and forth; you might recall the dialogue between Loretta and Ronnie in the Threshold Crisis of *Moonstruck*. The scene appears headed for a dramatic climax, but something unexpected intervenes which pops the rising tension in a comic way: Ronnie gets so mad he pushes the table over, smashing glasses and bottles, and grabs Loretta roughly. At that moment we are caught in a context that still pretends to be serious. The audience holds their breath. Loretta pushes away, shouting, "Wait a minute! Wait a minute!"—then kisses him fiercely. From Loretta, this is both unexpected and absurd, but it gives us the "Aha!" reaction. The tension is suddenly released, and we can laugh as Ronnie picks Loretta up melodramatically to take her to—"the bed!"

So, Samuel's burp here serves the same purpose, of breaking the tension and sending the scene in a new direction. We move in an instant from confrontation to forgiveness. That, I believe, is the essential message of Rachel's smile. It says,

"I got you, and now we're even. And it's okay." It is a gracious smile. In retrospect, we can see that Rachel's real want was not so much to punish Book as to regain her self-possession.

And after all, what does Rachel *really* want? This brings up an important point about beats and about every aspect of working with characters. At some stage between your first draft and your final draft you may sit down and analyze all of your character's motivations and beats with the formula: a want leads to an action.

$$\text{Want} \rightarrow \text{Action}$$

But this is really not the way that we normally experience people. In reality, it is the reverse process. We see the person's action and from that we infer the want, by sort of reading backward. If we are really honest with ourselves, we have to admit that we largely experience ourselves the same way. We seldom know what we want. We surprise ourselves all the time. We say yes when we had intended to say no. What's *that* about?

We want to experience our characters with the same freshness. Rachel is fresh and natural in this scene because she is not too aware of her want, even as she is acting it out. She is *living*, not following a script. In character-driven stories, the characters may range from very self-aware and deliberate to very unconscious and impulsive. Plot-driven movies have a fundamentally different code. Where the characters are functions of the plot, their wants tend to be up front, leading directly to actions. Somebody has hijacked two ballistic missiles and is threatening to blow up San Francisco—we've got to stop him! Then we have the strategy, the chess game, the chase. Want leads to action. It is in fact this exposure of the inner "mechanics" of decision-making that makes some action-genre characters feel so "constructed," and not like people we could meet. In character-driven stories, motives tend to be only semiconscious, discovered en route, because they hold the tension between a conscious mode and an unconscious need.

Rachel is acting on layers of wants, which range from the relatively conscious to the completely unconscious. Closest to the surface is the want of regaining some control in her life. If we could step into the scene and interview Rachel, she could probably say yes to that. Her needling comments are spontaneous and opportunistic rather than deliberated, but they are relatively conscious. Connected to this want and unleashed by it, but in a semisubconscious layer, is the want of getting back at this man who is unfairly and unsympathetically controlling her life. As Rachel acts on this want, she is probably not fully conscious of exactly what she is doing. She is simply following her impulse. But if we really pressed her, maybe ran the videotape of the scene back for her, she would probably ultimately admit that, yes, there was an impulse for retribution. We could all have a good laugh.

But then we come to the genuinely unconscious layer of Rachel's want. The question comes up in the audience's subtext: why has Rachel gone to all the trouble of finding out so much about John Book? Of course, it is a screenwriter's trick, and a clever one, to get out the exposition about Book's mode this way. But it still has to work for Rachel's character. It has to authentically come from her voice. So what's it about? She has obviously gone to some effort to pump Elaine for information. This fact slides by as incidental, inconsequential. Yet in reality it sets up this deepest level of subtext in the scene. The easiest way to get at this layer is simply to pay attention to our body-response during the scene. We can certainly feel something in our bodies while we're looking at the scene as it was ultimately shot and edited. This scene is where we first feel the chemistry between Rachel and Book—and the vibe, the interest, is coming from Rachel. But this is truly unconscious on Rachel's part. Falling in love with a brutal cop would be way out of her comfort zone.

The deep music of the beat structure—the fact that Rachel keeps pushing into Book's private territory, while he is unable to riposte—carries us rather effortlessly into the scene's subtext. We contact the characters' deeper feelings and wants. It is this subtext layer that brings the scene to life. Clearly, it is important for us as writers to be able to perceive and express those wants of our characters that are unconscious. How do we manage this without either burying the subtext too deep or, contrarily, making it too obvious?

The formulaic response would be that you always make the lovers of Act II antagonistic to each other in Act I. Yes, it sounds like a cliché, and it is a cliché. Here is one of those temptations we face as screenwriters: the easy way out. This solution *will* generally work. Plug in the conflict, plug in the erotic subtext. However, the formula is not going to help us contact Rachel as a *person*. Ideally, Rachel really comes alive on the computer screen as we write. We feel her feminine presence, and as she delivers her zingers we feel the subtextual eros—and we know it's right. And everyone else on the development team knows it's *right*. But in the reality of most screenwriting processes, the writer is trying to "hear" the characters amid a host of distractions. The director wants a rewrite for *this*, the star wants a rewrite for *that*, and they are placing contradictory demands on the screenwriter. Sometimes we need a way to step out and reconnect with the authenticity of the characters. How can we see that Rachel is attracted to Book without even realizing it herself?

The beats of Rachel's increasingly penetrating zingers do amount to "getting even" with Book. But "getting even" means something more than merely getting revenge. It also means "getting *equal*," establishing a situation of equality. By fighting back, Rachel is establishing her dignity and worth. It is her way of saying, "I am just as strong as you are, even if it is a different kind of strength." Maybe Rachel never had to fight for her dignity like this before. Book has presented her with a challenge. He in fact has acted as her threshold guardian to the wider world: are you ready for this world, or are you just a timid little thing? The spirit in her rises to the challenge, cutting right through her widowhood and mourning. She wants to show him—the spirit in her wants to show him (this is unconscious, after all)—that she is his equal, worthy of him and of this bigger life.

This single act of establishing herself as Book's equal is what opens up the possibility of romance between them and sets up the entire second act development of their relationship. Somewhere inside us, we are aware that love is only possible between equals. Unless the two people are ethically equal, there is no love. There may be other things—projection, infatuation, obsession, possession—but not something we could legitimately call love. Up to this point in the story, Rachel has been a victim. As long as she remains a victim, neither Book nor the audience will be attracted to her. As long as she is in victim-consciousness, there is no possibility of equality between them. The power is unbalanced. By stealing the beat Rachel rights that balance. Maybe it is Rachel's healthy instinct not to be a victim of circumstance. It is not in her character to be a victim even if it is her *mode* to be nonviolent. Stealing the beat is really the only way that she can *show* herself, and Book—and us—that she is not a victim. An unconscious and unintended consequence of demonstrating that she will not be a victim is that she reveals her involuntary interest in this man.

Without trying, Rachel and Book have crossed a threshold to a kind of intimacy. And suddenly, at the end of the scene, we can see them as a couple, as a family: the woman whose husband has just died and the man who has never had a family. This is a consequence of the beat structure of the scene. This new situation is underscored by the final frame of the scene, a tableau. The camera pulls back to a 3-shot, and we have the whole story subliminally seeded into our feeling systems. We have a perfectly balanced image of the ideal family group: the child in the center, the two parents leaning forward, creating a harmoniously circular or elliptical composition. As the last image of the scene, the shot has extra retention in our eidetic memory. They *are* a family for us now. As though mystically energized by this new bond, Samuel will, immediately in the next scene, miraculously discover the photo of McFee, triggering the outer plot crisis of the story.

I have gone into this small scene at great length to show how much dramatic impact a few simple beats can carry when they are well constructed. Here "well constructed" specifically means that the beats create a dramatic curve. This dramatic curve has a life and momentum of its own, and the "material" the beats are composed of is not merely conflict, not conflict about an issue external to the characters, but conflict that implicates the deepest layers of who the characters are. The screenwriter takes—and follows—the characters out of their comfort zones, not merely to "reveal character" in some general sense, but to discover the unacknowledged self in each awakened by the presence of the other.

The scene gets through the exposition effortlessly because the exposition is simply the *text* riding on the *subtext* of Rachel and Book's awakening attraction. The *deep music* of the beats takes us directly to the heart of the scene on a body-level. It is conveyed by the minute shifts in vocal tone and body language motivated by the beats. This subtext doesn't have to be spoken. We feel it where we need to feel it. The text then acts as a supportive layer to occupy our conscious minds. If we watch this scene in *Witness* with the audio turned off, and just attend to the "dance" between John and Rachel, we can hear this *deep music.*

Hanging Drama

Often the natural curve of tension and release fits neatly within the package of information we refer to as a scene. At other times however, it is important for the two *not* to coincide, for the dramatic business of the scene to be left hanging, unfinished. We are not always given an answer to the scene's dramatic question within the scene itself. Sometimes the answer is suspended, to be resolved in the following scene. This technique builds a lot of suspense and can almost literally pull an audience out of their seats toward the screen.

To a large extent, scene rhythm is a question of taste and style—the screenwriter's style and the director's style. There is no objective right or wrong here. Some people prefer a more self-contained style, others like to leave everything hanging and edgy. The chosen style is then going to interact with the story material, the idiom and the genre. *Witness* seems determined to work with self-contained scenes. Every major scene in the movie has a complete dramatic curve, including a bit of falling action at the end. In the major Story Steps of Threshold Crisis and Catastrophe, the parts of the story step's dramatic curve are articulated in separate scenes, down to a small Calm Before the Storm moment between the catastrophe and climax of the sequence. This approach contributes largely to the "classic" feeling that *Witness* evokes. Some people like this, others don't. This is not a judgment that one style works and another doesn't. It is a question of what is appropriate in a specific storytelling/stylistic context. *Terminator 2* often keeps the action running relentlessly from scene to scene, yet there are also carefully modulated moments where the pace slows down and the waves of tension and release are more congruent with individual scenes.

One place where it is a very good idea to leave the end of the scene hanging, that is, to end the scene without answering the dramatic question or releasing the tension, is between the outer plot catastrophe and climax. (To a lesser degree, this is also true of the catastrophe and climax moments within each Story Step.) To give one example of the highly effective use of the hanging scene ending, we could refer to the catastrophe/climax of *Trainspotting*. As in many end of Act II catastrophes, what the hero thought was the best thing that could happen—in this case, the successful negotiation of the drug deal—turns out to be the worst thing that could happen. Renton himself tells us at the end of this drug deal scene in the hotel: "For a moment it was all worth it. For a moment we were like brothers." Yet as soon as we come into the next scene in the pub, where the catastrophe occurs, we can feel that the money in the sack in the middle of the table divides rather than unites these false friends.

In the establishing moment of the scene in the pub, Spud naïvely offers what he plans to do with his share of the money. But the energy shifts when Begby gets up to buy a fresh round of beer, threatening to kill any of the others who would dare try and take off with the money. The stakes rise further when Sick Boy gets up to go to the john. Renton assures him that they wouldn't run out on a mate, but Sick Boy replies, "Why not? I would!" So that leaves Renton and Spud at the table to contemplate temptation. Renton *is* tempted. It is a moment of deep ambivalence and suspense; the scene could go in any direction. Then Sick Boy returns. Renton's chance to run with the money is gone, but the tension is still rising like a storm about to break.

Suddenly the storm does break. Begby savagely beats a man in the bar half to death. Spud tries to intervene and is slashed by Begby's knife. There is utter chaos, yet the scene is still building. The bloody Englishman on the floor is merely incidental to the dramatic conflict. The conflict is really between Renton and Begby as protagonist and antagonist embodying contrasting values. Renton had thought this drug deal would bring him freedom and happiness. Now Begby calls to him:

> Hey, Rentie boy! You bring me over a fucking kip.

For a moment, Renton hesitates. From resistance or from terror? Begby repeats the demand. Renton slowly gets up.

> And bring the fuckin' bag.

The beats that follow are nonverbal. Begby makes Renton hand him the bag, take out a cigarette, light it, and place it in Begby's mouth. Freedom has turned to slavery. We can feel the tension between them, and in the mirroring close-ups we can feel vividly on a gut level that if Renton doesn't change and get away from these people, he will end up as soul-dead as Begby. And right now Begby is in control. He exhales in Renton's face. Renton tries not to blink as the cloud of cigarette smoke hits him and surrounds him. *CUT.*

Nothing is resolved here. The tension is left hanging to be carried over into the next scene, which will be the climax of the movie.

Practicing with Beats and Scenes

Now is a good time to begin a variety of practices to work with identifying beats and shaping scenes. Successful writers are always writing. They are not waiting for a contract to be inked. Good writers have adjusted to the self-knowledge that writing is the way they discover, examine, question, reflect. They are writing for themselves, not for someone else's approval. Writing to write.

Writing can take many, many forms. I feel it is very useful to have a writing practice that is simply there to be formless: open, uncensored, and free. That clears the pipes, opens up the circuits. It is a great means for discovery. But right now we want something a little more focused. As I have suggested, in screenwriting we are always writing scenes. The scene is the concentrated arena where all of the structures and dynamics of drama can be found. A screenplay requires many kinds of scenes, so we want our practice with scenes to focus on how scenes move and what makes them work, while opening us to many different possibilities. Each screenplay will make its own demands, so we cannot afford to be rigid in our technique.

What makes a good scene? Some will say a good scene has to "grab us." That's more than a little vague. It begs the question: what grabs us? A lot of fire? A big conflict? A big revelation? Dramatic character change? These are all our projections onto the *idea* of a scene. A good scene is not necessarily a "big" scene, as I hope the close look at the small but rich hot dog scene in *Witness* demonstrated. A "big" scene may be a good scene—but it may not. A feature film is typically made up of between one and two hundred scenes. They cannot all be "big" scenes any more than an orchestra can play fortissimo all the way through a symphony. It would lack modulation. Rather, each scene has to be good in its own way. So it doesn't make much sense only practicing with "big" scenes. It is better to practice broadly with all kinds of material.

Internal Software: Imaginal Anthropology

A good way to practice is to learn how to see the beats in ordinary behavior and follow the movement of the beats to bring out a story. Here it is good to temporarily drop all expectations about what is dramatic or cinematic. We are going to start by looking at *life*.

Once a week, go somewhere you've never been before, somewhere outside your habitual patterns, outside your comfort zone. Just to observe and write. It doesn't have to be a mud-wrestling bar, midget show, or cross-dressing competition. Try a local clinic, union hall, hair salon, or dog grooming salon. Or hop on a city bus or suburban train and just let it take you somewhere. Now you are an anthropologist. Allow yourself to be drawn toward any interaction that interests you or seems to have potential. Find a place where you can sit unobtrusively and record what goes on. Of course, this is what writers have been doing in cafés for centuries. Get the dialogue as accurately as you can. Listen for ten minutes. Later, take the most interesting minute and transcribe the dialogue exactly as it was spoken.

Try to get a feel for the style of each person's language and what that tells you as an anthropologist. Meanwhile, record the specifics of body, gesture, clothing, and the details of physical objects and setting. How are objects used? How does each detail reveal something about the attitudes and values of the "characters"?

Continued

Some objects are *transactional*. That is, by being passed back and forth they describe a transaction between the two people. It may be a file or CD that is passed in one direction only, and may be the reason for the encounter. Sometimes salt shakers and other utensils are passed back and forth. The ostensible reason would be obvious, but these are also points of physical contact. People do it unintentionally, but nevertheless it makes them feel more at home with one another. We know that friends often try food from each other's plates, clearly indicating a level of physical comfort.

Writing on the spot while observing is better than tape recording and writing it later. It's okay to use an audio recorder, but don't let that prosthetic substitute for paying sharp attention. The best use of recorders is to help you render the dialogue verbatim later, including stutters, etc. But the tape recorder can be a crutch. Writing forces you to be very present, very focused. I think of the admonition of Eugene Delacroix to aspiring painters:

> An artist should be able to sketch a man falling from a ladder in the time it takes him to fall.

As you are "sketching," ask yourself what this interaction is all about. Who has the power in terms of urgency or status, and how can you tell? What is in the text of the "scene," and what is in the subtext? What are the people not saying to each other, what are they withholding? Is this an interaction of *persons* or *personas* (*social masks*)? If you sense personas, where are the people—are they hidden way down inside? Have they "checked-out"? Try to stay with the interaction until it terminates.

What you will have is some raw material. Don't worry about whether it is strong or flat or important. All of our interactions do have some form, are governed by form, starting with engagement and ending in disengagement. In between, no matter how banal, is the "stuff" of the interaction, which has its own form: gossip, argument, advice, entreaty, contract.

Take this raw material home and try the following steps:

- Work with the interaction and see how it forms itself into beats. This may not seem promising at first, but it may help to focus on: what was the interaction about? What was the beginning and the end? What catalyzed it, got it going? Did the "characters" cross a threshold to intimacy or confrontation? How was the interaction resolved?

Continued

Who broke the moment off? How? Why? When you can anchor these points, look at the steps that took the people from here to there. Look also at how they may have used body language and Freudian slips to express an inadvertent subtext.

- Using your own focusing or other introspective technique, find a point in the scene where *you* felt something, where *you* reacted in your body or through a fantasy that came up at that moment. You may have had a memory or association from your own life intrude. Let images come up around that response-moment. Just let your fantasy go and daydream what the scene may have "really" been about. Very often you will find yourself responding to something that was in the *subtext* of the interaction you witnessed. It is as though you have an intuitive "X-ray vision" that reveals who these people really are. Such intuitive responses are always "as if." They are not "clairvoyant" or meant to be taken literally. But they do often pick up underlying patterns, which are relayed to our conscious mind through our fantasies.
- Organize a new scene, using substantially the same text situation, but this time reshape the scene to bring out what you fantasized was in the subtext. Clarify and concentrate the stakes of the scene by eliminating activity that was trivial or redundant. Use the new scene as a launching point for a larger story in which these characters appear. Let your imagination run wild. The two ladies at the bakery might turn out to be part of a great melodrama, thriller, or satire—and perhaps they are.

The basic idea with this exercise in imaginal anthropology is to feel the shape of an observed event, use the beats to find the "dance" between the people, and then to put that dance into a new, imagined dramatic context.

As a second, related exercise, look at some movie scenes that have really touched you. If possible, look at both the screenplay version (from one of the web sites where they are available for download) and the final edited version, and do a script-to-screen comparison. Where are the beats as you read the scene? What has been added by the interpretation of the performers, especially via body language and gesture? Look at how ambiguity and ambivalence are handled.

One scene I find fascinating in this regard comes in the Core Crisis Story Step of *The Piano*. Ada enters George's cabin. George has no idea what she wants.

Has the piano been damaged? Of course Ada cannot *say* what she is doing there, but does she even *know* why she is there? The scene—and the entire drama—are about to move in a new direction. At what point does Ada seem to know what she wants, and how can we tell? How do the beats reveal this to us? Look at how the scene you choose to study is structured, how it builds through its beats.

Play with creating a new scene—different characters (a new Ada, a new George), a different situation—but with an analogous beat structure. For example, create a dramatic situation like this scene, set in the present time or the future. Don't worry if this is derivative; it's only an exercise. This exercise is like playing over a championship chess match to see how it works.

11

The Sixteen Story Steps

> The purpose of an exercise is to reduce and return: to narrow the area down and down until the birth of a lie is revealed and caught, if the actor can find and see this moment he can perhaps open himself to a deeper, more creative impulse.
>
> *Peter Brook*

A New Paradigm

THE IDEA OF THE SIXTEEN STORY STEPS—which approaches screenplays and their development neither from the perspective of plot points nor that of sequences, but in terms of *storytelling functions*—is new. But the Story Steps themselves have always been there. Screenwriters and directors have always used these steps, or we would not find them present in so many successful movies. It was something people found their way to intuitively, via the laborious process of decision making through which a screenplay is gradually refined. I have simply followed this same path of creative intuition. So the Sixteen Story Steps model is not something I have invented; I am simply articulating it in a conceptual form. No *concept* of this nature existed before that would allow filmmakers to identify this level of screenplay structure and work with it deliberately rather than stumble into it intuitivcly.

Because the Sixteen Story Steps model integrates all of the other models, it presents a very detailed set of keys to the entire development process. The Story Steps show us in *detail* how character and plot interact, how the story energy is moving through the three levels of the Story Molecule, and why the story must shift levels at specific points. The Story Steps reveal all of the heretofore invisible landmarks of the vast desert we call Act II, so that a screenwriter is empowered to cross that landscape without getting lost. They allow the development team to identify and verify where Act II must culminate in order to yield the most compelling and appropriate climax for the material. The Sixteen Story Steps manage to do all this because they don't get stuck at the surface level of how the screenplay presents itself, what the story *looks like*. They identify a structural level below that—the bones that make up the entire spine of the story. We could call it the *necessary grammar* of storytelling through film. We could equally call it the *grammar of necessity*, because the process of growth through crisis *does* have its own inherent structure and logic. This is true even when we experience it as chaotic—especially then, as we have seen.

Of course, there are pros and cons to conceptualizing. New concepts reveal flaws in old ways of thinking. Look at the most influential books on screenwriting, and their models of plot structure all show four or five "plot points" with a vague terra incognita in between, pictured either as a smooth curve or as jumpy peaks. Well, this is simply where we were at a certain stage in our understanding. Now that view comes to appear obsolete, because not only is it obviously incomplete, its incompleteness tends to distort the development process. Inordinate weight is put on a few "points." In the pressurized atmosphere of the blockbuster mentality, clobbering the audience with big action at the big points has tended to become a default mode. How one gets to these grandiose moments is often handled with less assurance.

A *point*, by definition, is without extension. But the major plot events in movies are sweeps of action, lasting eight to fifteen minutes of screen time. They have their own dramatic structure, beginning, middle, and end. So these major events or sequences (as we saw in the last chapter with the twelve scenes that comprise the Threshold Crisis in *Witness*) are certainly not mere points. In a movie, there are no static points: it is all a flow. The result of "plot point" thinking, along with other factors, has contributed to the widely held view that movies have become more coldly mechanical, even when they are mechanically constructed to be warm and fuzzy. And can we prove that movies are "better" today than they were in, say, 1958? If we stacked up a critics' list of the ten best films of that period against the ten best of any recent year, those of us who work in the business would have a sobering experience. After all, *Vertigo*, *The Searchers*, and *The Bridge on the River Kwai* make a pretty tall top of the batting order.

We can differentiate this new concept of Story Steps from the idea of plot points by means of the following observations:

1. Story Steps are not sequences or blocks of action as such. They are necessary storytelling functions. The story cannot be complete and coherent if functions are missing or damaged. Thus the key thing to look at is not the *content* of the action, but *whether it fulfils its function*.
2. Story Steps are not *points*. They move directly from one to the next without gaps. Therefore, the Story Steps, taken together, include *everything* that comprises the story's throughline. Subplots may fall outside this throughline, but the Story Steps will indicate better how and where the subplots connect to the throughline.
3. As a corollary to this, it is not the length or size of a Story Step that makes it work, but simply its function. Making it bigger will not necessarily make it better.

4. The Story Steps form a chain of cause and effect. We are not referring to cause and effect in character motivation, but in the logic of storytelling. For example, because the reaction of the threshold guardian in some way wounds the hero, she can for the moment no longer move toward her plot goal. Because movement toward the plot goal is impossible, the hero's frustrated libido seeks another outlet, and so on. Each preceding Story Step is the direct setup for the one that follows, and each following Story Step is the direct consequence of the one before.
5. From all this we must conclude that no single Story Step is more important than any other. They are all interdependent. Each must be just where it is for the story as a whole to have coherence, integrity, and power, and to appear to the audience as fully alive.

We shall go into each of these five points, and then look at *The Piano* as an example of how the Story Steps can work together to create a successful movie. Before we begin, however, it would be wise to give the reader a caveat or two. The first is to clarify what may appear to be a contradiction of earlier statements that I do not believe in the usefulness of "paint by numbers" approaches. Is this not what I am proposing here? It may sound as though I am offering magic wands or trade secrets that will relieve you of the creative risks that come with the territory of screenwriting. Well, it is important to demystify all this. Screenwriting books and seminars are normally advertised with catchy phrases called "bullets," just like any other product, from shampoos to sports cars. The bullets promote "21 Building Blocks," "23 Secrets to Make You a Great Screenwriter," "27 Orders of Mystical Initiation Leading to an Academy Award," etc. The implication is that if you don't know these specific secrets, you're screwed.

I certainly do not see the Sixteen Story Steps as magic. I simply see them as very useful. As creative professionals, we are interested in why our tools function the way that they do. That allows us to improvise successfully in new situations. So it is useful to know that storytelling is itself a language, one made up of actions rather than letters. Yet it has a grammar all the same. And I mean a grammar in the proper sense, in the sense that we learn that adjectives normally precede nouns while adverbs follow verbs. These are not "formulas"; they do not in any way restrict the content of the sentence. Rather, grammar is what gives language the possibility of having meaning at all. Grammar is an invisible, latent structure, a matrix. We take it for granted because it is ubiquitous. We never think about it, unless we want our writing to be special, significant, creative. Then we are forced to consider how we use language. And then the latent matrix of grammar floats up into view, like sugar crystals precipitating out of a clear solution. Think of the Sixteen Story Steps the same way.

The second caveat is the inverse of the first: do not confuse the grammar of storytelling with the content of the story. The decision whether the "quick sly fox" or the "quick red fox" jumps over the lazy brown dog is entirely up to you.

But it is helpful to know how the Core Crisis leads into the double bind, and how the double bind grows out of the Need versus Mode model, for without that, your Act II catastrophe will not work—and without *that*, your climax will not work. Remember sentence diagramming back in school? The Story Steps model will allow you to test and verify your throughline in the rich context of the models we have presented. Very importantly, they will provide an objective, shared language for the development team, allowing writers, directors, and producers to communicate more effectively. This puts you, whatever role you may play in the story development process, in a position of greater confidence, knowing that you can articulate how and why every scene fits in the context of a sequence and of the screenplay as a whole. There is nothing secret here. It is simply the fruit of many years' work on the real problems of story construction.

Uncovering the Bones

The discovery of the Sixteen Story Steps model came about because my colleague Tom and I were forced into it, necessity being the mother of invention and all that. In the mid-nineties there was growing international interest in thrillers, as thrillers were going mainstream and thriller storytelling strategies were starting to appear in many other kinds of movies. At that time, "thriller" began to take on a meaning beyond reference to the genre; it was expanding to become a general posture of using thrilling elements to entice audiences into a wide range of movies. It was no longer strictly a genre. And film and television producers in Europe were made increasingly aware, through the GATT (General Agreement on Trade and Tariffs, the foundation of the World Trade Organization) debates of the need to compete against a rising influx of American genre movies in their own markets. On both sides of the Atlantic, everyone wanted to know how to develop and write thrillers. We were invited to create workshops on the thriller, and it seemed like a good challenge.

It was at this point that Tom and I realized there was really nothing written about thriller. There was a whole shelf of books on horror movies, and another on film noir, both of which have different genre codes, development of action, and pacing than the thriller. We had put ourselves out on a limb and needed to come up with fresh and salient insights. As sometimes happens, we were tricked out of our comfort zone. We had to conceptualize what we knew about thriller in a few short weeks. Discussions with friends who had written thrillers yielded little insight. They confessed that they, too, were flying by the seat of their pants and just trying to make it "tighter" and "more scary, more thrilling." Thriller was said to be something you had to have a feel for. In fact, most writers were starting from a personal obsession, a derivative of a classic thriller, or with a collection of shocks and payoffs for the audience. They hoped that if the big moments really worked, the audience would let them slide from one major plot point to the next without walking out of the theater. It's not pretty, but it's the way many movies get made.

Working with a variety of thrillers we planned to show we were still, in the final days leading up to the seminar, trying to brainstorm our way into the meta-structure level of the thriller. We had all of our basic models to work with, which gave us this three-dimensional perspective. But they did not account for the special tightness of thriller construction. Each sequence or narrative step not only has to interlock with the ones before and after, but also has to set up or pay off twists in more distant parts of the screenplay. As our own mode was unraveling, I came up with a different way of questioning the thriller. I began to ask *negative* questions: what would make an otherwise workable script *fail* if it were removed or placed elsewhere in the story? Suddenly, features within Act II—common to all these movies, but as yet unnamed—began to emerge like a lost continent rising out of the sea in an old B-movie.

Throughout this book, we have been referring to the "spine" of the story. Lacking a detailed knowledge of the anatomy and physiology of this spine, people judge the shape of the spine by how it looks from the outside. This they do by means of what we call "step-outlines." Step-outlines are laid out according to the sequences that comprise the story. Coding systems identify the A-story, the B-story, and the subplots. Step-outlines are designed to get an overview of the screenplay and to judge whether it is "working." That judgment is as accurate and sophisticated as the concepts the development team can bring to bear on the information the step-outline gives them, concepts that are not explicit in the step-outline itself.

The problem with this is that sequences, as cinematic units, describe the action but do not reveal the bones. Cinematic units are not the same as storytelling units. Storytelling units in the spine of the story would articulate the dynamics that make the story work, not what the order of action on the screen is. Of course these two are related, but they are not identical. Especially in a period when there is increasing experimentation with nonlinear storytelling, the logic of the story and the order of action on the screen may diverge considerably. Stories are being pulled into many new shapes, but in the end they must still make meaning for the audience. If we are to discover the vertebrae that make up the spine of the story, we must speak the language of dramatic storytelling. Not: what is this sequence doing for me? But: what is *necessary*, given *my* story, the specific story I am trying to tell, to set up the catalyst? Do I need a hook, a prologue, a voice-over intro—and why? What *necessarily* connects the catalyst and Threshold Crisis? At what point must the primarily relationship be catalyzed? At what point must the backstory wound start impacting the present-time story? In which order do the three substories of the Story Molecule need to be paid off at the climax? This is what we mean by grammar of storytelling, the noun-verb-adverb stuff that allows you to make a coherent statement.

In other words, we are trying to get at the real essence of story structure for feature films, the structural elements that must absolutely be present, and must be exactly where they are, if the story is going to function dramatically. This is what we mean by *spine*. A spine is an organic structure made up of linked vertebrae. Vertebrae are not blocks or Lincoln Logs; they are not interchangeable. Each vertebra needs to be exactly where it is for the whole spine to be alive and function. Hurt one of the vertebrae and you hurt the entire story. Damage a couple of them and you probably kill the story.

Sequences as descriptive units in a step-outline are not *necessarily* the vertebrae themselves. It is a basic misunderstanding to confuse description with function, just as it is a basic misconception to imagine that a plot *point* is actually a point. Some development executives and screenwriters work with only two plot points and a climax. Others add a midpoint, but are unsure what it is supposed to do. Even with five major plot points, how much of the total screenplay is still unaccounted for? This is like trying to understand the workings of the whole spine by inspecting two neck bones, a shoulder blade, a lumbar, and a tailbone. At the worst, we have some studio readers flipping through the script to see if the plot points are where they're "supposed" to be. This does not lead the development into the deeper layers of the story where plot, character, and theme intersect. And some schematic models based on Campbell's Hero's Journey alone fail to take into account the basic differences between myth and drama. They are so eager to label every Guide, Witch, Ordeal, and Elixir (as though the more "mythic elements," the better the story) that they cease to be able to say anything productive about the inner dynamic and necessity of dramatic structure at all.

The best models don't tell us what to do, they facilitate our own process. Good models lead to productive development questions. Productive questions are, first of all, those that can be answered with some objectivity in reference to the story material itself. They help us see better what is really there. Productive questions do not lead away from the story into abstract theory, political correctness, or arbitrary page counts, but bring the story itself into focus. As we have emphasized before, asking questions opens up the development process. Flat judgmental statements shut the process down. They tend to close down discussion and creativity and the rapport in the team. When the openness of dialogue dries up, that tempts the "development demons" into power plays and other forms of acting out. This brings up a second aspect of productive questions: they lead us directly into the deeper layers of the story material. The writer is confronted more directly, for example, with the need/mode paradox of values on a gut level. The writer's journey is quickened in this way. Because so much of screenwriting requires the writer herself to confront and reconcile the character's conflicting values, bringing this into focus may actually save one or two screenplay drafts. It is a producer's dream

I imagine myself back once again in the Great Hall at the Field Museum in Chicago, where I loved to go as a kid, marveling at the huge skeleton of a brontosaurus, with its seventy-five-foot-long spine. Now, you and I each have a spine, and it has a certain number of bones. The number is not arbitrary because each vertebra has a special function to play in the whole. A spine is neither an abstract concept nor a convention. Each of those bones has to be right where it is. Think of the Story Steps as tracing the individual bones of that spine, showing how the nerves of the story radiate from each one to enliven the entire screenplay. Likewise, it is obvious that you cannot point to your own vertebrae and say, "These right here, these are my *favorite* vertebrae. But this other one, I could lose it and I wouldn't even notice." Your back would not work; you would be paralyzed. Why should we not expect the same to be true of the vertebrae in the spine of a screenplay? As with your backbone, we cannot take a Story Step out of the spine without harming the organic wholeness, logical coherence, and dramatic power of the screenplay. There is nothing mysterious about this. You will find it as natural and as deeply logical as your own body.

Certainly there are important variations in the emphasis, inflection, and size of Story Steps from film to film and genre to genre. Often in comedy, the emotional inflection or directional movement of a Story Step is inverted. For example, Story Step #12: The Breaking Point is the direct setup for Story Step #13: Catastrophe. It is a point of reversal in many stories. In a thriller, this reversal is most often characterized as: "What looked like the best thing that could happen turns out to be the worst thing"—as in *Seven*, when John Doe walks into the police station and gives himself up. But in comedy, the reversal that comes late in Act II is more typically: "What looked like the worst thing that could happen turns out to be the best thing." *Four Weddings and a Funeral*, for example, uses a two-part reversal to bring this off. The Breaking Point itself is the first reversal. This includes the funeral of Gareth, the character who was the embodiment of life-force and authenticity. We must recall that Gareth has died, specifically of a heart attack, in the middle of Carrie's wedding reception. So it is as though Gareth is acting out the feelings Charles cannot express. At the funeral, Matthew speaks the unvarnished truth about his friend. We can see all the refined persona masks slip as real feelings break through. Afterward, Charles walks by the river with his friend Tom. Here Charles reveals his desolation, that he had always waited for the perfect love—but maybe there's no point in waiting any more. So, the dramatic function of Gareth's funeral is specifically to bring Charles to this breaking point.

This is a reversal because Charles is abandoning his old mode of "kiss and run." The scene cuts immediately to the Catastrophe Story Step: Charles is marrying the wrong woman for the wrong reason. And just at this moment, Carrie shows up at the church, saying she is separated. The throughline question—"Will Charles act on his true feelings?"—has been built to a climax. This sets up the second part of the reversal: he does tell the truth, and Duckface decks him at the altar. Of course, we recognize that this is the best thing that could have happened to Charles. But it has been set up carefully, step by step. The breaking point is not arbitrary. It is the point where the old mode dies or is proven to be unworkable.

That is the *reason* for the reversal. Carrie's wedding has proven to Charles the failure of hiding his true feelings. Charles merely draws the wrong conclusion from this, and abandons his true feelings altogether. The emotional inflection of the comic breaking point is the opposite of that in *Seven*, but structurally it occupies the same place.

When we write step-outlines, what we are really trying to do is draw out this bone structure of the story. But if a step-outline is only a passive schematization, which doesn't take us below the surface, it doesn't really help us. The Story Steps reveal the structural elements of the screenplay, which is another way of talking about bones. "Structural elements" helps us differentiate from the other uses of the word "element." In development discussions, "element" can refer loosely to almost anything of attractive value, from a love-story subplot to a special setting or location, or a featured piece of technology that will create a "look." Sometimes the story development gets hung up on these extrinsic elements, which are each supposed to have a market value. The producer will say he likes the script changes, but we have to keep such and such elements. In one consultation I did on a thriller project, the elements the producers insisted on keeping, including a weak victim-hero, guaranteed that the project could not succeed. The reality of the screenwriter's workplace is that often, instead of the story finding its own integrity, story revisions must find their way into the spaces left by these non-story-based "elements." We can all use help getting a handle on this process.

Our use of "structural elements" here refers specifically to the bone structure. The Story Steps are *elemental* to the structure, the very basics. Working with them helps us stay on track in our writing. The Story Steps are essential if the audience is going to make the journey with the main character. When one is damaged or missing, what happens? Not only is there a gap in the coherence of the story, there is also a gap in the audience's rapport with the hero. The audience "falls out" of the story. When this happens, it is tough to get them back again. It is not simply a question of pacing. We do not need another chase or explosion. No, something is structurally missing that older models had not put their finger on.

Remember that the map is not the territory, nor is it a substitute for the journey. Models are not magic wands. If I have shared the origin of the Sixteen Story Steps model, it is to demystify it. My belief is that models should be few enough and general enough that you are stimulated to explore the variations for yourself. They should not intrude and micromanage your screenplay. At that point they take over too much authority from the creative process, which requires risk, the courage to be with uncertainty. The more detailed a model is, the later it should be used in the development process. While the other models can come into the development process early, the Sixteen Story Steps is most useful after the story has gelled, moving from treatment to script, and after the first screenplay draft has been written.

Working with the Story Steps

There will always be scenes and sequences on the screen, but the Story Step may be missing. The *function* may be missing. Each Story Step has its own development, its own beginning, middle, and end, its own dramatic curve. This weaves a warp behind the scenes and gives them their reason for being in the story. The climax or culmination of a Story Step will not always be a big moment. But once we know what to look for, it will become natural to work with them. A few samples from different parts of the plot curve will give us a start.

Each Story Step is a logical sequence, yet in itself it is a form without content. It is the logic of cause and effect: put your hand in the fire and you'll get burnt. That is an if/then proposition. The entire screenplay is a chain of such propositions unraveling from that first overarching proposition, the dramatic catalyst. The hero responds to that first *if*, precipitating a series of *thens*. The character does not know the content of the thens, and neither do we. This is why we have development questions, questions whose answers generate new questions on multiple levels. The story presents one set of if/then conditions: the story field of total possibility. The screenwriter presents another set, a personal perspective limited by blind spots. The two sets interlock in a sort of fractal pattern. We would find it truly beautiful if we, as writers, didn't so often feel lost in the middle of it.

What do we mean by "logical sequence"? How does that connect with the function of the Story Step? Each step, as a sequence, frames the action of the screenplay in such a way that the next step becomes a logical outcome, a logical necessity. If the first sequence is incomplete, there is no bridge to the next, no necessity. Necessity is the fabric of destiny: within ourselves simultaneously as it appears to come at us from the outer world. I may propose the *if*, while the outer world responds with the then. Or the world may pose the *if*, and I hustle for a response, a comeback.

- If somebody broke into your house. . . ?
- If your plane was hijacked. . . ?
- If you were bored, waiting in a station between trains, and you went into the john to take a pee, and at that moment two guys murdered somebody, but they didn't see you. . . ?
- If Johnny Camerreri scratched his head and asked you to marry him, and you happened to be a control freak who also wanted to have a proper married life. . . ?
- If you thought of yourself as a dedicated playboy, but then you met a woman and fell head over heels. . . ?

This process of responding to necessity is made cleverly and comically explicit in *Three Kings*. The mercenary soldiers, looking to heist millions in gold that Saddam has stolen from Kuwait, enter Iraq illegally. They overpower the guards in a village and search a bunker, liberating a prison full of Shiite rebels in the process. Not finding the gold, they drive on toward another bunker, leaving Saddam's soldiers and the rebels fighting each other. Now, during a break in the action, Troy wants to know what was going on back there: the Iraqi soldiers just ignored them, let them do what they wanted. Archie Gates responds by asking the others what is the most important thing in life. The answer is: necessity. People do what is most necessary at a given moment. The soldiers' necessity, Archie tells the men, is to put down the rebel uprising, which leaves the team of Americans free to do what they want. Here, in Act I, Archie's own sense of necessity is opportunistic and self-serving. But the outer world has yet to respond. In fact, he seems to be blithely tempting fate, and once they cross the threshold, the game plan goes to hell. Another factor, helping the Shiites, makes a claim on them.

Thus, in Act II of *Three Kings*, Archie is forced to declare, "The necessity has changed." In Act II, the soldiers must help the Shiites so that the Shiites will help them. This is already an important ethical shift from an arrogant interpretation of the old philosophy of self-reliance. And in Act III, Archie and his comrades are forced, and ultimately willing, to sacrifice the gold. At the climax, they use it as a bargaining chip in exchange for free passage for the rebels to a refugee camp in Iran. Thematically, *Three Kings* is about realizing what we really need, and how our perception of necessity grows with our character, our sense of value. Each Story Step has added its proposition, its logical sequence, to the development of the whole. Necessity—experience—forces Troy, Conrad, the Chief, and Archie to undergo a transformation of values. Because Archie realizes the real bunker was hidden behind the fake well, they have to go back to the village; because they go back, they are forced to take sides; because they take sides, Saddam's soldiers attack them; and on and on.

In story development, we speak broadly of an establishing sequence, a catalyst sequence, a catastrophe sequence. But it would be more to the point to speak of an *establishing function* and a *catalyst function*—or step. The function of the Establishing Story Step is to set up the story to the point where the plot is ready to begin. This includes setting the idiom, genre, pace, tone, and POV of the movie; establishing the story's Day World and its flaw; introducing the main character and nailing his mode; and providing an establishing incident that will lead immediately to the catalyst. Can you do all that in one sequence? Maybe, maybe not. Probably not. The Establishing Story Step includes hooks, prologues, and intros, as well as an establishing scene as such and the establishing or inciting incident. Each of these may be a different sequence, if we can attribute any sort of precise meaning whatever to the word "sequence."

"Sequence" tempts you to think in terms of a block of action. In reality, it's much more complex than that. Each Establishing Story Step will take the shape that necessity—the story's internal logic—dictates. The real question for us is:

what does *my* screenplay need to establish for the audience before the plot can begin? Does *my* story need a hair-raising opening hook where we see the first murder? Does *my* story need a voice-over intro that establishes a more distant POV, as is done in *American Beauty*? Do I want to show the end at the beginning to foreshadow a tragedy, as is also done in *American Beauty*? If I have multiple character throughlines, can I introduce them all in one establishing scene, or do I need separate establishing scenes for each character? Because the central characters in *American Beauty* were members of the same family, it was more effective to show them together. But because the dramatic world of *Short Cuts* is so dispersed, and the theme has to do with the pain of disconnection, a long sequence of intercut establishing scenes was needed. These are the real decisions we are faced with day after day.

Every Story Step in every screenplay demands to be treated individually. There are some situations where the function of the Story Step appears to be nailed by a single line of dialogue. But when we look more closely, we can see that twenty minutes of action was needed to set up that one line, to make that specific dialogue necessary and appropriate. Then, when we hear the character speak it, it rings true. For example, the second act of *Midnight Run* is long, rambling, and arguably contains action sequences which, though exciting in themselves, represent horizontal rather than escalating dramatic movement. There is a vague sense that you could lose one or two of these action sequences without greatly altering the story. However, there is a key point in the movie where Jack's fundamental conflict of values comes out in the open. This is Story Step # 11: Polarization of Values. It is one of the steps that create the double bind and must be hit clearly or the catastrophe simply will not resonate. The value attached to the mode and the value attached to the still-unconscious need are revealed to be irreconcilable. At this point the double bind closes like a trap. Recall that in *Four Weddings* this point occurs at Carrie's wedding reception, where Charles's mode of playing it safe and hiding his true feelings behind a charming façade has caused him to lose the woman he truly loves. How is this step handled in *Midnight Run*?

The Polarization of Values Story Step hits its culmination in a relatively short dialogue scene where Jack and the Duke are riding westward in a boxcar. As we come into the scene, the difference between the two characters is orchestrated immediately. Jack figures them to be in Arizona: "I think we're almost home." Of course, L.A. is not home for John Mardukis. For him, it means something else entirely: "I'm almost dead." The conflict is thus constellated. Who will take the beat first? Jack has created the illusion for himself (Story Step #10: Deepening) that he and the Duke can be pals on the road, friends even, and he can still turn him in and collect his bounty. Jack is in denial about the real consequences, and tries to convince the Duke (and himself) that he will be safe in a witness protection program. But the Duke will not let him hide. In the climactic dialogue of the scene, the Duke destroys the illusions:

Duke:

Serrano is the heroin dealer you told me about in Chicago? Who owned your buddies and destroyed your life. . . . That's Serrano? That's the guy you're takin' me in. . . . That's the guy that's gonna kill me?

(beat)

Hope it's a wonderful coffee shop, Jack.

And so the double bind is set. The values of money versus friendship, of status quo security versus deep integrity, are now polarized and are straining in opposite directions. Jack is still not ready to abandon his old mode, but it is crystal clear now that he cannot have both and will ultimately have a hard decision to make. This scene comes an hour and a half into the movie. It shows how a Story Step may culminate in a single line of dialogue. If we're not careful, we might identify the Story Step with the big moment that epitomizes it. But of course the moment is in the context of a scene and needs the entire scene to set it up. In reality, the values have been polarizing since the point where Jack and the Duke were momentarily caught by Serrano's henchmen, twenty screen minutes earlier. So in fact, this is a long but diffusely structured Story Step. Why, then, does it need to be so long?

Here is where we need to probe deeper into the function of the Story Step. The function of Polarization of Values is to crucify the hero in the tension of opposites, forcing the "grow or die" situation. This can only be effective if we have seen the values to have equal force. We know Jack is a stubborn, determined, and bitter character. The possibility that friendship could come to have an equal hold on him appears to be extremely remote. So what would we need to do (imagining this to be our story) to show this process whereby, in spite of himself, Jack is compelled to admit the Duke into his inner spaces? We need to see them go through thick and thin together, laugh together, establish trust and equality. We do see each save the other's life. We see the Duke affirm the bond of friendship when he could have abandoned Jack to the river. In sum, over those twenty minutes of screen time the bond is established as so real and vital for the audience that we cannot imagine how Jack can still speak of turning the Duke in. The audience is some steps ahead of Jack here. Those twenty minutes of action have established the value of friendship for Jack, though he has yet to admit it. We can see that Jack's entire life has led him to this point, as he sits brooding in the boxcar, unable to answer. The only way out of the trap is through making the leap to see the situation in a new way. It is a moment of existential crisis. This pushes Jack to the next Story Step (#12), Breaking Point, where we see how Jack reacts to the double bind. One Story Step leads directly into the next.

As another example, Story Step #14: Calm Before the Storm is typically brief. Part of its function is rhythmic, to give the audience a moment to exhale from the tension of the catastrophe before the action moves forward relentlessly to the climax. As we said earlier, the catastrophe is the point of highest dramatic intensity thus far in the story. Its tension is not going to be resolved, but suspended. But this is not only a mechanical moment of suspense. Each Story Step is the outcome or consequence of the one preceding. The Calm Before the Storm shows us the immediate consequence of the catastrophe. We see, directly or by implication, how these consequences impact on all levels of the Story Molecule. The inner conflict level often shows us whether the hero will grow or die. The inner (character change) climax in the overall ripple climax may in fact have already happened, as we may be shown by some small but significant change of behavior (Renton in *Trainspotting*). Or we may see that the hero is still locked in the old mode. Book is calmer and more centered as he puts the birdhouse back up. That is a good sign. Mills, on the other hand (in *Seven*), is cocky and aggressive as he and Somerset drive John Doe to the climactic rendezvous point. Definitely a bad sign.

Like all story steps, Calm Before the Storm must be handled individually. It is the outcome of all the steps that have gone before. At one extreme of brevity is the Calm Before the Storm in *Terminator 2*, which lasts only some seconds between the death of the good Terminator, played by Schwarzenegger, and the point where the bad Terminator, morphed into Sarah, stalks John for the last time. There is just one very quiet, suspended beat where John is hiding and the bad Terminator is trying to sense where he is. Here is the rhythmic beat. Significantly, it is precisely within this suspended moment that we see the "dead" hero switch over to "alternate power" and come back to life. This is a novel variation on the motif of death and rebirth.

But there is no uniform rule that says this Story Step must be brief. It is here in Story Step #14: Calm Before the Storm, between the catastrophe and the climax, that subplots may have to be resolved or additional exposition given to set up the climax. It is here that we find the false climax of *The Piano*, where Stewart enters George's cabin in the middle of the night and puts a rifle to his face. This scene culminates the love triangle subplot, but it is obviously not the main climax, since Ada herself is absent from the scene. And when we come back to *Midnight Run*, we find eight minutes of screen time elapsing between the falling action of the catastrophe, where Jack discovers that Marvin has indeed turned the Duke over to Jimmy Serrano's men, and the arrival of Serrano at the Las Vegas airport for the showdown. What is happening in those eight minutes? Most importantly, we see Jack drop his old loner mode and elicit the FBI's help to catch Serrano and save the Duke. This involves exposition about the plan, even the introduction of new characters. It could be argued that this is cumbersome, but I believe we are successfully carried through this Story Step by the change in Jack's character. Jack has a new life, and as Robert de Niro plays it, his energy is infectious: "I feel like a cop again!"

We approach each Story Step with flexibility and with our own story goals in mind. Is the Calm Before the Storm in *Terminator 2* "better" than the one in *Midnight Run* because it is shorter? The question itself is senseless. It could only make conceivable sense in the context of the entire story and in relation to the objectives that the development team has laid out for the movie. Other factors also impact the size and shape of Story Steps. These include the idiom and genre of the movie, as well as the way the story is being told (POV, plot structure, subplots, linear/nonlinear, etc.) and our own style as screenwriters. What we can expect to remain consistent are the order and functional content of the Story Steps. There are good reasons the Story Steps appear in the order they do. This is the deep, organic logic of stories. We ask the audience to go out on a limb with us when we try to mix vertebrae around. But within that logical order there is nevertheless an infinite world of storytelling possibility. Nonlinear storytelling in movies presents exciting challenges, because we are reordering the surface structure of the story (the temporal order of sequences and scenes on the screen) while constructing behind that a logical track of story steps the audience follows more or less subliminally. It is not surprising to see more filmmakers responding to this virtuoso Call to Adventure.

Individual Story Steps are already surprisingly complex, because through them we can glimpse the need/mode tension, the dynamics of the Story Molecule, and the Hero's Journey of the character all at work. But at the same time, looking at individual Story Steps is limited. The full picture only emerges when we see how all the Story Steps link together, how all those chunky-looking bones make a spine that flexes and moves and is *alive*. Therefore, we will take a film example we can follow all the way through from beginning to end. For this purpose, we shall use Jane Campion's *The Piano*. Keep in mind that this is simply an example. A still more comprehensive understanding would emerge from comparing the spines of twelve movies side by side, Story Step by Story Step. Hopefully, a discipline of working with these Story Steps will impact positively the way we develop movies in the future.

Traveling the Spine: *The Piano*

To properly frame this journey along the spine of Jane Campion's *The Piano*, let us begin by centering on our intention for doing so. What are we trying to get out of it? *The Piano* is a story that we know has already been produced into a successful movie. But we are not, in this context, interested in analyzing the movie as a finished product. We are interested in decision-making processes that go into shaping a story. We do not have access to the actual development discussions that took place, nor did Jane Campion have access to the Sixteen Story Steps paradigm. Nevertheless, those Story Steps are present. Whether conceptualized under another name or arrived at intuitively, the dynamic of the Story Steps shaped *The Piano*.

A movie is in a constant process of shaping until the final cut is approved, the lab work is done, the sound is mixed, and the film is released. It would be in bad taste to try to second-guess Jane Campion. What we can do, though, for the sake of our understanding, is to hypothetically reconstruct the development challenges implicit in the material itself. If *The Piano* came to us as a project in development, what would we need to consider from a dramaturgical/storytelling point of view, and how could the Sixteen Story Steps aid us in our work?

From a first look at the concept or treatment, we can already pick out salient features that will lead to cutting-edge development questions. "Cutting edge" here means important bifurcation points that will decisively alter the kind of film we end up with. The earlier a bifurcation comes into the development process, the greater the impact on the final result. Therefore, it is a prime development skill to know how to sort the core development questions from the secondary. In the case of *The Piano*, we are retrospectively identifying the core decision-making process that would have guided the story development. The core decisions, sometimes made subconsciously, focus on the unity of idiom, genre, storytelling structure, tone, and style. As always, story development questions are our best aid.

Question: What is the subject? What kind of story are we trying to tell?

- The subject has centrally to do with art. We can guess that from the title. The main character seems to be happy only when she is playing her piano. At those times she appears to take off in rapture. So we can expect art and artists to be central to the theme as well. The story has many traits of an "art movie." The Piano utilizes a common art movie device of announcing the theme at the opening through Ada's voice-over.

Question: What idiom and/or genre would most facilitate the story we have to tell? How can we ascertain this?

- The overall structure of *The Piano* concept is that of a melodrama. In melodrama, the world of the story is conceived as a kind of family. There is a limited horizon. The main character is a person yearning for freedom from the constriction of the family. This yearning is romantic and idealized rather than realistic and responsible. The throughline conflict then develops between the hero and the antagonist, who stands for the social status quo of the family. This is standard melodrama, and it all fits *The Piano*—but as a melodramatic *subplot.*
- The triangle of the three central characters also appears to embody this dynamic of the melodrama.
- Now, here is a cutting-edge question: is *The Piano* a melodrama with an erotic triangle whose main character happens to be an artist? Or is it a drama about an artist's conflict between art and reality, which uses the world of the melodrama as a metaphor? Of course, these are not mutually exclusive choices. It is a question of emphasis. But if we know that we are trying to market a drama about the artist's plight as a melodrama in order to reach a broader audience, then we can be aware all through preproduction and shooting of the particular balancing act we are performing.

- The opening is clearly "art movie," because it explicitly leads with the theme in the V. O. (voice-over).

Question: How do we plan to constellate the characters in the emotional network to support the choice of the melodrama structure?

- It is not a real love triangle, because Ada never loves Stewart.
- Furthermore, it is never clear whether Ada loves George, or only needs/tolerates him, or is propelled toward him unconsciously. Ada is rather wrapped up in herself, even after the climax. Perhaps George is more of a "transitional object," another way of identifying one of the functions of the guide.
- The other element in the love triangle is not Stewart, but the piano!
- Let's look at the *character web* of the story:

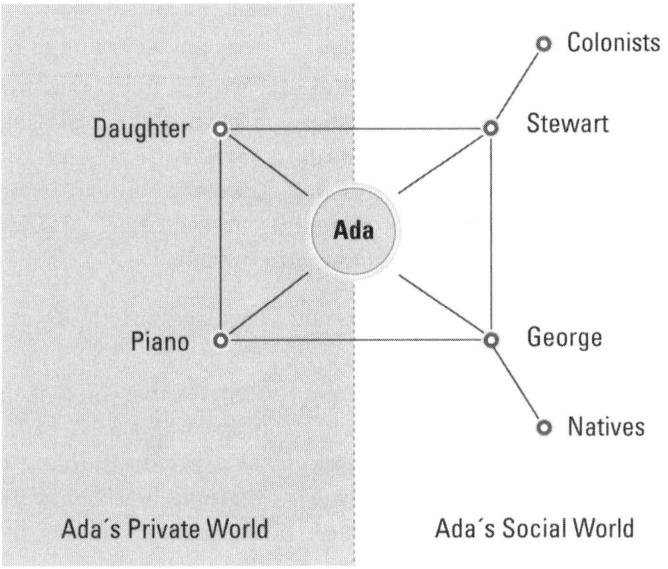

As the story begins, Ada's world contains only her piano and her daughter. All other persons are treated with hostility and suspicion. This split is so extreme as to be striking.

Question: How then can we identify Ada's mode in such a way that it unifies character, plot, and theme?

- What are actions that reveal attitudes? Around what central value do these actions and attitudes cluster? What we see is that Ada doesn't speak willingly to anyone but her daughter. She uses her daughter as a mouthpiece. Ada does not discuss; she makes demands. On the whole, her communication could be described as reactive tending toward passive-aggressive, rather than proactive and constructive. On the other hand, when she plays music she seems to enter a special sphere of art that lifts her above the world around her.

- Ada's daughter is also part of this special world. The worlds of art and childhood are linked in several ways. The daughter is also portrayed as wearing angel wings. As a first approximation of Ada's mode we could cluster the above around a value described as *spiritual flight* from the mundane world through her musical talent.
- The opposite of *spiritual flight* would be *earthy groundedness.*
- The object that embodies the mode value of "spiritual flight" is *the piano*. The object that embodies the contrary value, "earthy groundedness," is: *George*.
- Now, where does that leave the love triangle? Where does Stewart fit into all this? This question is very relevant to orchestrating the melodrama as a container for Ada's inner conflict, where the juice of the story appears to be.

We use the models to focus our initial impressions and to orient us to the story, the material on the desk before us, via questions that will take us deeper. We are neither analyzing nor criticizing the story. We are opening it up. We are taking the measure of it. These general observations could be made from a

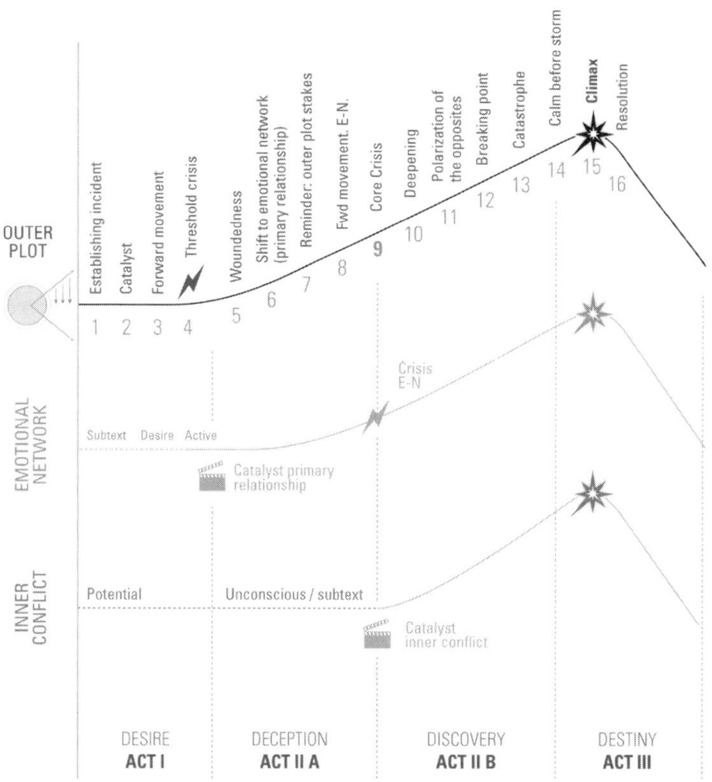

treatment-length version of the story. What is remarkable is that so often, when feeding such observations back to the screenwriter in a consulting session, the writer is just floored. She had not seen these aspects of the story at all. She had been following her own track with her own ideas about how it all fit together. Yet all of my observations are grounded in the story itself. This is not a question of who's right and who's wrong. We should not underestimate how much of a screenplay, especially in early drafts, is written intuitively, even unconsciously. I have simply traveled by an outer path to reach the same spot the writer arrived at by an inward way. Part of screenwriting is to realize clearly what we have actually written!

Movement #1: Story Steps 1–4

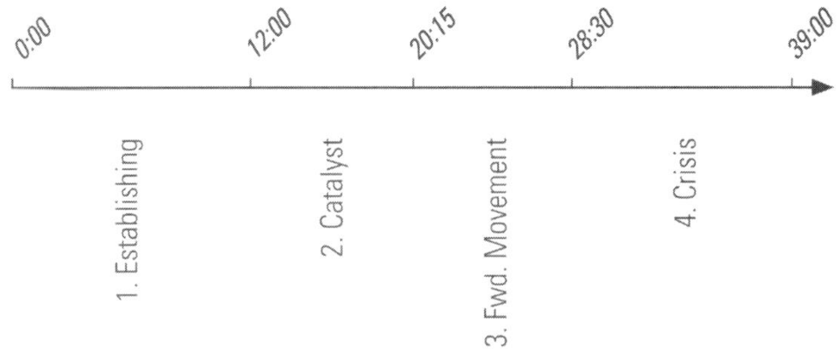

/ **First movement timeline: *The Piano*.**

Story Step #1: Establishing

The Establishing Story Step typically has two parts, an A and a B, identifiable in themselves, which both contribute to the establishing *function*. For reasons mentioned earlier, the first Story Step is very complex because it provides the audience's point of entry into the movie. Part A consists of those images and scenes we may use to open a movie, but which are not part of the main time frame of the story. The opening of the movie, which is to say the first minute or so, is a very compressed visual language that has an immediate impact on the viewer. The opening images receive special attention because they must grab the attention of the audience, establish a tone, and begin to direct the viewer's expectations. The opening may be highly evocative, like that of *Seven*, without indicating exactly where we are. Here are three kinds of openings used in Story Step #1-A that work as special doorways to lead the audience into the movie. They may or may not establish the Day World of the story. The *function* of 1-A is exactly to provide the opening.

- *Hooks*, normally very brief, function to pull the audience into the story on a visceral or emotional level

- *Prologues* give us backstory or exposition from a time frame before the main action
- *Introductions* may also give us exposition, but serve primarily to orchestrate a more distant POV

Story Step 1-A creates an entryway for the audience, orienting them to the language of this specific movie. Story Step 1-B is composed of the establishing scene, properly called, and an establishing incident that is the direct setup for the catalyst. Normally there is a shift in tone and style between 1-A and 1-B, signaled by the end of the opening musical theme and the establishing of a narrative rhythm for the first dramatic scenes. 1-A and 1-B together work to set the text, subtext, and theme for the movie.

The Piano has a prologue/introduction that lasts three minutes, opening with the obscure image from Ada's POV, peeking out at the world from between her fingers. Meanwhile, her voice-over begins to lay out the thematic territory of the story. As an opening strategy, this voice-over is rather direct. It is the evocative content of the monologue that creates the sense of fey mystery: the voice you hear is her mind's voice. She has *willed* herself not to speak, but she is not silent because of her piano. The images are also evocative, a montage that in fact prevents us from getting "grounded" in the space-time of the narrative. Where exactly are we? Who exactly are these people? The prologue ends with a scene at night where Ada can't help playing her piano in its packing crate. A sour-looking older woman intervenes, and Ada stops. This foreshadows the motif of the isolated artist versus an uncomprehending society. Thus ends the introduction, Story Step 1-A.

We cut to Ada and her daughter being unloaded on the beach in New Zealand. The entire voyage has been eliminated, and a time gap brings us now into the present time of the story. This is an efficient move to the establishing scene. Here we are introduced to the world in which the story will take place. The two sides of Ada's behavior are established: her aggressiveness toward the sailors on one hand, and the magic world of art she creates with her daughter on the other. Through most of the story, Ada is in one of these either/or extremes. One could say that Ada's behavior, in storytelling terms, is a risky aspect. Unless one identifies with her as an icon, one could fail to empathize with her. If we see her resistance and resentment as caused by a repressive patriarchy, we feel one way about Ada. Her wordlessness becomes a badge of universal female victimhood. If we expect moderate, adult behavior from her, we will feel another way. In any case, Ada is established as an arch-romantic melodrama heroine and an artist as "magical child."

The arrival of Stewart at the beach, accompanied by George and the natives, provides a natural setting for the establishing incident: the first encounter of the mail-order couple. Now, here may seem to be a subtle point, but it is in fact necessary to the articulation of the Act I setup. This is that there is not only a catalyst early in Act I, there are in fact *two* interlocking events: an inciting incident and a dramatic catalyst. The inciting incident gets the *story* going, in this case the story of Ada's marriage to a man she's never met. The catalyst gets the plot going. Story and plot are by no means identical. A story is a sequence of events with a beginning, middle, and end. A plot is a dialectical structure of growth through crisis. We do not have a Call to Adventure or throughline dramatic question until the catalyst. But the catalyst itself needs a context and a trigger to set it up. These are provided by the establishing incident. Immediately in this establishing/inciting incident of *The Piano*, the characters are orchestrated, and along with them the future conflict. Stewart is disappointed that Ada is "small." George is both earthy and empathic. The difference is not pushed in the audience's face, but laid in the subtext. This inciting incident in *The Piano* is very successful due to its economy of means. Because we have all the characters "onstage" together, all of the dynamics among them are laid out forcefully in three minutes of screen time. We already have the emotional network constellated.

Story Step #2: Catalyst

The prime function of Story Step #2: Catalyst is to establish the hero's plot goal and raise the throughline plot question, thus getting the outer plotline moving. The plot goal and plot question are two ways of expressing the same point. The throughline plot question will only be answered at the movie's climax.

Continuing in the same scene, we arrive at the dramatic catalyst at 12:30 into the movie.[34] Stewart will not take the piano with them, though Ada insists. Now, Stewart has already been "nailed" as lacking empathy. This, along with his brusque nervousness, makes his refusal seem cold and callous. We might note that there is never a discussion of a compromise, like moving the piano at least off the beach and away from the threatening tides. Why? In order to create a certain effect for the audience, the emotional impact of the shot a minute later where Ada looks down yearningly from the high bluff at the piano, alone and abandoned on the beach. This is a "beauty shot" that has a very peculiar erotic quality, especially as the piano from this high angle resembles nothing so much as a coffin. I mention this because very often when reading a script, certain moments like this stand out with a special, dreamlike quality. This is usually a clue to where the juice, the deepest motivation, is for the screenwriter—though, as with dreams, the meaning of the image may be largely unconscious. It is quite natural for the screenwriter's juice to be identified with the hero's Call to Adventure, but it also creates a blind spot for the writer.

Here is Ada's necessity, the if/then proposition. It is clear from the shift in the energy/tone in this shot that this is the Call to Adventure for her. What does Ada

34. All timings are referenced to the opening image of the movie.

want? Her piano. How does she want it? In an erotically tinged way, as a vehicle for spiritual flight above the mundane world. Also, in a high-romantic passion where love and death (the coffin) are commingled. Her throughline plot goal will include both the piano as object and the ecstasy state to which the piano is linked. So the outer plot throughline question may be stated as: *Will Ada be reunited with her piano*? ("Reunited" here will come to imply more than physical contiguity.)

Two points can be made here about how catalysts work, learning from *The Piano*. The first point refers back to the relationship between establishing incident and dramatic catalyst. This is that the catalyst is not *always* the bigger event. Yes, in *The Piano*, we could say it is handled in the "typical" way, where the sequence keeps building to the climactic point where Ada looks down from the bluff. The shape of the sequence underscores and places the audience's attention on the catalyst/call. But in other cases, often in thrillers, it is the establishing incident which is the "big" scene—the heist, deal, or killing—and the actual dramatic catalyst is a smaller moment in the falling action when the detective comes in to handle the case. Look at how these two steps are orchestrated in *Witness*. The inciting incident, the killing of the undercover cop in the train station washroom, is much more dramatic, and is given more screen time, than John Book's entrance. But until Book enters, we do not have a throughline plot question. The catalyst is a question of function: at what point do we have a main character with a Call to Adventure and a throughline plot goal?

The second point about catalysts is that the Call to Adventure is often repeated in order to give it greater emphasis. This is standard strategy in comedies because comic heroes are so reluctant. But this device can be found in many character dramas and melodramas, especially when the main character lacks the means to move immediately toward her plot goal. This is obviously the case with Ada. She is rather lost in an alien world, out of control of her destiny. And she can hardly fetch the piano herself. So after this first statement of the call, we have Ada's arrival at the house and her wedding photo in the rain. This part of the Catalyst Story Step is used to shade in Ada's new world, to fill in exposition. The local white women are shown as venal, infantile, and the wedding ceremony is a horror. The daughter is used as a way to give us backstory exposition about Ada, as well as to position her on a higher spiritual plane (the girl's "real" father was a famous German composer, the story about the bolt of lightning, etc.). This effectively shows us a Day World/Night World split externalized in the setting: heavy, earthy, sodden. We feel the weight of the rain and the mud. Ada, whose mode is spiritual flight, is already confronted with its opposite. This leads to the second statement of the call: Ada feels imprisoned by all this and sees the piano in her fantasy, also alone and seemingly endangered on the beach. This restatement of the call comes six minutes after the first, but together they are needed to fulfill the catalyst function.

Story Step #3: Forward Movement

As soon as we have the catalyst, not only do we have a throughline question (will Ada be reunited with her piano?), but we also have a more immediate plot question: what does the hero do *as a consequence* of receiving the Call to Adventure? The nature of the response is the hero's first beat, like Little Hans stepping out of his little hut and hitting the road to find his destiny. This is why we call this Story Step "Forward Movement." What we see at this point will define the plot as a chase, competition, investigation, and so on. This first beat in the forward movement will typically generate a part-throughline question that will frame the action for Act I.

How does Ada take the beat? By going to George and asking to be taken to the beach. George declines. Ada is insistent. A question of tone comes up here, in the "cute" moment where Ada and her daughter watch George saddle his horse. It is sort of funny, but also obtrudes as a "comic bit" patently designed to seduce the audience with its cuteness. Is this "good" or "not good"? The moment obtrudes because humor was not established as part of the palette of this melodrama. To bring in a stagey comic bit 22:00 into the movie is bound to stand out. In addition, it inadvertently points out to what an extreme the poor little girl is a narcissistic extension of her mother. It is only cute if you don't think about how symbiotically enmeshed the two are. The ambiguity of this bit is typical of *The Piano*'s multileveled complexity.

George finally relents and takes them to the beach. Beaches are of course symbols of freedom, both physical and spiritual. Ada is basically inviting George into her spiritual world. They share a moment of communion through the music while the little girl transforms "nature" (the wind-swept beach) into "art" (the many sand sculptures we are shown by the very high-angle aerial shot, itself a perfect visual expression of "spiritual flight"). This excursion will directly set up the Threshold Crisis, where George steals the beat. *The Piano*, for all its atmospheric moments, is closely plotted; notice that the crisis is a direct consequence of Ada's own insistent action, which already crosses the bounds of propriety according to the local Victorian mores. We can understand Ada's act here as reflecting her inordinate zeal for her music and, subtextually, her erotic connection to the piano. The scene also reveals how Ada's compulsion toward her piano creates a blind spot: she is blind to the impact her rapture has on George. (Or has something in Ada's unconscious already decided that George is the only man who can help her into life?) This zeal, which forms a blind spot in Ada's mode, is about to have unforeseen negative consequences. It will lead directly to George buying the piano.

Ada's erotically tinged compulsion carries her further, to carve a keyboard into the dining table. Stewart, with absolutely no sense of play himself, wonders why Ada would play a table. For a man who does not appear overtly stupid, he is sometimes obtuse enough to strain belief. Again, the audience either accepts Stewart via his iconic representation—what he stands for—or one may come to feel the dramatic cards are stacked against him. In other words, there is a didactic element in the story, where the characterizations appear tailored to fit a rhetoric about men and patriarchy. If this were our project in development, we might leave the script as is, but be very concerned about the nuances of the performance. If Stewart comes off as too one-dimensional, the whole texture of the drama will suffer.

George happens to be listening in the shadows at this moment to Stewart's complaint about the damaged table. This direct comparison of the two men leads us easily into the next Story Step. Before we move on, however, we should point out that Story Step #3 is normally where subplots are initiated. When we look at the forward movement of *The Piano*, we see that there are no subplots appearing at this point. Again, for all the atmospherics, the actual narrative development is quite compact and direct—like Ada. Turning this around, we could consider that a narrative this direct *needs* moodiness, needs the landscape to become another character, needs poetic spaces, so that the plot does not appear too flat and simple. Usually the screenwriter has reached this conclusion intuitively.

Story Step #4: Threshold Crisis

Story Step #4: Threshold Crisis contains both an attack from an antagonistic force or character against the hero's forward movement toward the plot goal, and a crossing of a threshold from a Day World into a Night World. One aspect or the other may play the leading role, depending on the requirements of the story, but both must be present to fulfill the Story Step's function of showing the audience that the dramatic conflict is now truly engaged and the hero is leaving her comfort zone. Consequently, we see the hero's mode begin the process of breakdown.

In the very next scene, George offers Stewart eighty acres of land in exchange for the piano. Thus the Threshold Crisis Story Step begins. There is no gap at all from the previous Story Step to this one. We have discussed elsewhere the detailed content of the crisis/threshold crossing. Here, let us see how the function of the Story Step shapes the action from within.

The Story Step has its own dramatic curve. The establishing moment of the Story Step is the offer of land for the piano. Without consulting Ada, Stewart agrees. The Threshold Crisis Story Step is catalyzed when Stewart volunteers that Ada could give George lessons. It is Stewart's idea, as though placed there in his head by George. Yet this is all consequential to Ada's drive to get her piano. The energy shifts into a higher gear of conflict in the next scene when Ada gets the news. Her protest becomes a fit of rage, but Stewart forces her to engage in the lessons. We have a physical threshold crossing as George has men carry the piano to his cabin. Then the energy turns inward. The scene where George has the piano tuned acts as a transition. As though hearing it from afar, Ada enters a pensive mood. A midpoint moment to the Story Step comes when Ada arrives at George's to inspect the piano and is surprised to find it in tune. She plays. There follows a brief scene at night where Ada tells her daughter a story of her father.

The story implies that this man, the girl's father, became frightened, presumably of the intensity of their relationship, or of Ada herself. At this moment Stewart looks in to say goodnight, but in fact the scene is used to foreshadow the intense erotic involvement that is to come with George. We move to the catastrophe/climax of the Story Step: at the first lesson, George kisses Ada's neck and offers her the deal. Ada can buy back her piano, one key per "lesson." As falling action, we cut to the daughter outside the cabin, first tormenting and then mothering a dog. The daughter is not merely taking out her frustration at being excluded, she is simultaneously mimicking Ada's own pattern of either/or behavior and providing a metaphor for the emotional tortures to come.

To summarize, through this Threshold Crisis Ada loses control. She is confronted by a threshold guardian who now controls her access to her piano. Her wound is a moral and ethical one: to have her own property taken from her and to be treated as a pawn of men. Through this attack, Ada enters a Night World that appears contrary to her Day World ideal. She wants spiritual freedom but is getting physical confinement. Her mode is starting to break down. The E-N relationship between Ada and George is also catalyzed by this same act. From this point on, they are bound together by the piano. George has been positioned as the threshold guardian who will become the guide in Act II, while Stewart is positioned as the unsympathetic husband who will become the actual antagonist of the melodrama subplot.

A side note on writer's process and writer's journey, using the example of *The Piano* because it provides rich material—but neither presuming to know anything about Jane Campion nor presuming to draw personal conclusions. We have in this story step the third small anecdote about the girl's father. Once again, Ada is placed "above" others. The man is described as frightened, but Ada herself is not. This is of course what is so one-sided about Ada's mode: it is both more and less than human. The normal range of human feeling is missing, for whatever reason, but there are special zones of feeling and experience that Ada can access. They are intense and carry an imperative that is connected with her musical daemon. In addition, the story about the father is completely ungrounded. This man, the father, is never given a name. There is no specific place or time mentioned, so these anecdotes float above the world of facts. They cannot be taken as true stories. They are elements of Ada's personal mythology, a mythology Ada seems to place between herself and reality.

This is a place where a screenwriter's work—or working with a screenwriter—gets very interesting. The double question that rises is this: how close is Ada's personal mythology to the writer's mythology, and how aware is the writer of the conditioning lens of her own personal myth? Is she able to do the inner work to put some perspective between herself and her character? If not, that identification could form a black hole into which the story development tumbles. Then strange things can happen: people (producers, studio execs, etc.) get their backs up and become stubborn as hell for no apparent reason. The story development or the project funding run into roadblocks. Where are the problems coming from? Some sort of psychic field may have been constellated in the real world by the author's identification with the character. It is one reason projects get cancelled.

Because all this is bound up with the question of complexes and the fields constellated by complexes, let's demystify complexes to the extent we can. Complexes are not "bad" in themselves. Complexes are first of all simply part of the psyche's means of organizing itself. They are inevitable. They may constellate either positively or negatively. Complexes organize experience by attracting it around "centers" or "attractors" within the unconscious. The problem is in the compelling nature of complexes. Under their influence, we make projections and behave compulsively. We cannot imagine what has gotten into us. It is hard to be objective when in the grip of a complex, because the attractor itself is unconscious, in the Night World, and thus invisible to us. As a result, we can act out rather blindly the signals sent from the attractor.

So expect that whenever the story touches a complex, the screenwriter will suddenly be very touchy. These areas need to be approached with respect and empathy. But sometimes they do need to be discussed, because they hold back the story. In the case of *The Piano*, we can see that the writer is doing or has done the appropriate work, because we do see Ada move away from her original mode through the story. She does grow through crisis. The stuff of Ada's fantasies helps us understand her mode. Yet we can also feel a powerful tug to identify the movie's POV with Ada's POV. There is so much juice here that it cannot all be contained, it seems, by the story. The power of an invisible attractor may in part explain, for example, the movie's ambivalent multiple ending.

This is part of the real work of screenwriting. Putting on the overalls and hard hat and going down into creative darkness means entering the proximity of the attractors, our own complexes.

Movement #2: Story Steps 5–9

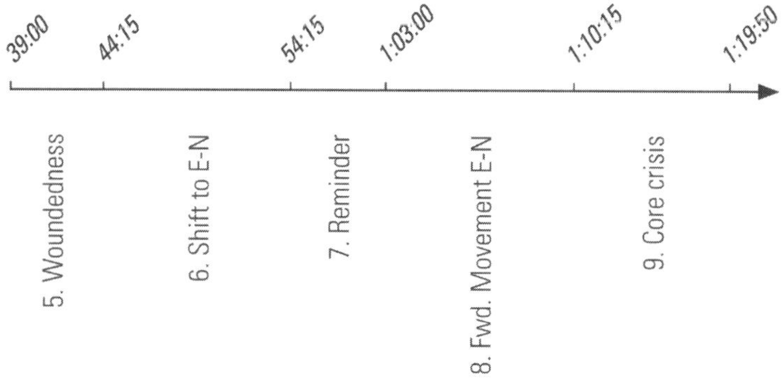

/ Second movement timeline: *The Piano.*

Story Step #5: Woundedness

Now we leave the familiar territory of Act I for the open spaces, the "steppes," of Act II. It is here that the Sixteen Steps paradigm really proves its value as an instrument of guidance. The first step into this new territory is actually quite simple: show us the consequence of the Threshold Crisis. This is what we mean by *woundedness*. First of all, show us what has changed for Ada. Let us see how she has been impacted by the attack of the threshold guardian, the loss of control, and the cracks appearing in her mode. Where is Ada now, in this Night World? And what is shifting for the other characters in the emotional network? The whole status quo situation of Act I has been destabilized, so we can expect movement.

The Piano handles this step in an oblique, indirect way. Specifically, Ada remains rather opaque while everyone changes around her. Why should the Story Step be handled in this way? The answer probably lies in the portrayal of Ada's character. If Ada shows too much moral outrage over the unfairness of George's "deal," it will be hard to believe the shift to the love story later in Act II. But if she shows too much acquiescence, her character becomes inconsistent. Given Ada's extreme introversion, it might be better to play her opaquely and let everyone else point to her through their reactions, their projections. We see it played this way on the screen, but let us appreciate that other possibilities were doubtless explored in earlier drafts.

Thus, Story Step #5: Woundedness opens not on Ada, but on Stewart, helping with preparations for the local drama club. The whole affair, like the angel with an axe (one of the children in costume playing with the prop axe), gives a violent and perverted impression. The paradox from the previous scene of the daughter's double-bind behavior with the dog gets an added motif, and the later violence is foreshadowed. A cut takes us back to the girl and the dog. It is the next piano lesson. She is forced to play outside and she doesn't like it. So, one element of woundedness in this film is a break in the symbiosis of mother and daughter. Inside, Ada plays while George watches from the bed. Later we see George, naked, wiping the piano with his shirt. This importantly reveals more about George's character. At the crisis, we might have seen him as an opportunist. Now it is clear that he is rather obsessed—and vulnerable, himself wounded by the impact of Ada on him. This is a key scene structurally, because it starts to open the story into George's POV, and detach us somewhat from Ada's. So, in this case, the characters who exhibit woundedness are specifically the daughter and George. This is an unusual treatment of the woundedness motif. In the falling action of the Story Step, Stewart asks about the lessons. Ada smiles. Here we see that among the dynamics shifting as a result of the crisis is the power balance between Stewart and Ada.

Woundedness is typically a brief Story Step. Obviously, the more time and energy we give to the hero's wounds, the more dramatic and thematic importance we give it. Dwell on it too much, and we risk making the character appear pathetic. It is, however, crucial to record the consequence of the crisis, or else the crisis itself is not fully real for the audience. But we usually tend to touch it in passing. What we really want to see is the hero's next move, her next action in the face of necessity.

Story Step #6: Shift to the Emotional Network (the Primary Relationship)

We shall recall that the story energy shifts to the emotional network ring of the Story Molecule at this point.* The way Story Step #6: Shift to the Emotional Network is typically played is that the hero's energy moving toward the outer plot goal is blocked as a consequence of the wounding at the Threshold Crisis, and his libido turns in another direction. That new direction is into the primary relationship, be it buddy, partner, or love interest. In an ensemble movie like *The Commitments*, conflict within the ensemble starts to take center stage. *The Piano* presents two variations on this motif, based on this story's own individual dramaturgy. First, as in *Moonstruck*, we have a character, George, who appears as the threshold guardian in Act I, but becomes the guide into the Night World of feeling in Act II. What is this Night World? Let's be clear: it is the world of Ada's unacknowledged universal need. Therefore it is neither sex nor infidelity as such. And why specifically George as the guide/lover? Because George is groundedness personified. It is not good sex that will transform Ada's character, but the fact that George forces Ada to acknowledge and make commitments to the bond that grows between them. So he is a guide to groundedness. The second variation is that the A-story and the B-story are coupled: Ada must go through George to get her piano back. Finally, because we have such a tight character web, we can expect to see a variety of conflicts developed within the ensemble, specifically the love triangle.

The shift to the emotional network begins when George escalates his sexual encroachment on Ada by lifting her skirt. His increasing provocations are a good cinematic way of showing us that the stakes are rising in the relationship. Each piece of clothing that comes off marks a clear progression. What are these stakes? If we missed the meaning of the earlier scene where George wipes the piano with his shirt, we might take the situation as out-and-out sexual predation. It certainly seems like it. Most of the Story Step is taken up with these scenes. Along the way, we have a parallel development of scenes in the wider emotional network. This parallel line also shows a progression: George with the native women who tell him he needs a wife, the daughter at the play rehearsal, a scene where Stewart asks George about the lessons. Here we have Stewart's first look of suspicion.

* See Chapter Nine: The Second Dramatic Movement section entitled *Rising Action, Rising Tension.*

The Story Step culminates in a scene where George offers Ada five piano keys if she will lie down with him. Now there is not only progression, but a qualitative shift in the dynamics of their relationship as well. George caresses her. Ada clearly doesn't like it. He notices, does not force things, and is unhappy. She leaves, and the scene and Story Step end on George's ambivalent feelings. This lets us know both that George is not a brute and that Ada has some new leverage. Notice that by ending the scene and the Story Step on George, we continue the crucial shift of the audience's POV toward him. This is done *because* George is the guide/lover. If he were simply the antagonist, a different strategy would be required. (Compare with *Raise the Red Lanterns*, which remains fixed in Song Lian's POV.)

The growing conflict between mother and daughter is still handled obliquely: the two are never shown in the same scene during Story Step #6, cinematically implying a separation.

Story Step #7: Reminder That Outer Plot Stakes Are Rising

As the audience's interest has become focused on the building relationship, it becomes a danger that the sense of the outer plot stakes may fade or diminish. The key balance the screenplay must achieve at this point is to establish that there are now two lines of growing conflict, the emotional conflict in the relationship and escalating "real world" plot conflict as well.

What outer-world stakes have been established in *The Piano* at this point? Clearly, the danger is that Stewart will find out about the sexual game between Ada and George. It has not yet been laid out, however, what Stewart might be capable of doing when he discovers the truth.

In fact, a double potential weakness of the story as it is developing appears here. One aspect is that Stewart does not make a very strong antagonist. His stiffness has a brittle edge. He has neither convinced nor forced Ada to become more intimate with him. As a consequence, the audience must infer from the subtext what is at stake. But the big aspect, if we reflect on it systematically, is that the throughline plot question, Ada's plot goal, centers on the piano. The question—will Ada be reunited with her piano?—only involves Stewart as a peripheral obstacle. Stewart is more the antagonist of a melodrama subplot, since it is George who is the main obstacle to Ada's plot goal at this moment. This takes us directly back to one of the cutting-edge development questions we asked at the beginning of this exploration of *The Piano*. The drama itself risks becoming vague and ungrounded. Therefore a reminder to set the outer plot stakes and establish a believable level of risk is even more essential here than in most films.

In a melodrama, the antagonist stands for the status quo values of the "family." The antagonist constrains the hero's yearning for freedom by self-righteously administering the code of the status quo. And, as in all dramas, it is the antagonist who determines how high the stakes and the conflict can rise in

Act II. Stewart is shown as a stick in the mud for sure, but we must recall that by taking in an unwed mother to begin with he has acted charitably in Victorian terms. His behavior with Ada up to now has been obliging, even deferential. We do not see Ada doing any of the normal chores a woman living on the frontier would be expected to do. Nor do we see Ada offering any form of acceptance toward Stewart.

Because Stewart is not yet seen to be a dangerous antagonist, something must now be done to raise the stakes. Here the Reminder Story Step resorts to a stock theatrical device: the play within the play. What is the content of the play? It appears to be some variation on the Bluebeard folktales, but staged as a "shadow" play, the shadows of the characters projected from behind onto a white cloth screen. In the play, the Bluebeard murderer chops off the heroine's hand. This certainly qualifies as an art movie device and a rather bald foreshadowing of the catastrophe. Is that enough to make you feel the plot stakes are rising? Not really. The real juice, however, is in the subtext of Stewart, Ada, and George sitting in the audience—though this still tells us nothing new about Stewart as an antagonist. George is one seat away from Ada, but Ada won't let him any closer. Stewart takes Ada's hand. George, clearly jealous, leaves. Ada smiles, aware of her own power over George. Maybe this combination of the play and the subtext will carry most of the audience. But we could also say from a narrative point of view that Stewart's passivity as an antagonist is the weakest aspect of the story's construction. This weakness of the antagonist may have its own negative consequences for the narrative later on in Act II.

The play sequence takes up the first half of Story Step #7. The second half of the Story Step shows us the next lesson. George appears naked, and wants to lie with Ada without clothes. The atmosphere is rather grave as the weight of what is at stake presses on both characters. This time the daughter is spying on them, so the stakes really are rising. In the following scene, Stewart finds the daughter playing sex games with native children and is furious. In the end, our perception of the outer plot stakes and the momentum of rising tension is much higher than it was at the beginning of Story Step #7.

These last two scenes bring up a point about interpreting Story Steps. Of course there is some interpretation involved. Someone could argue, for example, that the Reminder Story Step is comprised only of the theater sequence, while these last two scenes belong to the next Story Step, #8: Forward Movement in the Relationship. This is something to consider, because we do see a further escalation in that primary relationship, specifically that George is depressed with jealousy and his demands start to have a desperate quality. But we have to come back to the question of *function*. The function of this Story Step #7 is to remind the audience that the outer plot stakes are rising. In this case, as the two lines are coupled, the outer plot stakes are rising *because* of the shift in the emotional network. The play in itself is not enough to establish the level of risk. We need to see that Stewart is beginning to catch on. And we do see it, in his reaction to the girl's sex game. Stewart already knows, unconsciously, therefore this scene makes a more natural and forceful climax to the Story Step. And in fact, the scene where Ada lies with George is not *played* for the deepening of their relationship, or we would have held on that action longer. The emphasis is instead on the daughter's *discovery* of them.

Story Step #8: Forward Movement in the Relationship

The emotional network substory of the Story Molecule has been active since the crisis at the end of Act I. There, the primary relationship was catalyzed when Ada and George made the deal for piano lessons. We noted in Chapter Nine that in the first half of Act II, the line of the E-N development follows the same progression as the development of the outer plot in Act I: setup, catalyst, forward movement, crisis/threshold crossing. Story Steps #5 and #7 function to keep the new primary relationship anchored in the context of the outer plot. Otherwise there would be the danger, like that apparent in *Witness*, that the love interest could pull away and become a separate story, destroying the dramatic unity. Story Step #6 shows the main character's first move into this emotional territory, beginning to establish new dramatic stakes on this E-N level.

Now, Story Step #8 develops momentum and stakes for that relationship. It shows us the consequences *within the relationship* of the rising outer plot stakes of Story Step #7. In addition, it is the direct setup for the Core Crisis (Story Step #9), which, among other things, is the crisis/threshold crossing for this primary relationship. The prime function of Story Step #8: Forward Movement in the Forward Movement in the Primary Relationship is to bring the primary relationship up to the point of crisis, to demonstrate that a crisis will inevitably and immediately follow.

For forward movement in the E-N relationship, it is essential to know what is in the subtext of the primary relationship at this stage, because the energy in that subtext is now bubbling up to the surface. So we want to look ahead to the Core Crisis and ask what exactly is the threshold the two characters will cross (always a threshold of intimacy and trust), what new risk and opportunity come into play (crisis = risk + opportunity) at that threshold, and how this is a point of no return.

In the forward movement in the E-N relationship, the characters are still struggling to keep the energy of the relationship under control, hidden from themselves, each other, and the outside world. The tension of ambivalence becomes very great at this point: to deny, start a fight, even break things off. It happens in our own lives as well when we face a relationship threshold. These thresholds show their archetypal character because images and metaphors for the entire threshold pattern in general can occur in any given instance. Popping the marriage question can feel a lot like jumping out of an airplane the first time you went skydiving. Starting a new job can feel like the commitment of a marriage, and so on. The anxiety on the actual threshold evokes these fantasies, but the associated imagery belongs to the archetypal moment.

Story Step #8 brings the first major change in the direction of *The Piano*, and it is a real reversal: George unexpectedly sends the piano back. Now, on the face of it, we might not see this as a step forward into the relationship. We must understand that the tension is more than George can bear. The scene between George and Ada, which comes at 1:04:20 into the movie, is full of twists and is one of the most dramatically successful in the movie. Ada storms angrily to George's cabin. Where we might expect Ada to be pleased, even triumphant to finally have her piano, she is shocked, choking with outrage. George wants her to care for him. She cannot, and he tells her to go. In a second twist, Stewart intervenes at this point, trying to persuade George to continue the lessons. Stewart is not sure what it all means.

The Story Step culminates in a third and climactic shift, one which will set up not only the Core Crisis Story Step, but the entire rest of the story. The piano arrives and is set in place in Stewart's house. Finally, Ada has her own piano in her own home. But when Stewart asks her to play, Ada walks out of the house. This is *the* big shift in Ada's motive, though motive is much too conscious and ego-oriented a word to describe what is going on in Ada's psyche. Jane Campion finds an elegant cinematic metaphor instead. As the daughter, now clearly shifting allegiances toward Stewart, plays the piano, Ada stands staring into the rainforest. The camera moves in on her from behind, arriving finally on a CU of her chignon—then the image dissolves into an almost claustrophobically enclosed shot of the dense foliage, as if to say: "Ada's thoughts are as dark and tangled as the forest itself."

This moment has been prepared for us by the previous scenes, and thus does not come as a discontinuity in Ada's character. All of the Story Steps since the crisis have been building to this point. We have seen that even while George is raising the stakes, he is also making himself more vulnerable. As a result, the power in the relationship is shifting toward a balancing point between the two. Both George and Ada have established a certain kind of power, so there is now also the possibility of mutuality. It has proven useful to let Ada remain opaque. As a story, *The Piano* succeeds very well through indirection, through saying less and suggesting more, like Ada herself. We have been given just enough subtextual hints, but not more, to allow her shift of motive to feel believable. This scene makes a powerful setup for the Core Crisis immediately to follow, for we already see Ada physically moving away from the piano and toward another center of value.

Story Step #9: Core Crisis

The Core Crisis is a complex and subtle Story Step where all three levels of the Story Molecule intersect in a dynamic interaction. On the outer plot level, we have the pivot from the first half of Act II (Wounding and Recovery) into the second half (Setting the Double Bind). Each Story Step, as it clicks into place, provides a turn or shift in the narrative, but the Core Crisis can be justly considered the key pivot of the entire screenplay construction. Up to the Core Crisis Story Step, the story has been expanding outward with the growing relationships and mounting conflict. From the Core Crisis onward, though the plot stakes are still rising, the action starts focusing down with greater intensity toward the inevitable climax.

The greater intensity will come from adding the conflict of the inner levels of the Story Molecule to the outer plot conflict. This comes as the direct consequence of Story Step #8. On the E-N level, we have the crisis/threshold crossing in the primary relationship. This serves to drive the conflict of values to a deeper level, as the love interest now presents a value of equal intensity to the mode value. This will force a choice—and an existential crisis. Thus the Core Crisis also serves to catalyze the inner need/mode conflict. Where before this was a potential problem the hero tried by all means to put off and deny, now it becomes the "grow or die" situation.

These are the storytelling functions Story Step #9 must fulfill. How can all this be accomplished in one Story Step? Filmmaking (and thus screenwriting) is a shorthand language. As the Core Crisis Story Step opens, we see that the piano no longer means for Ada what it used to mean. She fiddles with the keys, trying to regain the touch. In fact, she caresses the keys with the back of her hand. We imagine her imagining herself caressed by George, or by whom? An extreme CU shows us a detail of a piano key, a heart and arrow simultaneously revealing a backstory wound and foreshadowing the love token Ada will send to George. The effect is not forced; there is a basic trust that the audience will get it. As though triggered by this reminder of past love, Ada immediately heads for George's cabin. The image, so simple in itself, has suggested a highly complex motivation. This is appropriate to both Ada's character and the theme, because though compelled, she is still floating, not yet grounded.

In melodramas, because the world of the story is defined as "family," most of the action, and most of the juice, resides in the emotional network. Therefore it is not surprising that the main emphasis in this Story Step is placed on the crisis/threshold crossing in the relationship of Ada and George, and the outer plot implications are spun out of that. Note that this threshold is marked by a physical boundary: the path through the wildness from Stewart's cabin to George's, with all of the overtones of exodus out of a bondage to a "promised land" that evokes. As this scene opens, the daughter is tugging at Ada's skirt to be allowed to come. Ada pushes her away. Moments later, Stewart finds the girl swearing a blue streak. When Stewart asks where Ada went, she screams, "To hell!" The stage is set for real trouble, while at the same time it catches the universal tone of urgent resistance that erupts within and without as an individual struggles to be born into her authentic life.

On a deeper level, the threshold is this: in the first half of Act II, Ada was compelled to go to George's in order to get her piano back. Now she has it, so why is she going to George's? Suppose we could catch Ada in the forest just now and ask her, "Ada, dear, do you really know what you're doing?" What would Ada's answer be? She knows that she is going to see George. But she is in such an agitated, compulsive state that it would be fairer to say that an imperative drive is acting through her rather than that she is doing it as a conscious volition. She does not know what will happen at George's. This is important for Ada's characterization. It really must be a threshold to the unknown for both Ada and the audience.

This determines the way the scene is played when she arrives. Like many of us, Ada is not conscious enough on such a threshold to order events. She can only participate in the compelling flow that carries her, and perhaps create the conditions where something happens that, in effect, carries out the work of destiny. The point, at such a threshold, is neither to be articulate nor elegant, but simply to get across, by hook or by crook. So Ada's inability to express herself here is eloquently expressive. The fact that she resorts to hitting George seems meant to suggest the primal depth of what drives her. *It* moves her life forward.

Just as Ada's violence finally gives her access to her passion, Stewart, as the threshold guardian, arrives outside the shack. The action rises as the clothes come off, but the movie has enough self-respect to stick to its premise and not use the sex gratuitously. The function of the Story Step is not lost. Of course, we know that the climax of intercourse is orgasm. But we do not get the orgasm. Where the orgasm would have been, we get a surprise: Ada speaks. This act reminds us of the opening, the question evoked at the prologue: why can't Ada speak? It also foreshadows the resolution, where we see that Ada has regained her voice. So, the pivoting function of the Core Crisis is fulfilled. The voice is our instrument of communication. Communication implies interaction with others, with all the conditionality, the give and take, of human life. Communion with others demands that we come down from the plane of the ideal and absolute. Baudelaire's poem *The Albatross* comes to mind as an expression of the torture the soaring spirit experiences when it must come to earth. It is a poem that evokes that melancholy and spitefulness toward the world common to Baudelaire's sense of "spleen," and comes out of the specific romantic culture of midnineteenth-century Europe. Ada might well have been familiar with it.

> Le Poète est semblable au prince des nuées
> Qui hante la tempête et se rit de l'archer;
> Exilé sur le sol au milieu des huées,
> Ses ailes de géant l'empêchent de marcher.
>
> (The poet is like that prince of the clouds
> Who haunts the storms and makes fun of the archer;
> Exiled to the ground, surrounded by jeers,
> His giant wings block him from moving about.)

Ada's unacknowledged need for grounding, for accepting the fundamental condition of incarnation, is pushing for expression. But has she indeed reached a point of no return? After all, there are real-world obstacles to her relation with George, one of them at this moment listening in the darkness below the floorboards. The conflict will get much worse before it gets better. And we can see in Ada's brusque manner as she dresses (in the next scene) that she is guarded and ambivalent. She will go back to the comfort zone if she can. Therefore it is important for the development of the conflict that George challenges Ada just now, saying that, if she is sincere, she must come again tomorrow. In a key cinematic moment of compressed visual imagery, George asks Ada if she loves him. At that instant, she looks at herself in the mirror. Her spirit is still circulating within the boxed frame of her own system. She is not open. Her next act, of pulling up George's shirt and kissing his chest, reinforces rather than contradicts this impression. Her action does not address George's question. We can read this from George's reaction: this is not the response he wants. He is not asking if she is sexually aroused, but if she is sincere; not if she desires him, but if she *loves* him. Now we have the throughline question for the relationship: *will Ada and George be together?*

In Story Steps #8 and #9, we have answered the question that framed the action for the first half of Act II: will Ada get her piano back? Yes, she will. But the twist that the piano has lost its value as the center of Ada's universe leads to a new question that will frame the action for the rest of Act II: will Ada choose George over the piano? The stakes have risen, because Ada has crossed the threshold of adultery in a Victorian society. And now her husband knows the truth. In the falling action that ends the Story Step, Stewart fumes as Ada plays delightedly in the bedroom, reunited for a beat with her daughter. Whatever malice or retribution Stewart has within him, we can guess that the storm is about to break.

The existential crisis Ada now faces is whether to accept the real love George offers, with the terrible conflicts, commitments, and limitations that will surely attend it, or retreat again to the beautiful but autistically enclosed world of her music. It will take the reminder of Act II to push her to the point of choice.

Movement #3: Story Steps 10–13

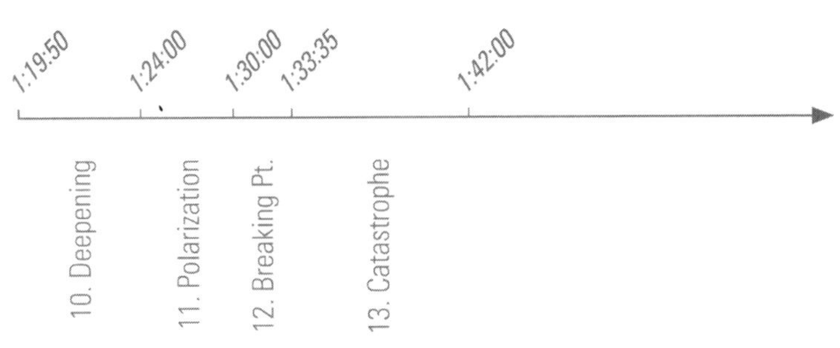

/ **Third movement timeline:** ***The Piano.***

Story Step #10: Deepening

In Story Step #10: Deepening, we must first of all show the consequences of the Core Crisis on the three levels of the story molecule. Then we must focus the conflict into the double bind that leads to the catastrophe.

The second dramatic movement has taken an external conflict (how can Ada get her piano?) and has opened up the feeling levels of it, awakening instinctual imperatives of both fear and desire. The new erotic wound has activated old wounds in relation to her former love and her wounded capacity to love at all. Though she has her piano now, she is still not "reunited" with it. Something larger is at stake now: can Ada succeed in coming back to real life? Can she fully inhabit her life? That small scene in the falling action of the Core Crisis Story Step, where Ada twirls around with her long hair flowing, laughing like a child, is deeply revealing of how much of Ada's life has been missing. We are never told what Ada's backstory wound is. We are rather presented with a pattern of wounds inseparable from Ada's extraordinary sensitivity. What we do see is that Ada behaves like a very hurt, *very* small child. This may be symptomatic of very early wounds, wounds to the infant's primal bond, before a child can even speak. If so, this is implicit in the story; it is part of the subtext. We are only given bits of context around why Ada in some past time took refuge in her piano. Now, this third movement drives Ada to the edge. Can she live? Can she accept life "on the ground"? This is the existential, live-or-die question that becomes active after the Core Crisis.

This is all bound up together with the piano. The piano has saved her life in the past, made life endurable, at the cost of placing her in a special zone insulated from further wounds and to that extent "outside" life. Now that same refuge has become her bane. Why must the piano be destroyed at the climax? For many people this remains a mystery, another impulsive act on Ada's part. But if the death of the piano is not part of a necessity, then the climax is a dramatic failure. Everything in this third movement is pointing directly to that climax, and derives its meaning from that climax, where the piano dies but Ada is born. If, when developing a screenplay, we forget for a moment where we are going, then we instantly lose the meaning of the journey. And conversely, if we forget the meaning of the journey, we instantly lose our way.

Story Step #10: Deepening first of all shows us the consequence of the Core Crisis. Where are the two characters in the primary relationship after crossing the threshold of intimacy? How does each one feel right at this moment? Even though we do not have a scene with George, we want to imagine him after Ada has left the cabin. And what has shifted in the larger emotional network that includes Stewart and the daughter? The big shift is that now everyone knows about the affair. Conflict is about to escalate.

Deepening means that the conflict is moving to this existential, "grow or die" level. At the same time, it also means that the quality of the outer plot conflict is sharpening. The hero is stepping into the double bind where the opposing mode and need values prove irreconcilable and pull apart, crucifying the hero in the middle. Part of the process is that the character does not yet realize the full dimension of the conflict and is by no means ready to face it. Ada *desires* George and is compelled by her desire. But her unconscious need is still precisely that: unconscious. Unable to face the daemon that is moving in the depths, the hero at this point typically goes into denial. She develops a fantasy that maybe she can somehow have both. In Ada's case, the fantasy is that she can have George as a secret lover, while maintaining her domestic life: Stewart, her daughter, and the piano. *We* can see that this is doomed, but Ada does not.

How are we shown that Ada has such a fantasy? (A fantasy is something interior, after all.) By the fact that she acts the fantasy out when she tries to sneak away to George's the next day. In *The Piano*, this is an especially short Story Step, because Stewart pops her bubble of fantasy immediately. He catches her in the woods and tries to rape her, but Ada is saved by the intervention of the daughter. The Maori have come into the house and are playing the piano. Stewart does not have the drive to consummate his attack. Instead he locks Ada in the house. In the falling action, we see Ada kiss herself in the mirror. Her daughter scolds her, and just wants to have life return to normal. This last beat underscores how dangerously disconnected Ada is. At this point she has primarily absorbed George (or her fantasy of him) into her "magical" world. Consequences? *What* consequences?

This story step lasts about four minutes onscreen. How can it accomplish its function of showing the hero's bubble of denial and destroying it all in four minutes? We recall that the same Story Step in *Midnight Run* took approximately twenty minutes to set up and pay off. The brevity is made possible because the action in this Story Step has been prepared in the step before. The key thing here is establishing that Stewart has observed the lovers. We know he must act, so the bubble is as good as popped before it has formed. Let us look at two hypothetical alternatives, which would have been less effective, but which might have been considered in earlier drafts.

One possibility would have been that the lovers are not discovered by Stewart at the Core Crisis Story Step. Then there would have been time to build Ada's fantasy of having it all. We would have had more of a "love story." But this would have taken more exposition time and very likely caused the dramatic intensity to dissipate because Stewart is already not a strong antagonist. You will have noticed that the Core Crisis Story Step does not come exactly midway through the movie, but begins later, at 1:10:15 in a film with total length of 1:55:15. As I said, we must treat the Story Steps flexibly, according to the needs of our own drama. Still, there is a challenge at this point: how to tell the rest of the story while hopefully remaining within the normal two-hour limit for theatrical release feature films. If the movie gets over that time limit, finding distribution may become much more difficult. An executive producer may be phoning us in the editing room to tell us no way, keep it under two hours or he will take control of the project and do the final cut himself. And . . . *The Piano* is not primarily a love story.

The other option is that Stewart does discover the lovers at the Core Crisis and breaks in on them immediately. What would be wrong with that? Well, there would certainly have been a fight in which the scene and the dramatic momentum would go over to Stewart and George. That would be wrong. It needs to remain Ada's story. Also, Ada would find herself with an immediate—but more superficial—choice to make. We have not yet developed the deepest level of conflict, which is the business of this third movement. Only the impossible double bind causes the deepest character change. It takes some time to put the character in the double bind and convey its meaning to the audience. So, in that case, Ada would be let off the hook rather than going all the way to the "grow or die" point. Giving the hero an easier way out is the solution often found in mediocre movies.

Story Step #11: Polarization of Opposites

When the hero's denial fantasy, which was a spontaneous effort on the part of the old mode to keep itself going, collapses, the tension of the opposites is revealed in all its naked, raw glory. This is the function of Story Step #11: Polarization of Opposites. Life tells us that a decision, a fork on the road, is at hand. A choice is forced upon us, but we are immobilized. Because no choice will relieve the tension, the stress builds to a breaking point. By that point, which way it breaks is out of our control. Some other power beyond the ego then decides.

Ada is locked in the house. She plays the piano in a trance. This is instructive, because it shows us how Ada has used the piano to escape into a safety zone. Stewart wonders at her. This is of course a parallel and evocation of George hearing Ada at the beach in Act I. It creates a subtext question: couldn't Stewart and Ada open up to each other, as George and Ada did? This is unlikely, however, because the fact that Ada has retreated or regressed into the piano is a danger signal for her. In the next scene, Ada caresses Stewart as he sleeps. He wakes. She continues exploring this until Stewart reaches for her, then she recoils. New scene, next day: the local women come to visit, and to bring the news that George is moving away. Ada now plays the piano with forceful dissonance. Here is the moment that the trap of the double bind swings shut, the polarization of opposites. It appears that Ada's options have been cancelled and her time has run out. The women leave, complaining about Ada's wild playing. But it is clear that music will no longer resolve anything for her.

In a restatement of the scene that opened the Story Step, we return to Ada caressing Stewart. He has trouble relaxing and enjoying it; he is simply too tense. This confirms that even if they were to try to make the best of things, they are temperamentally unsuited to each other. Ada cannot be with the man she loves while she is forced to be with the man she does not love, and to whom she cannot open herself. This is the way Story Step #11 is typically played in melodramas: the hero is trapped by the "family," just as he recognizes what freedom could really mean for him. It is at this point in *Trainspotting* that first Begby and then Sick Boy crash in on Renton just as he has started a new life in London without heroin. These situations are double binds: there is no apparent way out, but the character has to do *something*. No way out—unless he changes his way of seeing things.

Story Step #12: Breaking Point

The Breaking Point in *The Piano* is also very brief, a bit more than three minutes. Hearing that George is leaving, Stewart unboards the windows and opens the house. The child, in her angel wings, runs outdoors. Stewart tells Ada it's all for the best and that he must trust her not to contact George. She is free to come and go. He hopes that with time Ada will come to like him. When Stewart leaves for work, Ada removes a key from the piano, writes a love token on it, wraps it in cloth, and gives it to her daughter to take to George. The daughter refuses because they have promised not so see George anymore. But Ada insists, even to the extent of getting rough with the girl. Everything is in place for the catastrophe to be unleashed.

It is one of the strengths of *The Piano* as a narrative that both the crisis and catastrophe are precipitated by actions of Ada herself. The function of the breaking point is to show us how the character reacts to the double-bind situation. Because a character comes to identify with his survival mode, when that mode finally does break down, he really thinks he is gong to die. Panic reactions are common at this point, a last desperate attempt to save the dying mode. From the struggling ego's standpoint, this desperate outburst only succeeds in making things much worse. But paradoxically, the ensuing breakdown of the mode gives luck, fate—however we name that other factor in the psyche that has been buried in the shadow—the chance to create a new pattern.

Thus, we do not see Ada explain to her resisting daughter that this is just a goodbye present, and she can simply leave it at George's. The girl does not even need to speak to him. That would have made logical sense. Why does Ada instead behave so roughly that she constellates the girl's resistance? Ada's conscious motive is to send George this love token. But then it really would have been the end, wouldn't it? Another part of Ada, we could say, *wants* the mistake, *wants* the battle, the confrontation. In fact, perhaps no other course of action would have resulted in splitting her from Stewart and joining her to George. But if it was not a conscious action, who then was the actor?

The breaking point leads directly to the catastrophe, where it appears that Ada loses everything: the object embodying the mode value, the piano, as well as the object embodying the need value, George. She has broken the piano by removing a key from it, her finger is chopped off, and still she is separated from the man she loves. But notice how here, in Story Step #12, we see the resolution foreshadowed. Ada is already making the essential choice: to break the piano in order to affirm her connection to George. This is already the inner climax. A new identity has been born within her as a woman in conscious relation to another person, with whom she shares her innermost self. She affirms this in the face of the greatest conflict, enduring hardship and sacrifice on behalf of this value. In effect, this is why the daughter must deliver the package to Stewart instead. The self will out.

Story Step #13: Catastrophe

It was entirely without conscious intention on my part when I was developing this Sixteen Story Steps model, and it took a seminar participant to point it out to me later, but it is true: somehow the catastrophe turns out to be the unlucky number thirteen. The catastrophe is a complex Story Step that needs some time to unfold. It contains, as we have said, the point of highest dramatic intensity thus far in the narrative. It is the downward stroke that appears to be fatal. Very often, the catastrophe is a very major onscreen event, woe piling upon woe, as in *Dances with Wolves* and, to a lesser extent, *Witness*. One reason for this tidal wave of bad news is that the catastrophe happens on all three levels of the Story Molecule. We outlined this structure in *Witness*. John Book cannot stay with Rachel (E-N), discovers that Carter has been murdered (outer plot, E-N), ventilates his rage (inner), and, as a consequence, the killers discover where he is (outer plot). But sometimes the catastrophe happens more offscreen than on. In *Midnight Run*, it is the breaking point that is the big action sequence. Jack makes a last desperate attempt to elude the FBI and drives off into the desert. The catastrophe is delivered in the falling action: Marvin takes the Duke from Jack, Jack is caught by the FBI, and then he discovers that Marvin has sold the Duke to Serrano to be killed.

As always, the power of the Story Step is in what it means more than in what it looks like. And this meaning is always in the context of the whole drama, the stakes that have been set up through Act I and Act II. This is why establishing a clear need/mode conflict is essential. It is the only way the audience knows what the character has to lose. The catastrophe, we must keep in mind, is the Night of the Soul for Ada.

The Catastrophe Story Step begins when we see Ada's daughter take the other path, not the path to George's. The daughter's growing resentment toward Ada has been carefully developed throughout Act II, so her betrayal seems natural and inevitable. Though this girl is never given a name, she is fully three-dimensional and believable. My partner has pointed out that Ada in fact behaves like an abusive mother, using the little girl for her own narcissistic needs. So she takes the love token to "daddy" instead. As a consequence, Stewart rushes home in a rage. True, Ada's resistance is frantic, but the real ventilation of rage belongs to Stewart. As we know, he chops off Ada's finger. This brings up a delicate point in the orchestration of this catastrophe and of the narrative as a whole: Stewart is the active character here.

Now, it is normal that the antagonist takes the beat at the catastrophe. But it must remain Ada's scene. And the scene must convey more than simply the pathos of victimhood. The catastrophe leads directly to the climax, where the hero will have to be active enough to assert her new value in a way that resolves the throughline conflict. This is a general challenge in story development rather than an issue with *The Piano*. There is a balance needed between showing the suffering and collapse of the hero and showing the "resurrection" element that emerges as a consequence of the catastrophe. Added to this is the complexity that the hero's inner shift or inner climax may be revealed anywhere between Story Steps #12 and #15, depending on where it falls as appropriate to a given story. The simplest formula I have found as a guide to the balance needed here is:

> The hero's *mode* is shown to die,
>
> but the hero's *self* does not.

The specific challenge in *The Piano* is that both male characters are more active than Ada because in their society they have more means for action, and, in addition, Ada is portrayed as an extremely introverted and sensitive character. Stewart takes the beat in the scene, and there is no *action* by means of which Ada can steal the beat back again. Therefore, the storyteller (writer/director) must shift the beat on Ada's behalf. How is this to be done? At least in mainstream American filmmaking, the line is always: make the character *active active active!* It is one of those old saws honored more in theory than in practice. For how can we show the character at "ground zero" until we have revealed his incapacity to act? How can a character be reborn unless he is forced, in Campbell's words, to "bow or submit to the absolutely intolerable"? We as filmmakers are left with that tool which is the necessary expressive complement to activity: *interiority*. Interiority is just as magnetic as activity in a character. The power of every great close-up to take us into the soul of the character attests to this.

The Piano does not rely on a close-up, literally considered, but uses another device to take us closer to Ada in order to keep this her scene. It is the radical suspension of "narrative time" by going into "real time." This is a very common device used at the catastrophe. We watch Ada after her finger has been cut off: shock, disbelief, and a rather fey smile crossing her face. She gets up and staggers a few paces, struggles to appear normal, then finally sinks into the fathomless mud with her skirts billowing absurdly around her. It is like a drunken revision of the earlier shot in Story Step #8, standing at exactly the same spot, just before she crossed the threshold to George's at the Core Crisis. This evocation allows us to compare that Ada full of energetic impulse with this Ada full of despair. In the falling action of the Story Step, Stewart tells the girl to take the finger to George, threatening to cut off another each time they attempt to make contact. The real-time moment (actually slightly slow-motion) held on Ada as she makes those few steps manages to convey that her self is not utterly dead. She has borne witness to her truth and paid the price. Ada appears remarkably calm. We could interpret this as shock—or also as a recognition and acceptance of necessity.

The action of the Story Step closes with the daughter's arrival at George's, George's reaction, and an important scene between Stewart and Ada. Stewart talks deliriously to her. For perhaps the first time, we realize the depth of fantasy he has had about Ada. He climbs on her and wants finally to penetrate her, but her look chills him. He tells her he hears her "voice" in the wind, the frogs, the voice of nature. The way this Story Step is handled in *The Piano*, not only do the consequences of the catastrophe have time to sink in and penetrate the audience, but the narrative takes this moment to reveal an unexpected depth to Stewart's character. Just at the moment we want to hate Stewart, we are forced to empathize with him. Such cross-currents and inner contradictions in a character have been an important part of dramatic tradition and insight at least since Shakespeare. We see that, though he has kept it all inside, Ada has herself been a Call to Adventure for Stewart. What will Stewart do next? Are we witnessing Stewart cross a threshold here? Every character is somewhere on the journey. However, this moment is *also* necessary for us to understand Stewart's behavior in the next Story Step, which would otherwise appear unmotivated. This glimpse into Stewart's soul galvanizes us because the dramatic intensity is still rising, even in this interior moment. We have not yet resolved the conflict or answered the throughline questions.

Movement #4: Story Steps 14–16

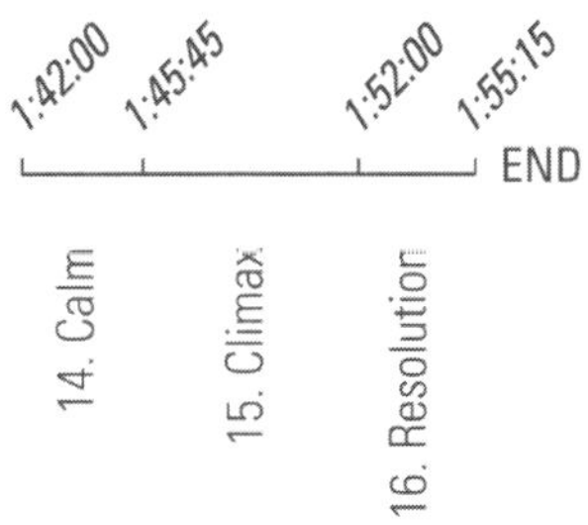

/ Fourth movement timeline: *The Piano*.

Story Step #14: Calm Before the Storm

Now we arrive at the point where this interesting story development problem must be resolved: we have two men who are in open conflict over a woman. The conflict has forced the possessive husband to violence. We have seen the lover swear vengeance, and we have a revelation of the depth of the husband's obsession with his wife. Therefore, we can expect further violence, a climactic confrontation between them. And yet that would be all wrong, because neither of the men is the main character. A big fight scene between them would upstage Ada and take the dramatic focus away from her. Bad idea. It would seem that the story has painted itself into a corner. Screenwriters are experts at getting themselves stuck like this. When we find ourselves as writers in such a trap, and realize *we* created that trap, we can appreciate that our shadow tricked us into it and there is something we can learn from it about our own mode and its blind spots. Then we may be able to find a uniquely creative way out of the corner.

We have commented that Jane Campion wisely chose to play this confrontation between the two men as an anticlimax. Let us look at how this works. We cut from the previous scene to find Stewart entering George's hut at night. He has a rifle. So the promise of violence set up in the previous Story Step is en route to fulfillment. Finding George in the dark interior, Stewart puts the gun to his face. Already, the audience starts jumping to all sorts of possibilities. It is an iconic moment subliminally remembered from hundreds of old Westerns and other action movies.

Then comes a twist so radical it seems to jump us into an absurd context. Instead of threatening George's life, Stewart asks if Ada has spoken to him. But Stewart says it *like* a threat. That keeps the visceral intensity rising while throwing us into new territory. We have no idea where the scene is going at this point. George is wisely mum. Stewart continues that he heard her voice in his head, and he quotes her: "I'm afraid of my will. Let me go. Let Baines save me." There is a beat held on George's reaction. And with that, Stewart leaves and goes out of the story. He leaves behind a suggestion that, as he possesses Ada's "voice," she is in some way still with him. So ends the Calm Before the Storm.

We can see that a key to making this work as an anticlimax, as well as keeping it Ada's throughline, is to bring Ada into the scene as an active character. No, she is not physically present, but having Stewart speak her lines has quite a surprising impact. Stewart almost sounds like a trance medium channeling Ada, and he may be convinced that he is doing exactly that. This plays on the power of woman as anima and muse, which is a subsidiary theme in *The Piano*. The point to be taken in terms of narrative construction, however, is that only by hearing Ada's "voice" are we prepared to go back to Ada in the next scene. Otherwise, our energy would be still caught up wondering what Stewart or George will do next.

This scene between Stewart and George resolves the love triangle subplot. Now we know that the husband will disappear from the picture and the lovers will be united. There are really no other subplots in *The Piano*. In fact, we may even be lulled into feeling that now the story is all over. The sense of irresolution here is quite vague. If we stopped the movie at this point and asked the audience what they guess will happen now, we probably would be met by looks of confusion. The reason for this is because, since the Core Crisis Story Step, the piano itself has gone into the background, and with it the main throughline. We need

Stewart to remind us that, though the love triangle is resolved, Ada still has to be "saved." Of course, it is a considerable liability in a story when the object embodying the core mode value is inert, even if it is a piano. It was certainly correct to resolve the melodrama subplot here in Story Step #14. But can it work to suddenly go back to the piano for the main climax?

Story Step #15: Climax

The structure of the last Story Steps of *The Piano* perplexes a lot of people. They take the melodrama subplot as the main throughline. But what then is the climax, since Stewart is now out of the story? There is indeed a thematic commentary about sexism, oppression, projection, and possession in the movie. But it is not the main issue in *The Piano*. If that were the subject, then a main character as unique as Ada would not have been necessary. In fact, in that case the Ada created by Jane Campion would be a liability, because as a character she adds so many other issues around creativity, introversion, and the survival of very deep early wounds. But while the adventure appears to "happen to" Ada, she herself is the one essential ingredient. It is all built around her.

Structure carries meaning and conveys meaning. As we come now into the main climax, the love triangle is already history. The Climax Story Step opens with an isolated, "thematic" shot of the angel wings washed in water. They appear to fly as much as float. Cut to Ada walking out of the house, her hand bandaged. We overhear a neighbor's voice say she is "shocked," which might be an oblique suggestion that Stewart has killed himself. In the yard, everything is packed up. George appears, surprisingly, in morning coat and top hat, as though he too needs to start a completely new life. Clearly, they are leaving. We might even think we were in the last scene of the resolution. This would surely be an unusual rhythmic element for a melodrama, to make us think the movie is over, then hit us with the real climax. It is a device taken from thriller structure. The first scenes lull us, with the exception of a few portentous hints: the wings in the water, the question of whether the piano is securely tied, and the plangent lament of the lone Maori woman on the beach as the long canoe pushes out through the surf.

But it is pure narrative pacing that finally alerts us on a gut level that something is coming. The boat paddles off. Now we could basically expect to see them go off into the sunset. Everything in the scene would seem to lead to that—another iconic moment. End of the movie. But again, having led us one way, the narrative gives us an unexpected twist. The shots of the chanting paddlers go on for a full minute of screen time. In the subtext, we begin subliminally to ask ourselves why we are still looking at this. The repetition, the *suspension*, starts to build up tension, yet we don't know about what. The story has utilized another stock genre-coded moment to spring us into unknown territory.

Then when Ada rises and signals that she doesn't want the piano, it feels fresh. Still, it is a narrative challenge to build from this point to an effective climax. Ask yourself: where can resistance come from that could be used to build the dramatic tension higher? George misunderstands her, tells her the piano is perfectly safe, they can have it fixed, and so on. Then one of the Maori argues that, no, the piano is bad luck. The daughter raises her voice insistently. Another full minute of screen time is used to build the conflict to the point where the piano finally goes overboard. Again, time is then slowed down and expanded. We enter Ada's POV as she watches the rope play out, as she makes the decision to stick her foot in the coil. . . .

When we see Ada pulled out of the boat and start to go down with the piano, it is suddenly apparent that this is the real climax, what all the action has been leading toward, that is, *Ada's* decision between the two values. The choice of setting for the scene creates a powerful metaphor. The ocean is a symbol for the unconscious. The piano is not broken up, or burnt, or sold. It is specifically *sent back* to the primordial collective unconscious. In the depth of the sea (sea as *symbol*) is not only death, but also the world of the archetypes, the wellspring of life, art, and beauty. It is in fact in the world of the archetypes that Ada took refuge at some time in the past. The links to that world gifted Ada with a prodigious musical talent, while simultaneously separating her from the mundane world of human concerns. Thus, Ada tied to the piano is not merely a picture of her immediate situation, it is a symbolic image of her old self. With the vivid directness of a nightmare, Jane Campion has externalized and condensed the core psychological and spiritual crisis into an effective dramatic and cinematic moment. It is truly a picture worth a thousand words. In order to save herself at this point, Ada must *choose* to let the old mode die.

This moment of decision is perhaps extravagantly drawn out. We first see Ada apparently content and complaisant as she goes down into the briny depths. If she stays like this, the old mode of escaping reality wins. Then, as though finally realizing what going down with the piano really means, she frantically tries to free herself. When she does, she has a wonderful rebirth. In an image sequence with an iconographic power equal to Botticelli's *Birth of Venus*, we see Ada's head break the surface, and we see her take her first breath.[35] Then the Maori men jump in to aid her and we see her supported by all these gigantic *putti*, the way a newborn whale is supported by the pod. We have a stunning collective of male midwives. It is as though a new mythology is also being born here, an entirely new set of images to describe possible relations between women and men, and between women and the masculine element in the psyche. The old complex of Western patriarchy is thrown over, so that the collective unconscious can bring up something new. As Ada is "birthed" out of the unconscious, her voice-over returns, telling us that her will chose life. "What a surprise and a gift that was."

35. This image of Ada's rebirth might be taken as a visual paraphrase of the poem by Jimenez quoted on p. 90 above.

Let us review the throughline questions in *The Piano* and the answers suggested by the climax. The most important question in *The Piano*, because it controls the others, is the inner conflict: will Ada's mode, so strong that it kept her from speaking, hold her in an aesthetic sphere apart from the world, or will her will choose to let her encounter life fully? The climactic action, aided by Ada's voice-over, tells us that she chooses life over death. On the emotional network level, this choice is reflected in how the love triangle plays out. Ada does not remain with Stewart because that relationship was against her will, and thus sterile. She will be with George because George, through his combination of instinct and empathy—his full humanness—was able to facilitate a path for Ada back to the "ground." We can see how this E-N level is a direct expression of the inner situation. The outer plot, more diffuse to begin with, posed the question: will Ada be reunited with her piano? And the answer to that is *no*.

Story Step #16: Resolution

The functions of Story Step #16: Resolution are to transfer the theme of the movie to the audience by showing us the consequences of the climax and to craft the final taste with which the audience will leave the movie theater.

Story Step #16, like #1, typically has an A-part and a B-part, and for a similar reason. The Establishing Story Step must act as a bridge for the audience into the movie, and here the Resolution Story Step must provide a bridge out of the movie. Both the very first and the very last images, because of their placement, comprise an especially condensed visual language. These images have an extra power to communicate. Both parts of the Resolution Story Step together perform the function of resolving and finishing the story, as well as bringing some form of closure to the storyteller's dialogue with the audience. But the two parts each make their own distinct contribution to the resolution function. Their combined effect is needed for a complete expression.

Story Step #16-A makes up the resolution, properly speaking. Here we see first of all the consequences of the climax on the three levels of the Story Molecule. On the outer plot level, as we said earlier, we see who is alive and who is dead, who is up and who is down, who is together and who is apart. In the context of a movie, these are not simply facts. These consequences are the means used to deliver the theme of the movie to the audience, full of implications. By showing us what has changed on the plot level, the climax is given time and space to sink in. And it is primarily through these outer indicators that we can see the nature and value of the growth through crisis the main character has undergone. Is she happier, stronger, calmer, saner? Has something from the shadow—from the Night World—been integrated into the personality? If so, that means something; if not, that also means something. Most commonly, we see that the character's identification with the old mode has died, but that which was a positive value has been integrated into a new attitude. Ada hasn't forgotten how to play the piano, but it is no longer the obsessive focus of her life. Finally, there is in the Resolution Story Step #16-A an ultimate beat in the primary relationship to bring closure to that. This final beat in the relationship may be used as a "curtain kiss." The power of the final kiss may be somewhat conventional, but that conventionality itself rests on the archetypal motif of the "Sacred Marriage."

In addition to the plot- and story-resolving aspect, there is also, as suggested by the curtain kiss/Sacred Marriage, a mythic level to the resolution. That is, one that brings the journey full circle. Bringing the journey full circle suggests completion on a more subliminal level. The most common way to do this is to physically bring the character back to a location or situation from the opening. This is a storytelling *function*, which may be accomplished in many ways, and not necessarily in a single defining moment. We notice that already in the Climax Story Step of *The Piano*, we have two full-circle elements: we see Ada leaving the island where in Act I she was arriving, and we have the reference to Ada's will, which takes us back to the opening voice-over monologue. The resolution will add other motifs to signify full-circle or closure. They, too, help define the meaning of the journey.

After the dramatic resolution itself, #16-B adds a more image/feeling component that we call the "final taste." Here we are talking about the very last images of the movie. What is the final taste you want your audience to walk out of the theater with? As with a movie's opening, the ultimate shape of #16-B: Final Taste is often crafted in the editing room, one of the last tasks of post-production. But it is the screenwriter's job to suggest the emotional and energetic quality of the final taste. It may be a single capping image, like in *Witness* where we see John Book's car, in long-shot (LS), headed back up the slope toward the city as Daniel strolls down the hill to resume courting Rachel. Life goes on. But it is also here that we may insert a stinger that suddenly reverses the emotional valence of #16-A: for example, we discover that the monster is not dead after all. Alternately, we may use #16-B for a thematic closure, where the audience is lifted *above* the immediate story by a voice-over and/or thematic images, as in *American Beauty* and *Terminator 2*.

How does The Piano handle both parts of the Resolution Story Step? #16-A lasts just under two minutes, opening on a close-up of Ada's hand, with a new prosthetic finger, playing a new piano. Then we are treated to something like a bourgeois idyll: Ada has a nice new house, her daughter is doing cartwheels on the lawn. Ada tells us in voice-over, as we see her walk along the porch with a black cloth over her head, that she is taking voice lessons. George approaches and kisses her, without lifting the black veil. This image evokes a famous painting by the surrealist René Magritte. In the language of images, the shot throws shadows on the idyll, suggesting that, despite the journey, the real Ada remains unknown even to herself—and/or that a man always prefers the fascinating "unknown woman" (the anima) to a real person. Story Step #16-A leaves us on this ambiguous note.

The ambiguity deepens in #16-B: Final Taste. Ada tells us that sometimes she dreams that she did *not* free herself from the piano, but instead went down with it. We see the rather gothic image of the piano at the bottom of the ocean, with the rope leading up to Ada's Victorian petticoats, floating like a strange flower on a stem. She tells us how peaceful and still it is down in her underwater grave as the camera tracks away, losing the image in a shadowy green murk. The End. Chilling as this image is, it is striking in its truthfulness, its psychological insight. The attractors that power complexes are tenacious, and sometimes we wonder if we can ever be done with them once and for all. And the answer is no. This final taste acts as a soft stinger because it reverses the felt-sense of the previous resolution.

Here we may emphasize that the Resolution Story Step does not necessarily mean a happy ending or the absence of ambiguity and shading. When we understand that there are two parts to the final Story Step, we can play them off one another to create complexity consistent with the complexity of the story we are telling. *American Beauty*, for example, shifts the resolution in the inverse direction. Story Step #16-A suspends the shock of Lester's sudden murder, repeating the shot over and over again, showing us each character's reaction. In this way it suggests what will happen to each of them in the future. Then #16-B lifts us to the plane of "eternity," simplicity and gratitude. The change in image quality between #16-A and #16-B both reflects and supports this reversal. In both of these movies, the ending has been crafted and fine-tuned to give us a specific final taste. We may find no words to describe it. That is not important. A movie is a movie. It works its own language.

I picked *The Piano* for this example because it is a fine film. For our purposes, it is accessible but certainly not simple. *The Piano* utilizes formulas of the melodrama genre to structure the narrative, to connect more readily with the audience, and to project interior conflicts into a visible cinematic universe. While much of the visual storytelling is subtle and multileveled, some of the melodrama elements, such as the gossipy neighborhood women, the Bluebeard play, and some of the characterization of Stewart, are handled so broadly as to verge on satire and self-referentiality. Perhaps those contrasts were necessary to the narrative texture of the whole. These are of course fine judgment calls. They are always made with no guarantee that the audience will respond to the result. In the absence of such guarantees, and in spite of test screenings, the movie eventually has to fly on its own power, with its own intrinsic qualities and virtues. However, we can craft the quality we put into the storytelling more effectively through tools like the Sixteen Story Steps.

Our models help us identify what is unique about *The Piano*, how it works, and why it works. Once we know the function of each Story Step, we can craft each one individually. A development meeting can focus on a five to ten minute Story Step rather than a shapeless hour-long stretch of Act II. We can see which

Story Steps are either weak or damaged, based on the secure criterion of whether they fulfill their storytelling function. On this basis, we could identify Story Steps #5 and #7 as the most questionable in *The Piano*. Story Step #5: Woundedness is dramatically risky because of the compromise needed in handling Ada's reaction to George's offer and the strategy of portraying this only indirectly, through the other characters. Story Step #7: Reminder That Outer Plot Stakes Are Rising has a weakness because the story is shifting to the love triangle subplot, thrusting the already diffuse outer plot throughline somewhat into the background. And the "art movie" technique of the shadow play may or may not create a sufficiently juicy and believable sense of impending outer plot stakes. With the Story Steps, we are in a position to evaluate these concrete observations in terms of our total story, our style, our audience, our market, and so on.

With *The Piano*, we are looking at a movie that has met its challenges remarkably well. It is indeed a paradoxical achievement: a character-driven genre movie. Of course, we have identified that, as an overarching strategy, *The Piano* in reality utilizes the melodrama structure as a cloak for a much more personal expression. Had *The Piano* been a traditional melodrama, we would not have had so much character development and change. Ada does make a real Hero's Journey, even if the outcome is uncertain. As we have noted, it is the inner conflict and throughline which controls the others, the E-N and the outer plot, in this movie. Melodramas tend to play mainly in the emotional network, while the consequences and climax are paid off on the outer plot level. Genre movies record the tension between the individual and society. Like the old Greek tragedies, violation of the collective norm is ultimately punished. The viewer's own ambivalence is played out in allegiances split between identifying with the anguished romantic hero and the desire for a return to the status quo order. Thus, normally we would not see the melodrama hero make such a full journey down into personal wounds and transformation. More commonly, we see the hero take some steps against outer constriction, and then either break away to freedom or be broken herself. *Raise the Red Lanterns* would be an instructive example of the traditional melodrama pattern.

We return to our observations that the Sixteen Story Steps paradigm takes us more quickly into the essential issues in developing our screenplays and allows us to work with the story on more concrete terms. After writing a draft, we are able to go back and look at how the scenes carry the Story Steps within them. By focusing our revisions on shaping the Story Steps, the scenes start to take care of themselves. The scenes and sequences find their necessary shape. In the end, we discover that it is the Story Steps that carry the scenes "on their back." The Story Steps, as the spine of the story, bear a hidden life the audience never sees directly but which informs the aliveness of the entire work. It would be wonderful to claim authorship for such an impeccable design. But no one designed or created the Story Steps. They are simply there, waiting for us to pick them up and use them.

12

The Creative Journey of Story Development

Insight occurs when, and to the degree that, one knows oneself.
—*Andrew Schneide*

IN REALITY, A SCREENWRITER does not work for herself alone. A successful screenplay is necessarily a team effort. Other members of the team—producers, directors, story editors, and so on—may come into the picture early or late, but the writer's work will obviously not arrive on the screen without a productive collaboration among the entire team. The creative journey ultimately embraces the system. The writer is at the center of this story development process. What follows may appear to be primarily addressed to the screenwriter, but it is understood that a development team is implicated. After all, it is that team's responsibility to bring a story to the screen. Either the team succeeds or the team fails.

Story Essence and Value

Screenplay development necessitates much creative destruction. It is a process, first of all, of mining or distilling the story to its essence, the essential dramatic truth it has to tell, then rebuilding the story out of that essence. This process takes as many drafts as it takes. There are many revisions in the script along the way, to clarify the throughline, tighten the action, concentrate the subplots, and so on. But from the perspective of the creative journey, these revisions, if they are to be productive, must be the fruits of *insight*. There are after all an infinite number of ways we can shift our scenes and characters around, until we get the feeling we are playing an endless game of 52-Pickup with our scene cards. The baffling, maddening truth about writing and rewriting your script is that until you have seized—or been seized by—the essence of it, your revisions may be only technical improvements, which leave the script worse off than it was before.

Good movies project an essence, like a perfume. It reaches into our bodies and feelings, into our thoughts and dreams. We tend to talk about these effects separately, but they all derive from that essence, which is both the source and the product of a powerful dramatic, thematic, and stylistic unity. Analysts and movie critics come along later and apply terms like "concept," "moral," "controlling idea," and so on. They get it on a head level. But as it hits us in the midst of long creative toil, essence is simultaneously visceral and elusive. Filmmakers themselves usually fumble for words or use an evasive smokescreen when asked to define their work. In great films, however, essence is projected as a quality of inevitability of every moment on the screen. In good films, it at least yields a clear and unified impression of a dramatic throughline. In less good films, we come away feeling that something is vaguely out of focus. Some aspects work, others don't—but we can't say exactly why.

The creative journey into the unknown, to find an original story or an authentic way of telling a commissioned work or adaptation, is a quest for this essence and is not satisfied until we have gotten as near as possible before committing the resources for the shoot. This process may even continue in the editing room. Essence is not the one-liner you pitch to a producer to make a deal. That may at best be an intuitive foretaste, perhaps the most evocative foretaste we can offer. At its worst, the pitch may be misleading, a delusion, mistaking the map for the territory, bringing back pictures before we have taken the trip. Essence is not what you put in at the beginning of the process, but what you get out at the end—if you are persevering in your intensity of encounter, and lucky. Essence is what comes out of working and struggling with the story, whether in the writer's solitude or in contentious studio development sessions.

Producers and studios are open to new visions, new kinds of storytelling. The openness is of course driven by the changes in the market and the saturation of the media environment. Screenwriters are also savvier than ever about box office trends, but has this led to a much higher proportion of excellent screenplays? Most people in the industry don't seem to think so. Part of this is due to producers' insecurities about risk-taking, but a large measure of the failure is a failure to track the story to its essence, being satisfied with something less. What producers and studio heads are looking for are not screenplays that merely "work" on a mechanical level and know how to integrate commercial elements. That only makes an average, workmanlike script. A studio throws away more of these scripts per week than the feature film output of the entire industry in a year.

What everyone wants are great *stories*, stories with originality, authenticity, and staying power: that elusive universal appeal that generates excitement, gets the movie successfully through the critical first weekend in the theaters, and continues to build an audience. This is the "call and response" we mentioned in an earlier chapter: the movie touches people deeply or in a special way. It hits the zeitgeist or reflects the audience to itself. Such a story has a personality, an identity. It feels alive and takes on a life of its own. Such a story is fashioned not mechanically, but in the creative fire.

A great story has a transcendental quality because the writer (or creative team) has transcended his craft, has gone beyond what he knows into what he does not know, and for which craft has been but a necessary preparation. The craft, the techniques and mechanics of the screenplay construction, must be learned and internalized until they become part of the writer. These are the preliminaries, our basic professional competence. Great stories, however, grow out of great intensity of encounter, contained and nourished by someone with both the analytic tools and the creative skills to sustain that intensity and bring it to fruition. If technique alone were sufficient, we would have many more great movies than we do.

We might summarize the creative quest for the essence of the story by a rough paraphrase of theologian Paul Tillich:

> The story's essence appears after the story itself has been lost in creative darkness and doubt.

Managing the Collaborative Process

Creative collaboration is not exactly a marriage, nor is it a love affair. Yet it can at times be reminiscent of both. It would be misleading to consider collaboration as a straightforward business contract; it is a relationship, with all the ramifications of that word. Furthermore, the relationship includes not only the persons involved, but also the screenplay itself as a semiautonomous "actor," which appears to have its own intentions and moods. After all, we cannot prove that the resistance, pleasures, or hide-and-seek maneuvers we experience while writing the script in fact belong to *us*, as our projections alone. Screenplays really do exhibit traits of living systems. The script confronts us with its own life and autonomy. It seems to have its own resistance, independent of the writer. For this reason, the concept of a "story field," which includes both the development team and the screenplay, is useful.

As in any relationship, each member brings to it his or her own perspective, expectations, anxieties, control fantasies, personal baggage, need/mode splits, and value systems. And as with any relationship, clear communication and a clear sense of boundaries tend to advance the relationship and its goals. This is not only a question of who is paying whom and the specific elements and deadlines written into the contract. Of course all parties wish the contract to be based on mutual trust and respect. But upon what is this trust itself founded? First of all, there is the professional competence of each member of the development team in his or her required role. Then there is the question of chemistry. Over the long haul of the project development, the dynamics of the relationship come to the fore, just as they do in any close relationship. These dynamics in their turn include not only conscious wishes and intentions, but an unconscious component as well. Let us recall that a screenplay is a task the outcome of which cannot be precisely known beforehand. It requires a descent into what we have termed the "story's unconscious," that larger set of possibilities inherent in the story material but which is not yet apparent to the development team. This descent into uncertainty can trigger or constellate the unconscious of everyone involved, and invariably does so in the forms of shadow projections, anxieties, defensive postures, and forms of acting out. An important question for the collaborative relationship becomes: are these the people with whom you want to take that journey? It is not always possible to tell before the contract is inked.

The issue of chemistry must be differentiated from what it is not. There is so much money and power involved in feature film production, such fantasies of desire and success when a single contract could potentially make one a millionaire, that the mutual seduction subtext cannot be ignored or left to operate in the shadows. People convince themselves that the chemistry is right because they *want* it to be right. Here we may do well to step back from the "personality ethic" of mutual seduction to a level of principle-based integrity of character, as the noted leadership consultant Stephen Covey suggests:

> [The principle-centered, character-based approach] says if you want to have a happy marriage, be the kind of person who generates positive energy and sidesteps negative energy rather than empowering it. If you want to have a more pleasant, cooperative teenager, be a more understanding, empathic, consistent, loving parent. If you want to *have* more freedom, more latitude in your job, be a more responsible, a more helpful, a more contributing employee. If you want to be trusted, be trustworthy. If you want the secondary greatness of recognized talent, focus first on primary greatness of character.[36]

With collaborative principles rather than personalities as a starting point, many of the process or chemistry difficulties that come up in screenplay development can be avoided or overcome. These include the upstaging and power plays that come in when members of the development team are anxious about their places in the status hierarchy—the sinking couches in producers' offices, the beverage rituals (Is Evian in or out? What does it say about you if you are not finicky about your espresso?), the writers' tantrums, and so on. Ploys for power tend to lead to development hell because they erode basic integrity and trust.

How do you demonstrate—first of all, to yourself—that you are a worthy and effective partner? Look at the responsibility you have taken on in the project, not in terms of the letter of the contract but in terms of the larger relationship. What are you willing to do to make this work? Where are you able to stretch or take on more responsibility for the sake of the project? Can you feel the edge of your shadow, where you may want to get out more than you put in? What core value governs your behavior in the relationship? The old saw, "Seek to understand

36. Covey, Stephen R., *The Seven Habits of Highly Effective People* (New York: Fireside/Simon & Schuster, 1989), p. 43.

before seeking to be understood," represents a basic core value for successful communication in screenplay development. It demonstrates *mutuality*.

Mutuality is a virtue in relationships, yet it contains a paradox, because when mutuality is forced it is no longer mutual. It may then become the enforcement of other agendas. Yet on the other hand, if mutuality is freely given, it may not be strictly mutual. One person's vision of "mutual" may not match the other's, though both are perfectly sincere. Each has his own sense of boundary versus shared space. We recognize the turmoil this causes in love relationships when one frustrated partner blurts, "I know you don't love me, because if you did, you would ____ !" Fill in the blank.

Thus, one of the individual responsibilities in a story development team is to sort out "perfect" mutuality from good-enough mutuality. Of course, perfect mutuality is not humanly possible to maintain through the ups and downs of a long-term relationship, and if it were, it could be a sign of an unhealthy symbiosis. When we see *moments* of perfect mutuality between trained artists, such as a jazz duo, a dance troupe, or a director and an actor, we recognize it as rare and extraordinary. Writers and producers are meant to contend with one another because they have different temperaments and perspectives on the project. The contention itself is part of the creative process. Given that, there is "fair" fighting that advances the project and there is "dirty" fighting that destroys rapport. Fair fighting, as in sports, is designed to bring out the best in both partners. One respects the rules of the game not out of fear of punishment but because one realizes it makes the sport more pleasurable. Aggression is tempered by this desire for the pleasure the sport affords. As in sport or love-making, power sharing enhances pleasure; domination is ultimately stultifying. Power sharing and clear communication are the best ways to signify mutuality in a professional relationship.

Here we return to a point, made much earlier, that asking good questions about the story opens the story up and furthers the development process, while judgmental statements tend to shut the process down. Over the course of this book we have identified the key questions that must be asked in order to open up the full potential of the screenplay material. We have marked out the territories into which those questions lead us. But evaluation is of course also central to our work. Evaluation means making judgments. So, how can we voice our judgments in ways that do not chill the creative energy? This is also part of adequate mutuality. The first way is to rephrase our judgments as questions wherever possible, in order to give an opening to our partners. "What does Sally want right now, I wonder. . . ?" rather than "Sally's action here is completely unmotivated. It's bullshit!" This brings us to a second way to make judgments that do not shut down the process: taking explicit personal responsibility for one's opinion. It makes a great difference to start a judgmental statement with "In my view. . . ." or "From my perspective. . . ." Again, an opening is left for our partners. This is power sharing. The collaborative relationship requires management of this kind because our actions have consequences. Yes, we might feel compelled sometimes to cry out "This stinks!" And we might be perfectly correct: the scene may indeed stink. But we want to be aware that this and all statements impact the relationship. We want to keep in mind our larger vision of the relationship and where we want it to lead us.

It was also for this reason, among others, that we introduced the psychological skill of *focusing*. Focusing is a boon to the communication process as well as to our creativity in general. Imagine: until recently we had the world split into a neat but illusory dichotomy of objective vs. subjective. *My* feeling was simply *mine*, beyond observation or question, locked inside my subjectivity. I defended it tooth and nail because it was *mine*. Now we are talking about gaining objectivity about our subjectivity, creating a middle ground where we can objectively attend to our subjectivity while it is happening—in real time. This objective-subjectivity is in fact the only genuine terrain for discussion in the arts. Each and every aesthetic choice, from a line of dialogue to the camera angle to the exact frame on which to cut a shot, is an act of objective-subjectivity. If we can open up the judgment "This stinks!" in terms of the felt-sense of that impression, we can turn a potential creative shut-down into a new world of creative possibility.

As you will have already surmised, there are real limits to our objectivity when working on a creative project, even when we have the best of intentions. We must objectively take into account the limits to our objectivity. This is true from the screenwriter right up through the studio boss. Therefore I take Stephen Covey's words, quoted above, as a laudable ideal and intention. They seem, however, to presuppose a human being who is pure ego, and whose will is coextensive with that ego. That is to say, there is no unconscious, no shadow. Such a being could theoretically have an ego identical to their persona mask: "I am exactly as I appear to be!" Such a being would be theoretically perfectible, if only. . . . "What I would do, I do not, while what I would not do—that I do!" cried the exasperated Saint Paul.

To put it another way, such a being could theoretically have an identical mode and need. But what we know from our work on characters is that mode and need are in opposition not because one is "wrong," but because this opposition expresses the fundamental polarity of our being. Further, psychological insight tells us that when the mode becomes more rigid, repressive, and dogmatically one-sided, the opposing force in the unconscious grows commensurately. The split deepens until it reaches a breaking point. While holding to our ideal intention, we want to carry it with humility and some skepticism. "The spirit is willing but the flesh is weak." Yes, but in that "weak flesh" there is not only fault. There is a countervirtue as well.

Thus, there will always be chemistry, with its subtle shadows of seduction and manipulation, as well as its special level of creative sharing, in collaborative relationships. We do our professional best to take responsibility, and that can keep us out of many troubles. But at the end of the day there still remains the dynamic of two or more distinct individualities. We do well to recognize and appreciate the differences between the members of the development team, beginning with differences in creative temperament. We have mentioned that the nature of producing tends to attract extroverts, while writers tend to be introverts. One focuses more on the product, the other more on the process. These are simply tendencies that may be noted. It is not an attempt to typecast or prejudge our partners. One of the values of teamwork is that partners can reinforce each other's strengths while compensating for the weak points. Screenwriters, for example, have their status quo modes, just as their characters do. Every mode has its blind spot, which is normally invisible to the person involved. If a competent partner can, instead of dumping on the writing, help the writer to see her blind spot, the script development can take a quantum leap forward. This of course can only happen under conditions of trust, taking us back to the basics of responsibility, mutuality, and clear communication. These relationship basics form a holding environment within which a dynamic "play space" can thrive.

Creative Chaos

The strong foundation of the collaborative relationship is set up in the earliest stages of script development. This is important, because the story team is about to cross a natural threshold in the creative process, one that puts strain on the relationship. The threshold comes when the screenwriter pulls the process down into chaos. Chaos enters when the story development ceases to go as planned. It gets off track because story elements are changing, because the throughline is lost, because deadlines are missed, or all of the above. Here the writer's and producer's perspectives begin to diverge sharply. The honeymoon is over. Yet just here is where the story has a great chance to come alive and reach its full potential. As we have said, the approved outline does not just break down inevitably, through a writer's Murphy's Law—it *must* break down. It is only at this point where we step off the map and into the territory. How much discomfort can a producer in this situation tolerate? That depends on the producer's preparations and expectations, how well he understands the creative process.

The pull toward chaos precipitates typical shifts in the dynamic between writer and producer (or story editor, development executive, etc.). What comes next may become a matter of some delicacy. The writer is now going into the Descent stage of the creative journey, the "elevator to hell," and may feel increasingly vulnerable and naked. The producer feels exposed as well, because in fact he is exposed. A blame game can start here. In addition, the conflict can take on the overtones of a family quarrel, for implicit in the structure of a development team is the potential for the projection of parent/child roles. The disappointed or angry producer can be overlaid by the writer with the unconsciously projected image of the disappointed and angry mother or father. This does not in itself mean that the screenwriter is neurotic. It means that the entire story development process is experiencing an *abaissement du niveau mental*, a lowering of the threshold of consciousness. We are headed down into the darkness of the creative mine. Don't forget your hard hat.

One of the great temptations for the producer at this point is to fire the writer, or at least threaten to do so. Many Hollywood features end up being worked on by a half-dozen listed and unlisted writers. But the first task, I believe, is to learn how to manage the shadows of creative darkness with the original team we have committed to. A new writer will not only unmake what the previous writer has done, but she will also come in with her own set of subjectivities and blind spots. Firing a writer is a serious judgment call, a last resort. It is not something to be used to relieve us of the anxiety of facing the unknown. Because guess what? The writer can be fired, but the anxiety will hang around like a hungry shark.

In fact, the more likely scenario will be for the development team to escape into escapism. This is the other great temptation in the face of creative anxiety. It involves a conscious or unconscious collusion on the part of the development team to take an easy way out rather than intensifying the creative encounter. Screenplay development is intense in any case, so let's be specific about what we mean. Escapism here means short-cutting the dramatic development by cutting to easier audience-reaction elements—more graphic violence and sex, for example—and inserting pumped-up stakes that are not intrinsic to the story's premise and need/mode thematic core. Escapism means not pushing the conflict all the way to the impossible double bind that forces a "grow or die" choice for the hero, but giving the character an easy, less authentic way out.

It takes some creative courage to stay the course with a story. It also takes the instincts of a hunter. The script is indeed undergoing profound shifts throughout all its revisions, as the word *re-vision* suggests. Which revisions are really taking the story in the right direction? This is what essence is about, the scent that keeps one on the right track. Revisions take us down through layers of dramatic truth. How do we know when we have hit bedrock? This is the point where a real understanding of the Need versus Mode model is invaluable. It not only defines the essential conflict both dramatically and thematically, but we can actually watch the need/mode dialectic move and express itself through all three dimensions of the Story Molecule. Once we have locked onto an irreducible conflict of opposites, we must be willing to follow the conflict to the bitter end and not let the hero out of the conflict before breakdown and breakthrough. Heading toward the hero's point of "grow or die" can feel a bit like the image of Slim Pickens riding the A-bomb in *Dr. Strangelove*. It is understandable that something in us wants to get away before it hits. Both as writers and as people, we don't know how it's all going to turn out. This is why we must talk about sustaining the intensity of encounter. It is the only way to come out at the end with a powerful dramatic unity.

Because the ground starts shifting under our feet, it is helpful for the team to have a set of core development questions that will help it find its way back to the main gallery of the creative mine when the lamps go out and it's pitch dark. My set of core questions, which I use with writers who have lost their orientation to the script, is as follows:

1. *Where is the juice in the story for* ***you****?*

   This is really the core question to ask every day when sitting down to write and when beginning each new scene. Moreover, each person in the collaborative team must ask themselves this question individually, because each may see the juice in a different place. Airing the differences may clarify divergent expectations, help build consensus, and enhance the vitality of the entire screenplay. If the juice is missing, so is the motivation to write.
2. *What about the story is:*
   - *Universal?*
   - *Unique?*
   - *Dramatic?*
3. *What do you love the most about your story, about your hero?*
4. *Where do you see the attitudes, modes, and values of*
   - *writer*
   - *hero*
   - *audience*

   intersecting and coming together?
5. *Speak* ***out loud*** *the dramatic/narrative premise in one to two sentences. How does it sound* ***today****?*
6. *Define the main character's mode (attitudes revealed by actions that cluster around a core value) as you understand it today.*

   Identify how your understanding of the hero's need/mode split has evolved since you first formulated it.
7. *What does this character need to learn about life?*
8. *How is the character getting in his or her own way?*
9. *Does character serve plot (genre stories), or does plot grow out of character (character-driven stories)?*
10. *Who else is in the world of this story?*
11. *Which character is the "moral center" or heart of the story? (It is typically* ***not*** *the main character.) What value does he or she embody?*
12. *What are the story's Day World and Night World? How can we see them?*
13. *What is scary/intimidating for* ***you*** *about this Night World?*
14. *Which character embodies the energies of the Night World, and what is his impact on the story?*

15. *How is the dramatic/thematic conflict reflected in tone, and how is the tone reflected in the style?*
16. *What myth/fairy tale does this story remind you of?*

This core group of questions serves to re-establish the working premise and give everyone a chance to get on the same page. They can in fact be turned to at any point in the development process, because there is no such thing as just going in to fix Act III. If Act III isn't working, that means the middle act has problems. And if the middle act has problems, then something was wrong in the setup. A faulty setup in Act I points back to the premise. It is all one gestalt, one living pattern. Change any element and you necessarily change the whole. It is never wrong to go back to the basics, which include the above questions as well as working with the models we have elaborated over the course of this book. This is the rhythm of mine- and mountain-creativity. We repeatedly need to come up for air to regain our bearings. Our work in the mine, hitting that seam of pure dramatic gold, depends on it.

Beyond the Creative Threshold

The greater part of this book has been concerned with a set of increasingly precise and detailed models and techniques to guide the left-brain, analytical side of our work. Now, with the creative journey, we are dealing with what *cannot* be objectively determined, but must be discovered and lived. Moving from outlines and treatments to the script, we are forced to discover what we think we have already invented. From this point on, the screenwriter is essentially on his own.

One thing we can expect to happen as we step from the map into the territory is that some of our personal attitudes and values will be challenged, knocked around, perhaps apparently destroyed. Like our characters, we have values which we have identified ourselves. That identification tends to give a feeling-tone of absolute certainty to the value. It may also be that we have overidentified ourselves with our main character and have projected our value system through that character. This situation will lead us into a creative double bind. Either, in order not to face the apparent threat to our own values, we will let our character off the hook before the point where the mode must break down—and then throw in some extra outer obstacles to make a flat climax appear to work—or we will go down with the ship and face the devaluation of our own value. In truth, the value itself cannot die. Only our identification with in can die. But try telling the screenwriter this when she is in the midst of an identity crisis and the script is falling apart!

What are you holding on to?
What is trying to be born?

Among the pieces of old programming that undergo review (to put it euphemistically) are our myths about efficiency and insufficiency. To grow up in Western society is to be inculcated with a belief in the value of efficiency and the corresponding devaluation of "wasting time." Efficiency is considered part of "getting it right," though it is not central—and can even be counterproductive—to creative work. Behind our ambitions to succeed as screenwriters, our views about revisions and rewrites are probably still influenced by our first experience of writing at the age of six. Remember that special "training paper," the one with the middle line? All the small letters had to exactly touch the middle line. If the teacher told us to do it over again, that meant we *didn't get it right*. When the teacher said that, we would feel ashamed. Revisions became associated with correcting mistakes, and that went with feelings of shame and unworthiness. Many grown-up screenwriters still carry this attitude.

Now, consider playwright and screenwriter Sam Shepard. The anecdote is reported that when Sam Shepard is working on a play, he writes the entire draft on canary-yellow legal pads. When he is done with the draft . . . he throws it away. The whole thing. Then he starts the next draft on a fresh canary-yellow pad, and when that's done, he tosses that one as well, so the story goes. Apparently, he trusts that if it's important, he will remember it and integrate it. He does this as many times as it takes until the play is ready. Many people hearing this anecdote react with shock, even outrage. Doesn't he save *anything*? How could he throw away valuable material? How inefficient! Is Sam Shepard *stupid*, that he gives himself so much extra work? Recently, there was an item that a well-known director, working with two very talented stars, used fifty takes on one particular scene. How inefficient, we might say. Does that mean the first forty-nine takes were wrong? Bad? This is the trap of the pseudo-myth of efficiency. If it takes you ten drafts to get your screenplay right, does that mean you are stupider than another writer who only uses three drafts?

Holding on to the value of efficiency will seriously impede our work as screenwriters because it acts as an inner threshold guardian. We need to be consciously aware of our attitudes rather than being unconsciously controlled by them. It is both truer and more productive to see revision simply as a way to develop the material. No shame need be attached. For the director who did fifty takes, it was a way of *ripening* the material by working on it and playing with it. Ripening it, bringing it to its full juiciness. Hopefully, when a producer asks for script revisions, everyone can take it in this healthy spirit. Within that context, we are free to ask for clarification. Remember, all aesthetic judgments are subjective-objective. There are no absolutes. Value is determined by context. That is to say, if a producer remarks that a scene is "not working," the statement has no absolute value. We must clarify: not working for whom? Not working in relation to what goal? Not working in relation to which other elements in the story? This specification keeps us in the play-zone of ripening the material. Clear communication around this is of course the responsibility of all parties.

Another cherished, culture-wide belief that undergoes deconstruction on the creative journey is: "Winning isn't everything—it's the *only* thing!" These words of football coach Vince Lombardi have emerged as perhaps *the* quintessential American proverb. We could call them the voice of the power complex. Once the premise is accepted as a *fact*, then Tonya Harding's attempt to break an Olympic figure skating competitor's knees is only a logical conclusion from the premise. However, Lombardi's proverb only works for win/lose situations. It is an attitude that is not interested in win/win. There has to be a loser, but who is the screenwriter going to beat? Is he going to beat the *story*? Beat the story into submission? There is in fact an organization that calls itself a "screenwriter's boot camp," which seems to promise just this—so deeply is this attitude ingrained in our society.

The attitude of conquering and the value placed on being a winner at all costs both miss the paradox that is central to creating, which could be better termed "victory through surrender." Sports and warfare metaphors may be appropriate to studio heads because the arena of box office grosses and market share does have winners and losers. But it is inappropriate to the act of creation, which is not fundamentally an act of aggression. Rather, creating is fundamentally erotic in nature. That is, it works by relating, bringing together, finding commonality, playfully unifying. Of course, there is a playful destruction along the way, just as people get their hair messed up when they make love. Our attitudes and beliefs, those mental hairstyles, are going to get messed up. Writing and revising is a process of opening up for the sake of uncovering a dramatic truth. It is an erotic surrender that is in no way a "giving up." So you write ten drafts and throw them away, like Sam Shepherd, before arriving at the final draft that expresses the dramatic essence of the story. Who's the winner? You are.

I say this lightly, but it is not easy to give up implicitly or unconsciously held beliefs. They make up our reality system, our survival mode. There is a struggle because, as we know, the old mode wants to hang on. Not only is it a habituation, it also serves to suppress or repress something else, a countervalue. Here it is especially valuable to ask:

> How is my present confrontation with one of my own cherished attitudes related to the story I am writing?

There is a process involved in stepping away from an attitude with which we have been overidentified, but which is no longer appropriate. Here, we can take some lessons from the structure of conflict in our screenplays. The first step is to bring the attitude out where we can see it. Perhaps the most effective way to do this is by learning to catch our shadow projections onto other people (including the characters in our screenplays). This step is already difficult and catalyzes conflict. Projections are unconscious, but we may create the conditions to observe them. We do this by using focusing techniques to sharpen our awareness of affect or emotional energy-charge: somebody suddenly makes me mad, or I feel betrayed, disappointed, cheated, or undervalued. The shadow quality we identify in the other person—manipulative, lying, power-hungry, conceited—is typically the opposite of an attitude, often unconscious, we hold about ourselves. If our affect-reaction is extreme, it is a sign or symptom that our cherished attitude or self-image is threatened. Why do we make shadow projections, anyway? It is often to locate something unpleasant away from ourselves. We spontaneously project it outward so we don't have to own it. It is equivalent to pointing to the splinter in our neighbor's eye rather than seeing the log in our own. In this case, if we can identify what shadow content we project onto another person, we may guess that we dis-identify from that projected quality and tend to identify with its opposite. It is helpful to lay these two polar attitudes out on paper, as we did with the Eight Worldly Dharmas.

The second step is to observe that there is an interplay of a pair of opposites going on, neither of which has an absolute value. By interplay, we mean that the opposites constellate or polarize each other. Behind the scenes, what appears to be irreconcilable in fact interpenetrates, like the yin-yang image. Each side contains its opposite in seed form. We may further trace back our own attitude to its roots: how did it come about that I have this attitude rather than the other? In one family or society, being as honest as George Washington and never telling a lie is the expected standard. But in other settings, other social worlds, it is completely understood that lying is necessary just to survive. That is not considered lying, but "getting along." In yet other social contexts, it is fine to lie to outsiders, but never to your father. At some point in life, the attitude we adopted was an important adaptation to our life circumstances, for whatever reason. We can appreciate that our cherished value brought us this far, to the point where we may transcend it for the sake of greater wholeness. For the greater wholeness lies in the interplay of opposites itself, not in one or the other side. This process of stepping back from one-sided positions to take in a bigger view is basic to living and writing creatively. To the extent that we can say yes to this process and incorporate it into our lives, we find our power to create move to a new level. We become increasingly "transparent to the transcendent." This phrase of German philosopher Karlfried Graf Dürkheim in this instance refers to seeing the more integral level of reality beyond the play of opposites. We begin to see the background of transpersonal being, the "love that moves the sun and the other stars,"* behind our endless personal squabbles. This makes us capable of perceiving and embracing higher levels of dramatic unity—of telling greater stories.

Realms of Creative Darkness

How can we describe the creative journey of the screenwriter in a way which opens up and enhances our understanding, rather than closing our minds with

* Final lines of Dante's *Divine Comedy*.

fixed notions about how it is supposed to work? In the first chapter, we launched some preliminary metaphors and images: that creativity is a cycle which takes us down like miners into the darkness of the unknown and brings us back with handfuls of creative gold (or coal, as the case may be); that the movement of creation is regressive; that it throws us into duality; that it gets heroic energies going as we face death and rebirth; and that it is always an act of *self*-creation. We understand that creativity engages our play-energy in seriously playful ways, in a rhythm of growth through crisis. And we could further picture the screenwriter's journey as a kind of alchemy: a transforming and transmuting of a mass of confused material into its essence. These are all metaphors. They are not to be mistaken for the territory of the creative unconscious. But the research of Stanislav Grof, Jean Houston, and a host of others has given us a sense that the unconscious is not merely a brute id. It appears to have realms, or levels, each with its own quality of experience, each with its own insights for the creative journey.

In the original research Grof and his colleagues did with LSD in the early 1960s, and later, using nondrug techniques to alter and enhance consciousness, they discovered transformations in the hallucinogenic/visionary experience of the unconscious. The trip would typically begin with acute alterations of sensation, which would dominate the field of consciousness: colors, shapes, smells, cartoon-like figures, and so on would swamp the senses. For most subjects, this phase was simply amazing fun. But it would not last. A spontaneous shift in the quality of the visions would occur. Images of a psychological nature would break into this stream of sensation, usually in a disturbing way: relived memories, phobias, regressive feeling states, extreme vulnerability, and self-destructive impulses were typical of this next phase. Naturally people would become alarmed and would often desire at this point to end the trip. This anxiety and resistance would lead to a "bad trip."

Grof, borrowing from the wisdom of myths, would have his experimental subjects accompanied by a guide who could help them talk through the difficult passages. If the subjects could let go of fear and observe the events without attachment, like Odysseus tied to the mast to listen to the Sirens, they would flow into a truly mythic dimension of experience. Here the subjects might find themselves living the myth of the crucified, sacrificed savior and undergo their own dismemberment and death, along with the death and rebirth of the universe itself. The feelings at this level could be called "ecstatically excruciating." Beyond this Night of the Soul, the subject would emerge to a sense of timeless, oceanic Being and report occurrences of cosmic consciousness, of consusbstantiality with each and all things and a harmony transcending life and death.

After establishing that these four levels of experience—which he termed the Sensational, Psychological-Tragic, Mythic-Dramatic, and Mystical-Unitive—were typical, Grof found analogies to the universal trauma of the birth process:

Sensational →	Emergence into the external world
Psychological →	Passage of the birth canal
Mythic →	Convulsive contractions of the uterus
Mystical →	Timeless uterine existence

The levels of the unconscious encountered in this research mark a regression, a return to the beginning by successive removals from ordinary "reality consciousness": rebirth via the experience of death and transcendence. Thus it represents another direct analogue to the cycle of the Hero's Journey, indicating how deeply that symbol seems to be encoded in our psyches.

And there is yet another analogy to be made here. Our coming into the world is often described mythically as a descent, the above schedule of transformations read in reverse through the birth process, from timeless unity through titanic convulsion and an arduous exodus to tumble into this world of existential separateness. When read in this *descending* order, we find a correspondence with the modes of storytelling described by Frank McConnell in his book *Mythmaking and Storytelling*: epic, romance, melodrama, and satire.

McConnell's work is important for understanding how movies communicate directly to the unconscious of the viewer and, taken together with the levels of consciousness described by Stanislav Grof, it can help us understand the realms of creative darkness we pass through on the screenwriter's journey. The hero in stories always stands for our libido—or energy—in relation to our creative selves.[37] McConnell, looking at many mythologies and folktale cycles, saw that there was a progression in the stories within each culture (the inverse of Grof's regression) from primal, fantastic origin-tales of the gods and mythic kings down to a shrunken but more human present. He found that this progression expresses itself in shifting modalities of storytelling: from epic to romance, from romance to melodrama, from melodrama to satire.

An epic tells of the origins of things, personified by the act of the semimythic king, in carving order out of chaos and founding a kingdom (king/kingdom = creator/creation). With the founding of the kingdom comes the establishment of ideal human values thought to be of divine origin, whether these be encoded in the Ten Commandments or the principles of chivalry of the Round Table. Likewise, our first creative impulses always carry the allure, the numinosity and prestige, of the archetypal Beginning. They come into the world trailing clouds of glory. Psychologically, our first relationship to a new story we are creating is thus highly idealized. Writers often see their stories as "perfect movies"—even before they start working on them! We could say that screenwriters first experience their stories in "Heaven," in a numinous semiconscious state, before they fall into "Time."

37. See Jung, C. G., *Symbols of Transformation* for Jung's discussion of the hero as a representation of psychic energy.

After *epic* comes *romance*. After the founding of the kingdom there is a fundamental shift: the kingdom must be defended, and the knight, whose stature and mission is no longer that of the founding king, takes center stage. Already the work of the primary creative impulse is done, and now its boundaries must be defined and elaborated. There is an ongoing battle against chaos without and inertia within, a constant fear of falling away from the ideal. The knight (Lancelot is the most famous example) or town sheriff (Gary Cooper in *High Noon*) draws his romantic quality from the tension between the divine and the human impulses, between duty and love, which he must carry, imperfectly reconciled, within his breast. The analogy carries over into the creative process as well. We carry on an infatuation with our story, usually until we have to face the first criticisms. Then we enter a difficult phase where we are sure our story is beautiful, powerful, and unique—but somehow people just don't see it.

The next transformation of storytelling modes comes with the shift from *romance* to *melodrama*.* As the outer boundaries of the realm become secure, there is already a sense of internal ossification and corruption that threatens to undo the society and its values from within. Thus the hero of the melodrama (as McConnell defines it) is the detective or reporter, whose stature and regard in the society is diminished in relation to the knight or the knightly sheriff, as the knight was diminished in relation to the king. The detective uncovers corruption in the heart of the society, but is powerless to eliminate the root cause of the evil. The highest houses, the guardians of virtue, are the most pestilent but are so entrenched in their power that they are impossible to bring down. The problems of false but cherished appearances, the deceptive tangle of images, and the pervasive sense of human perversity come to the fore. The ideals of the epic founders are now mere slogans coming twisted from the lips of publicity flaks. They have lost their original virtue and ability to inspire. The once-virtuous kingdom is sinking into shadow, and the detective-reporter can witness, point the finger, tell the tale. On the parallel level of the screenwriter's journey, the creative endeavor is discovered to be fundamentally and irrevocably flawed, to be human and no longer "divine." The screenplay no longer "works," and nothing we can do seems to be able to fix it. At this point the writer may feel disgusted with both his story and with the very act of writing.

Once the hero realizes the fundamental flaw in society, according to McConnell, he becomes an outsider. He may either become a prophet or a satirist. As a prophet, the hero may be a voice howling in the wilderness. Or he may alternately become a revolutionary who destroys the old society, or who departs from it to create a new kingdom based on new values: the start of a new epic. The other possibility for the outsider is to become a satirist, and satire is the end point of this descent, the cold laughter at society, at human foibles and faults, by one who has nothing left to lose. The satirist may in fact be a prophet or sacred

* The use of *melodrama* here denotes a storytelling mode according to McConnell's system. In this case it does not refer to melodrama as a genre.

clown, having been sprung out of the burst bubble of the society's closed vision into a much larger cosmos. Thus, through the satirist/clown/prophet, the sense of the holy may paradoxically return to the world. In the creative process, that satirist-energy represents the archetype of breakthrough after all faith in our creative virtue has been dragged down into the mud of developing the screenplay.

Epic	*Golden Age*	Inflated state of infatuated identification with our story idea
Romance	*Silver Age*	Creative duality: fear and desire elaborating and defending our concept while splitting into "creative persona" and "creative shadow"
Melodrama	*Bronze Age*	Descent into creative shadow, realizing that our own shadow is implicated in the story; obsession with flaws in the characters and the story; creative block
Satire	*Iron Age*	Breaking the neurotic personal reference or overidentification with the story or our hero, caused by our own transference, to see the story "as it is"

Inspired by critic Northrop Frye, McConnell correlated the four modes of storytelling in his program with the mythic "four ages of man" described by Hesiod. We may think of this descent as the "path of inertia and resistance." In both the creative process and the historical process, it describes metaphorically the falling away from the original creative vitality into solidity, heaviness, and corruption, from imperishable gold reflecting the sun to hard, black iron, the metal of weapons and killing, from the numinosity of the symbol into the rigidity of social forms, dogma, habituation, and unconscious repetition.

The descending "path of inertia and resistance" stands in contrast to the path of broadening perspectives that come to us out of the LSD and similar research into the levels of consciousness. We could call this latter the "path of initiation and ecstasy." The point is that both of these paths into the realms of creative darkness are involved in the screenwriter's journey. They both share the dynamic of breakdown and breakthrough. It is often said that there is no time in the unconscious, no before or after, no limitations of either/or. It is not a question of picking the path that appears more appealing. We are confronted with both and are asked to forge out of their contradictions a "union of opposites." It does matter how we handle these energies. The "path of inertia" can easily lead us to a sterile cynicism or a mechanical pragmatism that poisons our creative life. The "path of initiation and ecstasy" can lead us out of this world, away from engagement and compassion, and ultimately to irrelevance. The middle way toward the "union of opposites" we could call the path of "mindful writing." The mindful attention we pay to the inertia and resistances of the creative process, as well as to the phantoms, shadows, and ecstasies we experience, is where we find the real intensity of encounter which brings us through to creative insight.

The Structure of Creative Breakthrough

We can see that the screenwriter's actual journey is not a breezy bus tour through the Hero's Journey archetype. It is a real journey that entails real risks: the loss of certain attitudes, beliefs, and perspectives; the upsurge of repressed counter-values; and the possibility of failure. But, while it may feel chaotic, there is an implicit structure to it that is analogous to the Hero's Journey paradigm, as well as to the realms of creative darkness mentioned above. The archetypal cyclical structure does mark one of the soul's deep movements, that of growth via break-down and breakthrough. It should not be surprising that the same model depicts the process of creative breakthrough as well.

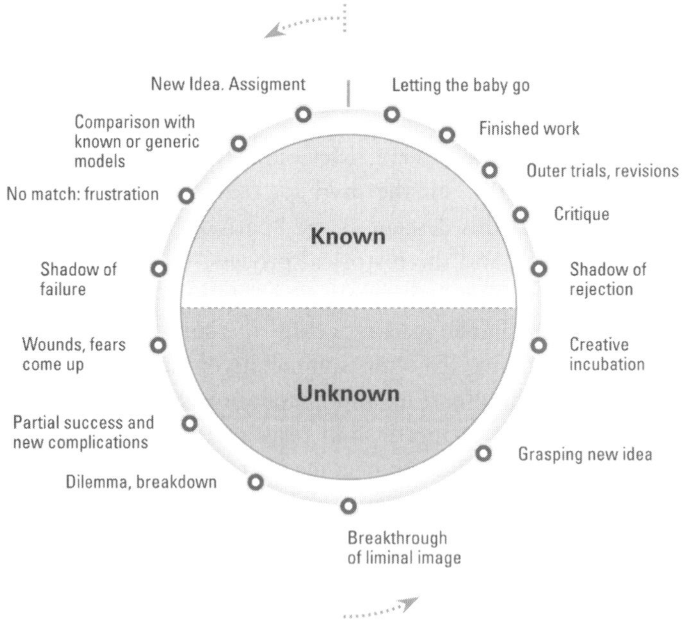

/ The Structure of Creative Breakthrough

Separation

In the context of the present chapter it is not possible to detail every step of this creative journey, but the broad outlines can be made visible. The creative journey begins with the writer's Call to Adventure, which may be a commission or the seeds of an original story idea. Stories are energy, and the appearance of a new story idea does not come into our lives as a simple fact. It comes as an energy impulse that may roar like a lion and command our attention, it may sneak up on us like a ghostly presence, or it may fall out of a bitter conflict in our present lives. The story idea itself is a precipitate of an antecedent psychic process. Something was already "brewing" inside. It is crucial for us to comprehend this fact because the real problems in the story's premise or in the execution of the screenplay can usually be traced back to that antecedent time when the author "dreamed" the story before becoming conscious of it. This is still true when the original idea is someone else's, like the producer who commissions a script based on his own original concept. And it is still true even when that concept is a genre story: thriller, romantic comedy, teen gross-out comedy, etc. The idea has always come from *somewhere*, a somewhere outside the spotlight of our conscious attention. The extra complexity of taking on a commission from someone else's original idea is that you are dealing with someone else's dream, a fact of which that person may be unaware.

To help bring this antecedent fantasy out into the development process where we can work with it, the first question I always ask a writer is to tell me about the original impulse to write the story:

- What was the place and time?
- What was going on at that moment in your life?
- What stimulus were you responding to?
- What was the energy quality or feeling related to that first impulse?

This helps both the writer and myself know where the juice is. The authenticity of the story for the writer is bound up with the first impulse, but typically this has already been covered over by other motivations and fantasies. And, as with every Call to Adventure, the creative impulse leads the writer into inflation and duality. Creative impulses bring enthusiasm, an aura of the Self with them. To be filled with creative energy can make us feel superhuman, even godlike (the ancient Greek word *enthusiasm* originally meant "to be filled with the god," manifested as heroic action, prophetic vision, etc.). After all, isn't creation the prerogative of gods? This aura can also make a writer imagine that he can operate on the screenplay without being touched and changed by it. This inflation will be punctured by the real problems the screenplay will pose. But creative inflation at the beginning is so universal that we must believe it to have its meaningful place in the cycle, to have an instinctive rightness of its own. And in truth, if a "divine" inflation and sense of authority did not accompany risky new endeavors, it is probable that human culture would never have evolved.

Inflation screens, at least for a time, the potentially paralyzing impact of duality. The moment desire appears, so does fear. Duality that is still unconscious to the writer makes itself felt as restlessness, as back and forth shifts between inflation and procrastination, between elation and despair. The work on the project has not even begun, and the poor writer is being tossed by the psychic waves. In fact, things are starting to move below the surface, in the depths of the psyche. The psychic status quo has already tilted out of balance and the ego is subliminally aware of a loss of security. Creative impulses activate the neurotic side of ourselves with the temptation to avoid pain by living on the surface of life. We may defend ourselves even against our creative calls, though we also long for them. The therapy for this is to learn to accept the call, to squarely face and work through our avoidance each day.

Setting concrete and achievable goals for our writing has a positive, grounding effect on our floating inflation and anxiety. It's good a way to give ourselves guidance. We could term goal-setting and structuring "left-brain guidance." Left-brain guidance also includes all of the concrete early story development work: identifying idiom and genre, writing story outlines, treatments, character bios, and so on. Depending on our creative temperament, we may also seek more intuitive, right-brain, creative guidance. I have seen writers work from improv practices, like those of Keith Johnstone; with cut-out and automatic writing techniques; with guided imagery, I-Ching, and tarot inspirations—and, of course, under the influence of drugs. There are two aspects to this movement toward intuitive, "unconscious" creation. Coupled with an awareness of the role of intuition and subliminal factors in the creation of a powerful story is often a desire to break free from the inhibiting logic of our Day World lives. We could call these two aspects "battling the father-complex" and "contacting the muse."

Setting goals for the screenplay and beginning the preliminary development work leads to comparison of the new idea with known models. If we are writing a genre movie like a thriller, we certainly want to know all about the thriller genre codes and how the thriller structure compares with the structure of straight character-driven drama. During this stage we will also be involved in researching our subject, the world of the story, and all of the objective and technical elements that will appear in the movie—how a construction crane or a laser gun works, how it feels to warp into another galaxy, how the sexual traffic of women from eastern Europe to the West operates. We may model our project on previous hit movies: "*Top Gun* on the high seas!" "*Godzilla* meets *Bambi*!" "*Die Hard* meets *All About My Mother*!" These are playful ways of exploring and defining the range of our idea.

The preliminary development tasks help in concrete terms to sharpen our concept and move it toward a viable dramatic premise. What are they doing in the dynamic of the creative journey? Models seed form-giving images in the psyche, images that will work behind the scenes in the creative process: conscious planning and unconscious scanning. Think of the value of dolls. Dolls are certainly not real children. Yet when we watch a small girl playing with a baby doll or Raggedy Ann, we see her modeling patterns of mothering interaction that will come into play in reality only many years later, while with the ubiquitous Barbie the girl may be modeling her future feminine persona. Story development models also have such a right-brain form-seeding aspect. Consider story development models and concepts at this early stage, like dolls, as containers for our creative fantasies. At the same time that it shapes and defines the dramatic premise, story development work gradually brings us out of our initial inflation without, hopefully, severing us from the sources of our creative inspiration. As professional screenwriters, it is important to temper our creative inflation before we must meet our creative threshold guardians, because meet them we must.

I believe Tom Schlesinger did important pioneering work in the area of the inner threshold guardians in the creative process. Our discussions around this topic over many years have been a central factor in our individual creative development. Tom's broad frame around the subject is that inner threshold guardians represent the limits of the writer's present sphere or level of development. This is of course a very personal area, yet we can recognize that there are psychological factors involved, and that they constitute lenses with specific perspectives through which we look at the world. Inner threshold guardians seem also to manifest as outer threshold guardians we encounter in life. Outer threshold guardians will appear whenever creative conflict surfaces in the story development team. Both are expressions of patterns or fields. Our position vis-à-vis the father complex, for example, draws to us certain kinds of inner and outer father experiences, which may take the forms of rejecting or ambivalent producers, and so on. Symptomatically, the inner threshold guardians typically manifest as:

- attacking or disparaging self-talk
- self-limiting beliefs
- unfocused, ambivalent, or anxious energy
- symptoms of great fatigue or illness
- unlucky accidents

The creative threshold mentioned earlier, where the screenwriter is hit hard by the experience of duality, may come while writing the treatment or after critique and feedback on it. It may also surface as she is writing Act I of the first draft of the screenplay. The writer may realize, for example, that the characters who are alive in her mind do not match the plot they are intended to inhabit. Uh-oh. The outline is breaking down, and with it so is the map the writer had hoped would lead her through creative darkness. This is what we mean by stepping off the map and into the territory. The point where the screenwriter must confront both herself and her collaborators with the bad news—that after all that development work, the screenplay is in trouble—is a harrowing one. The high hopes and inflated moods are crashing down into the dust.

Suddenly all our convictions around the project are wrestling with self-doubt. Can we really pull this off? Depending on the level of experience the writer has and the nature of the story he is writing—how much the story's issues map over onto the writer's issues—the desire vs. fear conflict can begin to strip away layers of self-esteem. Past wounds shoulder their way into consciousness as some of the ego's defenses break down under strain. The fear list grows: failure, rejection, humiliation, abandonment, homelessness, destitution, disease . . . death! As writers going through this, we probably know we are being hysterical and overreacting, yet nevertheless these emotions have dug their way into us and are blocking the flow of imagination. We are forced to confront the paradox we have repeatedly encountered in relation to the heroes of our stories: that *authentic creation* (like character growth) happens via descent, death, and rebirth. We must know that experience in order to write about it, it seems. We must experience for ourselves the split between who we think we are (the hot screenwriter) and who we really are (the vulnerable human being struggling with paradoxical feelings and loss of control). It is some consolation, though a rather abstract one, to know that this is precisely how our hero feels at this point in the story.

Here is where we really learn the truth of the adage we proposed at the opening of this book: that success as a screenwriter is predicated on how we handle fear. The bravado attitude of "no fear" is not a productive one. It is a way of radical dissociating from the feeling rather than proactively dealing with it. Fear is a fact. That we feel afraid is simply information that our system is giving us. We know it is paired with desire, "mutually arising," as the Buddhists put it. Going into denial about fear while putting a vice grip on desire only enmeshes us more deeply in the pair of opposites. Instead of being anxious, we become sociopathic narcissists: "My desire is the only thing that counts, the only reality!" The productive way to deal with fear is to *contain* it, that is, to allow yourself to feel it without identifying with the feeling. In fact, it is to contain both poles, fear *and* desire, pain *and* pleasure, winning *and* losing, without identifying with either. Not only is this the best way to personally survive the descent into creative darkness and uncertainty, it is also the quality that empowers us to empathize with all our characters, and thus to write their parts with equal authenticity. Stepping back from the pairs of opposites and containing them gives us power through flexibility. And that empathic union with our characters ultimately links us on a visceral level to our audience.

Descent

Whether we prepare by divesting ourselves of one-sided attitudes or not, we are descending. The Road of Trials in the screenwriting process includes all those revisions we make to "fix" the script. It seems that the hero is too soft to carry the plotline, so we go through the script toughening him up. A collaborator points out that the story needs more action elements in order to be a hot seller, so we toughen the character some more. Now we can see that the character appears too hard for the love story B-line. So we go through the love story scenes and sweeten him in those places. The producer tells us that the love interest isn't sexy enough, so we turn that into a role only J-Lo could play. This is like what happens when small children try to bake a cake to surprise mom on her birthday. The batter is too salty, so add more sugar. Now it's too sugary, add more salt. Now it tastes like neither fish nor fowl, so add some hot chili pepper. And now it's *really* disgusting! All sense of proportion—and *taste*—has gone out of it. As the screenwriter, we may have responded to all the critiques and suggestions because we are paid to do so, and because we are under deadline pressure. But three drafts into the screenplay we've got a real mess on our hands.

These increasingly labyrinthine complexities, where each proposed solution leads to further headaches, are typical during script revision. Meanwhile, where has the original story idea gone? The original creative impulse has been buried under lesser ideas, lesser because they have been Band-Aids. Officially, we have hung on to the original concept because it formed the basis of a contract. Yet whatever is left of it has been cut up and compromised. At this point, three drafts and perhaps a year into the project, we've got nothing left but scraps, a Frankenstein monster. We could turn the scraps into a thriller, we think. Why not? But we might just as easily make it a comedy. It's all absurd anyway. Each new proposal sounds flatter and more futile. The project is approaching breakdown.

This may be the point when the development team calls in a consultant or script doctor. "Our script is in cardiac arrest—*do something!*" Now, a consultant working from a basic plot throughline perspective may be able in relatively short order to identify the outer plot climax and, working backward, restructure plot points for the ends of Act I and II that will anchor a throughline leading to that climax. Then the plot can be said to be "working." However, what is often sacrificed in such a plot-salvage operation is character motivation, and with it the clarity and force of the need/mode opposition upon which the movie's theme is founded.

In my own experience, the problem, or symptom, the screenwriter presents is rarely the real issue. Yes, there have been some relatively straightforward cases that could be handled on the level of plot, character orchestration, subplots, dialogue, etc. Normally these are experienced writers who can at least articulate a localized problem clearly. More often, the writer presents a simple problem, but a brief discussion indicates that he is truly lost. Instead of one single, cogent answer to questions about the script, he gives two or three. He has presented a simple symptom, like fixing the dialogue, because he was embarrassed to admit the real situation. Therefore, I have developed a practice of differentiating between the *presented* level of the problem and the *effective* level of the problem. The presented problem is in the screenplay; the effective level is in the *system*: screenplay plus writer plus collaborators, in a field. The writer cannot find a solution because he literally cannot see what he is doing. This is where the writer's own blind spot, the one-sidedness of his mode, is having a decisive impact on his work.

Here, one wants to do some quick sorting to locate the problem via diagnostic questions:

- How severe is the screenplay problem? Is it localized to one scene, one relationship, or one level of the Story Molecule? Or is it systemic, affecting all three acts and all three levels of the Story Molecule? If the latter, it will be necessary to go back and rebuild the premise.
- Does the screenplay lack a full range of feeling? Is there a one-dimensional antagonist? If so, we can localize at least one major blind spot in the author.
- Now, regarding the screenwriter, to what extent is he or she implicated in the problem? Does he lack experience? Does she lack empathy? Does he appear capable of insight? Is she up to a direct and challenging dialogue?
- Who else in the system is implicated in the problem? Sometimes a writer is going nuts because of self-contradictory demands coming from a producer. Examples of self-contradictory demands are a "character-driven thriller," or a thriller with a weak victim for protagonist and a one-dimensional monster for antagonist.

The answers to these questions give a sense of how far the story is from bedrock, the essential dramatic and thematic truth it has to tell. Screenwriters at this stage of breakdown often no longer know what they want to say, which may in fact be a very good sign. It might mean that the story's *persona* has cracked and a deeper level of authenticity may be within reach. This is the point where discovering or uncovering the link between the main character's mode and the screenwriter's mode may bring about a sudden, cathartic breakthrough, a radical shift to a deeper level of honesty and conviction. The level of simple inevitability that signals dramatic unity may begin to shine through. But if the screenwriter is too resistant to look honestly at how she is mirrored in the story she has written, then we are usually back to a more superficial fix. There are limits, after all. A story consultant is not a personal therapist.

Such a creative crisis is often a "grow or die" point for a screenwriter in relation to the current project. There may be more than one such crisis as the writer opens up more and more to the transparent mirroring relationship between screenplay and author. This mirroring relationship is an intrinsic part of the creative process. It has nothing to do with "autobiographic" writing as we would normally think of it. The mirroring does not take place on an ego level of personal biography or personal tastes. We are talking here about: what drives me, really? What values do I stand for, do I *want* to stand for? What keeps me from being the person I always wanted to be? And what does all this have to do with my main character's insoluble need/mode conflict? We are referring to an expanding openness where we begin to recognize that *everything* mirrors some aspect of our being. When we can cross this creative threshold, we begin to see ourselves in all of the characters and situations, the dark as well as the light. We begin to see that psyche and world are mirrors reflecting one another. Then we as screenwriters are getting close to Shakespeare's "mirror held up to nature."

Initiation

Creative breakthrough for the screenwriter does not mean that all of the story problems will automatically be solved. And we must bear in mind that the screenplay itself is only one of the factors contributing to the success of the movie. Good script but wrong casting, or good movie but wrong release date, can also yield disappointing results. What creative breakthrough *does* do is make conscious the writer's deepest connection to the story, his deepest motivation. This is where the "controlling idea" is actually found. It is not in the script. It is a *transaction* between the writer and the script, just as it will later be a transaction between the movie and the audience. When the controlling idea appears, finally, after the original concept had been lost in creative darkness and doubt, we invariably get a better alignment of plot and character, action and theme. We find that now the three throughlines carried by the three levels of the Story Molecule support one another and reflect different aspects of the same theme. There is a new conviction, tested by experience this time, that we really know what this story is about and why we had to write it. It is a new, more complete, and more defensible vision of the screenplay and the finished film.

A new vision can lead to a new inflation: *now* we've got it! But while the solution may be in sight, the final draft has neither been written nor approved. The check is not yet in the mail. Coming around on the return arc of the journey, the writer comes to the return threshold with its guardians, termed by Joseph Campbell the "jury of sober eyes." These threshold guardians represent the energies of the Day World. They guard the status quo. Everyone has a stake in the story—the director, the producer, the studio, the stars, and any other collaborators—and these people may not be ready to be shaken up by the truth the writer has encountered. An executive producer may simply pull rank: "It's my way or the highway, fella." So, no matter how much strain and arduous work the writer has put in up to now, he must be prepared for a major struggle. These are now the writer's outer trials: to make visible in the Day World the truth that was discovered in the Night World.

Return

Once during a lecture, Joseph Campbell outlined the four options that face an artist here at the return threshold. The first option, he suggested, is to sell out. "If people don't want what you have, then give them what they want!" This makes perfect sense, unless one has really experienced a truth that is compelling and seems worth fighting for. The second possibility is to turn away from the battle and go back to a "safe" environment where our truth is not forced to confront the intransigence of the world, perhaps to an artist's retreat in Arizona, India, or Esalen. Third, one can act out: storm out of the meeting, tear up the script, destroy the disks—to hell with them! We notice that none of these three choices really work. Campbell's fourth option, then, is to "Give to those with ears to hear what you have to give." This may include the present production team, or it may not.

Campbell seems to be referring to artists, like painters, writers, and so on, who can afford to work on their own, and not screenwriters who are wedded to the huge collaborative—let's just say it, industrial—apparatus of feature filmmaking. But for those of us who choose to stay in this arena and fight for our new vision, there are reasonable steps we can take to prepare for the return threshold encounter. I would suggest that presenting a new vision for the script that follows long work, several drafts, breakdown and breakthrough, is a situation fundamentally different from pitching the original story idea. There is even more riding on it now. Everyone has committed enormous time and energy, and the entire system has undergone stress as the original concept has collapsed. This presentation must be as convincing as possible, foreseeing and addressing likely questions and objections up front.

The format of this book can itself be used as a model for both preparation and presentation of such a new vision of the screenplay. We would want to work through the story following the models first, to confirm that our new idea really is dramatically sound. Underground in the mine, after all, we find many shiny minerals that are not true gold. The Hero's Journey model gives us a gut sense of where the story must go, a cinematic vision of the Day World, the Night World, and some key dramatic moments. With the Need versus Mode model, we focus the mythic Day and Night Worlds into two opposing values whose conflict dramatically defines the main character. The Story Molecule then expresses the opposing values as outer plot conflict, primary relationship conflict, and inner existential conflict. Using the Story Molecule as a guide through the construction of the three throughlines, we want to see if the new screenplay concept will truly express what we intend.

For completeness, a presentation of a major new vision of the screenplay would cover these steps:

- Identify briefly and clearly the original premise to which the team had agreed.
- Summarize the revision process up to the present. What changes occurred, and why? What problems concealed in the original premise came to light and why were they unsolvable within the original paradigm?
- Take the meeting through the development models in relation to your new idea. The task here is to convince the others of the dramatic solidity and

richness of your vision. Why is it an improvement? Stay on task. The Need versus Mode and Story Molecule models are always the most relevant to a discussion of this kind.

- Ask your collaborators to hold their suggestions until you have finished. It is natural that they will be stimulated to new ideas of their own. It is important to be open, but not lose your track through interruptions.

Such a return threshold trial may put the development team's win/win intentions to a "grow or die" test. It is again a time to feel our responses without identifying with those feelings. This is just a constant practice. Do not take *anything* personally. It may be that everything meshes and your new vision meets with enthusiastic acceptance. Or people may need some time to take in a new story; they may appear ambivalent because they are wrapped up with these considerations. Or the development exec may tell you that you have a fine idea, but one that does not fit the target and audience for this production. These are objective-subjective decisions; "good" or "bad," "working" or "not-working," are strictly relative to the intended goals. If an executive producer is going to commit $20 to $30 million to a production, he must be satisfied according to his own criteria. The risk and responsibility for that decision are ultimately his. "Render unto Caesar."

Win/win does not mean compromise. It ideally means finding common ground where everyone gets what they want. We are always looking for the whole that is greater than the sum of its parts. This final stage of the story development process may still mean hunting for the magic synthesis that will yield a final script that thrills everyone. That outcome that is satisfying to all could be taken as an outer Sacred Marriage beat in the creative journey.

But before we lose the sense of that journey as we prepare to uncork the champagne, let us focus back on the level of process. The screenwriter who has taken the long road into creative darkness, suffered breakdown and breakthrough, and returned with a deeply touching story is *already* a winner, no matter what happens to the production. We want to keep that in mind, while we want to keep the objective requirements of the project as objective as possible. We are here to serve the story as it can be made into a film. Many writers, faced with concessions at this point, will wisely do what works best for the project, while saving the core of insights from their creative journey to be used on a fresh new original story. The inner gold we gain from having taken the journey is ours forever, if we keep it safe. We certainly do not want to throw away our inner gold out of resentment toward Caesar!

We come around full circle on the creative journey when we are ready to finish with the screenplay and let it go. We will move on to the next project and the cycle will begin all over again. I believe that it is equally important, in the long course of our creative productivity, to learn how to bring closure to a project as it is to get started. When beginning to outline and develop the screenplay, moving from our objective, analytical, "thinking about" mode into living and breathing the story was a major threshold crossing. Now, at the end, after months of wrestling in the dark with this sort of multiheaded monster, it is good to come back to a more objective perspective. Some screenwriters like to escape immediately to a cool-down spot, be it Mexico, Mallorca, or Marrakech. Other writers work on more than one project at once, especially those writing for TV, and may already be under deadline pressure for the next piece. These latter may feel that it is hardly worth their time to stop and reflect on what they have just accomplished.

Often we symbolize closure with a nice glass of champagne or a nice dinner out on the town. It is very good to celebrate. Yes, it is very satisfying for our egos. And, as the Sacred Marriage beat in the Hero's Journey suggests, celebration is a natural expression of the deeper sense of wholeness that comes from completing the cycle. Specifically, this point of termination allows us to reconnect with parts of our lives, both outer and inner, which had to be suspended or kept at arm's length while we were immersed in our work. Spouses and children who had to put up with our moods and whims, our coldness and indifference, deserve to be consciously invited back into our lives. Equally, that inner spouse, our muse, and the inner children and daemons who supported us through the work, who in fact fed us inspiration, also deserve their due. When we realize how ill-equipped our ego was to accomplish the work on its own, how much we relied on another force to carry us when we hit the creative wall, then the pride of our celebrations can be tempered by a note of thanksgiving.

Then there is the final question of what we could call "harvesting." What have we learned about the craft of screenwriting that we want to carry with us so we have it the next time we need it? For this I suggest some focused journal writing. It doesn't have to be long, but it is the time to really shine the spotlight on what we have done. Find your own approach to this, of course, but questions like the following are useful, especially if we are completely honest in our responses.

- What was most satisfying for me, and why?
- What was the biggest problem or challenge I confronted, and how did I solve it? Or, if I could not resolve it, how close did I get? Could I make further progress on that next time?
- What new screenwriting techniques did I learn or work on for this script?
- What new worlds did I encounter?
- If I could put it in a nutshell, what have I learned from writing this screenplay?
- Who was I when I began the project? Who am I now?

Taking the time and energy for such "harvesting" helps us ground the value of those long months of work in a form that will stay with us. It also signals a commitment to our inner creative resource, to our muse, that we respect it and take responsibility for our end of that creative relationship.

Resistance and the Journey

Now we come back to the starting point, the zero-point of the creative process: sitting with the unknown and the energies of fear and desire that arise when we face the unknown. That state of duality is part of the process and is not to be evaded, but embraced. Can we allow ourselves to experience all of the uncomfortable feelings, avoidant impulses, and self-talk that get in our way? A general term for all this flak is *resistance*. There are some insights about resistance that come out of therapy and are useful here, because both writing and therapy grow out of the same fundamental dynamics of human processes. When we feel the impact of resistance, we experience it merely as something brute and irrational. Whatever form it takes, it is simply "that which opposes me and stops my progress." But in therapy there are four different qualities of resistance which are distinguished: resistance at the beginning of therapy, resistance to what is coming up in the therapy itself, resistance to effecting real change as a result of therapeutic insights, and resistance to ending the therapy. Put into the terms of the Hero's Journey, they correspond to: refusal of the Call to Adventure, refusal of the Road of Trials, refusal of the Initiation, and refusal of the Return. Each of our resistances has an archetypal as well as a personal dimension.

Resistance at the beginning of therapy—or writing—has a lot to do with inertia. We get lost on the way to the first therapy session. We show up sheepishly ten minutes late for the second session. We miss the third session entirely. There are feelings of vulnerability before a stranger, confusion and embarrassment. We go through a constant inner dialogue between the part of us that wants to back out because (we rationalize) the situation isn't as bad as all that, and the part that wants to move forward. This is a fundamental resistance to commitment, with all that entails, and it may continue until we get hit with the first real insight that *engages* us. We have noted that writers go through a parallel period of resistance at the beginning of a new project, and at the start of each day's work. For some writers, it is enough to name the demon: "Oh, that's just my inertia, my laziness. Let's get on with it!"

But other writers really do need a few days to "heat up the cauldron," to clear the mundane junk out of the mind and build up enough creative "heat" and intensity to break through the inertia. Part of the necessary tension may even come from a sense of shame. If this helps a writer get where she is going, one cannot say it is wrong. Here we must know and acknowledge our own temperament, while realizing that resistance is a habit that propagates itself. Taking the plunge is also a habit that propagates itself, and as people who have chosen a path, we take on responsibility for our own habits. This is the stage where it is essential to really make strong erotic (in the broad sense) connections to our work, to let the story possess us and permeate us day and night: the locations, the characters, the historical research, the colors and textures. It is easiest to let our zeal become our discipline.

Resistance that comes up later, six months into the therapy process—or moving into Act II of the screenplay—may have an entirely different origin. The client and the therapist may have bonded and achieved a level of trust. Suddenly the client starts missing appointments. Here it is usually a resistance to what is coming up in dreams, memories, or daily life. Naturally the relationship with the therapist becomes implicated because of the intimacy and the unconscious projections present. Part of the issue may be trust itself. The trust bond may be shaken up because everything is changing inside; our old mode is on the Road of Trials. In-depth psychotherapy may reconstitute our very earliest childhood experience, wherein the events remain what they were, but they tell a different story. In screenwriting, there is something analogous that happens, usually as we are getting into the rising action of Act II of the screenplay. We realize that our outline no longer works. We have a deeper experience of duality. We know that the level of tension and risk is supposed to rise and so we are writing chase scenes or killings, but we realize that the writing is empty. We are just going through the motions. We are not ourselves in danger, and so we lack the feeling-tone, the intensity. Here we are constantly tempted to escape and steal a solution from *Fight Club* or some other movie. The writing becomes escapist and derivative. Escapist writing comes when a writer tries to escape from the feelings that are arising in the process. Meanwhile, inside we may have a mounting sense of panic and worthlessness. It is a crisis of commitment to ourselves. Here, above all, we must have the courage to tolerate the feelings of breakdown—and write out of those feelings, because this is what the protagonist is also feeling at this point in the story.

Resistance to implementing insights and resistance to finishing are both enmeshed in the story development process when the screenwriter enters a larger system composed of producers, directors, development executives, lawyers, and other people who all want to control the story for their own reasons. Not only are there contentions about what would legitimately make the story better, such as: should John Book and Rachel's love scene in *Witness* be shown or not? Would that place too much emphasis on their relationship and slow down the plot? And so on. The nuances of a scene may even determine whether the studio or the producers are sued and the movie's release imperiled. For example: several variations were reportedly shot for the ending of *Silkwood*, some making it more explicit, others less, that Karen Silkwood was murdered for disclosing plutonium disappearances at a Kerr-McGee plant. The final cut of the film had to be decided under great legal pressure from Kerr-McGee. In the end, a compromise climax was reportedly made over the objections of director Mike Nichols. When something like this happens, it can hurt a screenwriter or director deeply. All of the resistance and antagonism around making changes becomes a major boundary issue.

While these issues may be finally decided in the cutting room, they inevitably surface in preproduction and affect the script. Here part of the duality is that while the screenwriter is trying to get inside the story, or get the story inside her so that it can come to life, she is confronted with a host of demands imposed from the outside. Each person involved is often convinced that his own changes to the story are the imperative ones, and the ensuing power struggles can drag the whole project down. For the development process to work to everyone's benefit, it is first of all necessary to create a shared vision. At the very least, the shared vision should include an agreement on the premise, the idiom or genre, and the values of the story. It is also very helpful to have a shared language that can get at how the story is working beneath the surface, which is precisely one of the reasons for this book. The screenwriter can argue for her vision of the story, and find a solid basis for her argument by using the models we have presented here.

Finally there is resistance to termination. Often it is hard to know when to stop tweaking the screenplay. There are many breakthroughs that come to the writer, realizations about the characters, the plot, how it all fits together. Deeper understandings of oneself and human nature emerge as the writer gets closer to the truth or the essence of the story. But the writer's dearest truths may be torn to shreds in minutes during a story meeting. At least, that's the way it feels. Forward-thinking producers and development executives are coming to understand the benefits of building a spirit of creative alliance, in which everyone consciously sets their egoism aside for the sake of serving the story. But the writer may still experience inhibition and belligerence. This is the return threshold of the writing process, and as with any threshold, the experience of duality is heightened. It takes faith, courage, and stamina at this point to undergo the trial of the return threshold, which is to keep working on a screenplay one had thought finished, until *everyone* is satisfied. It requires discipline to keep letting go and opening up to the other perspective, the other possibility.

Our own resistance can block us from proceeding on our creative journey if we do not know how to engage with it constructively. If we think of our resistance as acting against us, as an autonomous antagonistic force, then we put ourselves in a double bind. It is our resistance after all. But if we are able to sit with the feelings and inner fantasies—the frustration, the claustrophobia, the self-talk, the inner pressure, the escapism—if we are able to tolerate these experiences and see through them, we can actually use resistance as a guide in writing. Increased resistance is the sign of a threshold. It marks a passage that must be negotiated with consciousness, a passage into or out of the liminal zone of creation. The danger is never so much in the resistance itself, but in the secondary avoidant behaviors we take up—snacking, drinking, talking on the phone, looking for a quick fix in a formulaic screenwriting guide—that turn resistance into dysfunctional patterns. Understanding that resistance itself is meaningful can help us face it directly.

Sustaining Creativity

Creative people are driven by their creativity and are fundamentally more open to the world than other people. These factors would suggest that creativity should be relatively self-sustaining. Yet we also know how often screenwriters and other artists get blocked. Creativity is not automatic. It is a relationship with our creative resource. Like every relationship, it requires responsibility and good faith. Good faith means not betraying a trust. Trying to force your dog to eat fish food brings out the dog's resistance, because it is inappropriate and the effort betrays a basic trust. It spoils the relationship. What does your creative resource have an appetite for? The answer is: it knows, and we have just to follow its lead. The creative intuition has a gradient of interests and fascinations that moves from the mild to the acute to the enduring. Our creativity knows how to move on that scale. It also cues us with certain felt-senses when on the trail of the archetypal and the numinous. It will lead us naturally to the more universal level of our art, where the eternal human situations and problems appear.

This movement toward the higher energy gradient is what Joseph Campbell termed "following your bliss." "Follow your bliss" has been much misunderstood by some who thought the phrase could be construed as "If it feels good, do it!" Bliss is akin to joy, which in an earlier chapter we differentiated from happiness. Bliss, as Campbell intends it, has not so much to do with the level of our ego appetites but with that which gives the very deepest sense of meaning and fulfillment to our lives. I believe Campbell took inspiration from an anecdote he often repeated about the Hindu saint Sri Ramakrishna. While visiting some friends, Ramakrishna was approached by a young woman who confessed that she simply could not bring herself to worship the images of Shiva or other gods. This made her feel unworthy and sinful. She could not explain her resistance. Ramakrishna asked, was there not *anything* she loved? The woman's eyes brightened immediately, and she told how she adored her baby nephew and took such delight in him. "Then worship that little boy," was Ramakrishna's counsel. The nephew was this woman's bliss. Bliss does not come from the ego, but it must be mediated by the ego.

What is your bliss as a screenwriter? What do you love to write? Political thrillers? Romantic comedies? Character drama? Develop your strength. Factors in the film business also encourage this. Writers, like actors, tend to get typecast. If a writer has had success writing a gritty urban drama or a sweet nostalgic period piece, she is more likely to be commissioned for another script in a similar vein than a different type of story. This is the risk-averse conservatism of the system. Why take a risk on an unknown when you can have a sure thing? This is a great opportunity for a writer—as long as this is where the bliss is. Most writers eventually want to expand in different directions. Then one can feel boxed in by one's specialty, even to the extent of getting severe writer's block.

Of course, this also suggests that it is important to be clear with yourself if screenwriting is *not* your bliss. If you don't just love it and everything about it, then be honest with yourself. If the bliss is there, you will feel fed by it even when you fail. The frustrations themselves will be taken as fascinating challenges to do better. That is a symptom of bliss. If, on the other hand, your *ambition* is wealth, fame, and success as a screenwriter but the *bliss* is not there for you, then there is not a high likelihood that you will succeed. The core motivation would be missing. Screenwriting is so competitive that people with strong core motivation have better chances. Core motivation means the pleasure and fulfillment intrinsic to the action itself. The activity facilitates a flow state[38] where we easily forget time, fatigue, even who we are, and leave our littleness behind. Screenwriting does not do this for everyone. It is demanding, collaborative, and rather technical compared with novels and other forms of writing and storytelling. Bliss is connected to destiny. It generates a positive feedback loop that perpetuates the pleasure of doing. So it is natural that bliss is central to our career choice.

In sustaining creativity, it would not be going too far to say that the story is our teacher. Learning how to learn from our stories enhances our long-range creativity. This means both learning technically from the demands of the screenplay and learning as human beings about life and conflict. As we have seen, these two are intimately related because when we are in creative darkness we do not know which technique will actually solve the story problem. A deeper link is missing, which prevents us from seeing the entire essential pattern. Yet the solution is already there, in the story field, which contains all combinations of possibilities relevant to the story. We cannot see it, but it is already there. Our creative intuition would scan and pick it out, were it not for a blind spot of our own. Thus the story is teaching us, the writers, about our own blind spots by forcing us to stumble into them and have to get out of them again.

Could we say, because of this, that there is an intrinsically *ethical* component to screenwriting? If we can look at this word "ethical" from an empirical, experiential perspective, rather than a collective moralistic one, then the answer is yes. Drama is about conflict. Conflict forces the characters to make choices. Those choices, whether conscious or unconscious, reflexive or accidental, are all based on values. Whether or not the value itself is absolute, the consequences of the choice are absolute. Young Detective Mills, in *Seven*, cannot help himself: he shoots John Doe at the climax. He has sealed his fate. Upon what *value* is he acting?

A collective morality might tell us that some values are good, while others are bad. And a movie may align itself with or against this collective position. But drama is not exclusively, perhaps not even primarily, concerned with categorical right and wrong. Drama is more concerned with the *process* that places the character in a double bind where he is forced to make a fateful choice. A situational, empirical ethic is created, since only that character must live that particular choice and its outcome. One character may obey the collective code,

38. Csíkszentmihályi, Mihály, *Creativity*.

but the consequences are tragic. Conversely, another *must* violate the collective morality for the sake of something of higher value. There would be no drama if there were not legitimate conflicts of value, just as there would be no need for politics if the right course of action were obvious to all. The story is our teacher in this domain of empirical ethics.

The screenplay forces *us* to make choices, and thus, like it or not, we find that the hero's ethical double binds implicate us as well. Though part of us might like to palm off our choices as simply market-based, the truth is that stories have their own internal logic that demands a certain integrity. Meaning, for example, that you must pay off what you set up, otherwise the story will not hang together. You must answer the throughline questions in some way that is consistent with the dramatic development and the implicit conflict of values. Some choices are questions of taste and aesthetic judgment. Do we need a certain graphic murder scene? Why or why not? Where does our own shadow of voyeurism come into play there? Some choices, though small in themselves, may profoundly impact the box office potential by changing the movie's rating. All of these many, many decisions reflect and challenge our set of values, our ethical sense. So while the screenplay is teaching us about the craft of screenwriting and about the pairs of opposing values that land our characters in ethical double binds, it is simultaneously teaching us about our own patterns of choices and the values behind them. When we take a moment to think about it, we can appreciate that screen-craft is life-craft. This is the power of storytelling.

Epilogue

Writing Practice Is Life Practice

We are not what we know. We are what we are willing to learn.

—*Council on Ideas*

WRITING PRACTICE IS LIFE PRACTICE. This, I believe, is the real foundation for sustained creativity. It is all practice in awareness. The natural place where these two sides, writing and living, come together and can be seen as one, is in a daily writing practice. The function of daily writing practice is to keep our awareness up. There are many formats that can be used for daily writing. The format is secondary. Very popular among writers is the "three pages per day" discipline promoted by Julia Cameron in *The Artist's Way*. Another format is to do ten minutes of "wild" writing in the morning. This could even be five minutes or three minutes. It can be done while waiting for a bus or in the dentist's office, as long as it is truly "wild," spontaneous, and uncensored.

While the formats can vary greatly, I think there are some principles that are important to making this writing practice work to promote awareness. First is *consistency*, to get up and write every morning, even when we don't feel like it. What comes out of avoidant or negative moods is often more interesting than when we are inspired. Writing through the "down" spaces also helps us accept and integrate them. Second is *openness*, writing without any fixed agenda but responding spontaneously to both inner and outer stimuli. Openness is instantaneous; it's a moment-to-moment thing. Openness is really the act of being totally present, alert to the minutest shifts in the movement of mind and being. It follows that if we want to be open, we have to let go of certain left-brain expectations. This is not literature. It doesn't have to be witty, wise, grammatically correct, or even coherent by collective standards. Let the writing find its own sense. This leads to a third principle: being nonjudgmental about what comes up. Do not be shocked, disgusted, or attached in reaction to what you write. Or rather, yes, be shocked, but do not *identify* with the shock. Look at it, work with it, inquire of it, write about it. What does my shock want to tell me? What value does my shock serve? It is all practice.

Many writing practices are addressed to the very large number of persons who want to become writers, either professionally or for their personal enjoyment. Writing games are designed to help people overcome their feelings of intimidation about writing, explore their creativity, and find their voice. One can explore absolutely everything in this way: one's family, early conflicts, favorite teachers, first sexual experience, scariest nightmare, and so on. However, much writing done in this vein gets stuck on an anecdotal level. It does not progress in vitality until we dedicate ourselves to moving on to the next level: looking *through* the events to what Gregory Bateson called "the pattern that connects." This is the level of *meaning*. Drama is not anecdote. Drama may *start* from an anecdote—someone borrows a pair of earrings from a friend and then loses them—but drama is concerned with the *meaning* of the anecdote. The meaning is spun out of the conflicts that arise from the loss of the earrings. Therefore, we want to differentiate between basic practices—like journal and "wild" writing, which help us open up our instrument—and somewhat more advanced practices that sharpen our dramatic awareness and skills.

Patterns That Connect

Three areas of life and writing that we can focus on to enhance our ability to perceive the dramatic are:

- proactively breaking old patterns
- learning to generate metaphors
- constructing dialectical need/mode constellations out of our own experiences

Proactively break old patterns. This starts with daily writing practice, and allowing ourselves to surprise ourselves. Let the practice emancipate itself from the page and proceed to small life patterns. Take a different route to work and see what happens. Spend two hours in a location you would never have thought to go: a dog salon, a union hall, a rodeo, whatever is out of the ordinary for you. But do it mindfully, noticing with empathy where you experience a threshold of discomfort, scorn, or fear. Take a bigger chance, and some weekend ride a train to someplace you've never been. Pick the location randomly. Feel the experience of arriving at a completely unfamiliar destination. Become a reporter: go into the coffee shop and engage a local resident in a conversation about life in this place. How is it socio-economically different than the place you came from? What are the particular concerns and conflicts of people here? How do the universal human experiences express themselves through the local and specific?

Then you may try proactively breaking larger patterns, especially around self-limiting beliefs. This can be dramatic. It might involve taking a very different stance with parents, spouses, friends, or children. You have always had a nagging feeling of sadness when your teenage kids leave the house without telling you where they are going, but you have never done anything to respond to that feeling. What are you hanging on to? What is struggling to be born? This is what Buddhist nun Pema Chödrön terms "leaning into the rough places" in our lives. That is a lovely, gentle term for it. If we can be gentle and loving with ourselves at the threshold to the unknown and not be eaten up by our inner threshold guardians, then we can begin to cross over into a larger life.

A personal experience of this came for me while I was a film student. It was a time of great urban upheaval: riots, cars and buildings torched, and an exacerbated sense of class and racial conflicts. As a suburban kid I felt intimidated by the inner city. At the same time, I was fascinated and drawn to it. It was clear to me that my reality could not forever exclude this reality. I was especially pulled to a region of old factories, warehouses, and scrap metal yards along the Chicago River. This place was antithetical to my own being (my mode), it seemed. One day I went there, taking my camera because I found the structures and shapes so fantastic. Probably the camera was also a kind of crutch—it gave me an excuse for being where I expected to be treated as an intruder. In a warehouse yard I was photographing stacks of wooden pallets whose end-pieces were painted red, yellow, and blue. Stacked up against the warehouse wall, these end-pieces created a pattern like a Mondrian painting. It was frankly beautiful. As I was engrossed, framing a shot, I heard heavy footsteps behind me.

"Hey."

I told myself to play it cool, but the hair was standing up on the back of my neck. I decided to pretend no one was talking to me and kept my eye to the camera's viewfinder.

"Hey. Whatcha doin'?"

The voice was as heavy as the man's footsteps coming toward me. I felt trapped, like I'd been caught trespassing. A dozen rational excuses flashed through my head, but when I turned to face the man behind me what came out instead was the simple truth. I was photographing the pallets because I found them beautiful, the arrangement of colors . . .

"Yeah?" he said, and paused. Long enough for me to project whatever into it. "Yeah, well, ya know why that is?"

And with that the ice was broken. He started explaining to me how the warehouse worked, what they stocked, and how they moved it. This all led to an explanation of why the pallets were color-coded the way they were. A relationship was established.

It was a lesson for me, that overcoming my fear and prejudice enough to cross a threshold and risk what might be on the other side could open me to other lives unlike my own. Having crossed that threshold, I would never go back. Something new was added to my repertoire of life-skills.

Learn to construct metaphors. Everything that happens in a movie is metaphorical, as are all stories in general. Stories are metaphors not because they don't mean what they say, but because they always mean more than they present. It may be impossible to tell a story that has only one literal level of meaning. Movies are especially metaphoric because the presented, "literal" level of the photographic image is so concrete. It looks literally real. There is no standard way in the cinema to make a simile, like "She is as white as a lily." This makes perfect *linguistic* sense, but in a movie, either we see her as a lily (which would be expressionism), or we don't.*

Strange to say, many people in our society have trouble with metaphors. Though we use metaphors unconsciously every day ("she's a couch potato," for example), when asked to work with metaphor consciously and deliberately, people get uneasy. The combination of rationalism, materialism, and literalizing fundamentalist beliefs in our culture promotes an overly narrow sense of what is true; true means that it's rational, observable, "common sense," or in the Bible. From the perspective of these attitudes, a metaphor appears as a lie and/or a kind of dangerous craziness. Once, on a book tour, Joseph Campbell was confronted by an aggressive, rationalistic radio host who boasted that he "always asked the tough questions." The host began the interview by asserting that myth is a lie. Campbell started to reply, explaining that myths are not lies but metaphors, expressive of human possibilities as understood in a given culture at a given point in time. As Campbell continued, he became aware that the host did not seem to know the meaning of the word metaphor. So Campbell, an old professor, turned the tables and asked the host to give an example of a metaphor.

After much delay and embarrassing dead air, the host finally offered:

"Okay. John Doe runs like a deer."

"No, that's a simile," Campbell explained. "The metaphor would be, 'John Doe *is* a deer!'"

"But that's a *lie!*"

"It's a *metaphor!*"

The two were still deadlocked when the show ended.

One practice with metaphor is to write down all of the similes you use casually in the course of a day—better yet, catch them live as you say them—and turn them into metaphors:

—I feel like a ton of bricks today.

—I *am* a ton of bricks!

The metaphor will immediately generate an image. See the image? It looks ridiculous and very comic. There will also be a felt-sense to it. Feel the felt-sense of "a ton of bricks."

* There is no standard way to construct visual similes and metaphors, which leaves creative space for filmmakers to invent solutions. A simile may be as local as: "Ada's thoughts are as dark and tangled as the rainforest itself" (see p. 403); a metaphor may be as vast as the forest embodying Ada's Night World.

—You treat me like a dog.

—I *am* a dog for you!

What a big shift comes with the movement to metaphor! The image and felt-sense of "dog" do not limit themselves to the ego's hurt feeling, but open out a world of their own. The dog wants to bark and run around. Metaphor is playful reality, with the richness we originally experienced as children.

Now that digital technology makes any conceivable image possible to render as cinematically real, it simultaneously makes any metaphor possible. The instantaneous digital transformation of the image is a new way to work with metaphor in movies. Consider the scene early in *The Fellowship of the Ring* where Bilbo the hobbit wants to see his precious ring one last time before leaving it to his nephew Frodo. At the same moment that Bilbo is seized by a monstrous feeling, his face morphs into a monster-version of itself. The effect is so brief as to be almost subliminal. It is an expressionistic metaphor that turns a character's inner feeling into a direct image. Tolkien's original text presents Bilbo's seizure by the power of the Ring as a simile. The movie turns it into a metaphor, a direct experience. Likewise, the dreary, eternally rainy city of *Seven* turns an oppressive feeling of pessimism and depression into a literal fact of the fictional world. Because such cinematic metaphors are forceful, fascinating, even shocking, we can expect them to be used more and more aggressively in the foreseeable future. Learning to play with metaphor will become a necessity if we do not want to be overwhelmed by the loss of reality-sense and cultural destabilization that will come along with the titanic inflation of the new imagery. We will be able to remember: "it's only a metaphor."

Constructing dialectical constellations of opposing need/mode pairs of values from our own experience is a much more complex activity. But behind the metaphors and images, a dialectical constellation is at the dramatic heart of the story. Articulating the oppositions in our own lives takes the earlier project of proactively breaking old patterns further into constellations with great dramatic potential. The potential for positive change in our own lives may also be dramatic.

What is a dialectical constellation? "Dialectical" refers to opposition, opposing forces in some sort of contact and dialogue. So a dialectic constellation is a constellation of opposing forces, laying them out so that we can see them clearly. It is a concept that grows naturally out of the Need versus Mode and Story Molecule models. We have noted that every character has his or her mode, and that to some extent the mode is always one-sided. That one-sidedness generates conflict with those who have opposing views. The hero and the antagonist have either opposing values or opposing attitudes about a shared value. An axis of opposition grows up between them. Likewise, the primary relationship character normally embodies the hero's unconscious universal need, a value that is the inverse of the mode value. There will be an axis of opposition between these two as well, an axis with a different emotional quality. But until the hero recognizes and integrates what he needs to learn, there will be opposition, as the climax of *Midnight Run* exemplified so well. Even true love never runs smoothly.

These basic insights can be applied to a wide range of systems. We could look at the need/mode split and the blind spots in corporate and other organizational structures. We could apply it to globalization or American foreign policy. Wherever there is a person or entity with positions and attitudes, there will be a mode we can define. And wherever there is a mode, we can also identify such axes of opposition and conflict. They are inherent in the system.

Now, most of us, most of the time, hold a variety of beliefs and attitudes we have "inherited" from those around us or from our life experience. Life moves so fast that we rarely have time to reflect on these positions. It is unavoidable. Then when we sit down to work on our screenplay and we can't make it work out, we are led to the discovery that some of our hero's attitudes map over onto our own. We get ourselves into a tight spot with the script, and that leads to an insight. But it is possible to do some of this work ahead of time, as part of a discipline of awareness. I say *some*, because we go through so many layers of learning when writing a script that we cannot say ahead of time where bedrock is. There will always be surprises.

The dialectical constellation process begins by simply identifying an attitude or position that we actually hold. The topic can be anything, but of course the greater the stakes or investment, the more we will get out of it. In the old days, they used to say never talk about sex, politics, or religion, so of course these are prime juicy territories. When we have identified an attitude, we may take that simply and nonjudgmentally as our status quo, where we are on that subject right now. The attitude contains a value with which our ego—our sense of "I"—is relatively identified. In relation to this position we shall lay out five other possibilities that are implicitly linked to the status quo (thus a total of six).

If we then personify these other positions, turn them into metaphors, we may quickly find that we have the beginnings of a drama, with a viable cast of characters and a plot trajectory.

We shall need an example of how this constellating process works. Through building the axes of opposition, we shall see tensions and inherent conflicts emerge. The dialectical constellation helps us envision where potential dramatic stakes are highest. An opening situation for a screenplay often appears very quickly, a situation full of dramatic potential.

A sample subject that comes to mind is the cloning of human embryos. This touches on sex, polities, and religion, which makes it a volatile topic. What comes up for you around this topic of cloning? Write a short statement that tells how you feel about it. That would be a starting status quo position.

Position #1: Person X (status quo/ego)—Let us say that "Person X" makes the following statement about human cloning:

Person X

> My attitude is that life is sacred and not to be tampered with. We should resist the temptation to play God. So I am against cultivating embryos for stem-cell research. There will always be some incurable illnesses, and death is anyway inevitable. Sometimes we need the grace to accept.

What values does this statement suggest? As we know from character development, finding exactly the right formulation for the mode value is itself a process of narrowing a range of close-but-not-quite terms. How about:

- upholding the sacred
- nonintervention
- respecting certain limits

None of these three possibilities really nails the statement completely, which is a sign that there is one or more deeper values connecting the presented attitudes.

—*See* a scene setting or a bare stage. *Imagine* a character to whom the above statement could belong. What does he or she look like/dress like? Take time to look closely at appearance, body language, and attitude.

—*Cue* that character to speak the lines. With what tone are they delivered? What does the character's body language express as he or she speaks? What is your own felt-sense as you listen? This gives us a base line for further exploration.

We'll consider Person X as equivalent to an ego. All of the subsequent positions are already inherently present in relation to this original position. The axes of opposition grow out of this original.

Position #2: Persona (or Person X's social mask)—The persona is that part of us that we want the world to see, our social mask. The mask serves to both conceal and reveal our identity. The persona is a complex related to the ego. However, in this process we may think of it as a separate character. This persona may or may not want to make his true position public. *Persona* makes the following statement:

Persona/Mask

> Everyone agrees that the market is still on the way down. But I was talking to my broker about it the other day and, you know, the biotech sector is looking good for growth. Of course, you've got to stick with the firms with solid basics, solid business ethics. No WorldComs for me, no thank you!

What values does this statement project?

- easygoing competence
- confident realism

- dependence on collective norms
- denial/self-delusion

Again, we have a territory of related attitudes that contains within it some value or related values. We note that this statement of the Persona diverges from that of Person X (the ego), and also that there is great complexity. The statement is not direct and frank. Does Persona tell us his concern about business ethics because that is an important value, because he thinks that is what we want to hear, or because he thinks that will maximize his own profits?

If we were developing a story, we could either play these as two sides of one character (Person X-Persona) or as two separate characters.

—Again, *envision* a scene or stage, and bring on the Persona character who has made the statement. How does the character appear?

—*Cue* the character and hear the lines from his or her own mouth. What is your felt-sense?

Persona figures typically conform to the expectations of those around them and avoid taking sides. Therefore, such characters usually are not placed on axes of opposition. In a movie, they become the secondary characters who represent the status quo: the neighbors, the townspeople, the guys at the office, and so on. In our constellation diagrams, we shall simply think of the Persona position as an aspect of Person X.

Position #3: The Shadow-Exaggeration of the ego's position now makes a statement. Referring back to Chapter Six, we saw that the antagonist in a movie very often shares a value with the hero's dominant mode value—but his attitude is different. The antagonist's attitude toward the value is much more one-sided and contaminated with the shadow side. It may be manifestly evil. Here, the Shadow-Exaggeration figure voices a similar-sounding attitude to Person X's, but taken to a polemic extreme.

Shadow-Exaggeration

> Man does not create life, God does. God endows man with in individual soul at the moment of conception. Human beings are not mice or guinea pigs to be used and flushed down the toilet! Anyone who performs, promotes, or supports human embryo cloning is doing *evil*. This arrogance of playing God has got to be stopped, by whatever means, whether by shutting down their labs by court order, or by force if necessary!

The Shadow-Exaggeration takes a similar position to the geo, but it sounds quite different. There is a subtle shift in underlying values. Attitudes we may identify:

- passionate activism
- strident self-righteousness
- "right-to-life"
- devout belief

—*See* a character whose words these are, and cue the character to speak the lines. How do you feel? Do you pick up any subtexts?

Often, we have observed, antagonists in movies carry this extreme of the hero's dominant mode value. We noted in an earlier chapter how Paul Schaeffer's (the police chief in *Witness*) crime is based on an abuse of police power, a shadow aspect of the same authority that is Book's mode value. This Shadow-Exaggeration character generates high stakes because his position is in fundamental conflict with all other positions, and the character declares a willingness to take action in defense of the attitude.

Position #4: The Positive-Inverse of Person X's position is the role often played by the anima/animus, the primary relationship character in a screenplay. He or she carries, in a positive sense, the value inverse to the main character's mode value—and thus potentially something the main character needs to learn about life. As opposites belong together for greater wholeness, they attract. There is a natural attraction between the ego's mode position and this one.

Positive-Inverse

> Evolution is a scientific fact. Look at how life on this planet has evolved over millions of years. That is miraculous in itself! If there is a divine being, evolution must also have been part of the divine plan, including this new challenge to guide evolution ourselves. I see it as a wonderful opportunity. Stem-cell research could change lives for millions by leading to the elimination of dreaded illnesses.

What are the attitudes or values that come through?

- pragmatic optimism
- naïve idealism
- compassion for suffering

As with all of these statements, there may be complex subtexts. This optimistic position may be that of a caretaker personality who just wants everybody to stop quarreling and be happy.

—*See* the character come on the scene. Don't try to prejudge or compare this character with any other. Don't try to pin the character as a love interest. Just observe what your imagination presents.
—*Cue* the line and get a felt-sense of this character. Sometimes when a statement is less extreme it is harder to pick out the attitude/personality. How do you feel about this person?

Position #5: The Negative-Inverse to the ego's position is another intrinsic part of the equation, one less often considered by writers. This position is a negative exaggeration of the Positive-Inverse that is typical of the primary relationship, meaning it takes Person X's original stance to the inverse polemical extreme.

Not only is it not in favor of respecting certain limits, it actively defies those limits. Its position is thus the diametric opposite of the Shadow-Exaggeration antagonist figure.

Let us hear a statement of this Negative-Inverse position:

Negative-Inverse

> Cloning is more pure, more beautiful. Sexual reproduction is all confused with sexual desire. Now we can let sex be the intimate pleasure it was meant to be and let reproduction be freed to serve its evolutionary purpose. Cloning is the way of the future. And it takes us back to our origins, because we started out as clones ourselves, left on Earth by master-beings who came from space. They have been waiting for us to reach this level so they can send us new instructions. We're almost there!

Apart from defying traditional limits and attitudes, what else emerges from this statement?

- belief in extraterrestrials
- taking an active part in a cosmic plan
- determined to draw attention and publicity

The Negative-Inverse would be the other logical direction to develop the antagonist. But because there is the "opposites attract" fascination, this character could also be orchestrated as a fascinating and seductive negative anima or animus, a love interest who takes Person X, the ego-position character, way out of his comfort zone.

—*Envision* this character in a setting. Make careful note of this character's self-presentation.
—*Cue* the lines. What fantasies are woven by or around these words? As always, pay attention to your felt-sense and any visual images that might come up.

If at this point we could identify the characters we have by values, it might look like this:

- Person X/ego: respecting certain limits
- Persona: easygoing pragmatic positivism
- Shadow-Exaggeration: rigidly upholding tradition by repressive means
- Positive-Inverse: naïve progressive idealism
- Negative-Inverse: defying traditional limits and attitudes

All of these other positions are structurally and logically implied by the ego's original position. They were there all along, like sugar crystals dissolved in water. Every attitude with which we as writers identify ourselves brings with it such an invisible crystal of internal oppositions. Of course, the same is true of each of our characters. What we have learned from working with the Need versus Mode model is that the more one-sided the ego's stance, the more tension there is in the entire structure. The crystal of opposing forces forms the core of the emotional network level of the Story Molecule. We could picture this as a pair of axes:

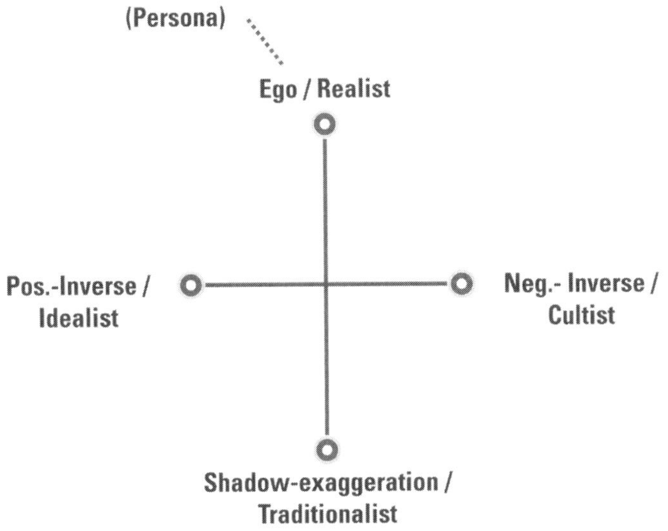

/ Axes of internal oppositions.

You may have noticed that we have just this sort of core constellation in *Witness*:

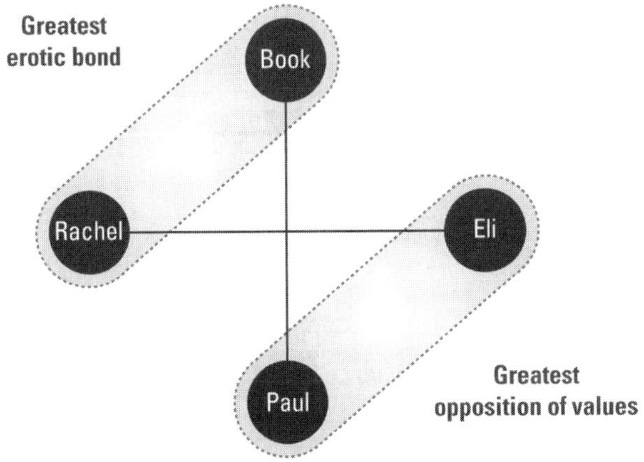

/ *Witness* opposing axes

Book and Paul are in conflict over incompatible visions of a value they have in common: power and authority. Book identifies with the positive and appropriate exercise of power and authority. Paul has used that same power corruptly to enrich himself. Rachel and Eli are likewise in conflict over differing visions of the Amish values they hold in common.

But you may have also noticed that the two positions that represent the most extreme opposition of values are actually Paul and Eli. Paul's value is: "Use whatever means necessary to get what you want!" Eli's is: "Violence is not permitted under any circumstances!" The line between Paul and Eli constructs the theme around violence vs. harmony, even though the two hardly have a scene together. It also highlights that the two lovers are squeezed between these opposing father figures.

Likewise, in the constellation we have just made around the subject of cloning, the values most deeply opposed are between the Shadow-Exaggeration of "rigidly upholding tradition by repressive means" and the Negative-Inverse position, "defying traditional limits." These are the two that will necessarily lead to violent confrontation, bombing of the sect's secret cloning lab, for example. Therefore we could reorganize the polarities of the crystal as follows:

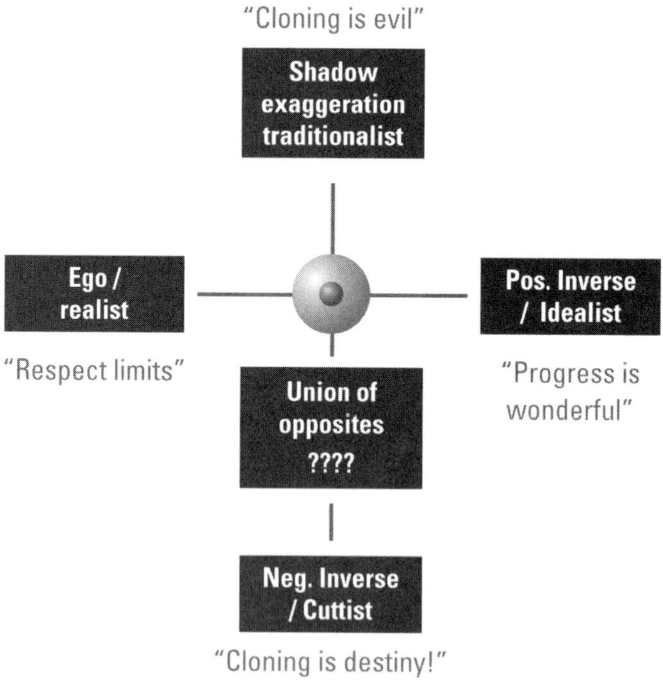

/ Cloning opposing axes.

We have seen that the ego position of Person X, along with the Shadow-Exaggeration and the two inverse positions, tend to form themselves into pairs of opposites that may be laid out in the form of a cross, or mandala. The middle of the cross is where the opposites intersect. The crossing point is a place of very special energy and meaning. Where the opposites unite, there is a possibility of reconciliation. But how can we picture this "union of opposites"—is it a character? Typically, the union of opposites, which cannot be logically represented, is a *symbolic* image, a metaphor. An image that resolves the tension of opposites is produced out of the depths of the psyche by what is referred to as the "transcendent function." The Sacred Marriage motif in the Hero's Journey is a symbolic image of the union of opposites. As it is also an image of wholeness, a way of representing the Self, the totality of the psyche.* The center position of the cross, where the union of opposites mysteriously appears, could therefore be taken as the voice of the Self within the constellation. While the symbol that appears there may be archetypal, we cannot program it mechanically without turning it into a stereotype. Some symbolic image will emerge, which will then exert a unifying and controlling influence on the entire constellation.

An example comes to mind from Mozart's opera *The Magic Flute*, which became a delightful film in the hands of Ingmar Bergman. *The Magic Flute*'s pairs of polar opposites fall into the same pattern as those in *Witness*. The pair of young lovers, in this case Pamina and Tamino, is crossed by two parental figures that appear to be irreconcilable. At the lower extreme is the figure of the Queen of the Night, who embodies the primordial, impulsive, chaotic matrix of life. At the other extreme is Zarastro, head of a masculine spiritual order dedicated to Light and Reason. The young lovers are tested, deceived, and initiated by these opposing forces.

But what is the power to reconcile primordial mother and primordial father in their eternal conflict? The opera's answer is: the magic flute itself. The magic flute has the power to soothe the violent and bestial and enchant the heart. Playing the flute, Tamino leads Pamina through all of the trials. Perhaps the magic flute might indeed be called "the voice of the enchanted heart." The flute also evokes the cosmic music of Orpheus, Krishna, and the Dancing Shiva—the music of Being. But it is still just a flute. We cannot nail it down without destroying its sublime power. The magic flute is a symbol that contains many meanings, yet transcends them all. Like music itself, it remains at least partly beyond our grasp.

In the opera, the magic flute and Mozart's music bring together and reconcile the pairs of opposites. Because *The Magic Flute* expresses itself in the idiom of myth and fairy tale, this manifestation of the Self can be made directly visible to the audience. The flute is magical and *charming*. It is *numinous*. This points to its root in the nonego dimension of the psyche, the dimension of the Self.

Now, what learning can we transfer from this example back to the worlds of screenplays and the dialectical conflicts in our own lives? Where do we look

* Refer back to the concept of the Self in the Initiation section of Chapter Three, p. 91.

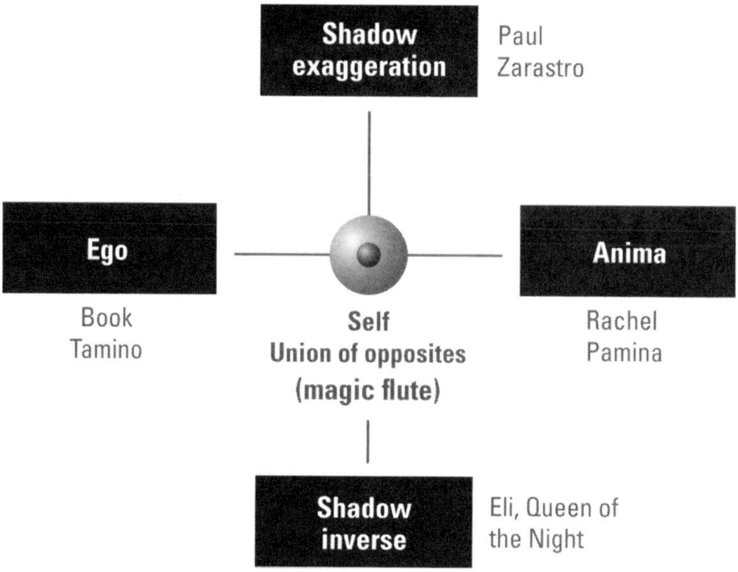

/ *Magic Flute* axes.

for the voice of the Self that reconciles opposites and relieves the banality of our daily squabbles? Often when writing, true symbols do come into our minds, offered by our unconscious. But we wonder how to incorporate them into the screenplay without seeming pretentious. First, let us go back to *Witness*, because of its deep-structure parallel to *The Magic Flute*. What might we see at the center of the cross, where the pairs of opposites intersect? What does the movie place in that position? (Keep in mind that the idiom of *Witness* is not that of myth and fairy tale, but rather an idiom of romantic realism. So whatever will appear at the center of the cross will have to fit the idiom.)

You see, we are now working at a very different level than the plot throughline, where we have Book at the center of the Story Molecule. Now we are looking at the deeper, symbolic structure of the story where Book, like Person X, takes up one of the opposing positions.

I believe that the center of the cross of *Witness* goes to Samuel. Though only a small boy, Samuel both catalyzes and reconciles the conflict in the story. By witnessing the murder, Samuel brings the hidden crime out in the open, and with it the hidden conflict between the values of Book and Paul *that already exists*. Likewise, Samuel constellates the pre-existent tension between the non-violent Amish way of life and the hyperviolence of the American city, that is to say, between our ideal of peaceful neighborliness and the disruptive reality of the shadow and its violence in our lives. And, at the climax, it is specifically Samuel's act of ringing the bell that brings about a resolution of the conflict. At this point Book is trapped; his "lone sheriff" mode has reached a dead end.

Paul has a pistol to Rachel's head and Book must give up. But Samuel's ringing of the bell brings the neighbors to witness—and thus Paul is overcome nonviolently. Dramatically, the movie gives the scene to Book, who is the hero. But the power, the power to resolve and reconcile, is Samuel's. He is the voice of the Self in the story.

Surely this is why Samuel is played as a "magical child." Samuel provides the movie's numinous moments, signaled by a specific recurring musical theme on the soundtrack. He exhibits none of the post-traumatic shock and affect a real child (or adult) would have after witnessing a brutal murder. Samuel is simply a little angel. Whether this interpretation was explicitly decided upon or was a product of creative intuition, a semiconscious gut feeling, is ultimately secondary. Samuel's dramatic function is to be the reconciler of opposites. The result is there on the screen. We might say that the Self will find a way to speak its peace. Ultimately, perhaps, what we call dramatic unity is grounded in the voice of the Self, through the reconciling symbols it presents to us.

Position #6: Union of Opposites—Finally, let us return to the dialectic constellation we started working with around the subject of cloning. What could we see at the center, there where the pairs of opposites come together?

We have to admit that we don't know what goes there, what will reconcile these opposites. Not *compromise*, but *reconcile*. The reconciling factor of the symbol comes from another level: a *magic* flute and a *magic* child. It is not a product of logical deduction. The pairs of opposing values could be logically deduced from the original Person X/ego position, but now we are stuck. We must move another, more intuitive level and wait for the unconscious to send up some image, feeling, hunch, or conviction. The pairs of opposites have served to put us in a tight spot—and that's just fine. It's just where we need to be. Now we are forced to ask for help beyond the ego's will that may only be found in the Night World of risk and adventure.

Whether this "makes sense" or not, I find an image floating up for me: the Star Child from the climax of Stanley Kubrick's *2001: A Space Odyssey*. The Star Child appears simultaneously wondrous and a bit monstrous. Wondrous because it is something absolutely new, unprecedented, immaculate, an Immaculate Conception. Monstrous because the image of an embryo without a womb is unnatural and uncanny. It appears so self-contained out there in the nothingness of space. And it appears monstrous, of titanic size up on the screen. On what does it live? To what does it relate? Is the Star Child coming to save the Earth, or destroy it? We may read the last image of *2001* either way. This is the image that spontaneously appears for me in the center of the mandala, and along with it I hear the lines from Yeats's poem "The Second Coming":

> And what rough beast,
> its hour come round at last,
> slouches toward Bethlehem to be born?

This is the creative intuition at work. Starting from a simple, "What's my attitude on such-and-such an issue?" the psyche is opening and deepening the material. Naturally, this image of the Star Child does not pragmatically resolve anything at this point. The story about cloning has yet to be told. It is not even a story yet. But even at this point, the central, symbolic image of the Star Child takes me down to another level beyond debate or political compromise. I am caught by the numinous, the miraculous, the uncanny that is at the heart of this potential story. It is the mystery of life itself. With the numinous image, the problem suddenly belongs to *me*. It is no longer just something I am thinking about on a head level, trying to "problem-solve." I am accelerating into creative darkness.

If we now want to follow this constellation work a step further, we might hypothesize that the surface constellation of opposing forces mirrors another constellation on the archetypal level that we are unable to look at directly, the level the Star Child came from. The cruciform play of opposites (itself an archetypal image) represents the logical possibilities within the present situation and simultaneously a "timeless" pattern of relationships. (The Oedipus complex is such a timeless pattern of relationships, repeated in family after family down through the ages.) The timeless pattern might be pictured as a myth or fairy tale. Bringing both the current and the mythic/archetypal levels together creates a three-dimensional "virtual" structure. The Star Child/magical child/magic flute not only holds the opposites together on the upper and the lower levels, it holds these two levels together as well. We might envision this totality as a "virtual" cube:

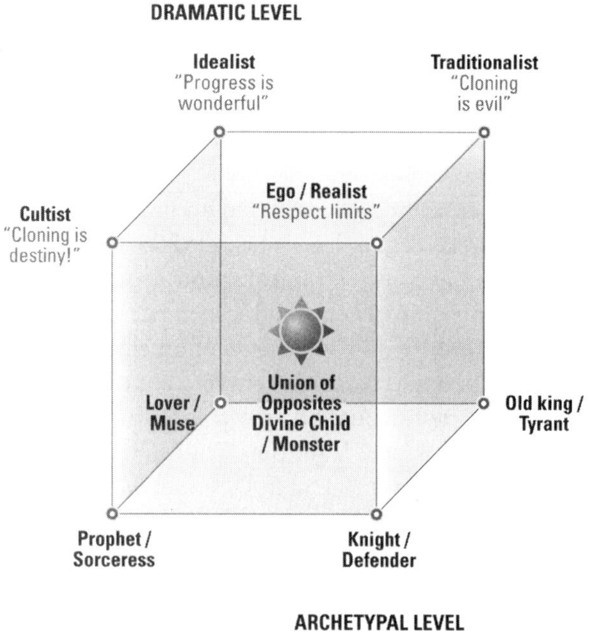

/ Cloning story virtual cube with union of opposites at center.

On the lower, subliminal, myth/fairy tale level, which reflects back the contemporary issue from the depth of the psyche, the traditionalist becomes the old king or tyrant, guardian of the old order. Person X's position of respecting certain limits becomes the figure of the knight who, like Lancelot, defends the realm but is susceptible to a conflict of duties. The idealist/anima becomes the lover who sees the potential for beauty and growth as more important than the old order. This figure may inspire and forge alliances, but she herself may be seduced by the greater determination of the two polar extreme antagonists. The space alien cultist becomes the prophet of a new order, or a sorcerer/sorceress with a power to bring the new and uncanny into being, for weal or woe. The energy these figures generate is already palpable because of the bonds of opposition between them.

Essentially the same drama may be told on either level, or a blend of the two. We orchestrate where we are vertically between the two levels partly by the choice of idiom, partly through the dramatic construction, and partly through the influence of symbols and motifs. *Blade Runner*, *The Matrix*, *Seven*, *Lord of the Rings*, and *Solaris*, though set in mythic landscapes, all reflect contemporary conflicts back to us. But you will have understood that it is not even necessary to deliberately pitch the screenplay on an overtly "mythic" level in order to get the theme across, since the lower (myth/fairy tale) cross of opposing figures always lies in the subtext of the upper.

At the center of the "virtual" cube, and radiating a mysterious influence in all directions, is the numinous figure of an ambiguous Divine Child. Positively, the Divine Child is Moses/Jesus/Buddha/Krishna. As a monstrous or deformed Divine Child, we might have an imp, moonchild, trickster, or beast of the apocalypse. All the other figures in the "virtual" cube have some unknown connection to this central symbol. Out of this will grow a narrative, taking Person X as the main character. Through the development steps we take in building the narrative, the conflictual relationships, threshold crossings, double binds, and climaxes will shed light on this central role of the Union of Opposites figure, like the roles of Samuel and the magic flute. As always, we discover the meaning of the story through the act of writing it.

The "virtual" cube implies a flow of energy up from the depths, shaping itself in our consciousness in the form of a story. We are talking about libido, life energy, the greater part of which is beyond our conscious control. Psychic influence may flow from the archetypal level into our existential space/time. For example, it could be that the current social debate about human embryo cloning has constellated or awakened corresponding energies in the field of the deep unconscious. But one could inversely hypothesize that archetypal constellations—irrepresentable as such but provisionally "tagged" by these mythic figures—*themselves* precipitate the "real" situation, that is to say, an emerging conflict over human embryo cloning in both collective and individual consciousnesses, giving rise to contention, debate, legal actions, mass demonstrations, TV features, and potential real violence.

The image of the Star Child was linked by Stanley Kubrick to the millennium. Periodically, as in the year 1400 and the year 1500, Western culture has gone through millennial mass hysterias. There is plenty of evidence for millennial mass hysteria today—the "rapture" movements, the *Left Behind* series of novels, the tone of "End of Days" in the subtext of the invasion of Iraq. Hysteria by its nature does not respect boundaries, so debate about stem-cell research and cloning might very well be infected by it. But what triggers, century after century, these millennial fantasies and collective disorders to begin with? When we begin to understand how intimately linked scientific breakthroughs are with the scientist's experience of the archetypal level,[39] then we are forced to confront the possibility that psyche, the soul, has a reality and force of its own.

If we assert that writing practice is life practice, we mean that when we examine any one of our real attitudes and open it up, we find these other positions secreted there, in us, invisible like sugar crystals dissolved in water. And when we can come to accept that we already carry these many attitudes as part of our human nature, without being aware that we do, it can help us approach situations of conflict in the real world with greater empathy and breadth of vision. We may find that we have a greater power to reconcile conflicting sides. It may help us number among those blessed who are the peacemakers.

The End Is the Beginning

Sustaining creativity, once we have a grasp of screenwriting technique, is a question of staying close to the creative edge between old and new, order and chaos, known and unknown. It asks us to focus on what matters—and at the same time to toss that playfully over our shoulder, to constantly destroy old forms as we generate new, to live with and contain the tension of opposites. The three processes we have highlighted here—proactively breaking old patterns, creating metaphors, and dialectic constellations—simply serve to make more conscious the operations that our creative intuition carries out subliminally every day. Working with them as part of a self-discipline helps to make our movement in and out of creative spaces more spontaneous and graceful. As background disciplines, they feed our more focused screenwriting activity by affirming what we deeply know: that we create out of abundance, not out of scarcity.

Even when we feel totally blocked and can't come up with a single idea, nevertheless the abundance is always there, like the mountain lake behind the dam. The water may be dammed up because we are out of rapport with the story. It becomes part of our creative journey to remove the dam and let the water flow again. There is no scarcity of water. We say that necessity is the mother of invention, but abundance is the very essence of creation.

39. See for example M.-L. von Franz's books *Number and Time* and *Projection and Re-collection in Jungian Psychology*.

Sustaining creativity in the context of a story development team, once we have embraced the win/win principles of responsibility, mutuality, and clear communication, is a practice of sustaining faith in the mission of the project, enough faith to tolerate the descent into creative darkness riding on waves of breakdown and breakthrough. It is a practice of supporting each other to do our best work, even if we experience discomfort in the process. One does not tell a woman in the throes of childbirth to stop simply because she experiences pain. Sustaining creativity is sustaining faith that we will get out of it what we put into it. These faiths are in turn founded on a basic faith in the "other" power in the soul, the voice of the Self that comes to us via the creative intuition and the power of imagination. It is clearly a long road into the unknown to create a new story, but if we are willing to persevere we will be rewarded with self-knowledge. And we shall never be bored.

At the end of the long road of creative work we encounter a symbol of the Self, like Mozart's magic flute, thrown up from the depths by the Self. That symbol is our personal Initiation, our boon, while it becomes likewise the key element that unifies our entire story, whether as magic flute, Divine Child, ultimate victory, or Sacred Marriage, adding a fascinating and numinous luster to the finished work. It is possible that at the heart of every fully achieved story is a symbol of the Self. This is certainly true of myths and fairy tales. How could this be the case if it were not the Self invisibly guiding us to discover itself?

What changes in screenwriters who have come around full circle on this journey of creation? The change I have observed in writers could be termed a deepening and centering of value structures in a way consistent with greater authenticity. There is a movement from received value—to *discovered* value—to *intrinsic* value.

Received values are the ones we have inherited from our upbringing and our society. Many of us, perhaps most of us, simply take that value-set for granted. In beginning writers, this tacit acceptance forms a bias that gets challenged by the work, especially the work of dis-identifying from the protagonist and giving some dimension to a flat antagonist. The writer begins to make *discoveries* that can feel momentous as she steps out of the bubble of what "everybody thinks." There is often a period of inflation by the antithetical values: "If what everybody thinks isn't really true, then the truth is that we've all been deceived!" This necessary stage of separation can feel both like adolescent revolt and like wandering alone in the wilderness. Some unfortunate screenwriters find too much stress in this process of separation and fall back into the status quo. They content themselves with living the "industry persona," and their work is marketable but lacks vitality and authenticity.

Those who keep working through many, many screenplays may happily arrive at a point of accepting all of their characters in their messy humanness at the same time that they find the rewards *intrinsic* to the act of writing itself.

They discover value to be intrinsic to the character and intrinsic to the situation. The value is neither imposed by society nor in rebellion from it. One could say that it is seeing the *is* beyond good and evil, a vibrantly experienced union of opposites. This is, I suppose, what we mean by "mature" in reference to the later work of master writers and directors. With each project we complete, we harvest something for our future work. The end of one cycle is already the beginning of the next.

You, as an individual screenwriter or person laboring with stories, may choose to work on this deeper level of the journey, or you may not. Yet the fact remains that a deeper dimension peeks out from the material and challenges us, entices us, to find it and express it. And, there is some level beyond our art: that elusive essence a perceptive audience may yet feel. What we put into the screenplay is more than what ends up on the page; the audience's total experience of the movie is more than what is up on the screen. Stories touch us on many levels. The task I have chosen has been to open up a full range of techniques and possibilities that you can take with you and use in your own way on your own projects. After that, the journey is yours.